D1577197

|
(

Pl
it

R
A
re

(
P
i
(

;
r

|

|

i

2

BROWNING

BROWNING

A Private Life

IAIN FINLAYSON

HarperCollins*Publishers*

HarperCollins*Publishers*
77–85 Fulham Palace Road,
Hammersmith, London w6 8JB

www.harpercollins.co.uk

Published by HarperCollins*Publishers* 2004
1 3 5 7 9 8 6 4 2

A catalogue record for this book
is available from the British Library

ISBN 0 00 255507 7

Set in Minion by
Rowland Phototypesetting Ltd,
Bury St Edmunds, Suffolk

Printed and bound in Great Britain by
Clays Ltd, St Ives plc

to Judith Macrae,
Good Friend and Good Samaritan

ACKNOWLEDGEMENTS

Stuart Proffitt originally commissioned this biography and thereafter continued to take a kindly, informed interest not only in the progress of the book but of its author. I'm profoundly indebted to Stuart, not only professionally but personally for many years of generous friendship. Philip Gwyn Jones took over the editorship of the book. Patiently and confidently he waited for my promises to be fulfilled. When a text was finally delivered, his editing was shrewd, detailed, and invariably correct, not only in matters of plain prose but in sensitivity to the expectations of the prospective readership, the colour of my writing, and the character of Browning as I chose to present it. Karen Duffy and Georgina Laycock, also of HarperCollins, were continually supportive in many ways beyond hope of adequate thanks. Deborah Rogers, my agent, kept faith in the quality of the work interminably in progress. I'm deeply grateful for her patience and perseverance with me over many years.

In Florence, while I was idling on the excuse of researching Browning's life there, Magdalen Nabb kindly gave me not only lodging but also her benign, level-headed friendship.

Dorothy Adibi, Simon Burt, Rachel Campbell-Johnson, Christopher and Mary Campbell-Johnson, Jenefer and Alan Cooper, Jane Crichton-Stuart, Beth Finlayson, John Goodbody, Judith Macrae, Mick and Alexandra Rooney, Erica Wagner, Vicki Woods, and Eddie Wyatt — all plentifully and uncomplainingly contributed their time, encouragement, and other resources to keep me going throughout the research and writing of this biography. In the last stages of writing and revision, Cheryl Davies and George Samios helped to give me a voice beyond ink and paper. My thanks to them goes beyond words.

Further thanks for careful work on text and index must go to Richard Betts, Matt Bevis, Michael Cox and Douglas Matthews.

I am sincerely grateful to the Society of Authors and the Royal Literary Fund for financial support. To Mrs Fiona Clark, in particular, my warmest thanks are due for her exemplary tact and very practical assistance.

CONTENTS

PICTURE CREDITS

PROLOGUE

H ENRY JAMES, a man of sound and profound literary and personal judgements, provided the most epigrammatic epitaph for Robert Browning. On the occasion of the poet's burial in Westminster Abbey, on 31 December 1889, he remarked: 'A good many oddities and a good many great writers have been entombed in the Abbey, but none of the odd ones have been so great and none of the great ones so odd.'

The immortal voice having been condemned to final silence by disinterested Nature, and the mortal dust committed to elaborate interment by a respectful nation, James reflected that only Browning himself could have done literary justice to the ceremony:

> 'The consignment of his ashes to the great temple of fame of the English race was exactly one of those occasions in which his own analytic spirit would have rejoiced, and his irrepressible faculty for looking at human events in all sorts of slanting coloured lights have found a signal opportunity . . . in a word, the author would have been sure to take the special, circumstantial view (the inveterate mark of all his speculation) even of so foregone a conclusion as that England should pay her greatest honour to one of her greatest poets.'

Browning's greatness and his oddity, his great value, in James' view, was that 'in all the deep spiritual and human essentials, he is unmistakably in the great tradition — is, with all his Italianisms and cosmopolitanisms, all his victimisation by societies organised to talk about him, a magnificent example of the best and least dilettantish English spirit'.

That English spirit does not, generally, delight in literary or psychological subtleties; nevertheless, stoutly and steadfastly, 'Browning made them his perpetual pasture, and yet remained typically of his race ... His voice sounds loudest, and also clearest, for the things that, as a race, we like best — the fascination of faith, the acceptance of life, the respect for its mysteries, the endurance of its charges, the vitality of the will, the validity of character, the beauty of action, the seriousness, above all, of the great human passion.'

James particularly distinguished Browning as 'a tremendous and incomparable modern' who 'introduces to his predecessors a kind of contemporary individualism' long forgotten but now, in their latest honoured companion, forcefully renewed. These predecessors, disturbed in the long, dreaming serenity of Poets' Corner and their 'tradition of the poetic character as something high, detached and simple' by the irruption of Browning, are obliged to measure their marmoreal greatness against Browning's irreverent inversions and subversions that blew the spark of life into those poetic traditions. But death diminishes the force and power of any great man until — James observed — 'by the quick operation of time, the mere fact of his lying there among the classified and protected makes even Robert Browning lose a portion of the bristling surface of his actuality'. The stillness of silence and marble smooths out the poet and his work. The Samson who would crack the pillars of poetry is subsumed into the fabric of Poets' Corner, of the Abbey, and of an Englishness that eventually, by force of the simplicity of its legends and the ineffable character of its traditions, stifles the vitality of the poet's words and corrupts the subtle colours of their maker.

'Victorian values' has become a loaded phrase in recent times, sometimes revered, sometimes reviled. At best, the epithet for an age has provoked a revived interest not only in eminent Victorians but also, perhaps more so, in their ethical beliefs and social structures — though in our current perceptions those values are often misunderstood and misinterpreted when set against present-day values, which in turn are too often misapprehended by interested parties seeking to adapt them to their particular advantage and to the confusion of their opponents. Henry James gives the cue when he states that Robert Browning was a modern. Browning survives in the 'great tradition' as a 'modern' and, in his earlier life, he suffered for it. Matthew Arnold characterized

Browning's poetry as 'confused multitudinousness', and at first sight it is often bewildering. To cite the rolling acres of verse, the constantly (though not deliberately) obscure references, the occasional archaisms, is but to highlight a few surface difficulties.

To anyone unfamiliar with or still unseized by Robert Browning, his reputation as a serious, intellectual, difficult, and prolific writer is an impediment to reading even the most accessible of his poems. To the extent that he was serious — as he could be — he was serious because of his insistence on right and justice and the honest authenticity of his own work. To the extent that he was intellectual, he confounded even the most thoughtful critics of his day, and only now, with the perspective of time that enables more objective critical understanding of Victorian themes and thought, can his poetry be more deeply appreciated. To the extent that he was difficult, he was difficult because of his paradoxical simplicity. To the extent that he was prolific — well, he had a great deal to say on a great number of ideas and ideals, themes and topics.

The length of much of Browning's poetry is daunting. The attention span of modern readers is supposedly more limited than that of the Victorians, though even the attention of the most persistent, discriminating intellects of the literary Victorians was liable to flag: George Eliot, noting advice to confine her own poetic epic, *The Spanish Gipsy*, to 9,000 lines, remarked in a letter of 1867 to John Blackwood, 'Imagine — Browning has a poem by him [*The Ring and the Book*] which has reached 20,000 lines. Who will read it all in these busy days?' The diversity, too, is intimidating: 'You have taken a great range,' remarked Elizabeth Barrett admiringly, 'from those high faint notes of the mystics which are beyond personality — to dramatic impersonations, gruff with nature.'

To understand Henry James's assertion that Browning was 'a tremendous and incomparable modern', it is necessary to understand the Victorian world as modern, as a dynamic, experimental, excitingly innovative age of achievements in exploration (internal and external) and advances in invention, but also as a time of doubts raised by experiments and enquiries. Browning himself is a prime innovator, an engineer of form, an explorer of history and the human heart, revolutionary in his art and of lasting importance in his achievements. One critic has suggested that Browning's masterpiece, *The Ring and the Book*, may be viewed as a 'heroic attempt to fuse Milton with Dickens, the modern novel with the epic poem'. Certainly, the comparison with Dickens is sustainable: Browning's poetry is conspicuously democratic, rapid, colloquial, and modern in its preoccupation with individuals and the social, religious, and political systems in which they find themselves obliged to struggle, to progress throughout the history of humanity's efforts to develop.

Words like 'develop' and 'progress' raise the matter of Browning's optimism, which is usually taken at face value to mean his apparently consoling exclamations on the level of 'God's in his heaven — All's right with the world', 'Oh, to be in England/Now that April's there', 'Ah, but a man's reach should exceed his grasp/Or what's a heaven for?', and so on. These are positive enough, and over-familiar to those who seek moral, theological, or nationalistic uplift from Browning. They have become the stuff of samplers and poker-work, tag lines expressive of a pious sentimentality ('It was roses, roses all the way . . .') he rarely intended, a jingoistic English nationalism ('Oh, to be in England . . .') he hardly felt, and a shining Candidean optimism ('God's in his heaven . . .') that was the least of his philosophy. Browning's poetry too often survives miserably as useful material to be raided and packaged for books of inspirational verse-in-snippets and comfortable quotations. This is a permanent fame, perhaps, but not Parnassian glory.

Browning's optimism was a more robust and muscular character-istic, deriving not at all from sweet-natured sentimentality or rose-tinted romanticism. Rather, it was rooted in a profound, passionate realism — naturalism, some claim — and tremendous psychological analysis that looked unsparingly, with a clear eye, at the roots and shoots of good and evil. Unlike most Victorians, Robert Browning was more matter-of-factly medieval or ruthlessly Renaissance in his assessments and acceptance of matters from which fainter, or at least more emollient, spirits retreated and who drew a more or less banal moral satisfactory to the pious, who tended to prefer the possibility of redemption through suffering. For some readers, suffering was quite sufficient in itself — a just reward and retribution for the sin or moral failure, for example, of being poor.

Browning's innate Puritanism, as Chesterton remarks, stood him in good stead, providing a firm foothold 'on the dangerous edge of things' while he investigated 'The honest thief, the tender murderer.' The early attempts of the Browning Society and others to construct a 'philosophy' for Browning, a redeeming and inspirational theological and ethical system to stand as firmly as that imposed by Leslie Stephen on Wordsworth, is bound to be suspect in specifics and should be distrusted in general.

That Browning was a lusty optimist is rarely doubted in the popular mind, but the evidence adduced to support the theory is too often selective and superficial. His optimism was in fact an appetite and enthusiasm for life in all its aspects, inclusive rather than exclusive, from the highest joy to the darkest trials. His optimism was an expression of endurance, of acceptance, of the vitality of living and loving, of finding value in the extraordinary individuality and oddity of men and women. Robert Browning is, in the judgement of G. K. Chesterton, 'a poet of misconceptions, of failures, of abortive lives and loves, of the just-missed and the nearly fulfilled: a poet, in other words, of desire'. Ezra Pound insists on Browning's poetic passion. *Men and Women*, the collection of poems that redeemed Browning from obscurity in middle-age, is a demotic, democratic piece of work that reflects his distance from his early reliance on the remote Romantic imagery of Shelley and adopts a firmer insistence on the mundane life of city streets and market-places.

This interest in the apparently tawdry, temporal life of fallible men and women somewhat disconcerted his more elevated, intellectual contemporaries. Of *The Ring and the Book*, George Eliot (who should have known better, and might have had more sympathy for the poem in her youth) commented: 'It is not really anything more than a criminal trial, and without anything of the pathetic or awful psychological interest which is sometimes (though very rarely) to be found in such stories of crime. I deeply regret that he has spent his powers on a subject which seems to me unworthy of them.' She was not the only contemporary critic to make such a point, or adopt such an aesthetic view: Thomas Carlyle declared the poem to be 'all made out of an Old Bailey story that might have been told in ten lines and only wants forgetting'.

In short, Browning shocked his contemporaries. The shock consequent on his choice of subject matter was perhaps compounded by the novelty of his poetic approach to its treatment. *Pippa Passes*, startlingly unlike in form to anything contemporaneous in English poetry, is regarded by Chesterton, aside from 'one or two by Walt Whitman', as 'the greatest poem ever written to express the sentiment of the pure love of humanity'. Like Whitman, Browning was responsive to the spirit of his age. For all his learning and his familiarity with the past, and for all his choice of antique subject matter and foreign locations, Browning is no funeral grammarian of a past culture, of spent history. His portrait of the Florentine artist Fra Lippo Lippi is as living, as vibrant, and as relevant as might be a current account of the life of the modern painters Francis Bacon or Damien Hirst. The speeches in *The Ring and the Book* might, with some adjustments, make a modern television or radio series examining a murder case from the points of view of all the protagonists. The form of serial views of one event was not new when Browning revived it from Greek classic models, but he infused it with modernity and it has since become a staple model for dramatists.

Browning did not bestride the peaks of poetry like a Colossus with a lofty and noble eye for the prospect at his feet. He rambled like a natural historian, peering and poking in holes and corners, describing minutely and drawing his particular conclusions; he visited the courtroom with a reporter's notebook, and the morgue with the equipment of a forensic scientist. He was an entomologist of humanity in all its bizarre conditions of being. His great subjects were philosophy, religion, history, politics, poetry, art, and music — a few more than even Ezra Pound later marked out as the fit and proper preoccupations of serious poetry. They were all encompassed in Browning's studies of modern society and the men and women of a universal humankind.

Browning's poetry is often of a period, but in no sense is it period poetry, nor is Browning a period poet. In this he differs from the more consciously archaic writers and works of the Pre-Raphaelites who admired him, strove to imitate him, and embedded themselves in a literary aspic. Whereas his successors became conscious, perhaps dandified and decadent, Browning himself was largely and serenely unconscious, vigorous, and often matter-of-fact. He had principles and opinions, at first devoutly and latterly didactically held. But Browning was learned and assimilative rather than rigorously intellectual. His poetry suffers often from obscurities that puzzle intellectuals because Browning was, above all, a widely and profoundly literate, well-read man.

Once he had absorbed a fact or a thesis, he subsumed it in his mind where it found useful and congenial company. Joined with a mass of other facts and theses, it became so inextricably enmeshed with its fellows that, when it was eventually pulled out to illustrate, embellish, or point up a phrase in Browning's work, it was comprehensible only — though not always afterwards, when he had done with it — to the mind of the poet. Being already so personally familiar with it, he thought nothing of its unfamiliarity to his readers. Chesterton regards this as the greatest compliment he could have paid the average reader. There are many who may feel too highly complimented. In this sense, his poetry is devoid of intellectual arrogance or one-upmanship. Perfectly innocently and without conscious affectation, Browning's work arises from and is coloured with what Henry James identified as an 'all-touching, all-trying spirit . . . permeated with accumulations and playing with knowledge'.

For all his modernity, now increasingly acknowledged and admired by literary critics, Browning has recently been somewhat neglected by literary biographers. 'What's become of Waring?' is a well-known line from one of his best-known poems. What, one may reasonably ask, has become of Browning? There is no lack of interest in him in one sense — in the sense of Robert Browning as one half of that romantic pair, the Brownings. The marriage of Elizabeth Barrett and Robert Browning remains a perennially seductive subject, and not only for biographers. One difficulty for the modern biographer is that Robert Browning's reputation has never quite lived down being cast as a great romantic hero, the juvenile lead, as it were, in Rudolph Besier's 1934 stage play *The Barretts of Wimpole Street* and subsequently in the Hollywood movie, where Robert Browning was played dashingly and dramatically by Fredric March. This has become his principal claim to popular fame. For various reasons, Robert has become the dimmer partner, Elizabeth the brilliant star. The romantic hero of fiction or drama is, in any case, generally only a foil for the romantic heroine.

There are big modern biographies of most of Browning's contemporaries, and more are published every year, but Browning himself is comparatively unknown to present-day readers. Elizabeth Barrett Browning is, to be realistic, the more immediately colourful and engaging character — the drama of her early years as a supposed invalid, the romance of her marriage to Robert Browning and their escape to Italy, the currently fashionable interest in her as an early feminist and as a radical in terms of her views on politics and social justice. Her husband, by contrast, is perceived as a more reactionary and conventional, a more prudish and private character. If judged solely by the quantity and quality of their letters to friends and acquaintances, his personality is less immediately engaging, and, for all his superficial sociability, more introverted and private.

In contrast to the relative scarcity of biographies of Robert Browning, there is an astonishing quantity of critical monographs and papers hardly penetrable to any but the Browning academic specialist. What has recently been lacking, is a chronological narrative of Browning's life as an upstage drama to complement the downstage chorus of critics of his work. This present book is a conventional, chronological biography of Browning. Despite the enormous and constant critical attention paid to Browning, and the number of books about Elizabeth Barrett Browning and the marriage of the Brownings, there have been few modern biographies that give themselves over mostly to the life and character of the man himself.

The standard late twentieth-century biography of Robert Browning that confidently, authoritatively, and entertainingly treats his life as thoroughly as his poetry is *The Book, the Ring, and the Poet* by William Irvine and Park Honan, published in 1974. *Robert Browning: A life within life*, Donald Thomas's biography, published in 1982, is the conscientious work of a scholar who combines a life of the poet with critical analysis of his work. Clyde de L. Ryal's 1993 biography, *The Life of Robert Browning*, is an attractive, authoritative literary critical work that provides an overview of Browning's life and work as a *bildungsroman* without the distraction of — for the purposes of his book — unnecessary domestic detail.

In this present biography, I have of course been heedful of as much recent biographical work on Browning as seemed to me relevant to my purposes — specific references are gratefully (and comprehensively, I hope) acknowledged — but I have not neglected earlier biographies in my search for such materials as Nathaniel Hawthorne might have characterized as the 'wonderfully and pleasurably circumstantial'.

A principal resource for any Browning biographer must be the official *Life and Letters of Robert Browning* (1891) by Mrs Alexandra Sutherland Orr, a close friend of the poet. Mrs Orr wrote her biography at the request of Browning's son and sister. Besides the obvious constraints of these two interested parties at her shoulder, she was writing, too, soon after Browning's death, as a close friend as much as a conscientious critic. She is thus, and naturally, tactful. Though she is not deliberately misleading, nevertheless she will occasionally suppress materials when she considers it discreet to do so, and will sometimes turn an unfortunate episode to better, more positive account than we might now consider appropriate. A close, long-standing friend of Browning's, William Wetmore Story, supplied Mrs Orr with details of their long friendship. On reading the published biography in 1891, he commented that it seemed rather colourless, but admitted that Browning's letters 'are not vigorous or characteristic or light — and as for incidents and descriptions of persons and life it is very meagre'. Subsequent biographers have supplied the deficit.

My second principal biographical authority is Gilbert Keith Chesterton, whose short book about Browning, published in 1903, is valuable less for strict biographical fact, which now and again he gets wrong, than for consistently inspired and constantly inspiriting psychological judgements about the poet and his work, which he gets right. Like Mrs Orr, Chesterton's value is that he was closer in time and thought to the Victorian age, more attuned to the Browning period and the psychology of the protagonists than we are now, closer to the historical literary ground than we can be. Chesterton's *Robert Browning* has never been bettered. It remains unarguably perceptive and uniquely provocative. Besides its near-contemporaneity to its subject, Chesterton's book is valuable because it evokes Browning's character with the very ironies and psychological inversions that Browning himself often employed in his poetry. Time and again Chesterton proposes the converse to prove the obverse, exactly as Browning could easily — with poetic prestidigitation — prove black to be white or red.

Two lively, thoughtful women — Betty Miller and Maisie Ward — have contributed more recent biographies that sometimes convincingly and sometimes controversially propose psychological and psychoanalytic interpretations of Robert Browning, his poetry, and his life. Their insights are regularly disputed, and perhaps for that very reason they regularly startle their readers out of complacency. They ask questions, raise points, that — right or wrong — are still worth serious consideration by Browning's critics and biographers.

I should also say that I have generally relied on earlier Browning criticism, which retains much of its vigour and sparky originality. This is by no means to belittle latter-day critics, many of whom write ingeniously and excitingly, but merely to indicate that for the purposes of this biography I have for the most part personally preferred period sources and contemporary authorities. An exception has to be made for *The Courtship of Robert Browning and Elizabeth Barrett*, Daniel Karlin's close and authoritative study of the love-letters that preceded the marriage. This book is indispensable to any modern biographer of Browning, not just for Karlin's detailed analysis of the voluminous correspondence but also for the tenderness and imagination he brings to its interpretation.

There is — or has been — a discussion about how far the biography of an objective poet is necessary, in contrast to the permissible biography of a subjective poet. Browning gave his own views on this in his essay on Shelley. Since Browning himself is generally reckoned to combine subjective and objective elements in his work, then it probably follows that a biography detailing the day-to-day activities of the poet may be as relevant as a critical commentary on his poetry. G. K. Chesterton remarked that one could write a hundred volumes of glorious gossip about Browning. The *Collected Letters of Robert Browning and Elizabeth Barrett Browning*, when the full series is finally published, will be exactly that. But for all the froth and bubble of Browning's social life, not a great deal happened to him — there is a distinct dearth of dramatic incident. One is inclined to sigh with relief, like Joseph Brodsky who says of Eugenio Montale, who won the Nobel Prize for Literature in 1975 for the poetry he had written over a period of sixty quiet years, 'thank God that his life has been so uneventful'.[1]

And yet, as Chesterton concedes of Browning biography, 'it is a great deal more difficult to speak finally about his life than his work. His work has the mystery which belongs to the complex; his life the much greater mystery which belongs to the simple.' By and large, my biographical preference has been for a straightforward (I won't say simple) chronological narrative rather than a series of thematic chapters.

And so, this biography is divided into three major sections. These large sections deal successively with three subjects associated with three themes: adolescence and ambition, marriage and money, paternity and poetry.

I like, too, the unfashionable Victorian biographical convention of 'Life and Letters'. Much of this book is based on the correspondence of Robert and Elizabeth Browning, from which I have quoted lengthily and freely. Where either of them have written personally, or their words have been otherwise recorded by others, I have often preferred to quote them directly rather than make my own paraphrase. Their own voices are important — the tone, the vocabulary, the tempo of the sentences, the entire texture of their poetry, letters, and recorded conversation: all contribute to our understanding of character. The Brownings' letters are not referenced to the various collections in which they have appeared over the years, since chronological publication of their complete collected correspondence is currently in progress. All dated letters will finally be found there in their proper place.

My reliance on previous biographical materials is deliberate. Far from studiously avoiding them, I have sedulously pillaged them. Biographies are a legitimate secondary source just as much as the first-hand memoirs of those who once saw Shelley, Browning, or any other poet plain and formed an impression that they set down in words or pictures for posterity. It might be argued that a scrupulous biographer who is familiar with all the details of his or her subject's life may indeed be better informed as to the subject's character than those friends and enemies who knew him in his outward aspect but were less intimately acquainted with his private life. An enemy of Browning's, Lady Ashburton, is a case in point. She formed a view of a Miss Gabriel that proved to be wrong. Lady Ashburton, to her credit, thereupon fell to wondering that two views of Miss Gabriel's character could be so contrary. As a starting-point for biography, her surprised surmise could hardly be bettered. Her latterly-held opinion of Robert Browning could have benefited from some similar consideration of his contrarieties.

'A Poet', wrote John Keats, 'is the most unpoetical of anything in existence; because he has no Identity — he is continually informing and filling some other Body.'[2] This remark, though referring to poets in general, seems to justify the view of Henry James and others that

Robert Browning the public personality and Robert Browning the private poet were two distinct personalities. When the biographer stops to point to an image or a word that is apparently autobiographical (or at least seems open to a subjective interpretation), it is because biography imposes a structure and perceives a coherence that the subject himself cannot fully be aware of. The literary biographer neither need be completely *contre* Sainte-Beuve, nor feel officiously obliged to seek biographical meaning in a text. And yet, of course, Robert Browning is one man, not a series of discrete *doppelgängers* inhabiting parallel universes. To quote Joseph Brodsky again, 'every work of art, be it a poem or a cupola, is understandably a self-portrait of its author . . . a lyrical hero is invariably an author's self-projection . . . The author . . . is a critic of his century; but he is a part of this century also. So his criticism of it nearly always is self-criticism as well, and this is what imparts to his voice . . . its lyrical poise. If you think that there are other recipes for successful poetic operation, you are in for oblivion.'[3]

I have avoided, so far as possible, attributing feelings to Browning or anyone else that they are not known to have felt. I have tried to suppose no emotions that are not supported by the statement of anyone who experienced them personally or observed them in others and interpreted their effects. I have stuck so far as possible to the facts insofar as they are known and can be supported, if not ideally by first-hand sources, at least credibly by reliable hearsay; and — where facts fail and supposition supersedes — by creditable biographical consensus and, in the last resort, my own fallible judgement.

Nevertheless, and despite all best intentions, biography is a form of fiction, and successive biographies create, rather like the monologuists in *The Ring and the Book*, a palimpsest of their subject. Like a Platonic symposium, all the guests at the feast will have their own ideas to propound. A biography, like a novel, tells a story. It contains a principal subject, subsidiary characters, a plot (in the form, normally, of a more or less chronological narrative), and subplots, and it unfolds over a certain period of time in various locations. It has a beginning, a middle, and an end, however much these elements may be creatively juggled. That the biographer is not his subject is the point at which the narrative takes on the aspect of fiction. The subject lived his or her life for, say, threescore years and ten, and — allowing for various forms of psychological self-defence — he or she may be regarded as the first authority for that life. Autobiography, however, is generally even more fiction than biography, even less trustworthy than biography. If we put not our faith in princes or poets, even less should we trust an apologist *pro vita sua*. As Jeanette Winterson puts it, 'autobiography is art and lies'.

Poetry, of course, may be said to be art and truth. The poet, even if he lies in every other aspect of his life, cannot consistently lie in his work. Robert Browning's poetry tells the truth not only about Robert Browning, but about the men and women he loved and the common humanity he shared with them and sought to understand. Says Chesterton, with an irresistible conviction and authority:

> Every one on this earth should believe, amid whatever madness or moral failure, that his life and temperament have some object on the earth. Every one on this earth should believe that he has something to give to the world which cannot otherwise be given. Every one should, for the good of men and the saving of his own soul, believe that it is possible, even if we are the enemies of the human race, to be the friends of God . . . With Browning's knaves we have always this eternal interest, that they are real somewhere, and may at any moment begin to speak poetry.

Lacking the vanity and hypocrisy of the age, Browning was blind to no one, and to the best and the worst of them in their inarticulacy he gave the voice of his own understanding, compassion, and love as few had done so sincerely since Chaucer, Shakespeare, and Burns.

PART 1

ROBERT AND THE BROWNINGS

1812–1846

ONLY ONE THING IS known for certain about the appearance of Sarah Anna Browning, wife of Robert Browning and mother of Robert and Sarianna Browning: she had a notably square head. Which is to say, its uncommon squareness was noted by Alfred Domett, a young man sufficiently serious as to become briefly, in his maturity, Prime Minister of New Zealand and sometime epic poet. Mr Domett, getting on in years, conscientiously committed this observation to his journal on 30 April 1878: 'I remembered their mother about 40 years before (say 1838), who had, I used to think, the squarest head and forehead I almost ever saw in a human being, putting me in mind, absurdly enough no doubt of a tea-chest or tea-caddy.'[1]

Many people have square heads. There is little enough to be interpreted from this characteristic, though to some minds a square head may naturally imply sturdy common sense and a regular attitude to life. A good square head is commonly viewed as virtually a guarantee of correct behaviour and a restrained attitude towards vanity and frivolity. Lombroso's forensic art of physiognomy being now just as discredited as palmistry or phrenology, we may turn with more confidence to Thomas Carlyle's shrewd and succinct assessment of Mrs Browning as being 'the type of a Scottish gentlewoman'.[2] The phrase is evocative enough for those who, like Carlyle, have enjoyed some personal experience and acquired some understanding at first hand of the culture that has bred and refined the Scottish gentlewoman over the generations. She is a woman to be reckoned with. Since we know nothing but bromides and pleasing praises of Sarah Anna's temperament beyond what may be conjectured, particularly from Carlyle's brief but telling phrase, we may take it that she was quieter and more phlegmatic than Jane Welsh, Carlyle's own Scottish gentlewoman wife whose verbal flyting could generally be relied upon to rattle the teeth and teacups of visitors to Carlyle's London house in Cheyne Walk.

Mrs Browning's father was German. Her grandfather is said to have been a Hamburg merchant whose son William is generally agreed to have become, in a small way, a ship owner in Dundee and to have married a Scotswoman. She was born Sarah Anna Wiedemann in Scotland, in the early 1770s, and while still a girl came south with her sister Christiana to lodge with an uncle in Camberwell. Her history before marriage is not known to have been remarkable; after marriage it was not notably dramatic. There is only the amplest evidence that she was worthily devoted to her hearth, garden, husband, and children.

Mrs Browning's head so fascinated Alfred Domett that he continued to refer to it in a domestic anecdote agreeably designed to emphasize the affection that existed between mother and son: 'On one occasion, in the act of tossing a little roll of music from the table to the piano, he thought it had touched her head in passing her, and I remember how he ran to her to apologise and caress her, though I think she had not felt it.'[3] Sarah Anna Browning's head was at least tenderly regarded and respected by Robert, her son, who — since he has left no description of it to posterity in prose or poetry — either refrained from disobliging comment or regarded its shape as in no respect unusual.

Mrs Browning was a Dissenter; her creed was Nonconformist, a somewhat austere faith that partook of no sacraments and reprobated ritual. She — and, nine years into their marriage, her husband — adhered to the Congregational Church, the chapel in York Street, Walworth, which the Browning family attended regularly to hear the preaching of the incumbent, the Revd George Clayton, characterized in the *British Weekly* of 20 December 1889 as one who 'combined the character of a saint, a dancing master, and an orthodox eighteenth-century theologian in about equal proportions'.[4] Before professing Congregationalism, she had been brought up — said Sarianna, her daughter, to Mrs Alexandra Sutherland Orr — in the Church of Scotland. One of the books that is recorded as a gift from Mrs Browning to her son is an anthology of sermons, inscribed by him on the flyleaf as a treasured possession and fond remembrance of his mother. As a token of maternal concern for her son's spiritual welfare it was perfectly appropriate, and might perhaps have been intended as a modest counterweight to the large and eclectic library of books — six thousand volumes, more or less — that her husband had collected, continued to collect, and through which her precocious son was presently and diligently reading his way.

Sarah Anna Browning doubtless had cause to attempt to concentrate young Robert's mind more narrowly. He had begun with a rather sensational anthology, Nathaniel Wanley's *Wonders of the Little World*, published in 1678, and sooner rather than later would inevitably discover dictionaries and encyclopedias, those seemingly innocent repositories of dry definitions and sober facts but which are, in truth, a maze of conceits and confusions, of broad thoroughfares and frustrating *cul-de-sacs* from which the imaginative mind, once entered, will find no exit and never in a lifetime penetrate to the centre.

But Mrs Browning's head, square with religion and good intentions, was very liable to be turned by kindly feeling towards her son and poetry. Robert, in 1826, had already come across *Miscellaneous Poems*, a copy of Shelley's best works, published by William Benbow of High Holborn, unblushingly pirated from Mrs Shelley's edition of her husband's *Posthumous Poems*. This volume was presented to him by a cousin, James Silverthorne, and he was eager for a more reliable, authoritative edition. Having made inquiries of the *Literary Gazette* as to where they might be obtained, Robert requested the poems of Shelley as a birthday present.[5] Mrs Browning may be pictured putting on her gloves, setting her bonnet squarely on her head and proceeding to Vere Street. There, at the premises of C. & J. Ollier, booksellers, she purchased the complete works of the poet, including the Pisa edition of *Adonais* in a purple paper cover and *Epipsychidion*. None of them had exhausted their first editions save *The Cenci*, which had achieved a second edition.

On advice, as being in somewhat the same poetic spirit as the works of the late Percy Bysshe Shelley who had died tragically in a boating accident in Italy but three years before, Sarah Anna Browning added to her order three volumes of the poetry of the late John Keats, who had died, also tragically young, in Rome in 1821. Her arms encumbered with the books of these two neglected poets, her head quite innocent of the effect they would have, she returned home to present them to her son. There being not much call for the poetry of Shelley and Keats at this time, it had taken some effort to obtain their works. Bibliophiles, wrote Edmund Gosse in 1881 in the December issue of the *Century Magazine*, turn almost dazed at the thought of these prizes picked up by the unconscious lady.

The Browning family belonged, remarked G. K. Chesterton, 'to the solid and educated middle-class which is interested in letters, but not ambitious in them, the class to which poetry is a luxury, but not a necessity'.[6] Robert Browning senior, husband to Sarah Anna Wiede-mann, was certainly educated, undeniably middle-class, and interested in literature not so much for its own sake — though he was more literate and widely read, it may safely be said, than many of his colleagues at the Bank of England — but more from the point of view of bibliophily and learning. There was always another book to be sought and set on a shelf. The house in Camberwell was full of them.

Literature and learning are not precisely the same thing, and Mr Browning senior, according to the testimony of Mr Domett, was accus-tomed to speak of his son '"as beyond him"' — alluding to his Para-celsuses and Sordellos; though I fancy he altered his tone on this subject very much at a later period'.[7] Poetry safely clapped between purple paper covers is one thing, poets are quite another — and an experimental, modern poet within the confines of one's own family is bound to be unsettling to a traditionalist, try as he may to comprehend, proud as he may be of completed and published effort. Mr Browning senior may initially have been more pleased with the fact of his son's work being printed and bound and placed in its proper place on his bookshelves than with the perplexing contents of the books themselves.

That said, introductory notes by Reuben Browning to a small volume of sketches by Robert Browning senior refer kindly to his step-brother's bibliophily and store of learning — however much at random and magpie-like it may have been acquired: 'The love of reading attracted him by sympathy to books: old books were his delight, and by his continual search after them he not only knew all the old books-stalls in London, but their contents, and if any scarce work were spoken of, he could tell forthwith where a copy of it might be had. Nay, he would even describe in what part of the shop it was placed, and the price likely to be asked for it.'[8] So, 'with the scent of a hound and the snap of a bull-dog' for an old or rare book, Mr Browning acquired learning and a library.

'Thus his own library became his treasure,' remarked Reuben Browning. 'His books, however, were confessedly not remarkable for costly binding, but for their rarity or for interesting remarks he had to make on most of them; and his memory was so good that not infrequently, when a conversation at his table had reference to any particular subject, has he quietly left the room and in the dark, from a thousand volumes in his library, brought two or three illustrations of the point under discussion.' The point under discussion, however esoteric, would rarely defeat Mr Browning senior's search for an apposite reference: 'His wonderful store of information,' wrote Reuben Browning, 'might really be compared to an inexhaustible mine. It comprised not merely a thorough scholastic outline of the world, but the critical points of ancient and modern history, the lore of the Middle Ages, all political combinations of parties, their descriptions and consequences; and especially the lives of the poets and painters, concerning whom he ever had to communicate some interesting anecdote not generally known.'

A portrait of Mr Browning senior, preserved throughout their lives by his children, was 'blue-eyed and "fresh-coloured"' and, attested Mr Browning's daughter Sarianna to Alfred Domett, the man himself 'had not an unsound tooth in his head' when he died at the age of 84. In his youth he had been a vigorous sportsman, afflicted only by sore throats and a minor liver complaint. Altogether, his general health and recuperative powers were strongly marked. Alfred Domett took these facts of paternal health and heredity seriously, on the ground that 'they have their significance with reference to the physical constitution of their son, the poet; which goes so far as to make up what is called "genius"'.

So far as Domett was aware, no cloud shadowed the home life of the Brownings: 'Altogether, father, mother, only son and only daughter formed a most suited, harmonious and intellectual family, as appeared to me.' Mr Browning senior, to Domett, was not often a physically significant presence: his friend's father, 'of whom I did not see much, seemed in my recollection, what I should be inclined to call a dry adust [sic] undersized man; rather reserved; fond particularly of old engravings, of which I believe he had a choice collection.' Mr Browning took pleasure not only in collecting pictures but also in making them. He was liable to sketch the heads of his colleagues and visitors to the Bank of England, a habit so much encouraged by his employers that hundreds of these whiskered heads survive to this day.

Mr Browning also wrote poetry of a traditional kind. His son in later life praised his father's verses to Edmund Gosse, declaring 'that his father had more true poetic genius than he has'. Gosse, taking this with scarcely too gross a pinch of salt and allowing for filial piety, kindly but rigorously comments that, 'Of course the world at large will answer, "By their fruits shall ye know them," and of palpable fruit in the way of published verse the elder Mr Browning has nothing to show.' The elder Browning's poetic taste was more or less exclusively for double or triple rhyme, and especially for the heroic couplet, which he employed with 'force and fluency'. Gosse goes on to quote the more celebrated son describing the moral and stylistic vein of the father's vigorous verses 'as that of a Pope born out of due time'. Mr Browning had been a great classicist and a lover of eighteenth-century literature, the poetry of that period having achieved, in his estimation, its finest flowering in the work of Alexander Pope. Though his son's early poetry, *Pauline* and *Paracelsus*, confounded him, Mr Browning senior forgave the otherwise impenetrable *Sordello* because — says William Sharp in his *Life of Browning* — 'it was written in rhymed couplets'.

Pope, according to the critic Mark Pattison, 'was very industrious, and had read a vast number of books, yet he was very ignorant; that is, of everything but the one thing which he laboured with all his might to acquire, the art of happy expression. He read books to find ready-made images and to feel for the best collocations of words. His memory was a magazine of epithets and synonyms, and pretty turns of language.' Mr Browning senior's satirical portraits of friends and colleagues are said to be very Pope-ish in expression, quick sketches reminiscent in their style of Pope's rhetorical (often oratorical) couplets. It is further said that he was incapable of portraying anyone other than as a grotesque. The sketch of his wife is certainly none too flattering.

This domestic, middle-class idyll, quiet-flowing and given muted colour by art, poetry, music, bibliophily and decent religious observances, was touching to Alfred Domett, who recollected his serene memories of the Browning family in the tranquillity that fell upon him after leaving public office in New Zealand and returning to London to look up an old friend now celebrated as an important poet and public figure.

Mr Browning, like his wife, became a Dissenter and a Nonconformist in middle life, though it had taken Sarah Anna Browning time and energy to persuade him from the Episcopal communion. In his youth, he had held principles and expressed opinions, uncompromisingly liberal, that had all but brought him to ruin — certainly had distanced him from the prospect of maintaining at least, perhaps increasing, the family fortune that derived from estates and commercial interests in the West Indies. His father, the first Robert Browning, had been born the eldest son in 1749 to Jane Morris of Cranborne, Dorset, wife to Thomas Browning who in 1760 had become landlord of Woodyates Inn, close to the Dorset-Wiltshire border, which he had held on a 99-year lease from the Earl of Shaftesbury. Thomas and Jane Browning produced five more children, three sons (one of whom died young) and two daughters.

Robert the First, as he may here be styled, was to become grandfather of the poet. He was recommended by Lord Shaftesbury for employment in the Bank of England, where he served for the whole of his working life, fifty years, from August 1769, when he would have been about the age of twenty, becoming Principal of the Bank Stock Office, a post of some considerable prestige which implied wide contact with influential financiers. This first Robert Browning was no man, merely, of balance sheets and bottom-polished trousers: at about the age of forty, he vigorously assisted, as a lieutenant in the Honourable Artillery Company, in the defence of the Bank of England during the Gordon Riots of 1780.

In 1778, he married Margaret Morris Tittle, a lady who had been born in the West Indies, reputedly a Creole (and said, by some, to have been darker than was then thought decent), by whom he sired three children — Robert, the eldest, being born on 6 July 1782 at Battersea. A second son, William, was born and died in 1784. A daughter, Margaret — who remained unmarried and lived quietly until her death in 1857 (or 1858, according to a descendant, Vivienne Browning) — was born in 1783. Nothing more is heard of Margaret, beyond a reference by Cyrus Mason, a Browning cousin, who in later life composed a memoir in which he wrote that 'Aunt Margaret was detected mysteriously crooning prophecies over her Nephew, behind a door at the house at Camberwell.'

The picture of an eccentric prophetess lurking at keyholes and singing the fortunes of the future poet is not conjured by any other biographer of Robert Browning. Cyrus Mason is not widely regarded as a reliable chronicler of Browning family history. He begins with his own self-aggrandizing agenda and sticks to it. His reputation is rather as a somewhat embittered relation who took the view that the poet Robert Browning and his admirers had paid inadequate attention and given insufficient credit to the more remote branches of the family. The contribution of the extended family to the poet's early education, he considered, had been cruelly overlooked and positively belittled by wilful neglect.

However, since the reference to Margaret Browning does exist, and since Margaret has otherwise vanished from biographical ken, a possible — rather than probable — explanation for this single recorded peculiarity of the poet's aunt is that she may have been simple-minded and thus kept in what her family may have regarded (not uncommonly at the time) as a decent, discreet seclusion. The extent to which they succeeded in containing any public embarrassment may — and it is no more than supposition — account for Margaret's virtually complete obscurity in a family history that has been otherwise largely revealed.

Margaret Morris Tittle Browning died in Camberwell in 1789, when Robert (who can be referred to as Robert the Second), her only remaining son, was seven years old. When Robert was twelve, his father remarried in April 1794. This second wife, Jane Smith, by whom he fathered nine more children, three sons, and six daughters, was but twenty-three at the time of her marriage in Chelsea to the 45-year-old Robert Browning the First. The difference of twenty-two years between husband and wife is said, specifically by Mrs Sutherland Orr, Robert Browning's official biographer, sister of the exotic Orientalist and painter Frederic Leighton, and a friend of the poet, to have resulted in the complete ascendancy of Jane Smith Browning over her husband. Besotted by, and doting upon, his young darling, he made no objection to Jane's relegation of a portrait (attributed to Wright of Derby) of his first wife to a garret on the basis that a man did not need two wives. One — the living — in this case proved perfectly sufficient.

The hard man of business and urban battle, the doughty Englishman

of Dorset stock, the soundly respectable man who annually read the
Bible and *Tom Jones* (both, probably, with equal religious attention),
the stout and severe man who lived more or less hale — despite the
affliction of gout — to the age of eighty-four, was easily subverted by
a woman whose gnawing jealousy of his first family extended from the
dead to the quick. Browning family tradition, says Vivienne Browning,
a family historian, also attributes a jealousy to Robert the First, naturally
anxious to retain the love and loyalty of his young wife against any
possible threat, actual or merely perceived in his imagination. Their
nine children, a substantial though not unusual number, may have been
conceived and borne as much in response to jealousy, doubt, and fear
as in expression of any softer feelings.

Jane Browning's alleged ill-will towards Robert the Second, Robert
the First's son by his previous marriage to Margaret Tittle, was not
appeased by the young man's independence, financial or intellectual.
He had inherited a small income from an uncle, his mother's brother,
and proposed to apply it to a university education for himself. Jane,
supposedly on the ground that there were insufficient funds to send her
own sons to university, opposed her stepson's ambition. Then, too,
there was some irritation that Robert the Second wished to be an artist
and showed some talent for the calling. Robert the First — says Mrs
Orr — turned away disgustedly when Robert the Second showed his
first completed picture to his father. The household was plainly a
domestic arena of seething discontents, jealous insecurities, envious
stratagems, entrenched positions on every front, and sniper fire from
every corner of every room.

Margaret Tittle had left property in the West Indies, and it was
Robert the First's intention that their son should proceed, at the age of
nineteen, to St Kitts to manage the family estates, which were worked
by slave labour. He may have been glad enough to go, to remove himself
as far as possible from his father and stepmother. In the event, he lasted
only a year in the West Indies before returning to London, emotionally
bruised by his experience of the degrading conditions under which
slaves laboured on the sugar plantations. Robert the Second's reasonable
expectation was that he might inherit perhaps not all, but at least a
substantial proportion of his mother's property, had he not 'conceived
such a hatred of the slave system'.

Mrs Sutherland Orr states: 'One of the experiences which disgusted him with St Kitts was the frustration by its authorities of an attempt he was making to teach a negro boy to read, and the understanding that all such educative action was prohibited.' For a man who, from his earliest years, was wholly devoted to books, art, anything that nourished and encouraged inquiry and intellect, the spiritual repression of mind and soul as much — perhaps more than — physical repression of bodily freedom, must have seemed an act of institutionalized criminality and personal inhumanity by the properly constituted authorities. He could not morally consider himself party to, or representative of, such a system.

Certainly as a result of the apparent lily-livered liberalism of his son and his shocking, incomprehensible disregard for the propriety of profit, conjecturally also on account of a profound unease about maintaining the affection and loyalty of his young wife — there were only ten years between stepmother Jane and her stepson — Robert the First fell into a passionate and powerful rage that he sustained for many years. Robert Browning, the grandson and son of the protagonists of this quarrel, did not learn the details of the family rupture until 25 August 1846, when his mother finally confided the circumstances of nigh on half a century before.

'If we are poor,' wrote Robert Browning the Third the next day to Elizabeth Barrett, 'it is to my father's infinite glory, who, as my mother told me last night, as we sate alone, "conceived such a hatred to the slave-system in the West Indies," (where his mother was born, who died in his infancy,) that he relinquished every prospect, — supported himself, while there, in some other capacity, and came back, while yet a boy, to his father's profound astonishment and rage — one proof of which was, that when he heard that his son was a suitor to her, my mother — he benevolently waited on her Uncle to assure him that his niece "would be thrown away on a man so evidently born to be hanged"! — those were his very words. My father on his return, had the intention of devoting himself to art, for which he had many qualifications and abundant love — but the quarrel with his father, — who married again and continued to hate him till a few years before his death, — induced him to go at once and consume his life after a fashion he always detested. You may fancy, I am not ashamed of him.'

As soon as Robert the Second achieved his majority, he was dunned by his father for restitution in full of all the expenses that Robert the First had laid out on him, and he was stripped of any inheritance from his mother, Margaret, whose fortune, at the time of her marriage, had not been settled upon her and thus had fallen under the control of her husband. These reactions so intimidated Robert the Second that he agreed to enter the Bank of England, his father's territory, as a clerk and to sublimate his love of books and sketching in ledgers and ink. In November 1803, four months after his twenty-first birthday, he began his long, complaisant, not necessarily unhappy servitude of fifty years as a bank clerk in Threadneedle Street.

A little over seven years later, at Camberwell on 19 February 1811, in the teeth of his father's opposition, Robert the Second married Sarah Anna Wiedemann, whose uncle evidently disregarded Robert the First's predictions. She was then thirty-nine, ten years older than her husband and only one year younger than his stepmother Jane. They settled at 6 Southampton Street, Camberwell, where, on 7 May 1812, Sarah Anna Browning was delivered of a son, the third in the direct Browning line to be named Robert. Twenty months later, on 7 January 1814, their second child, called Sarah Anna after her mother, but known as Sarianna by her family and friends, was born.

William Sharp, in his *Life of Browning*, published in 1897, refers briskly and offhandedly to a third child, Clara. Nothing is known of Clara: it is possible she may have been stillborn or died immediately after birth. Mrs Orr never mentions the birth of a third child, and not even Cyrus Mason, the family member one would expect to seize eagerly upon the suppression of any reference to a Browning, suggests that more than two children were born to the Brownings. However, William Clyde DeVane, discussing Browning's 'Lines to the Memory of his Parents' in *A Browning Handbook*, states that 'The "child that never knew" Mrs Browning was a stillborn child who was to have been named Clara.' The poem containing this discreet reference was not printed until it appeared in F.G. Kenyon's *New Poems by Robert Browning*, published in 1914, and in the February issue, that same year, of the *Cornhill Magazine*. Vivienne Browning, in *My Browning Family Album*, published in 1992, declares that her grandmother (Elizabeth, a daughter of Reuben Browning, son of Jane, Robert the First's second wife) 'included a third baby — a girl — in the family tree', but Vivienne Browning 'cannot now find any evidence to support this'.

It is known that Sarah Anna Browning miscarried at least once. In a letter to his son Pen, the poet Robert Browning wrote on 25 January 1888 to condole with him and his wife Fannie on her miscarriage: 'Don't be disappointed at this first failure of your natural hopes — it may soon be repaired. Your dearest Mother experienced the same misfortune, at much about the same time after marriage: and it happened also to my own mother, before I was born.' Unless Sarah Anna's miscarriage occurred in a very late stage of pregnancy, it seems improbable that a miscarried child should have been given a name and regarded, in whatever terms, as a first-born — but natural parental sentiment may have prompted the Brownings to give their first daughter, who never drew breath, miscarried or stillborn, at least the dignity and memorial of a name.

The small, close-knit family moved house in 1824, though merely from 6 Southampton Street to another house (the number is not known) in the same street, where they remained until December 1840. Bereaved of his mother at the age of seven, repressed from the age of twelve by his father and stepmother, denied further education and frustrated in his principles and ambitions in his late teens, all but disinherited for failure to make a success of business and to close a moral eye to the inhumanity of slavery, set on a high stool and loaded with ledgers in his early twenties, it is hardly surprising that Robert the Second sought a little peace and quiet for avocations that had moderated into hobbies. He settled for a happy — perhaps undemanding — marriage to a peaceable, slightly older wife, and a tranquil bolt-hole in what was then, in the early nineteenth century, the semi-rural backwater of Camberwell.

His poverty, counted in monetary terms, was relative. His work in the Bank of England, never as elevated or responsible as Robert the First's, was nevertheless adequately paid, the hours were short and overtime, particularly the lucrative night watch, was paid at a higher rate. There was little or no managerial or official concern about the amount of paper, the number of pens, or the quantity of sealing wax used by Bank officials, and these materials were naturally regarded as lucrative perquisites that substantially bumped up the regular salary. Though Mrs

Orr admits this trade, she adds — somewhat severely — in a footnote: 'I have been told that, far from becoming careless in the use of these things from his practically unbounded command of them, he developed for them an almost superstitious reverence. He could never endure to see a scrap of writing-paper wasted.'

He could count on a regular salary of a little more than £300 a year, supplemented by generous rates of remuneration for extra duties and appropriate perks of office. He may have been deprived of any interest in his mother's estate, but his small income from his mother's brother, even after deductions from it by his father, continued to be a reliable annual resource. Over the years, Robert the Second acquired valuable specialist knowledge of pictures and books, and certainly, though he was no calculating businessman and willingly gave away many items from his collection, he occasionally — perhaps regularly — traded acquisitions and profited from serendipitous discoveries.

In the end, though it was a long time coming, Robert the First softened towards his eldest son. That he was not wholly implacable is testified by his will, made in 1819, two years before his retirement from the Bank: he left Robert the Second and Margaret ten pounds each for a ring. This may seem a paltry inheritance, but he took into account the fact that Robert and Margaret had inherited from 'their Uncle Tittle and Aunt Mill a much greater proportion than can be left to my other dear children'. He trusted 'they will not think I am deficient in love and regard to them'. As a token of reconciliation, the legacy to buy rings was a substantial olive branch.

It may be assumed that the patriarch Browning's temper had begun to abate before he made his will, and that the Brownings had resumed some form of comfortable, if cautious, communication until the old man's death. There is certainly some indication that Robert the First saw something of his grandchildren — the old man is said by Mrs Orr to have 'particularly dreaded' his lively grandson's 'vicinity to his afflicted foot', little boys and gout being clearly best kept far apart. After the death of Robert the First in 1833, stepmother Jane, then in her early sixties, moved south of the river from her house in Islington to Albert Terrace, just beyond the toll bar at New Cross. In the biography of Robert Browning published in 1910 by W. Hall Griffin and H.C. Minchin, it is said that the portrait of the first Mrs Browning, Margaret Tittle, had been retrieved from the Islington garret and was hung in her son's dining room.

The most familiar photograph of Robert the Second, taken — it looks like — in late middle age (though it is difficult to tell, since he is said to have retained a youthful appearance until late in life) shows the profile of a rather worried-looking man. A deep line creases from the nostril to just below the side of the mouth, which itself appears thin and turns down at the corner. The hair is white, neatly combed back over the forehead and bushy around the base of the ears. It is the picture of a doubtful man who looks slightly downward rather than straight ahead, as though he has no expectation of seeing, like The Lost Leader, 'Never glad confident morning again!'. He still bled, perhaps, from the wounds inflicted upon him as a child and young man: but if he did, he suffered in silence.

As some men for the rest of their lives do not care to talk about their experiences in war, so Robert the Second could never bring himself to talk about his bitter experiences in the West Indies: 'My father is tenderhearted to a fault,' wrote his son to Elizabeth Barrett on 27 August 1846. The poet's mother had confided some particulars to him three days before, but from his father he had got never a word: 'I have never known much more of those circumstances in his youth than I told you, in consequence of his invincible repugnance to allude to the matter — and I have a fancy to account for some peculiarities in him, which connects them with some abominable early experience. Thus, — if you question him about it, he shuts his eyes involuntarily and shows exactly the same marks of loathing that may be noticed if a piece of cruelty is mentioned . . . and the word "blood," even makes him change colour.'

These 'peculiarities' observed in his father by the youngest Browning did not go unremarked by others who, with less fancy than his son to seek an origin for them, were content to observe and to wonder at this marvellous man. Cyrus Mason, as an amateur historian of the Browning family, speaks specifically of Robert the Second's 'imaginative and eccentric brain'. It seems likely that he is not only confessing his own bewilderment, which becomes ever more apparent as his memoir proceeds, but a general incomprehension within the wider Browning family. Inevitably, mild eccentricities of character become magnified by family and friends otherwise at a loss to account for the somewhat detached life of a man who is for all practical, day-to-day intents and purposes a conscientious banker and responsible family man, but whose domestic and inner life, so far as it is penetrable by others, exhibits a marked degree of abstraction and commitment to matters that harder, squarer heads would not regard as immediately profitable in the conduct of everyday life — 'Robert's incessant study of subjects perfectly useless in Banking business', to quote Cyrus Mason. Such minor aberrations are naturally inflated in the remembrance and the retelling, particularly when it becomes evident that such a man has become, indirectly, an object of interest and attention through efforts made by admirers or detractors to trace the early influences upon his remarkable son.

Mrs Orr tells us that Robert the Second, when he in turn became a grandfather, taught his grandson elementary anatomy, impressing upon young Pen Browning 'the names and position of the principal bones of the human body'. Cyrus Mason adds considerably to this blameless, indeed worthy, anecdote by claiming that 'Uncle Robert became so absorbed in his anatomical studies that he conveyed objects for dissection into the Bank of England; on one occasion a dead rat was kept for so long a time in his office desk, awaiting dissection, that his fellow clerks were compelled to apply to their chief to have it removed! The study of anatomy became so seductive that on the day Uncle Robert was married, he disappeared mysteriously after the ceremony and was discovered ... busily engaged dissecting a duck, oblivious of the fact that a wife and wedding guests were reduced to a state of perplexity by his unexplained absence.'

This story has the air of invention by a fabulist — Mr Browning, being a little peckish, might merely have been carving a duck — and earlier echoes of preoccupied, enthusiastic amateur morbid anatomists recur to the mind (in the annals of Scottish eccentricity, there are several instances of notable absence of mind of more or less this nature at wedding feasts); there is even a faint, ludicrous hint of Francis Bacon fatally catching a cold while stuffing a chicken with snow by the roadside in an early endeavour to discover the principles of refrigeration. The patronizing tone is one of barely-tolerant amusement, of reminiscence dressed up with a dry chuckle, of family anecdote become fanciful.

'Uncle Robert', in short, was held — more or less exasperatedly — to be something of a whimsical character. His seeming inclination to desert the ceremonies and commonplace observances of 'real life', of family life, for abstruse, even esoteric researches — all those books! — may be exaggerated, but the metamorphosis of memory into myth is generally achieved through the medium of an actuality. The pearl of fiction accretes around a grain of actuality, and in this case the attitudes and behaviour of Robert Browning, father of the poet, achieve a relevance in respect of his attitude towards the education, intellectual liberty, and the vocation of his son.

Robert the Second, frustrated in his own creative ambitions, did not discourage his son from conducting his life along lines that he himself had been denied. Cyrus Mason declares that, from the beginning, the 'arranged destiny' of Robert and Sarah Anna's son was to be a poet. His life and career, says Mason, were planned from the cot. The infant Robert's 'swaddling clothes were wrapped around his little body with a poetic consideration', his father rocked his cradle rhythmically, his Aunt Margaret 'prophecied [sic] in her dark mysterious manner his brilliant future', and women lulled him to sleep with whispered words of poetry. Whether unconsciously or by design, Mason here introduces the fairy-story image of the good or bad fairy godmothers conferring gifts more or less useful.

Allowing for the Brothers Grimm or Perrault quality of these images conjured by Mason, and his patent intention in writing his memoir to arrogate a substantial proportion of the credit for the infant Robert's development to a wider family circle of Brownings, there is a nub of truth in his assertion. There is some dispute as to how far it may be credited, of course. Mrs Orr merely states that the infant Robert showed a precocious aptitude for poetry: 'It has often been told how he extemporised verse aloud while walking round and round the dining room table supporting himself by his hands, when he was still so small that his head was scarcely above it.' Some children naturally sing, some dance, some draw little pictures and some declaim nonsense verse or nursery rhymes: Robert Browning invented his own childish verses. Doting family relations would naturally exclaim over his prospects as a great poet and genially encourage the conceit.

That he was raised from birth as — or specifically to become — a poet is improbable: more unlikely still is the assertion that he was raised 'poetically' by parents whose inclinations in the normal run of things were kindly and indulgent in terms of stimulating their son's natural and lively intelligence, but not inherently fanciful: they were respectably pious, middle-class, somewhat matter-of-fact citizens of no more and no less distinction than others of their time, place, and type. They were distinctive enough to those who loved them or had cause to consider them, but they were not — in the usual meaning of the word — distinguished.

They were what G.K. Chesterton calls 'simply a typical Camberwell family' after he sensibly dismisses as largely irrelevant to immediate Browning biography all red herrings such as the alleged *pied-noir* origins of Margaret Tittle (which may have been true), a supposed Jewish strain in the Browning family (now discounted, but which would have been a matter of extreme interest to the poet), and the suggestion, from the fact that Browning and his father used a ring-seal with a coat of arms, of an aristocratic origin dating from the Middle Ages for the family name, if not for the family itself.

Nevertheless, in thrall to the romance of pedigree and the benefits that may be derived from a selective use of genealogy, Cyrus Mason's memoir is motivated not only by a gnawing ambition to associate himself and his kinsfolk more closely with the poet Browning and to aggrandize himself by the connection, but also, vitally, to give the lie to the 'monstrous fabrication' by F.J. Furnivall, a devoted admirer and scholar of the poet Browning, that the Brownings descended from the servant class, very likely from a footman, later butler, to the Bankes family at Corfe Castle before becoming innkeepers. Cyrus Mason claims to trace the Browning lineage back unto the remotest generations — at least into the fourteenth century — to disprove any stigma of low birth. He even manages to infer, from some eighteenth-century holograph family documents, the high cost of binding some family books, the good quality of the ink used, and, from the evidence of 'fine bold writing', a prosperous, educated, literary ancestry. These elaborate researches were of the greatest possible interest to Cyrus Mason: they consumed his time, consoled his soul, confirmed his pride, and confounded cavilling critics.

Cyrus Mason was satisfied with his work, and it is to his modest credit that he has amply satisfied everyone else, most of whom are now content to acknowledge this monument to genealogical archaeology and pass more quickly than is entirely respectful to more immediate matters.

We consult Mason's book much as visitors to an exhibition browse speedily through the well-researched but earnest expository notes at the entrance and hurry inside to get to the interesting main exhibit. 'For the great central and solid fact,' declared G. K. Chesterton, 'which these heraldic speculations tend inevitably to veil and confuse, is that Browning was a thoroughly typical Englishman of the middle class.' Allowing, naturally, for his mother's Scottish-German parentage and his grandmother's Creole connection, Robert Browning was certainly brought up as a middle-class Englishman.

Chesterton's argument, scything decisively through the tangled undergrowth of genealogy and the rank weeds of heterogeneous heredity, becomes a spirited, romantic peroration, grandly swelling as he praises Robert Browning's genius to the heights, then dropping bathetically back as he regularly nails it to the ground by constantly reminding us that Browning was 'an Englishman of the middle class'; until, finally, he sweeps to his breathtaking and irresistible conclusion that Browning 'piled up the fantastic towers of his imagination until they eclipsed the planets; but the plan of the foundation on which he built was always the plan of an honest English house in Camberwell. He abandoned, with a ceaseless intellectual ambition, every one of the convictions of his class; but he carried its prejudices into eternity.'

Robert Browning's mother was no bluestocking: she was not herself literary, nor was she inclined to draw or paint in water-colours. Her husband did enough book collecting and sketching already. Though she had a considerable taste for music and is said to have been an accomplished pianist (Beethoven's sonatas, Avison's marches, and Gaelic laments are cited as belonging to her repertoire), she was very likely no more than ordinarily competent on a piano, though her technique was evidently infused with fine romantic feeling. Sarah Anna Browning tended her flower garden (Cyrus Mason remarks upon 'the garden, Aunt Robert's roses, that wicket gate the Robert Browning family used by favor, opening for them a ready way to wander in the then beautiful meadows to reach the Dulwich woods, the College and gallery') and otherwise occupied herself, day by day, with domestic matters relating to her largely self-contained, self-sufficient family. Other biographers beg to differ when Mrs Orr tells us that Mrs Browning 'had nothing of the artist about her'. In contrast to her husband, she produced nothing artistic or creative, but partisans speak warmly of her tender interest in music and romantic poetry. She possessed at least an artistic sensibility.

Mrs Orr remarks, cursorily but not disparagingly: 'Little need be said about the poet's mother', the implication — quite wrong — being that there was little to be said. Her son's devotion to Sarah Anna was very marked: habitually, when he sat beside her, Robert would like to put his arm around her waist. When she died in early 1849, he beatified her by describing her as 'a divine woman'. Most biographers and others interested in the poet Browning make a point of the empathetic feeling that developed between mother and son: when Sarah Anna Browning was laid low with headaches, her son dreadfully suffered sympathetic pains. 'The circumstances of his death recalled that of his mother,' says Mrs Orr, and adds, however 'it might sound grotesque', that 'only a delicate woman could have been the mother of Robert Browning'.

She was certainly religious, and none doubted that her place in heaven had long been marked and secured by her narrow piety, commonsense good nature, and her stoical suffering of physical ailments. Sarah Anna Browning endured debilitating, painful headaches, severe as migraines (which indeed they may have been). In contrast to her vigorously hale husband, she is portrayed by Mrs Orr as 'a delicate woman, very anaemic during her later years, and a martyr to neuralgia which was perhaps a symptom of this condition'.

Robert, her son, was not so delicate in health or attitude. He established an early reputation not only for mental precocity but vocal and physically boisterous expression of it. In modern times, his vigour and fearlessness, his restlessness and temper, might worry some as verging on hyperactivity. 'He clamoured for occupation as soon as he could speak,' says Mrs Orr and, though admitting that 'his energies were of course destructive till they had found their proper outlet', she discovers no inherent vice in the child: 'we do not hear of his having destroyed anything for the mere sake of doing so'. A taste for lively spectacle rather than wilful incendiarism is adduced as the motive for Robert's 'putting a handsome Brussels lace veil of his mother's into the fire' and excusing himself with the words, 'a pretty blaze, mamma' (rendered as 'a pitty baze' by Mrs Orr, prefiguring the lisping baby-talk that so rejoiced the ears of the poet and his wife when their own son, Pen, first began to speak).

To quiet the boy, Sarah Anna Browning's best resource was to sit him on her knees, holding him in a firm grip, and to engage his attention with stories — 'doubtless Bible stories', says Mrs Orr, as a tribute not only to Mrs Browning's natural piety, her vocation as a Sunday School teacher, and her subscription to the London Missionary Society but also, no doubt, to the improving effect of religion in general, Nonconformism in particular, and its associated morality. If, as Cyrus Mason suggests, Robert was raised to be a poet, quiet introspection was not a notable characteristic of his infancy — though music (he liked to listen to his mother play the piano and would beg her to keep up the performance) and religion (Sarah Anna Browning could curb her son's arrogance until quite late in his life by pointing out the very real peril and lively retribution awaiting those who failed in Christian charity) could soothe the savage child and bind them together, mother and son, in a delicate balance of love and apprehension. Maternal indulgence, too, was a reliable ploy: Robert could be induced to swallow unpleasant medicine so long as he was given a toad which Mrs Browning, holding a parasol over her head, obligingly searched for in her strawberry bed — a memory of childhood that never faded in her son's recollection.

A recollection of his mother's garden very likely informs the idyllic first section — 'The Flower's Name' — of the poem 'Garden-Fancies', a revised version of which was included in *Dramatic Romances and Lyrics*, published in 1845:

> Here's the garden she walked across,
>   Arm in my arm, such a short while since:
> Hark, now I push its wicket, the moss
>   Hinders the hinges and makes them wince!
> She must have reached this shrub ere she turned,
>   As back with that murmur the wicket swung;
> For she laid the poor snail, my chance foot spurned,
>   To feed and forget it the leaves among.[9]

As she walks with little Robert through her garden, talking to him, Sarah Anna Browning's gown brushes against a bush or hedge of box. She stops, hushes her words, and points out 'a moth on the milk-white phlox'. Here roses, there rock plants, elsewhere a particular flower with a 'soft meandering Spanish name' that inspires an ambition in the boy to learn Spanish 'Only for that slow sweet name's sake'. Above all, the roses 'ranged in valiant row' where Sarah Anna always pauses —

> . . . for she lingers
> There like sunshine over the ground
> And ever I see her soft white fingers
> Searching after the bud she found.[10]

There are any number of anecdotes that attest to a happy childhood and none that imply any serious cause for parental or official reprobation — saving only the exasperation of the Revd George Clayton who, in the course of a church service, had cause to admonish 'for restlessness and inattention Master Robert Browning'. The boy had been reduced by impatience to gnawing on a pew.

The question of Robert the Third's education was settled when his head became filled with so much random information that it increased what Mrs Orr describes as his 'turbulent activity' and it was thought desirable that he should be off-loaded for an hour or two every day into the care of a 'lady of reduced fortunes' who kept a dame school or local kindergarten. There, Robert's precociousness so dispirited the mothers of the other children in the school, who reckoned that Robert was getting all the poor lady's attention to the disadvantage of their own dullard sons, that they complained and demanded his removal. Thereafter, until the age of eight or nine, Robert enjoyed the advantages of a home education. His mother mostly took care of his moral, musical, and religious education, his father fired up his imagination with his own squirrelled store of learning and his inspired, fanciful methods of imparting it.

Robert the Second, thoroughly versed in the Greek poets, is conjured irresistibly in his son's poetic memory: the poem 'Development', first published in *Asolando*, probably dates from 1888 or 1889, and is often quoted to illustrate Browning's first encounter with Homer in 1817 or thereabouts.

> My Father was a scholar and knew Greek.
> When I was five years old, I asked him once
> 'What do you read about?'
>   'The siege of Troy.'

'What is a siege and what is Troy?'
                                   Whereat
He piled up chairs and tables for a town,
Set me a-top for Priam, called our cat
— Helen, enticed away from home (he said)
By wicked Paris, who couched somewhere close
Under the footstool, being cowardly,
But whom — since she was worth the pains, poor
    puss —
Towzer and Tray, — our dogs, the Atreidai, — sought
By taking Troy to get possession of
— Always when great Achilles ceased to sulk,
(My pony in the stable) — forth would prance
And put to flight Hector — our page boy's self.

Adds Browning,

This taught me who was who and what was what:
So far I rightly understood the case
At five years old:

And when, after two or three years, the game of Troy's siege had become familiar,

My Father came upon our make-believe.
'How would you like to read yourself the tale
Properly told, of which I gave you first
Merely such notion as a boy could bear?'

whereupon, at about the age of eight, Robert the Third opened Pope's translation of *The Iliad* and

So I ran through Pope,
Enjoyed the tale, what history so true?
Attacked my Primer, duly drudged,
Grew fitter thus for what was promised next —
The very thing itself, the actual words,

in Greek by the age of twelve. Thereafter, for a lifetime, there was no end to Homer and Greek and the worm casts of scholarship, the dream-destroying detritus of peckers through dust and texts, winnowers of grain from chaff, who tumbled the towers of Ilium more surely to rock and sand than the hot force of *vir et armis*, desiccating the blood of heroes and giving the lie at Hell's Gate to Hector's love for his wife.

'Development' raises questions as to whether Robert the Second was to blame for encouraging his son's learning through play and — strictly speaking — falsehood rather than, in Gradgrind fashion, sticking strictly to the facts:

> That is — he might have put into my hand
> The 'Ethics'? In translation, if you please,
> Exact, no pretty lying that improves
> To suit the modern taste: no more — no less —
> The 'Ethics'.

In no mistrustful mind of dry-as-dust nonagenarian scholarship, unburdened by the *Ethics*, bubbling with guiltless, childlike nine-year-old innocence of any distinction between accredited reality and mythological falsehood, between truth-to-fact and truth-to-fiction, Robert was sent to school.

Browning's biographers can become thoroughly intoxicated in the well-stocked cellar of fine vintage learning that their subject laid down from his earliest years and drew upon in draughts for the rest of his working life as a poet. He read everything and 'could forget nothing' — except, as he claimed later, 'names and the date of the Battle of Waterloo'. The boy's virtual self-education at home rather than his formal schooling informed a lifetime's poetry and play-writing. School was the least of it — a pretty perfunctory performance lasting only some five or six years. Robert boarded, from Mondays to Fridays, with the Misses Ready, who with their brother, the Revd Thomas Ready, kept an elementary school for boys at number 77 Queen's Road, Peckham.[11] It was reputedly the best school in the neighbourhood, highly regarded both in respect of pedagogy and piety. Mr Ready instructed the older boys while the younger boys, up to the age of ten, were physically and spiritually improved by the two Ready sisters, who sang the hymns of Isaac Watts as they oiled and brushed out the hair and brushed up the moral fibre of their charges. Robert attended the Ready school until he was fourteen.

His distress at leaving his mother was more than he thought he could bear. And what was it for, this dolorous separation? He later remarked to Alfred Domett,[12] whose two elder brothers had been at the Ready school, that 'they taught him nothing there, and that he was "bullied by the big boys" '. John Domett recalled to his brother Alfred for his memoir, 'young Browning, in a pinafore of brown holland such as small boys used to wear in those days, for he was always neat in his dress — and how they used to pit him against much older boys in a "chaffing" match to amuse themselves with the "little bright-eyed fellow's" readiness and acuteness at retort and repartee'. Robert distinguished himself not only by a smart mouth but also by occasional sharp practice: when the master's attention was diverted, he would close the Revd Ready's lexicon, obliging him to open it again to look for the word he'd been referring to. He also learned how to suck up to Mr Ready, composing verses that earned him some privileges and would have warmed the heart of the great Dr Arnold of Rugby. 'Great *bosh* they were,' Robert said, quoting two concluding lines:

> We boys are privates in our Regiment's ranks —
> 'Tis to our Captain that we all owe thanks!

and followed this piece of blatant toadying by reciting from memory to Alfred Domett, while they were walking by a greenhouse discernible behind the walls of the school playground, a disrespectful epigram he had also made:

> Within these walls and near that house of glass,
> Did I, three (?) years of hapless childhood pass —
> D—d undiluted misery it was!

He got his revenge, though, by taking off the Misses Ready in full Watts voice, 'illustrating with voice and gesture' the ferocious emphasis with which the brush would sweep down in the accentuated syllables of the following lines:

> 'Lord, 'tis a pleasant thing to stand
> In gardens planted by Thy hand
>
> . . .

> Fools never raise their thoughts so high
> Like *brutes* they live, like BRUTES they die.'

Mrs Orr, uncorseting a little in citing this anecdote, obligingly admits that Robert 'even compelled his mother to laugh at it, though it was sorely against her nature to lend herself to any burlesquing of piously intended things'. She quickly snaps back, though, Mrs Orr, remarking that Robert's satirical swipe — even if it demonstrated some falling away from 'the intense piety of his earlier childhood' — evidenced merely a momentary triumph of his sense of humour over religious instincts that did not need strengthening. His humour took a sharper, drier tone when, in 1833, some years after leaving the school, he heard of a serious-minded sermon delivered by the Revd Thomas Ready and commented:

> A *heavy* sermon — sure the error's great
> For not a word Tom utters has its weight.[13]

The quality of the education at the Ready school was probably perfectly adequate for its times and most of its pupils. If it threatened to stultify the brilliance of Robert Browning, and if his contempt for it has condemned it in the estimation of posterity, the fault can hardly be heaped on the heads of the diligent Readys. Robert himself, quickly taking his own measure of the school in contrast to the pleasure of his father's exciting, fantastic excursions into the education of his son, seems not to have bothered to make close friends with any of his slower-witted contemporaries, though he did dragoon some of his classmates into acting difficult plays, mostly way above their heads, some of which he wrote specially for them. He conspicuously failed to win a school prize (though, according to Mrs Orr, 'these rewards were showered in such profusion that the only difficulty was to avoid them') and took a somewhat *de haut en bas* attitude towards the school in general.

His satirical impulse was not entirely lacking in some grandiose, theatrical sense of his own superiority, to judge by Sarianna Browning's later description to Mrs Orr of an occasion when her brother solemnly 'ascended a platform in the presence of assembled parents and friends, and, in best jacket, white gloves, and carefully curled hair, with a circular bow to the company and the then prescribed waving of alternate arms, delivered a high-flown rhymed address of his own composition'. Such a performance was very likely not unknown at home.

It is hardly surprising that Robert was bullied at school, nor that he sometimes played up, nor that he learned virtually nothing that he later considered useful. If one of the purposes of such a school was to 'knock the nonsense' out of a boy, iron him out and apply his mind to the *Ethics* — as it were — there was a lot of knocking out to be done, since the boy Robert was immediately filled up again and creased with the learnedly fantastic 'nonsense' he got at home. 'If we test the matter,' wrote Chesterton, 'by the test of actual schools and universities, Browning will appear to be almost the least educated man in English literary history. But if we test it by the amount actually learned, we shall think that he was perhaps the most educated man that ever lived; that he was in fact, if anything, over-educated.'[14]

Robert's scorn for the Ready school (despite acknowledging, on the later word of Sarianna in 1903, that 'the boys were most liberally and kindly treated'), though perhaps fair enough in terms of his own needs, which the world and its books — far less an elementary school in Peckham and its primers — were not enough to satisfy, was conceived from what Chesterton acutely perceives as his elementary ignorance in one vital respect: Robert was ignorant of the degree to which the knowledge he already possessed — 'knowledge about the Greek poets, knowledge about the Provençal Troubadors, knowledge about the Jewish Rabbis of the Middle Ages' — was exceptional. He had no idea that he himself was exceptional, that the world in general neither knew nor cared about what he knew and, according to its own lights, got along without it very well. He never was wearied by knowledge and never was troubled by the effort taken to acquire it: learning was pleasure and increase, it never was a dispiriting chore or a burden to his brain. 'His father's house,' commented Sarianna Browning to Mrs Orr, 'was literally crammed with books; and it was in this way that Robert became very early familiar with subjects generally unknown to boys.' 'His sagacious destiny,' remarked Chesterton, 'while giving him knowledge of everything else, left him in ignorance of the ignorance of the world.'

The books Robert read 'omnivorously, though certainly not without guidance' before and during his schooldays are known mostly on the authority of Mrs Orr, who gives a part-catalogue of them. In addition to *Quarles' Emblems* in a seventeenth-century edition which Robert himself annotated, there may be counted 'the first edition of *Robinson Crusoe*; the first edition of Milton's works, bought for him by his father; a treatise on astrology published twenty years after the introduction of printing; the original pamphlet *Killing no Murder* (1559) [*sic*], which Carlyle borrowed for his *Life of Cromwell*; an equally early copy of Bernard de Mandeville's *Bees*; very ancient Bibles ... Among more modern publications, *Walpole's Letters* were familiar to him in boyhood, as well as the *Letters of Junius* and all the works of Voltaire.' Later, when Robert had sufficient mastery of ancient languages, Latin poets and Greek dramatists (including Smart's translation of Horace, donated by his step-uncle Reuben) crowded his mind together with Elizabethan poets and playwrights, scraps from the cloudily romantic Ossian (by James Macpherson, another poet who had difficulty separating fact from fiction),[15] Wordsworth and Coleridge (representatives of the English Romantics) and — to crown the glittering heap — the inimitable (though that stopped no one, including Robert Browning, from trying) poetry of Byron.

These works are not the end of it — hardly even the beginning. Wanley's aforementioned *Wonders of the Little World: or, A General History of Man in Six Books* forever gripped Robert Browning's imagination, its title-page advertising the contents as showing 'by many thousands of examples ... what MAN hath been from the First Ages of the World to these Times in respect of his Body, Senses, Passions, Affections, His Virtues and Perfections, his Vices and Defects.' Nathaniel Wanley, Vicar of Trinity Parish in the City of Coventry published his *Wonders* in 1678, in an age when reports of wonder-working strained credulity less than they might now. The book furnished Robert's poetry with morbid material for the rest of his life. He came across Wanley's *Little World of Wonders* pretty much as Robert Louis Stevenson came across Pollock's toy theatre and characters, 'penny plain and tuppence coloured'.

The *Emblems* of Francis Quarles, first published in 1635, was relatively wholesome by comparison, though as a work of intense piety and severely high moral tone, it naturally directed the attention of readers ('dunghill worldlings') to the dreadful consequences of any lapse from the exemplary conduct of early and medieval Christian saints. The text was decorated with little woodcuts of devils with pitchforks, the Devil himself driving the chariot of the world and attending idle pursuits such as a game of bowls. Mythology and folklore were mixed with biblical allusions, the whole rich in an extensive, imaginative vocabulary. We have more qualms today about exposing young minds to the grim, the ghastly, the grotesque and the gothic, even the fairy tales of Perrault, Hans Christian Andersen, and the brothers Grimm in the unexpurgated version, though children will generally seek out and sup on horrors for themselves. Robert Browning's early exposure to morbid literature and its fine, matter-of-fact and matter-of-fiction examples of casual and institutionalized cruelties, injustices, and fantastical phenomena was balanced by early immersion in more authoritative works, among them — notably — the fifty volumes of the *Biographie Universelle*, published in 1822, Vasari's *Lives of the Painters, The Art of Painting in All its Branches* by Gérard de Lairesse, and *Principles of Harmony* by John Relfe.

Mrs Browning contributed a worthy work of 1677 by Elisha Coles, *A Practical Discourse of Effectual Calling and of Perseverance* (the only book in the house, according to Betty Miller, to bear her signature)[16] and Cruden's *Concordance to the Holy Scriptures*. Mrs Miller comments that these two works of religious dedication testify not only to Mrs Browning's ingrained piety but point up 'something of the divided atmosphere in which Robert Browning was brought up. On the one hand he was given the freedom of a liberal and erudite library; on the other, he found himself, like Hazlitt, who counted it a misfortune, "bred up among dissenters who look with too jaundiced an eye at others, and set too high a value on their own particular pretensions. From being proscribed themselves, they learn to proscribe others; and come in the end to reduce all integrity of principle and soundness of opinion within the pale of their own little communion".'

This may be generally true, and not only of Dissenters; but it is too harsh when applied to the Brownings in particular. In this sense, as characterized by Hazlitt, it is difficult to believe that Robert the Second adhered quite as limpet-like as his wife to the rock of Nonconformism or that her son Robert's self-confessed passionate attachment in childhood to religion would not wane in the light of opinions other than those sincerely expressed by Congregationalists and other Nonconformists who were drilled into dutiful observance and stilled into attention by the 'stiffening and starching' style of the Revd George Clayton and the hectoring manner of Joseph Irons, minister of the Grove Chapel, Camberwell. Alfred Domett was reminded, in conversation with Dr Irons ('the clever but apparently bigoted High Churchman'), 'how we used to go sometimes up Camberwell Grove of a Sunday evening, to try how far off we could hear his father (Mr Irons, an Independent Minister or Ranter) bawling out his sermon, well enough to distinguish the words; and how on one occasion, taking a friend with him, they stood outside at a little distance and clearly heard, "I am sorry to say it, beloved brethren, but it is an undoubted fact that Roman Catholicism and midnight assassin are synonymous terms!".'[17]

The religion of the Brownings, the Congregationalism of the nineteenth century, was a moderate Calvinism, shading later to liberal Evangelicalism, that derived from the first Independents of the Elizabethan age. These spring-pure Puritans, persecuted in England, disclaimed any duty to the hierarchy of the Church over their duty to God and conscience. They sailed, some of them, into exile to found pilgrim colonies in New England, and others later came to power in the Cromwellian Commonwealth. The long history of Protestant dissent had been vividly, violently marked by persecution, fanaticism, exile, torture, death, and the blood of their martyrs persisted as a lively tang in the nostrils of zealous Nonconformists.

In the early years of the nineteenth century, dissenters from the established Church of England still suffered some remnants of political and social disability — legal penalties for attending their chapels were not abolished until 1812; they were subject to political disenfranchisement until 1832 and — fatefully for Robert Browning as the son of a Dissenter and not himself a communicant of the Anglican church — the ancient universities, including Oxford and Cambridge, until 1854 were open only to members of the Established Church of England. These were serious matters that inclined Nonconformists, most of whom belonged — in East Anglia, the South Midlands, the West country and South Wales — to the respectable working classes, to support the Liberal Party led later in the century by William Gladstone.

Nevertheless, there was a difference in practice between the proscriptive Puritanism bawled from the pulpit and the less rigid, more charitable observance of its dogma in the busy social life and generous-minded charitable organization of the Congregationalists who were as strong in the Lord as they were in the practical virtues of education, evangelism, care of the sick, fundraising bazaars, music, and self-improvement. Robert Browning was born in a period between the early, bleak, and joyless fervour of the seventeenth-century Puritans and the moral hypocrisy of the late Victorians, whose conformity to social conventions characterized virtually every deviation from the norms of Evangelical fundamentalism as either morally reprehensible or criminal, and probably both. In 1812, Mrs Grundy (who had been invented in 1800 by the playwright Thomas Morton as a character in *Speed the Plough*) was still a laughing-stock and had not then become the all-powerful, repressive deity of respectable late Victorian middle-class society. The domestic tone of the Browning household was nicely moderated between the mother's religious principles and the father's cultural enlightenment. In any case, there is no liberty like an enquiring mind that recognizes no limits, and the young Browning's mind was made aware of no obstacles, beyond the blockheads of school who temporarily impeded his progress, to the accumulation of knowledge.

The violent, at least turbulent, and colourful life of Browning's mind was tempered — though, more likely, all the more stimulated — by vigorous physical activity: he learned to ride and was taught dancing, boxing, and fencing,[18] and he walked about the surrounding countryside. It was two miles, a 'green half-hour's walk over the fields'[19] and stiles, past hedges and picturesque cottages, from Camberwell to Dulwich where, in 1814, the Dulwich Picture Gallery, attached to Dulwich College, had been opened. In that year, the two-year-old Robert was making his first picture of 'a certain cottage and rocks in lead pencil and black currant juice — paint being rank poison, as they said when I sucked my brushes'.[20]

London, as Griffin and Minchin take pains to describe, was by no means well furnished with public art galleries. Neither the National Gallery nor Trafalgar Square then existed. Dulwich Picture Gallery, designed by Sir John Soane, had been specially commissioned for the exhibition of some 350 European paintings — Dutch, Spanish, French, Italian, and English. Children under the age of fourteen were, according to regulations, denied entry, but somehow young Robert Browning was allowed to enter with his father, who, said Dante Gabriel Rossetti later in Paris, 'had a real genius for drawing — but caring for nothing in the least except Dutch boors'. This was not quite fair: Mr Browning also had a distinct relish for Hogarth grotesques. But it was true that, according to his son, Mr Browning would 'turn from the Sistine altar-piece' in favour of the Dutch artists Brouwer, Ostade, and the Teniers (father and son), who were amply represented at Dulwich.

The Dutch School did not detain the interest of young Robert, whose love of Dulwich was suffused, as he wrote to Elizabeth Barrett on 3 March 1846, with 'those two Guidos, the wonderful Rembrandt of Jacob's vision, such a Watteau, the triumphant three Murillo pictures, a Giorgione music lesson group, all the Poussins with the "Armida" and "Jupiter's nursing" — and — no end to "ands" — I have sate before one, some *one* of those pictures I had predetermined to see, a good hour and then gone away . . . .' Enthusiasm for favourites did not mean an uncritical eye for failures. Familiarity bred contempt for works 'execrable as sign-paintings even'. For a 'whole collection, including "a divine painting by Murillo," and Titian's Daughter (hitherto supposed to be in the Louvre)' he would 'have cheerfully given a pound or two for the privilege of not possessing'.

In his letter of 27 February 1846 to Elizabeth Barrett, Robert had asked the pertinent question, 'Are there worse poets in their way than painters?' There is a subtle difference in the 'melancholy business'; a poet at least possesses resources capable of being adapted to other things: 'the bad poet goes out of his way, writes his verses in the language he learned in order to do a hundred other things with it, all of which he can go on and do afterwards — but the painter has spent the best of his life in learning even how to produce such monstrosities as these, and to what other good do his acquisitions go? This short minute of our life our one chance, an eternity on either side! and a man does not walk whistling and ruddy by the side of hawthorn hedges in spring, but shuts himself up and comes out after a dozen years with "Titian's Daughter" and, there, gone is his life, let somebody else try!'

The point of this rushing reflection is only partly to do with art: it also makes a none-too-subtle reference to Robert Browning's seizing the moment, 'the short minute of our life, our one chance', with his beloved Miss Barrett, as he finishes with the line:

I have tried — my trial is made too!

But this is in the future. The boy Robert had only just begun, on first acquaintance with the Dulwich pictures, to try his hand at poetry, good, bad, or indifferent, excepting some early extemporized lines of occasional verse for domestic or school consumption. The critic — tutored by the work of de Lairesse — was being formed, but the artist was still mostly whistling, ruddy by the hawthorn hedges, on the way to Dulwich. It was difficult to know which way to turn, which vocation to pursue: painting and drawing, for which young Robert had a facility, inspired by his father and the works of de Lairesse; music, which he dearly loved, inspired by his mother, Charles Avison's *Essay on Musical Expression*, and two distinguished tutors — Relfe, who taught theory, and Abel, who was proficient in technique; poetry, for which he not only had an aptitude but also a taste fuelled in several languages (Greek, Latin, French, some Spanish, some Italian, German later, even a smattering of Hebrew in addition to English) by the great exemplars — Horace, Homer, Pope, Byron — of the art of happy expression.

In the event, at the age of twelve, in the very year, 1824, of Byron's death at Missolonghi, Robert the Third produced a collection of short poems entitled *Incondita*. The title, comments Mrs Orr, 'conveyed a certain idea of deprecation'; Griffin and Minchin suggest an 'allusion to the fact that "in the beginning" even the earth itself was "without form"'. The title may have been modest, but the principal stylistic influence — Byronic — was not, and at least one of the poems, 'The Dance of Death', was, on the authority of Mrs Orr, who was told of it, 'a direct imitation of Coleridge's "Fire, Famine, and Slaughter"' (1798). A letter of 11 March 1843 from Robert the Second to a Mr Thomas Powell, quoted by Mrs Orr, testified that his son had been composing verses since 'quite a child' and referred to a great quantity of 'juvenile performances', some of which 'extemporaneous productions' Robert the Second enclosed.

The sample sheet of verses, taken at the time and for some while after at face value, was subsequently identified to Mrs Orr by Sarianna Browning as 'her father's own impromptu epigrams'. The attempt to pass off the father's effusions as the work of the son is baffling, and Mrs Orr kindly directs us to suppose that 'The substitution may from the first have been accidental.' The letter is, however, valuable for its affirmation that Robert the Third was remarkably precocious in poetry and the credible information — borne out by his habitual practice in later life — that he deliberately destroyed all instances of his first efforts 'that ever came in his way'.

Sarianna being too young at the time — no more than ten years old — never saw the poetry of *Incondita*, but it impressed Mr and Mrs Browning to the extent that they tried, unsuccessfully, to get the manuscript published. Disappointment in this enterprise may have been one reason that led Robert to destroy the manuscript, but it had already got beyond him into the world: Mrs Browning had shown the poems to an acquaintance, Miss Eliza Flower, who had copied them for the attention of a friend, the Revd William Johnson Fox, 'the well-known Unitarian minister'. Robert, with an adult eye for reputation, retrieved this copy after the death of Mr Fox and, additionally, a fragment of verse contained in a letter from Miss Sarah Flower. He destroyed both.

Mrs Orr, though regretting the loss of 'these first fruits of Mr Browning's genius', supposes that 'there can have been little in them to prefigure its later forms. Their faults seem to have lain in the direction of too great splendour of language and too little wealth of thought', an echo of Mr Fox's opinion. Fox admitted later to Robert that 'he had feared these tendencies as his future snare'. Two poems, said to have survived from *Incondita*'s brief and limited exposure, are 'The First-Born of Egypt', in blank verse, and 'The Dance of Death', in tetrameters. They are certainly gorgeous, richly allusive, spare no wrenching emotion or sensational effect, and ascend to dramatic climax. A distinct gust from the graveyard scents the relentless progress of grisly calamities that would give suffering Job more than usual pause for thought.

Nevertheless, the Byronic, perhaps less so the Coleridgean, influences were not merely juvenile infatuations. In a letter of 22 August 1846 to Miss Barrett, Robert commented that 'I always maintained my first feeling for Byron in many respects ... the interest in places he had visited, in relics of him. I would at any time have gone to Finchley to see a curl of his hair or one of his gloves, I am sure — while Heaven knows that I could not get up enthusiasm enough to cross the room if at the end of it all Wordsworth, Coleridge and Southey were condensed into the little China bottle yonder, after the Rosicrucian fashion ... they seem to "have their reward" and want nobody's love or faith.' (The reference to Finchley as a place of ultimate pilgrimage is attributable to the fact that two days previously Miss Barrett had driven out as far as that fascinating faubourg.)

The death of Byron was as climactic in its effect as either of the surviving poems of *Incondita*, which take the fold of death as their theme. It may have been the stimulus that prompted the twelve-year-old Browning's manuscript. The fallout was great on other poets, other idealists, who subsided into plain prose and practical politics — it was the death, too, at least in England, of any idea of romantic revolution. Alfred Tennyson, we are told, memorialized the event by carving the words 'Byron is dead' on a rock near Somersby. He was fifteen. Thomas Carlyle, approaching thirty, felt as though he had lost a brother. It is not too much to say that the death of Byron had as profound an effect in England and Europe in 1824 as the death of President John F. Kennedy had for America and the world in 1963. It was like an eclipse of the sun that stills even bird song, or the silence after a thunderclap. There were few who were unaffected. 'The news of his death came upon my heart like a mass of lead,' wrote Carlyle to his wife Jane.

Equally tremendous was the year 1832: Goethe died, and so did Sir Walter Scott. Robert maintained a high regard for Scott the polymathic author, often quoting from him and occasionally reflecting Scott's work in his own poetry. The death of Keats in 1821 had been quickly followed by that of Shelley in 1822. Wordsworth was to die in 1850, and Heinrich Heine in 1856. These losses amounted, in the case of poetry, to the death of European Romanticism. 'Though it is by no means clear what Romanticism stood for,' the historian Eric Hobsbawm points out in a chapter on 'The Arts' in *The Age of Revolution*, 'it is quite evident what it was against: the middle.' Isaiah Berlin, in *The Roots of Romanticism*, supposes that, had one 'spoken in England to someone who had been influenced by, say, Coleridge, or above all by Byron', one would have found that 'the values to which they attached the highest importance were such values as integrity, sincerity, readiness to sacrifice one's life to some inner light, dedication to some ideal for which it is worth sacrificing all that one is, for which it is worth both living and dying'. This attitude, says Berlin, was relatively new. 'What people admired was wholeheartedness, sincerity, purity of soul, the ability to dedicate yourself to your ideal, no matter what it was.'

The middle, then, famously distrustful of extremes, did not apparently stand much chance, squeezed between the reactionary, traditional elements of the old order and the revolutionary, idealistic instincts of the avant-garde. Yet society has an irresistible tendency to compromise, to assimilate and settle into social stability — albeit radically altered, both right and left — when shaken by destructive events and stirred by disturbing philosophies. Nowhere is this more marked than in the mobile middle class, the eternally buoyant bourgeoisie, which confidently came into its own following the French and Industrial Revolutions.

This middle class was perceived by pre-Revolutionary enthusiasts as equipped with reason, sentiment, natural feeling, and purpose in contrast to the sterility, decrepitude, reactionary instincts, and corrupt clericalism of pre-Revolutionary society. The artificiality of the Court was in theory to be replaced by the spontaneity of the people — whereupon, of course, by the inevitable evolutionary law of society, the new society in practice naturally stiffened into a bureaucratic, bourgeois respectability, in its own time and triumphant style stifling fine romantic feeling with its own brand of philistinism. Revolutions, like romantic poets, die young. Byron astutely recognized that an early death would save him from a respectable old age.

G. K. Chesterton points to what is now known as the 'percolation theory' or the 'trickle down effect' that supposedly occurs when society is in some way shaken out from top to bottom or from bottom to top. Robert Browning, says Chesterton, was 'born in the afterglow of the great Revolution' — the French Revolution of 1789, that is — the point of this observation being that the Jacobin dream of emancipation had begun 'in the time of Keats and Shelley to creep down among the dullest professions and the most prosaic classes of society'. By the time of Robert's boyhood, 'a very subtle and profound change was beginning in the intellectual atmosphere of such homes as that of the Brownings . . . A spirit of revolt was growing among the young of the middle classes which had nothing at all in common with the complete and pessimistic revolt against all things in heaven or earth . . . On all sides there was the first beginning of the aesthetic stir in the middle classes which expressed itself in the combination of so many poetic lives with so many prosaic livelihoods. It was the age of inspired office-boys.'

With this famous portmanteau phrase, Chesterton sweeps together such marvellous boys as John Ruskin 'solemnly visiting his solemn suburban aunts', Charles Dickens toiling in a blacking factory, Thomas Carlyle 'lingering on a poor farm in Dumfriesshire', and John Keats, who 'had not long become the assistant of the country surgeon'. Add to these Robert Browning, the son of a Bank of England clerk in Camberwell. These men, born to fame but not to wealth, were the inheritors of a new world that gave them a liberty that, in Robert Browning's case, 'exalted poetry above all earthly things' and which he served 'with single-hearted intensity'. Browning stands, observed Chesterton, 'among the few poets who hardly wrote a line of anything else'.

The matter of poetry as Robert's sole vocation was mostly decided by the revelation of Percy Bysshe Shelley, the atheistical poet. The effect was tremendous. It was like coming across a hitherto unknown brother who had thought everything, experienced everything, accomplished everything that Robert Browning, fourteen years old, living in Camberwell, had as yet only dimly felt and begun to put, somewhat derivatively of admired models, into words. Robert had read the cynical, atheistical Voltaire without obvious moral corruption; he had read of the world's virtues and vices, irregularities and injustices, in the words of Wanley, Shakespeare, Milton, and in other works of dramatic historical fiction, without becoming contemptuous of virtue; he had read the sensational Byron without becoming mad or bad; he had read the waspish Horace Walpole without becoming overwhelmingly mannered. But the cumulative effect was bound, in some degree, to be unsettling. Shelley — who had, like young Robert, read Voltaire and encyclopedias, and who had consorted with Byron — ratcheted up the adolescent tension one notch too far.

Shelley's musical verse hit every note. With exquisite Shelleyan technique, all the airs that had been vapouring in Robert's head were given compositional form — delicate, forceful; and as the concert performance proceeded, Shelley's genius, his creative spirit, played out the great work of the ideal world in which infamy was erased, God rebelled against Satan, and in which — as Chesterton remarks — 'every cloud and clump of grass shared his strict republican orthodoxy'. All things in heaven and on earth proclaimed the triumph of liberty. 'O World, O Life, O Time,' Robert in later life apostrophized with deliberate irony

on the flyleaf of Shelley's *Miscellaneous Poems* given to him by his cousin
Jim Silverthorne, a book he vigorously annotated in his first enthusiasm
and then thought better of in his maturity when he tried, on 2 June
1878, to erase 'the foolish markings and still more foolish scribblings'
that 'show the impression made on a boy by this first specimen of
Shelley's poetry'. What he could not vehemently blot out or rub at or
scratch away or scribble over, he hacked at with a knife or finally —
all these obliterating resources being inadequate — cut out with scissors.
It seems an excessive reaction, some fifty years later, but the first enthusi-
asm had evidently come to seem itself embarrassingly excessive. Not
only did Robert not wish to remember it, he was determined to efface
it from memory — his own or posterity's — absolutely, though without
actually, as was his usual resort, burning the book to ashes. He could
burn his own poetry, perhaps, but not another's.

'Between the year 1826, when Browning became acquainted with
the work of Shelley, and 1832, when *Pauline* was written,' says Betty
Miller in *Robert Browning: A Portrait*, 'there took place in the life of the
poet a crisis so radical that everything that followed upon it, including
his marriage with Elizabeth Barrett, was qualified in one way or another
by the effects of that initial experience.' This sums up the biographical
consensus that began with Mrs Orr's pronouncement that Robert held
Shelley greatest in the poetic art because 'in his case, beyond all others,
he believed its exercise to have been prompted by the truest spiritual
inspiration'.

The souls of Keats and Shelley were identified in Robert's mind
with two nightingales which sang harmoniously together on a night in
May — perhaps his birthday, the 7th of May in 1826 — one in a
laburnum ('heavy with its weight of gold', as William Sharp says Brown-
ing told a friend) in the Brownings' garden, the other in a large copper
beech on adjoining ground. 'Their utterance,' says Mrs Orr, 'was, to
such a spirit as his, the last, as in a certain sense the first, word of what
poetry can say.' The image was no doubt prompted in Robert's mind
by Keats' 'Ode to a Nightingale'. At any rate, whether or not these birds
were the transmigrated souls of Keats and Shelley, as Robert reverently
convinced himself, they 'had settled in a Camberwell garden', says
Chesterton less reverently, 'in order to sing to the only young gentleman
who really adored and understood them'.

The major impact on the tender sensibilities of young Robert Browning was made by Shelley's *Queen Mab*, which later achieved a reputation, when issued in a new edition by the publisher Edward Moxon, for being that most horrid — indeed, criminal — thing, a blasphemous libel. 'The Shelley whom Browning first loved,' says Mrs Orr, 'was the Shelley of *Queen Mab*, the Shelley who would have remodelled the whole system of religious belief, as of human duty and rights; and the earliest result of the new development was that he became a professing atheist and, for two years, a practising vegetarian. He returned to his natural diet when he found his eyesight becoming weak. The atheism cured itself; we do not exactly know when or how.' In a letter to Elizabeth Barrett on 13 September 1845, Robert wrote of having lived for two years on bread and potatoes — a regime that, if strictly adhered to, would have tested the faith and asceticism even of the Desert Fathers.

Queen Mab is a lecture in poetic form to Ianthe, a disembodied spirit, on the sorry state of the temporal universe. Mab is a bluestocking fairy queen who takes intense issue with the various shortcomings of contemporary politics, conventional religion, and cankerous commerce, all of which are judged to be more or less hopelessly misguided when not actually corrupt. Queen Mab's denunciation convinces less by rational argument than by the irresistible force of her — Shelley's — convictions. She barely stops for breath (only now and then pauses for footnotes), fired by ideas and ideals that combine termagant intensity with tender sentiment, fiercely heretical in her inability to accept a creating Deity but spiritually softer in her recognition that there could be 'a pervading spirit co-eternal with the universe' which might or might not, according to religious belief, be identified with the supreme maker, sometimes called God.

In an aside, dealing with the matter in a footnote, Shelley argued abstinence from meat as a means whereby man might at a stroke eliminate the brutal pleasures of the chase and restore an agricultural paradise, improve himself physically and morally, and probably live forever in health and virtue. The spiritual and the corporeal were virtually synonymous. Shelley recommended himself and the pure system of his ideas to youth whose moral enthusiasm for truth and virtue was yet unvitiated by the contagion of the world. Queen Mab was pouring out a song which, if not of innocence, at least was addressing innocents. The force of Shelley's expression rather more than the systematic reason of his argument is still powerfully appealing to idealists, and most of his vehement agitprop (as it might be called today) speaks to succeeding generations even unto our own times — so much so that the utterances of Queen Mab sound not unlike the conventional wisdom of modern environmentalists, new-agers, and bourgeois bohemians. It is difficult for us now to appreciate the thrilling horror with which Shelley's words were received by his unnerved contemporaries who read not only blasphemy — bad enough — but revolution between, as much as upon, every irreverent line.

Vegetarianism worried Robert's mother; atheism worried the Revd George Clayton. Robert stuck to his beliefs for a while, but forgave himself his youthful excesses, characterizing them later in his life as 'Crude convictions of boyhood, conveyed in imperfect and unapt forms of speech, — for such things all boys have been pardoned. They are growing pains, accompanied by temporary distortion of soul also.'[21] He regretted the anxiety caused to his mother, whose strong-minded inclination that her son should not compromise his physical health was resisted by Robert's insistence that meat-eating was a symptom of spiritual disease and argued, presumably, 'what should it profit a man if he feed his body but starve his soul'. Besides, the new diet was also a symptom of liberty, a badge of freedom, a symbol of release from dependence.

Atheism served much the same purpose. That his speculative beliefs were sincerely held and admitted of no counter-persuasion from those who expressed concern for his physical and spiritual welfare was perhaps secondary to their practical effect. Robert Browning had got out into the world, and he would deal with it on his own terms. He might still be living within the narrow propriety of his parents' house, which increasingly rubbed at his heels and elbows, but he was his own man. Sarianna, his sympathetic sister, admitted to Mrs Orr that 'The fact was, poor boy, he had outgrown his social surroundings. They were absolutely good, but they were narrow; it could not be otherwise; he chafed under them.'[22]

Robert had left the Ready school at the age of fourteen, and for two years thereafter he was educated privately at home, in the mornings by a tutor competent in the general syllabus; in the afternoons by a number of instructors in music, technical science, languages (French particularly), singing, dancing, exercise (riding, boxing, fencing), and probably art.[23] In the evenings, if his father did not entertainingly contribute to the educational process, Robert worked at his own pleasure, voraciously reading, assiduously writing, sometimes composing music. None of his musical compositions have survived the incinerating fire he so loved to feed. Robert 'wrote music for songs which he himself sang', states Mrs Orr, citing three: Donne's 'Go, and catch a falling star', Hood's 'I will not have the mad Clytie', and 'The mountain sheep are sweeter' by Peacock. These settings were characterized to Mrs Orr, by those who knew of them, as 'very spirited'.[24]

Robert also acquired a social life, associating with three Silverthorne cousins — James, John and George, the sons of Christiana Wiedemann, Sarah Anna Browning's sister, who had married Silverthorne, a prosperous local brewer. All three were musically gifted and sometimes described as 'wild youths'.[25] The Silverthornes lived in Portland Place, Peckham. James came to be Robert's particular friend, and his name is written in the register of Marylebone Church as one of the two witnesses at the wedding in 1846 of Robert Browning and Elizabeth Barrett. James, who succeeded to the family brewery, died in 1852. To mark his passing, Robert wrote the poem 'May and Death' which lovingly commemorates the friendship between himself and James (called Charles in the poem).

In addition to association with cousins, Robert acquired improving acquaintance with, notably, Alfred Domett and Joseph Arnould (later to become Sir Joseph Arnould of the High Court bench of Bombay, but meanwhile something of a youthful radical and an admirer of Carlyle). Both were clever, ambitious young men of his own age, sons of established Camberwell families. He had, too, independent adventures. Stories are told — and credited by some — of his ramblings, following the tracks of gypsy caravans far across country. William Sharp, in his biography of Browning (1897), seems to think that Robert kept company with 'any tramps, gypsies or other wayfarers', though Mrs Orr in her more authoritative (less lyrical and very much less airily romantic) biography, published in 1891, quashes any suggestion that he caught them up or was detained in parleyings with them: 'I do not know how the idea can have arisen that he willingly sought his experience in the society of "gipsies and tramps".'

Both Sharp and Mrs Orr knew Robert Browning personally, and it must be admitted that the latter can lay claim to longer, more intimate and more extensive acquaintance with the poet. There is no doubting it from the tone of her book that Mrs Orr strives for a scrupulous fidelity to the facts — some of which, if deplorable, are omitted — but some caution is required when dealing with her inclination to polish the poet to his brightest lustre and to put the best and brightest face on failure. She can sometimes, in her emphases and suppressions, be inspired to what we now recognize as spin. However, Sharp invites comparison with Browning's poem 'The Flight of the Duchess' and a song which Robert heard on a Guy Fawkes night, 5 November, with the refrain, 'Following the Queen of the Gipsies oh!' that rang in his head until it found appropriate poetic expression years later. Chesterton sufficiently credits or relishes Sharp's literary association as to repeat it in his own biography. It seems likely that, whatever romantic fascination Robert may have had with the itinerant life of gypsies, they represented his then feelings of freedom as a desirable thing rather than as an actuality in his life or as an alternative to it. He had neither any incentive to run away with the 'raggle-taggle gypsies-o!', nor any inclination to inquire too closely into the reality of lives less privileged, in conventional terms, than his own.

There is talk, too, of Robert's taste for country fairs. This is elaborated by Griffin and Minchin, who charmingly describe how, 'For three days each summer the Walworth Road from Camberwell Gate to the village green — a goodly mile — was aglow after sunset with candles beneath coloured shades on the roadside stalls: on the Green itself, besides the inevitable boats and swings and merry-go-rounds, there was the canvas-covered avenue with its gingerbread booths, there was music and dancing, and best of all, there was the ever-popular Richardson's Theatre — appreciated, it is said, by the poet in his younger days. Peckham also had its fair, which was held just opposite Mr Ready's school; and Greenwich, noisiest and most boisterous of fairs, was close at hand.'[26] Again, with an implied note of reproof, Mrs Orr dampens any speculative fervour about Robert's bohemian instincts by insisting that 'a few hours spent at a fair would at all times have exhausted his capacity for enduring it. In the most undisciplined acts of his early youth, were always present curious delicacies and reserves.'

She is keen to return Robert to his books and his work, away from any suggestion of irreverent or — spare the mark — inappropriate interests and activities: 'There was always latent in him the real goodness of heart which would not allow him to trifle consciously with other lives.' Fifine might go to the fair, but Robert should stay home and satisfy himself with the habit of work as his safeguard and keep tight control of an imagination that, rather than mastering him, would serve him. This seems a little censorious, not to say apprehensive that Robert might have had yearnings that, if not severely restrained, would have led him into even more 'undisciplined acts'. We must close our eyes in holy dread at the very thought and be thankful that nothing unworthy soiled the blameless page he worked upon, far less sufficiently overcame his 'curious delicacies and reserves' to distract him from it.

Better to think of Robert no longer incited by his early adherence to Byron — that libertine and sceptic who roamed at large as much in the world as in his meditations — but at sundown, on the brow of the Camberwell hill (now known as Camberwell Grove), among the spreading elms, suffused with the spiritual light of Shelley and looking down, deliriously, on the darkling mass of London sprawled at his feet, lit by the new gas lamps. For the time being, Robert remained safely distant from the snares and entanglements of the beautiful but seductive city: so many lives to refrain from toying with, so much noisy, messy — maybe vicious — life to assault curious delicacies and reserves should he dare to descend to put them to the test. Byronism, as Chesterton remarks, 'was not so much a pessimism about civilized things as an optimism about savage things'. But now Robert was Byronic only in the dandyism of his dress. It was Shelley who suited his soul. And so, turning, Robert would go home to bed, sleeping in a bedroom that adjoined his mother's, the door always open between them, and to give her a kiss — every night, even in the worst of their disputes — before retiring. He never willingly spent a night away from home.[27]

Robert's fascination with and attachment to the natural as contrasted with the artificial world was innate. It took inspiration from his mother's intense sympathy with flora and fauna, if we are to credit W. J. Stillman, in his *Autobiography of a Journalist* (quoted by Griffin and Minchin), who states that Mrs Browning had that 'extraordinary power over animals of which we hear sometimes, but of which I have never known a case so perfect as hers. She would lure the butterflies in the garden to her, and domestic animals obeyed her as if they reasoned.' The Browning household at times approximated to a menagerie: Griffin and Minchin speak respectfully of Browning's learning early to ride his pony, playing with dogs, keeping pets and birds including a monkey, a magpie, and — improbably — an eagle. The collection of toads, frogs, efts, and other 'portable creatures' that is said to have filled his pockets gives some additional substance to the story already quoted that Mrs Browning induced Robert to take medicine by finding a toad for him in the garden. He could whistle up a lizard in Italy, chuck a toad under its chin in Hatcham, and later kept a pet owl in London as well as geese that would follow him around and submit to being embraced by the middle-aged poet.[28]

William Sharp describes Browning's occasional long walks into the country: 'One particular pleasure was to lie beside a hedge, or deep in meadow-grasses, or under a tree . . . and there give himself up so absolutely to the life of the moment that even the shy birds would alight close by, and sometimes venturesomely poise themselves on suspicious wings for a brief space on his recumbent body.' Sharp, in this pastoral mode, quotes Browning himself as having said that 'his faculty of observation at that time would not have appeared despicable to a Seminole or an Iroquois'.[29] His faculty of absorption and repose, in this imagery, would have done credit to a St Francis. His love for his mother's flowers — particularly the roses and lilies that later he would gather to send to Elizabeth Barrett — was perhaps one contributory factor in his brief vegetarianism.

In a letter of 24 July 1838 to Miss Euphrasia Fanny Haworth, he makes a significant confession: 'I have, you are to know, such a love for flowers and leaves — some leaves — that I every now and then, — in an impatience at being able to possess myself of them thoroughly, to see them quite, satiate myself with their scent — bite them to bits.'

This devouring quality of Browning's desire for sensation, to the extent of attempting to consume it literally in the form of vegetable matter, is remarkable. It is as though Browning's passion to possess the world could only be achieved by eating it, by incorporating it within himself. In *Pauline*, he recognized some of this when he identified

> a principle of restlessness
> Which would be all, have, see, know, taste, feel, all.

and he declared that,

> I have lived all life
> When it is most alive.

How apposite, then, to come upon the charmingly-named Flower sisters, Eliza and Sarah. It was to Eliza that Mrs Browning had confided the text of *Incondita* and it was Eliza, so taken with it, who had copied it for Mr William Johnson Fox, a friend of her father, Benjamin Flower, 'known', says Mrs Orr, 'as editor of the *Cambridge Intelligencer*'. Robert, encouraged by her enthusiasm for his poems, began writing to Eliza Flower at the age of twelve or thirteen.[30] She was nine years his senior. These letters, which she kept for her lifetime, were eventually and effortfully retrieved and destroyed — all but a few scraps — by Robert. It seems likely, even without the confirmation of the correspondence, that Eliza was his first, immature love, though the boyish, romantic attachment died out 'for want of root'. Sentimental love, if that was what it amounted to, subsided into a lasting respect and affection for 'a very remarkable person' who, with her sister, was responsible for a number of popular hymns such as 'Nearer, my God, to thee', written by Sarah Flower Adams and set to music by Eliza. These were composed for Mr Fox's chapel where Eliza 'assumed the entire management of the choral part of the service'.[31] Eliza, though Robert denied it, seems to have been the major identifiable inspiration for his second excursion into verse: the long confessional poem entitled *Pauline*.

Mrs Orr conventionally regrets that the headstrong Robert Browning was not sent to a public school where his energies might have been efficiently directed; but Griffin and Minchin take the more sensible view that a pre-Arnoldian public school education, if only and unrepresentatively to judge by the boy's experience of the Ready school, would have been been 'hardly encouraging ... Nor were public schools in good odour.' The reforms inspired by Dr Arnold of Rugby were a thing of the future.

Meantime, Robert's father in 1825 had subscribed £100 to the foundation of the new London University, an investment that brought no dividends but procured one particular advantage: since Mr Browning was one of the original 'proprietors', he was entitled to a free education for a nominee. Robert, his son, could be admitted to London University as a student. In contrast to Oxford, Cambridge, and the other ancient universities, which required subscription to the Thirty-nine Articles as a necessary prerequisite to admission, London University was non-sectarian, the education was less costly than at other academic institutions, and it was possible to combine the university education with private home study.

Robert was earnestly recommended by his father, describing himself as 'a parent anxious for the welfare of an only Son' who deemed admission to the University 'essential to his future happiness'. Furthermore, Mr Browning testified to Robert's impeccable moral character ('I never knew him from his earliest infancy, guilty of the slightest deviation from Truth') and to his 'unwearied application for the last 6 years, to the Greek, Latin & French languages'. Mrs Orr draws a discreet veil over the upshot, confining herself to the information that 'In his eighteenth year he attended, for a term or two, a Greek class at the London University' — he registered for the opening session, 1829–30 — and that 'It was at about the time of his short attendance at University College that the choice of poetry as his future profession was formally made.' The phrase 'short attendance' implies some length of time more than a week, which was the period Robert survived lodging away from home and his mother with a Mr Hughes in Bedford Square, and perhaps a little longer than the few months he endured the pedestrian German, Greek, and Latin classes for which he registered before quitting the college entirely. He was seventeen years old, an age at which, as Mrs Orr frankly acknowledges, he was naturally 'not only more restless, but less amiable than at any other'.

'The always impatient temper assumed a quality of aggressiveness,' she reports. 'He behaved as a youth will who knows himself to be clever, and believes that he is not appreciated, because the crude or paradoxical forms which his cleverness assumes do not recommend it to his elders' minds.' This is judiciously put. A little less indulgent is the bald admission that Robert 'set the judgements of those about him at defiance, and gratuitously proclaimed himself everything that he was, and some things that he was not.' School and college simply wearied him: the pedantic routine was stifling. It was not that he lacked aptitude for study, more that he lacked inclination to confine it to the well-worn track. Which is not to say Robert was unpopular: William Sharp quotes a letter from *The Times* of 14 December 1889, in which a friend loyally testified that 'I attended with him the Greek class of Professor Long, and I well remember the esteem and regard in which he was held by his fellow-students.'

Poetry was the thing — a foregone conclusion, at least according to Robert. Some attempts seem to have been made to promote the professions of barrister (chosen by his friends Domett and Arnould), clergyman (though Robert had given up regular church attendance), banker (employment in the Bank of England and Rothschild's bank being the family business), even desperately — it is said — painter or actor. For a short while, when he was sixteen years old, Robert attended medical lectures given by the celebrated physician Dr Blundell at Guy's Hospital. These are said to have aroused in him 'considerable interest in the sciences connected with medicine',[32] but perhaps more from a fascination with the morbid, since 'no knowledge of either disease or its treatment ever seems to have penetrated into his life'. At any rate, there seems to have been no positive belief that Robert might be suited to the medical profession. The tentative suggestions of anxious parents — the adamantine refusal of a strong-willed son — sulks and silences: it is a familiar-enough scenario, distressing to Mrs Browning, worrying to Mr Browning, a matter of some well-concealed anxiety, no doubt, to Robert Browning himself, who made a conspicuous effort to prepare himself for the profession of poet by reading Johnson's *Dictionary* from cover to cover.

Robert had become accustomed to the standards of early nineteenth-century suburban middle-class comfort, but he had been educated as a mid-to-late eighteenth-century gentleman, not only in the breadth of his acquired learning but equally in the departments of upper-class sporting activities such as riding, boxing, and fencing, the social graces of singing, dancing, music, and art, and the civilized values of a man of fine feeling in dress and deportment. The acquisition of these benefits was one thing — they required no financial outlay on his own part; to maintain them would be quite another. Refined tastes are generally expensive to indulge as a permanent style of life.

In his late teens and early twenties, Robert cut a noticeable figure: his appearance was dapper and dandified, verging in some respects on the Byronic, particularly in the manner of his hair, which he wore romantically long, falling over his shoulders and carefully curled. He was of middle height, neither tall nor short, slim, dark-haired, sallow-complexioned, brightly grey-eyed, charming in his urbane, self-confident manner. Robert presented himself to society as 'full of ambition, eager for success, eager for fame, and, what's more, determined to conquer fame and to achieve success.' He was a model of punctilious politeness, good-looking, light-footed and — remarked Mrs 'Tottie' Bridell-Fox, daughter of William Johnson Fox, of his appearance in 1835 to 1836 — 'just a trifle of a dandy, addicted to lemon-coloured kid-gloves and such things: quite "the glass of fashion and the mould of form".'[33] He grew, when able to do so, crisp whiskers from cheekbone to chin.

In the absence of an assured annual unearned income, Robert made up his mind to a calculated economy in his private needs: writing to Elizabeth Barrett on 13 September 1845, he would later comment, 'My whole scheme of life (with its wants, material wants at least, closely cut down) was long ago calculated ... So for my own future way in the world I have always refused to care' — though that was then, without any responsibility other than to his own material maintenance. The Brownings were not poor, but neither were they rich — they were generous not only in keeping Robert at home but equally in the confidence they displayed in allowing him to devote himself to writing poetry. They might, of course, have been merely marking time, hoping that something would turn up, catch Robert's attention, fire his imagination and provide him with a good living. But on the best interpretation, his parents were large-minded and great-hearted in their confidence that this was the right thing to do for their son in particular and for the larger matter of literature in general. There was not much prospect of any financial return on their expenditure: it could hardly have been regarded as an investment except in the most optimistic view, poetry then, as now, being a paying proposition only in the most exceptional cases — Lord Byron being one in his own times; Sir Walter Scott, who also benefited from his activity as a novelist, being another.

But no doubt Mr Browning would have looked back on his own career and felt again the sigh of responsibility, of inevitability, with which he had given up his own artistic ambitions for routine employment as a banker. Robert 'appealed to his father', says Edmund Gosse, 'whether it would not be better for him to see life in the best sense, and cultivate the powers of his mind, than to shackle himself in the very outset of his career by a laborious training foreign to that aim'. And, says Gosse, 'so great was the confidence of the father in the genius of the son' that Mr Browning acquiesced — though perhaps by no means as promptly as Robert Browning later convinced himself and Gosse to have been the case. But acquiesce he did. Whatever Mr Browning might have felt he owed his son, perhaps he felt he owed himself another chance, albeit at second-hand. It was an indulgence, no doubt, but Mr Browning was not a man to invite difficulties or disputes. It was also a matter of simple fact: Robert remained rooted at home.

William Sharp makes the point that the young Robert Browning is sometimes credited with 'the singular courage to decline to be rich', but that Browning himself 'was the last man to speak of an inevitable artistic decision as "singular courage"'. He had, says Sharp, 'nothing of this bourgeois spirit'. Money, for money's sake, was not a consideration — as his letter of 13 September 1845 to Elizabeth Barrett later testified. He would prefer 'a blouse and a blue shirt (such as I now write in) to all manner of dress and gentlemanly appointment'. He could, 'if necessary, groom a horse not so badly, or at all events would rather do it all day long than succeed Mr Fitzroy Kelly in the Solicitor-Generalship', though by 1845 that youthful insouciance was changing in the light of love and its prospective attendant domestic expenses and obligations. Nevertheless, for the time being, in 1830, he 'need not very much concern himself beyond considering the lilies how they grow'. Or how the roses might blow in his mother's garden.

In *Robert Browning: A Portrait*, Betty Miller reviews the Brownings' financial situation, pointing remorselessly to the comparatively humble origins of Robert's mother as the daughter of a 'mariner in Dundee' rather than aggrandizing her as the daughter of a more substantial ship owner, and playing down the status and salary of the Bank of England clerkship enjoyed by Robert's father. She also instances some contemporary critics who perceived Robert's lack of apparent professional middle-class occupation as disgraceful. The prevailing attitude of respect for what is now identified as the 'Protestant work ethic' was as incorrigible then as now: poverty was generally considered to be morally reprehensible and fecklessness was regarded as a moral failing. The 'deserving poor' (a fairly select minority of the hapless and the disadvantaged) received pretty rough charity, grudging at best and rarely without an attached weight of sanctimony.

An accredited gentleman with an adequate fortune might blamelessly lead a life of leisure and pleasure, but the Brownings pretended to no giddy gentility. They were of the middle class, and the men of the middle class contributed their work to the perceived profit (moral and pecuniary) of society and to their own interests (much the same). Faults in character evidenced by apparent idleness were probably vicious and not easily glossed over by any high-tone, high-flown talk of devotion to poetry or art as a substitute for masculine resolve or absolution from a moral and material responsibility to earn a decent living. There is in this a suggestion that a poet must be, if not effeminate, at least effete — in contrast to the virtuous character of the common man committed to his daily labour who takes his 'true honourable place in society, etc. etc.', as Robert himself remarked. He was not wholly indifferent to conventional social values and expectations.

His position as a family dependent, nevertheless, did not unduly worry Robert: he acknowledged his father's generosity and airily supposed that, with a little effort, he might make 'a few hundred pounds which would soon cover my simple expenses'; and furthermore he felt, too, 'whenever I make up my mind to that, I can be rich enough and to spare — because,' he wrote later to Elizabeth Barrett, 'along with what you have thought *genius* in me, is certainly talent, what the world recognises as such; and I have tried it in various ways, just to be sure that I *was* a little magnanimous in never intending to use it.' Robert could do it if he had to, but for the time being he didn't see, or perhaps acknowledge, the necessity — he continued never to know 'what it was to have to do a certain thing to-day and not to-morrow', though that did not imply any inclination to do nothing. As Edmund Gosse reported from a conversation with Robert in his later life, 'freedom led to a super-abundance of production since on looking back he could see that he had often, in his unfettered leisure, been afraid to do nothing'. For the time being, however, Robert settled back into the familiar routines of family life and his proper application to poetry. He gave up vegetarianism as damaging to his health and atheism as damaging to his soul. The prodigal had returned, though in this case he could barely be said ever to have been away.

In January 1833, Robert completed a poetic work entitled *Pauline: A Fragment of a Confession*. It had been written as the first item in a projected grander master plan conceived at Richmond on the afternoon shading to evening of 22 October 1832 when he had seen Edmund Kean, once a great actor, by then in decline and disrepair but still powerfully impressive even when debilitated by drink and tuberculosis, play Shakespeare's Richard III. The poem, consisting of 1,031 lines, took Robert three months to write. He was twenty years old. Chesterton's dry comment is that 'It exhibits the characteristic mark of a juvenile poem, the general suggestion that the author is a thousand years old.' Robert himself, in a note inserted in 1838 at the beginning of his own copy, remarks that, 'The following Poem was written in pursuance of a foolish plan which occupied me mightily for a time, and which had for its object the enabling me to assume and realize I know not how many different characters; — meanwhile the world was never to guess that "Brown, Smith, Jones & Robinson" (as the spelling books have it) the respective authors of this poem, the other novel, such an opera, such a speech, etc., etc., were no other than one and the same individual. The present abortion was the first work of the *Poet* of the batch, who would have been more legitimately *myself* than most of the others; but I surrounded himself with all manner of (to my then notion) poetical accessories, and had planned quite a delightful life for him. Only this crab remains of the shapely Tree of Life in this fool's paradise of mine, — R.B.'

If Christiana, Aunt Silverthorne, had not kindly and unpromptedly paid £30 for its publication (£26 and 5 shillings for setting, printing and binding, £3 and 15 shillings for advertising), *Pauline* might have experienced the fate of *Incondita* — burned by its author to ashes. As it was, Sarianna had secretly copied, in pencil, particularly choice passages during Robert's composition of the poem.[34] She knew already the irresistible attraction for her brother of a fire in an open grate. She, indeed, was the only other person in the household who knew that Robert had begun writing the work at all. But then, five months later, there it was, published by Saunders and Otley, born and bound and in the hands of booksellers in March 1833. The author remained anonymous. Readers might suppose it to be the work of Brown, Smith, Jones, even Robinson, if they pleased: Robert Browning perhaps wisely elected for privacy over fame, though possibly only, batedly, preferring to anticipate the moment of astonishing revelation.

The book fell, not by chance, into the hands of reviewers. The Revd William Johnson Fox had read *Incondita*, and had reacted with a response that, if it stopped somewhat short of fulsome praise, had not been discouraging. Fox had acquired, in the interim, the *Monthly Repository* which, under his ownership and editorship, had achieved a reputation as an influential Unitarian publication. Its original emphasis had been theological, but Fox was eager not only to politicize its content but equally to give it a reputation for literary and dramatic criticism. Space could be found to notice improving literature: ten pages had recently been devoted in January 1830 to a review of the *Poems* of Tennyson by the 24-year-old John Stuart Mill (editor of Jeremy Bentham's *Treatise upon Evidence* and founder of the Utilitarian Society, activities that had unsettled him to the point of madness until the poetry of Wordsworth restored to him the will to live). On receipt of a positive reply to the letter reintroducing himself — though he seems only to have been aware, to judge by his letter, that Fox contributed reviews to the *Westminster Review* — Robert had twelve copies of *Pauline* sent to Mr Fox, together with a copy of Shelley's *Rosalind and Helen* which, afterwards wishing to retrieve, he later used as an excuse to call personally on Fox.

Fox's review was delightful. It admitted *Pauline: A Fragment of a Confession* to be 'evidently a hasty and imperfect sketch'. Nevertheless, 'In recognising a poet,' wrote Fox, 'we cannot stand upon trifles, nor fret ourselves about such matters. Time enough for that afterwards, when larger works come before us. Archimedes in the bath had many particulars to settle about specific gravities and Hiero's crown; but he first gave a glorious leap and shouted *Eureka!*' Fox's own leap was of faith that he had discovered a true poet. Of the work of genius before him, he had no doubt: he recommended the whole composition as being 'of the spirit, spiritual. The scenery is in the chambers of thought; the agencies are powers and passions; the events are transitions from one state of spiritual existence to another.' There was 'truth and life in it, which gave us the thrill and laid hold of us with the power, the sensation of which has never yet failed us as a test of genius.' Tennyson had passed the Fox test of genius, and now so did Browning. Both had raised the hair on the back of his neck. Mrs Orr begs to differ in respect of Fox's acceptance of the 'confessional and introspective quality of the poem as an expression of the highest emotional life — of the essence, therefore, of religion'. But she gives her full approbation to the 'encouraging kindness' of the one critic who alone, discerning enough to cry *Eureka!*, discovered Robert Browning in his first obscurity.

Allan Cunningham in the *Athenaeum* noticed *Pauline* with some graceful compliments — 'fine things abound . . . no difficulty in finding passages to vindicate our praise . . . To one who sings so naturally, poetry must be as easy as music is to a bird.' This was gratifying stuff, gilding the Fox lily which scented the air Robert Browning breathed and which he acknowledged as 'the most timely piece of kindness in the way of literary help that ever befell me'.[35] Fox had, however, given a copy of *Pauline* to John Stuart Mill who, besides being Fox's friend and assistant on the *Monthly Repository*, contributed reviews and articles to the *Examiner* and to *Tait's Edinburgh Magazine*, where, in August 1830, in an omnibus review of some dozen books, Mill briefly dismissed the poem as 'a piece of pure bewilderment'.

This might not have been so bad as a glancing cuff at an author's head by a reviewer too pressed for time to have read the poem properly and too squeezed for space to give it more than a line. But Mill, either then or later, had taken trouble to read *Pauline: A Fragment of a Confession* very thoroughly, and more than once. At the end of his copy, on the fly-leaf, he made a long note presumably for his own reference. What he wrote was this:

With considerable poetic powers, the writer seems to me possessed with a more intense and morbid self-consciousness than I ever knew in any sane human being. I should think it a sincere confession, though of a most unlovable state, if the 'Pauline' were not evidently a mere phantom. All about her is full of inconsistency — he neither loves her nor fancies he loves her, yet insists upon *talking* love to her. If she *existed* and loved him, he treats her most ungenerously and unfeelingly. All his aspirings and yearnings and regret point to other things, never to her; then he *pays her off* toward the end by a piece of flummery, amounting to the modest request that she will love him and live with him and give herself up to him *without* his *loving her moyennant quoi* he will think her and call her everything that is handsome, and he promises her that she shall find it mighty pleasant. Then he leaves off by saying he knows he will have changed his mind by to-morrow, and despite 'these intents which seem so fair,' but that having been thus visited once no doubt he will be again — and is therefore in 'perfect joy', bad luck to him! as the Irish say. A cento of most beautiful passages might be made from this poem, and the psychological history of himself is powerful and truthful — *truth-like* certainly, all but the last stage. *That*, he evidently has not yet got into. The self-seeking and self-worshipping state is well described — beyond that, I should think the writer has made, as yet, only the next step, viz. into despising his own state. I even question whether part even of that self-disdain is not *assumed*. He is evidently *dissatisfied*, and feels part of the badness of his state; he does not write as if it were purged out of him. If he once could muster a hearty hatred of his selfishness it would *go*; as it is, he feels only the *lack* of *good*, not the positive evil. He feels not remorse, but only disappointment; a mind in that state can only be regenerated by some new passion, and I know not what to wish for him but that he may meet with a *real* Pauline. Meanwhile he should not attempt to show how a person may be *recovered* from this morbid state, for *he* is hardly convalescent, and 'what should we speak of but that which we know?'

This is raw, unedited — though by no means unreflecting — stuff, the sort of thing a reviewer or critic will write for himself before dressing it up or toning it down for publication. It shows Mill's mind working largely on spontaneous impressions, though — or therefore — fresh and certainly, in this particular instance, acute in literary and psychological insights into a poet whose name and very existence were unknown to Mill. Just six years older than Robert Browning, he was already making a name for himself in literary, political, and journalistic circles. Just as well, then, that Mill's notes were never polished up and printed. It was quite enough that Mill's annotated copy of *Pauline* was included among the review copies that Fox returned to Robert on 30 October 1833. It is surmised that Mill's words, when Robert read them, prompted his own holograph note on his own copy of *Pauline*, referring to the poem as an 'abortion' and as a 'crab' on the Tree of Life in his paradise. Robert refused to permit republication of *Pauline* for nigh on thirty-five years, acknowledging merely his authorship of the poem 'with extreme repugnance and indeed purely of necessity'. Not only the review copies were returned to him by Fox; the publishers also sent Robert a bundle of unbound sheets. Not a single copy of *Pauline* had been sold.

If Mill had been a little too harsh in his disparagement, Fox had perhaps been a little too generous in his praise. Mrs Orr pointedly says of Mill that, 'there never was a large and cultivated intelligence one can imagine less in harmony than his with the poetic excesses, or even the poetic qualities, of *Pauline*'; and she acutely recognizes that Fox 'made very light of the artistic blemishes of the work . . . it was more congenial to him to hail that poet's advent than to register his shortcomings'. Mill recognized what Fox did not: the poet's morbid self-consciousness and the self-seeking state of his mind, the poem as a sincere confession, and its power and truth as a psychological history of its author. For in truth, *Pauline* was written, says Mrs Orr, whose view is enthusiastically confirmed in turn by Betty Miller, in a moment of 'supreme moral or physical crisis'.[36] Nobody, then or since, has doubted this for a minute. Mill may have been right to suggest that the poet was barely convalescent, far less recovered, from his morbid state of introspection, of self-examination — for *Pauline*, real or imagined as Browning's confessor, occupied his attentions as a woman less than his own interesting condition as a young man, slicing himself into an infinity of thin tissue samples and inspecting the results under a microscope of forensic self-analysis.

Robert claimed *Pauline* to be 'dramatic in principle'. It is gorgeous in imagery, but it is dramatic in the sense that a philosophical inquiry by Plato is dramatic: a scene is set; time, place, and characters are perfunctorily established before it proceeds to discussion of a moral crisis or conundrum and its resolution. The poem is of course — in view of Robert's preoccupation with him — heavily influenced by Shelley (invoked in *Pauline* as 'Sun-treader' and 'Apollo'). Scholarly consensus has it that the dramatic principle of *Pauline* is a lyrical narrative inspired by the form of Shelley's *Alastor*, and deriving elements from that poet's *Epipsychidion*. Robert Browning confesses his guilty history to Pauline, who is made privy to disappointing experiences in life and disappointed experiments with living — the poet's loss of honour in disloyalty to all he held dear, to Pauline herself (who represents women he has loved, including his mother, representing familiar, comfortable domesticity), to a lapse from his inherited religious faith and the substituted creed of Shelley (who taught him to believe in men perfected as gods and the earth perfected as heaven), the sinking of the good estimation of his family (disappointed by his spurning of conventional education and a conventional career). It is a sorry catalogue, all in all.

The examination of the poet's soul reveals the accumulation of guilt and regret, initially a cause of despair and self-doubt that gradually evolves into a more positive source of self-confidence and optimism. Robert, in the course of *Pauline*, heals himself, though his renewal necessarily involves an alteration in personal consciousness. To become what he is, it has been necessary to be what he was. On a note of self-definition, he relinquishes his Shelleyan delusions; he returns to his love of God (with some qualifications and reservations), to his love for Pauline (and her domestic virtues and comforts), to art (Shelley, the 'Sun-treader', is installed in the firmament — a star in eternity — his ideals renounced but his supremacy as a poet maintained), and to himself in the space he has cleared for future manoeuvre. Read autobiographically, rather than as art, *Pauline* probably did an effective therapeutic job for the poet; as art, the poem is generally agreed to be a precociously subjective failure.

Robert's return to religion was not corseted by the narrow confines of Congregationalism. He sought out colourful, dramatic, evangelizing preachers whose theatricality appealed to his taste not merely for their rhetorical flourishes of eloquence, but for imaginative reasoning splendidly dressed with a generous garnish of allusions, references, myth, metaphor, and metaphysics. One of the most celebrated was William Johnson Fox himself, who spoke with a liberal tongue and conscience. Following on Fox's review of *Pauline*, Robert paid an evening call at Stamford Grove West, near Dalston in Hackney, where he renewed acquaintance not only with Fox but with Eliza and Sarah Flower, both nearing thirty years of age, who were living with him as his wards after the death of their father in 1829.

They hardly recognized Robert after four years: now almost twenty-one years old, he was a sight to behold — becomingly whiskered, elegantly gloved and caped, drily witty. The sisters had read *Pauline* and were interested to see the author. Sarah, in a letter of June 1833, remarked to a cousin that the 'poet boy' had turned up, 'very interesting from his great power of conversation and thorough originality, to say nothing of his personal appearance, which would be exceptionally poetic if nature had not served him an unkind trick in giving him an ugly nose'.[37] Quite what was wrong with Robert's nose is not specified, though perhaps it was merely less 'unmatured' than the poet who, Sarah considered, 'will do much better things'. Her estimation of *Pauline* was evidently more critical than that of her guardian, Mr Fox, though William Sharp suggests that the enthusiasm of the Flower sisters influenced Fox's own partiality for the poem. Sarah herself wrote poetry, so probably knew what she was talking about, and she had doubtless discussed *Pauline* with her sister Eliza, who was acknowledged to be an excellent critic.

Eliza Flower makes only brief appearances in Mrs Orr's *Life and Letters of Robert Browning*, but she acknowledges that, 'If, in spite of his [Browning's] denials, any woman inspired *Pauline*, it can have been no other than she.' Vivienne Browning offers the alternative suggestion, in an essay, 'The Real Identity of Pauline', published in the Browning Society notes in 1983, that Robert might have had in mind his Aunt Jemima, only a year older than himself, described by Mrs Orr as 'very amiable and, to use her nephew's words, "as beautiful as the day"'. But whoever may have been the model for Pauline is hardly relevant: she was, as Mill understood, 'a mere phantom'. Pauline was a womanly compound: if not Woman herself, she was at least a combination of friend, lover, Sophia, sister, mother, and even — since it is possible to identify some subtle adolescent homophile lines in the poem — the inspiration may sometimes, just as likely, have been Shelley as well as any woman. The point being, rather, that Robert probably felt some tender adolescent attraction to Eliza, who was nine years his elder — the first of the older women after his mother to engage his attentions and affections throughout his life. The poetic figure of Pauline, a mature figure of a woman with abundant dark hair and a rather sultry eroticism, very likely represented — personified — the sexual image, ideals, and desires that Robert was beginning to form for himself.

Eliza, who was in love with William Johnson Fox, was pleased to see Robert again, though her initial admiration was exceeded by his own self-admiration. She began to think, 'he has twisted the old-young shoot off by the neck' and that, 'if he had not got into the habit of talking of head and heart as two separate existences, one would say that he was born without a heart'. At any rate, any prospect of romance between them was fairly improbable, though they continued to be friends. Ever afterwards, Robert maintained for Eliza a sentimental friendship that was rooted in loyalty to his admiration for her music, respect for her mind, and tender affection for her goodness. She died of consumption in 1846, the year of Robert's marriage to Elizabeth Barrett.

For all Robert's later repugnance for *Pauline*, for all his thwarted attempts to recover the copy of the book that Mill had written in, for all his reluctance to authorize any further publication even of extracts from it in his lifetime, for all his resistance to inclusion of an amended version of the poem in a collected edition of his work in 1868, and for all revisionist tinkerings with the poem to render it fit for an edition of 1888, his dissociation from it could never be complete. The secret of his authorship soon leaked out and, in fact, initially did him some good. It brought him at least some limited literary recognition (albeit of a mixed nature) and established something of a style that twenty years later was recognized by the young painter and poet Dante Gabriel Rossetti, who had read Browning's *Paracelsus* and, coming across *Pauline* in the British Museum library, was astute enough to understand that it was by the hand of the same author — though he was careful enough to copy it out and ask for Browning's confirmation of authorship, which Robert duly supplied.[38]

Biographers of Browning now fall down a hole of unknowing for two years, pulling themselves back into the light of biographical day with some difficulty, finding occasional toeholds in scattered references throughout Browning's later work that give clues to his activities from publication of *Pauline* in 1833 to publication of his next production, *Paracelsus*, in 1835. William Sharp suggests that during this period Robert began to go out and about in 'congenial society', specifically citing new acquaintance with 'many well-known workers in the several arts',[39] including Charles Dickens and Serjeant Thomas Noon Talfourd, a notable lawyer — the title 'Serjeant' derived from his position in the Inns of Court as a barrister — who was to publish *Ion* in 1836 and several more blank verse tragedies that do not much detain the attention of posterity but gave pleasure in their own time. Talfourd was then famous, nevertheless, for his wide acquaintance with literary men, later on account of his elevation to the judiciary and his work as a Member of Parliament in securing real protection for authors' copyright, and always for his loquacity and conviviality.

If Robert did indeed meet Talfourd at this time, he would have been a good man for a young author to know — though Sharp says that Browning's first reputation among such company was as an artist and musician rather than as a poet, and residence south of the river in remote, rural Camberwell made night engagements impracticable. During the day, says Sharp, Robert consulted works on philosophy and medical history in the British Museum Library and very often visited the National Gallery (unlikely, since that institution did not open until 1838). Certainly Robert was fortifying his friendships with men like Alfred Domett, Jim Silverthorne, his cheerful young uncle Reuben Browning (who was an elegant scholar of Latin and an accomplished horseman), and he may at this time have joined a circle of young men who clustered around a Captain Pritchard of Battersea, who had met Robert when he was sixteen and had introduced him to the medical lectures given at Guy's Hospital by a cousin, Dr Blundell.

In the winter of 1833–4, at the age of twenty-one going on twenty-two, Robert found himself on an expedition to Russia, specifically to

St Petersburg, nominally as secretary to the Chevalier de Benkhausen, the Russian consul-general in London. How on earth he wangled this trip, how on earth indeed he made the acquaintance in the first place of the Russian consul-general — who 'had taken a great liking to him'[40] — is not clear, though Mrs Orr says that 'the one active career which would have recommended itself to him in his earlier youth was diplomacy . . . He would indeed not have been averse to any post of activity and responsibility not unsuited to the training of a gentleman.'

These remarks suggest that Robert was by then perhaps chafing and fretting at home even more than before and may have been thinking better of his decision to commit himself exclusively to poetry and financial dependence on his family. Mrs Orr does not spell out the reasons for this aspiration to diplomacy as a career, and there are no surviving letters from this period to add substance to speculation. William Shergold Browning worked as a Rothschild banker in Paris at this time, while his brother Reuben Browning, Robert's favourite uncle, worked for Nathan Rothschild in the Rothschild London banking house. It is tempting to assume a connection between international banking and diplomacy that could have brought Robert to the attention of the consul-general. At any rate, there must have been some personal recommendation and introduction, more likely to have derived from a family connection than any other.

Of the Russian expedition, of its official purpose and its immediate personal importance for Robert, we know next to nothing: Robert wrote regularly and lengthily to Sarianna, but he burned the letters in later life. He set off with Benkhausen, say Griffin and Minchin, contradicting by a few months Mrs Orr's version of an earlier, winter journey, on Saturday 1 March 1834. Early spring seems more likely; they would still be travelling through snow, but would reach Russia just as a thaw was setting in. They travelled, it is estimated, 1500 miles on horseback and by post carriage. In 1830, Stephenson's Rocket, a marvel of modern technology, had made the first journey on the Liverpool to Manchester railway, and The General Steam Navigation Company operated a basic, bucketing, piston-thumping packet service from London to Ostend and Rotterdam; but there the transport system ran, literally, out of steam. 'We know,' says Mrs Orr, 'how strangely he was impressed by some of the circumstances of the journey: above all by the endless monotony of snow-covered pine forest through which he and his companion rushed for days and nights at the speed of six post-horses, without seeming to move from one spot.'

'How I remember the flowers — even grapes — of places I have seen!' wrote Robert to a friend, Fanny Haworth, on 24 July 1838, '— some one flower or weed, I should say, that gets some strangehow connected with them. Snowdrops and Tilsit in Prussia go together'; and throughout Browning's work there are associations of this sort that testify to the power of his memory for detail: 'Wall and wall of pine' and, from the poem 'A Forest Thought':

> In far Esthonian solitudes
> The parent firs of future woods
> Gracefully, airily spire at first
> Up to the sky, by the soft sand nurst . . .

and so on until he reached St Petersburg where he looked at pictures in the Hermitage, no doubt as thoroughly and with as critical an eye as at the Dulwich Gallery.

In a letter to Elizabeth Barrett, on 11 August 1845, Robert described a play he had written, in about 1843, entitled 'Only a Player Girl': 'it was Russian, and about a fair on the Neva, and booths and droshkies and fish pies and so forth, with the Palaces in the background'. The play is not known to have survived either the destroying hand of time or that of the author. He says, furthermore, that at St Petersburg he met a Sir James Wylie who 'chose to mistake me for an Italian — "M. l'Italien" he said another time, looking up from his cards.' Others regularly made the same assumption, whether sincerely or satirically, taking their cue from Robert's sallow-complexioned, dandified appearance. Another acquaintance in St Petersburg, say Griffin and Minchin,[41] was a King's Messenger called Waring whose name Robert borrowed eight years later in *Dramatic Lyrics* to cover for the identity of Alfred Domett as the eponymous subject of the poem 'Waring' and imagined as,

> Waring in Moscow, to those rough
> Cold northern climes borne, perhaps.

Before leaving Russia, after an absence from England of some three months, Robert watched the solid ice crack on the frozen Neva and heard the boom of guns that accompanied the governor's journey on the now navigable river to present a ceremonial goblet of Neva water to the tsar. 'St Petersburg, no longer three isolated portions,' say Griffin and Minchin, 'was once more united, as the floating wooden bridges swung into place across the mighty stream, and the city was *en fête*'. Robert, presumably delighting in Russian fairs, which may have occupied his interest rather more than Mrs Orr would have approved, kept an attentive and recording ear open to the music of Russia, folk songs in particular. Fifty years later in Venice, by the account of a friend, Katherine Bronson, he was able to recollect perfectly and accurately sing some of these songs to the elderly Prince Gagarin, a retired Russian diplomat, who exclaimed delightedly and wonderingly at Browning's musical memory that, he declared, surpassed his own.[42]

In Russia, and shortly after his return to London, Robert had not overlooked his poetic vocation: besides storing up materials for future work, he wrote a number of poems — notably the grimly dramatic monologue 'Porphyria's Lover', with its quietly sensational last line; a sonnet, 'A Forest Thought', which most early Browning biographers and critics have passed by tight-lipped and with a sorrowful shake of the head; a song (beginning, 'A King lived long ago . . .') that he incorporated a few years later into *Pippa Passes*; a lyric (beginning, 'Still ailing, wind? Wilt be appeased or no?') that was later introduced into the sixth section of 'James Lee' (in *Dramatis Personæ*); and the poem 'Johannes Agricola in Meditation' (later published in *Dramatic Lyrics*), which might be thought of, in its theme of Calvinistic predestination, as Browning's equivalent of 'Holy Willie's Prayer' by Robert Burns. All these were submitted to Fox's *Monthly Repository* and accepted for publication. They appeared there, anonymously over the initial 'Z', from 1834 to 1836.

Whether to support his life as a poet or seriously to begin a diplomatic career, or simply to reinforce the independence that the visit to St Petersburg had probably aroused, Robert felt confident enough after his three months as aide or secretary, or whatever role he played in attendance to the Russian consul-general, to apply 'for appointment on a mission which was to be despatched to Persia'.[43] He was disappointed to be passed over, the more so since the response to his application had, on a misreading, appeared to offer him the position which in fact

— he learned only in the course of an interview with 'the chief' — was offered to another man, whom Robert damned in a letter to Sarah Flower, suggesting that 'the Right Hon. Henry Ellis etc., etc., may go to a hotter climate for a perfect fool — (that at Baghdad in October, 127 Fahrenheit in the shade)'.[44]

Still, to be realistic, the failure was maybe all to the good. Diplomacy was certainly a creditable profession for a gentleman, though that gentleman needed not only financial assets to back it up, at least in the beginning, and, to advance it, the social contacts that most successful young diplomats had either acquired on their own account at Oxford or Cambridge or naturally possessed through upper-middle-class and aristocratic family relationships. To cut a career as a diplomat was as difficult and expensive as to make progress as a barrister (Alfred Domett and Joseph Arnould were already finding this out in their first years as young lawyers) or gain promotion as a military officer in a regiment of any social consequence. The cost to the Browning family purse of maintaining Robert as an embassy attaché would have weighed even more heavily than keeping him at home as a poet. Maisie Ward supposes that the Silverthornes would have found a place for Robert in the family brewery, but 'this would have meant no less drudgery, no better future prospects than the bank, and if [Cyrus] Mason's view of the worldliness of the family is correct, they would certainly have aimed at something more socially acceptable'.

A certain sense of heightened social awareness is imputed to the Brownings by Maisie Ward and by Cyrus Mason: it may fall short of social snobbery, but attitudes and aspirations do tend to suggest at least an impetus towards gentility — what we now regard more positively as 'upward mobility'. Mrs Orr's definite and regular distaste for any possibility of Robert's being tarred by association with 'lowlife'; the horror with which Cyrus Mason (and other Brownings even into the mid twentieth century) regarded any suggestion that even distant ancestors might have been of the servant class; the gentleman's education that Robert enjoyed — these are pointers that perhaps speak more of prevailing social values in mid nineteenth-century England than of the particular case of the Brownings, though of course the Brownings were of the middle rank of the powerful middle classes that mostly subscribed without question to the desirability of self-improvement in their lives.

There were no awkward assertions of social superiority, however, to make any visitor to the Browning household feel ill at ease (Mrs Browning was no Mrs Wilfer, with her head tied up in a handkerchief and her aspirations affirmed in a superior sniff); it was a sociable house and many of Robert's friends have recorded warm memories of happy evenings there among good company. Cyrus Mason gnashed his teeth in the darkness of outer family, dismally nursing into old age his own exclusion from this cheerful company — more than likely, says Maisie Ward, he simply bored the Brownings to death — and took his revenge cold as his abiding bitterness when he wrote of the 'misty pride' that hung like a dampness in the 'genteelly dreary' Browning household and shrouded its inhabitants, whose single, self-absorbed concern was to develop a poet of genius to the obliteration of natural affection within the near family and shameful neglect of its extended members. The fact that Reuben Browning and the Silverthornes, close family, were welcome guests, and are known to have been generous to Robert, would tend to put paid to Cyrus Mason's more extreme accusations.

It is true, nevertheless, that Robert took the trouble to cultivate good acquaintance. A letter written in 1830 by Robert to a close friend, Christopher Dowson, refers to 'the unfortunate state of our friend P[ritchard]'.[45] Pritchard is not a significant figure in Browning's correspondence — the letters that have survived the conflagration of Browning's personal papers contain only minor references to him — and nobody but Griffin and Minchin is interested in poor old Pritchard as a character in Browning's life, either at this time or later. They describe him as 'a brisk, dapper, little, grey-haired sea-captain, with a squint and a delightful fund of tales of adventure'. He lived at Battersea, and it was his whim to keep his address a close secret. However, he was the focus of a set, known as 'The Colloquials', of young men into whose orbit Robert was attracted and with whom he struck up lasting friendships. Pritchard's 'elasticity of mind bade defiance to advancing years and enabled him to associate unconstrainedly with those who were very considerably his juniors', say Griffin and Minchin, and they further state that he had a chivalrous regard for women, to the extent of leaving his money to two maiden ladies on the ground that 'women should be provided for since they cannot earn their living'.[46] One of these maiden ladies was Sarianna Browning, who later inherited £1000 by Pritchard's will.

Through Pritchard, Robert met and associated with Christopher and Joseph Dowson, William Curling Young and his younger brother Frederick Young, Alfred Domett, and Joseph Arnould. The Dowsons knew Pritchard through shipping, their family business; Christopher Dowson later married Mary, Alfred Domett's sister; Joseph Dowson associated himself with the Youngs through business interests; in short, the group developed close family and business ties that bound them together longer than their youthful debates — their 'boisterous Colloquies', as Arnould later characterized them — about politics, poetry, theatre, philosophy, science, and the business of the group magazine, *Olla Podrida*, which they produced to publish their own essays, poems, and whatever other of their effusions pleased them. Robert himself contributed 'A Dissertation on Debt and Debtors', an essay which characteristically quoted from Quarles and uncharacteristically — for a man whose horror of debt was later well known and to become deeply ingrained — defended debt as a necessary condition of human life.[47]

A less regular member of the group was Field Talfourd, an artist and brother of Thomas Noon Talfourd, and it has been suggested that Benjamin Jowett, the future celebrated Master of Balliol College, Oxford, may have attended some Colloquial meetings — though his name is introduced more on the basis that he was then a native of Camberwell than on any sure evidence of his participation in the group's activities. The Colloquials seem to have been a kindly, good-natured set of young, middle-class men whose aspirations and ambitions variously took them into the middle ranks of the law, politics, and business, at home and in the service of the Empire. Several of them, notably Arnould and Domett, wrote poetry for the rest of their lives: Arnould, while at Wadham College, Oxford, won the Newdigate Prize for poetry; Domett turned out stuff such as *Ranolf and Amohia: a South-Sea Day Dream*, inspired by his Antipodean travels and career, not wholly disrespected by public regard in his own day but entirely unknown to present fame. Of them all, Robert was forever closest to Alfred Domett.

Diplomacy had not yet done with Robert Browning, though Robert may have all but done with diplomacy. In 1834, a young Frenchman presented himself to the Brownings. This was Count Amédée de Ripert-Monclar, then in his mid-twenties. He was socially affable, urbane, cosmopolitan, and intellectually impressive, literate in European art and poetry, and interested in finance. He had been recommended to William Shergold Browning, of Rothschild's in Paris, by the Marquis of Fortia, his uncle, who shared with William Browning an interest in literature. William in turn recommended young Ripert-Monclar to his brother Reuben in London, who introduced him into the Browning household. Ripert-Monclar claimed to be spending his summers in England, ostensibly for pleasure.[48] In fact, the young aristocrat was a Royalist, an active supporter of the dethroned Bourbons now living in England as a result of the French revolution of July 1830 that made Louis-Philippe, duc d'Orléans, King of France until he in turn was toppled in 1848. Ripert-Monclar, as he confessed to the Brownings, was acting as a private agent of communication between the royal exiles and their legitimist friends in France. He was not himself an exile, though it can be assumed that he was no favourite of Louis-Philippe. There is a suggestion that he may have been briefly held in jail in 1830. It was diplomacy of a thrilling sort — clandestine, subversive, and romantic.

Amédée and Robert struck up an immediate, intimate friendship: they talked no doubt of royalty and republicanism, though they probably discussed art and poetry more than politics; they would have talked of France, particularly of Paris, and Robert's French — already reliable enough to have enabled him to write part of *Pauline* in good French — would have become even more polished. The young Frenchman introduced Robert to the works of Balzac and the new French realist writers, he sketched his new friend's portrait, and at some point or other he suggested the life of Paracelsus, the Renaissance alchemist and physician, as the subject of Robert's next major poem. He then thought better of the idea, 'because it gave no room for the introduction of love about which every young man of their age thought he had something quite new to say'.[49] But too late, too late to withdraw the suggestion: besides, Robert had already dealt with love in *Pauline*, and there had been precious little profit in that. Better, perhaps, to steer clear for the time being, take another tack.

Though two or three months of preliminary research ('in the holes and corners of history', as Chesterton likes to put it) had been necessary, Paracelsus was already a familiar-enough character to Robert: there was the entry in the *Biographie Universelle* on his father's shelves; there was the Frederick Bitiskius three-volume folio edition of Paracelsus' works; there were relevant medical works to hand, including a little octavo of 1620, the *Vitæ Germanorum Medicorum* of Melchior Adam, with which he was already acquainted from his recent interest in medicine. By mid-March 1835, interrupting a work in progress called *Sordello*, which he had begun a couple of years earlier in March 1833, Robert had written a full manuscript entitled *Paracelsus*, a poem of 4,152 lines which was 'Inscribed to Amédée de Ripert-Monclar by his affectionate friend R.B.'. This dedication was dated 'London: 15 March 1835'. *Paracelsus*, divided into five scenes and featuring four characters, had taken Robert just over five months to complete. It was published at his father's expense by Effingham Wilson, of the Royal Exchange, on 15 August 1835. Saunders and Otley had declined the privilege of publishing the poem, and it had taken some trouble and influence to induce even Effingham Wilson, a small publisher, to undertake the job. Wilson published *Paracelsus*, says Mrs Orr, more 'on the ground of radical sympathies in Mr Fox and the author than on that of its intrinsic worth.'[50]

In a preliminary letter of 2 April[51] to William Johnson Fox, Robert requested an introduction to Fox's neighbour, Edward Moxon, printer and publisher of Dover Street, Piccadilly, 'on account of his good name and fame among author-folk, besides he has himself written — as the Americans say — "more poetry 'an you can shake a stick at"'. Moxon was a high-flying old bird to be expected to notice a fledgling fresh out of the nest and bumping near to the ground like Robert Browning. Thirty-four years of age in 1835, when he gave up writing his own poetry, Moxon was less distinguished as a poet than as a publisher and bookseller. Leigh Hunt wittily described him as 'a bookseller among poets, and a poet among booksellers'. The remark has stuck to Moxon, who in 1830 had established his business which quickly acquired a reputation for publishing poetry of high quality by a remarkable list of poets including Shelley, Keats, Coleridge, Lamb (who introduced many of them to Moxon), Southey, Clare, Wordsworth, and Tennyson, who became Moxon's close friend. Leigh Hunt remarked that 'Moxon has no connection but with the select of the earth', which was intended satirically but may have been true enough in literary terms, implying a discrimination that has proved itself in posterity and went far beyond the terms of mere business in Moxon's defence of his poets against the famous attacks by Lockhart and the rest of the Scots critics of *Blackwood's*, the *Edinburgh* and the *Quarterly* reviews.

On 16 April 1835[52] Robert again wrote to Fox to report on a visit to Moxon, whose 'visage loured exceedingly' and 'the Moxonian accent grew dolorous' on perusal of a recommendatory letter by Charles Cowden Clarke (who had been a close friend of Keats, and was now a friend of Fox) which Robert presented to him. This was not encouraging; even less encouraging was Moxon's view of the poetry written by some of Robert's tremendous contemporaries, far less a work by someone virtually unknown. Moxon gloomily revealed that *Philip von Artevelde*, a long dramatic poem by Sir Henry Taylor that had excited the *Athenaeum*, normally decorous, to rave enthusiastically in fifteen columns just the year before, had 'not paid expenses by about thirty odd pounds'. Furthermore, 'Tennyson's poetry', said Moxon, 'is "*popular at Cambridge*" and yet of 800 copies which were printed of his last, some 300 only have gone off: Mr M[oxon] hardly knows whether he shall ever venture again, etc. etc., and in short begs to decline even inspecting, etc. etc.' Poetry could no longer be relied upon as a paying proposition.

Robert offered to read his poem to Fox some morning, 'though I am rather scared of *a fresh eye* going over its 4000 lines ... yet on the whole I am not much afraid of the issue ... I shall really *need* your notice on this account'; and finished off his letter with some heavy humorous flourishes that included a discreet swipe at John Stuart Mill advising him not to be an 'idle spectator' of Robert's first appearance on a public stage ('having previously only dabbled in private theatricals'). *Paracelsus* was to be Robert's première, his big first night with the critics, who were invited to attend and advised to pay attention, 'benignant or supercilious' as Mill in particular should choose, but 'he may depend that tho' my "Now is the winter of our discontent" be rather awkward, yet there shall be occasional outbreaks of good stuff — that I shall warm as I get on, and finally wish "Richmond at the bottom of the seas," etc. in the best style imaginable.'

Paracelsus received mixed reviews from those critics who did not pass it over in silence entirely. The reviewer for the *Athenaeum* gave the poem a brief, lukewarm notice in 73 words on 22 August 1835, reluctantly recognizing 'talent in this dramatic poem' but warning against facile imitation of Shelley's 'mysticism and vagueness' in a work the reviewer found 'dreamy and obscure'. There was worse from some other reviewers whose notices Robert, if he did not take them to heart as guides to future good poetic conduct, at least bore as scabs on his mind and as scars in his soul. He still scratched at them a decade later. On 17 September 1845, in a letter to Elizabeth Barrett, he recalled 'more than one of the reviews and newspapers that laughed my "Paracelsus" to scorn ten years ago' and contrasted, in a further letter to her of 9 December 1845, 'that my own "Paracelsus", printed a few months before, had been as dead a failure as "Ion" [by Thomas Noon Talfourd] a brilliant success . . . I know that until Forster's notice in the *Examiner* appeared, *every* journal that thought it worth while to allude to the poem at all, treated it with entire contempt.' Fox contributed a tardy review in the *Monthly Repository* in November: Robert had read *Paracelsus* aloud to him and they had discussed the poem, so he had had the benefit of the poet's own industry, ideas and intentions to draw upon in his favourable notice, which declared the work to be 'the result of thought, skill and toil' and not — as the *Athenaeum* had judged it — a dreamy and obscure effusion. *Paracelsus* was not only a poem, declared Fox, but a poem with ideas.

His bold, informed defence of the poem had its effect: John Forster, in an article in the *New Monthly Magazine and Literary Journal* early in 1836, promoted Robert to Parnassus: 'Without the slightest hesitation we name Mr Browning at once with Shelley, Coleridge, Wordsworth.' A vacancy had recently occurred, since Samuel Taylor Coleridge had died in 1834. But Forster had needed little or no prompting from a sympathetic review by Fox. As chief dramatic and literary reviewer of the *Examiner*, he had already dealt generously with *Paracelsus* in that publication: 'Since the publication of *Philip von Artevelde*,' he wrote, 'we have met with no such evidences of poetic genius, and of general intellectual power, as are contained in this volume.' Forster closed his review of *Paracelsus* with these words: 'It is some time since we read a work of more unequivocal power than this. We conclude that its author is a young man, as we do not recollect his having published before.' He was evidently, perhaps mercifully, unacquainted with *Pauline*, now immured in the British Museum Library. 'If so, we may safely predict for him a brilliant career, if he continues true to the present promise of his genius. He possesses all the elements of a fine poet.' Forster, unlike

Fox, had not enjoyed the benefit of Robert Browning's acquaintance, and his review is all the more valuable for that reason. He assumed Browning to be a young man, though it was difficult to tell from the poem itself: to repeat Chesterton's line, Robert could have been anything between twenty and a thousand years old if the evidence of *Paracelsus* were the only criterion by which to judge his age.

Forster, says Mrs Orr, 'knew that a writer in the *Athenaeum* had called it rubbish, and he had taken it up as a probable subject for a piece of slashing criticism'. A young critic (Forster was twenty-three years old in 1835, only five months younger than Browning) will some-times adopt this tactic — an acknowledged means of getting on in literary society by bringing one's own talent more prominently to the attention of fellow-critics, editors, and publishers than the work being reviewed. However, intending to bury Browning, Forster paused to praise, though 'what he did write', says Mrs Orr, 'can scarcely be defined as praise. It was the simple, ungrudging admission of the unequivocal power, as well as brilliant promise, which he recognized in the work.'[53] This in turn is perhaps a little grudging of Forster's real recognition that here was a poet, perhaps not yet fully formed but promising great things. Robert himself, weighing the laurel crown awarded by Forster in the balance against the ashes heaped on his head by others, did not feel as pleased as he might otherwise have done if Forster's had been but one voice amongst a full chorus singing in praiseful tune. Though he privately enjoyed the wholehearted applause of family and friends for his 'private theatricals', his public reception, now that he had put himself stage front, was more problematical.

Paracelsus was important to Robert. If *Pauline* had been a preview, in theatrical terms, the aspiring player would have performed to an empty house before being hooked off the stage by dissatisfied critics. But now — as he himself had written to Fox — this latest poem was his 'first appearance on any stage'. It had been better, maybe, to start again and afresh. However, Robert specifically disclaimed in the preface any intention to promote *Paracelsus* as a drama or a dramatic poem. It was, he insisted, a poem and of a genre very different from that under-taken by any other poet. He warned critics off judging it 'by principles on which it was never moulded' and subjecting it 'to a standard to which it was never meant to conform'.

What he meant by this was his intention 'to reverse the method usually adopted by writers whose aim it is to set forth any phenomenon of mind or the passions by the operation of persons and events; and that, instead of having recourse to an external machinery of incidents to create and evolve the crisis I desire to produce, I have ventured to display somewhat minutely the mood itself in its rise and progress, and have suffered the agency by which it is influenced and determined, to be generally discernible in its effects along and subordinate throughout, if not altogether excluded.'

No doubt this sentence made his meaning entirely clear to his contemporaries. What in effect Browning did in *Paracelsus* was to divide the poem into five sections or scenes, each a monologue by Aureolus Paracelsus, 'a student', with occasional interruptions by three other characters — Festus and Michal, husband and wife, described as 'his friends', and Aprile, thought to be inspired by Shelley, described as 'an Italian poet'. These three took the roles, mostly, of auditors and some-times prompts, iterating his moods at a critical point in his life. In each section, Paracelsus examines the state of his own inner life. By means of the insights he successively gains, he is enabled to act.

Rather more clearly, in his preface to the poem, Browning defined its intended form: 'I have endeavoured to write a poem, not a drama: the canons of the drama are well known, and I cannot but think that, inasmuch as they have immediate regard to stage representation, the peculiar advantages they hold out are really such only so long as the purpose for which they were first instituted is kept in view. I do not very well understand what is called a Dramatic Poem, wherein all those restrictions, only submitted to on account of compensating good in the original scheme are scrupulously retained, as though for some special fitness in themselves and all new facilities placed at an author's disposal by the vehicle he selects, as pertinaciously rejected. It is certain, however, that a work like mine depends more immediately on the intelligence and sympathy of the reader for its success: indeed, were my scenes stars, it must be his co-operating fancy which, supplying all chasms, should connect the scattered lights into one constellation — a Lyre or a Crown.'

The poem is not notably dramatic, nor is it a linear narrative, nor is it lyric. It is light years away in its obscure allusions, recondite refer-ences, novel form, and difficult philosophy from the comparatively undemanding verse narratives of, say, Sir Walter Scott (who was never-theless considered difficult even by some contemporary critics) or, for that matter, the familiar brio and theatricality of Byron's verses. If it required strenuous mental effort from a perceptive critic, it stretched to incomprehension the limits of the common reader whom Browning, however flatteringly, expected to co-operate with him, engage with him, in the very creation of the poem. *Paracelsus* was, in the modern term, 'interactive' — it depended, as Browning said in his preface, 'more immediately on the intelligence and sympathy of the reader for its success'.

For the meantime, however, the common reader confirmed the most dolorous expectations of Moxon. The light-minded reader in 1835 preferred the sentimental verse of Laetitia Elizabeth Landon (who died in 1838 at the age of 36, styled herself in life for the purposes of authorship as 'L.E.L.', wrote several novels and copious poetry, attracted to herself a reputation for indecorous romantic attachments that caused her to break off her engagement to John Forster) and Felicia Dorothea Hemans (who was responsible in 1829 for the poem 'Casabianca' and its famous first line, 'The boy stood on the burning deck . . .'); preferred, too, gift books of mawkish poetry, and other such comforting, easily digestible products, after-dinner *bon-bons* or *bon-mots* that demanded no effort or response more than an easy smile, a wistful sigh, a romantic tear or any momentary rush of unreflecting, commonplace feeling. Nothing but the most banal expression of sentimental emotion was likely to succeed in the market for new poetry. Robert accepted that a work such as *Paracelsus*, even if lucky enough to find a publisher ready to print it, would be not only a short-term casualty of the early nineteenth-century crisis in poetry publishing but even, in the long term, might stand more as a *succès d'estime* than as a source of short-term financial profit or a lasting resource of popular taste. It would have to be enough in the mid-1830s that a few discriminating readers should read Robert Browning and — so far as they were able — appreciate what he was trying to do and say.

Paracelsus partook of the times not only in the experimental nature of its form, for the first half of the nineteenth century was an age of experiments and advances: it positively incorporated new thinking and new ideas and conflated them with the occult wisdom of the Renaissance, another distinct period of new thinking, new art, new science, and new technology. In *The Life of Robert Browning*, Clyde de L. Ryals[54] points to Browning's assimilation of late eighteenth- and early nineteenth-century scientific findings in biology, geology, and other sciences, to the extent that he was later to claim, very reasonably, that *Paracelsus* had anticipated Darwin's *On the Origin of Species* (published in 1859) by some quarter of a century. Objecting to an assertion that he had ever been 'strongly against Darwin, rejecting the truths of science and regretting its advance', Robert only had to look back to find 'all that seemed *proved* in Darwin's scheme was a conception familiar to me from the beginning: see in *Paracelsus* the progressive development from senseless matter to organized, until man's appearance.'[55]

Since all things are in nature, and Paracelsus was a natural philosopher and scientist, inexhaustibly desirous to plumb the secrets of nature (in Renaissance terms, an alchemist), it is hardly surprising that he appealed to Robert Browning as a bridge between science as it had been understood by the ancients and the perception of science by savants in his own age. Science itself was appropriate as a convenient vehicle for comment upon the facts of life that have always been known in one way or another, in one philosophy or another, but have been variously interpreted, when not entirely lost or forgotten or ignored, from generation to generation.

When Paracelsus died in 1541, he disappeared from the ken of all but the most esoteric scholars. Chesterton comments, wonderingly, on Browning's choice of poetic protagonists — 'the common characteristic of all these persons is not so much that they were of importance in their day as that they are of no importance in ours'. In his choice of Paracelsus, Browning's 'supreme type of the human intellect is neither the academic nor the positivist, but the alchemist. It is difficult to imagine a turn of mind constituting a more complete challenge to the ordinary modern point of view. To the intellect of our time the wild investigators of the school of Paracelsus seem to be the very crown and flower of futility, they are collectors of straws and careful misers of dust. But for all that', says Chesterton, 'Browning was right.' There could have been no better choice than Paracelsus, claims Chesterton, for Browning's study of intellectual egotism and, he says, the choice equally refutes any charge against Browning himself that he was a frigid believer in logic and a cold adherent of the intellect — the proof being that at the age of twenty-three Browning wrote a poem designed to destroy the whole of this intellectualist fallacy.

The entire poem is daringly experimental in form and philosophy: in both respects, it attempts to strip away the phenomenal world to reveal the noumenal world; to strip man of his physical integuments and reveal his psychical nakedness; to bare nature and reveal the natural. In the process, Robert Browning somewhat stripped himself psychologically bare: *Paracelsus*, for all his resolution after the personal revelations in *Pauline*, could not help but import some of his own state of mind and being into his work. Authors almost invariably write out of their own state of mind and being — there's no help for it except rigorous self-awareness which is difficult consciously to attain, improbable to try to impose, and almost impossible thereafter to maintain.

The last thing *Paracelsus* was intended to be was confessional, but as Betty Miller acutely points out, two of the characters in the poem — Michal (M for Mother) and Festus (F for Father) — can be interpreted as Mr and Mrs Browning. They speak 'out of the social and domestic environment of Robert Browning himself'. They 'reveal, and with a singular candour on the part of their creator, the attitude of Browning's own father and mother towards their brilliant, if ill-comprehended son'. In the discussions between the sober Festus, the gentle Michal, and the impatient, aspiring student Paracelsus, she says, 'we catch an echo of the family conflict that preceded . . . the renunciation of a practical for a poetic career'.

Anyone familiar even with the barest biographical details of Robert's life at this time, and beginning to read *Paracelsus*, will immediately grant the truth of Betty Miller's astute psychological insight. It is perfectly plain, the entire difficult crisis; there it is, unmistakably recognizable in the pages, more harrowingly true to the turbulent family emotions and Browning's own deepest feelings than any second-hand biographical fact and fancy can conjure. But then, too, as Ryals suggests, *Paracelsus* moves 'back and forth between enthusiastic creation of a construct or fiction and sceptical de-creation of it when as "truth" or mimesis it is subjected to scrutiny'.[56] With a poet as self-conscious at this time as Robert Browning, it should not easily be assumed that he would be unaware of using, even in disguise, his own life, its events and emotions;

that he was not capable of a conjuror's sleight-of-hand with a pack of cards, or an alchemist's trick of turning lead into gold; that he would not make and unmake even these materials — now you see them, now you don't; now lead, now gold — with as much ruthless facility as any others.

There is no real dispute, either, about Betty Miller's judgement that, 'In form, *Paracelsus* lies between the confessional of *Pauline* and the theatrical on which Browning wasted so many years. It is the closest of his early works to the dramatic monologues of his best period.' *Paracelsus* did not make money for Browning, but it profited his reputation mightily. Future works would be styled and recommended as being 'By the author of *Paracelsus*'. At the age of twenty-three, Robert Browning was a candidate for fame within London literary and theatrical circles. *Paracelsus* did not entitle him to a named and reserved seat in the Academy, far less the Siege Perilous at the literary round table; but he went confidently out and about, elegant and accomplished, affable and amusing, loquacious and learned, marked by those who mattered in the contemporary court of the London literati.

On 6 May 1835, the great actor-manager William Charles Macready was catching up with the most improving new books, reading 'the pleasing poem of *Van Artevelde*' that had so distressed Edward Moxon by its failure to recoup its costs. Reaching his London chambers, he found 'Talfourd's play of *Ion* in the preface to which is a most kind mention of myself'. Later in the day he called on the famously provocative young dramatic and literary critic John Forster, who was agitatedly considering a duel in Devonshire before thinking better of it.[57] Macready was forty-two years old, and had succeeded to the place vacated on the English stage by the death of the actor Edmund Kean, whose grotesque, pathetic last performance of Richard III at Richmond had so much impressed and inspired Robert.

Macready was less barnstorming than Kean, who had acted vividly in the best Romantic manner, and he was certainly more seriously, in terms of intellect and artistry, attentive to the texts he produced and performed. He was ambitious, not only personally but for the English stage as a whole. Kean's behaviour and attitudes, Macready considered, had brought the business of acting ('my pariah profession') into disrepute — though the low reputation of the English stage had never been higher than the sensational moral history of its best-known reprobates and its lowest hangers-on. It was Macready's duty, as a rectitudinous Victorian — and, as he privately admitted, a reprehensibly envious rival of the disgraceful Kean — to raise the cultural level of the theatre to the virtue attained by the finest of the fine arts, to the most salubrious literary heights; in short, to purge the theatre of its most vicious elements and inspire it to the highest moral and artistic standards.

This ideal represented Macready's conventional middle-class Victorianism crossed with his passionate egalitarianism, which, much as it reprobated the vile standards of the stage, also snobbishly scorned the high disdain and low virtue of society. Unfortunately for Macready, the English stage and its audiences resisted his energetic idealism.

On 27 November, Macready presented himself for dinner at the house of William Johnson Fox in Bayswater. 'I like Mr Fox very much,' wrote Macready in his diary entry for that day; 'he is an original and profound thinker, and most eloquent and ingenious in supporting the penetrating views he takes.' From which encomium we may take it that Macready and Fox harmoniously agreed, or amiably agreed to disagree, on most political, religious, and artistic matters. The evening got better still. 'Mr Robert Browning, the author of *Paracelsus*, came in after dinner; I was very much pleased to meet him. His face is full of intelligence. My time passed most agreeably. Mr Fox's defence of the suggestion that Lady Macbeth should be a woman of delicate and fragile frame pleased me very much, though he opposed me, and of course triumphantly. I took Mr Browning on, and requested to be allowed to improve my acquaintance with him. He expressed himself warmly, as gratified by the proposal; wished to send me his book; we exchanged cards and parted.' The acquaintance warmed to the degree that on 31 December, the last day of 1835, Browning and five other guests were regaled with a dinner at Macready's house where 'Mr Browning was very popular with the whole party; his simple and enthusiastic manner engaged attention and won opinions from all present; he looks and speaks more like a youthful poet than any man I ever saw.'[58]

Macready thought it noteworthy to write in his diary on 1 February 1836 that John Forster 'was talking much of Browning, who is his present *all-in-all*'. On 16 February, after one or two casual meetings, the acquaintance between Macready and Robert began to catch in earnest, to develop from personal friendship to professional association: 'Forster and Browning called, and talked over the plot of a tragedy which Browning had begun to think of: the subject, Narses — a victorious general in the time of the Roman Emperor Justinian. He said that I had *bit* him by my performance of Othello, and I told him I hoped I should make the blood come. It would indeed be some recompense for the miseries, the humiliations, the heart-sickening disgusts which I have endured in my profession if, by its exercise, I had awakened a spirit of poetry whose influence would elevate, ennoble, and adorn our degraded drama. May it be!'

Robert was not only balm for Macready's suffering professional soul; he found him personally soothing. Forster and the rest could be rumbustious and depressing: 'My nerves and spirits were quite quelled by them all'; but Browning's 'gentle manners always make his presence acceptable'.[59] *Paracelsus*, on the evidence of Macready's diary entry for 8 December 1835 — the day he finished reading the poem and set himself to considering it with the same professional eye of a player that he had brought to Talfourd's *Ion* — would not do as drama — (which Robert had never intended that it should). The 'main design of the poem', according to Macready, 'is not made out with sufficient clearness, and obscurity is a fault in many passages'. That said, however, he admitted the poem's 'most subtle and penetrating search into the feelings and impulses of our nature, some exquisite points of character, the profoundest and the grandest thoughts and most musically uttered. The writer is one whom I think destined for very great things.'

John Forster had been invited as a guest to Macready's New Year's Eve dinner at Elm Place, his house in the rural village of Elstree, and so it was by no remote chance that both Forster and Robert happened to be waiting with other Macready invitees earlier in the day at the 'Blue Posts' in Holborn, a boarding stage, for the same rumbling and bumping Billing's coach that Macready himself used almost daily in his journeys to his London chambers from his country home and back again. Mrs Orr says that the introduction between Forster and Robert took place at Macready's house, whereupon Forster inquired, 'Did you see a little notice of you I wrote in the *Examiner*?' From this point on, Forster and Robert seem to have been pretty constantly together. It was at Elm

Place, too, that Robert first met Miss Euphrasia Fanny Haworth, a neighbour of Macready's, a young woman some ten or eleven years older than Robert, interested in art and literature.

Narses was abandoned as a probable dramatic subject, and no more was heard of Forster's and Browning's interest in writing for the theatre, and for Macready in particular, until a few months later in 1826, when Macready acted in a production of Talfourd's *Ion* at Covent Garden. The first night, dedicated as a benefit night for Macready (who, after thirteen years, had just abandoned Drury Lane and its abominable manager Alfred Bunn), was on 26 May. Macready, having taken the principal role before a starry audience of literary and legal luminaries, social celebrities, politicians, and peers, was 'called for very enthusiastically by the audience and cheered on my appearance most heartily. I said: "It would be affectation to conceal the particular pleasure in receiving their congratulatory compliment on this occasion. It was indeed most gratifying to me; and only checked by the painful consideration that this might be perhaps the last new play I ever might have the honour of producing before them. (Loud cries of 'No No!') However that might be, the grateful recollection of their kindness would never leave me."'

Macready repaired after the performance to Talfourd's house in nearby Russell Square, where he 'met Wordsworth, who pinned me; Walter Savage Landor, to whom I was introduced, and whom I very much liked; Stanfield, Browning, Price, Miss Mitford — I cannot remember them all.'[60] There were some sixty people in all, crowding around one another in congratulatory mode. Macready was placed at the supper table between Landor and Wordsworth, with Browning opposite — which speaks well for Robert's own status in the company. Macready perhaps forgot or omitted to give some detail in his diary for this tremendous day, but Mrs Orr supplies the information that when Talfourd proposed a toast to the poets of England, Robert was included in their number, named by his host as the author of *Paracelsus*, and he stayed put in his chair while glasses were raised to him; according to Griffin and Minchin, Wordsworth 'leaned across the table and remarked, "I am proud to drink your health, Mr Browning!"'[61] This story is rubbished by Betty Miller, who points out that Robert had never much liked Wordsworth's poetry or his politics and would not have been particularly flattered by the grand old placeman's compliment — even if Wordsworth had been there to make it: he had gone home before the toasts were offered. The story has survived even the firm evidence that contradicts it.

Years later, on 24 February 1875, Robert wrote to the Revd Alexander B. Grosart to explain, with some embarrassment, why he had attacked Wordsworth in 'The Lost Leader', a poem published in *Dramatic Romances and Lyrics* in 1845: 'I *did* in my hasty youth presume to use the great and venerable personality of Wordsworth as a sort of painter's model; one from which this or the other particular feature may be selected and turned to account: had I intended more, above all, such a boldness as portraying the entire man, I should not have talked about "handfuls of silver and bits of ribbon." These never influenced the change of politics in the great poet; whose defection, nevertheless, accompanied as it was by a regular about-face of his special party, was to my juvenile apprehension, and even mature consideration, an event to deplore.'

Wordsworth had abandoned liberalism, Robert's preferred political position, and by so doing he had proved himself, in Robert's estimation, that most disgraceful and detestable thing — a traitor. Throughout Robert's poetical canon there are hissing references to the turpitudinous characters of turncoats. Unpleasant revenges, as unsparing as in Dante's Inferno, are invented for them.

> Just for a handful of silver he left us,
>   Just for a riband to stick in his coat —
>   Found the one gift of which fortune bereft us,
>   Lost all the others she lets us devote . . .[62]

There will be further occasions on which we will recognize that Robert Browning could be a good hater for the sake of conscience; this is one of the first and most significant. Wordsworth, heaped with honours, eulogized by friends and literary partisans such as Harriet Martineau, had become Poet Laureate in 1843. He had become, too, an object of absolute disgust for Robert, whose poem pulled no punches. This was not satire, this was not an elegant swipe: 'The Lost Leader' was a seriously-intended piece of lethal invective that found its mark not only through Robert's authentic outrage but through his authentic poetic voice. His counterblast has stood as long as Wordsworth's poetic reputation, and its venomous sting still poisons the old man in posterity.

There are other contradictions and misapprehensions concerning Talfourd's famous party, none of them too surprising. It was a party celebrating a significant occasion; it was a party boiling and roiling with writers, actors, quantities of poets, lawyers, and journalists; and if it wasn't an occasion for binding up old wounds and gouging open new ones, settling old scores and setting new grudges, for giving gossip and getting things wrong, then it can't have been much of a party. But in fact it was all those things and more — it was a wonderful party. The more it is recalled, the more legends it accretes. The *Ion* supper is a sort of early Victorian charabanc, standing room only, for every notable of the period bundled and bumped together and bowled along, fired by their own fissiparous energies. Robert was noticed by one of the guests, Miss Mitford, who never forgot how he looked that night. Ten years or more later, in a letter of 1847,[63] she wrote, 'I saw Mr Browning once and remember thinking how exactly he resembled a girl drest in boy's clothes — and as to his poetry I have just your opinion of it — It is one heap of obscurity, confusion and weakness . . . I met him once as I told you when he had long ringlets and no neckcloth — and when he seemed to me about the height and size of a boy of twelve years old — Femmelette — is a word made for him. A strange sort of person to carry such a woman as Elizabeth Barrett off her feet.'

'Femmelette', applied to a man or a woman, means a feeble creature, lacking force and energy, a languishing, listless person, in distinct contrast to Miss Mary Russell Mitford herself, who tended to be pert. In 1836, she was a successful, middle-aged dramatist associated with Macready (who had taken roles in her plays); essayist; sometime poet (set on that path by the encouragement of Coleridge), and famous as the author of the sketches and stories that were published in 1832 as *Our Village*. Her nature was generally sunny, though she was as capable as anyone — and possibly more than some — of asperity and decided views. Perhaps Robert merely struck Miss Mitford as a little insipid, as at least modestly reserved: it was not his manner then to be full-voiced or conspicuously hearty. He would stand up for himself when necessary, but his mode was essentially placatory, as would be evident later to Macready when he noted Robert's moderating, calming reaction to the impetuosity and hot-headedness of Forster.

The talk tended towards the literary and theatrical, and Macready 'overtook Mr Browning as they were leaving the house and said, "Write a play, Browning, and keep me from going to America." The reply was, "Shall it be historical and English: what do you say to a drama on Strafford?" '[64] The Earl of Strafford had been in Robert's mind, and even more to the fore in Forster's mind since he happened to be writing the lives of Strafford and other statesmen of the period of Charles I, the Civil War, and the Commonwealth. Forster had temporarily stalled on his biographies, due partly to some personal difficulties with the fascinating Laetitia Landon, and Robert had been assisting him with some of the literary work on Strafford. Forster's *Lives of the Statesmen of the Commonwealth* was published in parts between 1836 and 1839 and his *Life of Strafford* had been published just a few weeks before the *Ion* party. Strafford was very much *dans le vent*.

Robert, seized by the idea of a great play for a great contemporary actor, delivered a full text some ten months later in March 1837. It might have been sooner — he was a fast writer once he had settled on his subject and theme — had he not been simultaneously working on the poem *Sordello*, which he had begun shortly after writing *Pauline* and which had already been displaced, to an extent, by the intervention of *Paracelsus*.[65] Macready was willing to credit that *Strafford*, the play, would be his own salvation from some personal professional difficulties and rescue the English stage from the wretched condition into which it had sunk. Any play by Browning, for that matter, might do the trick, for he had surely seen John Forster's imaginative, puffing article in March, in the *New Monthly Magazine*, entitled 'Evidences of a new genius for Dramatic Poetry', which declared, among other emphatic assertions, that 'Mr Browning has the powers of a great dramatic poet' and that his genius 'waits only the proper opportunity to redeem the drama and elevate the literary repute of England'.

Macready, with his actor's head sunk into his hands, might have felt his spirits rise a little. On 3 August 1836 Forster told Macready that 'Browning had fixed on Strafford for the subject of a tragedy'. On 1 November, when Forster reported to Macready on the progress of Browning's play, he praised it highly, but Macready feared that the young critic and would-be biographer of Strafford might be 'misled as to its dramatic power; characters to him having the interest of action'.

However, '*Nous verrons!* Heaven speed it! Amen!' Despite pious senti-
ments, Macready began to feel faintly uneasy.

On 23 November, Macready confided to his diary that he 'Began
very attentively to read over the tragedy of *Strafford*, in which I find
more grounds for exception than I had anticipated. I had been too
carried away by the truth of character to observe the meanness of plot,
and occasional obscurity.' On 21 March 1837, when Macready and Robert
read through *Strafford* together, he felt his heart fail. He is frank in his
diary entry for that day: 'I must confess my disappointment at the
management of the story. I doubt its interest.' Familiarity did not
improve it. 'I am by no means sanguine, I lament to say, on its success.'

On 30 March, Macready read the play to Osbaldistone, manager of
Covent Garden, 'who caught at it with avidity, agreed to produce it
without delay on his part, and to give the author £12 per night for
twenty-five nights, and £10 per night for ten nights beyond . . . Browning
and Forster came in;' records Macready in his diary for 30 March, 'I
had the pleasure of narrating what had passed between Mr Osbaldiston
[*sic*] and myself, and of making Browning very happy.' Macready sug-
gested some further revisions that Robert 'was quite *enraptured* with.'
Forster said he was trying to induce Longman to publish the text of the
play. Robert asked if he could dedicate the play to Macready, who said
'how much I should value such an honour, which I had not anticipated
or looked for'. All of them, thoroughly pleased and in the highest good
humour with one another and their prospects, looked forward to the
production of *Strafford*, that most interesting new play by that great
new dramatic poet Mr Robert Browning, and a stage success on the
scale of, or surpassing, Talfourd's *Ion*.

Dramatists, even authors of books, will repress a grim smile when
they hear of a celebratory mood in which congratulations are exchanged
in circumstances such as these. Elation is excusable, euphoria is under-
standable — it is the very air that is breathed in a moment of head-
spinning optimism and rare agreement: it's like bouncing on a spring
mattress before the bed frame gives way and the whole company is
tumbled down, some coming off with worse bruises than others.
Macready held fast to his first and subsequent doubts about the stage
worthiness of the play that Osbaldistone's enthusiasm had made all the
more urgent to resolve. He went over the play laboriously with Robert

himself, and even drafted in Forster to meddle with the text and structure in an attempt to relieve *Strafford* of what he perceived as its 'heaviness' and stiffen what he felt to be its 'feebleness'. He had read it to his wife Catherine and his children, who were 'oppressed by a want of action and lightness; *I fear it will not do.*'[66]

Quarrels were not unfamiliar to Macready. On 12 April there was positively a dust-up between Macready, Forster, and Browning: 'There were mutual complaints — much temper — sullenness, I should say on the part of Forster, who was very much out of humour with Browning, who said and did all that man could to expiate any offence he might have given.' Forster, at Macready's behest, had been worrying for a while at the text of *Strafford* and — by Macready's account — seemed to agree with the great actor's cuts and alterations. 'He thought my view of the work quite a clear one, and in the most earnest spirit of devotion, set off to find and communicate with Browning on the subject — a fearful rencontre.' In fact, Macready seems to have been anxious to 'furnish Browning with a decent excuse to withdraw the play', to the extent of trying to find out if the actors who had been engaged were 'restive about their parts'. But no luck there: Macready was 'disappointed at their general acquiescence'. In his diary for 13 April, Macready acknowledged that, when Forster returned with Robert in tow, 'Forster ... showed an absence of sense and generosity in his behaviour which I grieved to see. There was a *scene.*'

Quite what the dispute was about is not entirely clear. Whatever offence had been taken by Forster, and whatever its cause, he blew up and — not for the first time — lost his considerable temper. This feature of Forster's personality was well known, and it was a worry to Robert, who confided in Macready 'how much injury he did himself by this temper'. The dispute ended when Robert 'assented to all the proposed alterations, and expressed his wish, that *coûte que coûte*, the hazard should be made and the play proceeded with'. This seemed satisfactory.

Until the next day. Macready wrote a detailed report in his diary on 14 April of how he found Robert at Forster's where the poet-dramatist 'produced some scraps of paper with hints and unconnected lines — the full amount of his labour upon the alterations agreed on. It was too bad to trifle in this way, but it was useless to complain; he had wasted his time in striving to improve the fourth act scene, which was ejected from the play as impracticable for any good result. We went all over the play *again* (!) very carefully, and he resolved to bring the amendments suggested by eleven o'clock this evening. Met Browning at the gate of my chambers; he came upstairs and, after some subjects of general interest, proceeded to that of his tragedy. He had done nothing to it; had been oppressed and incapable of carrying his intentions into action. He *wished to withdraw it.*' Macready sent Robert for Forster and they both came back. They turned over all the pros and cons, for acting the play, for not acting the play. Finally they all decided to go ahead with *Strafford*, though Robert asked for more time to complete his alterations. 'It was fixed to be done. Heaven speed us all!' wrote Macready at the end of a difficult day.

It was one thing to deal with writers and critics, but that was not the end of it for Macready or the fate of *Strafford*: hardly even the beginning. For as soon as it was decided to perform the play, the complications and intrigues of staging it took over. On 20 April, all Macready's doubts about the play recurred. He read *Strafford* again. He groaned. He sweated. He strongly feared its failure: 'it is *not good*.' He had had five days for his fears to be fed by the fact that Osbaldistone was on the verge of bankruptcy and had imposed 'parsimonious regulations'. That is to say, the production budget had been slashed to the bone. The actors were playing up. Miss Helen Faucit, a fine young actress, only twenty years old and already a popular favourite with audiences, complained to Macready that 'her part in Browning's play was very bad, and that she did not know if she should do it. She wanted me to ask her to do it. But I would not, for I wish she would refuse it, that even at his late point in time the play might be withdrawn — *it will do no one good.*'[67]

Even as he learned his own part, Macready's spirits fell further: he felt a certain obligation to Robert Browning that compromised his better judgement that he should withdraw for his own benefit; but he could not help hoping for an accident that should prevent performance, relieve his own decision to proceed, avoid the play and — worse — his own performance in the leading role being grievously hissed by a disappointed house, bringing down his own reputation as much as that of Browning to damnation. Browning might recover some ground and rescue himself with *Sordello*, but in his worst moments the worried actor considered that the inevitable failure of *Strafford* would mean it would be all up for the great Macready. 'It will strike me hard, I fear. God grant that it may not be a heavy blow.'[68] The sole chance for the play, he thought, would be in the acting: his own, at least. He had his doubts about the performances of some of his co-players.

And sure enough, the notices of the première of *Strafford* in the newspapers of 2 May, the morning after the first night, were nothing like as bad as Macready had anticipated: he was gratified to find them 'lenient and even kind to Browning. On myself — the "brutal and ruffianly" journal observed that I "acquitted myself exceedingly well".' When Macready called that day on Forster and found Robert with him, he told him candidly that 'the play was a grand escape, and that he ought to regard it only as such, a mere step to that fame which his talents must procure him.' It had been, in Macready's estimation, a narrow squeak. Some small ill-feeling still rankled between the three of them: Forster had written up the play in the *Examiner*, judging it more poetic than dramatic, which was to Macready's mind a 'very kind and judicious criticism', though the judiciousness thereof was evidently not to Robert's liking. Robert suggested that if Forster wanted any future tragedies, he should write them himself. Forster expressed himself hurt by Robert's 'expressions of discontent at his criticism' which Macready thought had, if anything, verged on indulgence 'for such a play as *Strafford*' and he was cross at Robert's ingratitude 'after all that has been done for Browning'.[69]

The first night, on 1 May, had been a triumph: a full house; the end of each act attended with the plaudits of an enthusiastic audience; calls of 'Author! Author' from a partisan claque to which Robert did not respond — it is not clear whether he was even in the house — so that the hubbub took some time to die down; the critics generally positive, despite some serious shortcomings in the staging and the general dilapidation of Covent Garden. William Sharp writes sadly that 'the house was in ill repair: the seats dusty, the "scenery" commonplace and sometimes noticeably inappropriate, the costumes and accessories almost sordid'.[70] The less said about the acting and understanding of the actors, the better: though Robert himself had something to say in remarks he made to Eliza Flower, who communicated them eagerly in a letter to Sarah Fox: 'he seems a good deal annoyed at the go of things behind the scenes, and declares he will never write a play again, as long as he lives. You have no idea of the ignorance and obstinacy of the whole set, with here and there an exception; think of his having to write out the meaning of the word *impeachment*, as some of them thought it meant *poaching*.'[71]

The exceptions were very likely Miss Faucit as Lady Carlisle and Macready as Strafford. Both had acquitted themselves well; she tender and affectingly pathetic, he majestic in bearing and bearded to resemble a Vandyke courtier of the period. Mr Vandenhoff as Pym had taken a purely perfunctory interest in his part, which he reportedly played with a nauseating, whining drawl; Mr Dale as Charles I was deaf as a post; and 'The Younger Vane', says Sharp, 'ranted so that a hiss, like an embodied scorn, vibrated on vagrant wings throughout the house'.[72] The part of the Queen, Henrietta Maria, was taken by Miss Vincent, fresh from her triumph at Drury Lane where she had played with Burmese bulls to the greatest satisfaction of her audiences. It was thus all the more to the credit of the play itself that it transcended these ignoble obstacles. The second night, when Robert sat 'muffled up in the pit to feel the pulse of the audience',[73] the house received the play with warm-enough applause.

And so on through to the fourth night's 'fervid applause' from an 'admirably filled house' and playbills announcing two further performances, one of which took place as advertised, the second fatally handicapped by the absence of Vandenhoff, who, having secured a better offer in America, jumped stage and took ship. He failed to turn up to play the important part of Pym, Strafford's principal antagonist. The performance was cancelled. The play's run was terminated. The precarious financial condition of the Covent Garden theatre collapsed entirely, and the promising young author, for his pains, got not a penny of his promised reward of £12 for even four, five, far less the projected first twenty-five nights, and he might whistle forever for the £10 for each of the ten nights further envisioned.

It was something, however, never mind if Robert had made little or no money from the play's performances, that Longman had at least published the text of his play on the occasion of the first night of *Strafford*, 1 May. The Brownings had not been required to dip into their own purse to pay for the honour, though neither the book nor the play brought any profit to either party. Five months later, Macready took over the management of the Covent Garden theatre from Osbaldistone with a troupe of good actors, and for two years thereafter indulged his mission and pursued his ambition to improve the English stage. Robert himself stuck for a decent while to the vow of renunciation he had made in the hearing of Eliza Flower: it was to be six years before he next ventured near a stage or a theatre except as a regular spectator.

The blank verse tragedy that was *Strafford* took as its principal character the English statesman Sir Thomas Wentworth, first Earl of Strafford (1593–1641), who from 1639 was chief adviser to Charles I. In 1640, Strafford was impeached by the House of Commons. On a Bill of Attainder, and with the assent of the king, he was executed on Tower Hill. The action, such as it is, of Browning's play — rather, the course of events from which the drama derives — is centred around the character of Strafford himself; his monarch, Charles I; his antagonist, John Pym, formerly Strafford's closest friend; and his would-be lover, Lady Carlisle. It is a drama of crossed loves and conflicted loyalties, passions and prejudices, public and personal: Strafford loves Pym, who considers himself betrayed by his friend's defection to the royalist cause; Strafford loves Charles I whose unworthiness and weakness betray his adviser's loyalty and send him to the block; Strafford is loved by the unhistorical character Lady Carlisle, whose devotion he does not perceive, blinded as he is by his fatal commitment to the king.

Strafford had not been a critical failure — that the production had abruptly stalled due to external circumstances was no fault of Robert Browning's, but the fiasco of the fifth night and the abrupt, untimely termination of the play's intended run has tended to colour posterity's judgement of its success. Of course posterity has also had an extended opportunity to judge the published text of the play and to review it in the light of developments in drama since 1837. It does not stand out conspicuously in the modern, revised history of the English theatre. It has enjoyed occasional amateur college productions, but it has never been professionally revived — nor is it likely to be. But for all that, *Strafford* in its time was well-enough received by contemporary critics and those playgoers who happened to see it before it fell off the stage into the pit of English literary and theatrical history.

Robert retired hurt — by the stage, by Forster, by the low conduct of venal and inadequate actors, by a general disgust — though his disappointment did not stop him associating with the many new friends he had made, frequenting the backstage green room when he attended the theatre, dining with Macready and Forster and Talfourd and the rest, all of whom welcomed his good company. He retired for extended periods to Camberwell where, in his room, succoured by his immediate family and surrounded by his familiar and fetish objects, pictures, and books, an idea for another historical play occurred to him. But mostly he set himself back to work on his interrupted poem, *Sordello*, which he intended to finish during a visit to Italy.

Prompted perhaps by his theatrical disappointments (it is good form to remove oneself abroad temporarily after an embarrassing dramatic disaster), and probably also to add colour not only to his own life but to his poetic work in progress, he embarked on his adventure in the afternoon of Good Friday, 13 April 1838. He sailed from London's St Katharine's Docks as the only passenger on the *Norham Castle*, a merchant vessel bound for Trieste on Rothschild business. It may be supposed that passage had been arranged for Robert by Reuben Browning.

The journey to Trieste, where he was dropped off by the ship's Captain, Matthew Davidson, took seven weeks. It was as terrible in its episodes of almost Byronic high drama as in constantly wretched periods of dispiritingly low seasickness. It took a full week of gales and snow before they even reached Start Point, Devon. On 26 April, they were off Lisbon; the next day they were sixteen miles north-west of Cape St Vincent. They passed the Straits of Gibraltar on Sunday 29 April, and on 6 May they came upon an upturned boat off the coast of Algiers. On 13 May, they were seven miles from Valetta; the next day they sailed close to Syracuse and were briefly becalmed on 16 May within sight of Mount Etna. It took another fortnight before they reached Trieste. The next evening, 31 May, Robert left by steamer for Venice, where he arrived early on the morning of 1 June.[74]

A letter to Fanny Haworth in Elstree is normally quoted in full in any account of Browning's life. It is worth repeating as a rare early example of Robert's narrative prose. It is dated 24 July 1838, by which time he was back in Camberwell. The introductory passage has been partly quoted already — 'I have, you are to know, such a love for flowers and leaves ... bite them to bits ... snowdrops and Tilsit ...'; it is a charming, literally flowery, preface to saying:

> You will see Sordello in a trice, if the fagging-fit holds. I did not write six lines while absent (except a scene in a play, jotted down as we sailed thro' the Straits of Gibraltar) — but I did hammer out some four, two of which are addressed to you, two to the Queen ... the whole to go in Book 3 — perhaps. I called you 'Eyebright' — meaning a simple and sad sort of translation of 'Euphrasia' into my own language: folks would know who Euphrasia, or Fanny, was, — and I should not know Ianthe or Clemanthe. Not that there is anything in them to care for, good or bad. Shall I say 'Eyebright'? I was disappointed in one thing, Canova. What companions should I have? The story of the ship must have reached you 'with a difference' as Ophelia says, — my sister told it to a Mr Dow who delivered it, I suppose to Forster, who furnished Macready with it, who made it over etc. etc. etc. — As short as I can tell, this way it happened: the Captain woke me one bright Sunday morning to say there was a ship floating keel uppermost half a mile off; they lowered a boat, made ropes fast to some floating canvas, and towed her towards our vessel. Both met half-way, and the little air that had risen an hour or two before, sank at once. Our men made the wreck fast, and went to breakfast in high glee at the notion of having 'new trousers out of the sails,' and quite sure that she was a French boat, broken from her moorings at Algiers, close by. Ropes were next hove (hang this sea-talk) round her stanchions, and after a quarter of an hour's pushing at the capstan, the vessel righted suddenly, one dead body floating out; five more were in the forecastle, and had probably been there a month — under a blazing African sun ... don't imagine the wretched state of things. They were, these six, the 'watch below' — (I give you the results of the day's observation) — the rest, some eight or ten, had been washed overboard at first. One or two were Algerines, the rest Spaniards. The vessel was a smuggler

bound for Gibraltar; there were two stupidly-disproportionate guns, taking up the whole deck, which was convex and [here Browning inserts three small drawings of the ship, noting ('All the "bulwarks," or sides at the top, carried away by the waves')] — nay, look you, these are the gun rings, and the black square the place where the bodies lay. Well, the sailors covered up the hatchway, broke up the aft deck, hauled up tobacco and cigars, good lord such heaps of them, and then bale after bale of prints and chintz, don't you call it, till the Captain was half frightened — he would get at the ship's papers, he said; so these poor fellows were pulled up, piecemeal, and pitched into the sea, the very sailors calling to each other 'to cover the faces': no papers of importance were found, however, but fifteen swords, powder and ball enough for a dozen such boats, and bundles of cotton &c that would have taken a day to get out, but the Captain vowed that after five-o'clock she should be cut adrift; accordingly she was cast loose, not a third of her cargo having been touched; and you can hardly conceive the strange sight when the battered hulk turned around, actually, and looked at us, and then reeled off, like a mutilated creature from some scoundrel French surgeon's lecture-table, into the most gorgeous and lavish sunset in the world: there — only thank me for not taking you at your word and giving you the whole 'story.'

The image of the loosed boat as a 'mutilated creature' turning to look at Robert Browning and his shipmates before reeling off into a luridly effulgent sunset is stunning — worthy of Mary Shelley's *Frankenstein*, published in 1818, or any of the tuppence-coloured gothic horrors in Wanley's *Wonders of the Little World*. Mrs Orr provides some supplementary detail, which Robert confided to Sarianna but withheld from Fanny as too sensational:[75] 'Of the dead pirates, one had his hand clasped as if praying; another, a severe gash in his head. The captain burnt disinfectants and blew gunpowder, before venturing on board, but even then, he, a powerful man, turned very sick with the smell and the sight. They stayed one whole day by the side, but the sailors, in spite of orders, began to plunder the cigars, etc. The captain said privately to Robert, "I cannot restrain my men, and they will bring the plague into our ship, so I mean quietly in the night to sail away." Robert took two cutlasses and a dagger; they were of the coarsest workmanship, intended for use. At the end of one of the sheaths was a heavy bullet, so that it could be used as a sling. The day after, to their great relief, a heavy rain fell and cleansed the ship. Captain Davidson reported the sight of the wreck and its condition as soon as he arrived at Trieste.'

Robert's letter to Fanny continues with a brisk itinerary: '"What I did?" I went to Trieste, then Venice — then thro' Treviso and Bassano to the mountains, delicious Asolo, all my places and castles, you will see.' Presumably Robert means that Fanny will see them if not first in poetical form in *Sordello*, then certainly in other poems in due course — Pippa would soon and significantly pass, in April 1841, through delicious Asolo. 'Then to Vicenza, Padua and Venice again. Then to Verona, Trent, Inspruck (the Tyrol) Munich, "Wurzburg in Franconia"! Frankfort and Mayence, — down the Rhine to Cologne, thence to Aix-la-Chapelle, Liège, and Antwerp — then home.' Robert here carefully blots out four lines, asking Fanny Haworth to 'Forgive this blurring, and believe it was only a foolish quotation: — shall you come to town, anywhere near town, soon? I shall be off again as soon as my book is out — whenever that will be.'[76]

It may or may not have been true that Robert had written only four for sure, no more than six, lines of poetry: while the *Norham Castle* passed through the Pillars of Hercules (Robert being hauled up to the deck by Captain Davidson and supported in his tottering, nauseous state so that he might see the tremendous Rock of Gibraltar), and skirted the north African coast, he wrote either now on this first journey to Italy, or later on a second trip, one of his best known poems, 'How they Brought the Good News from Ghent to Aix', written in pencil on the cover of Bartoli's *De' Simboli Trasportati al Morale*, according to Mrs Orr a favourite book and constant companion of Robert's.[77] Robert himself declared, in a letter of 20 October 1871 responding to an inquiry about the antecedents of the journey from Ghent to Aix, 'I have to say there were none but the sitting down under the bulwark of a ship off the coast of Tangiers, and writing it on the fly-leaf of Bartoli's *Simboli*; the whole "Ride" being purely imaginary.' This seems definite, but Robert could be often contradictory and sometimes plain wrong in his recollections about where and when and how a particular poem was written.

'We can imagine,' says Mrs Orr with a sympathetic shudder, 'in what revulsion of feeling towards firm land and healthy motion this dream of a headlong gallop was born in him.'

> I sprang to the stirrup, and Joris, and he;
> I galloped, Dirck galloped, we galloped all three . . .
> Behind shut the postern, the lights sank to rest,
> And into the midnight we galloped abreast.

Better, perhaps, to think of happier times, of Robert inspired by this floundering journey on the swell of the sea to recall the first journey into Russia, and hear again in the slap of water against the sides of the *Norham Castle* the rhythmic beat of his own and Benkhausen's galloping horses as they ran through northern Europe, their hooves thudding through the silences of white snow and green firs. He wrote, too, 'Home Thoughts, from the Sea', a short poem 'written at the same time, and in the same manner'[78] — in pencil on the cover of a book — a colourful riot of geography ('Nobly, nobly Cape Saint Vincent to the North-west died away'), history ('Bluish 'mid the burning water, full in face Trafalgar lay'), and triumphant English victory ('Here and here did England help me: how can I help England? — say') in eight rhythmic, rhyming, ringing lines.

Not much remains of first-hand information about Robert's first excursion to Italy and his journey home through Germany and the Low Countries. On his return, he was back in touch with William Johnson Fox, that great man who, as Robert wrote to Fanny Howarth in April 1839, 'is my Chiron in a small way', referring to him as the possessor of a 'magnificent and poetical nature'. Robert regarded Fox as 'my literary father' and took care to maintain the connection with him and his family. William Sharp[79] reports a reminiscence of Fox's daughter 'Tottie' (later Mrs Bridell-Fox), who wrote: 'I remember him as looking in often in the evenings, having just returned from his first visit to Venice. I cannot tell the date for certain. He was full of enthusiasm for that Queen of Cities. He used to illustrate his glowing descriptions of its beauties, the palaces, the sunsets, the moonrises, by a most original kind of etching. Taking up a bit of stray notepaper, he would hold it over a lighted candle, moving the paper about gently till it was cloudily smoked over, and then utilising the darker smears for clouds, shadows, water, or what not, would etch with a dry pen the forms of lights on cloud and palaces, on bridge or gondola on the vague and dreamy surface he had produced.'

Robert had spent two weeks in Venice out of his four in Italy, and images of his impressions would surface later in poems such as *Pippa Passes*, 'In a Gondola', 'A Toccata of Galuppi's', and — significantly for the time being — in the work in hand, *Sordello*, the poem that is confirmed as having been in the making since at least 1835, and probably for a while before, very likely soon after *Pauline*. Robert wrote to Fox on 16 April 1835, in a letter referring to *Paracelsus*, that 'I have another affair on hand, rather of a more popular nature, I conceive, but not so decisive and explicit on a point or two.' This 'other affair', *Sordello*, had already been subject to several revisions since its inception in or about 1833, and would again be revised to incorporate first-hand impressions of the Italian sites and sights still remaining, however much altered, some six hundred years after the thirteenth-century troubador (*trovatore* or, more literarily, *trouvère*) Sordello had walked and talked among them.

On the day of his departure for Italy, Robert had written to John Robertson, a friend who was connected with the *Westminster Review*, to say, 'I sail this morning for Venice — intending to finish my poem among the scenes it describes.'[80] *Sordello*, the poem, is also referred to in a letter to Fanny Haworth that Mrs Orr cannot date precisely but is likely to have been written in the summer of 1838 or 1839: 'I am going to begin finishing *Sordello* — and to begin thinking a Tragedy (an Historical one, so I shall want heaps of criticism on *Strafford*) and I want to have *another* tragedy in prospect, I write best so provided: I had chosen a splendid subject for it, when I learned that a magazine for next, this, month, will have a scene founded on my story; vulgarizing or doing no good to it: and I accordingly throw it up. I want a subject of the most wild and passionate love, to contrast with the one I mean to have ready in a short time.'[81] The plays he had in mind were to be *King Victor and King Charles*, and *The Return of the Druses*. With his hopes for the popular appeal of *Sordello*, and the prospective play devoted to a theme of 'the most wild and passionate love', it can be taken that Robert was aiming now at the wild hearts as well as the impassioned minds of the market for poetry and plays.

Which begs a question about the condition of his own heart: love, remarks Mrs Orr very astutely at this point, had played a noticeably small part in Robert's life. His adolescent feelings of affection for Eliza Flower were never very serious, nor likely to be taken very seriously, considering her long-standing devotion to William Fox. No woman — so far as we know from the scant evidence remaining of Robert's early years — detained his romantic attention or redirected it from the affection he maintained for his mother. Nobody else, for the time being, could count on being kissed goodnight every night by Robert Browning. Mrs Orr suggests that, in the absence of any personal experience of 'wild and passionate love', Robert turned to Fanny Haworth to supply the deficit, though what he supposed she might know of it is beyond conjecture. There was a lively sympathy, but no romantic feeling, between Robert and Fanny, and it would certainly have been indelicate, if not improper, for him to inquire too closely into the passions of an older, unmarried woman living cloistered at home with her mother. In a letter of April 1839, he tells Fanny direct, 'Do you know I was, and am, an Improvisatore of the *head* — not of the *hort* [*sic*] . . . — not you!'

In March 1840, Edward Moxon, at the expense of Robert's father, published *Sordello* — 'that colossal derelict upon the ocean of poetry', as even the partisan William Sharp is obliged to describe the poem. Alfred Tennyson read the first line:

Who will, may hear Sordello's story told,

and finally he read the last line:

Who would, has read Sordello's story told,

whereupon he famously said that the first line and the last line were the only two lines of the poem that he understood and they were lies since nothing in between made any sense to him. Douglas Jerrold, at the time a well-known playwright and later an original staff member and contributor to *Punch*, is said to have started reading *Sordello* while recuperating from illness. No sooner had he picked up the book than he put it down, saying, 'My God! I'm an idiot. My health is restored, but my mind's gone. I can't understand two consecutive lines of an English poem.' He called his family to his bedside and gave them the poem to read. When they sadly shook their heads and could make no more of it than he could himself, he heaved a sigh of relief and, confirmed in his sanity, went to sleep. Thomas Carlyle wrote to say that he had read *Sordello* with great interest but that Jane, his wife, wished to know whether Sordello was a man, a city or a book.[82]

It is as well to get these three memorably funny stories dusted off at the start. They live forever in Browning's life and legend, not just because they are sharply humorous or because they comfort our own confusion on reading the poem with the satisfaction of knowing that it confounded even the greatest intellects of its time, but also because they express a genuine, general bewilderment that explanations by critics of the poem's form and expositions by researchers of the poem's references have not wholly redeemed. *Sordello* has been incorporated into the fabric of English literature, but — still and all — its reputation persists, unfairly say some modern revisionary critics, as a notoriously difficult work, a monument to obscurity and a testament to tedium.

Robert Browning himself, says Sharp, came to be resigned to the shortcomings of *Sordello* as an accessible work of art: years later, 'on his introduction to the Chinese Ambassador, as a "brother-poet", he asked that dignitary what kind of poetic expression he particularly affected. The great man deliberated, and then replied that his poetry might be defined as "enigmatic." Browning at once admitted his fraternal kinship.' Sharp adds, rather nicely, that Browning's holograph dedication of a copy of *Sordello* to a later friend, the French critic Joseph Milsand, read: 'My own faults of expression were many; but with care for a man or book such would be surmounted, and without it what avails the faultlessness of either? I blame nobody, least of all myself, who did my best then or since.'

That was — and remains — simply true. George Santayana, in an essay, 'The Poetry of Barbarism', declares that if we are to do justice to Browning's poetry, we must keep two things in mind: 'One is the genuineness of the achievement, the sterling quality of the vision and inspiration; these are their own justification when we approach them from below and regard them as manifesting a more direct or impassioned glimpse of experience than is given to mildly blatant, convention-ridden minds. The other thing to remember is the short distance to which this comprehension is carried, its failure to approach any kind of finality, or to achieve a recognition even of the traditional ideals of poetry and religion.' This latter qualification is now more disputed than the preceding encomium.

However, the estimation of Browning's contemporaries was naturally foreshortened by the immediate, looming presence of *Sordello*, which had not then achieved the longer perspective of later critical perception nor the farther horizon of literary history. It was right under their noses. Sharp[83] characterizes the poem as 'a gigantic effort, of a kind; so is the sustained throe of a wrestling Titan'. He compares its monotony to 'one of the enormous American inland seas to a lover of the ocean, to whom the salt brine is as the breath of delight' — which is a pretty way of dressing up the word 'stagnant'. He regrets the 'fatal facility of the heroic couplet to lapse into diffuseness' and this, 'coupled with a warped anxiety for irreducible concision, has been Browning's ruin here'. Nevertheless, on the charge of *Sordello*'s obscurity, Sharp admits that 'its motive thought is not obscure. It is a moonlit plain compared to the "*silva oscura*" of the "Divina Commedia"' — a tract of open country compared to Dante's 'dark wood'.

It is irresistible, though irreverent, to think of comparing *Sordello* to the smuggler's ship that Robert came across on his voyage to Italy: the poem first setting sail on publication, heavily armed with emotion and erudition, fully ballasted with all the approved poetic paraphernalia, confident of successfully accosting and overwhelming readers and critics that cross its path, foundering on the unexpected obstacle of public bewilderment and upturned by a sudden storm of critical abuse, all hands dead, wounded, lost in attitudes of frightful prayer, finally righting itself and — with an ineffably battered dignity — turning to look mutely, uncomprehendingly at those critic-surgeons who butchered it and cast it adrift, reeling off into the sunset like a 'mutilated creature'. It is a painful metaphor for the unsuspected end of a brave adventure.

As Chesterton remarks,[84] *Sordello* is almost unique in literary history, in the sense that praise or blame hardly figured in its reception: both were overwhelmed by an almighty, universal incomprehension that stopped informed criticism in its tracks. 'There had been authors whom it was fashionable to boast of admiring and authors whom it was fashionable to boast of despising; but with *Sordello* enters into literary history the Browning of popular badinage, the author whom it is fashionable to boast of not understanding.' So far in his career, Robert's reputation as a poet and playwright had seemed to be advancing much in step with those of his contemporaries. *Pauline* had fallen stillborn and anonymously from the press, but since nobody had noticed, nobody had heard the dull thud, its failure made no difficulties, and it had had the useful result of attracting the interested attention and positive regard of William Johnson Fox. *Paracelsus* had obtained a reasonable critical reception, though the poem itself had not sold out its first edition; and *Strafford* had been received with general enthusiasm, though how it would have fared in a longer theatrical run could never be known. So far, so good, all things considered: one undoubted failure, two moderate successes, nothing to be ashamed of (though *Pauline* remained decently veiled and in a permanent purdah). But *Sordello* suddenly blighted this promise in the bud.

Chesterton perceptively and properly disputes and demolishes the persistent myth of *Sordello*'s unintelligibility: its literary qualities, when perceived and understood, render the poem clearer. As Sharp admits, too, 'its motive thought is not obscure' and is perceptible to intelligent critical analysis. The final verdict on *Sordello*'s appeal to posterity may be given by Ezra Pound, who, perhaps exasperatedly, exclaimed, 'Hang it — there is but one Sordello!' And yes, there is no getting round it — we could not now or for the future do without *Sordello*, any more than Robert Browning could then or later have done without it. Since Pound regarded Browning as 'my poetic father', it is not irrelevant here to refer to T. S. Eliot, who admitted that Pound himself, in his time, suffered from being simultaneously judged to be 'objectionably modern' and 'objectionably antiquarian'. The fellow-feeling and the sense of paternity that Pound bore for Browning is, in this sense, perfectly understandable.

The charge of Browning's wilful obscurity, though it does not begin with *Sordello*, is sometimes attributed to Browning's intellectual vanity and, by extension, arrogance. Chesterton speaks true when he says that 'throughout his long and very public life, there is not one iota of evidence that he was a man who was intellectually vain.' It is plain that, in his early career, he had little or no awareness that nobody knew as much as he did, and that that profound ignorance made him unaware that what was perfectly clear to Robert Browning was of the uttermost obscurity to almost everyone else. But that is a different matter: had he been aware of it, and had he made allowance for it, he would have committed a worse sin of being consciously condescending and patronising, of writing *de haut en bas* — which is one fault for which he is never successfully prosecuted.

'He was not unintelligible because he was proud,' says Chesterton, decisively and characteristically turning the difficulty on its head, 'but unintelligible because he was humble. He was not unintelligible because his thoughts were vague, but because to him they were obvious.'[85] And because they were obvious, he fell into that concision of expression, allusion, and imagery which Sharp perceives as a fault and which, admittedly, compounded the unintelligibility of the poem for his readers. If Browning is accused of intellectual complexity, it is paradoxical that that complexity derives from his efforts to reduce it to a simplicity that, in the event, was fully comprehensible — and then only intermittently — solely to himself. By not writing down to his readership, Browning's *Sordello*, says Chesterton, was 'the most glorious compliment that has ever been paid to the average man'. It is a compliment that has not, then or now, been easily understood or greatly appreciated. The compliment was rebuffed, indeed, by the *Athenaeum* on 30 May with reference to the poem's 'puerilities and affectations', and by the *Atlas* on 28 May which found *Sordello* full of 'pitching, hysterical, and broken sobs of sentences'.

Even Macready finally gave up on the book: 'After dinner tried — another attempt — utterly desperate — on *Sordello*; it is *not* readable.'[86] Only Fanny Haworth had much good to say for it, a kindness to which Robert responded gratefully in a letter to her of May 1840: 'You say roses and lilies and lilac-bunches and lemon-flowers about it while everybody else pelts cabbage stump after potato-paring — nay, not everybody — for Carlyle ... but I won't tell you what [Richard Monckton] Milnes told me Carlyle told him the other day: (thus I make you believe it was something singular in the way of praise — connu!).' In fact, it is pleasing to report that Carlyle did have a good word to say.

Nobody now reads *Sordello* — or if they do, not idly, not without a good reason, and rarely without a concordance conveniently to hand. This is fair enough: Robert himself, in later life, when asked to explain a reference in one of his poems, was obliged to reply that once God and Browning knew what he meant, but 'now only God knows'. And in modern times, quite aside from the poem's literary difficulties, its sheer length — divided into six cantos (or 'Books') it amounts to five or six lines short of a total of 6,000 lines — is a deterrent to the casual reader. Chesterton is kindly inclined to exonerate Browning, finally, on the grounds of innocence and inexperience: 'The Browning then who published *Sordello* we have to conceive, not as a young pedant anxious to exaggerate his superiority to the public, but as a hot-headed, strong-minded, inexperienced, and essentially humble man, who had more ideas than he knew how to disentangle from each other.'[87] Substitute, then, for Sharp's image of 'the sustained throe of a wrestling Titan', the idea of Robert Browning as a Laocoön entangled in the coils of serpents so intertwined that they become one indistinguishable, roiling mass. Robert, all unwitting, called up leviathans from the vasty deep of his unconscious mind and conjured them off the pages of his conscious reading, so that they devoured him.

'A very great part of the difficulty of *Sordello*,' instances Chesterton, 'is in the fact that before the reader even approaches to tackling the difficulties of Browning's actual narrative, he is supposed to start with an exhaustive knowledge of that most shadowy and bewildering of all human epochs — the period of the Guelph and Ghibelline struggles in medieval Italy.' Griffin and Minchin[88] say that, 'In 1844, when Browning landed at Naples, among the first sights that met his view were advertisements of the performance of an opera on Sordello', and that as late as 1910 (the publication date of their biography) 'in the windows of Italian bookshops, one may see paper-covered volumes on the legend of Sordello and of the Ezzelini family who figure so prominently in Browning's poem'. This is like saying an Italian arriving in London and seeing advertisements of the performance of a play on the Earl of Strafford would know instantly the historical treat he might expect from a stage version of the story, or that paper-covered volumes on the legend of Richard the Lionheart and Blondel the troubador would immediately engage his attention with a thrill of long familiarity.

Chesterton and others might later, with hindsight, excuse *Sordello* on several counts, but youth, except by the special indulgence of Mrs Orr,[89] cannot be one of them. In 1840, Robert was twenty-eight years old and henceforth, says Mrs Orr, 'his work ceases to be autobiographic in the sense in which, perhaps erroneously, we have felt it to be'. Erroneously, certainly, if we take it to be true-to-fact; not so far off the mark if we take it and interpret it, in the light of the known biographical facts about Browning, as perceptive emotional self-confession. His future work will, says Mrs Orr, be 'inspired by every variety of conscious motive, but never again by the old (real or imagined) self-centred, self-directing Will . . . in *Pippa Passes*, published one year later, the poet and the man show themselves full-grown. Each has entered on the inheritance of the other.'

Chesterton picks up this cue from Mrs Orr and runs with it a little further, saying that *Sordello* 'does not present any very significant advance in Browning on that already represented by *Pauline* and *Paracelsus*. *Pauline*, *Paracelsus* and *Sordello* stand together in the general fact that they are all, in the excellent phrase used about the first by Mr Johnson Fox, "confessional" . . . Browning is still writing about himself, a subject of which he, like all good and brave men, was profoundly ignorant.' And Chesterton, like Mrs Orr, recognizes *Pippa Passes* as a significant step forward not only in the technical development of Browning's poetry but in the personal development of the poet himself. Both speak in a new voice from another place.

Poetry was the principal string to Robert's bow; but he could not help pulling on another, trying to shoot a true arrow from it. As he had written to Fanny Haworth, it suited his way of working to keep several things on the go simultaneously. This is interesting to know, but nothing to make too much of: it is not uncommon — few writers conscientiously finish one job (book, play, poem or essay), dotting the 'i's and crossing the 't's, before committing themselves to the next. Writers tend to work on several (more than one, anyhow) projects in parallel rather than serially or consecutively, and none of them will ever be at the same stage of development at the same time. It is only pedants and plodders and publishers who insist that one cannot do two things (or three, or four or more) at the same time. Since *Strafford*, Robert had taken his opportunities to keep up and broaden his acquaintance with the theatre and those associated with it. The untimely death of *Strafford* had been a blow, but his fascination with the stage had not died with it. Somewhat smoke-scented, its feathers a little ruffled, shaking out the ashes and preening the charred tips from its wings, the phoenix of Robert's theatrical ambition was ready for another flight.

Macready, in his tenure as manager of Covent Garden (he reigned there from 30 September 1837 to 18 July 1839), was one focus of Robert's attention; another was the well-disposed William Johnson Fox. Between Macready and Fox, two substantial rocks in the social life of London, Robert was naturally pulled by the eddies and currents that flowed around and between them into contact with a wide literary, legal, political, and social acquaintance.

This included men such as Charles Dickens (exactly Browning's age and already prolific, with *Sketches by 'Boz', The Pickwick Papers, Oliver Twist*, and *Nicholas Nickleby* under his belt); Walter Savage Landor (the famously and intractably temperamental poet, dramatist, and polemicist, recently returned from Italy after bitter separation from his wife); Edward Bulwer (the fashionable novelist, playwright, and politician who was to become Bulwer-Lytton in 1843, when he inherited the great house Knebworth from his mother, and thereafter first Baron Lytton); Daniel Maclise (the Irish portrait and history painter); Leigh Hunt (who had personally known Byron, Shelley, and Keats and whom Robert liked for his childlike nature and because he had rescued Shelley's heart from the funeral pyre on the beach at Viareggio and now treasured it, along with a wisp of Milton's hair, in his collection of literary relics); John Forster, of course, who was by now a close friend of Dickens and was to become his biographer; Richard Henry (sometimes Hengist) Horne (adventurer, critic, sometime editor of the *Monthly Repository*, author of plays that were never acted); Richard Monckton Milnes (later the first Baron Houghton, a tremendous social swell of wide literary and political acquaintance who amassed a large library of pornography that included the thrillingly wicked works of the Marquis de Sade); the literary and legal lion Thomas Noon Talfourd; and other playwrights, critics, actors, and men and women of fashion who thronged the times, the theatres, the salons and the dinner tables of London.

From the time of *Strafford*, Robert became a regular diner-out: he seems, indeed, rarely to have refused a decent invitation. Such social activity was useful: having attracted the public eye, he was not about to drop out of its sight. Acquaintance with the author was more sought after than with his books: Robert was talkative, intelligent, personable, and — having got over early reserve in company — was by now confident in conversation and socially assured. By chance, fatefully, when dining at Talfourd's in 1839, Robert made the acquaintance of John Kenyon, described by Mrs Orr as being at that date 'a pleasant, elderly man', who turned out to have been a schoolfellow of Robert's father.[90] This encounter led to the reunion of Mr Browning and Mr Kenyon, who were as delighted with one another in their advancing years as they had been as schoolboys. This first meeting after so long a break prospered into an enduringly warm friendship with the whole Browning family. Mrs Orr quotes from a letter, dated 10 January 1884, from Robert to Professor Knight of St Andrews, some twenty-eight years after Kenyon's death: 'He was one of the best of human beings, with a general sympathy for excellence of every kind. He enjoyed the friendship of Wordsworth, of Southey, of Landor, and in later days, was intimate with most of my contemporaries of excellence.'[91]

At about this time — even the thorough Mrs Orr cannot put an exact date on it — the Brownings moved to a larger, three-storeyed house, Hanover Cottage, to be near Jane Browning, Robert the First's widow, who had moved nearby from Islington with her daughter Jemima and son Reuben. A letter conjecturally dated December 1840 by Robert to William Macready specifically states, 'we remove into a new house, the week after next, — a place really not impossible to be got at', and another to Macready, which on internal evidence must be dated no earlier than 1840, gives 'Hanover Cottage Southampton [St]' as Robert's address. The reference to Southampton [St] must be provisional. To Laman Blanchard, the author of *Offerings*, Robert wrote in April 1841 to advise him of his new address: 'if, in a week or two you will conquer the interminable Kent Road, and on passing the turnpike at New Cross, you will take the *first* lane with a quickset hedge to the right, you will "descry a house resembling a goose-pie"; only a crooked, hasty and rash goose-pie. We have a garden and trees, and little green hills of a sort to go out on.' Mr Browning's books, six thousand and more, were lodged in 'the long low rooms of its upper storey.'[92]

Robert's description of the house as 'resembling a goose-pie' has vexed many Browning scholars, who have scoured all of literature to discover an appropriate association. One might offer to this inquiry the eighteenth-century Scottish poet and *perruquier* Allan Ramsay, who became a bookseller in Edinburgh and promoted the city's first circulating library. He built a round house known as the 'Goose-Pie' on the lower slopes of the Edinburgh Castle hill, above what are now the Princes Street gardens. Perhaps — and it's not unlikely: Carlyle would have known them — Robert had read Ramsay's *The Tea-Table Miscellany*, a collection of Scottish songs and ballads, the first volume of which was published in 1723, or *The Ever Green* (1724), which contained Ramsay's revisions of representative work by the late medieval *Makars* of Scotland, notably the great poets Dunbar and Henryson. From Ramsay's editions of Scottish poetry Robert might have gone on to glean a little gossip about Ramsay's life, and a house known as the 'Goose-Pie' is striking enough to have stuck in anyone's memory to be retrieved later as an amusing and typically recondite reference.

Mr Browning's stepbrother Reuben, Robert's young uncle, was allowed to put up York, his horse, which Robert was encouraged to ride, in the stable and coach-house which was attached to the house and accessible from it. The horse was groomed by the gardener, who was also responsible, with Mrs Browning, for the large garden 'opening on to the Surrey hills'.[93] Sarianna spoke later of trees in the front of the new house, and Mrs Orr refers specifically to a white rose tree in the garden under which lived a toad which became so much attached to Robert that it would follow him about and suffer him to tickle its head. Hanover Cottage was larger than the family's previous house and is referred to in several literary memoirs of the period, always with affection and respect for the warmth of its welcome to Robert's guests.

After *Strafford*, Robert's brain teemed with ideas for further dramatic productions, including an adaptation of a ballad, 'The Atheist's Tragedy', just lately published by John Payne Collier (who in 1840 founded the Shakespeare Society and busied himself thereafter with falsifications and forgeries in folios of Shakespeare's plays that are the subject of academic debate to this day). His interest in the ballad was eclipsed by another rendering of it in dramatic form by Richard Hengist Horne in 1837, but no matter; there were other subjects. He wrote two plays, *King Victor and King Charles* and *Mansoor the Hierophant* (later retitled *The Return*

of the Druses), both of which were submitted to Macready for his atten-
tion and refused by the great actor.[94]

On 5 September 1839, Macready 'Read Browning's play on Victor,
King of Sardinia — it turned out to be a *great mistake*. I called Browning
into my room and most explicitly told him so, and gave him my
reasons for coming to such a conclusion.'[95] Robert was not best pleased:
Macready records in his Diary for 20 September a meeting with Forster
who 'told me of Browning's intemperance about his play which he read
to Fox, Forster, etc.'. On 6 August 1840, Macready was in another
dilemma: Robert had delivered the text of *The Return of the Druses*.
Macready sighed and despaired: 'with the deepest concern I yield to the
belief that he will *never write again* — to any purpose. I fear his intellect
is not quite clear. I do not know how to write to Browning.'[96] That he
evidently found something to say is evidenced by a letter from Robert
to Macready dated 23 August. It begins: 'So once again, dear Macready,
I have failed to please you! The Druzes [*sic*] return in another sense
than I had hoped.' On 12 August, Robert called on Macready and they
talked, Macready giving his frank opinion both on *Sordello* and *The
Return of the Druses* and 'expressing myself most anxious, as I am, that
he should justify the expectations formed of him, but that he could not
do so by placing himself in opposition to the world.' Nevertheless,
Macready promised to read the play again.

On 27 August, Robert called at Elm Cottage, Elstree, to retrieve his
manuscript. He came upon Macready before the great actor-manager
had finished his bath, 'and really *wearied* me with his obstinate faith in
his poem of *Sordello*, and of his eventual celebrity, and also with his
self-opinionated persuasions upon his *Return of the Druses*. I fear he is
for ever gone. He speaks of Mr Fox (who would have been *delighted*
and proud in the ability to praise him) in a very unkind manner, and
imputed motives to him which on the mere surface seem absurd . . .
Browning accompanied me to the theatre, at last consenting to leave
the MS. with me for a second perusal.'

In his letter of 20 August to Macready, Robert had vigorously
defended his play, in terms that it is not difficult to imagine he defended
it to others, to anyone who would listen indeed, and had finished
by hoping that *The Return of the Druses* might 'but do me half the
good "Sordello" has done — be praised by the units, cursed by the

tens, and unmeddled with by the hundreds!' The failure of *Sordello* and Macready's plain misunderstanding of the finer points of his plays, which Robert was more than willing to explicate and exculpate, had caused the poet-dramatist to lose some of his customary aplomb, and the old actor to doubt the man's sanity. Convinced of the inevitability of his future celebrity, Robert was anxious to promote it in poetry and in performance.

There is a note of panic in his attitude at this time, in his attempts to salvage a career that looked likely to be cut short by the incomprehensible incomprehension not only of the public but of his literary and dramatic peers. Little wonder that his behaviour and remarks (even about those he knew to be his supporters) might be somewhat intemperate and contributed to a reputation in the world that was doing him no good.

After yet another reading of Robert's 'mystical, strange and heavy play', Macready could not revise his original opinion: 'It is not good.'[97] He wrote to say as much to Robert, who, two days later, on 16 August, turned up to collect his rejected manuscript.

There was no lasting difficulty for the time being between the two men, no serious disruption of their sociability: Robert continued to attend Macready's plays, met him with mutual friends, dined with him. Mrs Orr supposes that Macready's *Diaries*, edited for publication, omit some of the detail surrounding the production of Robert's third attempt at a performable play — *A Blot in the 'Scutcheon* — which was produced at Drury Lane on 11 February 1843. This was some three years after Robert had written it, to judge by references in an undated letter to Macready that is likely to have been written before the end of December 1840. In this letter Robert says, in effect, third time lucky: ' "The luck of the third adventure" is proverbial. I have written a spick and span new Tragedy (a sort of compromise between my own notion [i.e. in the *Druses*] and yours — as I understand it at least) and will send it to you if you care to be bothered so far. There is *action* in it, drabbing, stabbing, et autres gentillesses, — who knows but the Gods may make me good even yet? Only, make no scruple of saying flatly that you cannot spare the time, if engagements of which I know nothing, but fancy a great deal, should claim every couple of hours in the course of this week.'

This is a conciliatory, even faintly humble letter. It certainly counts on Macready's patience and good grace, and concedes that some dramatic action might be required to hold the attention of the playgoing public. He is prepared to give Macready what he wants if Macready will take what Robert wants to give. Such diplomacy had become necessary: Macready was losing faith in his young dramatist. Robert's correspondence includes a couple of letters to Macready, dated 26 April 1842, in which he tries to drum Macready into stating his intentions towards not only *The Return of the Druses* but also *A Blot in the 'Scutcheon*.

In Macready's edited *Diaries* there is a curious silence about the play he calls *Blot* until 25 and 26 January 1843, when he refers to reading it. On the Saturday, 28 January 1843, there had been a reading of *Blot* during which the actors had laughed at the play. Macready told Robert of the actors' reaction and 'Advised him as to the alteration of the second act.'

On 31 January, Macready went to the Drury Lane theatre. 'Found Browning waiting for me in a state of great excitement. He abused the doorkeeper and was in a very great passion. I calmly apologized for having detained him, observing that I had made a great effort to meet him at all. He had not given his *name* to the doorkeeper, who had told him he might walk into the green-room, but his dignity was mortally wounded. I fear he is a very conceited man. Went over his play with him, then looked over part of it.' By 7 February, *Blot* was in rehearsal and Robert had recovered his temper. But there were difficulties looming. Macready, right up to the last minute, was considering significant alterations to the play that were resisted by Robert: on 10 February 'Browning . . . in the worst taste, manner and spirit, declined any further alterations . . . I had no more to say. I could only think Mr Browning a very disagreeable and offensively mannered person. *Voilà tout!*' But Macready thought that about a lot of persons who contradicted or even mildly discomposed him, so this judgement on this playwright at this time can be taken with a pinch of salt. Tempers, in any case, were short all round. The next day, Robert reappeared at the theatre. He 'seemed desirous to explain or qualify the strange carriage and temper of yesterday, and laid much blame on Forster for irritating him'. Macready 'directed the rehearsal of *Blot in the 'Scutcheon*, and made many valuable improvements', though the acting left something to be desired.

On 11 February the three-act tragedy *A Blot in the 'Scutcheon* was performed to no great acclaim. The play lasted three nights before it disappeared forever from Macready's repertoire. *The Times* shortly declared it to be 'one of the most faulty dramas we ever beheld', and on 18 February the *Athenaeum* unkindly laid into the play: 'If to pain and perplex were the end and aim of tragedy, Mr Browning's poetic melodrama called *A Blot in the 'Scutcheon* would be worthy of admiration, for it is a very puzzling and unpleasant piece of business. The plot is plain enough, but the acts and feelings of the characters are inscrutable and abhorrent, and the language is as strange as their proceedings.'[98] On 18 March, Macready records in his Diary: 'Went out; met Browning, who was startled into accosting me, but seeming to remember that he did not intend to do so, started off in great haste. What but contempt, which one ought not to feel, can we with galled spirit feel for those wretched insects about one? Oh God! how is it all to end?' One thing had certainly ended: the association and friendship between Robert and Macready, which was not resumed for some twenty years thereafter. When they did cross one another's paths, as happened on 4 June 1846 at a garden party, Robert cut Macready: '*Browning* — who did not speak to me — the *puppy!*'[99]

Most of the preceding account leading to production of *A Blot in the 'Scutcheon* has been told from Macready's point of view, taken from his *Diaries* (as edited for publication). Robert Browning's side of the matter is naturally somewhat different in detail and emphasis. Much later in life, he gave his own version to Edmund Gosse, and Mrs Orr[100] publishes in full a letter of 15 December 1884 to Frank Hill, in which Robert thanks Hill, then editor of the *Daily News*, for suppressing a paragraph referring to *A Blot in the 'Scutcheon* in an article about the theatre. What Robert had to say to Gosse pretty much corresponds with the frank account he disclosed to Hill. Additionally, a letter from Joseph Arnould to Alfred Domett substantially describes, from his own first-hand observation, the play's first night; and finally a letter from Charles Dickens recommending the play completes the full knowledge we have of this crisis in Browning's professional life before his personal life was about to be thrown into upheaval.

Macready, it should be understood by connoisseurs of the backstage drama to *A Blot in the 'Scutcheon*, was experiencing severe domestic as well as professional difficulties in the early 1840s, some of which were public knowledge, some of which were public gossip, and some of which were nobody's business but Macready's. When, in October 1841, he took over the management of the Drury Lane theatre, he needed new plays to add to his existing repertoire and John Forster, on 29 September 1841, had 'importuned' him to read *A Blot in the 'Scutcheon*. Macready, although doubtful of Browning's ability to write anything ever again, and despite his wavering faith in Forster himself, whose intemperate enthusiasms by now matched not only his intemperance of character but increasingly his intemperate taste for the bottle, read Browning's *Blot* and was not impressed. Forster, too, by now had his doubts about the play, which was dispatched to Charles Dickens for a third opinion. Dickens did not reply for a year. When he did, on 25 November 1842, Forster showed the great novelist's response to Macready. Dickens' letter read:

> Browning's play has thrown me into a perfect passion of sorrow. To say that there is anything in its subject save what is lovely, true, deeply affecting, full of the best emotion, the most earnest feeling, and the most true and tender source of interest, is to say that there is no light in the sun, and no heat in the blood. It is full of genius, natural and great thoughts, profound and yet simple and beautiful in its vigour. I know nothing that is so affecting, nothing in any book I have ever read, as Mildred's recurrence to that 'I was so young — I had no mother.' I know no love like it, no passion like it, no moulding of a splendid thing after its conception, like it. And I swear it is a tragedy that MUST be played: and must be played, moreover, by Macready . . . And if you tell Browning that I have seen it, tell him that I believe from my soul there is no man living (and not many dead) who could produce such a work.

This letter, as quoted by Forster in the biography he later wrote of Dickens, was not in fact known to Robert Browning until, some thirty years later, he read it in Forster's *Dickens*. This unqualified testimonial to the sublimities of *Blot* put Macready in a difficult position: Dickens' opinion could not be ignored. The plot and sentiments of *A Blot in the 'Scutcheon* had deeply affected Dickens not just as an objective critic, but subjectively for deep-seated reasons of his own that served to heighten his enthusiasm for the play, which took the eighteenth century for its setting and family pride as its theme.

Lord Henry Mertoun, a landowner, asks Lord Tresham for the hand of his sister, Mildred, in marriage. Tresham, delighted, agrees. When Tresham is told by an aged servant that Mildred has been entertaining a secret lover — identity unknown — in her room, he confronts this clandestine cloaked figure and they fight. In the course of the duel, the secret lover — Lord Mertoun himself, whose awe of his idol Tresham has inspired his covert activity — is fatally wounded. Tresham, overwhelmed by remorse, takes poison. Mildred, overcome by her own remorse, dies of grief in her brother's arms. The stage is littered with three corpses, and a fourth — the play itself — is dead by the time the curtain falls on it. This is to put the matter of *A Blot in the 'Scutcheon* a little bluntly: it is easy enough to render it ridiculous as melodrama; but the sentiment of pathos and the irony of self-righteousness were not fully realized in its principal characters, who lacked not for Shakespearean speeches but for Shakespearean credibility of character. This, then, is the play that Robert conceived when, two or three years earlier, he had written to Fanny Haworth, 'I want a subject of the most wild and passionate love.'

Joseph Arnould attended the play's first night, a lengthy account of which he wrote for the benefit of Alfred Domett in May 1843:

The first night was magnificent (I assume that Browning has sent you the play). Poor Phelps did his utmost, Helen Faucit very fairly, and there could be no mistake at all about the honest enthusiasm of the audience. The gallery — and of course this was very gratifying, because not to be expected at a play of Browning's — *took* all the points as quickly as the pit, and entered into the general feeling and interest of the action far more than the boxes, some of whom took it upon themselves to be shocked at being betrayed into so much interest in a young woman who had behaved so improperly as Mildred. Altogether the first night was a triumph. The second night was evidently presided over by the spirit of the manager. I was one of about sixty or seventy in the pit, and we yet seemed crowded compared to the desolate emptiness of the boxes. The gallery was again full, and again, among all who were there, were the same decided impressions of pity and horror produced. The *third* night I took my wife again to the boxes: it was evident at a glance that it was to be the *last*. My own delight and hers, too, in the play, was increased at this third representation, and would have gone on increasing to a thirtieth; but the miserable great chilly house, with its apathy and emptiness, produced on us both the painful sensation which made her exclaim that 'she could cry with vexation' at seeing so noble a play so basely marred.[101]

Arnould's letter also painted in the background, backstage machinations, and mischief-making that, as much as the obvious shortcomings of the play, contributed substantially to its failure. The fault was not all Robert Browning's, even allowing for the profundity of his anxiety that did him no good in the way it influenced his own behaviour towards Macready. Macready had his own agenda in respect of *A Blot in the 'Scutcheon* that contributed to its short, disastrous run, and it is possible that he deliberately undermined the play by orchestrating a bad reception for its performances.

Robert Browning's own scrupulously detailed version to Frank Hill of the *Daily News* in a letter of 15 December 1884 reads thus:

Macready received and accepted the play, while he was engaged at the Haymarket, and retained it for Drury Lane, of which I was ignorant that he was about to become the manager: he accepted it 'at the instigation' of nobody, — and Charles Dickens was not in England when he did so: it was read to him after his return, by Forster — and the glowing letter which contains his opinion of it, although directed by him to be shown to myself, was never heard of nor seen by me till printed in Forster's book some thirty years after. When the Drury Lane season began, Macready informed me that he should act the play when he had brought out two others — 'The Patrician's Daughter' and 'Plighted Troth:' having done so, he wrote to me that the former had been unsuccessful in money-drawing, and the latter had 'smashed his arrangements altogether:' but he would still produce my play. I had — in my ignorance of certain symptoms better understood by Macready's professional acquaintances — I had no notion that it was a proper thing, in such a case, to 'release him from his promise;' on the contrary, I should have fancied that such a proposal was offensive. Soon after, Macready begged that I would call on him: he said the play had been read to the actors the day before, 'and laughed at from beginning to end:' on my speaking my mind about this, he explained that the reading had been done by the Prompter, a grotesque person with a red nose and a wooden leg, ill at ease in the love scenes, and that he would himself make amends by reading the play next morning — which he did, and very adequately — but apprised me that, in consequence of the state of his mind, harassed by business and various trouble, the principal character must be taken by Mr Phelps; and again I failed to understand —, what Forster subsequently assured me was plain as the sun at noonday, — that to allow at Macready's Theatre any other than Macready to play the principal part in a new piece was suicidal, — and really believed I was meeting his exigencies by accepting the substitution. At the rehearsal, Macready announced that Mr Phelps was ill, and that he himself would read the part: on the third rehearsal, Mr Phelps appeared for the first time, while Macready more than read, rehearsed the part. The next morning Mr Phelps waylaid me at the stage-door to say, with much emotion, that it was never intended that *he* should be instrumental in the success of a new tragedy, and that Macready would play Tresham on the ground that himself, Phelps, was unable to do so. He added that he could not expect me to waive such an advantage, — but that, if I were prepared to waive it, 'he would take ether, sit up all night, and have the words in his memory by next day.' I bade him follow me to the green-room, and hear what I decided upon — which was that as Macready had given him the part, he should keep it: this was on a Thursday; he rehearsed on Friday and Saturday, — the play being acted the same evening, — *of the fifth day after the 'reading' by Macready.* Macready at once wished to reduce the importance of the 'play,' — as he styled it in the bills, — tried to leave out so much of the text, that I baffled him by getting it printed in four-and-twenty hours, by Moxon's assistance. He wanted me to call it 'The Sister'! — and I have before me, while I write, the stage-acting copy, with two lines of his own insertion to avoid the tragical ending — Tresham was to announce his intention of going into a monastery! all this, to keep up the belief that Macready, and Macready alone, could produce a veritable 'tragedy,' unproduced before. Not a shilling was spent on scenery or dresses — and a striking scene which had been used for the 'Patrician's Daughter,' did duty a second time. If your critic considers this treatment of the play an instance of 'the failure of powerful and experienced actors' to ensure its success, — I can only say that my own opinion was shown by at once breaking off a friendship of many years — a friendship which had a right to be plainly and simply told that the play I had contributed as a proof of it, would through a change of circumstances, no longer be to my friend's advantage, — all I could possibly care for.[102]

One can hear Robert, in the course of this letter, warming to his reminiscence, waxing again with the indignation that through long years had not seriously cooled in his breast. If sin there had been in this dolorous sequence of events, it was that Macready had finally, fatally, been false to friendship. The heat of this disgrace flares through the letter, and Robert remarks that 'my play subsists and is as open to praise or blame as it was forty-one years ago'. He is not about to encourage positively any latter-day production of the play: 'This particular experience was sufficient: but the Play is out of my power now; though amateurs and actors may do what they please.' In his account of an interview with Robert Browning on the subject of A Blot in the 'Scutcheon, Edmund Gosse gives the Browning version a dramatic, journalistic, jaunty air that somewhat plays up the admittedly farcical aspects of the business that, nevertheless, caused Robert real pain. And Mrs Orr, uncharacteristically, cannot resist a humorous touch: 'I well remember Mr Browning's telling me how, when he returned to the green-room, on that critical day, he drove his hat more firmly on to his head and said to Macready, "I beg pardon, sir, but you have given the part to Mr Phelps, and I am satisfied that he should act it;" and how Macready, on hearing this, crushed up the MS., and flung it on to the ground. He also admitted that his own manner had been provocative; but he was indignant at what he deemed the unjust treatment which Mr Phelps had received.'[103]

The version according to Gosse admits what Robert had confessed in his letter to Hill: that he was not merely deceived in his dealings with Macready, but that his disappointments were founded less on simple misunderstandings than on total ignorance. Macready's financial embarrassments only became clear to Robert on publication of the old actor's diaries, and only in the light of these revelations, he wrote to Hill, 'could I in a measure understand his motives for such conduct — and less than ever understand why he so strangely disguised and disfigured them. If "applause" means success, the play thus maimed and maltreated was successful enough: it "made way" for Macready's own Benefit, and the Theatre closed a fortnight after.'[104]

Robert's final excursion into the legitimate theatre was *Colombe's Birthday*, which he finished writing in March 1844 but which was not produced until 1853 — by Mr Phelps, as it happened, at the Haymarket Theatre, with Helen Faucit taking the role of the heroine. It played seven nights before vanishing forever from the boards of the London stage. The play had been originally written for Edmund Kean's son, Charles, who was performing at Covent Garden and who was looking for new parts to play. His wife, Ellen Tree, was designated for the part of Colombe. Kean offered, it is said, £500 to Robert for a play, though Robert himself speaks in a letter to Christopher Dowson of 'two or three hundred pounds'. But several complications got in the way of production. Kean wanted to postpone the play's performance until Easter the following year; the engagement at the Haymarket was to be for twelve nights only; Kean was off to Scotland; Kean was a slow studier of new roles (a failing that incited Robert's scorn as a fast-writing author). Robert was disinclined to 'let this new work lie stifled for a year and odd, and work double tides to bring out something as likely to be popular this present season'.[105] It was a disappointment that the play should not go immediately into production, particularly as Robert had been busy turning out other dramas — notably, *Luria* and *A Soul's Tragedy*, which 'I have by me in a state of forwardness'.

If *A Blot in the 'Scutcheon* had fragmented Robert's friendship with Macready beyond ready repair, *Colombe's Birthday* was to deal yet another devastating blow, this time to his friendship with John Forster. The play had been published by Edward Moxon as one of a continuing series of Browning's works, and it was reviewed by Forster on 22 June 1844 in the *Examiner*. Forster concluded his generally respectful review with the fatal words, 'There can be no question as to the nerve and vigour of this writing, or of its grasp of thought. Whether the present generation of readers will take note of it or leave it to the uncertain mercies of the future, still rests with Mr Browning himself. As far as he has gone, we abominate his tastes as much as we respect his genius.' That did it for Robert Browning — until, a year later, Forster apologized, 'very profuse of graciocities' as Robert reported to Miss Barrett on 18 September 1845, and so 'we will go on again with the friendship as the snail repairs its battered shell'. But the friendship was never the same, and much later there were no more than fragments of the shell strewn around to be trodden upon and utterly crushed.

To frustrate Macready's attempts to edit or alter the text of his plays in production and performance, Robert had had them printed by Edward Moxon, who eventually suggested publishing Browning's works at the expense of the Browning family as a continuing part work, a series of paper-covered pamphlets: 'each poem should form a separate brochure of just one sheet — sixteen pages in double columns — the entire cost of which should not exceed twelve or fifteen pounds.'[106] By using the same small, cheap type as was being used to print a low-priced edition of Elizabethan dramatists, Moxon could afford to offer bargain terms which Robert was quick to accept. The umbrella title of *Bells and Pomegranates* was, as usual, perfectly clear in its symbolism to Robert Browning, but he was obliged to provide some cues and hints to less erudite readers as to its origin. The perplexity of the general astonished Robert, but he finally, graciously explained that the intention was to express 'something like an alternation, or mixture, of music with discoursing, sound with sense, poetry with thought; which looks too ambitious thus expressed, so the symbol was preferred'.[107]

If this was still not clear enough, the reference to bells and pomegranates derived from the Book of Exodus, wherein is described the fashioning of Aaron the priest's ephod: 'And beneath upon the hem of it thou shalt make pomegranates of blue, and of purple, and of scarlet, round about the hem thereof; and bells of gold between them round about:/A golden bell and a pomegranate, a golden bell and a pomegranate, upon the hem of the robe round about.' (Exodus 28: 33–4) There is poetry in the rhythm of these words and in their symbols, in the alternating images around the hem of the garment worn by Aaron whose 'sound shall be heard when he goeth in unto the holy place before the Lord, and when he cometh out, that he die not' (ibid., verse 35). Robert further explained that 'Giotto placed a pomegranate fruit in the hand of Dante, and Raffaelle [Raphael] crowned his Theology (in the *Camera della Segnatura*) with blossoms of the same' — the fruit being symbolic of fine works.

The series of eight pamphlets was published over a period of some five years. It began in 1841 with *Pippa Passes*, a moderately long dramatic poem which Robert had written while he was finishing *Sordello* and after his trip to Italy. The second pamphlet, in spring 1842, comprised the text of an unperformed play, *King Victor and King Charles*. The third was *Dramatic Lyrics*, in November or December 1842. *The Return of the Druses* was the fourth pamphlet in January 1843. *A Blot in the 'Scutcheon*, the fifth, was published on the day of its first performance on 11 February 1843. *Colombe's Birthday*, published in March 1844, was the sixth pamphlet. The seventh in the series was a collection of short poems, *Dramatic Romances and Lyrics*, in November 1845. The final pamphlet, the eighth, on 13 April 1846, was the text of *Luria* and *A Soul's Tragedy*, two unperformed plays.

These successive publications were prefaced in the first, *Pippa Passes*, with a dedication to Thomas Talfourd. The complete dedication, later omitted except for Talfourd's name, expressed Robert Browning's hopes and aspirations and also alluded subtly and ruefully to past experiences: 'Two or three years ago I wrote a Play, about which the chief matter I much care to recollect at present is, that a Pit-full of goodnatured people applauded it: — ever since, I have been desirous of doing something in the same way that should better reward their attention. What follows I mean for the first of a series of Dramatical Pieces, to come out at intervals, and I amuse myself by fancying that the cheap mode in which they appear will for once help me to a sort of Pit-audience again.' The Pit-audience was to take its time — some twenty years — to applaud the eager poet-dramatist optimistic of acclaim and certain of celebrity.

A letter from Thomas Carlyle of 21 June 1841, acknowledging Robert's gift of a copy of *Pippa Passes* and of *Sordello*, suggested some difficulties ahead: 'Unless I very greatly mistake, judging from these two works, you seem to possess a rare spiritual gift, poetical, pictorial, intellectual, by whatever name we may prefer calling it; to unfold which into articulate clearness is naturally the problem of all problems for you. This noble endowment, it seems to me farther, you are *not* at present on the best way for unfolding; — and if the world had loudly called itself content with these two Poems, my surmise is, the world could have rendered you no fataller disservice than that same! Believe me, I speak with sincerity; and if I had not loved you well, I would not have spoken at all.'

Carlyle, in contemporary critical terms, was perfectly right, and much of what he had read of Robert's work was obscure to him. On those grounds, critical and public discontent with Browning's poetry was by no means a bad thing. His view that Robert had not yet come into full inheritance of his 'noble endowment' boiled down to a sort of headmaster's mid-term report — in simple terms, 'shows promise, could do better'. But of course, in Carlylean terms, it was not that simple. Carlyle continued sincerely but perhaps depressingly: his Scottish, rather Calvinistic, disposition assumed not only the value of struggle in itself but also the enhanced value of achievement as a result of it. What followed was virtually a moral sermon:

> A long battle, I could guess, lies before you, full of toil and pain and all sorts of real *fighting*: a man attains to nothing here below without that. Is it not verily the highest prize you fight for? Fight on; that is to say, follow truly, with steadfast singleness of purpose, with valiant humbleness and openness of heart, what best light *you* can attain to; following truly so, better and ever better light will rise on you. The light we ourselves gain, by our very errors if not otherwise, is the only precious light. Victory, what I call victory, if well fought for, is sure to you.

Excelsior! was Carlyle's hortatory word to Robert Browning who, if anyone, bore a banner with a strange, indecipherable device. Mocked and misunderstood, nevertheless the hero's way led upward through —

doubtless — a cold and lonely and desolate territory until the sunlit peak was reached. But even Carlyle recognized the difficulty. He kindly offered the weary wayfarer a short respite, a room for the night, as it were, where he could check his equipment, take his bearings, fully assess his commitment to the arduous journey ahead, consider the true philosophical meaning of the journey rather than be focused upon its artistic, symbolic value:

> If your own choice happened to point that way, I for one should hail it as a good omen that your next work were written in prose! Not that I deny you poetic faculty; far, very far from that. But unless poetic faculty mean a higher-power of common understanding, I know not what it means. One must first make a *true* intellectual representation of a thing, before any poetic interest that is true will supervene. All *cartoons* are geometrical withal; and cannot be made till we have fully learnt to make mere *diagrams* well. It is this that I mean by prose; — which hint of mine, most probably inapplicable at present, may perhaps at some future day come usefully to mind.

Carlyle concluded his letter, sugaring the salt, by admitting to Robert that, 'I esteem yours no common case; and think such a man is not to be treated in the common way. And so persist in God's name as you best see and can; and understand always that my true prayer for you is, Good Speed in the name of God!'

Whatever Robert may have thought then of this letter would surely have been tempered later by a letter of 17 February 1845 from Elizabeth Barrett. She had sent *her* poems to Carlyle, who had evidently offered her the same advice as he had given to Robert Browning, and indeed freely to every other poet except Tennyson: 'And does Mr Carlyle tell you that he has forbidden all "singing" to this perverse and froward generation, which should work and not sing? And have you told Mr Carlyle that song is work, and also the condition of work? I am a devout sitter at his feet — and it is an effort for me to think him wrong in anything — and once when he told me to write prose and not verse, I fancied that his opinion was I had mistaken my calling, — a fancy which in infinite kindness and gentleness he stooped immediately to correct. I never shall forget the grace of that kindness — but then! For *him* to have thought ill of *me*, would not have been strange — I often think ill of myself, as God knows. But for Carlyle to think of putting away, even for a season, the poetry of the world, was wonderful, and has left me ruffled in my thoughts ever since.' And whatever Carlyle might think about *Pippa Passes*, the conception of it was, to Miss Barrett's mind, 'most exquisite and altogether original — and the contrast in the working out of the plan, singularly expressive of various faculty'.[108]

Thomas Carlyle was from the beginning, and remained, an important friend to Robert Browning and a significant intellectual influence in his life. On 5 May 1840, Macready attended a lecture by Carlyle. What it was about he could not recollect, 'although I listened with the utmost attention to it, and was greatly pleased with it'.[109] The title and subject matter of the lecture, which Macready could not well recall, was 'The Hero as Divinity'. The second, on 8 May, he recollected very well: '"The Hero as Prophet: Mahomet"; on which he [Carlyle] descanted with a fervour and eloquence that only a conviction of truth could give. I was charmed, carried away by him. Met Browning there.' Macready had met Robert at the earlier lecture, too, three days before. Robert also attended the third lecture, 'The Hero as Poet'. This series of six lectures, the remaining subjects of which were 'The Hero as Priest', 'The Hero as Man of Letters', and 'The Hero as King', ran from 5 to 22 May. This lecture series, the sensation of the season, was published as that great and curious Carlylean work, *On Heroes, Hero-Worship, and the Heroic in History* in 1841.

Carlyle's first impression of Robert Browning had not been wholly positive. Forty years later, Robert, in a letter of 18 March 1881,[110] candidly admitted that Carlyle 'confessed once to me that, on the first occasion of my first visiting him, he was anything but favorably impressed by my "smart green coat" — I being in riding costume: and if then and there had begun and ended our acquaintanceship, very likely I might have figured in some corner of a page as a poor scribbling-man with proclivities for the turf and scamphood. What then? He wrote *Sartor* [*Resartus*] — and such letters to me in those old days. No, I am his devotedly.'

Carlyle, seventeen years older than Robert, might deplore his dandyism, but he admitted his young friend to be beautiful, striking in his facial features, and possessing a full head of dark, flowing hair. Besides, the 'neat dainty little fellow' professed a marked enthusiasm for the philosophy of the Scottish philosopher whose intellectual distinction in London literary society added a lustre to his otherwise gaunt, somewhat dour appearance. As Carlyle got to know Robert better, he formed a close personal attachment to him and a high opinion of his capabilities. To Gavan Duffy, the young Irish nationalist, Carlyle declared Robert Browning to possess not only a powerful intellect but, 'among the men engaged in England in literature just now was one of the few from which it was possible to expect something'. Browning, said Carlyle, responding in 1849 to Duffy's suggestion that the poet might be an imitator of Coleridge's 'The Suicide's Argument' (first published in 1828), 'was an original man and by no means a person who would consciously imitate anyone'.[111]

Robert and Thomas Carlyle had certainly met by 27 March 1839, when they are recorded as dining together at Macready's table.[112] In a letter of 30 December 1841 to Fanny Haworth, Robert tells her that he 'dined with dear Carlyle and his wife (catch me calling people "dear," in a hurry, except in letter-beginings!) yesterday — I don't know any people like them — there was a son of [Robert] Burns' there, Major Burns whom Macready knows — he sung "Of all the airts" — "John Anderson" — and another song of his father's.' This reference speaks confidently of some considerable intimacy and friendship beyond mere literary respect or intellectual hero-worship. In a letter to Robert of 1 December 1841, Carlyle lamented that, 'The sight of your card instead of yourself, the other day when I came down stairs, was a real vexation to me! The orders here are rigorous. "Hermetically sealed till 2 o'clock!" But had you chanced to ask for my Wife, she would have guessed that you formed an exception, and would have brought me down.' Carlyle goes on to invite Robert to pay visits on Friday nights for tea at six or half-past six. A letter of 1842 from Robert to Mrs Carlyle accepts an invitation to breakfast. Carlyle's letters to Robert in this period are those of a man corresponding with an intellectual equal and a friend interested in the common domestic matters of life as well as the more rarefied matters of the mind and the human condition. Browning had, wrote Carlyle to Moncure Daniel Conway, 'simple speech and manners and ideas of his own'. He was 'a fine young man . . . I liked him better than any young man about here.' And though Carlyle 'did not make much out of' *Paracelsus*, he conceded that 'that and his other works proved a strong man'.[113]

Robert not only rode into town to visit Carlyle at his house in Cheyne Row, Chelsea, but Carlyle rode out to Hatcham to visit the Brownings, whose decent domestic respectability he admired as much as the tidy trim of 'the little room' in which Robert kept his books. Perhaps Mrs Browning played the piano for him, perhaps Carlyle now and again burst into song. It was not unlikely — despite Elizabeth Barrett being convinced of his having 'forbidden all "singing" to this perverse and froward generation, which should work and not sing'. Robert revealed to her, in a letter of 26 February 1845, an occasion a couple of weeks before when Carlyle had abruptly asked him, 'Did you never try to write a *Song*? Of all the things in the world, *that* I should be proudest to do.' It may be that Carlyle was mindful of Andrew Fletcher of Saltoun's remark in 1703, 'I knew a very wise man so much of Sir Chr — 's sentiment, that he believed if a man were permitted to make all the ballads, he need not care who should make the laws of a nation.' If he could not make a song, Carlyle could at least sing one. Six months before, Robert had heard the sage of Ecclefechan, the prophet of Craigenputtock, the great Cham of Chelsea, 'croon if not certainly sing, "Charlie is my darling" ("my *darling*" with an adoring emphasis)'.

Of this enduring but improbable friendship, Chesterton puts the matter succinctly: 'Browning was, indeed, one of the few men who got on perfectly with Thomas Carlyle. It is precisely one of those little things which speak volumes for the honesty and unfathomable good humour of Browning, that Carlyle, who had a reckless contempt for most other poets of the day, had something amounting to a real attachment to him ... Browning, on the other hand, with characteristic impetuosity, passionately defended and justified Carlyle in all companies.'[114]

Dramatic Lyrics had been published, at Mr Browning senior's expense, in late November 1842. The pamphlet consisted of sixteen poems, four-teen of them new: 'Porphyria's Lover' and 'Johannes Agricola in Medi-tation' had already been published in the *Monthly Repository* in 1836. Moxon had suggested a collection of small poems for popularity's sake, and so Robert had collected up poems he had written over the past eight years, during and after his trip to Russia. 'Porphyria's Lover' (first titled 'The rain set in early to-night . . .') and 'Johannes Agricola' (first titled 'There's Heaven above . . .') are said to have actually been written in the spring of 1834, in St Petersburg. 'Cavalier Tunes', a set of three poems — 'Marching Along', 'Give a Rouse', and 'My Wife Gertrude' (later titled 'Boot and Saddle') — was probably written in the summer of 1842, arising out of Robert's background reading for *Strafford* and coinciding with the two-hundredth anniversary of the Civil War. *Sordello* and Robert's visit to Italy in 1838 had inspired 'My Last Duchess' (here titled 'Italy') and 'In a Gondola'. 'The Pied Piper of Hamelin' is said to have come from reading in his father's library. These, together with 'Waring', were to figure among Robert's most famous poems and, with 'Porphyria's Lover' and 'Johannes Agricola', are among the best known, best loved, and best studied poems in the English language, from high school to high table.

On first publication, Robert had been anxious to allay any interpretation of *Dramatic Lyrics* as expressing anything that might be construed as personal to the author. A plain disclaimer asserted: 'Such poems as the following come properly enough, I suppose, under the head of "Dramatic Pieces"; being, though for the most part Lyric in expression, always Dramatic in principle, and so many utterances of so many imaginary persons, not mine.' This was largely true in principle: the poems are not notably introspective but are mostly based on legend or history; they depend on dramatic action more than philosophical themes; and — with the exception of 'Cavalier Tunes' — they are distinctly flavoured with Robert's observations of nations and nationalities other than England and the English. The title of the collection also directs readers away from any psychological analysis: the poems are by an author recently known for dramatic works and the word *Lyrics* in the title specifically casts them back to the lyrical poetry of the Romantic poets. Of course, this is somewhat disingenuous — they are in a distinctively modern, Browning idiom.

Robert might have saved himself all the trouble of dissociating himself personally from the utterances in *Dramatic Lyrics* since the pamphlet attracted little or no attention from readers or critics. John Forster reviewed it, more or less admiringly, in the *Examiner*, writing that 'Mr Browning is a genuine poet, and only needs to have less misgiving on the subject himself.' But difficult, of course, to believe in one's genuine poetic ability when nobody else notices it or pays good money to read it. Perhaps Forster meant, however, that Robert had identified his true manner in *Dramatic Lyrics*. If so, he was right. The pamphlet proved definitively, for the first time, Robert's personal, inimitable mastery of the dramatic lyric and the monologue.

'The Pied Piper of Hamelin', a last-minute addition to fill up space in the volume, had been written for young Willie Macready, the actor's eldest son, when the boy was ill in bed. Willie liked to draw pictures and had asked Robert for something to illustrate. His retentive mind recalled a story about the death of the Pope's Legate at the Council of Trent from Wanley's *The Wonders of the Little World*. Willie's clever drawings inspired the final version of the improvised poem, now a nursery classic, which was perfectly designed to thrill an imaginative little boy:

> Rats!
> They fought the dogs and killed the cats,
>   And bit the babies in the cradles,
> And ate the cheeses out of the vats,
>   And licked the soup from the cooks' own ladles,
> Split open the kegs of salted sprats,
> Made nests inside men's Sunday hats,
> And even spoiled the women's chats
>   By drowning their speaking
>   With shrieking and squeaking
> In fifty different sharps and flats. (ll. 10–20)

The poem is a perfectly structured, perfectly paced, perfectly psychologically judged dramatic story, perfectly suited to the human voice — to recitation, which Robert loved. If we are to look for the cadences of his own voice in conversation, we may look no further than 'The Pied Piper'. Robert very likely enjoyed it as much as Willie. Indeed, it became one of his party pieces when entertaining at children's parties. The rhythms are important here, just as they are in another poem in *Dramatic Lyrics*: 'Through the Metidja to Abd-el-Kadr', said to have been composed on horseback in 1842. The thudding phrase 'As I ride, as I ride' resonates throughout the poem, just as effectively creating the sense of a rhythmic, steady gallop as the cadences of 'How They Brought the Good News from Ghent to Aix', published in 1845 in *Dramatic Romances and Lyrics*:

> Not a word to each other; we kept the great pace
> Neck by neck, stride by stride, never changing our place;
> I turned in my saddle and made its girths tight,
> Then shortened each stirrup, and set the pique right,
> Rebuckled the cheek-strap, chained slacker the bit,
> Nor galloped less steadily Roland a whit. (ll. 7–12)

If 'The Pied Piper' was aesthetically a great dramatic success, no less were other poems in the pamphlet. Robert had been impressed by Tennyson's poetry, though he preferred reality to Tennyson's romance. It is this insistence on reality, rather than romance or sentiment, that gives such power not only in the fantasy of legend to the ambiguously happy though unambiguously moral ending of 'The Pied Piper', but also to the grim amorality of poems like 'Porphyria's Lover' and 'My Last Duchess'. Both these latter poems concern the murder of women. It is possible that the murderers in both are mad — fantasists to whom reality is a mirage; but to suppose any such thing is to flinch from Robert Browning's insistence on character over the detail of narrative, in contrast to Tennyson's emphasis on story over characterization. Ian Jack makes this important point: 'Tennyson tells us that the old man who narrates the story is an artist, but we have to be told — whereas in Browning we would know from the smell of the paint.'[115] G. K. Chesterton had earlier made this point in a different way: Robert knew about painting, sculpture, music, and the rest because he had practised painting, sculpture, and music with his own hands.

And in these two poems of muted horror, just as in the poems of action and adventure, the unemphatic pace of the narrative underlines the matter-of-fact nature of the act and its matter-of-fact acceptance:

> Porphyria worshipped me; surprise
> Made my heart swell, and still it grew
> While I debated what to do.
> That moment she was mine, mine, fair,

Perfectly pure and good: I found
A thing to do, and all her hair
   In one long yellow string I wound
   Three times her little throat around,
And strangled her. No pain felt she;
   I am quite sure she felt no pain. (ll. 33–42)

And we, too, are sure: the tenor of the lines might do just as well for telling us that her lover was tying Porphyria's shoelaces as an act of humble homage. Just so the Duke, in 'My Last Duchess', refers to the death of his wife:

That's my last Duchess painted on the wall,
Looking as if she were alive. I call
That piece a wonder now: Frà Pandolf's hands
Worked busily a day, and there she stands.' (ll. 1–4)

Porphyria's lover waits quietly for the rain to stop and the wind to die down, the girl's 'smiling rosy little head' propped up on his shoulder.

And thus we sit together now,
   And all night long we have not stirred,
   And yet God has not said a word! (ll. 58–60)

Just so the Duke goes down to — possibly — dinner with his guest, calling attention casually on the stairs to another interesting work of art:

   Nay, we'll go
Together down, sir. Notice Neptune, though,
Taming a sea-horse, thought a rarity,
Which Claus of Innsbruck cast in bronze for me! (ll. 53–6)

The Duke gave commands and his wife died; Porphyria's lover wound her hair around her neck and strangled her: in neither case was there remorse or retribution; no police to break down the ducal door, no God to strike down Porphyria's murderous lover with a thunderbolt. Like Johannes Agricola, similarly complacent, the murderers may have felt:

> I have God's warrant, could I blend
>> All hideous sins, as in a cup,
>> To drink the mingled venoms up;
> Secure my nature will convert
>> The draught to blossoming gladness fast: (ll. 33–7)

The point about these characters — ruthless, cold, passionate, hot — is their natures, fully and subtly realized. Their actions depend upon in the act, and are informed in the aftermath, by their characters, and not vice versa. Murder is banal enough: it is the character who commits it who is the interesting subject, and Robert Browning is so much in complete control of the poem that gives the character to us fully-formed that we are largely unaware, on a first reading, of the artistry — the poetic authenticity, the artistic integrity — with which he does it.

Robert Browning, if his works were not often or generally read, was frequently and widely discussed among his friends. He breakfasted with John Kenyon, took six o'clock tea with the Carlyles, dined with Serjeant Talfourd, supped with Macready and William Johnson Fox. All these were social occasions that broadened his acquaintance and at which he was welcome for his confidence in conversation and aptitude for anecdote. Harriet Martineau, though mystified by *Sordello*, admitted that in conversation 'no speaker could be more absolutely clear and purpose-like' than Browning. 'He was full of good sense and fine feeling, amidst occasional irritability, full also of fun and harmless satire, with some little affectations which were as droll as anything could be. A real genius was Robert Browning assuredly.'[116]

Joseph Arnould, writing in 1845 to Alfred Domett, described a dinner party at which Robert was also a guest: 'Glorious Robert Browning is as ever — but more genial, more brilliant and more anecdotical than when we knew him four years ago.' And yet, and yet, in this year, 1845, the polished social performance was becoming tedious to Robert, as though he were Macready toiling through a familiar role, night after night, in the same company of players, speaking the same words, throwing in a few ad-libs, in a long run of a popular play. Too often, it felt like an exercise in public relations.

In 'Respectability', published in *Men and Women* on 10 November 1855, Robert wrote:

> How much of priceless time were spent
> With men that every virtue decks,
> And women models of their sex,
> Society's true ornament.

In a letter of 12 March 1845 to Elizabeth Barrett, he wrote, 'So you have got to like society, and would enjoy it, you think? For me, I always hated it. — have put up with it these six or seven years past, lest by foregoing it I should let some unknown good escape me, in the true time of it, and only discover my fault when too late; and now that I have done most of what is to be done, *any* lodge in a garden of cucumbers for me!' He does not 'even care about reading now', he confesses. 'But you must read books in order to get words and forms for "the public" if you *write*, and *that* you needs must do, if you fear God. I have no pleasure in writing myself — none, in the mere act — though all pleasure in fulfilling a duty, whence, if I have done my real best, judge how heart-breaking a matter must it be to be pronounced a poor creature by critic this and acquaintance the other!' He supposes Miss Barrett likes 'the operation of writing as I should like that of painting or making music ... After all, there is a great delight in the heart of the thing; and use and forethought have made me ready at all times to set to work — but — I don't know why — my heart sinks whenever I open this desk, and rises when I shut it.'

A month earlier, Robert had been writing to Miss Barrett about critics, trying to be fair-minded and even-handed in response to her inquiry about his 'sensitiveness to criticism'. What he had said then was, 'I shall live always — that is for me — I am living here this 1845, that is for London.' For himself — 'for *me*' — he writes from a thorough conviction of duty, and he does his best: 'the not being listened to by one human creature would, I hope in nowise affect me.' And yet, 'I must, if for merely scientific purposes, know all about this 1845, its ways and doings', and if he should take a dozen pages of verse to market, like twelve cabbages (or pomegranates, he might have said, but didn't) he had grown himself, he should expect to get as much as any man for his goods. If nobody will buy or praise, 'more's the shame ... But it does so happen that I have met with much more than I could have expected in this matter of kindly and prompt recognition. I never wanted a real set of good hearty praisers — and no bad reviewers — I am quite content with my share. No — what I laughed at in my "gentle audience" is a sad trick the real admirers have of admiring at the wrong place — enough to make an apostle swear.'

In this selfsame letter to Miss Barrett, a few lines previously, Robert had seized eagerly on her wish that they should 'rest from the bowing and the courtesying, you and I, on each side'[117] and given himself up to her — and their developing correspondence — entirely: 'I had rather hear from you than see anybody else. Never you care, dear noble Carlyle, nor you, my own friend Alfred over the sea, nor a troop of true lovers! — Are not these fates written? there!' These fates were written — what about Robert's own? The work — far less, or far more, the life, the entire fate of Robert Browning — seemed in 1845 to be in the balance: the achievement so far, what did it amount to? 'What I have printed gives *no* knowledge of me — it evidences abilities of various kinds, if you will — and a dramatic sympathy with certain modifications of passion . . . *that* I think — But I never have begun, even, what I hope I was born to begin and end — "R. B. a poem" —'. At most, 'these scenes and song-scraps *are* such mere and very escapes of my inner power, which lives in me like the light in those crazy Mediterranean phares I have watched at sea, wherein the light is ever revolving in a dark gallery, bright and alive, and only after a weary interval leaps out, for a moment, from the one narrow chink, and then goes on with the blind wall between it and you.'

This is the letter of a man whose lightning or lighthouse flashes illuminate his world fitfully and reveal himself, though captain of his own ship, becalmed on a dark flood. Robert's perplexity and discouragement was of long standing. In short, he was depressed: the weeks passed, Carlyle talked wisely and beautifully, there had been quarrels with Macready and Forster, the rarely positive critical response to his work was pleasing enough but misguided, the plays were defunct, the poems had sold disappointingly. On 9 October 1843 he wrote to Alfred Domett, who had thrown up the law and disappeared to the colonies, to New Zealand, 'People read my works a little more, they say, and I have some real works here in hand; but now that I could find it in my heart to labour earnestly, I doubt if I shall ever find it in my *head*, which sings and whirls and stops me even now — an *evening* minute by the way.'[118]

Perhaps to still his whirligig head, or to give it something substantial to dance around, Robert sailed for Naples in the late summer of 1844.

As is the case with his previous journeyings abroad, precious few relics survive to substantiate the itinerary or illuminate the events. There is some dispute as to whether Robert wrote the poems 'Home Thoughts from the Sea' and 'How They Brought the Good News from Ghent to Aix' on this voyage or on the first voyage to Italy — Robert himself said the one, then the other. And if he could not remember, then attribution by others is just as credible one way or the other. Mrs Orr is virtually the sole source of information for Robert's second trip to Italy, and she gives no circumstantial detail about how he met 'a young Neapolitan gentleman', by name of Scotti, 'who had spent most of his life in Paris' and with whom, very likely, Robert talked his proper French and improved his vernacular Italian. Quickly becoming good friends, they travelled together from Naples to Rome, Scotti helpfully haggling over their joint expenses. 'As I write', reported Robert in a letter to Sarianna, 'I hear him disputing our bill in the next room. He does not see why we should pay for six wax candles when we have used only two.'[119] One can see why Robert, who had learned to be careful of money, should warm to a man with a mind similarly concentrated on his own short purse. Says Mrs Orr of Scotti, 'he certainly bore no appearance of being the least prosperous'. In Rome, Scotti was judged by Countess Carducci — an acquaintance of Robert's father — 'the handsomest man she had ever seen.' But Mr Scotti 'blew out his brains soon after he and his new friend had parted; and I do not think the act was ever fully accounted for'.[120]

We could wish to pause there, at that sensational moment, to inquire further about the impoverished Signor Scotti and his suicide: he sounds just the man, and his death just the circumstance, to stop Robert in his tracks to add his friend and his end to his repertory company of characters fit for a poem. But all we know of Robert's time in Rome is that he visited Shelley's tomb in the New Protestant Cemetery, in commemoration of which he wrote the few lines on 'Fame' which form the first part of 'Earth's Immortalities', inspected the grotto of Egeria, the scene imagined by Byron of the supposed interview between King Numa Pompilius of Rome and the advisory nymph, and the recently restored church of Santa Prassede, close by Santa Maria Maggiore, where the tomb of Cardinal Cetive may have partly inspired the poem 'The Bishop Orders His Tomb at Saint Praxed's Church'. These are all occasions of the most tantalizing interest, and about which too little — if any — first-hand evidence exists.

We fall back upon Mrs Orr, too, for information about the journey home to Hatcham, via Livorno where he found Edward John Trelawny who had been an intimate of the poets Shelley and Byron. Trelawny might have been in a better condition to discuss the poets had he not been stoically — 'indifferently', says Mrs Orr — enduring a painful operation to have a troublesome bullet dug from his leg by a surgeon. Trelawny's cool fortitude struck Robert very much. That the veteran was able to talk at all, far less reminisce about poets and poetry, was very remarkable.

Robert returned from Italy in December 1844. During his absence, he had missed the much-acclaimed publication of Miss Elizabeth Barrett Barrett's *Poems* in the summer of that same year; but once back in Hatcham he read the volumes, which, if they had not in themselves been of the greatest interest, would certainly have caught — or been brought to — his attention on account of two delicately allusive lines that ran:

> Or from Browning some 'Pomegranate', which, if cut deep down
>   the middle,
> Shows a heart within blood-tinctured, of a veined humanity.

What, in 1844, did Robert know of Elizabeth Barrett Moulton Barrett? No more than anyone else, which wasn't much in the way of first-hand information, far less reliable gossip — though uninformed speculation (it was said that Miss Barrett was completely crippled, unable to move) was never short as a negotiable commodity. The poet, essayist, and former seafaring man Richard Hengist Horne, who had experienced enough maritime and military adventure to qualify him as a Baron Munchausen (except that most of his tales, like those of 'Abyssinia' Bruce, were largely true) put it about that she was in very delicate health and had lived for years hermetically sealed in her room, her only contact with the outside world being through the medium of letters very erudite and literary in tone. He was more authoritative than most, since she had recently collaborated with him on a two-volume book, *A New Spirit of the Age*, in which 'Orion' Horne, ably assisted by the contributions of others (including Robert Browning as well as Elizabeth Barrett) had aspired to make a general estimate of contemporary literature without, alas!, possessing much literary ability or even critical faculty himself.

In retrospect, from the distance of our own times, Horne's judgement in 1844, when the book appeared, was naturally coloured by the florid taste of his age, lengthily praising the likes of Talfourd, who is now not much more than a literary footnote to the period. But critical perspectives inevitably alter: to Horne's credit, he did rate highly those big guns who have survived as literary heroes: Carlyle, Macaulay, Tennyson, and Dickens — though he'd have found it difficult not to notice them respectfully at appropriate length; and he devoted generous space to the 'little known works of Mr Robert Browning', whose *Paracelsus* he praised over five pages and whose *Sordello*, at the length of a dozen pages, he sorrowfully judged would remain obscure but to have been treated unjustly by critics since the poem, in Horne's estimation, 'abounded with beauties'. And so, her hand dabbled in Horne's book, Elizabeth Barrett, the famously reclusive poetess, would have known not only of Mr Robert Browning's work but, less intimately, something of the poet himself.

In his book, Horne reflected upon his collaborator's invisibility among her contemporaries, supposing that future generations might doubt her very existence. But some, he knew, had actually seen her. Miss Mitford, for one, told him that Miss Barrett 'lies folded in Indian shawls upon her sofa with her long black tresses streaming over her bent-down head, all attention' while having her new poems read to her by an unnamed gentleman who, we suppose, must have been John Kenyon. Through the medium of Kenyon, then, we may also suppose that Robert learned more even than Horne gleaned from the gossiping Miss Mitford about the interesting lady poet who preferred to call herself Elizabeth Barrett Barrett rather than to use her full family name of Barrett Moulton Barrett. From Kenyon, Robert received a manuscript poem, 'Dead Pan', written by Elizabeth, and Kenyon was happy to communicate Robert's enthusiasm to its author.

In 1820, aged fourteen years, Elizabeth Barrett had privately published an epic, *The Battle of Marathon*, dedicated to her father, Edward Barrett Moulton Barrett. She had begun writing this at the age of eleven. Though imitative of the styles of Homer, Pope, and Byron, it was an impressive achievement — and would have been so if only by reason of its pastiche and precocious learning, far less as evidence of genuine poetic ability. This effort was followed the next year by 'Stanzas, Excited by Some Reflections on the Present State of Greece', published in the *New Monthly Magazine* (1821), and 'Stanzas on the Death of Lord Byron' in 1824. In 1826, at the age of twenty, she published an *Essay on Mind, with Other Poems*, the printing costs being paid by Mary Trepsack, a Barrett slave from Jamaica, who lived in the Barrett household. Elizabeth's correspondence with a family friend, Sir Uvedale Price, contributed substantially to Price's *Essay on the Modern Pronunciation of the Greek and Latin Languages*, published in 1827. On her own account, in 1832, she translated *Prometheus Bound* by Aeschylus, published with *Miscellaneous Poems* in 1833.

All these were given anonymously to the world, until she finally put her name to *The Seraphim, and Other Poems* in 1838, and followed these verses with occasional poems and translations published in *Blackwood's Edinburgh Magazine* and in the *Athenaeum*. In 1842, she published three hymns translated from the Greek of Gregory Nazianzen and 'Some Account of the Greek Christian Poets'. In 1844, there appeared her *Poems*, which famously included 'Lady Geraldine's Courtship' (the story of a beautiful, talented, high-born lady who chooses to marry Bertram, a low-born poet, rather than a suitor of her own rank) and, within that poem, the references to Robert Browning's own poems. Elizabeth Barrett was, by 1844, esteemed by the best and most influential literary magazines. Her classical and metaphysical learning, her poetic accomplishments, her mysterious reluctance to make any public appearances, all astonished and somewhat intimidated the literary establishment. There were some who muttered ungraciously about poetical obscurity and mysticism, but by and large her work was treated more reverently, more indulgently, than the irredeemable obscurities and impenetrable mystifications of Robert Browning's poetry.

Some three years before, John Kenyon had attempted to arrange a meeting between Robert and Elizabeth. He had enthusiastically told her about him, him about her; he had discussed his poetry with her, hers with him; and at one point this middle-aged romantic go-between had almost brought his plan to a satisfactory conclusion, only to have it frustrated by Elizabeth putting off the encounter with a perfectly plausible, believable plea of indisposition — though in fact, as she admitted, it was because of her 'blind dislike to seeing strangers'. Still, there it was — the reference to Robert Browning, in 'Lady Geraldine's Courtship', and in the best poetic company, his work linked favourably, equal in rank, with 'poems/Made by Tuscan flutes . . . the pastoral parts of Spenser — or the subtle interflowings/Found in Petrarch's sonnets'.

On 10 January 1845, Robert — having read the copy of Elizabeth's *Poems* given to Sarianna by John Kenyon, having punctiliously asked Kenyon if it would be in order for him to write, and having been assured by Kenyon that she would be pleased to hear from him — posted a letter from New Cross, Hatcham, Surrey, to Elizabeth Barrett at 50 Wimpole Street. The first sentence of his first letter to her is this:

> I love your verses with all my heart, dear Miss Barrett, — and
> this is no off-hand complimentary letter that I shall write, —
> whatever else, no prompt matter-of-course recognition of your
> genius, and there a graceful and natural end of the thing.

Several sentences further into the letter, Robert declares, 'I do, as I say, love these books with all my heart — and I love you too.'

And so it began.

But what was begun, and how was it begun? We know the upshot, the happy ending — the lovestruck drama has become the stuff of potent myth; but our sentimentality may misinterpret the beginning and our romantic predisposition may rose-colour our perceptions of the whole courtship correspondence as the simple singing of two flirtatious love birds, the coy cooing of two eroticized turtle doves. In *The Courtship of Robert Browning and Elizabeth Barrett*, Daniel Karlin points out that Robert, from his first letter, from the first sentence of that letter, knew what he was doing. Artless is the very last word that should be adduced to characterize Robert's letters. Different in kind to Elizabeth's, they are — insists Karlin — dramatic compositions. They may not be premeditated, but they are not spontaneous. Robert 'composes his love for Elizabeth in the same terms as he composes the action of his poems'. In all Robert's letters 'there is not a single casual allusion, there is not a single pointless digression; an all-embracing objective cannot tolerate unconnected images or associations. Elizabeth Barrett's best letters remind you of Byron; Browning's of St Paul.'[121]

Karlin makes the original and persuasive point — though some, enticed by the fairy-tale aspects of the Browning-Barrett courtship, will find it startling — that Robert, the composer of the initiating letter, stands behind Robert, the character in the letter, whose apparently impetuous, ornamental, gallant sincerity is deliberately presented. Elizabeth also has a role scripted by Robert: 'though', says Karlin, 'it is not made explicit until his second letter. He told her then, "your poetry must be, cannot but be, infinitely more to me than mine to you — for you *do* what I always hoped to do ... You speak out, *you*, — I only make men & women speak — give you truth broken into prismatic hues, and fear the pure white light, even if it is in me ...".'[122] And so Elizabeth's poetry, being pure white light, the very essence of her personality, is not dissociated from her being. In this sense, Elizabeth and her poetry are one, indissoluble, and thus Robert could write, 'I do, as I say, love these books with all my heart — and I love you too.'

Elizabeth thought this fanciful — 'an illusion of a confusion between the woman and the poetry', as she wrote much later to Mary Mitford. At the time, she remarked, 'Browning writes letters to me ... saying he "*loves*" me. Who can resist *that* ... Of course it is all in the uttermost innocence.' Nevertheless, her interest had been stimulated — tickled rather than touched, says Karlin — by this well-mannered, if superficially effusive, letter from a poet whose work she admired and who came well recommended by John Kenyon and Richard Horne, whose judgement she respected. The next day, the 11th, she replied. She responded rather formally as a fellow-poet, beginning by thanking 'dear Mr Browning, from the bottom of my heart. You meant to give me pleasure by your letter — and even if the object had not been answered, I ought still to thank you. But it is thoroughly answered. Such a letter from such hand! Sympathy is dear — very dear to me: but the sympathy of a poet, & of such a poet, is the quintessence of sympathy to me!'

Thus the correspondence — the long fuse, leading to the startling denouement — was sparked not simply by poetry but by the shared experience of being poets and, crucially, by the differences between them in that respect. Karlin defines this central concern: 'The ways in which each praised the other's poetry — Browning because Elizabeth Barrett seemed to him an examplar of "pure" poetry, she because of Browning's "power" and "experience as an artist" — rapidly acquired a personal as well as an aesthetic edge. Browning and Elizabeth Barrett were to debate their relative status up to and beyond the altar, and it was in and through this debate that their feeling for each other defined and developed itself.'[123]

It is not to be assumed, from Karlin's demonstration, that Robert set out deliberately to seduce Elizabeth, though it is plain that he was powerfully attracted by the idea of the woman he identified with her poetry. But they had never met, knowing each other only by literary repute and conversational hearsay. It did not seem improbable to Robert that they would meet. From the very outset he hoped, and very likely intended, that they would. He had been rebuffed (like many others) once: through John Kenyon, Robert had once come so close, 'so close, to some world's wonder in chapel or crypt, only a screen to push and I might have entered'.[124] Now, tantalizingly, Elizabeth offered some renewed basis for hope: 'Winters shut me up as they do dormouse's eyes; in the spring, *we shall see*: and I am so much better that I seem turning round to the outward world again.'[125] Their first letters were 'all in the uttermost innocence' because, by and large, Robert and Elizabeth were innocents — at least in love.

Neither of them, though they had not been short-changed in their experience of the complete love and whole trust of family and friends, had been properly *in* love. Robert had fancied himself in love with one or other, or possibly both, of the Flower sisters, though had perhaps only played with the fancy of being in love with them; and he had flirted a little — though not seriously, not with intent — in his lively, youthful, teasing letters to Fanny Haworth, whose mature heart may (but we don't know) have fluttered at the sight of his handwriting. Elizabeth's experience of love had been not dissimilar: as Robert was adored and indulged by his mother and father, so Elizabeth was adored with a profoundly protective love by her father, and she in turn deeply loved the large litter of her younger brothers and sisters. As Robert had felt comfortable in the company of older women and was drawn to the values of a good mind complemented by feminine virtues, so Elizabeth had found pleasure in the learned company and erudite correspondence of older men whose intellects interested her and held her attention perhaps more than their persons, though she was not unaware of — greatly valued, indeed — the attractive power of a confident masculinity.

Both Robert and Elizabeth possessed a generous nature and a vitality of expression which informed their everyday lives and coloured their personal letters. For all that Daniel Karlin emphasizes the underlying Pauline rigour of Robert's letters to Elizabeth, they possess a surface sheen of Robert's delight in the exercise of writing, certainly, but also of having found a receptive and responsive correspondent — importantly and excitingly, an intelligent woman. Robert wrote spontaneously and instinctively within that Pauline style, being amusing, intelligent, sympathetic, and responsive to the nuances of Elizabeth's less confident, more impressionistic replies. He was graceful, poetic, provocative, pressing, and often powerfully eloquent in images and assertive attitudes that displayed a degree of sophistication seemingly derived from a worldliness beyond Elizabeth's personal experience. In short, irresistible even without declarations of love. If she had her doubts and anxieties about the constantly reiterated word 'love', Elizabeth was at least allured by Robert's manner — 'you draw me on with your kindness'.[126]

At first, Robert and Elizabeth contented themselves more or less with thoughtful, tentative criticism of each other's work. She frankly admitted her faults (as they seemed to her): 'Headlong I was at first, and headlong I continue . . . guessing at the meaning of unknown words instead of looking into the dictionary — tearing open letters, and never untying a string, — and expecting everything to be done in a minute, and the thunder to be as quick as the lightning. And so, at your half word I flew at the whole one, with all its possible consequences, and wrote what you read.'[127] But, she further admitted, 'In art, however, I understand that it does not do to be headlong, but patient and laborious — and there is a love strong enough, even in me, to overcome nature.'

In Robert she recognized 'What no mere critic sees, but what you, an artist know, is the difference between the thing desired and the thing attained . . . You have in your vision two worlds . . . you are both subjective and objective in the habits of your mind. You can deal both with abstract thought and with human passion in the most passionate sense. Thus you have an immense grasp in Art . . . Then you are "masculine" to the height — and I, as a woman, have studied some of your gestures of language and intonation wistfully, as a thing beyond me far! and the more admirable for being beyond.'

This appeal for informed criticism, signifying that Robert, as a masculine poet, had much to teach Elizabeth as a feminine poet, was also about the differences between them, between men and women indeed, and Elizabeth rather tended to assume that she had at last found her great instructor, a kindred poetic spirit whose abilities, deserving of admiration, would communicate themselves advantageously to her own art and abilities. Simultaneously, her use of words — 'passionate', 'masculine' — was unconsciously provocative to Robert. He, just as Elizabeth had feared that he conflated her with her poetry and perceived a unity that she did not herself understand to be true, similarly felt that Elizabeth estimated him by his poetry and, in a letter post-marked 28 January, told her, 'you know nothing, next to nothing of me'.

He elaborated this in his next letter, post-marked 11 February, concluding: 'when I remember how I have done what was published, and half done what may never be, I say with some right, you can know but little of me'. Elizabeth accepted some of this letter, and protested the rest of it in her reply of 17 February: 'I do not, you say, know yourself — you. I only know abilities and faculties. Well, then, teach me yourself — you.'

And so it properly begins.

She had found out some small details already — Robert had offered to open his desk for her, that repository of things half begun, half finished. She was interested in the desk. She wrote: 'if I could but see your desk — as I do your death heads and the spider webs appertaining',[128] but he had not written of skulls and spider webs. In his reply, post-marked 26 February, Robert inquired, 'Who told you of my sculls and spider webs — Horne? Last year I petted extraordinarily a fine fellow (a *garden* spider — there was the singularity, — the thin, clever-even-for a spider-sort, and they are *so* "spirited and sly," all of them — this kind makes a long cone of web, with a square chamber of vantage at the end, and there he sits loosely and looks about), a great fellow that housed himself, with real gusto, in the jaws of a great scull, whence he watched me as I wrote, and I remember speaking to Horne about his good points.'

That might have been quite enough about spiders and intimations of mortality; but Robert continued, laying the skull to quiet contemplation of the view from the window in Hatcham and giving some intimate particulars of the room in which the skull reposed and Robert worked. 'Phrenologists look gravely at that great scull, by the way, and hope, in their grim manner, that its owner made a good end. He looks quietly, now, out at the green little hill behind. I have no little insight to the feelings of furniture, and treat books and prints with a reasonable consideration. How some people use their pictures, for instance, is a mystery to me; very revolting all the same — portraits obliged to face each other for ever, — prints put together in portfolios. My Polidori's perfect Andromeda along with "Boors Carousing," by Ostade, — where I found her, — my own father's doing, or I would say more.'

Robert had rescued the hapless Andromeda from his father's portfolio, from insalubrious company, and adopted her as his principal muse. Much has been made of this engraving after the painting *Perseus et Andromede* by Caravaggio di Polidoro — 'my noble Polidori' — which hung in Robert's room. Elizabeth naturally becomes identified with the captive Andromeda and Robert with her saviour, Perseus. Critics have had no difficulty tracing the powerful emblematic influence of Andromeda and the myth in which she figures throughout Robert's work. Put shortly, Andromeda was chained to a rock at the edge of the sea by her father as a sacrifice to a monstrous sea serpent. She was saved from death by the hero Perseus, who slew the dragon, released Andromeda, and married her. The figure of Andromeda appears first in *Pauline*:

> Andromeda!
> And she is with me: years roll, I shall change,
> But change can touch her not — so beautiful
> With her fixed eyes, earnest and still, and hair
> Lifted and spread by the salt-sweeping breeze,
> And one red beam, all the storm leaves in heaven,
> Resting upon her eyes and hair, such hair,
> As she awaits the snake on the wet beach
> By the dark rock and the white wave just breaking
> At her feet; quite naked and alone; a thing

I doubt not, nor fear for, secure some god
To save will come in thunder from the stars. (ll. 656–67)

By some interpretations, the young Robert Browning was saved from despair by Andromeda — superficially a Shelleyan, romantically eroticized image but, more profoundly, a symbol of the feminine, signifying creativity — who came to represent the power of poetry and, by extension, the timelessness and thus the immortality of art. Andromeda, in these terms, continued to influence Robert throughout his work of a lifetime, until finally — in the 'Francis Furini' section of *Parleyings with Certain People of Importance in Their Day*, a late (1887) poem — the emblematic image of a beautiful, naked woman in art is examined for its deepest significance which, towards the end of his life, Robert asserted to be a vision that ultimately leads us to God and, by implication, redemption. The poet or painter, by representing such an earthly image, one of many fixed immutable symbols, may, through the transmuting power of art, convey a sense of the spiritual in eternity to the modern, temporal, rational evolutionist.

Meanwhile, with his customary omnivorous appetite for experience and knowledge, Robert set himself to knowing and revealing himself to Miss Barrett. Elizabeth had all but said they might meet in the spring, and now, in his letter post-marked 26 February, Robert wrote on 'Wednesday Morning-Spring!' to announce signs of its approach: 'Real warm Spring, dear Miss Barrett, and the birds know it; and in Spring I shall see you, surely see you — for when did I once fail to get whatever I had set my heart upon?' Such confidence! Elizabeth replied the next day, wittily temporizing. 'Yes, but dear Mr Browning, I want the spring according to the new "style" (mine), and not the old one of you and the rest of the poets. To me, unhappily, the snowdrop is much the same as snow — it feels as cold underfoot — and I have grown sceptical about "the voice of the turtle," and east winds blow so loud. April is a Parthian with a dart, and May (at least the early part of it) a spy in the camp. *That* is my idea of what you call spring; mine *in the new style*! A little later comes my spring; and indeed after such severe weather, from which I have just escaped with my life, I may thank it for coming at all.'

Elizabeth's health, as usual, was her most useful, well-worn instrument for digging herself deeper into the life she had created for herself, and which allowed her pretty much to please herself. Illness enabled her to manipulate even, and especially, those she most loved to bind them to her own perceived, however irrational, benefit. To get her own way, she sacrificed much, but at some level she must have conceived the sacrifice to be worthwhile. In his own way, Robert too had established a *modus vivendi* that enabled him to suit himself as to when, or even if, he should do anything at any time not of his own choosing. He owed this considerable liberty to the largely passive indulgence of his parents and his sister, who, for whatever reasons of their own, colluded with him in the gratification of his personal desires, apparently against the prevailing social values of middle-class self-reliance and self-improvement. It is interesting to consider how these apparently opposed yet very similar character traits — there's no easily getting around the words 'selfishness' and 'ruthlessness' — contended to get their own way in the great things of their lives at the expense of their conventional personal comforts.

Among her family and friends, Elizabeth was considered 'delicate': at least they had become accustomed to her presenting herself as a semi-invalid and had collaborated in treating her as such. In a letter post-marked 6 May, Elizabeth recommended sleep to Robert on the ground that 'we all know that thinking, dreaming, creating people like yourself, have two lives to bear instead of one, and therefore ought to sleep more than others'; and for herself, 'I think better of sleep than I ever did, now that she will not easily come near me except in a red hood of poppies.' What we might now call her habit had been acquired over twenty-five years. In March 1845, Elizabeth was thirty-nine years old. Since the age of fifteen, and perhaps earlier, she had regularly been dosed with opium.

The Barretts, like the Brownings, had derived their fortune from the sugar plantations of the West Indies — though Robert's father had renounced the trade on moral grounds, while Elizabeth's father had continued to rely upon it for his income. Edward Barrett Moulton Barrett, who came to England in 1792 at the age of seven and married Mary Graham-Clarke on 14 May 1805, was the grandson of Edward Barrett (usually known as Edward of Cinnamon Hill), a hugely rich Jamaican plantation owner who died in 1798. Edward's father, Charles Moulton, was the son of another Jamaican family that also worked its plantations by slave labour. Charles seems to have been known for his savagery towards his slaves and, even for those times and in that place, acquired a bad reputation. Elizabeth, born to Edward and Mary on 6 March 1806, was formally christened with Edward, her younger brother by fifteen months, in February 1809. By that time, she had become known as Ba, an abbreviation for Baby — but the 'a' pronounced as in 'babby' rather than as in 'baby'.

At the time of Elizabeth's birth, the Barretts were living at Coxhoe Hall, near Durham, close to the Graham-Clarkes, but in 1809 Edward bought a property of some four hundred acres, Hope End, near Ledbury in Herefordshire, and moved his family (which by now included Henrietta, born on 4 March that year) to the house he almost immediately began — with an energy and taste for the exotic that William Beckford would have admired — to embellish, inside and out, in a Turkish style, to the extent of commissioning concrete and cast iron minarets from his architects. Edward's neighbours might mutter about grandiosity and flamboyance, even of *nouveau riche* vulgarity, but he didn't care; and Mary Barrett was captivated by a 'beautiful and unique' fantasy she thought worthy of an Arabian Nights story.

This extensive, expensive ornamentation of the house continued for nigh on ten years, in his absence as much as his presence. When Edward was not at Hope End, he was in London and Jamaica, attending to business. Mary's business consisted in almost constant childbearing and child rearing: after Elizabeth, little Edward (known as 'Bro'), and Henrietta ('Addles'), at regular intervals of about eighteen months came Sam (known as 'Storm', 'Stormy', or 'Stormie'), Arabella ('Arabel'), Mary (who died young, aged four), Charles, George ('Pudding'), Henry, Alfred ('Daisy'), Septimus ('Sette'), and — the youngest, born in 1824 — Octavius ('Occie' or 'Occy'). It was, by all accounts, not only a large but a mutually loving family, bossed by Elizabeth as the senior sister, and devoted to their sweet-natured, occasionally harassed mother. She in turn devoted herself to her dozen children, who occupied all her time. They were adored by their indulgent father, who took no great offence when his children were affectionately disrespectful. If anything, boldness and curiosity in his brood was encouraged: none of the children felt repressed, and they all looked forward eagerly to the fun they would have with him when he returned home from his business trips. They felt not just materially and emotionally safe, but, like little animals, secure in the predictable domestic routines and the regular disciplines of daily family prayers and other religious observances insisted upon by Mr Barrett. It was a fixed, solid world in which the Barretts, from eldest to youngest, were sure of their proper places — which did not exclude some natural jealousies and jostling for position — in the pecking order of Hope End.

If all this sounds like an idyll, it largely was. Hope End was an isolated rural property, deep in the agricultural west of the country, invisible from any road, silent but for bird song, and hedged from the outer world by dense foliage that to outsiders seemed oppressive. The Barretts lived in a quiet, secure, enclosed little world of their own, pretty much self-reliant and self-sufficient for their amusements. In this situation, Elizabeth discovered books at a very early age and her mother encouraged her to write about what she had read, nagging at her when her handwriting and critical standards didn't come up to scratch. Supervised by Mary, Elizabeth ate up novels by Maria Edgeworth and Walter Scott, and begged for more. When a tutor was brought in to prepare Bro for school at Charterhouse, Elizabeth eagerly shared the lessons with her younger brother and learned Greek with him.

In April 1821, Arabel, Henrietta, and Elizabeth fell ill with headaches, pains in their sides, and convulsive twitchings of their muscles. They were treated, on the best medical advice, with a tincture of valerian, whereupon Arabel and Henrietta quickly recovered. Elizabeth did not, and in June she contracted a case of measles. It is at this time that she seems to have decided that she suffered from 'natural ill health', and her symptoms increased not only in quality but in quantity. She described her constant headache and her recurrent paroxysms — her 'agony' — to her local and London doctors; how she swooned, the wild beating of her heart, her feeble pulse, the coldness of her feet, the constant pains in the right side of her chest that travelled round to her back, up to her right shoulder and down the arm. Margaret Forster succinctly describes how, 'From the onset of menstruation middle-class women were encouraged to regard themselves as delicate creatures who must take great care of themselves. Vigorous exercise was discouraged, rest encouraged. Every ache and pain was taken seriously.'[129] The result, too often, was a debilitated condition — a chronic invalidism at best;

at worst, symptoms resulting from hysteria or a narcissistic hypochondria that derived from or provoked the social attitude that women were naturally weak, dependent creatures. Illness was considered to be virtually the norm for upper- and middle-class women: to be 'pale and interesting' was quite the thing; robust health was not fashionable.

Elizabeth, whose health in childhood had been good, allowing for seasonal coughs and colds, nothing to worry about in normal circumstances, was prescribed purgatives that gave little or no relief. Advice, of course trustfully taken and dutifully observed, to confine herself 'in a recumbent posture' for long hours every day to a sofa or bed probably only reinforced her condition. Her paroxysms continued at the rate of three a day, though none at night, and she began to complain that her spine was 'swollen'. Though medical examination could detect 'nothing obviously wrong with the spine', she was put in a 'spine crib' — a kind of hammock suspended some four feet off the ground — just in case a disorder of the spine should develop. It was at this point that laudanum — dried and powdered opium dissolved in alcohol — was prescribed for Elizabeth, who took this universal panacea with just as much thought as we might take any mildly palliative over-the-counter nostrum or prescription drug today. A solution of opium or morphine enabled her to sleep in a 'red hood of poppies'. At first, the dose would have been mild, but in time she would come to depend upon taking up to forty drops a day, a serious quantity, and claim she could not do without it.

After a few months, Elizabeth recovered some of her usual high spirits. Her appetite improved, her symptoms of upper body pain and paroxysms abated, and she felt rested. But she continued to believe that she was truly suffering from a disease of the spine and, despite medical prognoses that she would make a complete recovery from ailments both real and imaginary, she behaved as though she were a chronic invalid with no hope of cure. Her body was as passive as her mind was active. For the next year, strung up in her spinal crib or recumbent on a sofa, she read voraciously, wrote quantities of gloomy verse, 'sickly' as she herself eventually characterized it, in the form of odes dedicated to her family, and continued her study of Greek. She read Shakespeare and the best modern poets — Byron, Shelley, Keats, Wordsworth — and became morbidly Romantic. She read Mary Wollstonecraft's *Vindication of the Rights of Woman* and became enraged about the sufferings of womanhood. Mary Wollstonecraft, in fact, affected her as deeply in her view of wedlock and subservience to men as Shelley's atheism and vegetarianism had affected Robert. Elizabeth rejected romantic love and marriage as a snare she should take care to avoid. Robert had rejected the prospect of marriage less philosophically, rather as an unlikely adventure which, even if he should find a compatible partner, he could not financially afford.

In common, too, with the young Robert Browning, Elizabeth Barrett had determined in her teens that to be a poet was an honourable profession, that poetry was real work of deep spiritual and high artistic value, that she herself could become a proper poet — 'one of God's singers'. Her ambitions extended far beyond the charming verses that young dilettantish women composed as prettily as they painted watercolours. Since Elizabeth's parents, like Robert's, were respectful of major poetry and serious poets, they made no difficulty about their eldest daughter's devotion to such a creditable art and encouraged her aspirations. From the age of eleven, after all, she had shown not just promise, but uncommon ability. However they might privately enjoy the lighterminded versifying of the other children, her parents and siblings soon learned that Elizabeth's poems were no laughing matter and to tread warily if ever tempted to take them lightly. By the age of twenty-one, Elizabeth was a published poet. She had proved the worth of her work to herself and enjoyed the regard of those who valued it. To buy time to pursue her high vocation and continue her scholarly studies, she insisted on respect for the importance of her work and indulgence for her precarious state of health.

Her physical condition had markedly improved: she no longer rode or walked great distances or played boisterously with the younger children as she had done before her first illness, but she did stroll around the house and the gardens of Hope End and tutored her younger brothers in Latin. For the best part of the day, however, she closeted herself in her room, writing and reading in bed until late in the morning and preferring not to join the rest of the family when visitors were entertained. Now that her physical frailty had become established, accepted by custom and usage, she no longer had to emphasize her mysteriously non-specific weakness by regular consultations with doctors: coughings and a susceptibility to colds were enough to provoke sympathy and promote a collective agreement within her family that Elizabeth should be protected from anything that might worsen her delicate state of health. For intellectual stimulation, she corresponded lengthily with neighbours, older gentlemen such as Sir Uvedale Price (author, in 1794, of *An Essay on the Picturesque*, which introduced a new aesthetic category), Sir James Commeline (a local vicar and classical scholar), and especially with Hugh Stuart Boyd, a scholar, translator, and poet who lived at nearby Malvern Wells. She fell half in love with Mr Boyd, who was sadly afflicted with blindness, the only man outside her family that she consented to see and to make the effort to visit. But Mr Boyd, a gentleman of some moderate private means, happened to be married already and the father of children.

Mary Barrett, exhausted by the birth of her twelfth child, Octavius, in 1824, distressed by the death of her mother, Grandmother Graham-Clarke, and suffering from rheumatoid arthritis, died at the age of forty-seven in October 1828. Elizabeth was twenty-two years old. As the oldest daughter, she might have been expected to take over the running of the Hope End household, but no such duty was imposed upon her. Instead, Aunt Bummy, Arabella Graham-Clark, an unmarried sister of Mary Barrett, came to live with the Barretts. She was forty-three years old, the same age as her brother-in-law, and capably took over the management of the household, so relieving Elizabeth of any domestic obligations. The death of his wife deeply affected Edward Barrett, who turned to religion for spiritual comfort.

On his trips to London he had fallen under the influence of the powerfully charismatic Scottish preacher Edward Irving who, by 1825, had started to go seriously off his theological head — and not quietly. Irving's big moment of revelation arrived when, sensationally, he predicted the imminent second coming of Christ. From 1828, he began teaching Christ's oneness with humanity in all its attributes and thus, heretically, to assert to his followers the sinfulness of Christ's nature. Edward Barrett's mind became infused with the Irvingite belief that salvation lay in purity, that translation to the next world, preferment in the afterlife, could be achieved only by remaining uncorrupted by this wretched and sinful world. Irving preached zealously to large crowds that flocked to hear his dramatic denunciations of the errors of turpitudinous humanity. His authority, he claimed, derived directly from God, whose mouthpiece he had become. As an instrument of the divine, Irving was regularly inspired to invoke the wrathful retribution of the Almighty upon the godless and the guilty.

Bereft of her mother, Elizabeth adhered emotionally to her father. They had always been close, though never dependent on one another. Edward Barrett's feelings towards his eldest daughter were sympathetic towards her physical fragility and psychological sensitivity. His general conduct as a good paterfamilias was not exceptional: he could be severe when necessary in his principles of good Christian conduct, and strict, though not abusive, about correcting any backsliding among the young Barretts, though he tended to be more indulgent towards Elizabeth than towards the rest of his children. But now Elizabeth became clinging, resentful of his business trips to London, anxious even when he was out of her sight at home. She wept pitifully when he went away and wept for joy when he returned safely. It is now generally accepted that, in the first years after his wife's death, Edward Barrett did not become abnormally possessive of Elizabeth: quite the reverse, in fact. If anything, it was Elizabeth who felt, however irrationally, abandoned and insecure to the extent that she became virtually reclusive and sought comfort to an unusual degree in the powerful protective presence and reassuring company of her father.

Mr Barrett, in turn, looked to his family for solace in his grief and loneliness. He was liable to fall into rages, justifiably or not, but he could generally put on a good-humoured face. If he was sometimes a beast, he was at least — like Dr Arnold of Rugby — a just beast. In whatever temper, thunderous or sunny, it was perfectly evident that he greatly missed his wife. As he turned inward upon himself and his children, so he excluded friends and barely tolerated the intrusions by various remote members of the Barrett and Graham-Clarke families. Like Elizabeth, he conceived a horror of visitors and refused to make visits to other houses. His children amply and affectionately returned his love for them, and so for a while their mutual need for security coincided. For the most part, harmony reigned throughout Hope End. Then, in 1830, just two years after the death of his wife, Edward Barrett's mother died. His shock was unspeakable. He had no words to describe the immensity of his loss. For that matter, the entire Barrett family was shocked to the extent that they were all shackled even more securely together in the isolated house and in their passionate, almost exclusive involvement with one another.

Edward Barrett was experiencing other difficulties, beyond the deeply wounding, irreparable losses in his private life. Some long-standing business and financial worries, caused by sustained mismanagement of his interests in the West Indies and a damaging lawsuit, were brought to a head by a slave rebellion in 1832 on the Jamaican plantations managed by his brother Sam. Additionally, the imminent prospect of the complete abolition of slavery (which eventuated in 1833) implied higher production costs and an inevitable tumult in the price of sugar. The monetary losses would be severe. Hope End, a significant drain on his resources (it was heavily mortgaged and creditors were pressing), would have to be sold. He kept much of the land, but the loss of the house was bad enough. It represented, even worse, a loss of his fundamental security in the world after the deaths of his wife and mother, and a serious loss of face — humiliating evidence of failure. If such precious things could so easily slip from his grasp, what might he lose next? In fact, Edward Barrett was far from ruined: the prospect before him was not that he would be a poor man, but he would no longer be a rich man.

The Barretts left Hope End on 23 August 1832. Mr Barrett had taken a large, comfortable house by the sea at Sidmouth in Devon, and the family settled more or less cheerfully, at least without protest, into their new lives. Elizabeth slept soundly, her appetite increased, and her cough was less troublesome: perhaps the sea air had something to do with the revival of her health, and probably, too, the stimulation of a new, more open and extroverted environment after the backwater of Hope End was beneficial. It was as though a heavy burden of gloom had been lifted from the Barretts. The whole family, buzzing around the beach and enjoying a more active social life, felt better and looked healthier. They received local visitors and returned their calls — all except Elizabeth, who refused to visit or be visited by anyone and mostly stuck to her books.

Bro, Stormie, and George, the older brothers, were by now judged by their father to be adult enough to prepare themselves for employment in the world. Bro, twenty-five years old, travelled to Jamaica to help his Uncle Sam, while Stormie and George, aged sixteen and nineteen respectively, left to attend Glasgow University. Elizabeth experienced her familiar feeling that, as soon as any of the family disappeared from her sight, she might never see them again, lose them altogether; but she put up a brave front, appeared compliant of inevitable changes in family life, and applied herself even more diligently to her proper business of reading and writing until the family situation should, with any luck, return to normal.

The three Barrett brothers returned to Sidmouth in 1835. At the end of the year Mr Barrett announced that, for the sake of his sons, the family would move immediately to London. George, who intended to become a barrister, would enter the Inner Temple, one of the Inns of Court; Bro (who had acquired first-hand experience of the West Indian estates) and Stormie (who stammered so badly that he could not take his viva voce examination and thus had failed to take his degree) would join the family business; and the younger boys would be properly educated. Elizabeth, who had found little intellectual stimulation in Sidmouth — not that she had made much effort to seek it out — was better pleased than not at the prospect of a literary life in London. For two years the Barretts lived at 74 Gloucester Place before moving permanently, in 1838, to 50 Wimpole Street.

London winters were cold, daylight turned a depressing grey, and dense, chilling fog hung like a malevolent yellow miasma about the streets, clutching at the throat and lungs. Elizabeth's health deteriorated. In contrast to the open situation of Sidmouth, the reflective light of the sea and the green of the surrounding Devonshire countryside, she felt immured, 'stuck to the fender', almost literally bricked in. There was hardly a leaf or a blade of grass to be seen except if she drove out to Hampstead Heath, which hardly qualified as real country. As for acquiring stimulating literary and intellectual acquaintance, her sole resource and only constant visitor was her portly, red-faced, fifty-two-year-old cousin, John Kenyon whose advantage, in addition to a kindly and sociable nature, was that his house in Devonshire Place was a notable focus for literary men and women. He contrived, with some difficulty, to introduce Elizabeth to Wordsworth, Walter Savage Landor, and — more successfully — Mary Russell Mitford, chatty and opinionated and well-connected with literary persons, who became one of her few close friends and a regular recipient, until her death many years later, of

Elizabeth's most personally confiding and wittily conversational letters.

As the result of a cold contracted in the winter of 1837–8, Elizabeth began to cough again. She continued to feel unwell into the spring. When she consulted the eminent Dr Chambers, he recommended even more rest, to the point that she was rendered virtually immobile, moving only from sofa to bed and back again, hardly stirring from her room, which was closely sealed from the least possibility of a draught. Despite all precautions, she caught another cold, and Chambers gravely diagnosed an affection of the lungs. In August 1838, he advised a change of climate. Elizabeth should winter somewhere warm, and Mr Barrett was persuaded, with some difficulty, that she should go to Torquay with her maid, Elizabeth Crow. During the three years of her convalescence at Torquay, usually attended by one or other of her brothers and sisters, Elizabeth was fairly constantly unhappy. She didn't like Torquay, she worried about the expense of it all, the climate was not particularly mild, and her health did not noticeably improve. At times, it took decided and distressing turns for the worse. She became increasingly reliant on laudanum to help her sleep. She wanted to be well for her father's sake, and strenuously put her mind to feeling better, but she was convinced she was dying.

Many explanations have been given for Elizabeth's chronic ill health: Betty Miller suggests that it derived from sibling rivalry, from jealousy of Bro. As a boy — it seemed to his elder sister — he was given the advantage by being sent to school to be properly, formally educated while she was obliged more or less to instruct herself. It is certainly true that Elizabeth was intellectually much cleverer than Bro. Mrs Miller's theory implies that Elizabeth was malingering: perceiving herself as largely powerless, she put on suffering and incapacity as a means to obtain control of her life and so avoid the domestic and social duties of a woman of her class (she never liked sewing, for example), perhaps even deliberately to restrict the possibility of being obliged to marry. Illness attracted and focused the attention of her parents, and the household was at least partly run on the basis of her requirements. She imposed what she called a 'rigid rein' upon herself in order not to be 'hurled with Phaeton far from everything human ... everything reasonable!'[130] In her own estimation, by imposing the restraint of immobility upon herself, she saved herself from acting upon the 'violent inclination' that remained in her 'inmost heart'. Elizabeth at least partly acknowledged that her ill health might be a desirable condition.

The modern consensus is that Elizabeth was truly ill. There seems little doubt now that she contracted a form of tuberculosis in her mid-teens and, as Daniel Karlin comments, 'Tuberculosis is an impression-able disease. Elizabeth Barrett's health fluctuated according to variations in climate and state of mind; she had periods of remission followed by crises, and the crises generally corresponded with times when she was under nervous strain. In these circumstances, there is little point in drawing distinctions between "physical" and "psychological" illness.'[131] This fits very well with Margaret Forster's view that 'It is impossible to over-emphasise how tension of any kind — pleasurable excitement just as much as unpleasant — had an immediate physical effect on Elizabeth. She was, as she described herself, "intensely nervous".'[132]

In February 1840, the Barretts learned that Sam had died in Jamaica at the age of twenty-eight. The loss of a brother struck Elizabeth down instantly. She became delirious, fainting into unconsciousness when she was not in an opium-induced sleep, and could be comforted only by her father, who came down to Torquay to stay with her for several weeks. He rallied her with pious exhortations. He urged Christian submission to God's will and invoked devotional feeling for His grace. She gave pious thanks for Sam's life and everything she had loved in him — his ami-ability, his goodness, his wit, his delight in dandyish dress — but it was difficult not to be overwhelmed by his loss. She made the effort, however, to such an extent that Mr Barrett was gratified by his beloved daughter's beauty of character as revealed in her staunch belief that love never dies, that Sam was but in another room, in another, better world, not dead to those who loved him. What she did not yet (if she ever did) know was that Sam had died — or so it was reported by missionaries who had worked to save his soul — of evil influences: the tropical climate, in part, but more perniciously of having resorted to native women and other carnal pleasures that had broken his health and imperilled his soul.

At about this time, Arabel and Bro had discovered romance. Bro's affair seems to have been the more serious of the two, or perhaps it was merely more advanced than Arabel's. Bro was thirty-three years old, an age at which his father had been married for eleven years and had sired eight children. Bro was refused paternal permission to marry. Mr Barrett set his face against any argument: he would hear no plea in favour of his son's proposed nuptials. This was not unexpected. First of all, the fact was that Bro had no money of his own and stood in no position to marry without financial support from his father. Secondly, there exists the possibility that Mr Barrett had reasonable objections to the proposed bride, though we know no grounds on which they might have been well founded. Thirdly, it was well known among the Barretts that Mr Barrett had adopted the Irvingite principle, bolstered by his own reading of the Bible, that a father exercised absolute authority over his children. It was his first duty to lead them from the paths of corruption, to save them from sin, to preserve their purity. He might grieve for Sam, but — and we may assume he knew the disgraceful details of the wage Sam had earned from sin — the circumstances leading to his son's spiritual ruin and consequent death would have surely confirmed his moral beliefs. For Mr Barrett to permit Bro to marry a woman who did not meet the exacting standards of the most rigorous morality would be to risk losing another son to perdition.

To an extent, from love, rather than from fear, the Barrett children were somewhat awed by the implications of their father's attitude: no suitor other than a saint would be worthy of any of them, and a saint would hardly be the most likely material from which a spouse might be made. They might privately, among themselves, poke affectionate fun at their father's protective concern for their spiritual salvation; but it was one thing to feel proud that they were special in his eyes, quite another when his interdict, as final as a ruling of the Last Judgement, frustrated their genuine emotions and commonplace desires. In a letter of 12 December 1845 to Robert Browning, Elizabeth summed up a situation that had unexpectedly arisen to affect her personally and to which she had once referred in jest to Arabel:

'If a prince of Eldorado should come, with a pedigree of lineal descent from some signory in the moon in one hand, & a ticket of good-behaviour from the nearest Independent chapel, in the other' . . .

'Why even *then*,' said my sister Arabel, 'it would not *do*.' And she was right, & we all agreed that she was right. It is an obliquity of the will — & one laughs at it till the turn comes for crying.

The rectitudinous Mr Barrett was not in principle opposed to the institution of marriage — he was himself a living testament to its virtues, beauties and benefits; but he was absolutely opposed to any occasion for sin, and, in that respect, an inappropriate attachment could not be countenanced. Where he suspected sin he generally discovered it. When one looks for devils, it is not difficult to find them. His religious principles had not descended upon him suddenly. There had been no voice in a thunderclap or vision in a lightning flash. He had experienced no moment of sudden revelation. They had waxed gradually within him, secreted like amber that, on exposure to the moral dilemmas of life, had hardened and trapped the insects of his intolerance. Irvingism had taken deep root, nourished by Edward Barrett's naturally devout Protestantism and his cautious, conservative Liberal politics. It was partly this slow evolution of his character into something grim and forbidding that inhibited the Barrett children from recognizing the process of transformation until it was too late to do anything to modify it. And so, by and large, it had become accepted as an element influencing their own lives.

The Barretts might admit that their father had their own good at heart, but that concept of the absolute good was utterly inflexible and did not yield to the more elastic idea of good as conceived by weaker characters. Edward Barrett's love was as oppressive as his ire. G. K Chesterton puts it precisely: 'He had, what is perhaps the subtlest and worst spirit of egotism, not that spirit which thinks that nothing should stand in the way of its ill-temper, but that spirit which thinks that nothing should stand in the way of its amiability . . . The worst tyrant is not the man who rules by fear; the worst tyrant is he who rules by love and plays on it as on a harp.'[133] In his deep anxiety about loss, to prevent any further harm to the Barrett family, he perversely suffocated the children by his insistence on the family's self-sufficiency, by his efforts to exclude any external threat to their well-being, and by his belief that they should be all in all to one another and be kept together.

Elizabeth, though strong-willed as a child, perfectly capable of throwing books and other objects around a room when she fell into a pet at being thwarted in her desires, did not as a mature woman challenge her father's authority directly in the matter of marriage. Instead, she secretly attempted to make over her own money to Bro so that he could marry as he pleased. She was foiled in this underhand strategy. Mr Barrett had no legal right to stop any of his children marrying, but his personal wishes and his threats to disinherit any of them who defied those wishes were intimidating enough. He would cut any of them off without a shilling and cast them out of his life — regretfully, no doubt, but unhesitatingly.

For one thing, Elizabeth was afraid of her father's anger and would not confront it directly. She could not in general bear, as she wrote to her brother George after her own marriage, 'agitating opposition from those I tenderly loved — & to act openly in defiance of Papa's will, would have been more impossible for me than to use the right which *I believe to be mine*, of taking a step so strictly personal on my own responsibility.' For another thing, she retreated into her perceived weakness less as a self-professed invalid and more as a helpless woman. To Robert Browning, who had lost his temper over Mr Barrett's apparent tyranny, she wrote on 12 June 1846: 'You said once that women were as strong as men, . . . unless in the concurrence of physical force. Which is a mistake. I would rather be kicked with a foot, . . . (I, for one woman! . . .) than be overcome by a loud voice speaking cruel words . . . being a woman, & a very weak one (in more senses than the bodily), they would act on me as a dagger would . . . I could not help *dropping*, dying before them — I say it that you may understand.' So much for the invigorating spirit of Mary Wollstonecraft's feminism. There was a third factor, however: Elizabeth, like the rest of her brothers and sisters, had been inculcated with a strong sense of family, and the Barretts were not only profoundly loyal to one another, they loved one another deeply. The children's loyalty and love for their father was no less real and no less committed than among themselves.

Bro, who had come to Torquay to be with Elizabeth, went sailing with three friends at midday on 11 July 1840. The sea was calm and the weather was fine, except for a brief squall that blew up suddenly in the afternoon. By nightfall, the boat had not returned. It never did. The Barretts explored every strategy they could devise to convince themselves that Bro could be alive. Every possible eventuality was examined and analysed until, at last and reluctantly, they gave up hope after three days. Bro's body was not discovered until three weeks later when it was washed ashore, with the corpses of one of his friends and the boatman, in Babbacombe Bay on 4 August. They were buried in a local churchyard two days later. Elizabeth despaired: she had quarrelled with Bro on the morning of the 11th. Her last words to her beloved brother had not been friendly. She convinced herself, too, that her illness had been the primary — the only — reason for Bro being in Torquay at all. He had stayed with her at her request, and she felt responsible for having kept him with her. It was her fault that he had been there, she reasoned, and so it was her fault that he had died. The blame was hers. Her guilt was fathomless.

For the three weeks between Bro's disappearance and his funeral, Elizabeth was scarcely conscious. Her mind, when not blank, was tormented — delirious visions of 'long dark spectral trains' and 'staring infantine faces' filled it; dreams were 'nothing but broken hideous shadows and ghastly lights to mark them', driving her, she said later, almost to 'madness, absolute hopeless madness'. For three months, she did nothing. Her father stayed with her, every bit as despairing and suffering as his daughter in their mutual loss. He returned to London in December. Elizabeth had finally felt strong enough to write a letter to Miss Mitford in October. Mary Mitford offered very practical comfort: understanding her friend's grief, empathizing sincerely with her loss, she tactfully offered Elizabeth a puppy from her own golden cocker spaniel's recent litter. It was a generous offer — such a dog was a very valuable gift — and Elizabeth at first refused. But she was persuaded to accept.

Flush, when he arrived in January 1841, was six months old and irresistibly pretty. Of course, he became thoroughly spoiled and as devoted to his new mistress as she to him. Vitally, Flush became the object of her adoring attentions; Elizabeth became responsible for this scrap of excitable animal life. Flush pulled her out of her self-absorption, relieving some of her guilt about Bro — though not entirely. She pushed the painful memory of Bro to the back of her mind, to inhabit some dark place where nobody was permitted to enter. For the rest of her life, she would not talk of him and others learned not to refer, within her hearing, to Bro or the tragedy at Torquay.

Elizabeth returned to London on 11 September 1841. Her three years' absence had been the most wretched of her life. The house in Wimpole Street, and her niche within it, seemed a haven of security from which she intended never again to be plucked and thrown into the difficult, dangerous world beyond it. Even to let anyone beyond Elizabeth Wilson (known as Lily), her capable and companionable personal maid who had replaced Crow, her immediate family and Flush into her room seemed unnecessarily hazardous. Not that visitors were encouraged or made welcome to the house at all: Mr Barrett, who had been reasonably outgoing, cheerful, and obliging in the days of his great prosperity, had withdrawn into himself as his resources had been depleted. His confidence had diminished and he turned, as it appeared to those who had known him in better days, gruff in manner with friends, grudging and curmudgeonly with strangers.

Elizabeth attributed his change of manner to shyness, about which she expressed some exasperation; but the truth of the matter was that Edward Barrett now felt inadequate. To compensate, he refused all occasions on which he thought he might not act with advantage — worse, be perceived to his disadvantage. Within his own house and family circle, he generally showed kindness and tenderness and was persuaded by Elizabeth to permit the amiable John Kenyon to visit and to meet Miss Mitford, who was also regularly admitted to Elizabeth's room. He was delighted with Mary Mitford, but his success with her did not encourage him to push his luck further with others, such as Mrs Anna Jameson, who thrust herself into 50 Wimpole Street in November 1844.

There was no keeping Mrs Jameson out. She had read and admired Elizabeth's latest publication, *Poems*, and nothing would do but that she should meet the author. Anna Jameson was not unknown in her own right among respected and respectable London society. Obliged to make her own living, she had established herself as a popular authority on art, travel, and literary criticism (mostly about women in Shakespeare and poetry), producing well-received, profitable books that enabled her to travel widely at a fast clip and in modest comfort to research more books on these improving subjects. Her works were not scholarly, perhaps, but they demonstrated some artistic taste and good sense; they were well researched at first hand, vividly written, and they sold well.

As a self-sufficient woman, Mrs Jameson was a convinced feminist in the Harriet Martineau mould, and naturally wished to exchange sisterly views with the celebrated Miss Barrett. She saw no good reason why this ambition should not be achieved, and so she politely left a note at 50 Wimpole Street announcing herself. But many people had left notes at the Barrett house, to no positive advantage. Mrs Jameson, turned away unsatisfied from the doorstep the first time, made a second attempt. She left another note, and this time she was admitted by Wilson. Elizabeth had read at least one of Mrs Jameson's dozen books and her curiosity about the woman's determination seems to have overridden her habitual inclination to close the door against even the most distinguished callers.

Anna Jameson was no beauty — Elizabeth, who paid close attention to physical appearance, noted that her complexion was pale and so were her eyes, she possessed no eyebrows to speak of, her lips were thin and colourless, and her hair was a very pale red. Carlyle briskly described her as 'a little, hard, brown, red-haired, freckled, fierce-eyed, square-mouthed woman'. But Carlyle was not one to varnish a plain portrait. He spoke as he found — and so, for that matter, did Mrs Jameson. She was Irish, which largely accounts for her colouring and partly for her character. Like Miss Mitford, Anna Jameson was of middling years. But with the coincidence of their ages, any resemblance to Miss Mitford ended.

Whereas Mary Mitford indulged Elizabeth's taste for writing and receiving long, confidingly effusive letters rapturously devoted, for the most part, to the incomparable beauties of Flush, his adorable character, and detailed accounts of his daily doggie activities, Anna Jameson spoke forth uncompromisingly and brusquely on all manner of matters within her competence, and they were many, including the subject of women's superiority of mind and the uselessness of what she called 'carpet work' to which the female sex was condemned and confined. 'Carpet work' was injurious to the female mind, she said, because it led, fatally, to the vapid habit of reverie. Elizabeth faintly protested this blanket condemnation, though she had never worked a carpet, far less knitted or plied a needle and thread, in her life. Mrs Jameson, taking stock of Elizabeth, generously made an exception for her on the ground that *she* might do carpet work with impunity because she could be writing poetry at the same time. Anna Jameson's vigorous, sharply intelligent, unreserved discourse, and the underlying kindliness of her nature, endeared her immediately, and so this good woman was admitted to the small, exclusive pantheon of Elizabeth's closest and most trusted allies. She could hardly have chosen anyone truer in friendship or more stout-hearted in the defence of her reputation and interests than Anna Jameson when such unqualified support was required and mattered most.

As Elizabeth's spirits improved, as her work became more widely known and widely appreciated, and as she took more interest in the activities and gossip of London's social, political and literary life — in response to her frequent letters, friends wrote back despatches from all these fronts and her chosen ambassadors reported to her in person — so her health also improved. In her letter to Robert of 5 March 1845, she wrote: 'I am *essentially better*, and have been for several winters; and I feel as if it were intended for me to live and not die, and I am reconciled to the feeling ... I am not desponding by nature, and after a course of bitter mental discipline and long bodily seclusion, I come out with two learnt lessons (as I sometimes say and oftener feel), — the wisdom of cheerfulness — and the duty of social intercourse.'

In her darker moments, Elizabeth felt she had been deprived of social and intellectual opportunities, ground to a husk in the mill of suffering, and she contrasted Robert's luckier, fatter experience of life to date: 'I do like to hear testimonies like yours, to *happiness* ... it is obvious you have been spared, up to this time, the great natural afflictions, against which we are nearly all called, sooner or later, to struggle and wrestle ... Remember that as you owe your unscathed joy to God, you should pay it back to His world. And I thank you for some of it already.' She made some judicious criticism of attitudes towards her: 'People have been kind to *me*, even without understanding me, and pitiful to me, without approving of me': and now Robert — 'How kind you are! — how kindly and gently you speak to me! Some things you say are very touching, and some, surprising; and although I am aware that you unconsciously exaggerate what I can be to you, yet it is delightful to be broad awake and think of you as my friend.'

Robert retorted in his letter post-marked 12 March that 'You think — for I must get to *you* — that "I unconsciously exaggerate what you are to me." Now, you don't know what *that* is, nor can I very well tell you, because the language with which I talk to myself of these matters is spiritual Attic, and "loves contradictions," as grammarians say ... but I read it myself and know very well what it means, that's why I told you I was self-conscious — I meant that I never yet mistook my own feelings, one for another — there! ... Do you think I shall see you in two months, three months? I may travel, perhaps.' That last, apparently throwaway but more probably well calculated, line had its effect. Elizabeth replied eight days later, ending her letter by saying, 'If you mean "to travel", why, I shall have to miss you. Do you really mean it?' She knew she was being pressed, that Robert's patience had been tried and was running short. This long letter of 20 March opened with the assurance that 'Whenever I delay to write to you, dear Mr Browning, it is not, to be sure, that I take "my own good time," but submit to my own bad time ... I have not been very well, nor have had much heart for saying so.'

The weather — 'this east wind that seems to blow through the sun and the moon!' — had been implacable and 'I only grow weaker than usual, and learn my lesson of being mortal, in a corner — and then all this must end! April is coming. There will be both a May and a June if we live to see such things, and perhaps, after all, we may. And as to seeing *you* besides, I observe that you distrust me, and that perhaps you penetrate my morbidity and guess how when the moment comes to see a living human face to which I am not accustomed, I shrink and grow pale in the spirit. Do you? You are learned in human nature, and you know the consequences of leading such a secluded life as mine — notwithstanding all my fine philosophy about social duties and the like — well — if you have such knowledge or if you have it not, I cannot say, but I do say that I will indeed see you when the warm weather has revived me a little, and put the earth "to rights" again so as to make pleasures of the sort possible.'

The letter goes on, very affectingly, very emotionally, and in important respects quite misleadingly, to summarize her life, to draw comparisons between Robert's full, heady experience of an active, happy life — 'You are Paracelsus' — and the life that Elizabeth has lived 'only inwardly; or with *sorrow*, for a strong emotion. Before this seclusion of my illness, I was secluded still, and there are few of the youngest women in the world who have not seen more, heard more, known more, of society, than I, who am scarcely to be called young now. I grew up in the country — had no social opportunities, had my heart in books and poetry and my experience in reveries. My sympathies drooped towards the ground like an untrained honeysuckle — and but for *one*, in my own house — but of this I cannot speak.' Here Elizabeth drew a veil over the memory of Bro.

It was a lonely life, growing green like the grass around it. Books and dreams were what I lived in — and domestic life only seemed to buzz gently around, like the bees about the grass. And so time passed and passed — and afterwards, when my illness came and I seemed to stand at the edge of the world with all done, and no prospect (as it appeared at one time) of ever passing the threshold of one room again; why then, I turned to thinking with some bitterness (after the greatest sorrow of my life had given me room and time to breathe) that I had stood blind in this temple I was about to leave — that I had seen no Human nature, that my brothers and sisters of the earth were *names* to me, that I had beheld no great mountain or river, nothing in fact. I was as a man dying who had not read Shakespeare, and it was too late! do you understand? And do you also know what a disadvantage this is to my art? Why, if I live on and yet do not escape from this seclusion, do you not perceive that I labour under signal disadvantages — that I am, in a manner, as a *blind poet*? Certainly, there is a compensation to a degree. I have had much of the inner life, and from the habit of self-consciousness and self-analysis, I make great guesses at Human nature in the main. But how willingly I would as a poet exchange some of this lumbering, ponderous, helpless knowledge of books, for some experience of life and man, for some . . .

And here she gives up, helpless and speechless after such a powerful passage of self-confession and self-revelation. She felt, perhaps, she had gone too far and cut it off with a bathetic moral banality — 'But all grumbling is a vile thing' — promptly followed by a pious platitude

— 'We should all thank God for our measures of life, and think them enough for each of us.'

We can read all this more objectively than subjectively, Elizabeth wrote it with passion, some element of self-pity and, in the light of what we now know about her early life, some self-delusion and self-dramatization. To take only the most glaringly self-serving example, if she had been lonely it had been through her own choice to avoid company. The impression she gave (by omission rather than direct statement) of being all but a solitary orphan child brought up by the fairies, was hardly fair to her two devoted parents or the eleven younger brothers and sisters who doted upon their demanding older sister. She might have felt solitary from time to time, she might have longed to be less alone sometimes, she might have felt intellectually isolated, but rarely could she have felt lonely in a social sense. At some cost to others, Elizabeth had bought time and space for her reveries, for her inner life, beyond which the Barretts buzzed like bees in the domestic environment, conscientious and generous in their efforts to care for her health, keep her amused, run her errands, and cater to her every comfort.

Nevertheless, there can be little doubt that what she wrote on 20 March 1845 was true to her deepest feelings, to her perceptions of her situation, if not strictly accurate as to domestic reality and psychological truth. The letter also seemed to mark a real and profound desire that she should move towards a more active life, that time was no longer on her side — 'I, who am scarcely to be called young now'. In March 1845, on her thirty-ninth birthday, she entered her fortieth year, though the anniversary merited no mention in her letters to Robert. There is a suggestion, in Elizabeth's appeals to Robert to make the imaginative effort to *understand*, to believe her self-assessment, after her observation that he distrusted her, that personal revelations had by now become necessary and that Robert, himself free to move, represented some hope (not yet quantifiable) of her own release to her personal benefit and the benefit of her poetry.

On the contrary, Robert, surfeited with being active in the world, understood that inwardness and seclusion were desirable and essential conditions for creative activity, for the poetic art, and that the products of the cultivated imagination were of more value than mere representations of reality. Elizabeth's 'lamentable disadvantage' was in fact her most priceless advantage. Robert valued very highly the 'visionary utterances' in Elizabeth's poetry and exalted her professed 'disadvantage' above what Daniel Karlin characterizes as 'the process of interaction between the mind and "external influences" out of which his own "dramatic" poetry was made.'[134] Elizabeth had the measure of Robert and his poetry when she wrote on 17 April, 'I have a profound conviction that where a poet has been shut from most of the outward aspects of life, he is at a lamentable disadvantage. Can you, speaking for yourself, separate the results in you from the external influences at work around you, that you say so boldly that you get nothing from the world? You do not *directly*, I know — but you do indirectly & by a rebound. Whatever acts upon you, becomes *you* — & whatever you love or hate, whatever charms you or is scorned by you, acts on you & becomes *you*.' No critic was ever more acutely perceptive about the well-springs of Robert's work than Elizabeth.

Her estimations of his character were, at this early stage, less sure — though, to be fair, she was working with inadequate information. Elizabeth had read Robert's poems, but she had not yet fully read the man. The two were not, as he had warned her, to be confused. Robert had provided some personal information about himself and his family, of course, and she had gleaned a little more from John Kenyon and Miss Mitford: the former biased in Robert's favour, the latter mildly prejudiced against him. The curtain had been rung up on the play, but neither of the principals had yet made their first entrances. They were still exchanging dialogue as offstage voices.

The preliminary scenes had been carefully set, principally by Robert. He had posed himself solitary at his desk with spiders and skull; he had pictured himself amidst a glittering crowd of celebrated men and women — a wealth of writers, an amplitude of artists, a surfeit of society beauties — weary of their dinner tables and ballrooms. Elizabeth had already conjured him, largely through his poetry, as a heroic figure, and Robert himself had impressed upon her his resolve in getting his own way in whatever he set his heart and mind upon gaining. What she did not yet fully understand, but had begun to suspect, was that he had cast her, sight unseen, as his leading lady, the romantic heroine. There were several objections to this, and she managed to play for time whenever Robert pressed for a meeting. Robert at first tended to assume that she deferred a face to face encounter on account of her invalidity, which, not having inquired too closely of Kenyon for particulars, he took to be greater and more debilitating than it was. In Robert's letter, post-marked 13 May, he wrote to say, 'I ask you *not* to see me so long as you are unwell or mistrustful of — No, no that is being too grand! Do see me when you can, and let me not be only writing myself.'

In her reply to Robert post-marked 16 May, she protested: 'But how "mistrustfulness"? And how "that way?" What have I said or done, *I*, who am not apt to be mistrustful of anybody and should be a miraculous monster if I began with *you*!' She excused herself: 'I have made what is vulgarly called a "piece of work" about little; or seemed to make it. Forgive me. I am shy by nature: — and by position and experience by having had my nerves shaken to excess, and by leading a life of such seclusion, . . . by these things together and by others besides, I have appeared shy and ungrateful to you. Only not mistrustful.' She relented: she said that if Robert cared to come to see her, he could come. It would be her gain, she said, and not Robert's. She did not normally admit visitors because, she wrote, 'putting the question of health quite aside, it would be unbecoming to lie here on the sofa and make a company-show of an infirmity, and hold a beggar's hat for sympathy.' To the extent that she did exploit her condition of health, she was obscurely repulsed by it herself and thus certain that others would also be disgusted.

It is a convention that romantic and operatic heroines, especially if pale, languorous, and dying of consumption, should be beautiful, and so it is sentimentally assumed that Elizabeth was chiefly worried by the effect her looks might have on Robert. It is difficult to conceive a more banal idea than that Elizabeth, hearing Robert's footsteps on the stair for the first time, should primp herself, pinch her cheeks for a little colour, and have Wilson, her maid, fuss with her hair to present herself to best advantage. She possessed no idea of herself as a tragic heroine, and still further from her mind was any concept of herself as a flirt, a coquette. Personally, she affected no mystery. To whatever extent she had been invested with glamour and mystery, that image of beauty unrevealed had arisen in the minds of others from her curious reclusiveness and invisibility. Conscious of public interest in her, and perhaps aware that her disinclination to put herself obligingly on show only served to fuel that curiosity, she feared, if anything, a constant troop of rubber-necking visitors curious to inspect her as a sort of freak show.

More to the point, Elizabeth worried that Robert would find her colourless in person, tongue-tied, less interesting than her poetry. He would be disappointed in her. 'There is nothing to see in me;' she warned him, 'nor to hear in me — I never learnt to talk as you do in London; although I can admire that brightness of carved speech in Mr Kenyon and others. If my poetry is worth anything to any eye, it is the flower of me. I have lived most and been most happy in it, and so it has all my colours; the rest of me is nothing but a root, fit for the ground and the dark.' The most he could expect should be 'truth and simplicity for you, in any case; and a friend. And do not answer this — I do not write it as a fly trap for compliments. Your spider would scorn me for it too much.'[135]

Having consented to a meeting, Elizabeth promptly took fright and retreated a little, disingenuously procrastinating not on her own account but by offering Robert an excuse for delay, a mediator, or the opportunity to create an obstacle to his visit. In her letter post-marked 16 May she reminded Robert that he had not been well, that he had had a headache and a ringing in his ears, and she entreated him 'not to think of coming until *that* is all put to silence satisfactorily. When it is done, ... you must choose whether you would like best to come with Mr Kenyon or to come alone — and if you would come alone, you must just tell me on what day, and I will see you on any day unless there should be an unforeseen obstacle, ... any day after two, or before six.'

Robert in turn had his anxieties. In his Friday evening reply post-marked 17 May, amusingly as he thought, he played with Elizabeth's alleged 'mistrust' of him — not that he would make away with the Barrett cloaks and umbrellas downstairs, or publish a magazine article about his meeting with her, rather that she mistrusted his 'common-sense, — nay, uncommon and dramatic-poet's sense, if I am put on asserting it! — all which pieces of mistrust I could detect, and catch struggling, and pin to death in a moment, and put a label in, with name, genus and species, just like a horrible entomologist; only I won't, because the first visit of the Northwind will carry the whole tribe into the Red Sea — and those horns and tails and scalewings are best forgotten altogether.' Robert then conjured an elaborately facetious encounter between himself and an imaginary Mr Simpson, an avid admirer of Mr Browning's poetry who earnestly wishes to meet its maker and is disappointed in the banality of Robert's conversation about the weather and politics and makes his excuses to leave after five minutes, saying to himself, 'Well, I *did* expect to see something different from that little yellow commonplace man.' Robert then said that he would call on Miss Barrett — allowing for any adverse circumstances — on Tuesday at two o'clock.

Elizabeth, discontented with his letter, replied the same day that 'I shall be ready on Tuesday I hope, but I hate and protest against your horrible "entomology."' Robert's light-hearted little fantasy of Simpsonism had not been well received by Elizabeth, who crossly considered that 'you, who know everything, or at least make awful guesses at everything in one's feelings and motives, and profess to pin them down in a book of classified inscriptions, ... should have been able to understand better, or misunderstand less, in a matter like this — Yes! I think so. I think you should have made out the case in some such way as it was in nature — viz. that you had lashed yourself up to an exorbitant wishing to see me, ... (you who could see, any day, people who are a hundredfold and to all social purposes, my superiors!) because I was unfortunate enough to be shut up in a room and silly enough to make a fuss about opening the door; and that I grew suddenly abashed by the consciousness of this. How different from a distrust of *you*! how different!'[136] Elizabeth and Robert had both, by this point, worked themselves up to such a pitch of apprehension that their hypersensitivity crackled like static electricity in the air between them. Of the two, Elizabeth was only marginally the less confident. Mr Barrett had been squared — he did not object to 'Ba's poet' paying her a visit so long as he did not have to meet him. In any case, Mr Barrett, like his sons, was usually out during the afternoons, until about seven o'clock. From two to six was the quietest part of the day in the house. It wasn't likely, in any case, that anyone would burst unexpectedly into Elizabeth's room: she saw her brothers and their noisy friends 'only at certain hours' and, she later told Robert, 'as you have "a reputation" and are opined to talk in blank verse, it is not likely that there should be much irreverent rushing into this room when you are known to be in it.'[137] At three o'clock in the afternoon of Tuesday 20 May 1845, Robert was led up the stairs and shown into Elizabeth's room. He left ninety minutes later, at half past four. Robert afterwards noted the date and time and length of the first meeting, as he would note all subsequent meetings, on the envelopes of Elizabeth's letters.

And that was all he noted. Neither Robert nor Elizabeth directly referred in their letters, then or later, to what passed between them during their times together in her room. It is as though the letters are one dialogue, the conversations quite another. They seem rarely to have overlapped, or flowed into one another; at most, the letters may have continued discussions initiated verbally, but the written correspondence is remarkably self-contained. Perhaps, after all, Robert and Elizabeth at first confined themselves to polite 'Simpsonisms' about the weather and politics. We can make some guesses, but we not know. We know, nevertheless, what Robert saw when the door closed behind him and he sat down to talk privately with Elizabeth. The room she had described to a Devonshire friend, Mrs Martin, on 26 May 1843, would not have substantially changed over two years:

> The bed, like a sofa and no bed: the large table placed out in the room, towards the wardrobe end of it; the sofa rolled where a sofa should be rolled — opposite the arm-chair; the drawers crowned with a coronal of shelves fashioned by Sette and Co. (of papered deal and crimson merino) to carry my books; the washing table opposite turned into a cabinet with another coronal of shelves; and Chaucer's and Homer's busts in guard over these two departments of English and Greek poetry; three more busts consecrating the wardrobe which there was no annihilating; and the window — oh, I must take a new paragraph for the window, I am out of breath.
>
> In the window is fixed a deep box full of soil, where are *springing up* my scarlet runners, nasturtiums, and convolvuluses, although they were disturbed a few days ago by the revolutionary insertion among them of a great ivy root with trailing branches so long and wide that the top tendrils are fastened to Henrietta's window of the higher storey, while the lower ones cover all my panes.

For the occasion of Robert's first visit, Elizabeth had made at least one adjustment to the decor of the room: she had taken down his portrait (reproduced from Horne's *New Spirit of the Age*) from the wall where it normally hung with portraits of Wordsworth, Tennyson, Carlyle, and Harriet Martineau. 'In a fit of justice', she also took down the picture of Tennyson.

The room, rich with crimson, was dimly lit: blinds were partly pulled against the afternoon sun, and the ivy (a gift from John Kenyon) further filtered whatever light was left. In this crepuscular atmosphere, perhaps she intended to blend with the shadows and fade, half-glimpsed, into the general obscurity she had pulled around herself. To complement this chiaroscuro, she would have been wearing a black silk summer dress (for winter, she wore black velvet), in perpetual mourning for Bro. Since she never went out, her complexion would have been pallid, in stark contrast not only to the deep black of her dress but to the glossy black of her thick hair, a mass of ringlets framing her small, worn face in which her eyes were sunk like 'two dark caves'. She looked at Robert directly, caught his gaze, when he made his first entrance, but thereafter, for several months, she averted her eyes from his. Elizabeth reclined on her sofa, a small figure in a large dress. Robert sat on a chair drawn up close to her sofa. He conversed in his confident, resonant voice; she replied in her thin, high, reedy voice. On his sixth visit, on Saturday 28 June, and thereafter, Robert would bring flowers from his mother's garden, roses especially, their fresh colour and heady scent filling the room with — he deliberately intended — a reminder and invocation of the living world outside.

The result of their first meeting was satisfactory: their letters, each thanking the other for the encounter, will not, however, satisfy those readers who wish for an immediate *coup de foudre*: 'I trust to you', wrote Robert immediately afterwards, 'for a true account of how you are — if tired, not tired, if I did wrong in any thing, — or, if you please, *right* in any thing — (only, not one more word about my "kindness," which, to get done with, I will grant is excessive) ... I am proud and happy in your friendship — now and ever. May God bless you!'[138] Elizabeth replied the next day, the Wednesday morning: 'Indeed there was nothing wrong — how could there be? And there was everything right — as how should there not be? And as for the "loud speaking," I did not hear any — and, instead of being worse, I ought to be better for what was certainly (to speak of it, or be silent of it,) happiness and honour to me yesterday.' And, her fears allayed, she looked forward to seeing Robert again: 'But you will come really on Tuesday — and again, when you like and can together — and it will not be more "inconvenient" to me to be pleased, I suppose, than it is to people in general — will it, do you think? Ah — how you misjudge! Why it must obviously and naturally be delightful to me to receive you here when you like to come, and it cannot be necessary for me to say so in set words — believe it of your friend, E.B.B.'[139] So far, so good — but no further. One letter is missing from the courtship correspondence, which is otherwise entire: the sixteenth letter from Robert to which Elizabeth replied on Friday evening, 23 May. The letter no longer exists, having been deliberately destroyed by Elizabeth. What it contained, we do not know, only that Elizabeth read it 'in pain and agitation'.

The supposition has been, by some who wish it to have been so, that it contained a proposal of marriage. Perhaps it did — there is no telling for a certainty that it did not, though Daniel Karlin's close analysis of the letters immediately following the initial meeting and Elizabeth's letter of 23 May tends to cast doubt upon the traditional interpretation. My own view is that a proposal of marriage is most unlikely. Robert was rash in his letter, undoubtedly — but not that rash. It is much more likely that Robert's letter touched, too prematurely and too precipitately, upon Elizabeth's most vulnerable point of self-estimation, misunderstanding and misinterpreting her perception of herself, possibly expressing overt and over-confident love for what she could not yet find to love in herself. Robert had trampled on sacred ground. A truth she could not face — would not face — was forced upon her and she felt, very acutely, the violation, the attempted ruin, of everything she had so carefully constructed to protect herself.

This is what Elizabeth wrote:

I intended to write to you last night and this morning, and could not, — you do not know what pain you give me in speaking so wildly. And if I disobey you, my dear friend, in speaking (I for my part) of your wild speaking, I do it, not to displease you, but to be in my own eyes, and before God, a little more worthy, or less unworthy, of a generosity from which I recoil by instinct and at the first glance, yet conclusively; and because my silence would be the most disloyal of all means of expression, in reference to it. Listen to me then in this. You have said some intemperate things ... fancies, — which you will not say over again, nor unsay, but *forget at once*, and *for ever, having said at all*; and which (so) will die out between *you and me alone*, like a misprint between you and the printer. And this you will do *for my sake* who am your friend (and you have none truer) — and this I ask, because it is a condition necessary to our future liberty of intercourse. You remember — surely you do — that I am in the most exceptional of positions; and that, just *because of it*, I am able to receive you as I did on Tuesday; and that, for me to listen to 'unconscious exaggerations,' is as unbecoming to the humilities of my position, as unpropitious (which is of more consequence) to the prosperities of yours. Now, if there should be one word of answer attempted to this; or of reference; *I must not ... I will not see you again* — and you will justify me later in your heart. So for my sake you will not say it — I think you will not — and spare me the sadness of having to break through an intercourse just as it is promising pleasure to me; to me who have so many sadnesses and so few pleasures. You will! — and I need not be uneasy — and I shall owe you that tranquillity as one gift of many. For, that I have much to receive from you in all the free gifts of thinking, teaching, master-spirits, ... *that*, I know! — it is my own praise that I appreciate you, as none can more. Your influence and help in poetry will be full of good and gladness to me — for with many to love me in this house, there is no one to judge me ... *now*. Your friendship and sympathy will be dear and precious to me all my life, if you indeed leave them with me so long or so little. Your mistakes in me ... which *I* cannot mistake (— and which have humbled me by too much honouring —) I put away gently, and with grateful tears in my eyes; because *all that hail* will beat down and spoil crowns, as well as 'blossoms.'[140]

Ruling out a proposal of marriage, Daniel Karlin does not doubt that Robert's letter had contained a direct, definite declaration of love for Elizabeth.[141] For various deep psychological reasons, she had to believe that Robert's 'unconscious exaggerations' in this regard (and she had warned him of such in the past, saying 'you unconsciously exaggerate what I can be to you') were now no less inappropriate ('unbecoming to the humilities of my position, as unpropitious . . . to the prosperities of yours'). The nub of the matter would seem to have lain in the complex concepts of 'humility' and 'distrust' that both Robert and Elizabeth needed to define between themselves before they could make any progress in the relationship that Robert avowed he wanted and that Elizabeth, from whatever emotions of self-doubt, felt as yet unable to consider possible. She, proud of her 'headlong' attitudes and tendencies, found herself for once outstripped by Robert's headlong dash. The image here is not so much Andromeda chained to the rock of her suffering and self-abasement, and being rescued by Perseus dropping from the sky, as Atalanta being overtaken in speed by Hippomenes, she rather than he dropping the three golden apples of 'thinking, teaching, master-spirits' to stop him in his pursuit of her. The prize for Hippomenes, should he win the race with her, would be Atalanta's hand in marriage — for Elizabeth, in her own case and for all sorts of reasons, an unthinkable conclusion.

Robert's response was to write immediately to Elizabeth, respecting — we have to suppose — the embargoes she had so firmly put on any references to whatever had caused her pain in his last, offending letter. Robert had been profoundly shocked by her response to that letter. He had miscalculated badly — 'no wonder if I *bungle* notably' — and somehow he had to make a wrong situation right. He did not doubt for a moment that Elizabeth meant what she had said: she would absolutely refuse to see him again if he persisted in the line he had taken. Yet he had to make some attempt to justify himself, to give some credible explanation as to why he had written as he had — 'intemperately' as it had been perceived. He would not excuse himself — he had gone thus far, too far as it appeared — but rather he would apologize for any 'misunderstanding' (as he conceived it to be) and positively make his motives clear.

Sensibly, instead of writing about his feelings for Elizabeth, he wrote of his own feelings about himself. If Robert stood accused of knowing too little about Elizabeth's feelings and mistreating them through ignorance, then she should understand how little she knew about his, fiery as a volcano and frozen as Tartarus: 'for every poor speck of a Vesuvius or a Stromboli in my microcosm, there are huge layers of ice and pits of black cold water'. The point he had tried to make, he assured her, derived from no gallant condescension or mock humility, 'for I really believe you to be my superior in many respects, and feel uncomfortable until *you* see that, too . . . I am but a very poor creature compared to you and entitled by my wants to look up to you.'[142] Robert thus emphasized the violence of his feelings being occasionally and unpredictably eruptive in comparison with the deepest ice-bound caverns that lay fathomless in his organism and in his work.

It may be inferred that in the letter that had so disturbed Elizabeth, Robert had vehemently — volcanically — based his profoundest admiration (which may be interpreted as love) for her upon his own abasement, and exalted her superiority so highly that she could not help but feel she was, personally and in her poetry (between which Robert made no distinction), being praised so far beyond her own poor estimation of herself that she could only deeply distrust his sincerity. Thus the quarrel conflated personal and poetic issues that were so inextricably linked in Robert's and Elizabeth's mutual estimations of their feelings about each other that they now had to seek and achieve some middle ground on which they could agree to meet as equals, mutually respectful of one another's art, able to learn from one another's virtues and abilities, rather than as master and pupil or mistress and petitioner. The crisis was, on a descending scale of visibility, about artistic status — about their respective stations on Parnassus; about literary and personal identity; about the strengths and weaknesses of men and women; and about the relative strengths and weaknesses of Robert Browning and Elizabeth Barrett themselves. From the poetic, to the personal.

To the extent that Elizabeth understood Robert's letter of apology and explication, she mended the quarrel in her letter of reply on Sunday, 25 May: 'I owe you the most humble of apologies dear Mr Browning, for having spent so much solemnity on so simple a matter, and I hasten to pay it; confessing at the same time (as why should I not?) that I am quite as much ashamed of myself as I ought to be, which is not a little.' On the face of it, this is contrite, but Robert had been badly shaken by her reaction and he took his warning. From time to time they discussed the quarrel in their exchange of letters, Elizabeth reiterating her residual sense that she had felt Robert to be stronger than she ('I felt the mastery in you by the first word and first look'[143]). For long enough, she continued to be impressed by 'the prosperities' of his position in the world as a healthy man and as a great poet, contrasted with 'the humilities' of her situation as a housebound invalid and as an inadequate poet. She continued to envy the wider experience of the world that Robert easily gained, the experiences that gave his work the width, depth, and the vitality of real men and women that she considered to be elements of its greatness.

And so, treading warily in the aftermath, Robert and Elizabeth continued to meet and to correspond. They stuck mostly to discussing poetry. At her request, Robert helped her to polish up her translation of *Prometheus Bound*. He showed himself to great effect, and so to her great admiration, as learned in Greek scholarship (almost as able as Elizabeth, though she would never have said so), though he was careful to confine his criticism to troublesome points of translation and not to trespass on Elizabeth's poetic style. In turn, and also at her request, he showed her, among other items of his work in progress, one poem in particular, 'The Flight of the Duchess', which was about to be published in *Dramatic Romances and Lyrics*, part 7 of the *Bells and Pomegranates* series. Robert entreated her to correct his work, to admire it of course, but to add to the virtue of the work by contributing her own creative vision to ornament its beauties.

She hesitated, she fell back upon her professed perception of the distance between herself and Robert. 'To judge at all of a work of yours, I must *look up to it,* — and *far up* — because whatever faculty *I* have is included in your faculty, and with a great rim all around it besides! And thus, it is not at all from an over-pleasure in pleasing *you*, not at all from an inclination to depreciate myself, that I speak and feel as I do and must on some occasions; it is simply the consequence of a true comprehension of you and of me — and apart from it, I should not be abler, I think, but less able, to assist you in anything. I do wish you would consider all this reasonably . . . and consent not to spoil the real pleasure I have and am about to have in your poetry, by nailing me up into a false position with your gold-headed nails of chivalry, which won't hold to the wall through this summer.'[144]

Nevertheless, despite such doubts, she was inevitably drawn into becoming the first critic of Robert's work and offered detailed and lengthy suggestions for alterations to 'The Flight of the Duchess' which Robert largely incorporated into the poem. He was thrilled: this was an exciting, positively creative element in his partnership with Elizabeth, and their work together steadily bridged the distances that had existed between them. Nothing, for any artist, is more intoxicating than this close, detailed consideration of work with a trusted and sympathetic collaborator, where the only end is to achieve a polished, finished artefact through a professional and personal partnership. The relationship is profoundly deepened and becomes more clearly defined. The object of attention becomes a third party in the collaboration, and in this case 'The Flight of the Duchess' became significant not only as the focus of critical attention but by its subject matter.

At the risk, again, of disappointing those romantics who have been inclined to anticipate the development of the relationship between Robert and Elizabeth, it has to be acknowledged that Daniel Karlin is correct when he states that 'the first poem he submitted to her has a special significance — though not for the reasons which have tradition-ally been given'.[145] The first nine sections of 'The Flight of the Duchess' (amounting to about a quarter of the finished poem) were published in *Hood's Magazine* in April 1845. The full version, in 926 lines, was published in *Dramatic Romances and Lyrics* on 6 November 1845. Robert is thought to have conceived and begun writing the poem three years before, in 1842, and in a letter of 15 April 1883 stated that the first inspiration for the poem 'originally all grew out of this one intelligible line of a song that I heard a woman singing at a bon-fire Guy Faux night when I was a boy — *Following the Queen of the Gypsies, O!*'[146] Robert's poem, set in medieval times, tells the story of a young, beautiful duchess unhappily married to a cold-hearted, contemptuous husband.

> She was active, stirring, all fire —
> Could not rest, could not tire —
> To a stone she might have given life! (ll. 174–6)

Her spirit is all but broken by the mean-mindedness of the Duke. She languishes under his miserable repression, his petty tyranny, until, one day, an old gypsy woman enters the castle while the Duke is out hunting and revives the Duchess with a vision of freedom, of 'liberty to breathe and feel naturally', of emotional, sexual, and social self-expression unfettered by conventional civilized values. With the aid of the Duke's retainer, the narrator of the story, the Duchess flees with the gypsy crone to a life in the natural world in which she can renew herself spiritually and fulfil the potentialities of her active nature.

The parallels in the poem with Elizabeth's and Robert's situation are superficially appealing, but it would be premature to apply them to the circumstances of the summer of 1845. The popular belief is that Robert intended the poem to persuade Elizabeth to marry him and run off with him, or run off with him and marry him — take your pick as to the more likely sequence of events. 'But', Karlin points out, 'the dates do not fit; Browning had the idea for the poem in 1842, and wrote most of it long before he began to correspond with Elizabeth Barrett; and, even if he had not, the early period of the courtship is wholly unsuited to the kind of strategy which he is supposed to have adopted. For the first few months, after all, Browning was not trying to persuade Elizabeth Barrett to leave Wimpole Street, but to let him in; nor could Mr Barrett, who had barely been mentioned so far, have sat for the portrait of the Duke — he was not yet a tyrant in Browning's eyes, but the respectable guardian of a fragile treasure.'

Rather, suggests Karlin, 'Browning seems to have used "The Flight of the Duchess", not by design, but opportunistically . . . Browning may well have realized, in the aftermath of his disastrous love-letter, just how well-suited the poem was to his continuing propaganda campaign on the subject of Elizabeth Barrett's superiority to him.'[147] Karlin does not discuss the effect of the poem on Elizabeth's emotions, but Margaret Forster supplies the deficit: 'The Flight of the Duchess' 'appealed to Elizabeth in every possible way since it was in praise of passion, of true love, and opposed to the sanctity of man-made marriage vows.'[148] It may also be suggested that the idea of freedom, of liberation into the wide world, of a fuller expression of an active nature, coincided with Elizabeth's growing frustration with the confinement in which she had placed herself and persuaded others to indulge as her natural condition.

She was not likely to run away from Wimpole Street with the 'raggle-taggle gypsies-o!', but the stirring example of the Duchess may well have stimulated her own fancies, and the fact is that the more her mind was stimulated in meetings and correspondence with the active mind of Robert Browning, the happier she began to feel and the more effort she began to make, as a conscious resolution in her own mind, to 'get on' — to benefit from her renewed energies. That summer, she began to visit John Kenyon's great house in Devonshire Place and to take short, faltering walks — 'as well as most children of two year's old' she ruefully remarked in a letter to her brother George — in Regent's Park. She recruited her strength by drinking milk and exposing herself to the sun. At home in her room, she even moved from her sofa to a chair loaned to her by Kenyon. The effect was dramatic. She looked better, felt better.

Robert, who had begun urging her to persevere in the slow business of taking more exercise, eating better, getting out in the summer air, was delighted. He was less successful in his advice that Elizabeth should give up her opium habit. Either she genuinely had become dependent on the drug after twenty-four years' consumption, or she would not — through fear — abandon the laudanum bottle. Either way, it amounted to the same thing: so long as she was convinced that the drug did her positive good — and she positively liked opium — the most that could be hoped was that she would, in time, be persuaded to moderate the daily dosage. For the meanwhile, opium was the least of her concerns. It was not a problem. Robert's fussing about it annoyed her: it was a vexation to her that he 'should care so much about the opium!'.

In her letter post-marked 18 July, Elizabeth wrote to Robert to say 'that Papa and my aunt are discussing the question of sending me off either to Alexandria or Malta for the winter. Oh — it is quite a passing talk and thought, I dare say! and it would not be in any case, until September or October; though in every case, I suppose, I would not be consulted ... and all cases and places would seem better to me (if I were) than Madeira which the physicians used to threaten me with long ago.' Contrary to his position in former years, her father had this time strongly opposed any such trip, at first forbidding it and finally giving grudging permission only under heavy pressure. Elizabeth's aunt, Mrs Jane Hedley, her friend, John Kenyon, and her brother George united in their determination that she should recruit her health in a dry, sunny atmosphere. Dr Chambers, called in to give a professional opinion, diagnosed a very slight affection of Elizabeth's left lung. He positively recommended the benefits of a warm, dry, sunny climate, and Pisa in particular, as likely to be of most benefit.

Plans for Elizabeth to winter abroad were not unusual, though she had resisted them in previous years. She was already preparing herself for her adventure when she wrote to Robert on Saturday, in a letter post-marked 28 July, to assure him 'that if I get better or worse ... as long as I live and to the last moment of life, I shall remember with an emotion which cannot change in its character, all the generous interest and feeling you have spent on me — *wasted* I was going to write ... I shall never forget these things, my dearest friend; nor remember them more coldly.' Daniel Karlin cites these words as 'the first indication that Elizabeth Barrett had begun, even tentatively, to think of Browning as he thought of her; and, appropriately enough, it comes immediately after a slighting allusion to Mr Barrett.'[149] She had written that 'Papa says sometimes when he comes into this room unexpectedly and convicts me of having dry toast for dinner, [he] declares angrily that obstinacy and dry toast have brought me to my present condition, and that if I *pleased* to have porter and beefsteaks instead, I should be as well as ever I was, in a month!' Four weeks later, in August, Mr Barrett cropped up again as a subject in a letter from Elizabeth to Robert:

Every now and then there must of course be a crossing and a vexation — but in one's mere pleasures and fantasies, one would rather be crossed and vexed a little than vex a person one loves ... and it is possible to get used to the harness and run easily in it at last ... my own sense of right and happiness has never run contrariwise to the way of obedience required of me ... while in things not exactly *overt*, I and all of us are apt to act sometimes up to the limit of our means of acting, with shut doors and windows, and no waiting for cognisance or permission. Ah — and that last is the worst of it all perhaps! to be forced into concealments from the heart naturally nearest to us; and forced away from the natural source of counsel and strength! — and then, the disingenuousness — the cowardice — the 'vices of slaves'! — and everyone you see ... all my brothers ... constrained *bodily* into submission ... apparent submission at least . . . by that worst and most dishonouring of necessities, the necessity of *living*, everyone of them all, except myself, being dependent in money-matters on the inflexible will . . . do you see?[150]

Whatever Robert saw, given this impressionistic sketch of the domestic situation at 50 Wimpole Street, it was shaping up as a shocking vision, quite the opposite of his own experience of a loving and liberal father, generous in all things within his means. There were details she could have given of how, in order to enjoy anything approximating to a private life, or blameless pleasures such as a picnic with young friends, the Barrett children were obliged to resort to subterfuge and plain deception. But the phrase 'vices of slaves' implied, however extravagantly, their moral degradation and necessary deceitfulness. Having characterized a tyrant, Elizabeth now began to soften the picture, bringing up the background into focus to set the foreground figure in moral context. The fault lay not in Mr Barrett's true heart but in the evil of the system to which he so sternly adhered:

But what you do *not* see, what you *cannot* see, is the deep tender affection behind and below all those patriarchal ideas of governing grown up children 'in the way they *must* go!' and there never was (under the strata) a truer affection in a father's heart . . . no, nor a worthier heart in itself . . . a heart loyaller and purer, and more compelling to gratitude and reverence, than his, as I see it. The evil is in the system — and he simply takes it to be his duty to rule and to make happy according to his own views of the propriety of happiness — he takes it to be his duty to rule like the Kings of Christendom, by divine right. But he loves us through and through it — and *I*, for one, love *him*!

The letter then went on to describe, very fully and very movingly, the prolonged grief and permanent guilt Elizabeth felt in respect of Bro's death at Torquay and her father's tenderness towards her in her emotional agonies at that time. These pages of the most intimate outpouring of emotion she would not have revealed to anyone outside the family but Robert were proof positive that she counted on his fully understanding her and, furnished with this knowledge of her deepest heart, that he could be trusted to support her in her feelings of abject worthlessness and self-abnegation. Her father, she said, had never reproached her for having persuaded Bro to stay with her in Torquay. Daniel Karlin tartly, but not unfairly, comments that 'Mr Barrett, if he had any knowledge of his daughter's character, would have known that he had no need to say anything to reproach her; she would do the job for him. Still, Elizabeth Barrett chose to give him credit for his silence, and to offer it to Browning as evidence of his fundamental affection.'[151]

Elizabeth did not necessarily, consciously, intend to provoke another declaration of love from Robert, but that was what she got in his reply post-marked 30 August. Perhaps conscious of having laid the burden of her sorrow upon him, and anxious lest Robert should be disinclined to bear with her, she had ended her account of Bro's death with the words, 'it is gravely true, seriously true, sadly true, that I am always expecting to hear or to see how tired you are at last of me!' What Robert now had to say to that is the closest we can get to the declaration in the letter Elizabeth had burned. Now he felt confident enough — courageous enough — to defy her interdict and renew his avowal:

I believe in *you* absolutely, utterly — I believe that when you bade me, that time, be silent — that such was your bidding, and I was silent — dare I say I think you did not know at that time the power I have over myself, that I could sit and speak and listen as I have done since? Let me say now — *this only once* — that I loved you from my soul, and gave you my life, so much of it as you would take, — and all that is *done*, not to be altered now: it was, in the nature of the proceeding, wholly independent of any return on your part. I will not think on extremes you might have resorted to; as it is, the assurance of your friendship, the intimacy to which you admit me, *now*, make the truest, deepest joy of my life — a joy I can never think fugitive while we are in life, because I KNOW, as to me, I *could* not willingly displease you, — while, as to you, your goodness and understanding will always see to the bottom of involuntary or ignorant faults — always help me to correct them. I have done now. If I thought you were like other women

I have known, I should say so much! — but — (my first and
last word — I *believe* in you!) — what you could and would
give me, of your affection, you would give nobly and simply
and as a giver — you would not need that I tell you — (*tell*
you!) — what would be supreme happiness to me in the event
— however distant.[152]

Elizabeth's response the next day was to accept as lastingly sincere
what she had earlier distrusted and rejected out of hand as extravagantly
fanciful. 'I asked for silence — but *also* and chiefly for the putting away
of . . . you know very well what I asked for. And this was sincerely done,
I attest to you . . . What I thought then I think now — just what any
third person, knowing you, would think, I think and feel. I thought too,
at first, that the feeling on your part was a mere generous impulse, likely
to expend itself in a week perhaps. It affects me and has affected me,
very deeply, more than I dare attempt to say, that you should persist
so.'[153] Robert's attitude towards Elizabeth's emotional self-indulgence
was robust: he set about rallying her spirits, insisting that she took too
much fault upon herself, that her father's forgiveness was as excessive
as her guilt — since she had little or nothing to reproach herself with
in reality, so she deluded herself about Mr Barrett's generosity in for-
bearing to blame her. Her positive duty towards herself, her father, and
to Robert lay in recovering her health. And so Robert, in his constant
belief that she could be well, supported Elizabeth in her decision and
desire to go abroad: it was her duty to do so.

The benefit to her health was not Elizabeth's sole reason for wishing to
avoid the winter weather in London: she wanted to leave Wimpole
Street. She had begun to believe that her happiness as well as her health
depended upon escape from the evils of being a burden to herself and
to others. If her ill-health was not to be remedied, the sojourn in Pisa
would confirm her as a chronic invalid. Her father, who wished his
daughter to devote herself to himself and God, would be satisfied. If
she put her health to the test in Pisa and recovered her strength, she
would prove that she could live a relatively normal, active life. Robert,
who wished his beloved to commit herself to him, would be satisfied.

By the end of September, Mr Barrett's attitude towards Elizabeth had moved from cold to icy: he complained, she wrote to Robert, 'of the undutifulness and rebellion (!!!) of everyone in the house — and when I asked him if he meant that reproach for *me*, the answer was that he meant it for all of us, one with another . . . I had better do what I liked: — for his part, he washed his hands of me altogether.'[154]

By mid-October, the Pisa plan had been abandoned. George Barrett had indignantly confronted his father, who had said that Elizabeth might go to Pisa but only under his heaviest displeasure. Elizabeth, hearing of this, had been forced to decide whether to go and bear the weight of Mr Barrett's displeasure, which would have fallen, too, on George and her sisters. She decided to stay. 'And so,' she wrote to Robert on a Tuesday, in a letter post-marked 14 October, in her aspect as the shackled Andromeda of Wimpole Street, 'tell me that I am not wrong in taking up my chain again and acquiescing in this hard necessity.' The result was that Elizabeth now plainly understood that her father loved her less than she had believed, and that Robert loved her more than she had been willing to accept. He had, barely two weeks before, told her explicitly what he most desired and what his dream was for himself.

Robert fully understood Mr Barrett's pathology to be not merely aberrant but positively harmful, not only to himself but also to his eldest daughter. He had said as much, and more, in a letter post-marked 25 September to Elizabeth:

I think I ought to understand what a father may exact, and a child should comply with . . . but now, and here, the jewel is not being over-guarded, but ruined, cast away . . . And you ask whether you ought to obey this no-reason? I will tell you: all passive obedience and implicit submission of will and intellect is by far too easy, if well considered, to be the course prescribed by God to Man in this life of probation — for they *evade* probation altogether, though foolish people think otherwise. Chop off your legs, you will never go astray; stifle your reason altogether and you will find it difficult to reason ill . . . In your case, I do think you are called upon to do your duty to yourself; that is, to God in the end . . . Now while I *dream*, let me once dream! I would marry you now and thus — I would come

when you let me, and go when you bade me — I would be no
more than one of your brothers — *'no more'* — that is, instead
of getting tomorrow for Saturday, I should get Saturday as well
— two hours for one — when your head ached I should be
here. I deliberately choose the realization of that dream (— of
sitting simply by you for an hour every day) rather than any
other, excluding you, I am able to form for this world, or any
world I know — And it will continue to be but a dream ...
You know what I am, what I would speak, and all I would do.

From the extinction of the Pisa plan arose not only the dream of
love but its confirmation and the possibility of its consummation in
marriage. Robert moved steadily towards the realization of his dream,
and Elizabeth, more realistic now about her dilemma, allowed him to
do so without serious let or hindrance. By January 1846 they were
discussing the possibility of eloping together and living in Italy. The
principal obstacle to their fleeing was — ludicrously as it may seem to
us now, but a matter of deepest concern to Robert and Elizabeth, both
morally conventional — the shame of the social opprobrium they would
inevitably bring upon themselves. What would people say? Even more
immediately, what would Mr Barrett say? Though his love had been
exposed as malignant, though his authority had been undermined, his
anger was still powerful enough to give Elizabeth pause for thought and
occasion for apprehension.

Though Robert had declared his love and Elizabeth had not repudi-
ated it, nevertheless he found himself still battling to raise her self-esteem
and convince her that she was worthy of his devotion. With the same
exemplary patience as he had encouraged her to improve her physical
health, to take a step further every day, so he worked to raise her
self-regard. She protested that she turned all she loved to dust and ashes.
Given half a chance, she implied, she could topple empires, bring them
crashing to ruin at a touch. By attaching herself to Robert, she would
destroy him. It was her duty to protect him by refusing him. Robert
did not make the mistake of attacking these pessimistic fantasies of
wickedness, knocking them down directly: rather, he gradually eroded
them. He abased himself, declaring himself to be poor stuff, and exalting
Elizabeth as a rare prize. She would be doing him great honour by

loving him, trusting him. He protested, time and again, his enduring love until she came to believe in it, and by so doing he subtly presented himself less as inadequate and undeserving than as an immovable rock, as a heroic, enduring lover, as a man perfectly capable of surviving whatever threat she imagined as potentially inimical to his well-being and of transfiguring it into a benefit. That might be so — Robert could be persuasive; but Elizabeth remained apprehensive, perhaps to an excessive degree, about one very tangible threat: the terrible Mr Barrett.

Robert the hero was all for confronting the tyrant, bearding the ogre in his own house. Since Mr Barrett did not permit his children to issue formal invitations to their friends to meet the rest of the family, only those with a family connection, such as John Kenyon, and those authorized by Edward Barrett were permitted to visit. Robert proposed that he should write to Mr Barrett, informing him of his intentions towards Elizabeth. That would be the honourable thing to do. Robert never liked hole and corner strategies, and both he and Elizabeth disliked deceit. But Elizabeth counselled against any such letter, and was not above some desperate hypocrisies of her own, directed towards Robert. She had small confidence in his ability to triumph in a trial of strength against Mr Barrett. In order to forestall any direct conflict, she deliberately played up the authority her father still exercised over her in particular and his household in general.

This was both true and false: Elizabeth spoke warmly to Miss Mitford of the gratitude and pleasure she felt in her father's nightly visits to her room when they prayed together. She inverted her feelings when she characterized these nightly prayers to Robert as a distressing ritual forced upon her against her wishes. Then, too, she emphasized to Miss Mitford how much she hated her father being away, while stressing to Robert how he kept her his captive. Of course, these dissimulations might well have been just as much to do with the conflict between her fear of freedom with Robert and a sense that her father's rule had become habitual. Like a deeply institutionalized long-term prisoner, she may well have been sincerely ambivalent about the possibility of release. She put on her chains again and fretted when they chafed.

She knew that her liaison with Robert would be regarded by her father as a moral crime. The more she and Robert persisted in it, the more reprehensible it became; and the more reprehensible it became, the more need there was to conceal it. Trapped in this vicious circle, shame about deception and fear of discovery might eventually sour even the most virtuous love. In this sense, Robert might have been right in his preference for facing up to Mr Barrett, and Elizabeth probably underrated Robert's fortitude, his ability to counter the negative effects of Mr Barrett's love with the positive good of his own. Elizabeth was a special case: Mr Barrett loved his other children, but his eldest daughter combined and represented everything he most valued. She had stayed uncomplainingly — by her own choice, indeed — in her own room with her books and her pen for most of her life; she had opted voluntarily to retire from the wicked world, conducting her social relations mostly by correspondence; she had spoken of romantic love in terms of such disparagement that her father and others would have found it difficult to believe that she would ever consider it appropriate for herself. In short, she had become a paragon of all the virtues, a monument to modesty, sheltering under her father's protective wing.

Suppose she now turned all this on its head by confessing she had fallen in love with a young, penniless poet and intended to run off with him? To be fair to Edward Barrett, he may have become a tyrant unawares — his motives were not innately cruel, but their effects created great unhappiness. Such a volte-face by his forty-year-old invalidish daughter would have smashed all his certainties into smithereens. It would have been as though Elizabeth had committed a form of moral suicide — tumbled as deep into the abyss as any fallen angel. Elizabeth knew the consequences: her father would remake himself, more ironclad and more pitiless than ever, and she would be cast out permanently from his love. And so she tried to see the matter from his point of view and to make Robert see, though he thought the worst of Mr Barrett, that he knew only his wrong side — 'his side of particular wrongness' — and that better knowledge of her father would alter his view. She acknowledged Edward Barrett's peculiar principles to be wrong: but it is worth repeating that she perceived the evil to lie more in the system to which he adhered than in the aberrations of the man himself. If Robert were to be brought to a point of such understanding and toler- ance, however, it would only come through the persuasion of Elizabeth: she had no intention of allowing Robert and her father to take a walk around one another, far less to exchange letters. She knew perfectly well that her father would rather see her 'dead at his foot' than married.

And so they went on — Robert protesting that letters once, and sometimes more than once, a day and afternoon meetings every few days were not enough. By January 1846, a year had passed since his first letter to Elizabeth. Their letters and conversations now dwelt less on poetry than on themselves and their feelings for one another: they liked to reminisce, in a rather self-congratulatory tone, about the development of their love, how right it was that they had not loved before, how unworthy they were of one another's great goodness and great genius, how they filled the deepest reaches of one another's needs. The word was love and both knew it fully for the first time. They knew it, but they did precious little about it beyond holding hands and exchanging kisses. Their excitement, however intense, all-devouring, incandescent, was stalled not only by conventional social propriety but by their own hesitations about what to do about their love.

Elizabeth's brothers and sisters had naturally noticed that her room was often filled with flowers in season and, without seriously suspecting anything as improbable as their sister having fallen in love, they joked about the regularity of Robert's visits. Robert had met and charmed Henrietta and Arabel at 50 Wimpole Street, and had been introduced to George on social occasions at John Kenyon's house, but he had met none of the other brothers. He had never met Edward Barrett, who in any case would not have wished to meet Robert. Edward Barrett had nothing against Robert; he had nothing against Mrs Jameson either; he had nothing against the man in the street, for that matter — simply, he had no particular wish to make casual acquaintances. Mary Mitford, not noted for her discretion, was no wiser than the Barretts about the importance to her friend of Robert's visits. Since she disliked Robert, thinking him lacking in manliness, she attached no significance to the fact that Elizabeth had stopped mentioning his name — indeed probably took some satisfaction in the omission. Elizabeth was confident enough that her increasing health and spirits would be attributed by family and friends — all great gossips — to natural causes rather than to her love for Robert, though she took particular care to conceal her feelings from John Kenyon, who, she convinced herself, possessed almost supernatural powers of perception. She particularly distrusted his spectacles: he slept in those spectacles, she thought, and through them he saw everything. So concerned did Elizabeth become about the remotest possibility of revelation that she virtually ordered Robert not to tell his parents or Sarianna about their intentions and plans. He protested, but obeyed.

Towards the spring of 1846, Robert began to suffer more than usually from severe headaches. Elizabeth recommended various remedies: he should take a break somewhere warm; he should take more vigorous exercise in the fresh air; he should take up smoking; he should drink black coffee; he should drink wine; he should steep his feet in mustard baths; he should take opium. Robert said that the best remedy would be for her to marry him, and for the sake of her health and his happiness they should both live in a warm climate. Elizabeth, pressed to give him a decision, did not say no. She did not say yes, either, but replied rather inconclusively that she would not fail him and said that when summer came, they 'would see'. Robert took this qualified acceptance to be as good as an affirmative. Elizabeth played along, delighting in long, detailed discussions about what sort of marriage ceremony they might have — she didn't care about an extravagant trousseau or an elaborate white dress, indeed she could well dispense with all such folderol — and about where they might live.

The question of where they might live was more amusing than how they might live. Mr Browning could not afford to support Robert and Elizabeth, and Mr Barrett would not. They gravely considered how little money they could live on, Robert citing his ingrained habits of frugality but questioning the reasonableness of expecting Elizabeth to be so calculating in her personal economy. Elizabeth had reassured him: 'you cannot despise the golds and gauds of the world more than I do, and should do even if I found a use for them. And if I *wished* to be very poor, in the world's sense of poverty, I *could* not, with three or four hundred pounds a year of which no living will can dispossess me. And is not the chief good of money, the being free from the need of thinking of it?'[155] In fact, she possessed about £8,000 in government stocks, which returned a dependable annual income of anything between £160 and £180, paid in quarterly instalments. In addition, she was entitled to 'ship money', an annual dividend of some £200 from shares in the *David Lyon*, a merchant ship trading with the West Indies. Elizabeth was sure, too, that she could earn something from her poems — she calculated on sales to magazines bringing in about £100 a year.

Nevertheless, money was a serious question — not only from the point of view of trying to live on Elizabeth's small income, but also from the fact that a necessarily clandestine marriage without a legal settlement beforehand, in order to preserve secrecy, meant that Elizabeth's unsecured property would, under the law, become the property of her husband to do with exactly as he pleased. Elizabeth would be putting herself wholly in Robert's hands and her money entirely in Robert's power. The fact that her income was relatively small was not the point, nor was it much to the point that Elizabeth absolutely trusted Robert to do what was right. The accusation could be made — and was in fact made later — that Robert had married for mercenary reasons, that he was little more than an unscrupulous fortune hunter. On the contrary, Elizabeth said, financially she was no great catch: people were more likely to say that *she* had taken Robert in.

As Robert had airily supposed some years before that he could make money if he chose, so he now said that some part of him wanted to be able to make fifty thousand pounds and build a house. It was a despicable ambition, he admitted, but still, he'd like to be able to prove that he could do it. Though he had hardly earned more than pocket-money in his life, part of him had surely hoped, with some justification, for financial success as a playwright; part of him had surely hoped, with less optimism, for financial success as a poet. A good-enough living could be made from hack work — book reviewing, essays, novels, travel writing, art criticism; but such work mostly depended on cultivating editors and influential patrons in London. A man intending to live abroad would effectually be removing himself from this source of income.

But, if necessary, Robert could find work, would find work, not only to support himself and Elizabeth but in order to satisfy Mr Barrett — and others, such as Miss Mitford, who had questioned his want of masculine resolve in not holding down what they would have considered to be a proper job — of his best and most honest intentions. There were two objections to this: Elizabeth would never allow Robert to compromise himself by giving up the writing of poetry as his sole occupation; Mr Barrett would never allow Robert, poor as Diogenes or as rich as Croesus, to marry Elizabeth under any circumstances.

All this discussion amounted to castles in the air, absorbing enough and entertaining enough, when combined with the delicious debates about how they loved one another — how much, in what manner, what might be the nature of love, whether Elizabeth was loved for her poetry, for her invalidism, for her real worth, though was not that worth overestimated? — until at length Robert was moved to declare 'I love you because I *love* you.' That was definite, without qualification, but of course open to interpretation as to the motive for love . . . and so it could have gone on forever had not Robert's efforts to encourage Elizabeth to get well and strong paid off by the summer of 1846. Elizabeth recognized that her improved health meant that she would no longer be able to delay committing herself not only to a firm plan of action, but also to a fixed timetable.

The more she procrastinated, throwing obstacles in the way, the firmer Robert became. Of course it was settled, she would tell Robert, she would not fail him, of course not, but what if they left things as they were for another year, until next year's summer or autumn? Certainly, said Robert, he would be willing to wait twenty years if Elizabeth thought it best, but since she asked his opinion, he thought that 'every day that passes before *that day* is one the more of hardly endurable anxiety and irritation, to say the least; and the thought of another year's intervention of hope deferred — altogether intolerable!'[156] What would Robert feel if she should die as a result of their elopement? Robert replied, firmly, that he would take that risk rather than lose the probability of the best fortune in fear of the barest possibility of an adverse event. Robert realized that Elizabeth respected his authority — indeed, would only be moved by the exercise of it. He would employ it honourably, not to force her into any course of action against her will but to strengthen her resolve to carry through the plan, to realize her desires, and to reassure her that the plan could be successfully accomplished.

They had settled on travelling to Italy, but how to get there and, once there, where in Italy to go? After prolonged discussion, they selected Pisa — perhaps with a slight sense of irony — as their destination. Rather than incur the expense of a direct sea voyage, they opted for the cheaper alternative: to cross the Channel by steam packet, travel through France, and thence to Pisa. Aunt Jane Hedley, who was staying with the

Barretts that summer, was pleased to see Elizabeth in such glowing health, and said as much to Mr Barrett, who replied, ungraciously, that on the contrary she looked sullen. This year, as last, Jane Hedley aired the idea, after some prompting from Elizabeth, that her niece should go to Italy for the winter. John Kenyon, as before, supported the idea and Anna Jameson, when she heard of it, offered to accompany Elizabeth since it coincided with her own intention to travel to Italy in September. Robert and Elizabeth were sorely tempted to confide their real intentions to Mrs Jameson, though finally they thought better of any disclosure. And so Mrs Jameson was no wiser than anyone else: she had met Robert, but had no idea that he knew Elizabeth, far less visited her regularly.

When Robert and Elizabeth met on 30 August, Elizabeth again vacillated. Her panic had been steadily rising: her own guilt and anxiety provoked her to look for suspicion in everyone — bustling and busy Aunt Jane, the boisterous Barrett brothers, her tenderly affectionate sisters, John Kenyon (who had fortunately broken his spectacles and therefore could see less well), and particularly she looked for any glimmer of comprehension in her father. They were all, except her father, probably too busy with their own lives to inquire too minutely into Elizabeth's. The Hedleys were in London for a lavish family marriage, and Henrietta was having difficulties of her own with her father over a suitor, Surtees Cook. Nevertheless, a guilty secret may preoccupy one's mind so entirely that sudden discovery seems certain. During a meeting with Robert on 30 August, cut short by an unexpected interruption by John Kenyon, Elizabeth had once again tried to delay. Robert, who had been obliged to pretend to Kenyon that he and Elizabeth were mere acquaintances, lost his temper in the letter he wrote with more than his customary candour the next day:

> I wonder what I shall write to you, Ba — I could suppress my feelings here, as I do on other points, and say nothing of the hatefulness of this state of things which is prolonged so uselessly. There is the point — show me one good reason, or show of reason, why we gain anything by deferring our departure till next week instead of to-morrow, and I will bear to perform yesterday's part for the amusement of Mr Kenyon a dozen times over without complaint. But if the cold plunge *must* be taken,

all this shivering delay on the bank is hurtful as well as fruitless
... You tell me you have decided to go — then, dearest, you
will be prepared to go earlier than you promised yesterday —
by the end of September at the very latest. In proportion to
the too probable excitement and painful circumstances of the
departure, the greater amount of advantages should be secured
for the departure itself. How can I take you away in even the
beginning of October? We shall be a fortnight on the journey
— with the year, as everybody sees and says, a full month in
advance ... cold mornings and dark evenings already. Everyone
would cry out on such folly when it was found that we let the
favourable weather escape, in full assurance that the Autumn
would come to us unattended by any one beneficial circum-
stance.[157]

Elizabeth's reply, post-marked 1 September, sympathized with
Robert's difficulty about having deceived Mr Kenyon, but also re-
proached him, a little peevishly, with a complaint: 'I have not given you
reason to *doubt me* or my inclination to accede to any serious wish of
yours relating to the step before us. On the contrary, I told you in so
many words in July, that, if you really wished to go in August rather than
in September, I would make no difficulty — to which you answered,
remember, that *October or November would do as well.* Now *is* it fair,
ever dearest, that you should turn round on me so quickly, and call in
question my willingness to keep my engagement for years, if ever? Can
I help it, if the circumstances around us are painful to both of us? Did
I not keep repeating from the beginning that they *must* be painful? Only
you could not believe, you see, until you felt the pricks.'

Having disburdened herself of what she felt to have been unfair
pressure, Elizabeth then reaffirmed her resolution but passed the final
responsibility to Robert: 'I mean to say only, that I never wavered from
the promise I gave freely; and that I will keep it freely at any time you
choose — that is, within a week of any time you choose ... May God
bless you always. *I* am not angry either, understand, though I did think
this morning that you were a little hard on me, just when I felt myself
ready to give up the whole world for you at the holding up of a finger.
And now say nothing of this. I kiss the end of the dear finger; and when

it is ready, I am ready; I will not be reproached again. Being too much your own, very own, BA. Tell me that you keep better. And your mother?'[158]

Robert had been ill, stricken with one of the worst headaches of his life — not surprisingly, perhaps, considering the tensions of the situation now coming to a head and which, the least of its effects, was causing trouble between himself and Elizabeth. And then Flush was stolen, snatched from their heels by professional dog thieves while Elizabeth and Arabel were out shopping. Between the shop and the carriage, Flush suddenly disappeared. The little spaniel had been taken and ransomed once before, so Elizabeth knew the procedure for getting him back. She knew exactly where to go: against her father's wishes, she bravely went personally by carriage to the sinks of Shoreditch to negotiate with the thieves. After some difficult moments, Flush was returned for a ransom of twenty guineas. For a woman who, until two years ago, had barely been able to take a walk in the park, this adventure was a remarkable display not only of determination and courage but of strength and energy.

Robert made the serious mistake of underestimating the sentimental importance Elizabeth attached to Flush. Flush had bitten him twice, which may have had a little to do with Robert's reaction, and he argued, agreeing with Mr Barrett for once, that it was morally wrong to pay money to thieves for the return of stolen property. This high moral principle of resistance to evil was judged callous by Elizabeth, and they quarrelled. How would he feel if it had happened to her? Would Robert refuse to pay a ransom for Elizabeth if she were kidnapped? He would pay, Robert replied, but then, for however long it might take — fifty years if necessary — he would hunt down and shoot the perpetrators. This was satisfactory to Elizabeth, who started talking again of the plan to travel to Pisa.

What with Robert's short but acute illness and the drama involving Flush, there might be no end to events and illnesses that conspired to postpone the departure. A little ironically, it was an intervention by Mr Barrett himself which precipitated a crisis that forced Robert and Elizabeth finally, after all their doubts, delays, diffidence, and dilatoriness, to act decisively. On 9 September, Edward Barrett announced that the Wimpole Street house was to be thoroughly cleaned and redecorated.

This was not entirely unexpected: it had been discussed for long enough, though nothing had been done about it; but now it was to be done promptly, so promptly that the entire family would be required to move for a month, probably longer, to lodgings in Dover, Reigate, Tunbridge, it didn't much matter where, without delay. George was instructed to arrange the details. Elizabeth wrote instantly, on Wednesday night, 9 September 1846, to Robert:

> 'Now! — what *can* be done? . . . Decide, after thinking. I am embarrassed to the utmost degree, as to the best path to take. If we are taken away on Monday . . . what then? . . . Therefore decide! It seems quite too soon and too sudden for us to set out on our Italian adventure now — and perhaps even we could not compass — Well — but you must decide for both of us. It is past twelve and I have just a moment to seal this and entrust it to Henrietta for the morning's post. More than ever beloved, I am
>
> Your own BA. I will do as you wish — understand.'

Robert replied immediately when, at midday on Thursday morning, 10 September, he received Elizabeth's note. '"I will do as you wish — understand" — then I understand you are in earnest. If you *do* go on Monday, our marriage will be impossible for another year — the misery! You see what we have gained by waiting. We must be *married directly* and go to Italy. I will go for a licence today and we can be married on Saturday. I will call tomorrow at 3 and arrange everything with you. We can leave from Dover &c., *after* that, — but otherwise, impossible! Inclose the ring, or a substitute — I have not a minute to spare for the post. Ever your own R.' Robert then thought better of rushing to obtain the licence — 'I will go tomorrow, I think . . . there are fixed hours I fancy at the office — and I might be too late.' Elizabeth wrote the same day, Thursday, to reassure Robert of her resolve to go through with the marriage and to calm matters a little: 'do not be precipitate — we shall not be taken away on Monday, no, nor for several days. George has simply gone to look for houses — going to Reigate first. Oh yes — come tomorrow. And then, you shall have the ring . . . soon enough and safer . . . But come tomorrow, come. Almost everybody is to be away at Richmond, at a picnic, and we shall be free on all sides. Ever and ever your BA.'

Robert and Elizabeth met, at Wimpole Street as arranged, on the

Friday afternoon of 11 September to plan, in fine detail, their movements over the following few days. The licence had been obtained that morning, and now the ring was secured. It was their ninety-first meeting; their marriage, the next day, would be the ninety-second, and the last, after which there would be no partings.

On the morning of Saturday 12 September 1846, Elizabeth Barrett left 50 Wimpole Street with her maid, Lily Wilson, dressed as though going out merely to pay a visit to a friend. The weather was fine and sunny and the distance along Wimpole Street to the turn into Devonshire Street was little more than two hundred yards. Before they had walked that far, Elizabeth all but fainted and had to be revived with sal volatile at a nearby chemist's shop, to which Wilson managed to support her. The two women staggered the five hundred yards further to Marylebone Street where, at the fly-stand, they obtained a hackney carriage to take them to St Marylebone Parish Church in Marylebone Road, facing the York Gate entrance to Regent's Park, no more than a couple of minutes away by foot. They arrived at a quarter to eleven to find Robert waiting with his best man, his cousin James Silverthorne, outside the church.

'What a wild, dreadful, floating vision it all looks like, to look back on it now!' Elizabeth wrote later to Henrietta.[159] The ceremony was of the plainest. In the silent church, witnessed only by Wilson and James Silverthorne, Robert and Elizabeth exchanged their marriage vows and were pronounced man and wife by the vicar. When required to sign the register, Elizabeth's hand faltered: 'Three times I tried to write my name and could not form a letter, and someone said, I remember, "Let her wait a moment," and somebody else thrust in a glass of water.'[160] At half past eleven the newly-wedded couple prepared to leave.

In her letter to Henrietta, Elizabeth described the succeeding moments with humour and composure: 'Always it *does* make us laugh, for instance, to think of the official's (the man with the wand in the church) attitude and gesture of astonishment as he stood at the church door and saw bride and bridegroom part on the best possible terms and go off in separate flies. Robert was very generous and threw about his gold to clerk, pew-openers, etc., in a way to convict us of being in a condition of incognito.' They had been accompanied to the door by the man with the wand who 'hazarded, between two bursts of gratitude, a philosophic sentiment about "marriage being a very serious event in one's mortal life"; — this as we left the church. And there he stood in the door way, his speech scarcely ended on his lips; ... mouth wide open in surprise! Never had he seen anything more remarkable than *that*, in the whole course of his practice!'[161]

Of Robert's marriage, G. K Chesterton declares, 'The manner in which Browning bore himself in this acute and necessarily dubious position is, perhaps, more thoroughly to his credit than anything else in his career. He never came out so well in all his long years of sincerity and publicity as he does in this one act of deception ... He was breaking a social law, but he was not declaring a crusade against social laws ... One of the best and most striking things to notice about Robert Browning is the fact that he did this thing considering it as an exception, and that he contrived to leave it really exceptional ... At a supreme crisis of his life he did an unconventional thing, and he lived and died conventional. It would be hard to say whether he appears the more thoroughly sane in having performed the act, or in not having allowed it to affect him.'[162]

Mrs Orr defends the secrecy surrounding the marriage in somewhat similar, though more cautious, terms: she makes the best of an exceptional expedient without recommending it as a general practice. She understands the circumstances without ascribing any credit to Robert beyond a praiseworthy devotion to Elizabeth's good: 'The engaged pair had not only not obtained Mr Barrett's sanction to the marriage; they had not even invoked it; and the doubly clandestine character thus forced upon the union could not be otherwise than repugnant to Mr Browning's pride; but it was dictated by the deepest filial affection on the part of his intended wife.'[163] There is a hint here that Mrs Orr places the principal responsibility for the clandestine marriage on Elizabeth, though it is excused on the ground that 'there could be no question in so enlightened a mind of sacrificing her own happiness with that of the man she loved; she was determined to give herself to him'.

Robert went home to New Cross after the marriage and there he wrote a letter to Elizabeth that Daniel Karlin characterizes — properly, most will think — as 'the only letter of his in the whole correspondence which is — almost — free of artifice and affectation, free of *pressure*; which is direct and serene both in its praise and its self-regard ... This letter is a consummate expression of the rhetoric of Browning's love for Elizabeth Barrett — its gestures of deference and self-reproach, its powerful use of language to scorn the use of language — but it is the one occasion on which, within the limits of the rhetoric, Browning comes close to what, in "One Word More", he says is the aim of every artist who "lives and loves": "to find his love a language/Fit and fair and simple and sufficient".[164] What Robert wrote and sent to Elizabeth at 1 p.m. on his wedding day was this:

> You will only expect a few words — what will those be? When the heart is full it may run over, but the real fulness stays within.
>
> You asked me yesterday 'if I should repent?' Yes — my own Ba, — I could wish all the past were to do over again, that in it I might somewhat more, — never so little more, conform in the outward homage to the inward feeling. What I have professed ... (for I have performed nothing) seems to fall so short of what my first love required even — and when I think of *this* moment's love ... I could repent, as I say.
>
> Words can never tell you, however — form them, transform them anyway, — how perfectly dear you are to me — perfectly dear to my heart and soul.
>
> I look back, and in every one point, every word and gesture, every *silence* — you have been entirely perfect to me — I would not change one word, one look.
>
> My hope and aim are to preserve this love, not to fall from it — for which I trust to God who procured it for me, and doubtless can preserve it.
>
> Enough now, my dearest, dearest, own Ba! You have given me the highest, completest proof of love that ever one human being gave another. I am all gratitude — and all pride (under the proper feeling which ascribes pride to the right source) all pride that my life has been so crowned by you.
>
> God bless you prays your very own R.
>
> I will write tomorrow of course. Take every care of *my life* which is in that dearest little hand; try and be composed, my beloved.
>
> Remember to thank Wilson for me.

PART 2

ROBERT AND ELIZABETH

1846–1861

ROBERT WOKE THE MORNING after his wedding day feeling perfectly well. His headache had gone. He had of course by now told his parents about Elizabeth. Mrs Browning said she would write to Elizabeth when she felt a little better, and Mr Browning expressed his delight. It was no doubt delightful, also, to assist Robert on this happy occasion by lending or giving him £100 to enable his son and the new Mrs Browning to run off together to Italy.

Equipped with ready money, Robert ran around in something of a tizzy, making the necessary travel bookings, though Elizabeth had to correct his mistakes about which railroad company was which, draw his attention to their different timetables, and suggest which Channel crossing would be the most suitable. His sense of etiquette, too, required refinement. Robert was all for putting 'At Home' or 'In Italy for a year' on their visiting cards, until Elizabeth told him to content himself with just their names. The announcement of their marriage in *The Times*, on 21 September — the day fixed for the departure of the Barrett household from Wimpole Street to Little Bookham near Leatherhead in Surrey, where George had found temporary accommodation for them, and by which date the Brownings would be gone from England — was another cause for concern: Elizabeth insisted that the date of the marriage should not be mentioned, lest it should reveal the clandestine nature of the ceremony. She had declared to her former maid, Crow, that she cared nothing for social etiquette, but now she was vexed by Robert's lack of it.

There were other difficulties. Robert refused to call at Wimpole Street on the scrupulous ground that he would not ask for his wife under her maiden name. Elizabeth was equally adamant that nobody in the household should know — or, more precisely, be told directly — that the marriage had taken place. It was impossible that Robert should turn up asking for Mrs Browning. What the Barretts did not know for sure, they could deny with perfect truth and propriety. Wilson of course knew, but it could not be allowed to go further. As to the arrangements for Elizabeth's departure from Wimpole Street, Robert was instructed that she could leave only during the hours of late morning or early afternoon. Since Arabel habitually slept in Elizabeth's room, an early departure would be so unusual as to alert Arabel and arouse suspicion.

Robert had urged Elizabeth to travel light, and somehow she and Wilson managed to smuggle 'a light box and a carpet box' out of the house and into a cab. The cab driver took the boxes to the railway office for later collection under the name of Browning. Robert and Elizabeth arranged to meet on Saturday 19 September at Hodgson's bookshop in Marylebone Road between half past three and four o'clock. They would then proceed to Vauxhall Station where they would pick up their luggage and board the five o'clock train for Southampton, where they would arrive at eight o'clock and immediately board the night boat for Le Havre. Robert was right to have thanked Wilson in his letter: without Wilson, it would have been impossible for Elizabeth to have married, far less got as far as Hodgson's bookshop a week later. Wilson was coming with them: she was a resourceful young woman, utterly trustworthy, devoted to Elizabeth and sympathetic to the romance in which she found herself involved, at some personal risk. She was embarking on an adventure whose outcome was as unknown to her as it was to her employers.

With Flush, Elizabeth and Wilson quietly left the Wimpole Street house while the rest of the Barrett household were all in the dining-room with their minds on nothing but their dinner. Robert was waiting for his wife, her maid, and her dog in Marylebone Road. When they were all packed into a cab, the Brownings took off for married life. The timing was tight, but the travel arrangements all synchronized perfectly and they landed safely in France the next morning. They rested for the day at Le Havre. It had been a rough, miserable trip, but Elizabeth survived it better than either she or Robert had expected. They were all tired, of course, but there had been no crisis of ill health. At nine o'clock on the evening of Sunday 20 September, they took a diligence through the night to Rouen, on their way to Paris. Elizabeth, by now thoroughly excited by the novelty of it all and made feverish by the thrill, at last began to flag in energy.

In Paris, Elizabeth urged Robert to send a note to Mrs Jameson at the Hôtel de la Ville de Paris where she had said she would be staying. And so Robert wrote, very succinctly: 'Come and see your friend and my wife, E.B.B. — Robert Browning'. On receiving and reading the sensational words of the note, Anna Jameson rushed to the Brownings' hotel. This was a significant moment for Robert and Elizabeth — their first revelation to anyone since their marriage of their new status. Mrs Jameson was delighted to see them, astonished by their news, unable quite to make up her mind about her first impressions of Mr and Mrs Robert Browning. Elizabeth seemed, she reported in a letter describing the meeting to Lady Noel Byron, 'nervous, frightened, ashamed, agitated, happy miserable'. Mrs Jameson, for her part, 'sympathized, scolded, rallied, cried and helped'. She obviously realized that Elizabeth was exhausted and persuaded her to rest. The cumulative effect of Mrs Jameson's reaction was very positive: she was the kindest of hearts and a most capable pair of hands.

The Brownings moved to Mrs Jameson's quiet hotel, where Elizabeth quickly recovered her energies and enthusiasms. Paris was perfect as a honeymoon city, Elizabeth was able to visit the Louvre, walk along the banks of the Seine, eat in restaurants — things she had never done, nor had ever expected to do, in her life. Always with her was the cheerful, knowledgeable Mrs Jameson and the voluble, enraptured Robert, who carried her upstairs and downstairs and sat with her during the dusky evenings, watching the stars high above the Paris rooftops — as she reported to Arabel — and talking, endlessly talking, about what they should do, what poetry they should write in Pisa, or merely prattling and talking lovers' nonsense.

Anna Jameson, thoroughly fascinated by the drama to which she had become attached, was very willing to agree, at Robert's request, that she should travel with them to Pisa. She was sure she had saved Elizabeth's life and that Robert would make a mess of things without her assistance. And so she took upon herself virtually every aspect of managing their progress to Italy, relishing the responsibility and indulging herself in the pleasure of observing how both Robert and Elizabeth opened like flowers towards one another, making it impossible to condemn such happiness.

Others were less generous. Before leaving London, Elizabeth had directed that all correspondence should be forwarded to Orléans, and her anxiety grew as they approached the city. She dispatched Robert to inquire whether any mail had arrived, and he returned with 'a great packet of letters'. Before opening them, she sent Robert away. The contents of the letters were disappointing, but no big surprise to Elizabeth. Her father's was as bad as could be expected — and, if possible, worse in the cold reality of the words with which he harshly and unsparingly condemned, disinherited, and considered her now dead to him.

The letter from George was surprisingly hard-hearted. She had 'sacrificed all delicacy and honour' and had left the family to bear all the sorrow and blame of her actions. George declared that he wanted nothing more to do with her. Letters from the rest of her brothers were similarly outraged: she had insulted them, their father, and the family pride. Henrietta and Arabel, on the contrary, were thrilled, glad that the masculine Barrett pride, which had oppressed and repressed them too, had been dented. John Kenyon had written to Robert and Elizabeth jointly to say that they had done the right thing, that he sympathized with their feelings for one another, and that, had they asked his advice beforehand about the marriage, he should have advised it. Miss Mitford had also written to say how glad she was to hear the news and that, had she been asked, she would have stood by Elizabeth at the church. The support of John Kenyon (which Elizabeth particularly valued), of Miss Mitford, and of her sisters went some way to compensate for the brutality of the letters from her father and brothers. But not entirely. Elizabeth burst into tears and it took Robert some hours of tender solicitude to comfort her.

From Orléans, the party travelled by rail to Lyons, and from there, in a downpour of rain on a rather squalid little steamboat, down the Rhône to Avignon. Elizabeth bore the rigours of the journey well, though the emotional turmoil at Orléans had distressed and weakened her spirits. After resting a day at Avignon, they travelled to Vaucluse, then on to Aix, and finally to Marseilles, where they embarked on a French steamboat for Livorno. Elizabeth was well enough to stand on deck with Robert to admire the dramatically rough sea and wonder at the Italian coast as they approached Genoa, where the boat laid up for twenty-four hours. While Mrs Jameson went off sightseeing with her niece Gerardine, who had accompanied her from Paris, Robert and Elizabeth took a short walk to marvel at 'strange and noble' old palaces and churches richly wrought with gold, marble, and porphyry: 'Beautiful Genoa — what a vision it is!' The next day, after another night of rough seas, they reached Livorno, from where it was only a short train journey to Pisa and the end of a long, wondrous journey.

At Pisa, the Brownings could at last be on their own — virtually for the first time. Anna Jameson had busied herself about them for some three weeks, settling them down like chicks in a nest. Her doubts about how they would manage were more practical than those of Wordsworth who, hearing that 'Robert Browning and Elizabeth Barrett have gone off together', mordantly remarked, 'Well, I hope they may understand one another — nobody else could!' Mrs Jameson, romantically and sentimentally, thought them wonderfully suited: 'If two persons were to be chosen from the ends of the earth for perfect union and fitness, there could not be a greater congruity.' There is only a cigarette paper between the sense of her view and that of Wordsworth, though in spirit they are poles apart. Mrs Jameson acknowledged a perfect, poetic, loving union of high minds, beautiful souls and congruent tempers; yet, she could not help but admit privately to herself — and openly in a letter to Lady Byron — certain reservations of a practical nature as to the fitness of these two extraordinary persons for ordinary life:

> With all the abundance of love and high principles, I have had now and then a tremor at my heart about their future. He is full of spirits and good humour and his turn for making the best of everything and his bright intelligence and his rare acquirements of every kind rendered him the very prince of travelling companions. But (always buts!!) he is in all the

common things of this life the most impractical of men, the most uncalculating, rash, in short the worst manager I ever met with.

Mrs Jameson, herself a very capable traveller and manager, had the broad-tempered grace to recognize a well-meaning, even intrepid fellow, capable of intelligent improvisation, adept at making the best of a bad job; but these virtues — generously credited to Robert — were not, perhaps, in Mrs Jameson's estimate, a substitute for sound judgement in difficult circumstances when a little forward thought and planning might have avoided a bad job altogether. Her perception was perhaps broadly correct in the novelty of the present circumstances, but later would have been unjust as Robert capably came to terms, albeit and too often fretfully and pedantically, particularly in the matter of money, with his management responsibilities as a married man.

Mrs Browning was not much better; indeed, on consideration, decidedly and altogether a dead loss: 'She, in her present state, and from her long seclusion almost helpless. Now only conceive,' wrote Mrs Jameson, her lively mind and good heart perceiving, with perhaps more relish than might be admitted, 'the menage that is likely to ensue and without FAULT on either side. For the present our first care is to get her into some comfortable lodgings.' The second was, so far as possible, to wean Elizabeth off her dependence on morphine. Having brought 'our dear invalid, in safety, to what she fondly calls her home,' Mrs Jameson found her to be 'still helpless' though looking 'wonderfully well, considering all the fatigue undergone. Under her husband's influence & mine she is leaving off those medicines on which she existed, ether, morphine, etc., etc. I am full of hope for her.' This regime continued, under Robert's supervision. On 8 February 1847 he was able to write to Arabel and Henrietta Barrett that 'Ba sleeps admirably — and is steadily diminishing the doses of morphine, quite as much as is prudent.'

Finally obliged to be about her own business, Mrs Jameson, with Gerardine in tow, bustled away in early November to Rome to inspect paintings and monuments for a book she intended to write. She left Mr and Mrs Browning — he allegedly impractical, she supposedly helpless — installed in 'rooms close to the Duomo and leaning down on the great Collegio [Ferdinando] . . . Three excellent bed-rooms, and a sitting room matted and carpeted, looking comfortable even for England.' So reported the new Mrs Browning in a letter to Miss Mitford, boasting — not quite incidentally — that 'Mrs Jameson says she won't call me improved but transformed rather.'

They were both, Robert and Elizabeth, transformed. After three months of marriage, Elizabeth wrote to her sister Arabel: '(Remind dear Minny [the Barrett housekeeper] of what I said to her once about angels — *I have found my angel.*) I have a full satisfaction for earth, and a hope for over the grave — I mean the *infinite hope*, since for some finite ones there seems room still upon earth. And I remember always, how in our dreary marriage at Marylebone Church, he pressed my hand which lay in his, declaring to me forever the union bound oath . . . we have hope in that which is infinite. Therefore, taking all in all, I am beyond comparison happier now than ever in my life I was. Who would have prophesied that to me six years ago?'[1] Her mind, for quite a while after reaching Italy, dwelt upon her narrow escape from the tomb: literal or metaphorical, it would have been much the same.

'I was buried . . .,' she wrote later to Mrs Martin, a Devonshire friend of the family, thinking of her former condition in Wimpole Street: 'A thoroughly morbid and desolate state it was, which I look back on now to with a sort of horror with which one would look to one's graveclothes, if one had been clothed in them by mistake during a trance.' She was sensible enough to admit that the fault was not entirely her own, that she and the rest of the Barrett family had colluded to create and perpetuate this morbid state: 'my family had become so accustomed to the idea of my living on and on in that room, that while my heart was eating itself, their love for me was consoled, and at least the evil grew scarcely perceptible. It was no want of love in them, and quite natural in itself: we all get used to the thought of a tomb.'

Elizabeth was at first largely confined to the apartment in Pisa, but the very different circumstances of marriage, and her husband's vigorous ambitions for her, strengthened her body and soul. Her room in Wimpole Street was a living memory, but the rooms in Pisa were a living reality: 'here,' she wrote to Mr Boyd in November 1846, 'the constant companionship and tenderness of the best and most gifted of human beings, has transfigured life to me . . . If the world ended for me at this moment, I may now say the grace of life with satisfied lips, having tasted so much of its sweetness. It was worth the endurance and even the survival of all my trials, to have lived these last two months — so much do I thank God for them. My health improves still, too.' Robert wrote to Thomas Carlyle from Florence in May 1847, in perfect confidence not merely that he had preserved Elizabeth's life, but that, 'Through God's providence, all has gone with us better than my best hopes. My wife, in all probability, will become quite well and strong. She only feels weakness, indeed, and may be considered well, except for that. I believe — from the accounts from England, and from the nature of the place in the country to which she was to have been removed a day or two after that on which we determined to leave England — that this winter would have ended the seven years' confinement without my inter-vention.'

They learned quickly how to order meals to be sent in from the local trattoria ('traiteur', as Elizabeth called it) and were delighted with the simplicity of their domestic economy: 'we like, both of us, this way of living, free from domestic cares and the ordering and cooking of dinners'. They agreed entirely about subsisting on fish as well as 'a little chicken and plenty of cayenne, and above all things pudding'. They both turned away from beef and mutton, as they would regularly during their self-imposed exile from England, and loathed the very idea of a Saturday hash. At dinner they drank local wine, 'an excellent kind of claret ... it is a light wine, you know, and not heating — the famous Chianti', as Elizabeth explained, in travel guide terms, to her sisters. They were much taken, also, with the novel custom of drinking — Wilson, too — their Italian claret out of tumblers instead of wine glasses. The light Chianti did not make Elizabeth feverish, as port used to do, though she did not give up her port, a wine which Robert professed never to have cared for, and she put up very little opposition to him slyly refilling her glass to the point that, 'I never being famous for resisting his invocations, am at the end of dinner too giddy to see his face and am laid down at full length on the arm chair and told to go to sleep and profit by the whole.' These pretty domestic habits were relayed regularly and at length in Elizabeth's letters to the Barrett sisters still living in Wimpole Street.

But the winter in Pisa, for all Elizabeth's epistolary high spirits, had been difficult: by mid-December, hard frosts and light snow — the first for five years, said the Pisans — had struck the city. 'The snow is on the Duomo,' wrote Elizabeth to her sisters on 19 December 1846, 'interposing between the yellow marble and blue sky; and the mountains are powdered with snow — yet the sun burns, burns, Robert says, to a degree of making him sick when he walks in it.' Elizabeth had occasionally been out, to judge by her delight in the incongruity of women walking in the streets 'with furs and parasols together'. Before the sudden onset of winter cold, she had found strength enough to walk far enough from their rooms to be impressed by the 'majestic, silent city, built of marble and backed by purple mountains', and in a letter of 19 November to Mr Boyd she reported having seen the 'gorgeous' Duomo, the Campo Santo, and the Leaning Tower. She had sat 'in the sun to watch the lizards — and the other morning Robert caught me a gigantic grass-hopper exactly like Anacreon's'. This reference to the Anacreontic grasshopper harked back to a quotation she had referred to in a letter to Mr Boyd in 1832: 'We deem thee blessed, O cricket, when on the tree tops, having drunk a little dew, like a king, thou singest.' If the grasshopper sang when drunk on dew, Elizabeth was singing to all who would listen about the intoxication of the sights, sounds, and scents of Italy.

The weather had been fine until mid-December, with Elizabeth unable to bear even a shawl in the hot sun; but now she and Robert huddled around pine wood fires roasting chestnuts and talking, at first sufficient and exclusive unto themselves, during a prolonged honeymoon period that ended only when Elizabeth balked at being so coddled. She recognized her own limitations: 'I was not at all well soon after I came to Pisa, and frightened poor Robert out of his propriety.' She was initially charmed by his solicitous attentions: 'We heap up the pine wood — that is, he does — he is so afraid of my suffering: indeed I am afraid too: for if I were to be ill after all, I feel I should deserve to be stoned for having married.' Nevertheless, her own ambitions and will were strong: 'But I shall not be ill — the cold will go off in a day or two; and even as it is, it is different from English cold. In the bedroom, for instance, where there is no fire, not a sign is there of frost on the window; and the air is not sharp and metallic like that which cuts away the breath — it is a different air altogether. I sleep well, and all day sit half in and half out of the fire, so that I shall do well, I dare say. To give me dressing room, Robert goes out into the cold, at morning and evening, like the kindest person in the world which he is — it makes me ashamed.'

Pisa is today not the most exciting of Italian cities, and tourists tend to explore not much further than the Campo Santo. It was duller still, perhaps, in 1846, being then a recommended resort for northern convalescents, who took their pallid complexions, delicate constitutions, congested lungs, and hacking coughs painfully along the streets. The economy of Pisa had shrunk since its glory days as a prosperous and powerful Renaissance city-state, once proud, predatory, warlike, and busy with the building of great ships. The city now depended largely on its reputation as a sanatorium for rich invalids. Robert spoke of Pisa, without enthusiasm, as 'this strange silent old city': it was certainly quiet; too quiet, perhaps, to gratify even mildly vivacious spirits who looked for more than a formal weekly reception at the governor's, and another given by a resident baroness, as the giddy heights and centre of social life. It was dolorous to find one's principal excitement in the *memento mori* of funeral processions. Once might be a novelty, twice might be interesting, but by the time the third, fourth, and subsequent cortèges had passed, the fascination might be expected to wear off.

The regular procession of the monks — sometimes all in black, sometimes all in white (according to the order), chanting in procession, carrying torches, escorting the corpse laid out on a bier open-faced except for the flimsy decency of a veil — became worse than monotonous: the funerals became, indeed, morbidly attractive. They thronged past the forty-seven windows of the Collegio Ferdinando on their way to the nearby cathedral, and Robert could hardly resist them. 'Ah, don't go to the window!' entreated Elizabeth, who never liked funerals in any case and whose mind dwelt less now on tombs and grave clothes. She was repelled by 'such horrible coarse chanting . . . Like the croaking of Death itself.' 'I can't help it, Ba — it draws me,' her husband would say, fixed on the sight despite his own dread, as he remarked, again, how the crucifix preceded 'the dumb Dead' and thought how he 'would rather like it' to be done in his own case.

The Brownings had taken their rooms until mid-April, and — said Elizabeth — they were sorry for it: 'four months would have been better than six for Pisa; and the Italian spring beginning in February, we might just as well have spent it in Florence for instance, as here. Not that we do not like Pisa — but there is little to see in it, and the country, so far as walkers usually penetrate, is very monotonous.' Robert asserted that he took no pleasure in his solitary expeditions for exercise along the Arno: 'he has an extravagant fancy (oh! even I call it unreasonable) that, except this walk for his health, he will go nowhere without me — "cannot enjoy it" — and thus he quite lives by my chair. What I cannot do he will not!' So wrote Elizabeth.

For his own part, Robert declared that he was never so happy in his life. He considered it 'the greatest advantage to us to be shut up in this seclusion without any distractions — that we have learnt one another better by it, than we should have done if we had taken the usual course of married people who live so for three weeks or a month, and then proceed to other amusements'. This honeymoon period, according to Robert, should be the tenor of the rest of their lives together; and indeed they had been tumbled precipitately into the novel reality of their changed lives from the first moments of their flight from England.

Though written much later, conjecturally in the summer in of 1853, and first published on 10 November 1855 in *Men and Women*, Robert's poem 'A Lovers' Quarrel' is located not only contemporaneously in the countryside around Bagni di Lucca but looks back — we may imagine — for its first images and emotions to the first weeks and months of new and contented marriage in Pisa:

> Dearest, three months ago!
> When we lived blocked-up with snow, —
>   When the wind would edge
>   In and in his wedge,
> In, as far as the point could go —
>   Not to our ingle, though,
> Where we loved each the other so!
>
> Laughs with so little cause!
> We devised games out of straws,
>   We would try and trace
>   One another's face

> In the ash, as an artist draws,
>
> Free on one another's flaws,
>
> How we chattered like two church daws! (ll. 15–28)

They agreed wonderfully well, 'apt to talk nonsense with ever so many inflections and varieties, and sitting here tête-à-tête, are at times quite merry'. Robert, said Elizabeth, made her laugh until she could laugh no more: 'such spirits he has, and power of jesting and amusing — alternating with the serious feeling and thinking; and never of a sort to incline him to leave this room for what is called "gaieties".' Robert might have been satisfied, on his own testimony, with this state of affairs, but Elizabeth reckoned that for her husband, at least, 'when we are in places where there will be more to see within reach, it will be better for him'. Though Elizabeth had been calling their constant company with one another — to the exclusion of any visitors — 'rather a trial', Robert had graciously replied that 'it could only be so in cases of unreal or fanciful attachments'. They were very devoted, earnestly solicitous of one another's well-being.

And so they dallied, reading Italian and French novels, interrupted only by occasional visits from a Professor Ferucci from the university. This gentleman, though 'too much at the University to spend time on any person', arranged for the Brownings to use the university's library. He insisted on speaking French, and spoke warmly of English scholars, esteemed English Latin as best and English Greek as foremost. He threatened to bring his wife to see Elizabeth; but this — and the threat of irruptions by other ladies announcing their eagerness to visit Mrs Browning — seems to have been discouraged. Robert himself, meeting an acquaintance in the street, specifically said he did not return visits and he spoke with dread of the prospect of social life among the English colony at Florence. They had taken an unaccountable dislike of the English abroad, perhaps wary of their gossiping curiosity and possibly on account of their solid reputation for frivolity and boorishness.

Pisa, despite the fact that Shelley had felt more deeply rooted there than anywhere, could be only an interlude. There was a limit to the pleasures of the flat city which, though rich enough in literary associations, was short of literature. The Brownings subscribed first to an Italian library, at the cost of eight pence a month, and continued to persist in reading exciting French novels and dull, soulless contemporary Italian fiction until, reckless of the extra expense, they paid a larger subscription to a better library that provided not only more interesting novels but delivery of a daily French newspaper, the *Siècle*. When they had read the newspaper, they read Balzac, Dumas, the wicked novels of Eugène Sue — among them, the sensational *Mystères de Paris* — and Stendhal together, discussing the merits and demerits of each. Robert was disinclined to value a story, even one of Balzac's, merely for the sake of a story. Style counted for much. Stendhal's *Le Rouge et le Noir* was judged by Robert to be 'exactly like Balzac in the raw — in the material and undeveloped conception'. They read and wrote and talked, and among their topics there was a great deal of vaporous, inconclusive discussion about what to do, and where to go.

The Brownings, despite Mrs Jameson's frank doubts and serious apprehensions, were proving themselves unpredictably practical. They had learned a great deal, and quickly, about housekeeping in Italy. Mrs Turner, a kindly acquaintance about whom nothing further is known, had taken Wilson in hand and escorted her round the shops to buy coffee, tea, and sugar, showing her 'how to do some small marketings'. Since Wilson had no Italian — though she quickly acquired a facility in the language — this was no small comfort. The easy commercial duplicity of Italians came as a surprise to the Browning innocents. Elizabeth commented to Arabel: 'We have made great discoveries here on the arts of housekeeping and house-taking, and have had our eyes unsealed to the abominable impositions practiced upon us. Cheating is systematized in Italy to a most frightful extent; and nobody sees any harm in what everybody does. Foreigners are considered the lawful prey of the nation ... You will be amused to learn that Robert and I are held to be "millionaires" in our neighbourhood.'

They found that their landlord had not been above a bit of under-hand dealing with them, talking up the price that the Brownings had paid for their rooms and causing a neighbouring landlord to match the boast by swearing that the Brownings would have paid even more to him had he been willing to renege upon a commitment to his tenant, Major L—, the result being, wrote Elizabeth, that 'Major L—'s wife — who thereupon being a woman of masculine understanding (and superstructure besides) walked about Pisa, abusing Mrs Browning in good set terms — for being unladylike, and I know not what. Robert was furious and would write a note and present his compliments and deny the facts broadly.' Elizabeth does not sound as morally offended as her husband by what probably amounted to little more than neighbourly one-upmanship between rival *padrones*. The offence taken by the wife of Major L—, possibly more serious, is described with some amused relish to her sisters while Elizabeth washes her own hands clean of the matter, faintly protesting her personal unfamiliarity with anything so businesslike as 'taking houses'. Robert, however, clearly felt his honour impugned and his instinct was to clear the good name and assert the good repute of the Brownings among those who might be prompted to consider and discuss it unfavourably on the word and hearsay of Mrs L—.

The Brownings recognized that they had been 'cheated in weight and measures, besides the price of every single thing; and we have been paying twice as much as we should have paid'. Never mind that Italy was wonderfully cheap compared with England: 'We hear now,' wrote Elizabeth, 'that, for two hundred and fifty pounds a year' — which was just about fifty pounds less than their income — 'we might and ought to live in excellent apartments, and keep our own carriage and two horses; and a man servant to boot: and we see how this might be done easily. At Florence too the cheapness is wonderful — only one must understand a little. Wilson opens her eyes at the system of iniquity worked out in such detail, minute by minute.' Money was a matter of deep concern. Elizabeth, if not frivolous about money, was less conscientious than her husband about minor expenses and paying bills on time. She had borrowed £70 from Minnie, the Wimpole Street housekeeper, and as much again from Arabel. These debts troubled Robert's conscience so much that they were promptly repaid.

His punctiliousness about ready settlement of his debts, even the most minor — and his caution, bordering on parsimony in small matters — would have gladdened the heart of Mrs Jameson, who had despaired of Robert's practicality. She had indeed noted, with pleasure, what Elizabeth described as 'our miraculous prudence and economy'. Elizabeth laughed at it, but Robert was as grave about money as a bank clerk balancing the books to the penny. She remarked, later, that 'There never was any one who looked round a corner with a more imaginative obliquity, when the idea of money difficulty is suggested in any form, than Robert does. It is we who remind our creditors of their claims on us instead of its being the other way.' Embarrassment — or the prospect of it, at any rate — did not greatly trouble Elizabeth. When a remittance from Rothschilds bank did not arrive precisely on the due date in the summer of 1847, Robert was alarmed and began to imagine some train of inevitable calamitous consequences. Bohemianism, at least in its *me ne frego* attitude towards the weighty matter of money, did not become Robert, who took his domestic duties and responsibilities seriously.

'Oh what a fuss we had to be sure,' wrote Elizabeth to her sisters. 'Because if something happened, and something followed, and something else didn't follow, why we should be "embarrassed" — how dreadful to be sure! I asked him to put my sofa pillow right, and give me the second volume of Dumas' last novel. He declared that my insouciance was by no means laudable, that I wanted someone to take care of me — and that I would ask for a second volume just in the same tone of voice if beginning a course of starvation, and didn't know where to get bread. I answered that the book was amusing and it might be so — but that as at present I didn't feel even hungry and believed that there was every prospect of dining at three o'clock, I could not see any necessity of working myself into a state of frenzy. Of course the letter came next day and justified all my impertinence.' Fate, in Elizabeth's view, could not harm her if she dined that day.

Though she might abominate 'fuss' about money, though she might wriggle and be pert about the reliability of income, and disclaim any *petit bourgeois* feelings of embarrassment about money owed or owing, it was a matter that required to be put on a sound footing. John Kenyon, in London, had taken it in hand so far as to experience some bad moments in discussion with Mr Barrett, and Elizabeth was properly appreciative. Her husband, being considered a ruthless fortune hunter by the Barrett men, could hardly put himself forward as the man to secure her capital and income; her brothers, for the time being prejudiced against their sister and her marriage, could not be expected to intercede with their father and act with best feeling in her interest; it would have been insensitive, perhaps, to instruct a lawyer or other man of business to deal with Mr Barrett. So the matter fell to Kenyon, who put himself forward as intermediary.

In her letter of 31 March to her sisters, Elizabeth wrote: 'We must see Mr Kenyon if possible — that dearest, best friend to us! When I talk of his being kind, the word seems to mock itself for being so miserably inadequate. A good deal lately while I have been lying here, I have thought of him and of the noble generous goodness which he has exercised towards me and mine, in a measure uncalled for, unsolicited, unexpected. Sympathy was all we asked him for, or thought of receiving, and he gave us head and heart and both warm hands, and thrust himself into most unpleasant positions for a man of his delicacy, rather than lose sight of an interest of mine by one moment's shrinking. Oh, I have been thinking it all over — and do you know, Henrietta, I did not even encourage his kindness when it showed itself in this form. I hate so these money-questions, though relating to my own income. But dear, admirable Mr Kenyon was stopped by nothing. I cannot tell you, you cannot be aware, of the full extent of his goodness and excellence: but I measure it at its height and depth, and am sensible to it with an increasing gratitude.'

Kenyon, besides securing Elizabeth's income, substantially added to it three years later by allowing her and Robert a pension of £100 a year, paid at the rate of £50 every six months, from his own pocket. The only point on which he had failed was to reconcile Mr Barrett to Elizabeth's marriage. Mr Barrett, reportedly, had no profound objection to Robert Browning. His wrath was all for his daughter: she had married when he had preferred that Elizabeth 'should have been thinking of another world'. The world she had chosen effectively excluded her not only from the world to come but — more immediately — from her father's.

Kenyon's gift, when it was offered and accepted, was a substantial sum. Though it did not make the Brownings rich, and often the payments were not made promptly, it greatly eased their financial position and allowed them to live modestly. Nevertheless, despite Elizabeth's irreverence about Dumas taking precedence over dinner, the general question of money was a constant in their new life, and Robert took particular care that they should live within their means. Budgeting was a matter of real, day-to-day concern, to the point that even their local library subscription was reckoned a luxury. Elizabeth recklessly pressed for a piano. Mrs Jameson had admired Robert's playing as 'full of science and feeling' and Elizabeth talked long and hard about her own love of music. But she argued in vain: Robert, consulting his weekly account book, scrupulously kept and from which bills were made up and paid weekly, reprobated such 'a foolish expense' and would not hear of a piano in Pisa, though he relented later in Florence.

On 12 March, Elizabeth suffered a miscarriage. She had not been aware of her pregnancy at all, much less that she was five months advanced into it: but so she was informed by Dr Cook, who attended her and who said that all might have been well had he known in time, six weeks earlier, when she had first begun to suffer regular 'sudden violent pains which came on in the night, relieved by friction and a few spoonfulls of brandy, and going off as suddenly as they came'. Wilson had herself suffered acute abdominal pains in late January and been treated by Dr Cook, called in by Robert, despite her reluctance to see a doctor. She had been dosing herself with pills and potions for what she supposed to be bilious disorders, and finally collapsed. Her illness had disturbed Elizabeth, who wrote to Miss Mitford on or about 8 February: 'For myself, the brightness round me has had a cloud on it lately by an illness of poor Wilson's . . . She would not go to Dr Cook till I was terrified one night, while she was undressing me, by her sinking down on the sofa in a shivering fit. Oh, so frightened I was, and Robert ran out for a physician; and I could have shivered too, with the fright. But she is convalescent now, thank God!'

During Wilson's convalescence, from what had been diagnosed as an inflammation of the stomach brought on by the effects of seasickness and aggravated by the unfamiliar spicy foods she had been eating in Italy — all that cayenne pepper, perhaps — Elizabeth had learned how to nurse her maid, mostly through Wilson's example of nursing Elizabeth herself. This was a novelty after forty years of never having had to give a thought to how to look after herself: as she wrote to Miss Mitford, she had 'learnt how it is possible (in certain conditions of the human frame) to comb out and twist one's own hair, and lace one's very own stays, and cause hooks and eyes to meet behind one's very own back, besides making toast and water for Wilson'. When Elizabeth, too, began to suffer acute pains, Wilson knew that they were not like her own. With some native wit lacking in her employer, she began to suspect pregnancy and, though Elizabeth had moderated her intake of morphine, became concerned that the drug might lead to a miscarriage. The pains did not abate, and Wilson finally plucked up courage to warn Robert of her suspicions.

Robert was aghast: he insisted that Dr Cook be called in. Elizabeth refused to see him: 'I was frightened out of my wits,' she confessed, 'by the suggestion about the morphine, and out of my wit about the entreaty about Dr Cook.' In any case, to avoid such fuss, she was unwilling to consider her present pains as unusual — she had, after all, been accustomed to discomfort for years. These present symptoms could not be significantly different. She suggested writing to — indeed, did write to — her London physician, Mr Jago, to put her case as a hypothesis for his opinion, before recognizing the absurdity of such a stratagem. Robert insistently pressed for Dr Cook: Elizabeth persistently put him off. The pains abated, and in the hiatus of the next few days, the calm before the storm, there was an uncomfortable stand-off. When Elizabeth again felt 'unwell', she allowed Dr Cook to be sent for. 'He came . . . declares he found the room at seventy, a scandalous fire, a wrong posture, and my pulse very irritable: laid me down on the sofa — commanded cold tea.' The pains returned the next day, much worse, but Elizabeth bore them stoically: 'I have had worse pain, I assure.' But the day after, she miscarried.

Elizabeth survived what Mrs Martin, writing to her from Devonshire, tactfully referred to as the 'Pisan "crisis"': indeed, she was more astonished than alarmed by it, furious at her own stupidity, irritated by her own *naïveté* — 'deepest innocence of ignorance' — in which she had mistaken the signs and symptoms of pregnancy for cold and colic, which Robert had thought she had caught from Wilson. Her strength had revived in the six months since marriage to such an extent that Robert, in this emergency, was in a worse state than his wife. Dr Cook ordered Elizabeth to remain in 'one position in bed' for three days, during which she was 'not suffered to move'. He could treat the wife, but there was nothing physic could do for the husband, who, when finally admitted to Elizabeth's room, 'threw himself down on the bed in a passion of tears, sobbing like a child'.

Dr Cook suggested that the pregnancy might have been more beneficial than not, in respect of Elizabeth's general health, and indeed she herself felt that the experience had greatly relieved her chest. She felt better, even hopeful and confident for the future, but Robert's state was pitiful. He was filled with the worst misgivings, with a sense that 'We are rebellious children, and He leads us where He can best teach us.' This awed, if commendable, sense of the Almighty and His inscrutable teachings was less consoling than it might have been when Robert began to consider the number and variety of dangers into which He might lead his children before their lessons had been thoroughly learned. Robert took more heed of these than Dr Cook's brisk assurances that all was well. To the wonder of the doctor and Wilson — 'I never saw a man like Mr Browning in my life,' said Wilson, and Dr Cook made a remark to the same effect — he hardly left Elizabeth's side for six days, neglecting to eat or sleep, tenderly rubbing away her pains, talking with her, reading to her.

On 31 March, she was able to walk, 'all dressed and ringleted', from one room to another. Passing a looking-glass, Elizabeth saw herself 'a little blanched, but otherwise rather improved than not!!' Both her own and Robert's spirits had revived, and they were talking again about going to Florence for a few weeks before resorting to Bagni di Lucca, recommended by Dr Cook as cooler in summer months than the city. 'When I am once able to get out in the carriage (and I dare say I shall, by the beginning of next week at any rate) there will be no bounds to the strength I shall gain, and, as it is, we have the window open. The air seems to float its balmy softness into you. Oh, such air! Observe, that if I am weak again (I think I hear someone saying — "There! Ba's weak again, you see") observe, it's quite a different thing from the prostration arising from disease ... the strength returns quite fast, hour by hour.' Robert was just as determined that Elizabeth should be well: his confidence matched and fed her own. His principal concern was for his wife — he could bear a miscarriage as well as she. In this case, to judge by his attitude in future cases, his care was all for Elizabeth. The loss of a putative child was nothing compared to the life of the beloved mother.

During the nights after the miscarriage, Wilson had slept on a sofa in Elizabeth's room, reminding Elizabeth of how Arabel had sometimes slept on the sofa in her room in Wimpole Street. Memories of her life in London, of family and friends still dear to her, filled her mind. At four every morning, the bells of Pisa pealed out and their rhythms, she wrote, rang her dreams apart. The bell-founders of Pisa had a well-merited reputation for fine work: 'let no one say as much for the bell-ringers,' commented Elizabeth drily. They were not only incompetent, their efforts were, when all the bells of all the churches in the city were shaken and clashed together, indescribably discordant. The *Pasquareccia* particularly affected her: it was the fourth and best-toned of seven bells which, Murray's *Handbook to Northern Italy* informed readers, pealed from the summit of the Leaning Tower. It was tolled on the occasion of criminals being taken to execution, and Elizabeth described it to Mr Boyd as sounding with 'a profound note in it, which may well have thrilled horror to the criminal's heart'. Its tone 'dropt into the deep of night like a thought of death. Often have I said "Oh how ghastly," and then turned on my pillow and then dreamed a bad dream.'

The bell perhaps reminded her of the accusations of 'criminality' levelled at herself and her husband by the Barretts of Wimpole Street. She had written regularly to her sisters, with whom relations had been quickly put on a sure, affectionate footing and on whom she relied for news of the household — for there was no news to be had from her brothers, who had condemned not only Elizabeth for deceit but her sisters, too, for connivance in deceit. They were all blameworthy enough, in the view of the Barrett men; but far and above the women's duplicity and foolishness stood the infamous deceit of Robert Browning himself. The Barrett brothers were hotly indignant at what amounted, in their estimation, to criminality: Robert had no money of his own, they reasoned, and so he had calculatedly married it. Since George had steadfastly maintained that no one should marry on less than an income of £2,000 a year, it was hardly logical to complain that Robert had married for a tenth of that. If anything, according to George's reasoning and assessment of his brother-in-law's cunning character, that sacrifice of a better prospect elsewhere might have stood rather in favour of Robert's *bona fides* than not and assured him of Robert's best intentions. George relented early in 1847, and the other brothers mostly came round thereafter.

If the Barrett brothers' shock and sharp condemnation of treachery was a rumble of thunder that shook the domestic scene in London and reverberated in Elizabeth's ears in Pisa, the fury of the father rocked the domestic firmament in Wimpole Street like the wrath of a minor deity. It was felt by everyone who remained after Elizabeth had gone. Those of the family who were supposed, unjustly, to have known of Elizabeth's flight, far less colluded in it, were punished: Arabel was given a smaller bedroom and an uncomfortable bed; Henrietta, to judge by family hearsay, had a book thrown at her by her father from the top of the stairs for her trouble, and either it was well enough aimed to hit her and knock her down or she slipped, dodging it, and fell downstairs. Hurricane gusts of rage followed, one after the other, until Mr Barrett subsided and refused to hear any mention, then or ever again, of Elizabeth's name. She, on the contrary, could never hear enough of him.

'Do write to me soon,' begged Elizabeth of Henrietta, 'and let me know whether my darling Arabel has her room yet, and whether Papa is kinder to her.' The improbable reply was that Papa was 'in high spirits and having people to dine with him every day'. This, though perhaps welcome on one level, was possibly even more unsettling on every other. As much to soothe her own spirit, it may be assumed, as perhaps to mitigate the temper of the tyrant, Elizabeth wrote frequently to her father, but received never a word of reply because he never read a word of what she had to say in defence of her behaviour and her attempts to reconcile him to her marriage and flight.

To Mr Boyd, on 21 December 1846, Elizabeth wrote to ask whether Arabel visited him 'properly, — that is frequently?' Arabel, it occurred to Elizabeth, might be in need of some consolation and support herself, some resort happier than the conditions in the Wimpole Street house: 'It is a grief to me that she should be treated coldly on my account, — and the injustice is rampant, as she knew nothing, you know, of the marriage. For myself, I am wounded, — yet feel myself justified, both by the hardness there, and the tenderness here. Completely spoilt and happy, I may write myself down. Now, everything I ever said to you of my husband, seems cold and inadequate! He is my compensation for the bitterness of life, as God knows and you knew.'

In the immediate dispiriting circumstances of family hostility, as much as in consideration of the beneficial effects of the Italian climate on her health, Elizabeth wrote at the end of March to say, 'you must see, dearest Henrietta and Arabel, how foolish and imprudent it would be for us to go to England this summer. There is the expense, for one thing, of going and returning: for you would not like me to run the hazard of a winter in England.' On 17 April the Brownings set out for Florence, much regretted by their *padrone*, who had taken a careful interest in Elizabeth's state of health and 'hoped fondly to the last that I might have a relapse, so as not to be able to go'. This sincere and honest expression of concern (though mostly self-concern) sped them on their way, 'not unconsolable perhaps for having got away. Robert declares that, if we had staid on there much longer, we should have fallen fixed into barbaric habits, and that on returning to civilized life we should with difficulty have extricated ourselves and been apt to cry out unawares, "Lady Londonderry, shall I give you a mug of coffee?" — or, "will you be good enough to thump with your fist on that door?" — (because at Pisa, there was not a bell in our rooms, and Wilson was summoned by a knock — it was our only way.)'

The route the Brownings finally chose had evidently been the cause of prolonged consultations and earnest discussions. A letter of 1 April from Robert to Mrs Jameson details, exhaustively, their 'travelling-projects'. He wrote: 'Had the weather permitted, we might have made the circle of Sienna, Colle and Volterra, and returned here, to leave again, by Prato and Pistoja [Pistoia] for Florence. In that case, we should have seen enough of Tuscany for the present, and be ready for Bologna and the north.' Elizabeth's illness prevented them from venturing so much, 'and we now mean to return from Florence, when the heats oblige us, to the Baths of Lucca as a safe place, — and as our road will be via Pistoja then will be time for that visit, and now (on thought) for Volterra and Sienna, as we go to Florence . . .' The letter continues with all the interest of a consultation with a booking clerk at a Thomas Cook office, attempting to coincide the plans of the Brownings with Mrs Jameson's own itinerary, to plot their courses so as to meet at various cities on various dates. It is a remarkable — if tedious — document, evidencing Robert's pedantic attention to the details of their journey and, very likely, by implication, his care and solicitude on the road itself once everyone was launched on the trip. The upshot was that the Brownings would arrive at Florence six days before Mrs Jameson.

Robert's principal care was, naturally, for Elizabeth's health — though Elizabeth herself was as liable to be insouciant about travel and going out as she was about money: nevertheless, writing to her sisters from Florence in April, she acknowledged that 'absolute rest does such infinite good, it is worth persisting in through every sort of temptation. And then Robert says "Don't be drawn into going out, Ba, I beseech you" — and it seems better to wait now in order to enjoy perfectly hereafter and escape the risk of adding more painful anxiety to what he has already endured about me.' Rather for the sake of her husband's anxiety — 'he is so dreadfully nervous when I am in the least unwell' — than for her own, she acquiesced: even if 'Otherwise, and if I thought only of myself . . . I should not mind being thrown back a week or two for the sake of a degree of delightful imprudence.'

The coach journey from Pisa to Florence had been tiring — perhaps imprudent — enough, but there was no help for it: 'The coupé we took in the diligence did very well, but was by no means equal to a coupé in a French diligence, and though I lay half the time, or more, across Robert's knees, the shaking made itself felt, and we regretted the private carriage which was nearly engaged when the Diligence people seized on us. Still it did very well, and the country with vine-festooned plains and breaks of valley and hill — ridges of mountain and sweeps of river — was far more beautiful than I expected between Pisa and Florence. As to Florence, I could see it only in our rapid passage to our hotel, across one of the bridges of our old dear yellow Arno; and when Robert had carried me into the Hotel du Nord and laid me down on the sofa, I could only wait for coffee and dream of being in the city of the Medici.'

The next day Robert went looking for an apartment. Better informed by now, as he thought, about Italian commercial attitudes, he took rooms in the via delle Belle Donne, a street running off the Piazza Santa Novella, for two months. Though short term, and not the best address in town, it was a better deal than he had negotiated at Pisa: the rent amounted to four pounds a month — a little less than the £1 6s 9d a week they had paid in the Collegio Ferdinando — and included 'every thing'. Elizabeth listed the elegant advantages to her sisters: 'linen, plate, china, etc., and this time, every thing is in order. We have real cups instead of the famous mugs of Pisa, and a complement of spoons and knives and forks, — nay we have decanters and champagne glasses! We have come to the remote extreme of civilization. As Wilson says succinctly, "it is something like!"'

The longed-for piano — a grand one, a German one, at a rental of some ten shillings a month (including the hire of music) — was installed, and Elizabeth pleasurably resumed her habits of lolling on a spring sofa ('the most delightful of possible sofas') and in a spring chair. Dinners, sent up at three o'clock from the nearby trattoria, cost 2s 8d a day, and included 'soup and three dishes, besides vegetables and pudding or tart. Every thing hot and well cooked, and there are three of us.' Wilson, very much the third party, 'dines after us, and something is always left for supper'. One of their dinners, on 30 April, consisted of 'Vermicelli soup — turkey — (not a whole turkey, but the third of one at least) — Fish (sturgeon) — stewed beef (done something like fricandeau), mashed potatoes — cheese cakes.' They took each day what they were sent, rather than ordering specifically. Wine was a separate matter: 'Robert pays three pence or four pence a bottle for what he drinks. My port, he will never touch, let me ask him ever so.'

These domestic dispositions having been made to their satisfaction, Mrs Jameson, with Gerardine (known familiarly as Geddie), arrived on 23 April, the Friday after their arrival and a day earlier than expected; but the good, excitable woman could not have let the date — the anniversary of Shakespeare's birthday — pass without doing it the due honours in the company of her 'two poets'. The Brownings, passing a quiet evening at home, were celebrating the occasion in their own way — assuming they had even remembered it. Elizabeth, recumbent on her spring sofa, and Robert at the piano were surprised to be interrupted: 'a voice said "upon my word here's domestic harmony!" and lo! Mrs Jameson stood in the room!' The Brownings jumped up to embrace her. She had brought a bottle of wine from Arezzo, and news from Rome. 'So we had coffee and supper together for the travellers,' reported Elizabeth, 'and a very joyous evening on all sides; and she cried out as usual "Oh, that inexhaustible man!" meaning Robert, — to which I rejoined, "and think of the stream running just the same for these six months past, ever since we parted!"'

Mrs Jameson and Gerardine stayed in Florence for a week, installed in a bedroom in the house and dining with the Brownings. This was a novelty: 'Think of our doing hospitality for a week!' Although the Brownings were now able to dine like civilized beings, with all the proto-Podsnappery of proper cutlery, crockery, napery, and glassware, quite in the London manner of Wimpole Street, Elizabeth had become used to the Italian informality of their housekeeping. She presided prettily over her table, and perhaps experienced a stab at her heart as a hostess when Robert mismanaged the carving; but this was their first attempt at entertaining and Mrs Jameson was good-natured to the point of indulgence. 'Observe,' Elizabeth wrote to her sisters, 'the difference of the possibilities of social life here and in England — No fuss, no need of arrangement or money.' Only a little money, that is: a dinner for five cost 4s 6d from the trattoria, and they were 'served excellently — green peas, asparagus — everything'. When they should come to England to visit Henrietta, they would expect only English mutton chops and port wine, she commented smugly, emphasizing too that such a dismal, prosaic English dinner would cost more.[2]

Over dinner, they discussed art, politics, and matrimonial matters — primarily the interesting question of the Brownings themselves. At home and abroad there was a general suspicion, amounting to a charge, that Mrs Jameson had personally arranged the marriage. Coincidence did not seem likely — stretched, indeed, credulity — that she could have met the Brownings in Paris and travelled with them to Pisa without pre-arrangement. Mrs Jameson told them that 'people write to her who never can be persuaded, but that she managed the whole.' Those who censoriously waved the finger would exclaim, 'Oh, it is discreet of you to deny it.' Those who roguishly wagged their bonnets at her, would cry, 'Of course you would deny it!' — adding, guilefully, 'of course you need not to me. You would never shake my conviction.'

Mrs Jameson, as a 'high-minded, true, generous woman', had a ready and honest answer to such calumnies: 'I tell you the truth. If I had had the least thing to do with it I should have considered it a great honour. But I knew nothing, suspected nothing.' 'To which,' wrote Elizabeth to Arabel and Henrietta, 'people shake their heads over writing paper of various sizes', not being as familiar as she and Robert were with Mrs Jameson's high-mindedness, generosity and devotion to truth. She was delighted to see the interesting couple still loving and in good spirits: 'I am sure she looked on in utter astonishment, while Robert seized on me to place me on the sofa.' But Robert was forever snatching up his wife to carry her about from doorway to sofa, upstairs and downstairs, from carriage to chair. This, and other expressions of devout care for his wife, combined with Robert's affable volubility and fine sensibilities, impressed Mrs Jameson mightily. 'She told me before she went away, "that every hour of her intercourse with him, from first to last, had raised him higher in her estimation and her affection." Dear Mrs Jameson!' wrote Elizabeth, recommending her sisters to treat this kind partisan gently when she returned to London for publication of her work, a book on Roman art, in July or August.

Meanwhile, Mrs Jameson and Gerardine usefully employed their time in Florence: they were busily out and about from early morning, assimilating and assessing great works of Italian art, leaving Elizabeth, much to her annoyance, lolling on her spring sofa, under Robert's absolute interdict — which was what his earnest concern amounted to — about going sightseeing with the Jamesons. Despite Dr Cook's assurance that she was perfectly capable of activity, and the almost irresistible lure of the Venus de Medici only two or three streets away, Elizabeth preferred to be just to Robert; she chose to run no risks and bided her time, which was no more than the week of Mrs Jameson's visit. When she and Gerardine had gone, on their way to London to confound sceptics with the news that the Browning marriage was proving an unqualified success, Robert hired a carriage to take his wife on a tour of the city.

The visions that met Elizabeth's eyes enraptured her: 'Florence,' she wrote on 26 May in her last letter to Mr Boyd before his death, 'is beautiful, as I have said before, and must say again and again, most beautiful.' The wonder of it all prompted her to a lengthy description, rich in detail, for the blind scholar: 'I have seen the Venus — I have seen the divine Raphaels — I have stood by Michael Angelo's tomb in Santa Croce — I have looked at the wonderful Duomo! This cathedral!! After all, the elaborate grace of the Pisan cathedral is one thing, and the massive grandeur of this of Florence is another and better thing — it struck me with a sense of the sublime in architecture. At Pisa we say, "How beautiful," — here we say nothing — it is enough if we can breathe.' Breathlessly, she urged him, 'Tell me everything you want to know — I shall like to answer a thousand questions.'

A thousand questions begging for answers, we may take it, crowded in her own mind. As much as the city's treasury of art, the city itself and its river enchanted her: the Arno, apparently now less yellow than on Elizabeth's arrival, 'rushes through the midst of its palaces like a crystal arrow; and it is hard to tell, when you see it all by the clear sunset, whether those churches and houses and windows and bridges and people walking, — in the water or out of the water, — are the real walls and windows and bridges and people and churches. The only difference is that, down below, there is a double movement, — the movement of the stream besides the movement of life.'

Life for the Brownings took on a brisker pace in Florence than in Pisa. They were still perfectly self-sufficient for company, but no longer dreaded or discouraged the intrusion of visitors. It was by now clear to themselves, clear to Mrs Jameson, who would in turn make it clear to everyone else, that they should — as Elizabeth had said — 'think of the stream running just the same for these six months past'. The marriage was as substantial, the Brownings were as firm in their foundations, as any church and house and bridge and wall reflected in the Arno — sceptics could not make the actuality disappear by throwing stones at its reflection in the public eye and rippling it away: the stream and the marriage flowed on just the same, six months and more later, as at the beginning.

The rooms they had taken for three months in the via delle Belle Donne, in the heart of the city, soon became insupportable on account of the heat, which, beginning to rise in May, reached unbearable indoor temperatures that, in the absence of any breath of cooling wind, mounted to the high 70s Fahrenheit. After their 3 o'clock dinner, Robert wheeled a great chair into his shadowed dressing-room, sat his wife down in it, bathed her forehead and her hands with eau-de-Cologne, and fanned her devotedly. It was a little less torrid in the shadows of the streets in the late afternoons:

'Now, Ba, do you want to be cool?'

'Yes, very particularly.'

'Then take my arm and come down stairs: there's quite a bath of cool air at the bottom of the house.'

'Oh — and for you to carry me up again! No, no, it isn't worth while.'

'But it *is* worth while, and I shall like to carry you — Now come, dear! take courage and come.'[3]

In the street, Elizabeth found the activity and the coolness had 'excited' her 'into an adventurous humour'. They walked along Trotto del asino, which Robert, who sometimes had a literal, heavily punning humour, liked to call Trot the Jackass Street. Out in the air, she felt stronger and could sometimes walk as far as the nearby Piazza Santa Novella and the Baptistery where they, like many others, enjoyed the *passeggiata* of elegant Florentines, most of whom had things to discuss and gossip about other than the poetry of Dante which the Brownings liked to debate between themselves.

Art, architecture, and fashion also occupied their attention. The Duomo was rapturously described by Elizabeth to Henrietta as 'this cathedral! so grand it is, with its pile of tessellated Domes — the massiveness glorified with various marbles — the porphyry crossed with the dim green serpentine — the white and black heightening and deepening one another. Think of a mountainous marble Dome, veined with inlaid marbles — marble running through marble: like a mountain for size, like a mosaic for curious art — rivers of colour inter-flowing, but all dimly.' The Brownings liked the deep romance of strong and sombre colours: they were delighted when a bolt of cloth, sent by Henrietta from London to be made up by Wilson into a fashionable dress for Elizabeth, turned out to be a becoming dark green.

Art, for Robert and Elizabeth, was a sublimely serious business. Neither were they disposed to giddiness in the matter of bonnets: Elizabeth, in her sisterly chatterbox manner, reported to Henrietta in this same letter of 16 May 1847 that she had ordered another drawn white crape bonnet, pretty and practical in the dusty atmosphere of Florence, 'washable like a pockethandkerchief' [*sic*] and cheap 'at the expense of a few pennies — (Seven pence a cap!)', rather than the extravagant 'fancy straw (Tuscan) worn a good deal here' which Robert objected to — though on what grounds (cost, utility, or fanciness) Elizabeth did not say. Robert also disliked the vapidity of pale colours, 'those fainting-away blues and pinks and lilacs and greens'; so his taste plainly did not run to the frivolous. Elizabeth indeed noted to Henrietta that Robert 'hates ribbons and prefers everything as simple and quiet as possible'. She fell in with his preferences, even to the extent of wearing her hair in a Grecian plait at her neck and changing her gloves without demur when he pointed out to her that they were disgracefully grubby and had a hole in them besides.

The heat became almost intolerable as May melted into June and July. The Brownings discussed alternatives, including the Tirol, but settled finally — at Elizabeth's insistence — on a trip to a more local, more easily accessible altitude, to the sublime wilderness, the trackless forests of rocky Vallombrosa, with the intention of lodging for two months at a Benedictine monastery there with the noble monks, all of whom, Elizabeth assured Henrietta, came from the best aristocratic families of Italy. There was a difficulty, aside from any consideration of expense: the noble but misogynistic monks would willingly consent to lodge Robert, but on no account would they admit women. 'They . . . will leave Wilson and me on the outside with other unclean beasts.' The Browning expedition set off, first by carriage and then transferred to a more antique form of transport: Robert rode on horseback, while Wilson and Elizabeth and the luggage bumped along on a sledge ('i.e. an old hamper, a basket wine-hamper — without a wheel') drawn by white bullocks, two of them, says Elizabeth in one account, four in another.

Equipped with a letter from the Archbishop of Florence to the abbot granting Elizabeth and Wilson permission to stay, Robert was confident of his ability to negotiate an accommodation with the abbot. But the abbot was adamant: the two women, a stench in the abbot's nostrils, were turned out of the guest lodgings after only a few days to return to Florence, there to suffer the summer heat like St Lawrence on his gridiron. Elizabeth complained that, besides all other humiliations, she had been half-starved — the food had been inadequate and virtually uneatable anyhow — and she took her petty, possibly petulant, revenge by putting her foot inside the door of the monastery and stamping it on the ground, thereby — she hoped — profaning it forever. But there had been compensations: Elizabeth had been in 'an ecstasy of admiration at the sublimity of the scenery'. She had been exhilarated by the super-naturally silent woods of Vallombrosa, the sight of soaring eagles, and by surviving the wild thrill of being pulled up precipitous, roadless mountains at four o'clock in the morning. By the time they returned to the city, she was tired as much by emotion as by exertion. She stayed at home while Robert went out doggedly into the furnace of the streets to look for another, cooler set of rooms.

He came across a suite of six rooms and a kitchen at a good address:

the *piano nobile* of the Casa Guidi, across the river in Oltrarno, close to the point at which the via Romana and the via Maggio terminate in the piazzetta S. Felice. The apartment, not overlooked by any other windows, enjoyed a view of the Palazzo Pitti, then inhabited by the Grand Duke Leopoldo II, with whom, Elizabeth proudly declared, she would not exchange residences. The entire barracks-like façade of the Pitti Palace dominated the parade ground of the Piazza Pitti. Casa Guidi, opposite the grey wall of the church of S. Felice, is a wedge-shaped building, not notable for the charm of its external architecture. Inside, however, in the first floor apartment, all was height and space, airy on account of high, floor-length windows. There was a small stone balcony or terrace just wide enough for the Brownings to walk along arm in arm, and all thankfully cool even when the temperature outside reached 86 degrees. The furnishings, too, were generous — relics of a Russian prince: mirrors, marble console tables elaborate with carving and gilt, armchairs upholstered in striped satin.

Robert rented the rooms for two months, until October. They settled in delightedly. Elizabeth was allowed to 'sit all day in my white dressing gown without a single masculine criticism, and as we can step out of the window on a sort of balcony terrace which is quite private, and swims over with moonlight in the evenings, and as we live upon water-melons and iced water and figs and all manner of fruit, we bear the heat with an angelic patience.' Elizabeth never managed to like figs, neither their look nor their taste, but she was generously, if naïvely, pleased that the Italian people should have such a paradisal diet of fruit for its cheapness as much as for the benefit of their health. When the lease of the Casa Guidi apartment ran out, their landlord demanded a higher rent. Robert, overconfident about his ability to beat down the price, mishandled the haggling and, for his sticking over two *scudi*, a matter of less than ten shillings, found himself obliged to remove his wife, Wilson, and their belongings to rooms in via Maggio, where they stayed some ten days until Elizabeth complained of the cold and its effect on her health; whereupon they returned to the Piazza Pitti, to small, sunnier, furnished rooms — a 'little baby-house' Elizabeth called it — for six months.

Their original intention had been to move from Florence, perhaps to Rome for the winter, but Elizabeth had become pregnant again. She miscarried in the second month, early in March 1848, her physician, Dr Harding, citing port wine as a cause and Robert identifying excessive letter-writing as another. Despite the reassuring fact that Elizabeth recovered her health quickly enough, and her general condition was no less robust than it had become during their time in Italy, the Brownings abandoned any idea of leaving Florence, which in any case they increasingly liked for its beauty and, far from incidentally — a constant motive indeed — for the relative cheapness of its luxuries when compared to Rome. As soon as Elizabeth could bear to move outdoors, they drove out in a carriage, drawn by two horses and attended by a coachman, to the fashionable open parks of the Cascine, bordering the Arno, where Elizabeth was delighted to see 'the elms as green as ever they mean to be, and the grass like emeralds, and the pheasants all alive and flying'.

In April 1848, their former landlord being willing to take them back (he had in fact been disappointed to lose them at all), they were able to secure the first-floor apartment in Casa Guidi again — the former suite of the last Count, remarked Elizabeth. What was now Casa Guidi had originally belonged to the Ridolfis. Part of the building had been bought from them in 1618 by Count Camillo Guidi, secretary of state to the Medicis; the adjoining building was acquired in 1650, and the two houses were combined in the later eighteenth century. The *piano nobile* was divided into two apartments in the 1840s. The arms of the last Guidi were in *scagliola* (a design in glued gypsum with a polished surface of coloured stones or marble dust intended to resemble marble) on the floor of Elizabeth's bedroom.

The Brownings had this time taken the rooms unfurnished. They didn't greatly repine the loss of the elaborate furniture — they felt it 'rather to suit our predecessor the Russian prince than ourselves' — though this left the question of replacing it. Fortunately, antique furniture was cheap and in plentiful supply due to the political situation, which had somewhat cleared the city of faint-hearted English expatriates eager to sell up and be gone in fear of imminent violent revolution. But rich, otherwise reasonable people are forever running like chickens before republican revolution overwhelms their certainties and political uncertainty disturbs their comfort. They are willing to cut their losses and take to their expensive heels unimpeded by anything but their jewels. In a letter to Henrietta of 7 March–1 April 1848, Elizabeth wrote scornfully and reassuringly that 'Many of the English are flying from Florence — tranquil as Florence is, and absurd as all fear is.'

In such circumstances, the intrepid Brownings decided in April 1848 to keep on the Casa Guidi apartment at a rent of twenty-five guineas a year (less by half than the guinea a week and more they had paid for the rooms furnished) and to fit it out in a buyer's market. Robert had grandiose tastes, despite their declared deprecation of the Russian prince's ornate furniture. To Henrietta, in letters of April and June 1848, Elizabeth declared that 'Sometimes, in joke, I call him an aristocrat — I cry out "*à bas les aristocrats*" — because he really cares a great deal about external things — perhaps it is an artist's sense of grace that he has, only that I choose to make fun of it.' Robert did certainly care about maintaining a *bella figura*: it spoke of decency, respect (for the self as much as for others), a seriousness in the matters of everyday life, a respectable and conscientious attitude towards his responsibilities. The fact that a good appearance pleased the senses was perhaps another matter, not altogether subsidiary. His wife was apparently a little more bohemian. Just as she could be more carefree about money, so she could care less than her husband about wearing a pair of grubby gloves. 'For instance,' she wrote to Henrietta, 'about houses, and furniture, and horses and carriages, he is far more particular than I ever was or can be. Then I laugh — and then he says it is for my sake. So it may be, and is, ungrateful that I am — only that he certainly looks to the things minutely, — he has a feeling about them, not altogether Spartan.'

Furnishings, for all Robert's particularity, were acquired more haphazardly than perhaps they intended. They discovered, after an inventory, that they 'had eight sofas, and only six chests of drawers'. Robert had taken a fancy to drawers, Elizabeth to sprung sofas. Robert conceived the idea that Elizabeth's bed should be of ducal proportions and importance — all gilding, curtains and carving. 'We have been extravagant enough to place a glass above the drawing room fire — not very large, but with the most beautiful carved gilt frame I ever saw in my life. Two cupids hold lights at the lower part. It belonged to the French Chargé d'affaires — from whom we have bought many other things. For our drawing room chairs — pure antique — Gothic, rather, black, carved wood.' Later there was a fuss about curtains, of white muslin, for the bed and the windows. Elizabeth's bedroom was finally and lavishly furnished with rare and beautiful chests of drawers, walnut and ebony, inlaid with ivory and embellished with gilt. From a convent, Robert acquired a great bookcase adorned with carved angels and demons to hold their library, which could now be sent for from England to fill it. Pictures would later be added — trophies brought home by Robert from foragings and ferretings in and around Florence, in dusty, improbable shops and stores. Burrowing in a corn store a mile outside Florence he discovered five paintings that were misattributed by a local dilettante in art, Mr Seymour Kirkup, as being from the hands of great, though then ‚unfashionable and underrated names of the Renaissance — Cimabue, Ghirlandaio, Giottino, and some, if not by Giotto, at least Giottesque. Whatever they might be, dealt and sold and bartered over the centuries, revolutionary in their time, they looked very fine — part of the very fabric of the Renaissance city — hanging on the walls of the Guidi, who were known to have been patrons of Masaccio.[4] These art works would later become the subject of a Browning poem, 'Old Pictures in Florence'.

The expense of time and money in moving around from one set of rooms to another had been thoroughly harassing for the Brownings, though they had managed to furnish the Casa Guidi rooms lavishly on a low budget: their costs amounted to the income, more or less, from their writings for the last two years — Elizabeth's earnings mostly, since there was little enough, if anything, coming in from sales of Robert's own published work. Throughout it all, for half a year and more of upheaval and uncertainty, Robert had kept his temper. Elizabeth, candidly admitting her own share of fault, glad of his lack of reproach, suggested that 'any other man, a little lower than the angels, would have stamped and sworn a little for the mere relief of the thing — but as to *his* being angry with *me* for any cause except not eating enough dinner, the said sun would turn the wrong way first.' Evidently, even after a year of marriage, her husband's equable temperament (at least in respect of his wife) still had the capacity to astonish her, perhaps in contrast to the more explosive tempers of her father and brothers.

Social life would have been difficult enough to establish and maintain, considering their various removals, even if they had been much inclined to seek out new friends and acquaintances. But, as Robert wrote on 29 June 1847 to Fanny Haworth, after ten weeks in the city 'We know next to nobody, — Powers the sculptor, we see every now and then, and have made a pleasant acquaintance with the Hoppners, the old friends of Byron.' Hiram Powers, an American sculptor, had been in Florence some ten years, since 1837. Within a few weeks of the Brownings' arrival in Florence he sought them out and fell into the habit of visiting them regularly for coffee and conversation. Elizabeth described him to Mrs Jameson, who evidently knew Powers' work well enough, on 7 August 1847. Her first impression, never to alter thereafter, was 'of a most charming simplicity, with those great burning eyes of his'. And later, on 1 October, she was able to tell Miss Mitford that Powers had become 'our chief friend and favourite, a most charming, simple, straightforward, genial American, as simple as the man of genius he has proved himself needs to be'. His wife was amiable, and between them they had 'heaps of children from thirteen downwards, all, except the oldest boy, Florentines'.

What Robert thought of Hiram Powers is not recorded, though it can be assumed that Powers' 'charming simplicity' was as much to his taste as to Elizabeth's, and his status as a long-standing friend of the Brownings speaks well of their mutual compatibility. Then, too, Elizabeth's recommendation of Powers as 'the man of genius' sorted very well with Powers' own estimation of himself and his art. Nathaniel Hawthorne, visiting Florence in 1858, met Powers, who talked 'very freely about his works, and is no exception to the rule that an artist is not apt to speak in a very laudatory style of a brother artist.'[5] Richard Belgrave Hoppner, lately British consul at Venice, came equipped with poetic credentials of the highest order: he had indeed known Byron, who had described him as 'a thoroughly good man'. He had also known Shelley, who had described Mrs Hoppner as 'a most agreeable and amiable lady'. She would at least have interested Robert Browning as a woman who had successfully tempted Shelley from his vegetarian habit by plying him with thick collops of roast beef.

Occasionally, friends from England passed through Florence and visited the Brownings with some welcome news of home. There were literary tourists, too, such as George Stillman Hillard, an American writer and reviewer who called to pay particular homage to Mrs Browning the poet, whose 'tremulous voice often flutters over her words like the flame of a dying candle over the wick. I have never seen a human frame which seemed so nearly a transparent veil for a celestial and immortal spirit.'[6] This was very satisfactory, perfectly poetic, though perhaps Elizabeth was merely feeling less energetic that day, and seeming a little more frail than usual. She herself felt very well. Elizabeth described Hillard, thenceforward a regular visitor, in kindly terms to Miss Mitford as 'an American critic who reviewed me in [the old] world and so came to *view* me in the new, a very intelligent man, of a good, noble spirit'.

Hillard was not the only one to notice Elizabeth's characteristic but somewhat misleading appearance of physical frailty and the gratifying luminosity of her spirit. Another new friend, Mary Boyle, a niece of Lord Cork, who was lodging with Lady Morgan in a sumptuous villa, declared that she had never seen 'a more spiritual face, or one in which the soul looked out more clearly from the windows'. As to Elizabeth's form, Mary Boyle noted it as 'so fragile as to appear an etherial covering'. On the contrary, Robert was at pains to assure Elizabeth's sisters that his wife was blooming, with colour in her rounded cheeks, a strengthened voice, and even 'her general comparative . . . shall I dare to write it . . . plumpness.' Nothing could have been better for her health and spirits than her marriage and translation from foggy London to sunny Italy. Robert believed very sincerely — and had so written in a letter to Thomas Carlyle — that their marriage had saved her life.

Their days were topped and tailed by Powers, who might call in the morning, and by Mary Boyle — 'A very vivacious little person,' wrote Elizabeth to Miss Mitford on 1 October 1847, 'with sparkling talk enough' — who liked to drop in on the Brownings at nine o'clock in the evenings to gossip, eat hot chestnuts, and drink mulled wine until midnight. By 8 December, according to a letter of that date to Miss Mitford, Elizabeth had discovered Mary Boyle to be a 'poetess by grace of certain Irish muses'. The Brownings also found her to be kind, cordial, and — greatly to her credit — able to make Robert laugh. Just as well that company came to call on the Brownings, because they were disinclined to go out and about in search of it. Or at least Robert was, despite Elizabeth's efforts to send him out to concerts or a play of Alfieri's; the most he would do was take Flush for a walk, 'yet we fill up our days with books and music (and a little writing has its share), and I wonder at the clock for galloping.'[7]

An acquaintance less transparent than Hiram Powers or Mary Boyle was the Revd Francis Sylvester Mahony, a former Irish Jesuit, otherwise known as Father Prout, the name under which he first contributed articles to *Fraser's Magazine*. He might have aspired to a cardinal's hat — he claimed — had it not been — he confessed — for his conviviality. Father Prout, witty and worldly, liked a pipe and a drink. He had taken a fancy to Robert Browning, who had first fallen in the way of this curiously wandering jobbing journalist and man of letters (and, more than likely, other less literary concerns) in London in the 1830s as a friend of Dickens and Thackeray. Thereafter, Father Prout tended to pop up like a pantomime figure, in a metaphorical puff of smoke, at interesting times in Robert Browning's life. Interesting enough for Robert to have remarked to Elizabeth in 1846 how he had first met Prout, nicknamed the Lion, 'in strange out of the way places roaring wildly'. Father Prout had even seen Robert without salutation, he had said, in various parts of Europe, and certainly Robert had seen Father Prout whenever the sight was least expected, as Elizabeth reported: 'Well — while we travelled across France, my fellow-traveller laughed a little as he told me that in crossing Poland Street with our passport, just at that crisis, he met — Father Prout.'[8]

Known to few enough now as the author of 'The Bells of Shandon', Prout had most recently been discerned standing at nine o'clock in the morning upon a rock, wrapped in a cloak and gazing out to sea as the Brownings reached the port of Livorno on their way to Pisa. 'Good heavens, there he is again!' Robert had exclaimed, '— there's Father Prout.' Elizabeth was startled by the 'extraordinary "dramatic effect"' made at that moment by Father Prout. In time, the Brownings came to feel a little haunted and daunted by this ubiquitous literary cleric. Father Prout, on his way to Rome, happened upon Robert in the street and kissed him full on the mouth — a good deal to Robert's surprise, as Elizabeth commented to Henrietta. Spontaneously helpful, enthusiastically generous, Father Prout — whose words were usually more bitter and wittily scathing than his nature — had offered to send a letter of introduction from Rome to the Grand Duke's librarian at the Pitti, 'who is said to be a learned man and will give us access to men and books here,' wrote Elizabeth to her sister. Father Prout was not above gossiping about his celebrated acquaintance: a reference to 'Robert Browning with his gifted wife' now being in Florence made the pages

Robert Browning; oil painting by Michele Gordigiani, July 1859, Florence thereafter.

The Three Roberts: Robert Browning (1749–1833) and Margaret Tittle (1754–89), grandfather and grandmother of the poet; Robert Browning (1782–1866), the poet's father, sketched in crayon by his daughter Sarianna, Paris, *c.*1860; Robert Browning the poet, sketched as a young man, in an engraving by J.C. Armytage.

Robert Browning; a portrait in water-colours, pencil and chalks by Dante Gabriel Rossetti, completed in Paris, 1855.

Clockwise: Robert's friends: William Charles Macready the actor-manager, bust by William Behnes, 1844; Alfred Domett, 1836; John Kenyon.

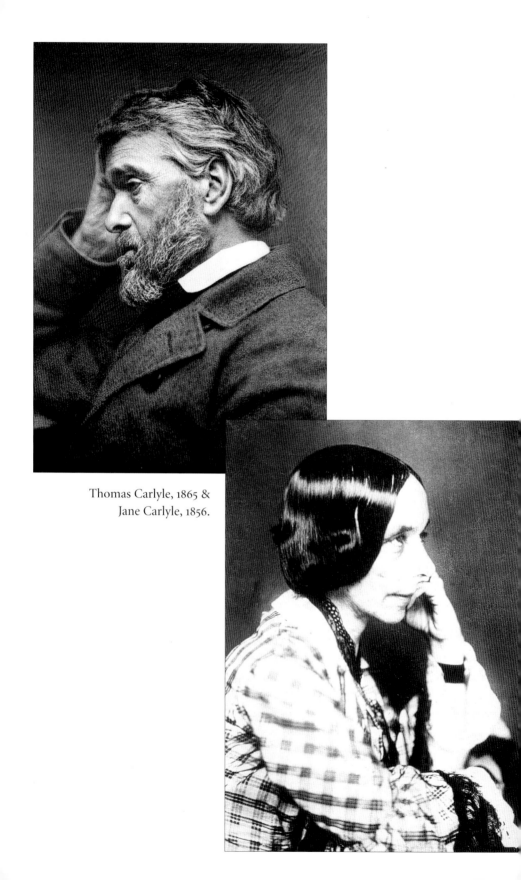

Thomas Carlyle, 1865 &
Jane Carlyle, 1856.

Flush, a golden cocker spaniel,
a gift to Elizabeth Barrett from
Mary Russell Mitford (herself
pictured right from a drawing
by F.R. Say of 1837).

50 Wimpole Street, home of
the Barrett family. The house
no longer stands.

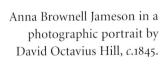

Anna Brownell Jameson in a
photographic portrait by
David Octavius Hill, *c*.1845.

Elizabeth Barrett Browning in her prime.

No.	When Married.	Name and Surname.	Age.	Condition.	Rank or Profession.	Residence at the Time of Marriage.	Father's Name and Surname.	Rank or Profession of Father.
117	12th September 1846	Robert Browning Elizabeth Barrett Moulton Barrett	of Full age	Bachelor Spinster	Gentn	Saint Paul Deptford St Marylebone	Robt Browning Edwd Barrett	Gentn Gentn

Married in the *Parish Church* according to the Rites and Ceremonies of the Established Church, *by Licence* by me, *Jno. Woods Goodhake Curate*

This Marriage was solemnized between us, *Robert Browning.* *Elizabeth Barrett Moulton Barrett* In the Presence of us, *James ....* *Elizabeth Wilson*

The marriage certificate from St Marylebone, 12 September 1846.

A sculpture of the clasped hands of Robert Browning and Elizabeth Barrett Browning, by Harriet Hosmer, 1853.

Casa Guidi, the house in which Robert and Elizabeth lived for most of their years in Florence.

Robert Browning sketched in pencil by his son Pen, 23 January 1853 – with the inscription in a parental hand 'I done this for Dear Papa'.

Elizabeth and Pen photographed in Rome, 1860.

of Galignani's *Messenger*, a Parisian newspaper distributed in Florence, in an extract from Prout's regular 'Letter from Italy' that he contributed to Dickens's *Daily News*.

Father Prout had been full of interesting, hopeful news about the former Cardinal Mastai Ferretti, Pope Pius IX, known as Pio Nono, who — Prout had written in the *Daily News* — appeared to have restored the golden glory days of Haroun al Raschid. Allowing for some journalistic conflation, not to say historical and theological confusion, Prout had expressed a general feeling of optimism in Italy about the tendency towards liberalism and national regeneration. Pio Nono, who had been elected to the throne of St Peter in 1846, gratifyingly began his tenure of office as a reformer by granting the Papal States a constitution, political amnesties in the prisons, and freedom of the press. There were hopes that the forces of Italian unity would regard him as a figurehead.

Robert, while still in Pisa, hearing that the British were thinking of sending a government minister and mission to Rome, had written on 31 March 1847 to an acquaintance, Richard Monckton Milnes, suggesting that he would be glad and proud to be secretary to a proposed British embassy and to 'work like a horse in my vocation'. He specifically referred to Pio Nono as 'this fine fellow' and — from the advantage of his viewpoint in Pisa — 'one sees more clearly than elsewhere that — why, only that England needs must not loiter behind the very Grand Turkian policy, but send a minister before the year ends'. Robert's revival of diplomacy as his 'vocation' is surprising, though considerations of a wife, perhaps children in the future, and the necessity of keeping a family fed and housed in Italy may have prompted desperate measures. In the event, the diplomatic mission was never sent and, though probably not for that reason alone, nothing came of Robert's claim on the patronage of Monckton Milnes.

In Florence, a city heavily freighted with a famous history, it was morally instructive and visually exciting, altogether pleasing, now that Italy was awaking from three centuries of quiescence and inertia, to watch that history being revived in latter-day terms as a new form of Renaissance. The dough of what would be known as the Risorgimento was being puffed up from the raw flour of popular resentment against foreign rule

by the effervescence of yeasty constitutional reforms, the water of politi-
cal liberty, and the honest salt of the people (though Tuscans, for
historical and tight-fisted reasons, preferred not to season their bread,
thus avoiding a tax on salt), the whole to be baked by nationalist
revolution as a traditional Tuscan loaf — symbolic of the greatness
Florence had once known as foremost of Renaissance cities, and that
Italy had known as the heart of the Roman Empire. The dough was
almost proven; the oven was already heating. The glory of the past could
be restored. *O bella libertà! O! bella!*

The Brownings were all for it: in a letter of September 1847, Elizabeth
commented favourably on Pio Nono, in whom so many progressive,
libertarian hopes resided: 'we are glad to be here just now when there
is new animation and energy given to Italy by this new wonderful Pope,
who is a great man and doing greatly . . . Think how seldom the libera-
tion of a people begins from the throne, *a fortiori* from a papal throne,
which is so high and straight. And the spark spreads! here is even our
Grand Duke conceding the civil guard, and forgetting his Austrian
prejudices.'

The Grand Duke was Leopoldo II of Tuscany, who had succeeded
his father Pietro Leopoldo I in 1824. He owed his official ducal position,
and thus some political loyalty, to his Habsburg cousins. Italy in the
first half of the nineteenth century was, as the great Austrian statesman
Metternich had slightingly but realistically remarked, a 'geographical
expression' rather than a nation. But, defined geographically, allowing
for some border areas of ambiguity, it was self-evidently a territorial
unit with obvious natural frontiers — the sea on three sides, the Alps
on the fourth. The divisions were largely internal — political (no two
Italian city states or regions were constitutionally alike), linguistic (every
district had its dialect, impenetrable to any outsider) and social (the
enduring Italian concept of local loyalties, *campanalismo*). Religion (a
universally observed Catholicism) rather than politics (historically
regional and factional) was the uniting element.

In the mid–1800s, a strongly aspirational but still inchoate national
consciousness, more a matter of historic, nostalgic memory and of a
pervasive present sentiment than deriving from an identifiable focus, or
based on any solid core, did exist among Italians. The country, defined
by its natural boundaries, had fallen into a long somnolence after about

1500, losing its commercial and cultural primacy, partly as a result of its failure to coalesce its eighty squabbling, self-interested city states into a national state capable of prospering politically and economically. Italy in the mid-nineteenth century was a backwater, a poor, overpopulated territory. It took Napoleon Bonaparte to pull down the old order in Italy, to force the peninsula back into mainstream history, to introduce Italians to the exciting and novel concepts of liberty, equality, and fraternity, and to awaken them to the benefits of industrialization and strong centralized government.

In 1815 the Congress of Vienna had undone much of Napoleon's work when it had attempted to reimpose pre-Napoleonic conditions and the old political boundaries on Italy. The prototypical Kingdom of Italy, established by Napoleon and centred on Milan (which was now reoccupied by Austrian troops), dissolved back into its constituent elements and most of the Napoleonic laws were repealed. The Italians were generally delighted to be rid of a foreign French Emperor, but they resented, just as much, the imposition of another authority, the Austrian Habsburgs. The Pope was restored to his estates, the Bourbons to Naples, and the Savoys to Piedmont. Various Habsburg cousins and collaterals were dispatched to rule the duchies of Tuscany, Parma, and Modena, while Lombardy and Venetia were annexed to the Habsburg Empire. A united Italy was denied to Italian liberals, inspiring them to a decade, from 1820 to 1831, of frustrated, badly co-ordinated revolts in Naples, Piedmont, Modena, Parma, and the Papal States.

A radical patriot hero, Giuseppe Mazzini, exiled in 1831 for his republicanism (though often thereafter he made regular, dashing reappearances in Piedmont), arose under the banner of *Giovane Italia* [Young Italy] and attracted a firebrand following, though more cautious spirits preferred the prospect of a confederation of Italian states under the presidency of the Pope. Pio Nono — young, good-looking, well-spoken, canonized after his death — seemed an admirable, perhaps God-given, candidate: even Mazzini supported the papal reforms on the ground that the smallest concessions could lead to even greater ones. Mazzini, alive to the cohering element of religion, preached national unification as a religious duty. He also understood the Italian popular psychology, and encouraged *festas*, songs, all sorts of enthusiastic public demonstrations of gratitude, to build up the national consciousness and keep the impetus towards nationalism flowing as freely as wine and music.

Once loosed, the flood of popular sentiment would gush and run irresistibly in the direction of freedom. Continual insurrection — in whatever form, so long as it kept the people conscious of their power and how to use it in executing God's purpose — was the key to liberty. Mazzini understood this perfectly.

In 1847, Grand Duke Leopoldo II was bending, temperamentally and politically, with the wind of current nationalistic sensibilities, and his anxieties would soon result in a grant to the Tuscans of a constitution on the papal model, with an assembly, a *consulta*. For the time being, by re-establishing the *Guardia Civica*, he had conceded the right of the Tuscans to their own armed guard. Leopoldo II not only had the wit to acknowledge the intense and probably irresistible pressure of local and more widespread patriotism, but was in any event disinclined to rule through repression. So long as the Tuscans were politically quiet and materially prosperous ('*sono tranquilli*' — they are quiet — he commented mildly and cautiously when complimented on the comfort and contentment of the Tuscans), he saw no need for the force of Austrian bayonets. He was no radical, but a wary liberalism did not go against his personal grain.

He was perfectly agreeable to his government asserting Tuscan independence against Austrian interference (though occasionally he would feel obliged to arrest a token insurrectionist) while resisting populist pressures for a unified Italy. He was personally a modest, moderate man and a pious Catholic; he liked his role in Florence, as well as a quiet life. Florence under his rule became, indeed, so tolerant of dissent that moderate liberals — who included some of the greatest writers of the day: Ugo Foscolo (who died in 1827), Giacomo Leopardi (who died in 1837), and Alessandro Manzoni (whose influential novel, *I Promessi Sposi*, achieved its final form in 1841–42) — found a less repressive haven in Florence than elsewhere in Italy. Mazzini had urged the people to accept such ducal indulgences with pleasure, and so they did.

The enlightened, delicately balanced rule of Leopoldo and the consequent comparative calm of Florence, as much as the city's natural beauty and the glory of its cultural history, had attracted many foreign tourists and residents. Florence in the 1840s was a substantial city of some

100,000 inhabitants. Jews and Protestants were tolerated, the police were less intrusive and repressive than elsewhere in Italy, the universities were famous for the high quality of their education, and poverty seemed less evident in Florence than elsewhere. Communications were improving; railway tracks were being laid all over Tuscany, and festooned alongside them was the new system of telegraph wires.

Alterations were also being made to the historical centre of Florence. Monumental architectural relics and artistic remnants of its past were everywhere, now illuminated by modern gas lighting. Leopoldo himself had gathered with a crowd of citizens in via Maggio on the first night that the lights were turned on. There, with a noisy and important flutter and rustle, they opened their newspapers to test the claim that they would be able to read the *Gazetto di Firenze* at a distance of seventeen arms' length from the new gas lanterns. Immemorial streets were widened, a road and pedestrian promenades along the Arno were constructed, existing buildings were improved, new statues of old Florentine artists and writers were erected in the Uffizi, and housing was built for the poor. Everything delighted the eyes, every prospect pleased the senses, and liberal sensibilities could be freely expressed.

The foreign presence was substantial and tended to sympathize with the rising tide of *italianità*, which, due to the moderating influence of Leopoldo's dynastic connection to Austria and his conciliatory attitude in Italy, was slower in Tuscany than in other regions, Piedmont particularly, to develop into nationalism and a corresponding demand for full political independence. There was little or no perceptible resentment among the indigenous Florentines at this form of occupation by *stranieri*, this more subtle form of colonialism by foreign residents and tourists.

In mid-September, the Brownings celebrated their first wedding anniversary. Robert indeed celebrated it all the time, twice a month at least — somewhat to Elizabeth's confusion, since she could never quite remember the date herself, but it so happened that the actual day, 12 September 1847, coincided with a significant Florentine *festa*. They had a dress circle view of the Florentine political stage. They drew up their chairs to a window overlooking the Piazza Pitti to watch the drama, in all its high operatic style, played out by the principals and a vast chorus assembled against the great backdrop of the Palazzo Pitti. Elizabeth wrote rapturously to her sister, Henrietta, on the day after her anniversary and the coincident *festa* to celebrate the establishment of the civic guard at the Pitti. Forty thousand strangers (historical shorthand for a very large number) from all over Tuscany thronged into Florence to join with the Florentines in their pageantry: 'for above three hours the infinite procession filed under our windows — with all their various flags and symbols, into the Piazza Pitti where the Duke and his family stood in tears at the window to receive the thanks of his people. Never in the world was a more affecting sight — nor a grander if you took it in its full significance.' Among the processing ranks of the magistracy, priesthood, peasants, nobles, and soldiers fraternizing with the people, 'came the foreigners, there was a place for them; and there are so many foreign residents here, that it was by no means unimportant to admit their sympathy, — French, English, Swiss, Greeks (such a noble band of Greeks!) all with their national flags'.

Propped up on 'a throne of cushions piled up on a chair' in the window, from which she had a full view, Elizabeth waved her handkerchief until her wrists ached. Robert waved his handkerchief, too, and from every window in every wall there was nothing but fluttering handkerchiefs and jubilant faces. Generous hands threw down drifts of flowers and contributed a constant patter of laurel leaves on the parades below; and then there was the noise, 'the clapping of hands, and the frenetic shouting, and the music which came in gushes, and then seemed to go out with too much joy, and the exulting faces, and the kisses given for very exultation between man and man, and the mixing of elegantly dressed women in all that crowd and turbulence, with the sort of smile which proved how little there was for fear'.

It was a little different a few months later, in February 1848, though there was still no cause for fear. Constitutions had been granted by the King of Naples, the King of Piedmont and, on 17 February, by Grand Duke Leopoldo. Naturally, there was another celebration to mark this significant surrender of power to the people. The Brownings, alerted, were once again entertained by a considerable fuss in the Piazza Pitti: '"Ba, Ba," says Robert at the door, "come this moment out here — I want you to see something." What in the world is the matter now, thought I — I went to the window — and there, with vehement bursts of acclamation, was the Grand Duke's carriage in the midst of a "milky way" of waxen torchlights. You would have thought that all the stars out of Heaven had fallen into the piazza.'[9]

They settled in at the window, sustained by sandwiches, to enjoy the sight of the Palazzo Pitti, described by Elizabeth as 'drawn out in fire' while 'the people pour along the streets in that quaint effusion of joy and sympathy, so touching to the stranger'. Robert was inclined to a more sanguinary view. The new civic guards liked to parade in all the splendour of their uniforms, complete with gleaming epaulettes and shining helmets. On one of these occasions, Robert noted particularly their weaponry. He murmured, 'Surely, after all this, they would *use* those muskets?'[10] That the fireworks of a *festa* might turn into real firepower was a disquieting thought in an apparently equable political situation. Elizabeth, for her part, had taken a liking for the unassuming little Grand Duke and, for the time being, reposed perfect faith in his best intentions:

> Good Grand Duke! I clapped my hands with all my heart at him. Such an excellent constitution he has given to Tuscany, with every religious distinction abolished at one sweep; and this by his free will and after long reflection. Nights after nights he has spent, they say, without sleep, in painful thought — and his face expresses it. I like him and I like his face. Well — you see, at the close of a festa-day, he thought he would go privately to the opera, for repose and refreshment — in order to which, he *walked there*, and only would have his carriage to return in. At the opera, however, he was recognized by somebody — and not a note more of music was listened to, through the vehement shouting — while at the door the people provided with torches, met him and carried him home to the Pitti in a triumph. The poor Duke, quite taken by surprise and overcome, wept, we hear, like a child. Well done people — wasn't it? In the illumination we set two wax candles at each of our five windows, which ruined us 'gloriously.' Think of that![11]

Other English residents were less indulgent towards the good little Grand Duke, though rather on social than political grounds. Thomas Adolphus Trollope, brother of the novelist Anthony Trollope and son of the redoubtable writer Fanny Trollope, who had recently come to

Florence to live in some splendour with Thomas at the Villino Trollope, was perhaps typical. Leopoldo II might do well to be lenient politically, but in matters of personal appearance and parties such benign latitude was not at all *comme il faut*. Not at all the done thing. The behaviour of guests at the weekly receptions at the Palazzo Pitti was, in Trollope's fastidious estimation, abominable. Leopoldo, said Trollope, ran 'the worst drawing room in Europe'. The English were bad enough, the men seizing plates of *bonbons* and tipping the contents into their pockets, the English ladies doing the same into their handkerchiefs; but they were moderate compared to the Tuscans. The Duke himself was 'about as bad and unprincely as well can be conceived. His clothes never fitted him and he always appeared to be struggling painfully with the consciousness that he had nothing to say.'

Thomas Trollope was not the only one to be disparagingly snobbish. Sophia Hawthorne, wife of the American novelist Nathaniel Hawthorne, was positively rude: Leopoldo looked to her 'like a monkey, most ugly and mean', and of course he possessed that unfortunate Habsburg physical characteristic, 'that frightful, coarse, protruding underlip, peculiar to the court of Austria'. Faugh! Leopoldo was really too common: vulgar, disgraceful, and disreputable; quite bourgeois, in contrast to the aristocratic tone of a city that had bred and favoured the ambitious Medici bankers, princes and patrons of art so admired by the Anglo-Americans.

Robert had a better intellectual grasp of Italian and Florentine history than any of them: he had made something of a study of it in his poetry and plays, and what he had read did not incline him to any great indulgence in works such as *Sordello*, *Luria*, and some shorter poems, notably — in 1845 — 'The Italian in England'. Elizabeth's unbridled enthusiasm for the artistic beauties of the city was one thing; the historical dungheap of princely brutalities and political treacheries, the cynicism of courtiers, and the religious persecutions of the medieval and Renaissance republics that had also nourished the artistic flowering of painting, sculpture, architecture, and scholarship, was quite another. Robert, as an outsider who kept his distance from the day-to-day lives of Italians as much as from detestable English tourists, took lessons from history that the Tuscans and their foreign partisans had forgotten, or preferred to interpret in different terms and by different criteria. For the time being, the Tuscans were more easygoing, better disposed towards Leopoldo than some foreign residents, though no less satirical. They liked him well enough for his general kindliness, and recognized that they were better treated and better off than most Italians elsewhere, but he was undoubtedly slow and dull in his manner. Sometimes known with guarded affection as *Babbo* [Daddy], *Il Granduca* was more usually and entertainingly known as *Il Granciuco* [the Great Ass].

The Brownings, except for friends such as Mary Boyle, Hiram Powers, and a few others who were gradually admitted to their small circle, made something of a point of keeping themselves to themselves. They were in no hurry, perfectly resistant indeed, to button themselves into a plush Florentine expatriate society. Elizabeth declared that they 'struggled to keep out of it with hands and feet' until it was recognized that 'nothing could be made of us'. Robert, though perfectly amiable and volubly conversational in congenial society such as he had frequented in London, could appear rather intimidating among the unknown quantity of expatriates. Thomas Trollope respectfully, though perhaps a shade smartingly and resentfully, noted this when he wrote, 'The tag-rag and bobtail of the men who mainly constituted that very pleasant but not very intellectual society were not likely to be such as Mr Browning would make intimates of. And I think I see in memory's tragic glass that the men used to be rather afraid of him. Not that I ever saw him rough or uncourteous to the most exasperating fool ... but there was a quiet lurking smile, which, supported by very few words, used to seem to have the singular property of making utterers of platitudes and the mistakes of *non sequitur* for *sequitur* uncomfortably aware of the nature of their words within a very few minutes after they had uttered them.'[12] It is difficult to resist the feeling that Thomas Trollope himself had subliminally felt — or been made to feel — uncomfortable by Robert's manner.

The Brownings, when they sought out company — or, more usually, company sought out the Brownings — tended to prefer the less artificial manners, better cultivated tastes, democratic attitudes, and workmanlike occupations of artistic, expatriate American painters and sculptors. They were less inclined to frequent the society of what was condemned by a snobbishly high-principled Tory and high-minded anti-liberal resident, the novelist Charles Lever, as 'a miserably mended class of small English' and others who dedicated themselves simply to pleasure in the hardly original form of card parties, private theatricals, and picnics, when they were not gambling or dancing. A little later, with more experience of the tone of Florentine expatriate society after four years in the city, Elizabeth declared it to be 'worse than any coterie society in the world'. If gambling or dancing were all, she did not object to it, but she reckoned it as ultimately corrupting: 'if there's an end, why, so much the better; but there's *not* an end in most cases, by any manner of means and against every sort of innocence'. Their American acquaintance included, early in 1848, the sculptor William Wetmore Story and his wife and children. Story soon afterwards left Florence for Rome, but returned in the autumn and from then on the Storys and the Brownings were to become close and lasting friends.

Closer to hand, right above the Brownings' heads in fact, in the second-floor apartment, lived Mr and Mrs David Ogilvy, described by Elizabeth to Miss Mitford in April 1850 as 'cultivated and refined people'. Mrs Ogilvy was a sensible, rather stern-minded Scotswoman married to an upper-middle-class Scotsman, who indulged a taste for poetry (her own as well as other people's). It may have been in their favour that they were not English. Mrs Ogilvy struck Elizabeth as 'a pretty woman with three pretty children, of quick perceptions and active intelligence and sensibility'. The friendship between the Brownings and the Ogilvies, neighbourly from July 1848 when the latter arrived at Casa Guidi and thenceforward epistolary when they left Florence in 1852, lasted thirteen years.

We are obliged to the regularity of Elizabeth's letters to Eliza Ogilvy for details and confirmation of events in the domestic life of the Brownings, and in particular for the information, confided from one mother of young children to another, about the attitudes of Robert and Elizabeth towards children, and in particular towards the development of their own son. Rather curiously, there is no indication, now or later, that the Brownings looked to Italians for company, social or intellectual. They did not make much effort with any nationality, for that matter, but Italians seemed remote and difficult to get to know behind their surface exuberance, and perhaps the Brownings may have wished for them in vain and from afar. On 15 July 1848, in a letter to Mrs Jameson, Elizabeth commented, 'As to Italian society, one may as well take to longing for the evening star, for it seems quite as inaccessible.'

Wilson, who had been their maid of all work (except for the heavy duties undertaken by a charwoman) and cook (until they engaged an assertive but first-class Italian cook named Alessandro), was more successful with her effort among Italians, though she mostly came into contact with them in the way of the small daily commerce of shopping and running errands. To her immense credit, she took the trouble to study an Italian grammar and quickly gained a grasp of the language at least sufficient to increase her confidence when dealing with haberdashers and street market traders and others useful in domestic matters.

Lily Wilson became, indeed, more Italianate than her employers when she had got over some initial aesthetic shocks: Elizabeth wrote to Henrietta on 7 July 1847 to tell her that 'Wilson has at last . . . ventured into the [Uffizi] gallery: but she only went to the door of the Tribune, being struck back by the indecency of the Venus. I laughed — laughed when she told me. She thinks she shall try again, and the troublesome modesty may subside — who knows? but really the sight of that marble Goddess and Titian's (painted stark, just overhead,) were too much at first.' In February 1848, Elizabeth reported to Henrietta that 'Wilson herself is blooming in health and spirits. She is getting naturalized — talks Italian and understands it, with a little licence in the grammar. She is contented enough with Florence.' Contented enough, apparently, in 1848 to get herself engaged to marry a Signor Righi of the Ducal Guard, a most respectable and fine-looking man whose family lived in nearby Prato.

Politically, 1848 was a significant and turbulent year in European history. Leopoldo's grant of a constitution to the Tuscans in February may have been a *sauve qui peut* tactic in view of the decision in January by King Bomba, Ferdinando II di Borbone, King of Naples and the Two Sicilies, to grant a constitution to Sicily in the face of popular revolt. Carlo Alberto, King of Piedmont-Sardinia, and Pio Nono at the Vatican followed that example. In the space of five days, twenty thousand Austrians, commanded by the redoubtable Marshal Radetzky, were driven out of Milan by the outraged Milanese, who were supported by Tuscan civilian volunteers and members of the Tuscan *Guardia Civica*. Venice, too, rose in revolt and the city was hurriedly evacuated by the occupying Austrians, who heard the Venetian Republic being proclaimed at their backs.

Carlo Alberto became front man for a national movement towards independence, and so the Tuscans marched off from their triumph in

Milan to join the Piedmontese and to meet Radetzky again at Curtatone and Montanara, where they were defeated by well-drilled, well-led, professional Austrian forces. What was left of the Tuscan forces limped home. A week after the celebrations marking the Tuscan constitution, the French constitutional monarchy of Louis Philippe was replaced by a republic. There was nationalist revolution in the states of Germany and, in mid-March, an uprising in the very heart of the Habsburg Empire, in Vienna itself. The old European certainties, the old monarchical orders, were crumbling. It was in such uncertain circumstances that many English expatriate residents fled precipitately, abandoning their houses and furniture.

In the event, as an ill wind that blew the Brownings some good, prices for rented accommodation fell and furniture to fill the Casa Guidi apartment was cheap and plentiful. Flight to the safety of England was premature: Florence was virtually an island paradise in a sea of troubles. Elizabeth, commenting on the general exodus to Miss Mitford on 15 April 1848, wrote: 'The English are flying from Florence, by the way, in a helter skelter, just as they always do fly, except (to do them justice) on a field of battle. The family Englishman is a dreadful coward, be it admitted frankly.' By mid-July, when she wrote to Mrs Jameson, the faint hearts had departed: 'Florence just now, and thanks to the panic, is tolerably *clean* of the English — you scarcely see an English face anywhere — and perhaps this was a circumstance that helped to give Robert courage to take our apartment here and "settle down".' Altogether, for brave hearts like the Brownings, Florence was as good a place as any, probably better, to be in difficult times.

Robert and Elizabeth, in no mind to run 'helter skelter', took continental uprisings in their stride: 'we talk and laugh and enjoy the world as much as if it were not turned topsy turvy. What an extraordinary state of times to be sure! Every morning as Robert goes to the post and to look at the newspapers, I say "Bring me back news of a revolution!" And generally he brings me back news of *two!*'[13] There was another *festa* in Florence — 'a grand Florentine illumination' — this time to celebrate the news that Austria had been thrown out of Lombardy. There had been a less harmonious disturbance under their windows the night before, when 'there was a loud shouting in our piazza — a great crowd had seized upon the arms of Austria, suspended on the house of the ambassador, and burnt them with a shriek of curses under the palace windows! then gave a "Viva Leopoldo secondo" and dispersed peacefully. I was not in the least frightened, nor had any reason for being so.'[14]

The letter to Henrietta goes on to make soothing noises about the personal safety of the Brownings and to brush lightly against the question of social equality. On the whole, Elizabeth was firm on the principle of a man's right to his property, and cautious on the strict principle of egalitarianism (though she favoured meritocratic advancement). Retention of a system of titles seemed inoffensive as 'an inexpensive mode of recognising public services — so much better than any money way, and as good as the inch of coloured ribbon in the button hole? *Hereditary* distinction, is a different question.' Fiercely, and rather rhetorically, she declared: 'Let the notion of privileged orders perish as it ought.' Robert and she, said Elizabeth, agreed nearly on all these points, 'but here and there we have plenty of room for battles'. The Brownings were republican in their political professions and principles:[15] Elizabeth had her reservations about the French system and suggested to Henrietta that, 'My idea of a republic is for every born man in it to have room for his faculties — which is perfectly different from swamping individuality in a mob.'

After the *festa* on their first wedding anniversary, she had begun to write a long poem on the theme of Italian liberation, which, when she submitted it to *Blackwood's Magazine* in 1848, was entitled 'Meditation in Tuscany'. It was incorporated into the still longer, still more fervid poem *Casa Guidi Windows*, which she completed and published in 1851. Making considerable allowance for the romantic paraphernalia of the poem and the poetic afflatus of its metaphoric imagery, it colourfully represents in extreme terms the principles that Robert, at least, professed more moderately and more cautiously in the bumping reality of their everyday lives in Florence, and later in their visits to Paris. Elizabeth always tended to more passion in the defence of her political bridgeheads.

Robert had been writing little or nothing in — far less about — Italy. Both he and Elizabeth had tinkered only with existing poems. Whatever letters Robert was writing at this time, they were either minimal or, if more than we yet know about were written, few have survived.

Elizabeth, despite Robert's despair for her health, was forever writing long letters to her sisters and other friends, for hours every day; and it is to this bright and indefatigable correspondence that we owe most of our information about the Brownings in Italy. In any event, there had been little time for concentrated literary work. The marriage itself (however harmonious), and settling into their new lives (however haphazard), had sopped up their days and energies like bread absorbs gravy. They were content enough, however Elizabeth might worry and protest about her husband's reclusive mood; but there were some inevitable tensions, mostly well concealed and indirectly expressed in the extreme courtesy and care they took for one another and their joint welfare. Their days had been marked, very largely, by events external to their personal lives, punctuated by *festas* rather than by poetry.

The mild beauty of spring again gave way to the torrid heat of summer. By late June the temperature in the shade reached eighty degrees and more, and only by closing all the windows, shutters, and pulling down the blinds — at Robert's insistence — could they reduce the indoor daytime temperature to the low seventies. They had intended to spend summers in England, but such an expense was not to be considered, either last year or this, in view of the money they had laid out in rents and furnishings; and so on 17 July, in the cooler air of evening, they set out for Fano, which lies on the eastern coast between Rimini and Ancona, for the pleasure of its sea and mountain air. Their itinerary had been planned with all Robert's customary precision, however Elizabeth makes it sound like an impetuous rush — she and Robert would 'take up our carpet bag and Wilson and plunge into the mountains in search of the monasteries beyond Vallombrosa, from Arezzo go to St Sepolchro in the Apennines, and thence to Fano on the seashore, making a round back perhaps (after seeing the great fair at Sinigaglia) to Ravenna and Bologna home'.[16]

They had relied on Murray's guidebook for their information about the desirability of Fano as a summer resort. Elizabeth, reporting on 24 August from Florence to Miss Mitford, was indignant: 'Murray, the traitor, sent us to Fano as "a delightful summer residence for an English family," and we found it uninhabitable from the heat, vegetation scorched with paleness, the very air swooning in the sun, and the gloomy looks of the inhabitants sufficiently corroborative of their words, that no drop of rain or dew ever falls there during the summer. A "circulating library" "which doesn't give out books," and "a refined and intellectual Italian society" (I quote Murray for that phrase) which "never reads a book through" (I quote Mrs Wiseman, Dr Wiseman's mother, who has lived in Fano seven years), complete the advantages of the place, yet the churches are beautiful, and a divine picture of Guercino's is worth going all that way to see.' They fled after three days down the coast to Ancona, which was beautiful but might have been better visited 'when there is a little air and shadow', and a little more variation in the available diet would have been welcome. With only the company and comfort of Mrs Wiseman, mother of Dr Wiseman, then a Roman Catholic bishop but soon to become Cardinal Nicholas Wiseman, they stayed a week, 'living upon fish and cold water'.

Their ill luck dogged them. There was no fair at Sinigaglia that year, and Ravenna, on which they had finally pinned their hopes since Robert had once taken a fancy to live there, was as hot as anywhere else, with the further positive disadvantage that 'the marshes on all sides send up stenches new and old, till the hot air is sick with them'. When they were denied entry to Dante's tomb, for want of official authorization, they disgustedly packed up and went home by way of the Apennines, which were admittedly sublime and beautiful, and sank back into their chairs at Casa Guidi declaring that 'Florence seemed as cool as an oven after the fire.' They had been away three weeks. '*Un bel giro*' — a fine trip — Elizabeth commented with amused asperity.

One positive thing resulted from the excursion to Fano. Probably while at Ancona, Robert wrote a poem of fifty-six lines, in eight stanzas, 'The Guardian-Angel: A Picture at Fano'. Its immediate subject was Guercino's *L'Angelo Custode*, which occasioned not only nostalgic references to his friendship with Alfred Domett but also to the three visits he had made with Elizabeth to sit in the chapel of the church of San Agostino to look upon the painting, 'And drink his beauty to our soul's content — My angel with me too.' The poem is a personal reflection, autobiographical rather than strictly historical, and critics, principally Betty Miller,[17] have found in it a revelation of Robert's circumstances at that moment — nostalgic for old friends, for the irresponsibility of youth, and for a former home and family exchanged for the present responsibilities of living in a foreign land with a wife not only in delicate health but in the first months of her third pregnancy. Guercino's guardian angel bends tenderly, protectively over a little child, clasping the infant hands in prayer. The effect, to modern sensibilities, is more than a shade sentimental — as Mrs Miller suggests, more appropriate to nineteenth-century romantic piety than to more robust eighteenth-century tastes or the more cynical ones of our own time. But evidently the sentiment powerfully affected Robert Browning at that moment and moved him to express its meaning for him in poetry.

William Irvine and Park Honan agree with Betty Miller's interpretation: 'the poem expresses his lassitude and frustration'.[18] The visit to Fano had been trying and disappointing, and nigh on two years of marriage had taken up time and energies he might have given to poetry. This was perhaps weighing on him as a frustration. During his courtship of Elizabeth, Betty Miller points out, Robert had looked forward to poetry as 'a real life's work for us both' and, for his own part, '*I* shall do all, — under your eyes and with your hand in mine, — all I was intended to do.' The greater works were to follow. The marriage was supposed to be a spur to great poetic achievement. What Irvine and Honan describe as Browning's 'vigorously operating self-confidence and basic independence of early ties' had been tested to a considerable degree by the radical choices he had made in his career and his marriage. There was nothing to be regretted in either case; but an angel's care would be welcome, not just for the inner, vulnerable child but for the adult, troubled man.

> If this was ever granted, I would rest
>   My head beneath thine, while thy healing hands
> Close-covered both my eyes beside thy breast,
>   Pressing the brain, which too much thought expands,
> Back to its proper size again, and smoothing
> Distortion down till every nerve had soothing,
>   And all lay quiet, happy and suppressed.

'Suppressed', of course, has a slightly different meaning — or is interpreted rather differently as repressed — in our post-Freudian society. Whatever Robert hoped to 'suppress' flowed out nevertheless in this poem, which perhaps served (as much as one might recall a dream a few days later) to express rather than repress the feelings Guercino's picture had evoked and thereby to lay them quiet and happy in the achievement of a poem and the articulated acknowledgement that the 'deep joy' of a happy marriage in his heart nevertheless did not still the perversity of his head. For all sorts of reasons, personal and professional, the Guercino painting is perceived as a deep disturbance to Robert Browning's peace of mind.

Shortly after their return Robert fell ill — psychosomatically, it is tempting to think — with an ulcerated throat and an associated fever. His sound constitution was not usually susceptible to illness, except for regular headaches. He had been ill for nearly a month on 10 October when Elizabeth reported the crisis to Miss Mitford. Robert refused to see a doctor, but Father Prout happened to be in Florence and, 'knowing everything as those Jesuits are apt to do', was at hand to diagnose the fever as having 'got ahead through weakness' and to prescribe a physic, 'a potion of eggs and port wine', which he mixed with his own pharmaceutical hand, much to the horror of Alessandro, the Brownings' cook, 'who lifted up his eyes at such a prescription for a fever, crying, "O Inglesi, Inglesi!"' The medicine worked. Robert slept and his pulse rate fell. 'I shall always be grateful to Father Prout, always', declared Elizabeth. Father Prout had taken charge, reassured Elizabeth that her alarm was groundless, and jokingly called her 'a *bambina*' — a little girl, a baby — for her terrors. The tonic effect of 'Mr Mahoney [*sic*], the celebrated Jesuit, and Father Prout of "Fraser" ... of whom the world tells a thousand and one tales' could not have been kinder, more comforting, or more cheering than 'the salutation of angels.'

Father Prout came to doctor and stayed to talk. His manner might be a little cynical, his manners a little rough ('not refined in a social sense by any manner of means'), but on first close and constant acquaintance he was entertaining as 'a most accomplished scholar and vibrating all over with learned associations and vivid combinations of fancy and experience — having seen all the ends of the earth and the men thereof, and possessing the art of talk and quotation to an amusing degree'. The patient recovered, but the physician — though supposedly on his way to Rome — lingered. To Henrietta, on 19 November 1848, Elizabeth wrote exasperatedly that Father Prout had fallen into the habit of

spending every evening with the Brownings: 'Oh, it's a settled thing —
he is our man of the mountain, whom Sinbad carried on his back . . .
all our evenings, so happy and tranquil, are absolutely done for, ground
to powder, smoked to ashes.' Father Prout liked to talk, smoke, and
expectorate into a spittoon, all copiously, for three hours and more at
a stretch. Elizabeth, putting herself to no great trouble to make any
contribution to this symposium, lay on a sofa and permitted herself to
be called 'Ba', while Robert was forced to make conversation with the
contradictory cleric — 'and this for a person who however full of talent
and reading, is by no means near to him on the ground of sympathies
of any sort even literary. Never were two clever men more unlike —
ways of thinking, ways of feeling, ways of imagining, all most unlike.'

When Father Prout finally left, well satisfied by another of his 'Attic
evenings with Browning and Ba!', there was 'a general burst of indig-
nation and throwing open of doors to get rid of smoke and malice'.
Robert, 'sorely tried between his good nature and detestation of the
whole proceeding', was repulsed in any effectual inclination to rid him-
self of their burden by Father Prout's 'sublime confidence' that noted
no hesitancy or lack of reciprocal ardour. Indeed, he proposed to return
from Rome as quickly as possible to stay two months more at Florence
'and spend every evening with Ba!' Elizabeth was indulgent enough to
admit his essential kind-heartedness and basic Christian principles, but
oh! — regrettably — Father Prout was undeniably a bore and a boor:
'it is the defect in delicacy — conventional or otherwise . . . which
prevents him from perceiving at a glance that the constancy of his
evening visits is an excess — to say the least of it. Still, one likes the
human nature of the man.'

'We have been obliged with quantities of Father Prout,' wrote
Robert, with dry understatement, on 3 December to Richard Henry
Horne. The occasion of this, the first known substantial letter by Robert
Browning from Florence, was a matter of some delicacy and considerable
importance to Robert. At first he is disarmingly, airily chatty, and later
he comments on some subsidiary information of merely personal record,
including the fact that Mr Samuel Phelps, the actor, had surprisingly
requested permission to revive *A Blot in the 'Scutcheon* on the London
stage and that the performance had been scheduled for the Wednesday
before the letter to Horne. 'As nothing worse can well come than *did*

come, I care very little about the event, — always wishing Phelps well, of course, and the play, too, for one or two friends' sake moreover, yours preeminently, staunch supporter of mine that you always were.' There was also to be a new edition of Robert's poems, for which he had done his best 'at correcting enough and not too much'. Notable omissions in this second edition were *Pauline* (sparing Robert's own *amour propre*) and *Sordello* (sparing his readership's patience). Sandwiched between the bread and butter of these remarks is the meat, the principal cause of the communication.

Eliza Flower had died in 1846, and at that time Robert had written a short letter from Pisa to her sister, Sarah Flower — who had married, to become thereby Mrs William Bridges Adams — saying 'that I should be glad to have my letters back . . . not being sure all such boyish rubbish had not been at once properly disposed of . . . No answer came to this — and I don't think I had written a week before a letter arrived from you [Horne], describing a horrible raking up of the correspondence in general.' Robert had intended to deal with the vexing matter when he next visited London, but now he had received news of the death of Mrs Adams. The poem he had given Eliza, *Pauline*, had been burned by Robert, but there had been a collection of earlier poetic effusions besides — oh! besides, dreadfully! — the letters: 'one day Eliza told me to my amazement and discomfort that she had "still by her somewhere safe," all the letters I had written to her — "never being used to destroy a scrap of any such thing" — moreover producing on some occasion or other, a sort of album-book in which were entered "poem" this and "poem" the other, duly transcribed from my delectable collection aforesaid.'

In this embarrassment and conjuring the possible horrors that the death of Sarah Adams might precipitate — she might have been projecting 'one of those hateful memoirs' — Robert asked Horne to act for him in retrieving the album-book and the letters. Robert balked, for the time being, 'at availing oneself of the law, which overhauls these ungodly appropriations, I believe', but his agony, at the thought of 'these things being raked up, a long day off, when one dies', is very apparent. In the event — however great a quantity of other letters and poems have survived to haunt the shade of Browning — the letters to Eliza Flower and all but a few scraps of the poetry she preserved, rake for them as many scholars may, are not yet known to that 'long day off' and latter-day makers of 'hateful memoirs'.

The end of the year found the Brownings putting up curtains, laying down carpets, and waiting for their books to arrive to fill their great 'rococo bookcase of carved angels and demons'.[19] Setting themselves up had been a slow business. 'You see,' Elizabeth wrote to Mrs Martin on 3 December 1848,

> being the poorest and most prudent of possible poets, we had to solve the problem of taking our furniture out of our year's income (proceeds of poems and the like), and of not getting into debt. Oh, I take no credit to myself; I was always in debt in my little way ('small *im*morals,' as Dr Bowring might call it) before I married, but Robert, though a poet and dramatist by profession, being descended from the blood of all the Puritans, and educated by the strictest of dissenters, has a sort of horror about the dreadful fact of owing five shillings five days, which I call quite morbid in its degree and extent, and which is altogether unpoetical according to the traditions of the world. So we have been dragging in by inches our chairs and tables throughout the summer, and by no means look finished and furnished at this late moment, the slow Italians coming at the heels of our slowest intentions with the putting up of our curtains, which begin to be necessary in this November tramontana. Yet in a month or three weeks we shall look quite comfortable — before Christmas; and in the meantime we heap up the pine wood and feel perfectly warm with these thick palace walls between us and the outside air.

The political *tramontana* was blowing something worse than cold air beyond the walls of Casa Guidi, whipping at the nerves of people outside in the piazza, and whistling around the ears of the Grand Duke in the Palazzo Pitti. The Brownings, looking out, were falling into despair about the progress of the 'war'. Miss Mitford was informed that 'it is painful to feel ourselves growing cooler and cooler on the subject of Italian patriotism, valour and good sense; but the process is inevitable'. Their coolness was increased by the appointment by Leopoldo II, in mid-October 1848, of a new government. The Austrian faction at

Leopoldo's court had taken heart from Radetzky's victories. The radicals countered with calls for Leopoldo to dismiss his current government and to beef up its replacement with stronger men more committed to the Italian nationalist cause.

Giuseppe Montanelli, a law professor from Pisa University and a veteran of the uprising against the Austrians in Milan and at Curtatone, was made Prime Minister. Montanelli then urged that Francesco Guerrazzi, a radical Livorno republican lawyer, man of letters, and ardent supporter of Mazzini, should be appointed to the new ducal government as Minister of the Interior. Guerrazzi, who urged the establishment of a constitutional assembly for Tuscany, was presumably the instrument by which Leopoldo would be levered out of power and deposed. Elizabeth was scathing: 'The child's play between the Livornese and our Grand Duke provokes a thousand pleasantries. Every now and then a day is fixed for a revolution in Tuscany, but up to the present time a shower has come and put it off. Two Sundays ago Florence was to have been "sacked" by Leghorn [Livorno], when a drizzle came and saved us.'

Elizabeth could become fierce in her disappointment and withering in her contempt. She looked, like any romantic heroine, for a hero. Strong men were wanted in Italy as much as in France: brave men, good men, sensible men were not lacking, but oh! for some strength! 'If Louis Napoleon had the muscle of his uncle's little finger in his soul, he would be president and king; but he is flaccid altogether, you see, and Joinville stands nearer to the royal probability after all. "Henri Cinq" is said to be too closely espoused to the Church, and his connections at Naples and Parma don't help his cause. Robert has more hope of the *republic* than I have: but call ye this a republic?'

Guerrazzi showed his mettle when, in January 1849, Leopoldo II was outmanoeuvred on several political fronts and sent his family to Siena before he himself abandoned Florence on 30 January. On the night of 7–8 February, dressed as a woman, Leopoldo fled Siena and sailed for Gaeta in the Kingdom of Naples, where the Pope, Pio Nono, having escaped in late November from the violence in Rome (he had declared war on Austria before fleeing, and had invited the support of the French), was already lodging in comparative safety. Their proximity in exile was rather an irony, since Pio Nono, who had become increasingly conservative, had threatened to excommunicate the members of any constituent assembly that might meet in Rome, and might well have been inclined to impose the same sanction on a Tuscan assembly agreed to by Leopoldo II. Caught as a soft liberal between the rock of Austrian aggression and the hard place of the papacy's conservatism, Leopoldo may have been glad enough to keep his head down and out of the firing line. Guerrazzi, for his part, may have been mildly sorry to see Leopoldo go: the Grand Duke at least represented some residual legitimacy, and power generally needs to be soundly grounded in order to endure.

Elizabeth's reaction to these events was local and parochial. Writing from 10 to 20 February to Henrietta, she reported from her window to say that 'this Tuscany of ours is swaying from left to right and from right to left, and the Grand Duke has gone to Siena, and the English ships are at Leghorn to protect English interests, and the English ambassador is writing threatening letters in the journals about what he shall do if insults are offered to the English'. For his pains, the windows of the nearby Ridolfi Palace, the residence of the English ambassador, were smashed. 'And the Florentines talk in their piazzas, of how they mean, if the Grand Duke doesn't come back either to-morrow or next day, to — plant a "tree of liberty" — there's a sublime scheme!' Elizabeth declared herself to have less reason to be afraid than the Florentines, the 'revolutionary party' being 'simply the more noisy and vehement of the population, and headed entirely by strangers from Leghorn'.

Nothing to do with the Florentines, of course, who were 'an amiable, refined, graceful people with much of the artistic temperament as distinguished from that of men of genius — effeminate, no, rather *feminine* in a better sense — of a fancy easily turned into impulse, but with no strenuous and determinate strength in them'.[20] Guerrazzi, to Elizabeth's mind, was 'a traitor ... false as falsehood'. Mazzini, though 'virtuous and heroic ... is indiscreet and mistakes the stuff of which the people is made, if he think to find a great nation in the heart of it. The soldiers refuse to fraternize with the republicans, and Robert saw a body of them arrested the other day.' She did not give the new republic 'more chance of standing than a straw in a storm has'. There were rumours of 'Piedmontese and Austrian armies on their way to Florence'.

She complained again of the Florentines' lack of strength — intellectual or moral — and of the lack of honesty, of union, of zeal: 'here, there are men only fit for the Goldoni theatre, the coffee houses and the sunny side of the Arno when the wind's in the north'. This insistence on manly strength preoccupied Elizabeth. Concluding the letter to Henrietta, she wrote: 'Weak men may be "pulled up", but strong ones are more easily and deeply touched, be very sure; and women are happier in their relations to strong men than to the inferior class, let the latter be ever so manly in the hunting field, and manageable at particular crises of stupidity. *That* I always thought, and now thank God, I know it.' Robert was, very fortunately, a man of genius.

Guerrazzi moved quickly to fill the vacuum caused by Leopoldo's absence. On 12 March a provisional government, established by Guerrazzi, Montanelli, and Giuseppe Mazzini, was voted in by Florentines and Tuscans. The excitement in Florence was intense. On that very day, a tree of liberty was indeed planted outside the Browning door in Piazza Pitti and another grand *festa* took place, including, as Elizabeth observed, the usual trappings of bells and whistles, military music, civic dancing, and singing, with an additional novelty — chants of *viva la repubblica!* and 'the firing of cannons and guns from morning to night'. There was no question of the Brownings moving from Florence, even if they wanted to — which they did not — or even if they could, which was unlikely: Elizabeth must have known by early January that she had successfully brought her third pregnancy to a late critical stage, and by February that she had brought the baby to full term. On 9 March 1849, three days after her forty-third birthday, and three days before the pro-republican *festa*, she gave birth to a fine, healthy boy.

The period of labour had been long, some twenty-one hours, beginning at about five o'clock in the morning of 8 March and continuing until some fifteen minutes after two o'clock in the morning the next day. From all accounts, Elizabeth endured the pain nobly and stoically, never once crying or crying out. Robert, who sat by her, holding her hand, as much as he was allowed, but mostly in a continual fret behind the thick wall and double wooden door, fearing that the lack of any sounds from the bedroom could only mean the worst, was kept informed by regular bulletins from Dr Harding, who shuttled back and forth between wife and husband with words of comfort and reassurance.

These meant little or nothing to Robert, consumed as he was by an unalloyed anxiety for Elizabeth's health and survival. The sound of the baby's bawling was very welcome, but it was another seven hours before he was allowed to see for himself, at nine o'clock on the morning of 9 March, that Elizabeth and the baby were both well and doing better than he — or indeed Elizabeth — had ever dared to hope. Elizabeth believed the reality of it only when she heard it herself from Robert, who handed the baby to her; and he believed it only when he saw for himself and finally trusted to the truth of what Dr Harding had tried to tell him.

'Now all is over,' Robert wrote immediately to Miss Mitford on 9 March, 'the babe seems happy in his cradle and Ba *is*, I suppose, the very thing you call happy — this is God's reward for her entire perfectness to me and everybody but herself.' To Henrietta and Arabel the same day, at four o'clock in the morning, Robert wrote: 'Dr Harding assures me that, without flattery, the little creature is the very model of a beautiful boy.' The beautiful boy had a big voice and he was already calling for the wet-nurse the Brownings had engaged to breast-feed him. Elizabeth would happily have breast-fed the boy herself, but Dr Harding advised against such a thing and she gave in to his caution. Wrote Robert, 'Babe . . . is now feeding like a hungry man.'

They were both, Robert and Elizabeth, immensely proud of the size and weight, the clear, fair, beautiful skin and all-round robustness of the baby. To Miss Mitford, on 30 April, Elizabeth described him as 'a lovely, fat, strong child, with double chins and rosy cheeks, and a great wide chest, undeniable lungs, I can assure you'. To Henrietta, on 2 May, she declared that 'Robert calls him sometimes "a little Bacchus," he is so rosy and round.' The birth itself had been lengthy but uncomplicated. Elizabeth had strong-mindedly reduced her reliance on morphine in line with Mr Jago's previous medical advice, and here was the result, the reward — a healthy son rather than a puny, sickly, mewling baby more like a changeling than a human child. Above all, she had at last performed 'the highest natural function of a woman' and done it without fuss, exactly like a normal healthy mother.

The wet-nurse — *la balia* — was something to behold. Signora Biondi was a *donna grassa*, stout and jolly and rosy, with brimful breasts, the incarnation of a perfect nursemaid. Elizabeth described her to Miss Mitford as 'quite uninjured by intellectual cultivation — she doesn't even know *the names of the months*'. Ignorance, however, never stopped her prattling from dawn to dusk in voluble Italian to the baby, who apparently understood her perfectly. The Brownings paid her by the month and provided her with a nurse's costume. 'Here in Italy it is generally arranged so,' wrote Elizabeth authoritatively to Henrietta:

It consists of a large uncut Tuscan straw hat with long blue streamers — gowns trimmed with blue ribbons (blue is a *boy's* colour, pink a girl's), white collars, smart white aprons, made of muslin, pockethandkerchief etc. For the winter she is to have a black beaver hat and black feathers. We like her very much. She is frank and honest, and full of mirth and good humour, and very fond of baby — whom she compliments upon not being at all like an English child.

'What did she mean by *that*?' I asked, not immediately perceiving the compliment.

'O, c'e qualque cosa di strana!' in all those English children, but this child is like a true downright Italian! Wilson and I in our patriotism set up defence and glorification of English children, but she shook her head, there was something unpleasant about them 'qualque cosa di strana'.

The nurse was also prone to exclaim, '*O, questo bambino è proprio rabbioso*' — which might have meant that the baby was furious or bad tempered, but more likely meant insatiable in his demands, forever hungry and irrepressibly clamorous for the breast. The only household member who was not immediately besotted with the boy was Flush, who would not be appeased but sulked and barked and crawled under furniture and dropped his ears for two weeks and refused to have anything to do with anyone, far less with the interloper, until finally he accepted the situation and 'patronised the cradle'.

In the late stages of her pregnancy, Elizabeth had brooded a little more than usually on her father. He was never far from her thoughts, and she constantly asked for news of him from her sisters. The latest appeal had been in February: 'Speak of dearest papa always.' Her sisters were safely sympathetic, her brothers had been appeased to various degrees, but Edward Moulton-Barrett had not come round. The separation from him had lasted long enough, surely. In a letter to Mrs Martin from Pisa on or about 20 October 1846, Elizabeth admitted: 'Always he has had the greatest power over my heart, because I am one of those weak women who reverence strong men ... I have loved him so and love him. Now if he had said last summer that he was reluctant for me to leave him, — if he had even allowed me to think *by mistake* that his affection for me was the motive of such reluctance — I was ready to give up Pisa in a moment, and I told him as much.'

Still, she had chosen to leave one strong man for another, and this one immediately proved the strength of his fatherhood: 'I do like men who are not ashamed to be beside a cradle.' Robert walked along the balcony of the apartment with the baby in his arms, tossed him in the air, and declared he would give his life for him — as once he had declared he would give his life for his wife's. He would have given the baby's life for hers, too. He had doubted, beforehand, that he had the paternal instinct and when Elizabeth caught a cold a couple of days before the birth and felt unwell, his nervousness for her reached such a pitch that he wished the child might mystically disappear without harm to her. But now that both were safe and prospering, and in the pride of paternity, he cut a few strands of the baby's dark hair, soft as the down on a duckling, to send to his mother.

Before the memento could reach the child's grandmother, there were letters from Sarianna, three of them: the first in February to say that Sarah Anna Browning 'was not well'; the second in March to say that she 'was very ill'; the third — delayed until Sarianna was assured by a letter from Florence that Elizabeth and the child were well — to congratulate the Brownings on the birth and to say that Sarah Anna had died. Sarianna had softened the blow, so far as that could be possible, delivering it by stages. In fact, Sarah Anna had died even before the second letter was written 'of an unsuspected disease (ossification of the heart)', as Elizabeth put it later to Miss Mitford; of 'serious apoplexy', as Sarianna afterwards identified it to Alfred Domett.[21] Her heart had given out ('poor, tender heart, the last throb was too near', wrote Elizabeth) before being allowed by her doctors to know that her first and only grandson had been born and that he had survived. For that matter, Sarah Anna had never even met Elizabeth. Whatever she knew of her son's marriage had been gleaned over the two and a half years since Robert had left home and across the distance between New Cross and Italy. Of course Robert and Elizabeth had intended to visit England every summer, but what with one thing and another — money for one, time and Elizabeth's health for another — and now . . .

Elizabeth now had to rally to the support of her husband. She wrote on 1 April to Sarianna to lament their common loss, 'for I too have lost', and to thank Sarianna for her 'consideration and admirable self-control in writing those letters. I do thank and bless you. If the news had come unbroken by such precaution to my poor darling Robert, it would have nearly killed him, I think. As it is, he has been able to cry from the first, and I am able to tell you that though dreadfully affected, of course, for you know his passionate love for her, he is better and calmer now — much better . . . No day has passed since our marriage that he has not fondly talked of her. I know how deep in his dear heart her memory lies.'

So deep, indeed, that Elizabeth had never seen, as she put it to Miss Mitford on 30 April, 'a man so bowed down in an extremity of sorrow — never. Even now the depression is great, and sometimes when I leave him alone a little and return to the room, I find him in tears. I do earnestly wish to change the scene and air; but where to go? England looks terrible now. He says it would break his heart to see his mother's roses over the wall, and place where she used to lay her scissors and gloves. Which I understand so thoroughly that I can't say, "Let us go to England." . . . It has been very painful altogether, this drawing together of life and death. Robert was too enraptured at my safety, and with his little son, and the sudden reaction was terrible.' No less terrible was the thought in Elizabeth's mind that her recent pregnancy had been the cause of Robert's separation at the last from his mother. She wrote as much, very frankly, to Sarianna: 'Very bitter has it been to me to have interposed unconsciously as I have done and deprived him of her last words and kisses — very bitter — and nothing could be so consolatory to me as to give him back to *you* at least.'

Though Elizabeth was urging Robert to visit his sister and father without her, he insistently refused and continued to weep over the letters from Sarianna for weeks, at least into the beginning of June. He would drop heavy tears over them, reported Elizabeth to Sarianna, then 'he treasures them up and reads them again and again'. He paid less attention to the baby than before, though not to the point of neglect or — as might have been — blame. 'Poor little babe,' Sarianna was told, 'who was too much rejoiced over *at first*, fell away by a most natural recoil (even *I* felt it to be *most natural*) from all that triumph. But Robert is still very fond of him, and goes to see him bathed every morning and walks up and down on the terrace with him in his arms.' For all that paternal pleasure might have been a consolation, 'Robert's nursing does not mend his spirits much.' He was pained to the deepest level of his being. His appetite failed, his sleep was disturbed and altogether, by the summer, he appeared to Elizabeth 'quite worn and altered'. She began to fear his complete nervous collapse. Elizabeth, for her part, was ready to move forward: she remarked to Sarianna, albeit wrapping it around with a great deal of sincere sentiment, 'we have to live after all'.

In these circumstances, Elizabeth took the initiative herself. Since Robert would not go to England, yet very much longed to see his father and sister, she suggested to Sarianna that she and Mr Browning should visit them in Florence: 'If your dear father can toss and rock babies as Robert can, he will be a nurse in great favour.' But meantime, until the New Cross Brownings decided whether to make the trip or not in the autumn, she managed somehow or other — mostly by insisting that the baby could do with some cooler air — to talk Robert into leaving the city. They decided to scout a suitable location ('most shadow at least expense') for the summer, to which end they left the baby with Wilson and Signora Biondi and embarked on an excursion by boat along the coast, sighting the 'white marble mountains' of Carrara, passing through olive forests, vineyards, acacia avenues, and chestnut woods, 'glorious surprises of most exquisite scenery', to Spezia, which 'wheels the blue sea into the arms of the wooded mountains'. There they visited Shelley's house at Lerici. The place, recalling Shelley's death by drowning, was painful to both of them — to Elizabeth on account of the memory of her brother, Bro, having drowned; to Robert on account not only of the death of his mother but also the pain that his Shelley-inspired enthusiasms for atheism and vegetarianism had brought her in his intemperate youth. They were not sorry to find that lodgings there were too expensive.

They wandered a little thereafter, always discovering local prices exceeded their purse, until Elizabeth persuaded Robert to consent at least to look at Bagni di Lucca. He had conceived the strongest prejudice against these Baths of Lucca, taking them for a sort of wasp's nest of scandal and gaming and expecting to find everything trodden flat by the continental English. But Elizabeth wanted to see the place, 'because it is a place to see after all. So we came, and were so charmed by the exquisite beauty of the scenery, by the coolness of the climate and the absence of our countrymen, political troubles serving admirably our private requirements, that we made an offer for rooms on the spot, and returned to Florence for baby and the rest of our establishment [Wilson, Signora Biondi, Alessandro and Flush] without further delay.' For the season of four months, the rooms, 'in the highest house of the three villages which are called the Bagni di Lucca, and which lie at the heart of a hundred mountains sung to continually by a rushing mountain stream', cost them £12 and they hoped to stay until the end of October. If the cost of living at Florence was delightfully cheap, it was even cheaper at Bagni di Lucca, so they told themselves that there was 'no extravagance in coming here'.[22]

Before returning to Bagni di Lucca, the Brownings stayed long enough in Florence to have the baby baptized on 26 June at the French Evangelical Protestant Church, which was in fact the chapel of the Prussian Legation at Florence. Their son's name, they decided, would be Robert Wiedemann Barrett Browning — Robert for at least three previous generations of Brownings, Wiedemann in honour of Sarah Anna Browning's maiden name, Barrett for Elizabeth's family. Elizabeth herself had suggested the inclusion of Wiedemann (at first with two 'n's, though the second one was later dropped). Nothing could have pleased Robert more. As he wrote, very tenderly, to Sarianna, 'I have been thinking over nothing else, these last three months, than Mama and all about her, and catching at any little fancy of finding something which it would have pleased her I should do, — yet I never was struck by the obvious opportunity I had of doing the honor in my power, little as it was, by keeping up the memory of that dearest of names — the name, beside, of her own father and mother, whom she loved so much, and of dearest aunt, too — who must have had that feeling for it, or she would not have called one of her own children by it . . . Ba told me I should greatly oblige *her* by not only giving the child that name but by always calling him by it, when he is old enough: she thinks the name very pretty in itself . . . and so it shall be. It is of course a very insignificant instance of Ba's sympathy with me, — still I mention it because it gratified me more as coming from her, than from anyone else.'

Robert's letter from Bagni di Lucca, on 2 July 1849, enclosing the certificate of birth and baptism, asked his sister, in his usual precise, somewhat fussy way, to have it 'properly registered ... as difficulties sometimes arise from omissions or negligent entries'. He had by now mostly recovered his delight in the beefy baby, describing how 'I fancied him of a worse temper than he turns out to be, for he is always merry and laughing and never cries without reason: he is very fat and well and cannot fail to profit, one would think, by the delightful change from the burning heat at Florence to the delightful cool of this place.' Everyone thought the baby 'remarkably flourishing', but between father and lively son, between Robert and the flourishing world indeed, there still lay a primitive shadow.

The liveliness of the joyful boy, the consolations of the contented wife whose intent it was to restore her husband to life and health, the regenerative value of the spiritual and physical natural beauties of Bagni di Lucca, should all have salved his soul: all this, he knew, 'ought to be unmixed pleasure to me, but is very far from it'. Sorrow is necessarily exclusive, and Elizabeth had sense enough to let Robert take time for himself, to heal in his own way. To feel happiness in the present seemed, perversely, a rejection of recent sorrows. Acknowledging in himself this denial, this self-sacrificing alienation, this severing of his attachments to his wife and son who represented life in the face of death, Robert drew breath and roused himself to a deliberate course of action. Like a convalescent recovering from a long illness, he declared to Sarianna, 'I do a plain duty in taking exercise and trying to amuse myself and recover my spirits.' Friends and acquaintances from Florence descended upon Bagni di Lucca, some of them bringing their children and babies with them, though none so fine as little Wiedemann, as they had decided to call him to distinguish between Robert *père* and Robert *fils*. What the baby later decided to call himself, they had not for the time being reckoned on.

Bagni di Lucca was, in normal times, a popular pleasure ground for the Florentine foreign colony. The topmost village, Bagni Caldi, where the Brownings lodged, was the most remote, accessible only on foot or by donkey; the village below was Alla Villa, the site of the Duke of Lucca's summer retreat; the third and lowest village, Ponte, had developed into something approximating a spa, a sort of miniature Baden-Baden.[23] Ponte, then, was Vanity Fair, the scandalous pit of frivolity and gaming that the Brownings, literally and metaphorically, rose over and dwelt above. Though Bagni di Lucca was quieter than usual that summer, and not so thronged with the addle-headed, pleasure-bent English (who by now were mostly back in England) the Brownings had so taken against, nevertheless it was ornamented — as it was every year — by the presence of Charles Lever, the Petronius, the arbiter of fashion, the master of ceremonies who presided over the customary seasonal amusements at Ponte.

He ascended to visit the Brownings, who liked him more than they had expected, since Elizabeth could not get through his novels and had anticipated less than she got in actuality from the author himself, who turned out to exhibit 'A most cordial, vivacious manner, a glowing countenance, with the animal spirits somewhat predominant over the intellect, yet the intellect by no means in default; you can't help being surprised into being pleased with him, whatever your previous inclination may be.'[24] Despite his apparent cordiality on this occasion, Lever — possibly dismayed by the liberalism and intimidated by the intellectualism of his hosts — did not take advantage of the acquaintance to renew it later in Florence. The Brownings descended from their 'eagle's nest' at least once to hear 'lectures on Shakespeare' by a Mr Stuart ('who is enlightening the English barbarians at the lower village'). To make his discourse more brilliant, and to the delight of Robert and Elizabeth, he gratifyingly cited Mrs Jameson as an authority on his subject.[25]

Otherwise, they were beyond the casual penetration of other people and beyond all but the most occasional newspapers carrying worrying intimations of the violent world they had left behind for a season. They filled their days with walking long distances through chestnut woods, up hills and down again, Elizabeth protesting that Robert's instinct to swing her up in his arms would be as likely to do her an injury as she would herself by attempting a steeper than usual climb on her own feet. There was a particularly notable adventure as far afield as Prato Fiorito, a mountain five or six miles distant, which they reached on donkeys and mountain ponies, escorted by three guides.

They gasped as they carefully negotiated narrow paths that fell away into frightful ravines; they gaped at the mountain ('pile the houses of London one upon another in a great heap and try to climb them!'); but they contrived to scramble up without incident. At the top, they sat down with the guides for a picnic of cold chicken and ham and tart. 'Wasn't it daring of us to take Baby? He was the least tired of the party, and never cried once throughout the ten long hours (six on donkey and back) — came home laughing and talking to himself, though burnt red with the sun, poor little darling, and didn't seem over-shaken or bruised the following day, as well he might be.'[26] For that matter, the Brownings were recuperating nicely from the shaking and bruising of their emotional traumas. Elizabeth herself had never felt better, and Robert was making good progress towards health and strength, recovering from his dispiriting grief and beginning to care passionately again about his own immediate family.

'Wasn't it daring of us to take Baby?' Henrietta might have thought so if she had been consulted before rather than after the event. But all that summer the baby had enjoyed his freedom; he had gurgled to himself and anyone else who took the trouble to listen; he had rolled around on floors, grass meadows, and his mother's shawl; laughed fit to burst at the tossing of horses' heads; splashed around like a chubby cherub in water and sunlight; pulled the ears of a remarkably tolerant Flush, who consented even to be ridden like a pony; and cut his first tooth. He looked now, Elizabeth decided, in consultation with Wilson, less the image of Robert than before: his face was fining down to the Barrett oval, though the mouth and chin were decidedly Browning, a perfect facsimile of Papa's.

The only dispute between Robert and Elizabeth was the language used with little Wiedemann, who could now recognize and make attempts to say words like 'Mama' and 'Papa'. Robert reproached Elizabeth for talking to the baby in Italian. Since it was his intention that the boy should be brought up as an Englishman — a principle with which Elizabeth generally concurred in point of theory, though less reliably in everyday usage — he hated the idea of his son not speaking English from the first. 'Robert being highly patriotic, you are to understand,' Elizabeth commented mockingly to Henrietta in September that year, 'and especially when the farthest from England.' The principle, then, was sound, however often practicality conspired to corrupt it. 'But as the balia talks incessantly to our child from morning till night, and he hears necessarily nothing but Italian therefore, except from Robert and me — even Wilson being forced to speak before him in Italian, to the balia and Alessandro — I really don't see that we should assist the development of his intelligence by confounding him with another language.' Time enough for Wiedemann to learn English when he went with them to England — next year, as they intended — and besides, 'We have heard of a child two years old, who stood stock still between the two tongues, and couldn't get on with either.'

Whether or not this information was well founded, it evidently seemed conclusive to Elizabeth, who had her own ideas about infant education and the limits of freedom allowed to a child. She was, in infant education, as in her politics, libertarian. Wiedemann was pretty much allowed to do as he liked; and if he came to some small grief in the course of it, as when he rolled too boisterously in a carriage and cracked his head, Elizabeth only laughed at Robert's alarm and his rush to pick him up and inspect him for damage. When Robert said, crossly, 'Really, Ba, I can't trust you,' she retorted that babies' heads were not made of Venetian glass. There had been a standing joke between Elizabeth and Henrietta that she was not to pick up the baby by his head. But it was not all insouciance in the business of bringing up baby: it was a vital matter, of the first importance, and much discussed.

On the Brownings' third wedding anniversary, 12 September 1849, 'baby came in to me with a rose in his fist, stretching it out for me to take; and then he took another to Robert. (That was dear Wilson's contrivance.)'[27] To Henrietta, Elizabeth also wrote at this time that 'Since our marriage we have lost some precious things ... he, the earthly presence of an adorable affection ... I, some faith in attachments I had counted on for tenderness and duration; but you may thank God for us that we have lost none of the love, none of the belief in one another ... and that indeed we have consciously gained in both these things. There is more love between us two at this moment than there ever has been — he is surer of me, I am surer of him: I am closer to him, and he to me. We live heart to heart all day long and everyday the same.' It may have been then, in this spirit of overwhelming feeling, that Elizabeth broached the subject of honouring in poetry the memory of those loved and lost. She knew Robert's distaste for 'personal' poetry and his disinclination to write any such thing, but it was a fit subject for conversation, as much between husband and wife as between poets; and, in the circumstances of his recent loss, there might be some release or consolation in commemorative verse, however often she had heard him speak disapprovingly of it during their courtship. But, as Betty Miller points out, Robert 'was reluctant to compose as much as an epitaph for his mother's tombstone', and indeed did not do so.[28]

Many years later, Robert Browning, in a letter of November 1864 to Julia Wedgwood, recalled that 'one morning I happened early to say something against putting one's loves into verse: then again, I said something else on the other side, one evening at Lucca, — and next morning she said hesitatingly "Do you know I once wrote some poems about *you*?" — and then — "There they are, if you care to see them," — and there was the little Book I have here — with the last Sonnet dated two days before our marriage.' The roll of poems in manuscript, if we take Robert's word in this letter, was given to him as he stood at a window looking out at a mimosa tree and a little church court. How it was done and how Elizabeth spoke, he still remembered: 'How I see the gesture, and hear the tones.' Robert noted that 'Afterward, the publishing them was through me.' They were included, under the title 'Sonnets from the Portuguese', in the two volumes that comprised the second edition of Elizabeth Barrett Browning's *Poems* published in 1850 by Chapman & Hall. Robert, in 1864, wrote of these sonnets as 'wonderfully beautiful ... I do not know of any utterance that has the same sort of thrill in it as they have — not that others have not felt it, but it is rarely given to express and experience at once that sort of feeling. Generally the life and the art are two things; at least, it seems to me an exception when they are so much one as they are with her.'

Elizabeth noted at the time only that Robert 'was much touched and pleased'. Those forty-three poems, 'that wreath of Sonnets put on me one morning unawares', were a gift, nevertheless, that weighed upon him, he recalled, as 'a strange, heavy crown'. The burden of the sonnets, whatever he meant later — perhaps the weight of love — at the time revealed to him depths of Elizabeth's love that he had not yet fathomed, and they opened to him a fuller, greater woman. He knew her again as one whose being he'd thought he had understood but who was still, even yet, fully to be known. The sonnets called Robert back to his wife from his mother:

'Guess now who holds thee?' — 'Death,' I said — but, there,
The silver answer rang . . . 'Not Death, but Love.'
    [Sonnet i, ll. 13–14]

They conspired a little over publication. The sequence's title, they decided, was to be 'Sonnets from the Portuguese', which might be taken, *prima facie*, as meaning from the Portuguese language, but in fact concealed a private reference to Elizabeth herself as 'the Portuguese'. Coming as the sonnets did, in the second edition of her *Poems*, after the poem 'Catarina to Camoëns', their placement referred by implication to Robert's loving fancy that associated the Catarina of the poem (which had affected him to tears) with Elizabeth. And since Catarina was Portuguese . . . *ergo*, Elizabeth! This little conceit, that the title of the sonnet sequence should be purposely ambiguous, pleased them both so immensely that afterwards Robert declared uncharacteristically that he never cared whether it should be unmasked or not.

There is another ambiguity — let us not call it deliberate obfuscation — about the sonnets. It is now generally credited that Robert's letter to Julia Wedgwood, placing the event at Bagni di Lucca in the summer of 1849, is the truth of the matter; but Betty Miller in a succinct footnote conveniently cites the contradictory versions put about by the Brownings themselves: 'E.B.B. held that this episode took place in Florence, in 1850. R.B. told [Edmund] Gosse that it was at Pisa in 1847, that the Sonnets were pushed "into the pocket of his coat"; and [F.J.] Furnivall that it was in "spying about" that he found the "tiny roll of paper." Julia Wedgwood and two others were told that the event took place in [Bagni di] Lucca in 1849: Miss Swanwick, that the poets "had been wedded two years" before it happened and R.B.'s daughter-in-law, that he found "the roll . . . in the top bureau drawer that first winter of their marriage".'[29] The versions given to Furnivall and Robert's daughter-in-law seem the most improbable: it was a point of honour between Robert and Elizabeth that they never read one another's writings without permission: 'I never see her letters, nor she mine, lest we should lose freedom in writing of each other.'[30] And to George Barrett, in a letter of 16–18 July 1853, Robert again emphasized his own discretion: 'I never read Ba's letters.' There is no question, however, about the date of composition of the sonnets: they were written in London in 1846, during the course of Robert's courtship of Elizabeth, though concealed from him until after the marriage and from everybody else until, soon after being shown to Robert, their formal publication.

The Brownings returned to Florence in mid-October when the weather in the mountains began breaking up, turning misty and chill. After a fatiguing journey, Elizabeth was 'very glad to get back to our chairs and tables, and I am ignoble enough to be not sorry that I can walk out without having to go up and down a ladder — or the equivalent of a ladder: and yet the dear mountains and silences, how I miss them.' They were back to something other than silence, certainly: in their absence, beyond their mountain fastness, Europe had not been notably quiet. Wilson had been worried on a particular point: Signor Righi, to whom she was engaged, had not been in touch with her. It turned out that he had been ill and Wilson fancied, as she confided to Elizabeth, he had 'suffered some vexation about the Grand Duke'. Righi had 'made no proof of heroism in fidelity toward the sovereign; and though averse at heart to Guerrazzi's revolution, was submissive to it in fact'. The Grand Ducal guard had been suspended and Righi had retired to Prato, to the family shop. The business was doing well enough to support the family, and Righi was imminently expected to show his face in Florence, but Elizabeth had her doubts. She wished Wilson well, but at times she could wish her own comfort and convenience even better. What would she do without her? For the time being, as it turned out, she did not have to worry about doing without Lily Wilson, who was disappointed by Righi. He kept his distance until the prospect of a wedding faded and died.

History, always busy, had not taken a holiday. Carlo Alberto had taken on the Austrians again in February, but was decisively knocked back at Novara on 23 March and forced to abdicate in favour of his son, Vittorio Emanuele. On 12 April, just a month after the birth of the Browning baby, there was a counter-coup in Tuscany. The collapsing government in Florence was taken over by the nervous municipal authorities, who arrested Guerrazzi and formally invited Leopoldo II to return from his self-imposed exile. Leopoldo postponed his less than triumphal re-entry into Florence until the end of July, shortly after the

Brownings left the city, having first taken the precaution of sending advance Austrian troops, mostly Hungarians and Croats, to occupy the city and put down any residual resistance. Before leaving for Bagni di Lucca, Elizabeth had watched the Austrians — some twelve thousand, and more to come, she told Henrietta — entering Florence. There was no *festa* that day: the crowd that gathered to watch 'shrank back to let them pass, in the deepest silence — not a word spoken, scarcely a breath drawn'. She and Signora Biondi — Wilson was out and Robert was at the Post Office — had run out on the balcony to watch as 'up from the end of the street and close under our windows came the artillery and baggage-waggons — the soldiers sitting upon the cannons motionless, like dusty statues'.[31]

The Italian nurse was distraught: '*Ah, signora, fa male di vedere questo. Sono brutti questi Tedeschi.*' ['Ah, madam, this is a bad thing to see. These Germans are nasty.'] Elizabeth, for her own part, felt her throat swelling with grief and indignation. She wished herself a thousand miles away. Florence was intolerable, a sad, melancholy place to be. It was partly the fault of the soft '*femelette*' Tuscans, of course, but she did not hesitate to single out the principal villain: 'As to the Grand Duke, he is made of the stuff of princes — faithless and ignoble.' Robert arrived back home to tell her that 'the Austrian General's proclamation is up — "Invited by your Grand Duke —!" So it is confessed at last, — the Duke has done it all. Wretched, infamous man. That ever I should have felt compassion for that man!' She was sincerely outraged: 'I, individually, give up the Grand Duke . . . I shed some tears when he went away, and could cry for rage at his coming back.' Robert, she admitted, had given up on Leopoldo 'a long time ago'.

Those who had been saddened to see the Grand Duke go were now saddened to see him return with Austrian support that made a mockery of his previously moderate rule and which, at a stroke, destroyed any shred of credibility he might have invoked from his past credit in Florence. Whether by personal choice or under Austrian instruction (it didn't now matter which — the public perception would have been the same in either case) he began to behave perhaps less badly in Tuscany than others were behaving elsewhere in Italy, but badly enough in contrast to his previous reputation for leniency. The constitution he had granted and had promised to protect was abolished in 1850. Press censorship was tightened, nominally at least. Tuscan patriots were imprisoned, and Leopoldo made a point of reviewing a ceremonial parade of Austrian troops in the Cascine on the occasion of the Emperor Franz Josef's birthday. Besides disbanding the Ducal Guard, he accepted honorary command of an Austrian regiment known as the Grand Duke of Tuscany's Dragoons, and approved the appointment of an Austrian general to the supreme command of the Tuscan army. Though the Risorgimento continued to burn like a slow fuse, it would be five and more years before Count Camillo Cavour, a statesman hero, more moderate, more cunning perhaps, than firebrands and firecrackers like Mazzini and Garibaldi, would make himself known as a potential political saviour. It would be to Cavour that Elizabeth would finally pin her next best nationalist hopes, her libertarian enthusiasm, and her patriotic support.

While Italy smouldered, the Brownings decided to rekindle the flame of their poetry. It was about time, Elizabeth reckoned. They had done little or nothing for three years. Robert's poem at Ancona, her own 'Meditation in Tuscany', and some editing of existing work for new editions: it didn't amount to much for two normally prolific poets. It wasn't as though either of them could afford — creatively or financially — to be idle. Elizabeth, more than Robert, had begun to fret as long as a couple of years earlier. On 8 December 1847, in her first happiness and while working on her 'Meditation in Tuscany', she had written to Miss Mitford to comment on a mutual friend who had seemingly fallen to 'pining in an access of literary despondency . . . *That*,' wrote Elizabeth firmly, 'only proves to me that she is not happy otherwise, that her life and soul are not sufficiently filled for her woman's need. I cannot believe of any woman that she can think of *fame first*.' She reprobated, very sternly, 'a vain and bitter longing for prizes, and what prizes, oh, gracious heavens! The empty cup of cold metal! *so* cold, *so* empty to a woman with a heart.' Fame, then, was not to be the spur. Duty to art and literature, rather, was the thing to set them going again; that and the need to repair the recent injuries they had both suffered. 'Being too happy doesn't agree with literary activity quite as well as I should have thought,' Elizabeth had remarked to Miss Mitford.

In Bagni di Lucca, she had begun, from her own anxiety and none too subtly, to nag at herself and at Robert: 'What am I to say about

Robert's idleness and mine?' she lamented on 1 October to Mrs Jameson. 'I scold him about it in a most anti-conjugal manner, but, you know, his spirits and nerves have been shaken of late; we must have patience. As for me, I am much better, and do something, really, now and then.' So Elizabeth had been working a little at poetry during the summer, and presumably hoped to communicate her fervour like a fever, by contagion or infection, to Robert as a means of doing him good. Fever had been on her mind in any case. There had been an outbreak of cholera in London and she had been worried for the health of her friends and of the Barretts, who (all except 'dearest Papa!') had decamped to Worthing.

In the Casa Guidi rooms, Elizabeth set herself to preparing a new second edition of her poetry that would include 'Sonnets from the Portuguese' and be published in 1850. From the beginning of November (whether on account of the weather, the baby, the work, or another pregnancy) she didn't leave the house for two months. Robert sat down to write *Christmas-Eve and Easter-Day*, which would be published on 1 April (appropriately, Easter Monday) 1850. He had certainly begun to write the poem by 9 January 1850, on which day Elizabeth wrote to Miss Mitford to say plainly, 'Robert is engaged on a poem, and I am busy with my edition.' Robert's poem resolved, or at least clarified, many of his religious difficulties and represented a major clearing-out of old psychological and theological lumber from the attic of his past. The theme — a debate about various forms of Christian worship, to put it too baldly — may have been suggested by Elizabeth or, at least, have been inspired by her more decisive religious views and tastes as to how her religion should be expressed, conducted, and observed.

The source usually cited in favour of her influence over this poem is from her letter to Robert on 15 August 1846 in which, after a discussion they had had about 'the many coloured theologies of the house', and the form their marriage service should take, she stated her unwillingness 'to put on any of the liveries of the sects'. God's truth, the truth as God knows it, she said, must be something so different from the various opinions about truth, 'these systems which fit different classes of men like their coats, and wear brown at the elbows always!'. Scornful of sectarianism, nevertheless she 'could pray anywhere and with all sorts of worshippers, from the Sistine Chapel to Mr Fox's, those kneeling and those standing. Wherever you go, in all religious societies, there is a little to revolt, and a good deal to bear with ... Still you go quickest there, where your sympathies are least ruffled and disturbed — and I like, beyond comparison best, the simplicity of the dissenters.' Not that the dissenters are by any means beyond criticism:

> Well — there is enough to dissent from among the dissenters — the Formula is rampant among them as among others — you hear things like the buzzing of flies in proof of a corruption — and see every now and then something divine set up like a post for men of irritable minds and passions to rub themselves against, calling it a holy deed — you feel moreover bigotry and ignorance pressing on you on all sides, till you gasp for breath like one strangled. But better this, even, than what is elsewhere — *this* being elsewhere too in different degrees, besides the evil of the place ... I would prefer, as a matter of custom, to pray in one of those chapels, where the minister is simple-minded and not controversial — certainly would prefer it ... The Unitarians seem to me to throw over what is most beautiful in the Christian Doctrine; but the Formulists, on the other side, stir up a dust, in which it appears excusable not to see. When the veil of the body falls, how we shall look into each other's faces, astonished, ... after one glance at God's!

This declaration had much impressed her suitor, and thus they had established between them, Robert and Elizabeth, that they were both dissenters by taste and inclination — she more firmly, perhaps, than he, who had gone over the years from the pious dissenting religion of his parents to Shelley-inspired atheism, thence to liberal Evangelicalism and whatever variations on a religious theme seemed most attractive and compelling in friends such as Fox the Unitarian and Carlyle the Transcendentalist. Now Robert thought to settle the matter as much for the sake of his deceased mother, his committed wife, and his son who should imbibe his parents' religious principles, as for his own sake. *Christmas-Eve and Easter-Day* is by no means Robert Browning's last word on his religious position, but it defines pretty well what he made of it at the time of composition and — it can reasonably be supposed — under the recent tremendous and controversial impact that *The Life of Jesus*, a translation into English by George Eliot, in 1846, of David Friedrich Strauss's *Das Leben Jesu*, had made not only on Robert Browning but on European Christian society and its traditional theologies as a whole.

The basis of Strauss's book was an analysis of the gospels that led him, as a central element in his thinking, to reject miracles as historical facts and, thus, to demythologize the gospels. A. S. Byatt, in an essay, 'Robert Browning: Incarnation and Art',[32] published in 1991 in *Passions of The Mind*, states succinctly: 'Strauss's great argument was that the New Testament History contains mythic truth, akin to the truths of other myths, or to the abstract truths of philosophy, in an incarnate form in human lives and stories.' Victorian society was becoming less secure in its Christian faith. Whether that insecurity had arisen as a natural result of debate, or a naturally-arising insecurity had sparked debate, there was a continual ferment about religion in general and Christian belief in particular. Strauss blew upon the religious coals with what seems to us now to be some cold, commonsensical air.

In their day, Strauss and the German biblical scholars of the 1830s provoked as much perturbation among the religious orthodoxies that adhered uncritically to the New Testament as Charles Darwin caused, a little later in 1859, when the publication of *The Origin of Species* contradicted the prevailing theological view that the books of the Bible in general, and the Book of Genesis in particular, were records of historical fact. Darwin's work in natural science was a powerful correlative to the philosophies of radical revisionist theologians. In his *Autobiography*, Darwin expressed the inevitable (though painful) personal conclusion that his researches had forced him to acknowledge that: 'the more we know of the fixed laws of nature, the more incredible do miracles become ... I gradually came to disbelieve in Christianity as a divine revelation ... Beautiful as is the morality of the New Testament it can hardly be denied that its perfection depends on part on the interpretation which we now put on metaphors and allegories.'

Browning's poem is a dramatic narrative in two parts, the first often lightly satirical, fantastical, and jaunty, as though 'levity only exists because of the strong conviction ... so it runs lightly over, like foam on the top of a wave.' The voice in the first part is reflective, looking back on the past; the two voices in the second part state Browning's present position, which was broadly congruent with Elizabeth's: critical of sectarianism. There is sharp realism, entirely human observation, in the scenes and characters conjured up in *Christmas-Eve*, which opens in the chapel of a dissenting congregation into which the narrator turns for shelter from the rain. The preacher is stupid and dull, the chapel-goers are churlish and physically grotesque, and so the narrator walks out into the fresh air to commune more reverently with nature, unmediated by any prescriptive form of service or ignorant interlocutor. A rainbow appears; a divine form (Jesus, impliedly) snatches up the narrator in his robe and he is transported mystically, magically, first to Rome and the 'miraculous Dome of God' propped 'with pillars of prodigious girth' that is the Vatican, thence to a lecture hall in Göttingen, home of the Higher Criticism of the Bible. Realizing that absolutism is wrong, the narrator opts for a liberal attitude that allows every sect and sectarian to possess, in his or her own way, a portion of the truth, a thread of the wondrous robe. He finds himself back where he began, in the chapel, reconciled to the congregation he had previously despised before his vision.

Easter-Day is considerably less light and substantially less satirical. It is a parleying between two voices. One complains how difficult it is to be a Christian, how insecure a man's faith may be, and how necessary God's help in sustaining it. Nature worship is all very well, in its way, but the sinews need to be stiffened by mortifications. The other voice suggests ways in which the Christian faith may be maintained and secured. The one, doubting, voice inclines towards asceticism; the second, more moderate, proposes that Divine Love is present also in modest pleasures. A vision of the Last Judgement is vouchsafed to the conjured character of the narrator of the first part, *Christmas-Eve*, and a choice is offered to him: heaven or hell. Both are states of the soul's continued being after the corporeal body has been cast off. The narrator opts for the beauty of the natural world, which turns out to be but a promise of heavenly beauty, a facsimile. As his way of life in this finite, virtual reality that is but a simulacrum of infinite beauty, the narrator chooses knowledge and art, the intellectual life. This, too, is exposed as inadequate in and by itself to inspire man to grace. Finally, the narrator turns to love, which he now perceives as the means through which the infinite beauty and the infinite love may be attained. It is love that lights the world and art and the mind.

The sternly ascetic tone of *Easter-Day* was, as Elizabeth pointed out, unlike her husband's attitude in his real, everyday life. The 'I' of the poem and the poet himself should not be regarded as identical, no matter how closely Robert's religious beliefs corresponded with those expressed in the poem. In a letter of 4 May 1850 to Mrs Jameson, Elizabeth praised her husband's *'faculty'* — 'he can do anything he chooses' — but she had complained to Robert of the *'asceticism'* in the second part', to which he had replied that it was *'one side of the question'* and she understood that 'it is his way to *see* things as passionately as other people *feel* them'. *Christmas-Eve and Easter-Day* was a formidable achievement, for the most part respectfully received by the few reviewers who noticed it and for the remaining part neglectfully received by the public who declined to buy it. Two hundred copies were sold in the two weeks after publication, but few thereafter. Copies were still available in the 1860s. Though the publishers, Chapman & Hall, had taken it on at their own risk — and so, unusually, this time it had cost Robert nothing in monetary terms — neither his prestige nor his purse was much profited by the work, which had been mainly beneficial in the matter of salving his own soul and his lingering grief over the death of Sarah Anna Browning.

A. S. Byatt, in the essay referred to above, quotes Browning's remarks to Mrs Orr as she recorded them in her *Handbook to the Works of Browning* (1885), and suggests that 'his position is not far from that of Strauss, or even with a touch of extra scepticism'. Browning said: 'I know the difficulty of believing . . . I know all that may be said against it [the Christian scheme of salvation] on the ground of history, of reason, of even moral sense. I grant even that it may be a fiction. But I am none the less convinced that the life and death of Christ, as Christians apprehend it, supply something which their humanity requires; and that is true for them.' Humanity, he declared, requires Christ. 'The evidence of Divine Power is everywhere about us; not so the evidence of Divine Love. That love could only reveal itself to the human heart by some supreme act of *human* tenderness and devotion; the fact, or fancy, of Christ's cross and passion could alone supply such a revelation.' Byatt points out that Browning's position, so stated, 'could be seen as an uneasy half-way house between a warm faith clung to, and the cold truth of an empty universe of law. It gave Browning a way to study what it means to be human and incarnate with, and in some cases without, the idea that infinite loves could, in fact or fancy, inhabit finite human hearts.' It might also be thought that Browning was balanced between the optimistic Epicurean and pessimistic Pascalian views of the universe; the one warm and welcoming, in which man may trust in a dissolution back to the friendly elements from which he came; the other fearful and awe-ful, the prospect of extinction merely, of nothing beyond but an eternally silent, infinite space.

These were serious matters, and they seriously bothered Robert Browning. But neither religion nor politics much disturbed the mind of William Wetmore Story, who returned with his family from Rome that autumn of 1850 to Florence. William Irvine and Park Honan astutely point out that 'Story's career is a Henry James novel that Henry James never wrote. Fortunately, he did write the biography. The theme is a variation on *The Portrait of a Lady:* the discovery of Europe, art, and happiness descends as a catastrophic interruption on a conventional America success.'[33]

In his biography of Story, Henry James conceded the novelistic potential: 'The old relation, social, personal, aesthetic, of the American world to the European ... is as charming a subject as the student of manners, morals, personal adventures, the history of taste, the development of a society, need wish to take up ... They came from a world that was changing, but they came to one likewise not immutable, not quite fixed, for their amusement, as under a glass case; and it would have quickened their thrill to be a little more aware than they seem generally to have been that some possible sensations were slipping away for ever, that they were no more than just in time for the best parts of the feast, and that a later and less lucky generation might have as many regrets as surprises.'[34]

Story, born in Salem, Massachusetts, in 1812, was 'upwards of thirty' when he abandoned a distinguished career as an academic lawyer for sculpture. In 1846, he was commissioned, as an amateur of figure modelling and painting, to make a public monument and statue to commemorate his father, Mr Justice Story of the US Supreme Court, who had died that year. Story consented on the condition that he should go to Europe and 'see what had been done in these ways'. He returned home, sketched his ideas for the monument, which were accepted, and took up his profession of law again. In eight months, he wrote an additional volume to supplement his existing work on contract law and a two-volume biography of his father. 'I was haunted, however, by dreams of art and Italy, and every night fancied I was again in Rome and at work in my studio. At last I found my heart had gone over from the Law to Art, and I determined to go back to Rome.'[35]

In 1848, he did exactly that. Story's choice of Rome over Boston was, James asserts, fully mature in the sense of what he had renounced, and with a 'lively intelligence, though doubtless with some admirably confused ideas . . . in respect of what he preferred'. It was, nevertheless, a decided and stubborn intelligence: 'It was William Story's advantage that he was, by the turn of his mind, sure — as he was also afterwards sure, almost always sure, of many things, with plenty of the love of discussion that makes our certainties sociable. . . .'

On their way from Genoa to Rome, stopping off in Florence for a few weeks, Story and his family first encountered the Brownings. To his constant friend the poet James Russell Lowell, from Rome on 21 March 1849, Story wrote, 'The Brownings and we became great friends in Florence, and of course we could not become friends without liking each other . . . He is of my size, but slighter, with straight black hair, small eyes, wide apart, which he twitches constantly together, a smooth face, a slightly aquiline nose, and manners nervous and rapid. He has a great vivacity, but not the least humour, some sarcasm, considerable critical faculty, and very great frankness and friendliness of manner and mind.' As to Mrs Browning, Story observed her just as particularly: Elizabeth 'used to sit buried up in a large easy chair, listening and talking very quietly and pleasantly, with nothing of that peculiarity which one would expect from reading her poems. Her eyes are small, her mouth large, she wears a cap and long curls. Very unaffected and pleasant and simple-hearted is she, and Browning says "her poems are the least good part of her." '[36]

Simple-heartedness is attracted to simple-heartedness, perhaps, and mutual recognition in that respect would have endeared them, the one to the other. As to Robert's lack of humour, among strangers, in male society particularly, it was admittedly sometimes wooden at best, forced when necessary, jocular rather than witty; but in the company of women it showed itself to better effect. Elizabeth and Robert laughed together often; Mrs Jameson came away from Robert delighted with his humour;

and Mary Boyle could not have made him laugh if he had not some capacity for recognizing humour and responding to it unaffectedly. But we are reminded of Thomas Trollope's assertion that Robert was stiff with men he did not know well, and Story was writing, in the letter to Lowell, after first acquaintance with Robert, who might well have been more guarded than he later became. If that might be a fault, it was transcended by other virtues that recommended him to Story's liking and friendship. Robert himself respected his new friend very highly, to the extent that he wrote to Thomas Carlyle on 10 June 1850 to recommend him, should Story care to call on Carlyle during a short visit he was then making to England.

In Rome, Mrs Story discovered an old friend from her former life in Boston: the Marchesa d'Ossoli, formerly Margaret Fuller, now married to Angelo Ossoli, an impoverished ('*decaduto*', Henry James politely puts it) but good-looking Roman aristocrat. If they were not actually married, they were supposed to be, since they had produced an infant son together. The Marchese was sadly possessed of no great intellect himself and sensibly deferred to his wife in conversation. But, as Elizabeth kindly characterized him, Ossoli was 'gentlemanly and amiable'. He made less impression on the Brownings and American friends than his celebrated wife, who, though at a loss, like everybody else, to understand the overall title of the poems, had enthusiastically reviewed Robert's *Bells and Pomegranates* as literary editor of the *New York Tribune* and had written of Elizabeth Barrett Browning as being 'above any female writer the world has known'. This, by itself, would have recommended the Marchesa d'Ossoli to Robert's whole heart; a further recommendation, from Elizabeth's point of view, was that she had known and could report at first hand about her meetings with George Sand (the nom de plume of Amandine Aurore Dupin) in Paris. Henry James, in his biography of Story, looks upon Madame Ossoli a little quizzically: 'Would she ... with her appetite for ideas and her genius for conversation, have struck us but as a somewhat formidable bore, one of the worst kind, a culture-seeker without a sense of proportion, or, on the contrary, have affected us as a really attaching, a possibly picturesque New England Corinne?'[37]

Corinne, whose adventures in the eponymous novel (1807) were narrated by Madame de Staël, arrived in Tuscany after a period in

Scotland. Her feelings were best prefaced by a quotation from Milton: ' *"Combien est terrible,"* dit Milton, *"le désespoir que cet air si doux ne calme pas!" Il faut l'amour ou la religion pour goûter la nature.'* Margaret Fuller had followed Corinne's instincts. She had found the solace of love in Italy, and she neither neglected her bracing religion nor forgot her profound taste for nature in Tuscany, whence she fled in the last months of 1849, to escape the fall of the republic in Rome. Her religion was Socialism (abhorrent to the Brownings, who believed it to be incompatible with liberty) and her philosophy was inspired by the progressive literary and romantic Transcendentalism of Ralph Waldo Emerson and Thoreau, who were influential among the mid-nineteenth-century Concord circle and the Brook Farm community in Massachusetts. In Boston, she had been the first editor of *The Dial*, the organ of New England Transcendentalism. She professed ardent feminist views and was open to passionate friendships with other women.

In Italy, her ideal heroic philosopher and statesman was Mazzini, and in the final days of the republic in Rome she had worked tirelessly as a nurse while her husband had fought physically in the ranks of republican defenders. During their six months in Florence, she visited the Brownings regularly and came to 'love and admire them both more and more, as I know them better. Mr Browning enriches every hour I pass with him, and is a most cordial, true and noble man.'[38] La Ossoli in turn impressed Elizabeth as 'A very interesting person ... far better than her writings — thoughtful, spiritual in her habitual mode of mind; not only exalted but *exaltée* in her opinions, and yet calm in manner. We shall be sorry to lose her.'[39]

The loss was greater than Elizabeth, and other friends of the Ossolis, could have imagined. A few days after this letter, Margaret spent her last evening in Florence with the Brownings. It was not the best or liveliest of occasions. 'Such gloom she had on leaving Italy. So full she was of sad presentiment! Do you know she gave a *Bible* as a parting gift from her child to ours, writing in it *"In memory of* Angelo Eugene Ossoli".'[40] Margaret's talk of forebodings and omens was fixed on a prophecy that her husband 'should shun the sea, for that it would be fatal to him'. A better omen, Margaret thought, was that the ship the Ossolis were shortly to sail on for America was called the *Elizabeth*. Margaret had written to the Brownings from Gibraltar, Robert reported on 16 August 1850 to John Kenyon. They had received a 'sad strange letter, but most affectionate, telling us how disastrously the voyage had proceeded thus far, the captain had died of smallpox . . . she had tended the dying man, whose sufferings had been horrible'. The letter had 'ended by bidding us write what should be the first thing to meet her at home. You see what *did* meet her, and the more particular accounts that have reached us are simply heart-rending.' Within fifty yards of the American shore, the *Elizabeth* had foundered in a sudden storm. The Ossolis, all three of them, were drowned.

Robert, to judge by the tone of his letter to Kenyon, was sincerely harrowed by their deaths and, even more, by the details he learned of the tragedy — so much so that he had kept them to himself for as long as possible in order not to distress Elizabeth, who, on 28 July, 'two months advanced towards confinement', suffered her fourth and most serious miscarriage. She had miscarried for the third time at about Christmas 1849, but had quickly recovered her health and spirits. This time it had been much worse. Robert assured Kenyon that they had 'good, prompt medical assistance' and that Elizabeth was now out of danger, 'wonderfully better indeed', though she had lost more than a hundred ounces (more than five pints) of blood in the course of twenty-four hours, making it necessary for Dr Harding to pack ice around her body to stop the haemorrhaging. 'Not one in five thousand women would suffer to the same extent,' the doctor had told Robert.

When Elizabeth was able to travel on 31 August, the Brownings and their household went by train to Siena. Robert had earlier rented a villa on Poggio dei Venti, a windblown hill a couple of miles outside the city, and there they spent the rest of the summer. Elizabeth's fertility, in her early forties, and against all expectations, is very striking. Since her marriage, she had been almost constantly pregnant: this last was the fifth pregnancy. So many miscarriages might have depressed any woman, but Elizabeth seems to have suffered no discernible lasting psychological damage. She and Robert must have been disappointed on each occasion, but since miscarriage had become almost habitual, they evidently came to terms with it; and, of course, there was the boy — Wiedemann, the wondrous child they had brought fully to life — every day more delightful.

Wiedemann preferred the name Pennini, or Penini (shortened to

Pen), for himself when he was able to pronounce it. There is some dispute as to how he acquired the diminutive. It hardly sounds like a corruption, even in Pen's baby talk, of Wiedemann, though that is the theory usually subscribed to. Nathaniel Hawthorne, in his *French and Italian Notebooks*, in an entry of 9 June 1858, writes confidently that boy was called 'Pennini for fondness ... a diminutive of Apennino, which was bestowed upon him at his first advent into the world because he was so very small, there being a statue in Florence of colossal size called Apennino.' Mrs Orr gives a ladylike snort at this interpretation: the boy was of normal size, and 'Apennino could by no process congenial to the Italian language be converted into Penini.' Her view is that it doesn't matter, having not 'much bearing on his father's family history'.[41] And so dismissing all idle speculations, she passes to the much more important topic of Pen's precocity and delightfulness.

Pen was charming when he was not crossed; angelic when he was indulged — which was constantly. His parents played with him end-lessly, bought him toys that they themselves showed him how to work, though they were sometimes as much a mystery to the parents as to the child (Robert got on his knees one Sunday morning, as 'a religious duty', to learn how to spin a top), and Elizabeth dressed him elaborately. In the summer of 1850 he was reluctantly but finally weaned from Signora Biondi's brimful breasts only by the expedient of smearing the nipples with bitter aloes. Pen was an energetic, healthy child and so, when he fell briefly but alarmingly ill with sunstroke shortly after his mother's last miscarriage, Elizabeth was distraught.

She frankly admitted that the boy was spoiled. But what did 'spoil-ing' mean? Its result, at least, was indiscipline. Both she and Robert, Elizabeth admitted to Miss Mitford, had no desire to court unpopularity with Pen. Robert, too, may have fondly recalled the licence afforded to him by his own parents, his father particularly. Pen himself seems to have been generally sweet-tempered and sunny-natured except when thwarted in any desire, whereupon he could — and would — scream dreadfully. When he wasn't shouting, he was singing. Elizabeth, in her letters, wrote a very great deal about the wonderful child. She couldn't give her friends and her sisters enough charming details about his activi-ties and accomplishments, though one can hear more than enough about them.

On 6 April 1850, Henrietta had married her longtime suitor, Captain Surtees Cook. He had been patiently courting her for five years. By marrying, Henrietta inevitably invoked the wrath of her father in precisely the same terms as Elizabeth had done, though Arabel and Henrietta's brothers were more sympathetic and supportive of Henrietta than they had been of Elizabeth. Rather inconsistently, Elizabeth expressed some minor disapproval: she did not think (exactly as her brothers had doubted Robert Browning) that Captain Surtees Cook could really afford to marry. But the deed was done — though none of the Barrett brothers, in deference to their father, had attended the wedding — and Elizabeth was full of plans for the domestic economy of the newly-weds. The ideal solution, naturally, would be that they should come to Paris or Florence where the living was cheap and their income would stretch, Elizabeth believed, to three or four times the extent it would in England. Henrietta doubted that she could live outside England, but Elizabeth was dismissive of such 'sublime' patriotism. And besides, there was the question of the weather. England, it was well known, had the world's worst climate. It was almost inconceivable that Henrietta could not see that France or Italy — or Brussels or Heidelberg, if it should come to that: anywhere but England — offered every benefit.

If Henrietta would not come to Florence, then plainly the Brownings must pay a visit to England. John Kenyon, in the summer of 1850, had offered to pay their travel expenses, but Robert had refused. In his letter of 16 August that year to Kenyon, he had been properly grateful for the kind thought, but refused it on the ground that, 'Our finances are straitened certainly, nor will this new doctor's bill improve them, but we have economised of late ... All my life I have elected to be poor, and perhaps the reason, or one among other reasons, may be that I have a very particular capacity for being rich ... so that there is no poor-spiritedness in my choosing to bound my wishes by any means, seeing that fortune could not easily supply me with means which I could not, if I pleased, outgo, at one stride, by my wishes ... be assured I could so effectually turn those moneys to account that not one unprofit-able penny should cumber my pocket at the year's end. But it was decreed otherwise ... Bless you, we are rich and excellenza'd and signo-ria'd all over Florence, and I patronise art in a way.' What this embar-rassed levity seems to mean is that being poor or rich is no great matter.

Robert is rich enough in all things but money, the least thing, and an excess of money will never be enough. But there is here, too, an echo of Robert's father who, from the purest motives and to the strongly-professed pride of his son, had given up an inheritance and had chosen to be poor.

In 1851, however, the Brownings took stock of their finances again and decided that their position, taking into account the income to be got from sub-letting the Casa Guidi apartment in their absence, was not so pinched as to make the long-promised visit to England impossible. At the beginning of their residence in Italy, they had fretted at the delay in getting back to London, but now they were, on the contrary, distressed by the very idea of returning even for a visit. Elizabeth regarded the thought of England as abhorrent, and would have preferred to meet Arabel and Henrietta and Robert's father and sister in France, or at least on the southern English coast.[42] However much they looked forward, albeit with some anxiety, to seeing their families again, they were eager to find some intellectual stimulation in Paris rather than London. Florence had come to seem a little stifling, a little cramped. Socially, it was lively enough, but hardly a literary Parnassus. Elizabeth was highly regarded as a poet by votaries in Florence, but her professional repu-tation — past and present — was higher still in England.

In 1850, her name had been promoted by the *Athenaeum* as a candi-date for the Poet Laureateship after the death of Wordsworth in April that year. The suggestion, at first made anonymously in late April (by a sub-editor, novelist, and friend of Robert's, Henry Fothergill Chorley), was the trigger for the *Athenaeum*'s campaign *against* the Laureateship as a meaningless, offensive, intellectually servile appointment that no self-respecting poet should consider. The only remedy, declared the *Athenaeum*, was abolition of the title altogether. It was in this context that Elizabeth's name had been put forward by the press. In the event, the Laureateship was awarded to Alfred Tennyson, whose standing was at its highest after publication that year of *In Memoriam*. Robert was not considered at all, even satirically. Elizabeth herself, should the post continue, preferred Leigh Hunt, if one discounted his lack of delicacy and good taste, on the ground that he was a great and good man who had been long neglected by the world.[43] The revised edition of Elizabeth's *Poems* had been published in London six months previously but had made little impression on reviewers. But now in May 1851, when the Brownings set off, her great poem *Casa Guidi Windows* was to be published and she had hopes of its success.

Having assured themselves that Elizabeth was fit and well, they travelled from Florence by coach for Mantua, thence by rail for Venice, on the first leg of their circuitous journey home — if that was what London might still be. In Venice, Elizabeth found herself 'between heaven and earth ... Never had I touched the skirts of so celestial a place. Do you know, when I came first I felt as if I never could go away. But now comes the earth side. Robert, after sharing the ecstasy, grows uncomfortable, and nervous, and unable to eat or sleep; and poor Wilson, still worse, in a miserable condition of continual sickness and headache. Alas for these mortal Venices — so exquisite and so bilious!'[44] Elizabeth and Pen, on the contrary, fattened and flourished. Robert's discomfort was as much due to a financial crisis as any physical debility. He had written from Venice to his uncle, the banker Reuben Browning, on 5 June. On 12 June, lest the first letter had gone astray, he wrote again in plain distress to try to discover 'what monies of mine have been paid into my account, or not paid'.

John Kenyon's bi-annual payment of £50, due to be credited in June (Kenyon, though reliable about these payments, could be unreliable about their promptness), was necessary to meet 'the Bill I had drawn in Florence, payable at the beginning of June', and another bill had been due to be met by a payment of 'Ship Div[iden]ds (which have never yet been so late in payment)'. The bills would be covered by 'a reserve we have, of £200 in the Bank, — set apart for the very purpose of meeting such emergencies'. The ship dividends, an investment greatly depended upon by the Brownings, amounted to £120, besides which there was a bank dividend, amounting to some £44, due in July. Reuben had accepted Robert's bills, but had — in the manner of a banker — expressed 'generally the informality of using an expired credit'. The main thing now was to obtain Reuben's official authorization for £50, which Robert could draw upon later at Lucerne, 'as otherwise I shall be in the greatest difficulty — not knowing anyone there'.

Besides, there was the immediate question of Schielin's, the Venetian bankers', commission charges of 1 per cent at Venice (twice as high as the rate in Florence) and more still for interest charges, 'in addition to the clever "dodge" of having no *napoléons d'or* ready, two days ago, when I went for my money — and then telling me this morning when I returned for them — that the value having risen *since then*, I must pay more for them — as indeed I did.' This sharp banking practice was all the more outrageous since the day before 'being a Festa was *no day* at his Bank'. The day after this letter, 13 June, the Brownings left Venice and proceeded to Padua (with a side trip to Arqua to view Petrarch's house and tomb), Brescia, Verona, and Milan, crossing the Italian lakes by steamer, and thence to Lucerne via the snows of Mount St Gothard. At Lucerne, with only a few francs to spare, Robert found to his horror that the ship-money amounted only to £50. He 'fell into a despondence about the bread we should get to eat for the next six months — and there was nothing for it but to give up lakes and mountains and come straight to Paris'.[45]

The Brownings, with Wilson and Pen, arrived in Paris at the end of June. Forgetting the *belle chiese* of Florence — there might well be churches just as lovely in Paris, but that city was famous for more material pleasures — Elizabeth wrote on 7 July to John Kenyon that 'we have beautiful shops instead, false teeth grinning at the corners of the streets, and disreputable prints, and fascinating hats and caps, and brilliant restaurants, and M. le Président in a cocked hat and with a train of cavalry, passing like a rocket along the boulevards to an occasional yell from the Red ... I like it all extremely, it's a splendid city — a city in the country, as Venice is a city in the sea.' They had settled in a 'comfortable quiet hotel, where it is possible, and not ruinous, to wait and look about one'. They had looked for the hotel they had stayed in on their first visit to Paris but mistook it for another which they liked well enough to stay. In Paris, they happened to meet Alfred Tennyson and his wife — on their way to Florence, as it happened — who invited them to tea at their own hotel nearby. Elizabeth, '(though tired half to death with the Louvre) rose up from the sofa in a decided state of resurrection, and acceded at once'. The Brownings were 'gratified — charmed ... Nothing could be warmer, nothing more pleasant'. The next day Tennyson — (who had been reading Robert's poems aloud the previous evening) and his charming wife called again. The Brownings happened not to be at home, so they in turn called on the Tennysons. They 'were all friends at once', to the degree that Tennyson pressed the Brownings to stay at his house at Twickenham for as long as they were in England and to the extent of his giving them a note to this effect for his servants. They had no intention of taking Tennyson up on his offer, but 'We took the note — it is an autograph at once of genius and kindness. How few ordinary men would have acted so! For, observe,' Elizabeth noted to Henrietta on 21 July, 'he had met Robert only twice or thrice in his life at London dinners and soirées. There had been no previous friendship. We are both pleased and touched to the heart.'

As to the prospect of England, the closer it loomed the more doubtful it seemed. Were it not for Arabel in London and Henrietta in Somerset, neither of whom could conveniently travel to France, they would not go. Robert's father and sister had said they would come to Paris to visit them there. 'I feel here *near enough* to England, that's the truth,' Elizabeth remarked to John Kenyon. 'I recoil from the bitterness of being nearer. Still, it must be thought of.' Robert, as Elizabeth reported to Mrs Ogilvy on 25 July, had 'lost his spirits from the moment of crossing the Alps and grew so unwell in Paris, fell into such a state of morbid nervousness, that at last I resolved on persuading him against going to England at all. The idea of taking his wife and child to New Cross and putting them into the place of his mother, was haunting him day and night, and I was afraid to think how it might end.' But it was thought of, despite the dread, and so it was done. They arrived in London in the third week of July and lodged in rooms Arabel had found for them in Portman Square before moving, for the rest of their two-month stay, to an expensive, gloomy apartment at 26 Devonshire Street, close to Wimpole Street, where they were 'miserably off' and Elizabeth couldn't 'tuck myself in anyhow'.[46]

Robert chose to go to New Cross alone — there is no account of this visit — and returned in better spirits: 'He is himself again.' Elizabeth was visited by Arabel and those of her brothers who were then in London — 'they came to us instantly'. Henrietta came up to London from Taunton with her own baby son to spend a week with them. Following on family, came a tidal wave of friends — 'Robert and I have not eaten an uninterrupted meal since we came': they included Barry Cornwall (the pen-name of the poet Bryan Waller Procter), Miss

Mitford, John Kenyon (who invited Robert and Elizabeth to dinner where they met — Elizabeth for the first time — Thomas Carlyle and his wife Jane), John Forster (who also took them to dinner), Chorley of the *Athenaeum*, and Mrs Jameson. Most of these struck Elizabeth as 'younger than I expected — especially Carlyle, with his slim, active figure and thick bushy hair'.

With Mrs Jameson, the Brownings visited the Great Exhibition at the Crystal Palace in the teeth of Carlyle's grumbles that it was 'a dreadful sight. There was confusion enough in the world without building a chrystal [*sic*] palace to represent it', and they heard the celebrated actress Fanny Kemble 'read Hamlet, with that face and voice of hers so various, deep and touching in vibrations. The reading struck and charmed me, and I could not criticize, as Robert does who is more learned.' Mrs Kemble returned the compliment and called on the Brownings, leaving — too late — cards of free admission to her performance. Wilson, naturally, seized her chance to spend ten days or a fortnight with her mother, who lived near Sheffield. She left Pen with Elizabeth, to the dismay and bewilderment of both since they had naturally assumed that Wilson would take Pen with her until she flatly refused the request. It was difficult to tell which of them missed Wilson the most.

It was an exhilarating business, this social whirl. Robert was delighted and energized by London literary life, easily and quickly picking up the threads of the friendships and pleasures he had let drop on his marriage and weaving in a few more. Elizabeth commented to Mrs Jameson that it was 'pure joy' to him. She, too, was dazzled by the brilliance and warmth of the fêting they both experienced, though from her 'first step ashore . . . into a puddle and fog' she had begun to cough even before reaching the city. Robert had abandoned London and all that it held in the way of society and prospects for his career principally because of his wife's health. It was very apparent, no matter how she delighted in Robert's enthusiasm, that she would never be able to acclimatize herself to the bad air of London and the climate of England, even in summer, no matter how she had recovered her health in Italy. This visit could only be temporary.

The interest of their friends was one thing: no difficulties, not even the natural curiosity of a gossiping society to see how the romantic lovers had fared, spoiled their reception. All was gas and gaiters, gilt and gingerbread. Quite other was the strain of family life. Elizabeth and Pen had been introduced to Sarianna and Mr Browning. Sarianna became virtually indispensable as an aunt to her nephew and as a friend to her sister-in-law, while Grandfather Browning formed as strong an attachment to Pen as he had to his own son. There was no unease, only warmth and affection, with the Brownings of New Cross.

The principal trouble lay in Wimpole Street, where Elizabeth, taking all possible precautions to avoid meeting her father, visited with sister Arabel. There was some residual frostiness from her brothers, all but George, with whom the Brownings became fully reconciled. The ice was still impenetrably thick in respect of her father. There was one heart-stopping near miss when Mr Barrett returned home unexpectedly from his office in the City and Elizabeth hid in Arabel's room from his footsteps on the stair. Robert regarded this closest of calls as 'imprudent to excess'. The end of it was that both Elizabeth and Robert wrote to her father and received in return a 'violent and unsparing' reply accompanied by a packet (sealed with black wax) containing all Elizabeth's letters which, for the past five years, Mr Barrett had saved up unopened for want of an address 'where he should send them'. That, then, however distressing, appeared to be final.

There was another, rather galling matter to be taken care of. On 23 September Robert wrote to Edward Chapman, his publisher, to ask that separate accounts for his own and Elizabeth's books should be sent to them every half year, at Christmas and in June. 'On the whole, everything seems tolerably satisfactory in the sale of the different books — even of mine, which will, I doubt not, succeed in the long run — but I am vexed at the ill luck of *Christmas Eve* etc. Was the price [six shillings] too high? Could anything be done by judicious advertizing at the seasons the book treats of? Could one put in some illustrations, even now? I might get you a few good ones.' Robert was at last, rather late in the day, thinking more practically about his popularity, and this question of appealing to the public, not only by judicious planning of publication strategies but — more — of acknowledging the public taste in poetry, clearly had begun to work in his mind and to influence his approach to his work.

On the morning of Thursday 25 September, the Brownings left London by train for Newhaven, where they intended to take the afternoon steamer for Dieppe and, next day, the train for Paris. This, as Robert had informed Thomas Carlyle in a letter of 23 September, was the cheapest route. Carlyle took the opportunity to travel with them. The job of negotiating Carlyle through the noise, smoke, population, and general turbulence of the multitudinous, transcendental universe to land him safe, but suspicious, at his destination, Lord and Lady Ashburton's house in Paris, took all Robert's management skills. Battling with a cold that might have been influenza, Robert magnificently managed the sage's tickets and manoeuvred his luggage, fought for seats for Carlyle and his own family, smoothed his friend's passage through customs, supervised payment of his bills, and generally wrestled with the world while Carlyle, impressed by Robert's exertions and voluble cheerfulness under pressure, blandly and magisterially sat peacefully at a distance from any strenuous effort and blithely smoked his cigar.

Elizabeth was much struck by the great man. To Mrs Jameson on 21 October, she wrote: 'Are you aware that Carlyle travelled with us to Paris? He left a deep impression with me. It is difficult to conceive of a more interesting human soul, I think. All the bitterness is love with the point reversed. He seems to me to have a profound sensibility — so profound and turbulent that it unsettles his general sympathies.' Which, being interpreted, probably meant generally perverse and sometimes crabby, albeit for good and perfectly understandable philosophical reasons that set him at odds with the rest of the world. To Miss Mitford, the next day, she remarked, 'Highly picturesque too he is in conversation. The talk of writing men is very seldom as good.'

'Robert,' reported Elizabeth to Mrs Jameson, 'is in good spirits and inclined to like Paris increasingly', though it had taken him some troublesome running around for two weeks to get himself and his household settled in suitable lodgings, described by Robert to Carlyle in a letter of October 1851 as 'pretty much what we looked for — a place somewhat more out of the way than was desirable — but sunny, cheerful, airy and quiet'. They had what Elizabeth described to Miss Mitford as 'a slip of a kitchen, and no passage, no staircase to take up the room which is altogether *spent* upon sitting and sleeping rooms'. This accommodation, on the sunny side of the street, consisted in fact of 'pretty cheerful carpeted rooms — a drawing room, a dressing and writing room for Robert, a small dining room, two comfortable bedrooms and a third bedroom upstairs for the *femme de service*, kitchen, etc.'. They kept themselves warm that cold winter by enormous fires, and the 'lack of passages or staircases to catch one's death in' was not to be regretted.

Elizabeth was delighted to get back to continental standards: 'Talk of English comforts! It's a national delusion. The comfort of the continental way of life has only to be tested to be recognized . . . The economy of a habitation is understood in Paris. You have the advantages of a large house without the disadvantages, without the coldness, without the dearness. And the beds, chairs and sofas are perfect things.'[47] Their address, with the advantage of a terrace Elizabeth described as being big as a garden overlooking the street, was 138 Avenue des Champs Elysées; the price of their accommodation was 200 francs a month, about £8, four times the cost of their Casa Guidi rooms. They added to their household a maid (the *femme de service*), Desirée, who cleaned and cooked; she also made cakes for Lady Elgin and Mme Mohl — the English-born wife of the orientalist Julius Mohl who came for tea and to discuss spiritualism and Shelley — as well as dinners for the Brownings.

The prospect of stimulating society was excited by an invitation to the Monday evening receptions, between eight and twelve, at Lady Elgin's in the Faubourg St Germain. Reputedly, she kept one of the best houses in Paris. Her late husband, the Earl of Elgin ('the marble man — "fixed statue on the pedestal of shame" as Lord Byron called him without reason', Elizabeth commented to her brother George), had distinguished himself as a diplomat and an acquisitive connoisseur of art by transporting a considerable quantity of Greek statuary from the Parthenon to London, at first intending it as an ornament to his own house and grounds. A morning dress was *de rigueur* in the salons of Paris: 'One dresses up to the throat, as in Italy, but with the head bare, they tell me,' Elizabeth reported to Henrietta. Robert had persuaded Elizabeth to leave off her caps, in any case. But Lady Elgin's 'reception', for all her prodigality (in addition to the usual weak tea of the Paris salons, 'she gave us bread and butter'), was small beer, hardly intoxicating. There the Brownings 'saw some French but nobody of distinction', a result disappointing to Elizabeth who had — in trembling anticipation — 'expected to see Balzac's duchesses and *hommes de lettres* on all sides.'

Better might be the Friday evenings at Madame Mohl's in rue du

Bac, 'where we are to have some of the "celebrities," I believe, for she seems to know everybody of all colours from white to red'. Mme Mohl, formerly Mary Clarke, though born in England, had received a French education and had learned from her former association with the famous Mme Récamier how to run a fashionable salon. Augustus Hare, in *The Years with Mother*, described her memorably as she appeared in 1857, 'a most extraordinary-looking person, like a poodle, with frizzled hair hanging down over her face and very short skirts'. William Wetmore Story vividly pictured her talk as 'all her own; nobody was like her for a jumble of ideas and facts, which made her mind much like her clothes, topsy-turvily worn.'[48] Elizabeth liked Mme Mohl very much.

More exciting yet, Carlyle had promised to obtain, on his return to London, a letter from Mazzini for the Brownings as a passport to the presence of George Sand, famous throughout Europe and America as a romantic novelist and playwright, and notorious as a married woman who had conducted notable affairs with the poet Alfred de Musset and the Polish pianist-composer Frédéric Chopin. Elizabeth had heard that the great woman 'is seldom at Paris now. She has devoted herself to play writing, and employs a houseful of men, her son's friends and her own, in acting privately with her what she writes — trying it on a home stage before she tries it at Paris.'[49]

Robert had gossiped too, a little more sourly, in a letter of October 1851 to Carlyle: 'We heard quantities about her the other night — from what may possibly be an authentic source — how she has grown visibly aged of a sudden (like Mephistopheles at the Brocken when he says he finds people ripe for the last day) and is getting more resigned to it than she had expected, seeing that with youth go "a Hell of Passions" — (which is all she knows about it). Meanwhile, the next best thing to youth, and the Hell and so on, is found to be strenuous play-writing. She writes in the country and her friends rehearse, test effects, prophesy of hits or misses of the Paris auditory; whereat she takes heart and writes again, points this, blunts that: one might as well or better, try and make articles for Chapman's Review, certainly!' By mid-November, however, it was said that George Sand would be in Paris by the end of the month, and Elizabeth was determined not to let slip this rare opportunity to meet with her.

Elizabeth had developed a cough and had given up most of her evening excursions, though she insisted that Robert should go forth and put himself in the way of congenial company. She had noted his socia-bility in London and knew that high-minded social diversions suited his temperament. In any case, 'we might as well be at Florence if he shuts himself up here as he does sometimes for days together'.[50] At these receptions, *chez* Lady Elgin, Mme Mohl, and Mme Buloz, Robert met literary men and sometimes women — writers and critics and politicians — great names enough, including Eugène Sue, Emile de Girardin, and Alphonse de Lamartine, though the topmost tuft, Victor Hugo, con-stantly eluded him. George Sand, it seemed, might elude Elizabeth, who, in despair over the difficulties involved in approaching her, urged a reluctant Robert to subtle strategies that he tried hopelessly to resist. George Sand had been to Paris, had gone from Paris. A M. François, a pretended intimate friend of the lady, had failed to present Mazzini's letter, suggesting that Robert should leave it at the theatre instead. 'Robert refused. Robert said he wouldn't have our letter mixed up with the love letters of the actresses or perhaps given to the "premier comique to read aloud in the green room, as a relief to the Chère adorable," . . . Robert was a little proud and M. François very stupid; and I, between the two, in a furious dissent from either.'[51]

It was too bad. The glamour of George Sand grew ever more fascinat-ing in Elizabeth's eyes, burnished to an ever more blinding dazzle by the cut and polish of gossip, some of which she imparted to Miss Mitford in her Christmas Eve letter: 'She is said to have appeared in Paris in a bloom of recovered beauty and brilliancy of eyes and the success of her play, "Le Mariage de Victorine," was complete. A strange, wild woman certainly . . . She has just finished a romance, we hear, and took fifty-two nights to write it. She writes only at night. People call her Madame Sand. There seems to be no other name for her in society or letters.' It took almost two months more for the Brownings to make another attempt on Madame Sand. On 11 February, Elizabeth took the matter in her own hands, accompanying the sacred letter from Mazzini with a note signed by both Brownings but in fact written by Elizabeth, 'as seemed right, being the woman'. Madame Sand was in Paris 'for only a few days, and under a new name, to escape from the plague of her notoriety. People said to us: "She will never see you; you have no chance, I am afraid." But we determined to try. At last I pricked Robert up to the leap, for he was really inclined to sit in his chair and be proud a little. "No," said I, "you *shan't* be proud, and I *won't* be proud, and we *will* see her. I won't die, if I can help it, without seeing George Sand." So we gave our letter to a friend who was to give it to a friend, who was to place it in her hands, her abode being a mystery and the name she used unknown.'[52] The message was sent out like a spark in the dark.

George Sand replied very gracefully on 12 February, agreeing to receive the Brownings four days later, on the Sunday, at 3 rue Racine. Nothing would stop Elizabeth now, not even Robert's uppermost concern for her health and, perhaps under the surface, his concern for her reputation and virtue. He was always cautious about the people Elizabeth should meet. The mysterious Madame Sand was — for all her fame and for all the tongue and finger wagging — an unknown and perhaps dangerous quantity. The Sunday night was cold, the air was sharp. They struggled over the visit, and Elizabeth won by pointing out 'that one might as well lose one's life as one's peace of mind for ever, and if I lost seeing her I should with difficulty get over it. So I put on my respirator, smothered myself with furs, and, in a close carriage, did not run much risk after all.'[53]

But it is at considerable risk that we encounter our idols in the flesh. George Sand was shorter and stouter in life than in legend. Elizabeth at first humbly stooped to kiss her outstretched hand, but was instead raised up and kissed on the lips by the lady. Her fabled beauty was not as it had been advertised: 'There is no sweetness in the face, but great moral as well as intellectual capacities — only it never *could* have been a beautiful face, which a good deal surprised me . . . We sate with her perhaps three-quarters of an hour or more — in which time she gave advice and various directions to two or three young men who were there, showing her confidence in us by the freest use of names and allusions to fact. She seemed to be, in fact, *the man* in that company, and the profound respect with which she was listened to a good deal impressed me.'[54]

More than her voice, which tended to rapidity and monotony, Elizabeth was struck by an element of scorn in her attitude, a disdain of pleasing and a contempt for coquetry, which underlay her surface kindness and pity. Elizabeth liked her rather than loved her. She 'felt the burning soul through all that quietness, and was not disappointed in George Sand'. But Elizabeth was often determined to find what she wanted to find. Having made such a fuss about visiting George Sand, then George Sand should be, if not in person, in soul at least, more than satisfactory. An ardent spirit was what Elizabeth had wished for. Robert kissed Madame Sand's small, well-shaped hand; Madame Sand kissed Elizabeth again, and invited the Brownings to return the next Sunday, excusing herself from returning their visit on account of 'a great press of engagements'.

When they saw her again, Madame Sand was silent and subdued, but pretty much as before in her aspect as Aspasia: 'She sate, like a priestess, the other morning in a circle of eight or nine men, giving no oracles, except with her splendid eyes, sitting at a corner of the fire, and warming her feet quietly, in a general silence of the most profound deference. There was something in the calm disdain of it which pleased me, and struck me as characteristic. She was George Sand, that was enough: you wanted no proof of it.' Her very lack of communication and enthusiasm was evidence of a finer mettle than those who sought its lustre. Robert, not looking for much beyond common courtesy and decent manners, was less impressed. He was, indeed, offended. 'Robert observed that "if any other mistress of a house had behaved so, he would have walked out of the room." — but, as it was, no incivility was meant.'[55]

They parted very kindly, with George Sand calling Elizabeth 'chère Madame', kissing her again, and looking forward to another meeting. The proposed third meeting was foiled for Elizabeth: when they called at rue Racine, the lady was not at home. But Robert on his own encountered Madame Sand some half-dozen times, once in the Tuileries, where she walked with him, her hand resting prettily on his arm, the whole length of the gardens. On that occasion, she was looking less well and was overdressed ('*endimanchée*') in 'terrestrial lavenders and supercelestial blues'.[56] Neither the style nor the colours were to Robert's taste, and nor was the lady herself: a long passage in Elizabeth's letter of 7 April to Miss Mitford acutely summarizes her attitude to George Sand, much overlaid and occasionally conflicted by Robert's own disdain for Sand's company and for the company she kept:

> I could only go with Robert three times to her house, and once
> she was out. He was really good and kind to let me go at all,

after he found the sort of society rampant around her. He didn't like it extremely, but, being the prince of husbands, he was lenient to my desires and yielded the point. She seems to live in the abomination of desolation, as far as regards society — crowds of ill-bred men who adore her *à genoux bas*, betwixt a puff of smoke and an ejection of saliva. Society of the ragged Red diluted with the lower theatrical. She herself so different, so apart, as alone in her melancholy disdain! I was deeply interested in that poor woman, I felt a profound compassion for her … a noble woman under the mud, be certain. *I* would kneel down to her, too, if she would leave it all, throw it off, and be herself as God made her. But she would not care for my kneeling; she does not care for me. Perhaps she doesn't care for anyone by this time — who knows? She wrote one, or two, or three kind notes to me, and promised to 'venir m'embrasser' before she left Paris; but she did not come. We both tried hard to please her, and she told a friend of ours that she 'liked us;' only we always felt that we couldn't penetrate — couldn't really *touch* her — it was all in vain.

There is regret in this passage for something more than just George Sand: more than Robert, Elizabeth recognized the withdrawal of the woman, of the artist, of the creator from the riffraff world that beseeched her, besieged her. She had hoped, in her heart, for a sympathy of sorority that was not offered. Perhaps her perception of George Sand's isolation sounded an echo of her own isolation and withdrawal before marriage, and her wish for Sand to be 'herself as God made her' brought home to Elizabeth her own fortunate circumstances in which she had been released into life by 'the prince of husbands'. George Sand was still lost — Elizabeth had been found. She could not be reached, could not be touched — she had retreated too far in upon herself and there dwelt alone. This was painful to Elizabeth as a woman, as it could not be to Robert who was simply offended by George Sand's swinish, sycophantic court and the apparent bad manners of his hostess.

To Mrs Orr, years later, Robert remarked that he 'fully shared his wife's impression of a want of frank cordiality on George Sand's part; and was especially struck by it in reference to himself, with whom it seemed more natural that she should feel at ease. He could only imagine that his studied courtesy towards her was felt by her as a rebuke to the latitude which she granted to other men.'[57]In Robert's view, George Sand was not interested in friendship with another woman such as Elizabeth, and was offended when she perceived a disdain to match her own in a man and a poet such as Robert, who was prepared to pay her the courtesy of simple politeness rather than the compliment of elaborate, deferential court. He makes too much, in retrospect, of Elizabeth's perception of George Sand's 'want of frank cordiality'. In a letter of 28 February 1852 to her brother George, Elizabeth excused any coolness: 'There was not the least intention on her part of being otherwise than most cordial to us — and the confidence she showed us was fuller of compliment than any banality of mere manner could be.'

More to Robert's taste was a new friend. Joseph Milsand, a French literary critic, had written an article, highly appreciative of Robert's work, in the 15 August 1851 number of the *Revue des Deux Mondes*, a leading literary and intellectual journal owned by François Buloz, whose wife's salon Robert occasionally attended. On 15 January 1852, Milsand would publish an equally appreciative article on the work of Elizabeth Barrett Browning, together with his estimation of two other poets, John Edmund Reade and Henry Taylor. The article on Browning's poetry was the second of a series on the broad subject of 'La Poésie anglaise depuis Byron', the first having been devoted to Tennyson.

Such praise, deriving from a sympathetic understanding of current English poetry in general, and Robert's in particular, had entranced Elizabeth. She wrote to inform Miss Mitford on 12 November 1851: 'there has sprung up in France lately an ardent admiration of the present English schools of poetry, or rather of the poetry produced by the present English schools, which they consider *an advance upon the poetry of the ages*, Think of *this*, you English readers who are still wearing broad hems and bombazeens for the Byron and Scott glorious days!' Milsand's perceptions were exciting and generous enough to move Robert, writing to Edward Chapman on 16 January 1852 to remind the publisher of his promise to supply a regular six-monthly account of the sales of the Brownings' books, to suggest that, should Chapman have read the article, and should he care to 'prefix to an advertisement of *Christmas Eve*, an opinion from a journal . . . why not take your extract from some real authority in the matter — such as the admirable critic in question?' There was no question that anything useful could be extracted from English reviewers.

Robert's first meeting with Milsand had come about, probably, early in December, through an introduction, says Mrs Orr, by 'Mrs Jebb-Dyke, or more directly by Mr and Mrs Fraser Corkran, who were among the earliest friends of the Browning family in Paris'.[58] Fraser Corkran was the Parisian correspondent for an English newspaper, the *Morning Chronicle*. His wife, Henrietta, was a devout spiritualist. Griffin and Minchin give a fuller account, not necessarily conflicting but more circumstantial in its detail, that proves the acquaintance to have ripened by early January. Miss Mitford had recently published a book of memoirs, *Recollections of a Literary Life*, in which she had written very pleasantly about the Brownings. Her dear friends would have been altogether charmed, had it not been for an unfortunate reference to Elizabeth's beloved brother Bro, whose death was still a wound in her heart. Elizabeth's friends and family knew better than ever to mention it in her hearing. There had been much sorrow and no blame in the event, wrote Miss Mitford, but Elizabeth had conceived 'a natural but a most unjust feeling that she had been in some sort the cause of this great misery'. It was this feeling that had cast 'the shadow that had passed over that young heart'.

The Brownings had not yet seen Miss Mitford's book: they heard about it accidentally in January from a friend who had attended a lecture at the Collège de France, where 'the professor [of comparative literature], M. Phalaret Chasles, in the introduction to a series of lectures on English poetry, had expressed his intention of noticing Tennyson, Browning, etc., and E. B. B. — "from whose private life the veil had been raised in so interesting a manner lately by Miss Mitford".'[59] Milsand had noticed the biographical details that had been lengthily extracted on 3 January in the *Athenaeum* and had approached Robert to ask whether the information might be too painful to Elizabeth to bear repeating in his own article for the *Revue des Deux Mondes*. On Robert's advice, Milsand dealt obligingly with the passage from Miss Mitford's book, which could not be ignored in any serious study, presenting it 'garbled and curtailed as seemed best to the quoter', and omitting the reference to Bro and the supposed effect his death had had on his sorrowing sister.

Miss Mitford, on receipt of Elizabeth's terrible, pained letter of reproach, lengthily explained herself and abjectly apologized. She was of course forgiven, though the hurt was irretrievable. The damage had been done, and Elizabeth accepted it well enough, even mockingly in a letter of 18 March 1852 to Mrs Ogilvy, describing how her Uncle Hedley and Robert had attended the lectures by M. Chasles, who, 'not finding the Mitford story sufficiently romantic for his ends, embroidered deeply with gold and silk, and produced a tragedy about a fiancé, which would have done honour, Robert says, to Dumas himself. Not one word of truth from beginning to end, but the most picturesque details (en revanche) including the "waving of handkerchiefs," the consolations received "in farmhouses," and final residences in "magnificent palaces of the Medici," called Casa Guidi.' Robert himself was not spared by M. Chasles, who characterized him as 'ce poète obscur, mystique ... du reste célèbre'. The French, it was reported to the Brownings, were offended by the indelicacy of this whole exhibition. Elizabeth herself didn't care what might be said of her work, 'But my *me* should be safe until I am dead ... Surely one may love Art, yet keep the door shut.'

Milsand, who was to remain a close friend of Robert's for the rest of his life, was regularly welcomed at what Robert referred to as their 'little bandbox apartment',[60] and Elizabeth appreciated his interest in herself and her son. She characterized Milsand somewhat ambiguously in a letter to Sarianna: 'What a perfect creature he is to be sure! He always stands in the top place among our gods ... he wants, I think — the only want of that noble nature — the sense of spiritual relation; and also he puts under his feet too much the worth of impulse and passion, in considering the powers of human nature. For the rest, I don't know such a man. He has intellectual conscience — or say — the conscience of the intellect, in a higher degree than I ever saw in any man of any country — and this is no less Robert's belief than mine. When we hear the brilliant talkers and noisy thinkers here and there and everywhere, we go back to Milsand with a real reverence. Also, I never shall forget his delicacy to me personally, nor his tenderness of heart about my child.'[61]

Insofar as these remarks are decipherable, Elizabeth would seem, for all her praise of Milsand's admirable intellectual sensibilities, to have regarded him as rather a dry stick, not given to 'impulse and passion' in his own life. Mrs Orr takes issue with Elizabeth's indulgent attitude towards 'impulse and passion', tapping her knuckles lightly but firmly. Milsand, writes Mrs Orr, 'would never have agreed with her as to the authority of "impulse and passion," but I am sure he did not underrate their importance as factors in human life.'

The beginning of Robert's serious-minded friendship with Joseph Milsand coincided more or less with a commission from Edward Moxon, his former publisher, to write a preface to twenty-five letters by Shelley that Moxon had acquired at a Sotheby's auction and intended to publish as a supplement to an existing epistolary collection. Robert, who had discussed the matter with Moxon in London, started work on his essay on Shelley soon after arriving back in Paris and completed it in December 1851. *Letters of Percy Bysshe Shelley* was published early in 1852. It was neither the lasting success nor the instant *coup d'estime* that both Edward Moxon and Robert Browning had hoped for. All but one of the letters were quickly revealed to have been spurious and the edition was promptly withdrawn. This was a substantial blow; worse was the information that Robert's later researches, in 1858, turned up about the conduct of Shelley, his hero, towards Harriet, his wife. They had not parted by mutual consent, as Robert had supposed, but rather she had been deserted by Shelley. Robert, apprised of the truth by Harriet Shelley's own letters, continued to love the poetry of Shelley though not, as before, the man himself, however his conduct might be excused. The radiance of the Sun-treader would be dimmed. The entire enterprise had been fated to be an exercise in disillusion.

Browning's essay on Shelley does not confine itself to Shelley alone of all his tribe: it is about poets, poetry, and very much about Robert Browning himself. Right from the start, he distinguishes two types of poet, congruent with the mid-nineteenth-century classification of poets into subjective and objective writers. Firstly, the objective poet is the maker, 'the fashioner; and the thing fashioned, his poetry, will of necessity be substantive, projected from himself and distinct'. The objective poet will endeavour 'to reproduce things external . . . with an immediate reference, in every case, to the common eye and apprehension of his fellow men', whereas the subjective poet 'is impelled to embody the thing he perceives, not so much with reference to the many below as to the one above him, the supreme Intelligence which apprehends all things in their absolute truth, — an ultimate view ever aspired to, if but partially attained, by the poet's own soul.' The work of the objective poet speaks for itself, and we no more need a biography of this type of poet than we need a map of his world. The objective poet, the Shakespeare, passes from the world, his work remains and is largely self-sufficient without reference to the life of the maker.

The case of the subjective poet is otherwise: 'in our approach to the poetry, we necessarily approach the personality of the poet; in apprehending it we apprehend him, and certainly we cannot love it without loving him. Both for love's and for understanding's sake we desire to know him, and as readers of his poetry must be readers of his biography also.' The life of the subjective poet, the Shelley who is primarily and autobiographically concerned with conveying personal experience and feeling, concerns us more deeply. Critical division into subjectivity and objectivity, which originated among German critics of the late eighteenth century, had largely been abandoned by latter-day scholars. In their own time, the terms were ridiculed by the art critic John Ruskin, who characterized them as 'two of the most objectionable words . . . ever coined by the troublesomeness of metaphysicians'. Some remnants of the distinction may survive — or may be revived — in contemporary concepts of 'readerly' and 'writerly' authors as defined by the French linguistic critic and semiologist Roland Barthes.

Throughout Browning's essay on Shelley there runs a bitter thread of resentment against critics whose brutality and ignorance hinder rather than help the creative faculty of the poet in its development. Milsand perceived both the objective and subjective poets at work in Browning's own work. Browning himself, being both introspective and extroverted in his life as in his work, aspired to Shelleyean subjectivity while also fashioning an objective world, dramatic and palpable, adducing the loftiest from the lowest. The aspirational in Browning's poetry was founded very firmly in man's inevitable fallibilities. In his work, Browning found the courage — intellectual and personal — to know the individual soul, to cherish it in its imperfections and in its struggles, not always successful, towards the highest attainments, in whatever form those may take. They will always be approximate, and therein perhaps lies Browning's realism. The poet, the man, the universe — all are in a constant state of development, of striving, of becoming. The subjective poet, Browning suggested, was religious, ever moving towards the light of revelation. 'I shall say what I think,' Browning declared, '— had Shelley lived, he would finally have ranged himself with the Christians.' But Shelley had 'died before his youth ended'. He had died, leaving his 'poetry as a sublime fragmentary essay towards a presentment of the correspondency of the universe to Deity, of the natural to the spiritual, and of the actual to the ideal ... I prefer to look for the highest attainment, not simply the high, — and, seeing it, I hold by it.' After all, we can but do our imperfect best.

Young men make mistakes. Of Shelley, Browning wrote decidedly, 'Let the whole truth be told of his worst mistake.' So do old men, but Robert was of a different mind when it came to the mistake of his own father, who had arrived in Paris with Sarianna in November 1851. Writing to her brother George on 4–5 December 1851, Elizabeth reported that Robert 'has been absorbed between his father and sister (whom he had to carry about Paris from morning till night when they were here) and the Shelley edition — which is off his hands today'. There had been discussions about whether to return to Florence, and the visit of some three weeks by Sarianna and Mr Browning had added weight to the debate between Robert and Elizabeth. On 12 November 1851, Elizabeth had written to Miss Mitford to remark on the collective affection felt by all the Brownings for one another: 'They are very affectionate to me, and I love them for his [Robert's] sake and their own ... Little Wiedeman ... is adored by his grandpapa; and then, Robert! they are an affectionate family and not easy when removed one from another. Sarianna is full of accomplishment and admirable sense, even-tempered and excellent in all ways — devoted to her father as she was to her mother; indeed, the relations of life seem reversed in their case, and the father appears the child of the child.' Robert and Elizabeth had discussed what should happen when the lease of the Hatcham house ran out in the spring of 1852: if they decided to stay in Paris, the hope was that they might establish Mr Browning and Sarianna there too, 'if no other obstacle should arise'.

While in London, on his visit to New Cross, Robert may have been first made aware of a developing tenderness between his father and an attractive lady, middle-aged and twice-widowed, the mother of three grown-up children, who lived nearby with her parents at Hatcham. Mr Browning had fallen into the habit of 'waving his hand and looking with great earnestness' at Mrs Von Müller every day as he punctually passed her house on the way to and from the Bank of England. This had been going on since at least December 1850. These neighbourly courtesies led to Mr Browning's offering to escort the lady home when he met her in the street, and to an impulsive proposal of marriage not long thereafter. Mrs Von Müller was happy to accept. The bargain was cemented by impassioned, imprudent love letters written by Mr Browning to his 'dearest Minny', who evidently felt secure enough in the ardour of her elderly suitor to confess, confidentially, a little indiscretion.

Before marrying Captain Von Müller, an Austrian military man, Minny had not been perfectly assured of the death in Spain of her first husband, a Mr Meredith, also a military man. This was a tremendous shock to Mr Browning, who now considered his position closely with respect to Minny, the possibly bigamous widow. Had Mr Meredith been certainly dead? Even if such were the case, Minny's incertitude had not stopped her deciding that her own perceived best interests had lain in a second, possibly precipitate, marriage. He decided, after much moral and even theological agonizing, that Mrs Von Müller had been guilty, if not of crime, then of gross error. Minny was much wounded by this calumny, which Mr Browning subsequently retracted. But still he was very much troubled. Robert would have to know sooner or later: the question of marriage, after all, was very present, pressing indeed; but the memory of his wife, so dear to the son, must not be desecrated. There must be no question of betraying that holy woman by her relict being enamoured of another. In this frame of mind, Mr Browning evidently decided to represent himself as the wronged party, as a man pursued by an unscrupulous widow whose dark secret revealed her as an unconscionable adventuress. And, in truth, Robert very likely found no difficulty in believing this version of the matter. His father's diffidence, unworldliness, sense of honour, and devotion to his family, as Robert remembered all these things, would have spoken in his favour without further proof being required of Mr Browning's injured innocence. Robert, not unreasonably, took his father at his word and took his part.

On 1 November 1851 Mrs Von Müller received a letter from Robert stating that his father had informed him of 'the manner in which she had annoyed him, and of the persecution he had undergone for some time'. Mr Browning himself, no doubt encouraged and convinced by this filial support, himself then wrote to Mrs Von Müller to break off the match on the grounds of her confessed bigamy and her misconduct from the time she was a girl: 'Has not your whole career, from your running away from school, to your settling at New Cross, been one continued series of anything but respectable?'[62] At the instigation of her son-in-law, Samuel Sutor, a prosperous shipowner, and no doubt fired by her own indignation as much as the rage of her family, Minny Von Müller brought a suit against Mr Browning for substantial damages on the grounds of breach of promise and defamation of character. The matter for the time being hung fire until the next year, the trial date having been set for 1 July 1852.

Meanwhile, Robert and Elizabeth revealed their knack for witnessing political revolution at first hand, and for obtaining a comfortable view of the proceedings as one might take a *première loge* for a performance at the opera. The Paris spectacle was as exciting — if not more so — than the festal Florentine variety. Louis Napoleon, born Charles Louis Napoleon Bonaparte in 1808, the nephew of Napoleon I, had been elected President of the French Republic in 1848. His constitutional three-year term was due to expire in December 1851. Louis Napoleon was not inclined to step down. The constitution could not be altered, and so, with the support of sections of the army, he organized a successful *coup* in Paris. On the night of 1 December, his troops seized strategic points throughout the city, suppressed the press, and closed down all printing operations. The constitutional Assembly was dissolved, universal suffrage was declared, and new elections were promised. In 1852, by universal plebiscite, the empire was restored and its new emperor, by popular vote, was Louis Napoleon III. All in all, it was a quiet revolution that lasted almost twenty years, until September 1870, when Louis Napoleon III was overthrown by republicans.

The national and foreign apprehension before the *coup* was worse than the actual event. Elizabeth, by now an experienced observer of simmering political ferment and sudden revolutionary upheaval, was — as usual — casual and confident in her assurances to brother George and sister Henrietta that reports in the English press were exaggerated. Troops processed along the Champs-Elysées, to be sure, and there was a distant noise of cannon, as threatening merely as a thunderstorm. 'Where is the danger, as long as one stays in the house?'[63] On 13 and 14 December, Elizabeth wrote again to calm Henrietta's nerves: '*Don't believe the Times*. To talk about "carnage" is quite absurd. The people never rose — it was nothing but a little popular scum, cleared off at once by the troops . . . My dearest Henrietta, what really *would* frighten me, would be the thought of going to London in January — Thank you. I choose Louis Napoleon's cannons rather.' The day following the night of the *coup*, 2 December, was very thrilling, very theatrical: 'the entrance of the troops into Paris . . . was very grand — the military music and the shouting of the people, as the president rode under our windows, the manoeuvering of the splendid cavalry, the white horses, glittering helmets, all that "pomp and circumstance," might well move older children than our babe. He was in the most enthusiastic state of effervescence, screaming and shouting out to the soldiers. You know he is a most excitable child at all times.'

Elizabeth had commented to George Barrett, in a letter of 4–5 December, that Louis Napoleon was 'a bold man, to say the least of him. He may be shot dead from a window at any moment. "A madman," some people call him, but certainly a bold man.' Some regarded Louis as a traitor — though not Elizabeth Barrett Browning, who admired strength and prompt action, the attributes of a hero. 'I confess myself to be carried away into sympathy by the bravery and promptitude of his last act. Call it perjury, usurpation of rights, what you will — call it treason against the constitution, which it assuredly is.' The constitutionality of the *coup* might be questioned, she admitted, but if it expressed the wishes of the people against the will of the assembly . . . 'There's a higher right than legal right, we all feel instinctively, — the living people are above the paper constitution. Therefore if Napoleon is loyal and true in his appeal to the will of the people and in his intention of abiding by the issue of the approaching election, "je fais acte d'adhesion," I, for one, and hold him justified to the full extent of his revolutionary act. But I wait to see. One can't quite trust a man in his position, and with the Napoleon blood in him, which he evidently has to the ends of his fingernails — My sympathy with his audacity and dexterity, is rather artistical sympathy than anything else — just as one cries "Bravo" at a "tour de force".'

This rousing, romantic appeal to George, when repeated in whatever terms to Robert, fell like dust on a desert. To Elizabeth, the *coup* and all its implications were of the greatest possible interest, consuming pages of her letters to all her friends and family — she could have composed a full chronicle of the *coup* by the time she had written and bundled up all her correspondence into a manuscript. She was puffed up with a political fervour that, however sublimely communicated to her friends and siblings, was deflated in her domestic environment. In a letter of 30 December to Mrs Ogilvy, she noted limply that 'Robert and I do not agree on this subject with our usual harmony, I must confess to you. I expect him to come round in time, and perhaps he expects the same of me ... He sympathizes with some of the fallen, though not, when you come to examine the assembly. He always hated the Buonapartists, and expects no good out of him, with such a "galère".'

Elizabeth was scornful of Robert's apparent lack of concern and — more, perhaps — his lack of obvious political passion. His restraint drove her to an extremity of impatience. Since Robert professed himself at first disinclined to think much about, far less analyse the situation, he confined himself mostly to a hatred not only of Louis Napoleon, but of 'all Buonapartes, past, present or to come, but then he says *that*', Elizabeth wrote to Mrs Jameson on 12 April 1852, 'in his self-willed, pettish way, as a manner of dismissing a subject he won't think about — and knowing very well that he doesn't think about it, not mistaking a feeling for a reason, not for a moment. There's the difference between women and men.' Mme Mohl had confessed to Elizabeth 'that she liked exaggerations because she hated the President. She is a clever shrewd woman, but most eminently and on all subjects a woman; her passions having her thoughts inside them, instead of her thoughts her passions. That's the common distinction between men and women, is it not?'[64]

Pen, hardly a man yet, was fully enthusiastic, constantly and gratifyingly shouting '*Buono, buono*' at any military demonstration. The Browning household opinions steadily became louder and more animated, from pistol fire to cannon shot, as newspaper report succeeded newspaper report, rousing Elizabeth's rage. The ignorant lies of the

English newspapers — as such she assessed their reports, particularly and monstrously *The Times* — drove her to emotional outbursts. But, as she wrote to Mrs Ogilvy, 'The English never understand the French in the first place ... that's a matter of course.'

George Barrett was assailed by fire from both barrels of the dispute when, following letters from Elizabeth, Robert himself wrote mordantly on 4 February 1852: 'I daresay you fancy us in the middle of noise and bustle, as indeed we are — but our little nest hangs at the far end of a twig in this wind-shaken tree of Paris, and the chirpings inside are louder than the bluster without.' The cold weather had done as much to keep the Brownings indoors as the revolution. Robert admitted that he and Elizabeth had agreed 'on the difficulty of the position with the stupid, selfish and suicidal Assembly', but 'when Louis Napoleon is found to cut the knot instead of untying it — Ba approves and I demur. Still, one must not be pedantic and overexacting, and if the end justifies the beginning, the illegality of the step may be forgotten in the prompt restoration of the law.'

The reasonable tone of this letter contrasts with Elizabeth's view of Robert's 'self-willed, pettish' way in conversation. Elizabeth's opinions, in the view of her lawyer brother and her law-abiding husband, were not only ill-founded in terms of constitutional legality, but plainly contradictory of her previously professed republican principles and sympathies in Italy. But she would have it that Louis Napoleon was bold rather than bad; that the people — whose will was paramount — had chosen him; that the Assembly had been wrong, in the teeth of Louis Napoleon's popularity with the people, to reject an amendment that would have given him another term as president; she even insisted, when Louis was declared Emperor, that the spirit of the *coup* was republican. Elizabeth's flat denial of facts that, when admitted, might lead to correct conclusions, greatly puzzled the rational Robert and the judicious George. To George, Robert commented: 'Is it not strange that Ba cannot take your view, not to say mine and most people's, of the President's proceedings? I cannot understand it — we differ in our appreciation of facts, too — things that admit of proof.'

Margaret Forster, in her perceptive biography of Elizabeth Barrett Browning, takes the view that, however boldly Elizabeth might hold her fireside opinions against the knowledge of those who had experienced the situation in the streets, however proud she might be of holding her own point of view, she and Robert 'were both fascinated that they could argue and differ so hotly, breaking their "usual harmony" and yet feel no rift. Elizabeth felt that it was a triumph to hold such opposing views and yet not come to blows.' Intellectual differences were 'absurdly unimportant compared to emotional ones.'[65] This view is borne out by Elizabeth's own assessment of the marital relationship in a letter to her sister: 'Oh Arabel — "have we quarrelled?" "How often have we quarrelled?" We are famous for quarrelling, are we not? That is because we love one another too much to be content with temporising — It seems foolish to talk of such things — but for a man to love a woman after six years as he loves me, could only be possible to a man of very uncommon nature such as his — I cannot tell you what his devotion and tenderness are to me at every hour.'[66]

At this point we may turn again to Robert's poem 'A Lover's Quarrel' for his own view of the Browning quarrels (always bearing in mind that these lines are poetry and not simple self-confession) and understand, a little, the hurt suffered by seeming betrayal of what he considers a lapse in his wife's good judgement; the reproaches he might make on that score of her self-betrayal of 'the beauteous and the right', on which he himself depends and is guided; and the sorrow — amounting to grief — at a separation of hearts akin to death:

> Dearest, three months ago
> When we loved each other so,
> > Lived and loved the same
> > Till an evening came
> When a shaft from the devil's bow
> > Pierced to our ingle-glow
> And the friends were friend and foe!
> . . .
> Love, if you knew the light
> That your soul casts in my sight,
> > How I look to you
> > For the pure and true
> And the beauteous and the right, —
> Bear with a moment's spite

When a mere mote threatens the white! (ll. 78–84, 99–105)

. . .

Foul be the world or fair
More or less, how can I care?
   'Tis the world the same
   For my praise or blame,
And endurance is easy there.
   Wrong in the one thing rare —
Oh, it is hard to bear!(ll. 78–84, 99–105, 113–19)

Margaret Forster's convincing assessment is also supported by Betty Miller, who points to the development of Elizabeth's natural self-confidence and assertiveness within marriage: 'It was only gradually, testing herself out in the intimacy of marriage and discovering herself the stronger, that she had come to accept the responsibilities and privileges of that position as her natural due. This was all the easier for her in that, the first-born of a large family, she had early acquired the attitude, solicitous and mildly domineering, of the elder sister: six years older than her husband, the temptation seems to have been to treat him, at times, with the humorous firmness applicable to a spirited but inexperienced younger brother. The passage of the years reinforced perceptibly this self-opinionated aspect of her character. "Gentle yet pertinacious in difference" is how H. F. Chorley describes her; ". . . at once forbearing and dogmatic, willing to accept differences, resolute to admit no argument". She was proud of her own independence in this respect.'[67] For his own part, Robert was willing enough to be led emotionally, to submit complaisantly in the minor daily matters of life, in the sense that in most things he tended to give pride of place to his wife's emotional welfare and happiness. Intellectually, he recognized — just as Elizabeth did — that men and women did not only think differently but approached the great questions of life, and no less the small ones, from different angles, by different paths, and that the emphases given to any subject by a woman would not necessarily be those given to it by a man.

The facts in the current case were, in Robert's view, that the authoritarian rule Louis Napoleon imposed, the autocratic decrees he issued, the violent suppression of any dissent — all these — were clearly contradictory of promises he had made. Louis Napoleon did, in time, attempt to prevent any impetus towards further revolution by liberaliz-ing the Empire so that, by 1870, France had become a partial democracy. But for the time being, there was a strict censorship not only of the press but, by a sort of collective, self-imposed caution, even of the intellectual, conversational salons of Paris, where people, voluntarily or involuntarily, held their tongues. Arrests were made by the thousands, and people one knew, one had talked to, were liable suddenly to be snatched up and to disappear. It was not, by French political standards, a reign of terror, but it was close enough to cause a not irrational fear and put a curb on unconsidered conversation.

The fate of a friend, Eugène Pelletan, was a case in point. He had promised to bring Alphonse de Lamartine, the poet-statesman who had taken a leading role in the 1848 revolution, to see the Brownings, but had failed to turn up as appointed. Robert and Elizabeth learned that Pelletan had been 'caught up by the Government and sent off to [the prison of] Saint-Germain to "faire le mort" on pain of being sent further [i.e. deported]'. Elizabeth was really very sorry, but not much surprised. His 'delight in talking battle, murder, and sudden death' had been amusing but incautious.[68] Pelletan, when he later became a French deputy, took the trouble to denounce poetry: 'In our age of sceptical maturity and republican independence,' he declared, 'verse is a superan-nuated form. We prefer prose, which, by virtue of its freedom of move-ment, accords more truly with the instincts of democracy.'[69]

It is at this point in the Brownings' domestic partnership that most biographers introduce the differences between Robert and Elizabeth in the question of Pen's upbringing. There were times during the first stages of the coup d'état when it was dangerous to walk in the streets (both Robert and Joseph Milsand had experienced worrying moments), but whenever possible Wilson would take Pen out and about with her. When they came back, Wilson would tell Elizabeth that people turned to look at the child. As well they might. It would have taken more than a casual glance to tell whether the fantastical Pen was a boy or a girl. Elizabeth loved fashion for herself, though she pretended that her sober but modish new dresses were for Robert's pleasure rather than for her own gratification, and in Paris she liked to dress little Pen even more extravagantly than in Florence.

To Henrietta, on 2 November 1851, she wrote to give a thrilled and particularized account of her own 'fashions' and then of Pen's: 'we have bought him a white felt hat, white satin ribbons and feathers — really the prettiest hat I ever saw, and he looks lovely in it — with a trimming of blue satin ribbon inside at each cheek. Then he wears trowsers now! — that is out of doors. Such ridiculous tiny trowsers up to his knees: and long white knit gaiters. It's a beautiful costume, and he is much admired, I assure you. People stare at him, Wilson says, and turn around to stare again.' Later, in Florence, Pen made much the same head-turning impression: 'His grace and golden ringlets draw so much attention in the Cascine that Wilson swears she is abashed by it.'[70] Pen's appearance put even the almost unlimited admiration of the Florentines for *bella figura* to the test.

To her brother George, Elizabeth wrote on 2 February 1852 to impart ever more delightful details about the wonderful boy: 'Little Wiedeman grows more and more a darling. He never ceases talking the most extraordinary mess of a language you can imagine! and is most amusing to us all . . . We don't teach him yet to say grace or even regular prayers. I am so afraid of tying up the pure free spirit in formalisms, before he can understand significances. But he understands perfectly that God is good and makes him good and gives him gifts — And quite of his own accord, the other day, after breakfast, he said, turning his bright face up to the ceiling and lifting his right hand, — "Thé buono — grazie a Dio" [Good tea — thanks be to God]. And now he does it constantly, quite out of his own head, I assure you.' Nobody needed assurances by this time of Elizabeth's delight in Pen's precociousness. When he spoke, it was with a lisp that rendered even more peculiar his jumble of speech in three languages — Italian, French, and English, though he preferred Italian. Miss Mitford, when she had met Pen in London, had been appalled not only by the boy's bizarre linguistic babble but, more, that his English parents generally spoke with him in Italian rather than English. And now he had added French to the various vocabularies that he mispronounced.

Elizabeth was serenely, sublimely, unperturbed by Pen's indiscipline not only in language but in his general behaviour. She loved the boy unaffectedly and regarded as 'too pagan' the conventional view that a surfeit of love might spoil a child. Robert had some reservations on this point, as on several others, and occasionally told the boy off for misbehaviour, whereupon Pen would run to his mother, lip trembling, and his mother would send him running back to kiss his father and to be comforted. He was excitable in any case, even Elizabeth admitted as much, but few excitements were denied him. In a letter of 24 January 1853 to Mrs Ogilvy, Elizabeth declared that 'Robert has rather a passion than a love for the child. If I spoil, he spoils doubly — and I must tell you that I suffer pangs of jealousy just now, having been "pushed from my stool" where I used to be preeminent in the little creature's affections, somewhat too early I think.'

To whatever extent Pen might transfer some of his attentions to his father over Elizabeth, who admitted she clung 'to the infantile ways', for the time being Robert had little influence over Elizabeth in the matter of Pen: her insistence on pampering the boy — dressing him up, keeping him childish and virtually androgynous for as long as possible — was resistant to any paternal reservations and protests. Robert wanted Pen to speak English; Elizabeth persisted in speaking to him in Italian, and both Robert and Wilson generally gave way to her in the matter of language. Robert's deference to Elizabeth in these emotional matters was very characteristic of their relationship at this time: symptomatic, indeed, of the way it had developed since their marriage. After a series of slight illnesses, little inexplicable fits, in the autumn and winter of 1851–2, Elizabeth became alarmed for Pen and moderated her distrust of 'formalisms' to the extent that Wilson's advice, to the latter's relief, was accepted and she was allowed to impose a more regular regime, a more conventional structure, on the boy's daily life, that gave them all a quieter time.

Besides Robert's reverence for Elizabeth's strengths as a wife, as a mother and as a woman, he was always conscious that her health was more fragile than often it seemed in her everyday activity. She had survived five pregnancies in foreign countries; had walked, ridden, or been carried up and down mountains; had gone out and about in society to an extent that would have seemed fantastical to her only a few years before; had continued her career as a poet throughout marriage and motherhood; had thoroughly enjoyed two revolutions under her very own terraces in Florence and Paris; and through it all she had never felt better. More often than not, she had deferred to Robert's constant concern for her health and well-being. If and when he resisted her intemperate desire to go out in the cold or among crowds, she generally acceded to his wish and conceded that he might be right. Nevertheless, her heart and mind were very occasionally, and very strenuously, fixed otherwise, and nothing that God, man, or her husband could do would persuade her to stay quietly at home: an exhausting expedition she made with Mrs Jameson to a military fête in Paris in May 1852 was a case in point.

The winter of 1851–2 in Paris — exceptionally cold, and more than usually wet — had restricted her activities and she had begun to cough. Elizabeth blamed the weather, as she always did, but Margaret Forster perceives a more sinister decline in her health from this point: 'anyone with a bronchial condition suffered. But it was also true that from now on Elizabeth's cough is mentioned much, much more frequently in her letters, whatever the climate . . . No doctors were called in so there are no medical reports at this juncture but the frequent accounts of a cough, breathlessness, congestion, occasional chest pain and attacks of fever would indicate acute bronchitis verging on bronchopneumonia.'[71]

She was certainly using a respirator — an inhaler — that winter, to relieve her lungs and chest whenever she ventured out in the cold air. It had been produced from her muff as a curiosity for the inspection of George Sand, whose own lungs were none too robust. The respirator, however interesting, was not a success. Madame Sand, looking at the item with disdain, had proclaimed 'life wouldn't be worth the trouble of such precautions' and Elizabeth had immediately put it back in her furs. When she enquired about Madame Sand's own health she was told ' "Je ne me porte pas bien," . . . "but as to that, I never think of it except when I'm asked" — which was perhaps a way of saying "Don't ask." She nevertheless looked very well that day — Brilliant eyes, certainly, and a smile which outflashed them — only so rare a smile!'[72] Just so could Elizabeth wave aside enquiries as to her own health, and just so could she too look brilliantly well and gay, a fervid sheen glazing an underlying fragility. Some admirers took this for a shine of spirituality.

In May 1852, James Silverthorne died. James, Robert's favourite cousin and best man at his wedding, had been a particular friend, and his mother, Aunt Christiana Silverthorne, had generously paid for publication of *Pauline*. The Brownings had been close friends with the Silverthornes, closer at any rate than they had been with most of the extended Browning family. Sarianna wrote to give the news to Robert and asked that he should come to the funeral. Considering the special family bonds, Robert decided to go. Elizabeth, suddenly frightened, begged him to stay in Paris. There would be enough family at the graveside, after all, she suggested. Whether on account of the prevailing politics in Paris, or the entire family's recent minor bouts of illness, or a combination of both, or for any of half a dozen other reasons, she veneered her own accumulated emotional panic with a concern for Robert's own emotional state and projected it out on him.

The funeral could only, surely, revive memories of his mother's death. Moreover, what use was a morbid hovering at the graveside over that which was gone? She declared that, 'in no paroxysm of anguish could I identify or appear to identify the dust there and the soul there'. Later, in Rome, she frankly confessed her repugnance: 'I am horribly weak about such things — I can't look on the earth-side of death — I flinch from corpses and graves, and never meet a common funeral without a sort of horror. When I look deathwards I look over death, and upwards, or I can't look that way at all.'[73] It would surely be too distressing for Robert to go. Elizabeth's own distress was very apparent. She looked so pale, so anguished, that he abandoned his plans to go alone to London. Writing to Arabel, Elizabeth blamed Sarianna for even suggesting the idea. She admitted Sarianna to be 'good and true, affectionate and generous', but in this she had been unaccountably obtuse. Sarianna, 'not made of the same stuff as Robert', could have no notion 'of what he would suffer in going'.

There was, however, and soon enough, another painful occasion for suffering that could not be avoided. On 1 July 1852, Robert's father appeared before Lord Campbell and a Special Jury in the Court of Queen's Bench at Guildhall as defendant in the case brought by Mrs Von Müller. The defendant's counsel was Mr Willes; the plaintiff was represented by Sir Alexander Cockburn. The proceedings of this action to recover compensation in damages for a breach of promise of marriage were reported in *The Times* the next day. Neither Robert nor Elizabeth was present. They arrived in London on 6 July and read the newspaper's odious but accurate account (as everybody else had done, including the Barretts of Wimpole Street), which spared the Brownings no embarrassment in the details and no humiliation in the verdict. The humorous tone of the court proceedings and the subsequent press reports reduced the case to farce: the 68-year-old defendant had wooed the 45-year-old plaintiff in some fifty compromising love letters that began delicately and tenderly in December 1850 — 'My dear Mrs. Von Müller' — but quickly became warmer to the point of being deeply amorous — 'My dearest, dearest, dearest, dearest, dearest, dearest much-loved Minny'.

The packed courtroom enjoyed the letters very much, shrieking with laughter when tasty extracts were read out by the plaintiff's barrister, while Lord Campbell was very taken with the style and intelligence of Mr Browning's love letters, which also referred in an informed manner to matters of theology. Only one interpretation, however, could be put upon them; even Mr Browning's counsel was obliged to admit it and offer in mitigation the plea that his client was 'a besotted old man', a 'poor old dotard in love', and that this was 'an idle and trumpery case'. To minimize the seriousness of the matter, though perhaps not substantially helping his client, Mr Willes compared Von Müller v. Browning to that celebrated but farcical case of Dickensian fiction, Bardell v. Pickwick.

Lord Campbell took a sterner view of it as 'a very gross case'. The dotard's doting, however indulgently it might be considered, nevertheless had led to a proposal of marriage and subsequently a withdrawal of that proposal accompanied by serious allegations that could be interpreted as defamatory. Evidence was given to prove Mrs Von Müller's irreproachable character, and her first husband's death certificate was produced as proof that he had died some two months before her second marriage. Evidence on the other side was given, and accepted by Lord Campbell, as to the hitherto exemplary life of the defendant. He might, without blame, have thought better of the marriage and prudently withdrawn his offer to Mrs Von Müller, but it was plain that Mr Browning had acted 'in a most cowardly manner'. Mrs Von Müller had been disappointed in her expectations and was entitled to damages. The jury retired, found for the plaintiff, and damages were set at £800 — a figure calculated as neither too large in the particular circumstances of the case nor too small as to impute any blame to the plaintiff for misconduct.

Since Mr Browning's salary as a clerk in the Bank of England was certified in court to be 'about £320 a year', £800 was, for all the court's care to fix a reasonable level of compensation, a considerable sum of money. Neither Mr Browning nor Robert could pay it, so discussion turned to whether they would pay it at all. Talking it over among themselves, the Brownings decided that an appeal would only bring further unwelcome publicity. Even as it was, the embarrassment was acute. Cyrus Mason, who feeds like a buzzard on the entrails of the Brownings in the aftermath of the case, says that one of the letters read out in court had 'begged for a glove or some portion of dress which his sweetheart had worn, that it might be treasured as a token of affection; following the reading, Uncle Reuben on reaching Rothschild's, found his office table piled with soiled gloves, old shoes, stockings, crumpled caps and handkerchiefs, with a card announcing that the worn articles were sent by the "old lady of Threadneedle Street"' — by her employees, anyhow, the merrily callous wags of the Bank of England.[74] The most immediate solution seemed to be that Mr Browning and Sarianna should promptly remove themselves to live permanently in Paris, beyond the jurisdiction of the court, thus putting themselves out of the way of having to settle the damages awarded to Mrs Von Müller. Robert took three days to escort his father and sister to Paris, to make them 'tolerably comfortable' in an apartment in the rue de Grenelle, close to the Louvre, and entrust them to the care of Mr and Mrs Fraser Corkran.

The effect upon Robert was unspeakable. He returned from Paris thoroughly harassed. The whole thing had been deplorable. He had believed his father's account of the matter and, on that basis of trust, had written the unfortunately pompous letter to Mrs Von Müller which, together with Mr Browning's own letter of renunciation, had been read by her son-in-law, Samuel Sutor, whose own filial outrage had prompted the case which had now resulted in appalling, public ridicule. Robert, whose jealously guarded privacy had been so brutally and facetiously torn to shreds, was as inconsolable as his father, whom, nevertheless, he did not greatly reproach and continued to love and pity. The old man fell briefly into a depression, but within six months, according to Robert, who wrote to John Kenyon on 16 January 1853, he was 'well, as ever — of all his old spirits — strange, in one sense, not in another. He reads at the Library and draws at the Louvre, having got leave for both, goes book-hunting as of old, "shaping his old course in a country new," like Lear's Kent. My child sends him real letters, all his own, conception and execution alike, which gladden his heart and so, *"This, all!"* as the last letter sensibly ended.'

Robert's letter also informed Kenyon how the particulars of the Von Müller matter had been, God willing, concluded in London. 'Those people applied — *She*, to the Principal of the office, the Attorneys to the governor of the Bank, and more than once. They were briefly answered that the Bank knew nothing of my father's private business. Seeing the failure there, they have actually written to our own lawyer, who sends the letter to me, and here it is to say that if we will pay *their costs* we need not pay the plaintiff's damages, she never having had any intention of claiming them! They have her in their power, of course. They add, that my father may return to his home forthwith, they having no intention whatever to molest him. "Springes to catch woodcocks!"''

Robert's reaction was that 'They will just take their last revenge in an outlawry, which we must put up with, as with much worse. And meantime, to guard against any ill chance, I shall advise my father to send in his resignation, which, it has been communicated to him, the Bank will accept, and allow him to retain two thirds of his salary "with which they hope he may live comfortably abroad" — very kind and handsome of them, certainly. And thus far ends, if God please, this strange and calamitous visitation which has grieved me as few things could.'

When Robert returned from Paris to the rooms he and Elizabeth had taken in Welbeck Street, he was exhausted: 'the vexation of it all is immense', Elizabeth remarked to Henrietta. She had had her own vexations. For one thing, Wilson had asked for an increase in salary from sixteen guineas a year to twenty. Considering what Lily Wilson had done and continued to do for the Brownings, and considering the current rates of salary for a lady's maid, this was far from unreasonable. Wilson was in fact underpaid by about two guineas. Elizabeth told her they couldn't afford the extra four guineas, that she considered the demand greedy and ungrateful, indeed that it was evidence of Wilson's lack of devotion. Was not Wilson loved by the Brownings? In response, Wilson intimated that she might pack her bags, look for another situation, and refuse to return to Italy. In fact, she went to Sheffield for three weeks instead of the usual fortnight[75] to visit her mother. While there she evidently thought better of her ultimatum and came back to London on 3 September, much to Elizabeth's relief.

Henrietta had come up from the country, though heavily pregnant with her second child, and was lodged nearby. Arabel was still in Wimpole Street, where Elizabeth visited her, careful as ever to avoid being seen by her father. She spotted him once in the street, but hid herself in time, ducking down another street. Taking her courage in both hands, she finally decided to write to him to announce her presence in London and to beg him to see her. She might have known better. Back came a letter so humiliating to her that she could hardly bear to read it. To Henrietta, she confided: 'It was, I confess to you, with a revulsion of feeling that I read that letter, written after six years, with the plain intention of giving me as much pain as possible. It was an unnatural letter, and the evidence of hardness of heart . . . is unmistakable.' Mr Barrett would consent to forgive her only on her admission of error and repentance of her folly. It was clear, at last, now that all hope was extinguished in her heart, that her sentimental longing for her father to relent — and more, to embrace her back as a married woman and mother into his love and into his family — had been utterly, and for so long, in vain.

Her own heart hardened, and anger replaced affection. 'I have a child myself. I know something of the parental feeling. There can be no such feeling . . . There never can have been any such . . . when that letter was produced. Certainly the effect of it is anything but to lead me to *repentance*. Am I to repent that I did not sacrifice my life, and its affections to the writer of that letter?'[76] Elizabeth's own fear of her father had infected Pen, who trembled and began to believe that the Wimpole Street house was inhabited by a 'mitaine' (in French, meaning a fingerless mitten) — a made-up word evidently meaning a sort of ogre, who only came out at dusk, since he and his mother always had to leave the house before six o'clock. Better that Pen should be afraid of the 'mitaine', Elizabeth commented, than of the truth as it stood about his maternal grandfather.

Now that the desperate situations concerning their respective fathers had been resolved — both conclusively, but neither very satisfactorily

— Robert and Elizabeth turned to the consolation of their friends. There were plenty of them. Writing to John Kenyon, Robert was able to say, 'I felt all those spark-like hours in London struck out of the black element I was beset with, all the brighter for it!'[77] Besides visits to Kenyon, who introduced them at his house in Wimbledon to the celebrated novelist and poet Walter Savage Landor (whose characterization of Louis Napoleon as 'a man of wonderful genius' was delightful to Elizabeth), there were the Carlyles to see. Elizabeth being mostly and irritatedly confined with Pen to the rooms at 58 Welbeck Street, and Wilson having taken herself off in a huff to Sheffield, Jane Carlyle thrillingly brought the great Italian patriot Mazzini, 'with that pale, spiritual face and those intense eyes full of melancholy illusions', to visit her. 'Oh, such a fuss the Brownings made over Mazzini this day,' wrote the testy Mrs Carlyle. 'My private opinion of Browning, is, in spite of Mr C[arlyle]'s favour for him, that he is "nothing" or very little more, "but a fluff of feathers!" *She* is *true* and *good*, and a most *womanly* creature.' The general consensus is that Mrs Carlyle had taken against Robert when, obliviously holding a hot kettle in his hand while absorbed in conversation, she had asked him to put it down — which he did, on her new carpet. The mark it left was indelible. 'See how fine he has grown,' said Mrs Carlyle. 'He does not any longer know what to do with a kettle.' Carlyle himself was more tolerant: 'Ye should have been more specific,' he told his wife. Jane Carlyle, unappeased, grew to like Robert less and less, and even reconsidered her opinion of Elizabeth, who did not endear herself further on subsequent occasions.

Better disposed towards the Brownings were, of course, old friends such as Richard Monckton Milnes, with his new wife and new daughter, and the Tennysons, whose son Hallam's christening Robert attended in September, when he held the baby for quite ten minutes, occasionally tossing him in the air with all the expertise he had acquired when bouncing Pen. He was sorry to have had no time to see John Forster, but he called with Elizabeth on Fanny Haworth and her mother, and none too surprisingly (though there might have been another involuntary exclamation — 'Good heavens!') the ubiquitous Father Prout turned up. Touchingly, Robert made up the quarrel between himself and old Macready, whose wife had recently died. In a letter of 23 September, Robert impliedly referred to the death of his mother and recalled 'happy days when I lived in such affectionate intimacy with your family: and if some few of the idler hopes of that time came to nothing, at least all the best and dearest memories of a friendship I prized so much remain fresh in my heart as ever — else it would be too sad *now*'.[78] Robert could later in his life be a good hater where he thought he recognized malice, but in these days in London, when friends and memories of former times came crowding companionably back, he was moved by old, fond sentiments and inclined to let bygones be bygones. Macready had had his own difficulties, Robert acknowledged, and he retained a fondness for the old actor-manager and their association.

There were interesting new acquaintances, too, such as the Christian Socialist novelist Charles Kingsley (who had recently published the reforming novel *Alton Locke*); the American poet James Russell Lowell (a friend of the Storys); John Ruskin, author of *The Stones of Venice*, and his young wife Effie — lovely, elegant, but not very intelligent and soon, scandalously, to run away with the painter John Everett Millais. The Irish poet William Allingham introduced Robert to Dante Gabriel Rossetti, the young Pre-Raphaelite artist who had conceived an intelligent passion for Robert's poetry. Astonishingly, Rossetti had read the anonymously-published *Pauline*, and had become convinced that only the author of *Paracelsus* could have written it. He wrote to Robert, who confirmed his brilliant intuition, to tell him that he had, in his admiration, transcribed *Pauline* in its entirety from the British Museum copy.

Robert also renewed friendship with the elderly William Johnson Fox, who had given up the pulpit for politics and currently lived comfortably in a large house in Regent's Park. Fox wrote delightedly to his daughter on 16 July 1852 to say, 'I had a charming hour with the Brownings yesterday; more fascinated with her than ever. She talked lots of George Sand, and so beautifully. Moreover she silver-electroplated Louis Napoleon!!!'[79] The shade of Eliza Flower, some six years dead but still lively in the memory of the two men who had loved her, no doubt hovered, unacknowledged, over Elizabeth's enthusiastic gossip.

The English weather, not to say the constant social effort, was beginning to affect Elizabeth's health. 'For the last ten days I have suffered much from a tearing cough, and cannot leave the house except at intervals. Such a climate! We are much too late, and have been caught in the fogs and winds.'[80] Tardily, the Brownings set off for Paris on

12 October. There they found Sarianna and her father in the sympathetic hands of the Fraser Corkrans, who seemed delighted with Mr Browning's simplicity and his grandfatherly attitude towards their own children. Elizabeth, too, was touched by the old man's 'simplicity and affectionateness', as she described it to Arabel. He seemed in low spirits, lost and bewildered: 'He can't understand any of it . . . struggles against facts and necessities . . . said dolefully that "he knew it had been a trouble to me." "*Of course it has,*" said Robert, "*What did you imagine?*" ' Elizabeth was gentler, assuring him that 'I wasn't troubled at all and rather liked it upon the whole.'[81]

They stayed a couple of weeks, taking a little time to tidy their domestic affairs and for Elizabeth to satisfy her desire to see the new Emperor Napoleon III's ceremonial reception into Paris. The weather and the spectacle, both, were brilliant. Louis Napoleon, according to the excited report made to John Kenyon by Elizabeth in November, 'showed his usual tact and courage by riding on horseback quite alone, at least ten paces between himself and his nearest escort, which of course had a striking effect'. Both Elizabeth and Pen waved their handkerchiefs very loyally. Pen shouted and Louis Napoleon 'took off his hat to him directly'. Whether Robert took out his own handkerchief to do anything with it but blow his nose, or wave it under his nose, Elizabeth — not quite unaccountably — does not say.

They were reluctant to leave Paris and its pleasures, but another winter there could not be considered. The common sense of this was almost immediately apparent when they set out on the long and arduous journey back to Florence. They had chosen their route over the Alps for economy's sake, but the expense to Elizabeth's health was considerable. The journey, to use Elizabeth's own word, was 'disastrous'.[82] The high, cold air of the Mont Cenis pass caught at her throat and lungs, causing paroxysms of coughing, and some trouble about accommodations *en route*, which forced them to sleep for three nights in their clothes, exhausted all of them and almost did for Elizabeth. They stopped so that she could catch her breath at Turin, where a fire was kept burning for most of the night in her bedroom and Robert, almost mad with worry, tenderly nursed his wife. After resting for a couple of days, they continued on to Genoa, staying there for ten days. At first Elizabeth seemed worse than ever until, as if by a miracle, the drier, warmer southern air calmed and revived her. The coughing moderated and 'every breath', she felt, 'brought the life back to me'.

Margaret Forster, consulting modern medical advice, quite rightly dismisses as 'unjustified' some suggestions that 'Elizabeth's dramatic recovery means that her illness was psychosomatic'. Though she could show psychological dependency — on strong men, on opiates, even on the continued childishness of her son, which kept the question of her own ageing unconsciously at bay — she was no hypochondriac in later life, and not inclined after marriage to displace anything she could not cope with, consciously or unconsciously, into chronic illness. As Forster concludes: 'Chronic bronchitis, even without spreading to the lung tissue and becoming bronchopneumonia, has a direct, acknowledged connection with wet, cold weather and even with city life (especially city life in Victorian times.) The kind of journey the Brownings had undertaken, most of it in draughty carriages, quite obviously exacerbated Elizabeth's condition. Without modern antibiotics the only beneficial treatment for this condition was to remove the patient to a warm, dry atmosphere, which was precisely what Robert did. But of course her recovery was more apparent than real. The likeliest diagnosis is that patches of infected tissue remained scattered throughout her lungs, dormant but ready to become inflamed at the slightest provocation.'[83]

On 14 November 1852, Elizabeth wrote to Sarianna to rejoice in her pleasure at being in her own house again. The comfortable rooms and the familiar furniture of Casa Guidi looked exactly as they had left them. So, rather less gratifyingly, did Florence. Elizabeth adapted quickly to familiar routines, but Robert took longer to wind down. After the exciting sensations, sometimes exhilarating, sometimes alarming, of being tossed about in the complicated oceans of Paris and London, Robert felt — not unnaturally — deflated, becalmed in a backwater. 'Robert has been perfectly demoralised by Paris, and thinks it all as dull as possible after the boulevards: "no life, no variety." Oh, of course it *is* very dead in comparison! but it's a beautiful death, and what with the lovely climate, and the lovely associations, and the sense of repose, I could turn myself on my pillow and sleep on here to the end of my life; only be sure that I *shall do no such thing*.'

They would return to Paris in due course, they decided, but meantime their plans were to stay in Florence until they could let Casa Guidi again, whereupon they would go to Rome, either by Christmas or in the spring. There was some talk of yellow fever in Rome, and on account of Pen's health Elizabeth would prefer to remain safely in Florence for the time being, until 'Roman fevers' had abated. She reported herself to be well and happy. She had nearly lost her cough and had got quickly to her feet, walking out at dusk to inspect sunsets over the Arno, becoming familiar again with the beloved sights of the beautiful city.

By 24 November, when Elizabeth wrote to John Kenyon, Robert was still disconsolate: '[he] said most strongly that the place is dead, and dull and flat, which it is, I must confess, particularly to our eyes fresh from the palpitating life of the Parisian boulevards'. Robert had, however, renewed acquaintance with Hiram Powers, who was currently in 'the crisis of removal to a new house and studio, a great improvement on the last, and an excellent sign of prosperity of course'. Powers was working on a couple of massive, monumental marble statues — a heroic 'Washington' and a charming 'California'. It was time that the Brownings, too, did some work. Elizabeth decided that she and Robert should impose upon themselves something of the regular routine they had settled on for Pen. Robert rose at seven o'clock, Elizabeth a little later. It took them a while to adjust to the day and get dressed, but by nine o'clock they were at breakfast with Pen, who was then taken out shopping or visiting or to the parks and gardens by Wilson. Robert thereupon retired to his desk in a little sitting-room on one side of the dining-room, while Elizabeth arranged herself on a sofa in the drawing-room, on the other side. The doors were shut between them and they worked, each alone, not communicating with one other, until three o'clock when it was time for dinner. Afterwards, in the late afternoon or the early evening, Robert would go for a stroll in the streets and piazzas.

To a friend in Florence, Isa Blagden, Elizabeth wrote in the winter of 1852–3: 'You can't think how we have caught up our ancient traditions just where we left them, and relapsed into our former soundless, stirless hermit life. Robert has not passed an evening from home since we came — just as if we had never known Paris. People come sometimes to have tea and talk with us, but that's all.' Robert himself wrote to Joseph Milsand on 24 February 1853: 'We live wholly alone here, I have not left the house one evening since our return. I am writing — a first step towards popularity for me — lyrics with more music and painting than before, so as to get people to hear and see.'[84]

At this time, he was in touch with Edward Chapman about proofs of the revised third edition of Elizabeth's *Poems* and ruefully considering his own publishing history: 'I condole with you about my own bad job — I'll be bound you haven't sold a copy of *Christmas Eve*; yet I heard only last week about its success in America. Things may mend, however.'[85] Robert was clutching at a straw. His American success had been small. Published by Ticknor, Reed, and Fields in 1849, a two-volume edition of Browning's *Poems*, containing *Paracelsus* and *Bells and Pomegranates*, had attracted little critical attention and few sales. Between 24 November 1849 and 22 April 1856, 1,500 copies of Browning's *Poems* were printed. *Christmas-Eve*, not an obvious bestseller, ran no risk of being pirated by profit-minded publishers and was not formally published by Ticknor until 1864. Whatever American success Robert was referring to must have been a small sale of copies imported from London for enthusiasts and fellow-poets such as Longfellow. Such reputation as Robert did have in America was mostly as the husband of the celebrated Elizabeth Barrett Browning.[86]

Elizabeth was writing a long poem, *Aurora Leigh*; Robert was writing the poems that would be collected under the title *Men and Women*. In Paris, in a fit of enthusiasm for work, or perhaps of remorse and anxiety that he had done little or no writing at all for years, he had made a resolution to write a poem a day. It is generally and genially believed that in the first three days of January 1852, in Paris, he wrote, successively, 'Love Among the Ruins', 'Women and Roses', and 'Childe Roland'. On 4 January he gave up his New Year's resolution — as most of us do. The dates of composition of these three poems, which are among his most famous, are a matter of dispute among scholars. The legend is well known and, as a legend tends to be, is widely accepted as a pleasing story. But Robert himself was contradictory in later years, just as he would sow confusion about the occasion on which he first read Elizabeth's 'Sonnets from the Portuguese'. He wrote on 5 June 1854 that the poems were not written before 1853. In 1866, Robert said he wrote 'Childe Roland' in Paris. Eleven years later, in 1887, he is said to have remarked that, 'one year in Florence I had been rather lazy; I resolved that I would write something every day. Well, the first day I wrote about some roses, suggested by a magnificent basket that some one had sent my wife. The next day *Childe Roland* came upon me as a kind of dream. I had to write it, then and there, and I finished it in the same day, I believe.'[87]

Whatever the truth, wherever and whenever these three poems had been composed, Robert had written very little in recent years. In Paris, aside from the 'Essay on Shelley', and almost certainly 'In Three Days' (a short poem written to mark the time he had been in Paris, briefly but unusually absent from Elizabeth after the Von Müller case), he had probably written only three other poems. 'The Heretic's Tragedy', in 90 lines, is a farce about Jacques de Molay, the last Grand Master of the Knights Templar, who was burned at the stake in Paris in 1314; 'Respectability', in 24 lines, took a swipe at sexual hypocrisy and admitted true love even if it were — shades of George Sand! — considered illicit by the morality of established institutions; and 'A Light Woman', in 56 lines, a confession made to 'Robert Browning, you writer of plays' as 'a subject made to your hand' by a man who seduces his friend's promiscuous mistress to save the friend from harm. The seduction was not difficult — but at what cost to the 'saviour', no hero to his friend, thus playing with souls? In a few lines, Browning lightly and amusingly covers three themes in three poems that it would have taken a Balzac or a George Eliot several three-volume novels to cover. These poems, which are lit and scented by the flare of fire and brimstone and the gas lamps of the Paris boulevards, were to be included in *Men and Women*.

There were new faces that winter in Florence. Two of them promptly presented themselves in the drawing-room of Casa Guidi, much to Elizabeth's delight: 'We have had visits from the attachés at the English embassy [the British legation] here, Mr Wolf [Henry Drummond Wolff, later knighted], and Mr Lytton, Sir E[dward] Bulwer Lytton's son, and I think we shall like the latter, who (a reason for my particular sympathy) is inclined to various sorts of spiritualism, and given to the magic arts. He told me yesterday that several of the American rapping spirits are imported to Knebworth [the Lyttons' house in Hertfordshire], to his father's great satisfaction. A very young man, as you may suppose, the son is; refined and gentle in manners.' This pleasing young man, still only in his early twenties, was Edward Robert Bulwer Lytton, later to become, almost by default, a statesman, viceroy of India, and first earl of Lytton. Like his father, Edward Lytton combined politics and diplomacy with a taste and facility for literature. As 'Owen Meredith', he published several volumes of lyrical, Byronic verse that have come to be rated by posterity as mildly accomplished, ornate, and a little verbose.

Lytton, who wrote 'Genius does what it must, and Talent does what it can', had the good, though regretful, grace to recognize in later life that his accomplishments as a statesman had been more distinguished than his attainments as a poet. Lytton *père* had made efforts to dissuade Lytton *fils* from poetry; but Edward Lytton — who later preferred to be known as Robert Lytton — resigned himself to the fact that poetry, like cheerfulness, would keep breaking through, and was not to be resisted. The young Lytton had been encouraged in his poetic ambitions by John Forster, whose influence balanced — evidently even outweighed — the discouragement of the father. Sir Edward Bulwer-Lytton had himself combined a vigorous political profession with a second, parallel career as a prolific and fashionable novelist, though his works after 1842 took a turn first towards the occult (in *Zanoni* and *A Strange Story*) and then, in 1871, towards an early form of science fiction (in *The Coming Race*). He later also became a founding member of the Society for Psychical Research, which attracted a number of eminent literary persons to its proceedings.

Young Lytton was bound to be attractive to Elizabeth. Robert, too, seemed to like him. To John Forster, in a letter of 15 April 1853, he wrote that 'One can hardly imagine a more interesting and attracting young man.' His manners were charming without being affected; his conversation was clever and amusing; his social connections were impressive (though Elizabeth put no trust in princes and was no snob, she liked the polish of a well-bred young man); his energetic youthfulness was stimulating, and his interest in spiritualism was apparently more than merely fashionable. Elizabeth herself was becoming more and more fascinated, both in theory and in practice, by the supernatural. In London, on a visit to Fanny Haworth's mother, she had been excited at the prospect of encountering there 'Lord Stanhope and his crystal ball'. This potent object, when consulted, prophesied the spirit of the sun for the Brownings.[88]

Elizabeth had already conceived an interest in mesmerism, an early form of hypnotism first developed by and named after Friedrich Anton

Mesmer, an Austrian physician who had died in 1815, and had attempted to put herself in a suitable state of mesmeric receptivity. To Henrietta, in a letter of 21 February 1848, she had written: 'Tell my dear dearest Arabel that if she will come to me in a current of mesmeric influence, I shall be sure to be susceptible — so encourage her in it.' She was eager to extend her range of supernatural experiences; but Henrietta and Arabel were less interested in mesmerism than Elizabeth, whose reading and researches had already led her to the arcane metaphysical theories of the eighteenth-century Swedish mystic and scientist Emanuel Swedenborg.

In Paris, Henrietta Corkran had talked positively about the spirit world, recommending it to Elizabeth, who quietly expressed her own interest, and to Robert, who loudly reprehended it as humbug and charlatanism. Lady Elgin ('a most earnest enquiring woman') had talked seriously and thrillingly on several occasions of spiritualism. On one Saturday evening in late January 1852, Lady Elgin and George Thompson, a celebrated campaigner against slavery, visited the Brownings in Paris. To her brother George, in a letter of 2 February 1852, Elizabeth described how Lady Elgin, as usual, 'told us all sorts of supernaturalisms, which charmed me. Just think of my ill luck, George! That Mr George Thompson who sate by my side three quarters of an hour once, and conscientiously bored me with his American experiences of martyrdom for the slaves, knew all about the "Rappists", had heard the spirits "rap," knew how a spirit gave a kiss to one lady and an autograph to another — was ready to swear to all these facts from personal knowledge, and I might have heard him swear, and didn't!! I call this the extremity of ill-luck, don't you?' Elizabeth, conveying her vexation lightly, had in fact been sincerely disappointed to have missed, through simple ignorance, such an opportunity for first-hand spiritual enlightenment.

The 'Rappists' were a celebrated trio of American sisters — Anna Leah, Margaret, and Catherine Fox — whose ability to communicate with spirits in the afterworld had created a rage for amateur and professional table-tapping, automatic spirit writings, séances at which spirits could be induced to make utterances through receptive mediums and even, best of all, manifest themselves by means of ectoplasmic substances. Tables rocked, spirits knocked, tapped and rapped, flowers and household objects flew unassisted through the air, transcendental trumpets and ghostly guitars sounded, and the veil between the quick and the dead, between mortals and the dear departed, was rent. It was too thrilling. Heads were turned as often and as readily as tables. Irresistibly, the rage for spiritism or spiritualism infected Americans nationwide and was avidly taken up by Europeans. It was mostly an Anglo-American craze in Europe: Italian and French Catholics already enjoyed a supernatural element in their religion. Spiritualism appears to have arisen among mid-nineteenth-century Protestants synchronously with the rise of popular interest and intellectual faith in scientific research, and a corresponding discrediting of traditional Christian beliefs by scholarly critics such as Strauss. In the spirit of the times, spiritualists — who were often socially progressive to the point of crankiness in diet and personal habits of bodily purity — sought to employ scientific methods to give credence to their claims that spiritualist phenomena provided proof of a life after death.

For Lady Elgin to discuss spiritualism with Elizabeth and the likes of Mme Mohl was to preach to the converted or, at very least, to the credulous; to speak of it to sceptics was to invite trouble: 'We had Lady Elgin here last Saturday evening again, and the evening did not go off half as well as usual —, because of a decided dyspathy between her and Mrs Jameson — Lady Elgin is a great spiritualist with a leaning to Irvingism and a belief in every sort of incredible thing. While she talked of a communion of souls, Mrs Jameson began to talk of private madhouses — in a way which made my blood run cold — I really thought there would have been an explosion between the two women, and that Robert and I, who agree so admirably with Lady Elgin, (for whom I bear quite an affection) would never carry the evening to an end safely. Lady Elgin *did* say — "Perhaps you think me mad." ' Her ladyship evidently adhered to the spiritual dogma of Edward Irving, a former Church of Scotland minister who, believing that the apostolic succession had not yet been completed, founded the Catholic Apostolic Church, in which he sought guidance from ancient prophets with whom he and his congregation communed. Irving's spiritual beliefs survived his death in 1834.

Elizabeth, describing this unfortunate evening, in a letter of 13–14 May 1852 to George Barrett, credits Robert with some sympathy towards Lady Elgin. He had clearly, at this early stage, taken no definite position on spiritualism. He neither believed nor disbelieved, and evidently kept his mind partly open — though leaning towards scepticism — for as long as possible. In a letter of 2 June 1853 to Mrs Ogilvy, Elizabeth reported that 'poor Robert ... declares with his last breath that until he sees and hears with his own eyes and ears, he will give credence to nothing.' This amounted to spiritualist agnosticism rather than spiritist atheism. He could not be pushed or persuaded one way or the other until a case had been made that would satisfy his strict evidential standards.

Robert was casually interested, as he could be in anything even mildly grotesque, though it would be exaggeration to describe his attitude as one of active curiosity. Nevertheless, it was difficult to avoid the subject, considering the company he kept. Another new acquaintance in Florence that year was Frederick Tennyson, possessed of an independent income and views that, putting it mildly, tended towards eccentricity. He was forever on the lookout for the Second Coming, believing it to be imminent. He had married an Italian wife, a pleasant and patient Sienese woman who produced several children and proved herself a capable housekeeper and mother. She gave Elizabeth useful tips on household economy. Robert liked Frederick every bit as much as he had come to like his younger brother, Alfred. By the summer of that year, Frederick had become a regular fixture at Casa Guidi. To Joseph Milsand, Robert wrote, 'I have a new acquaintance here, much to my taste, Tennyson's elder brother, a very earnest, simple, and truthful man, with many admirable talents and acquirements. He is very shy. He sees next to no company, but comes here and we walk together.'[89]

'We quite love him,' wrote Elizabeth to George Barrett on 2 July 1853. 'He used to come to us every few days and take coffee and smoke (I graciously permitted the smoking) and commune about books, men and spirits till past midnight.' Lytton, Powers, and Tennyson, wrote Elizabeth on 2 June 1853 to Mrs Ogilvy, had become the Brownings' 'familiar spirits'. Frederick's belief in spiritualism, and a lot more besides, made Elizabeth feel 'almost a sceptic by comparison. He's a man to believe in a muffin's turning crumpet because of a devil on the left hand side; and to think it *nothing surprising.*' It took a lot more than a supposition of devils to surprise Robert, too, which probably did something to endear Frederick to him; besides, there was Frederick's 'elemental' poetry — amounting to 'two great volumes of poems (not published, understand)' — which Robert did not despise and in which Elizabeth, on reading some of it, found 'much fancy and sweetness'.[90] A year later, though, she felt able to add nothing very positive to this initial opinion: 'he has the poetical element, the melody, the richness of vocabulary — but he seems to me to see, feel, think, speak nothing distinctly. It's all a haze — a golden haze certainly.'[91]

In April 1853, Mrs Theodore Martin — the actress Helen Faucit, much admired by Robert for her professional abilities — produced Robert's play *Colombe's Birthday* at the Haymarket Theatre in London. To Edward Chapman, Robert had written on 5 March that 'Theatrical matters chop and change, and this may come to nothing sooner than something — but if there were to be any sort of success, it would help the poems to fetch up their lee-way, I suppose. Hadn't you better advertize, in that case? — You know best, of course.' Despite his lack of confidence that anything could ever go right and according to plan with a theatrical performance, the prospect of a new production was a boost to Robert's morale and an encouragement to persist with his current work on *Men and Women*. He went so far as to tell Chapman, 'Meantime, I shall give you something saleable, one of these days — see if I don't.'

Both the Brownings doubted whether the play could be a popular success. Robert, in a letter of 31 January to Mrs Martin, had told her to 'do what you think best with it', advising her to get a copy of the last, authoritative edition from Chapman and Hall and follow the corrections in that copy 'as they are important to the sense'; but otherwise, 'as for the condensation into three acts — I shall leave that, and all cuttings and the like, to your own judgment — and, come what will, I shall have to be grateful to you, as before.'[92] Elizabeth was more bothered than Robert, who had entirely handed over artistic judgements to its leading actress and producer, seemed to be. 'I care much more about it than Robert does . . . I should like it to succeed, being Robert's play, notwithstanding. But the play is subtle and refined for pits and galleries . . . a dreadful rumour reaches us of its having been "prepared for the stage by the author." Don't believe a word of it. Robert just said "yes" when they wrote to ask him, and not a line of communication has passed since. He has prepared nothing at all, suggested nothing, modified nothing. He referred them to his new edition, and that was the whole.'[93]

Robert confirmed this himself to John Forster in a letter of 12 April: 'all I heard of proposed adapting was that the theatres want the five to be made *three* acts. I bade them do so, by all means. In fact, one may suppose oneself dead and quiet and let the bustling care for you now as they will have to do soon enough — if they *do* care at all. I told Miss Faucit to do just what she liked, and dare say she will do neither more nor less, one whit, on that account. I always liked her.'

Helen Faucit's production ran for seven performances. Elizabeth commented, 'Yes, Robert's play has succeeded, but there could be no "run" for a play of that kind. It was a "succès d'estime" and something more, which is surprising perhaps, considering the miserable acting of the men. Miss Faucit was alone in doing us justice.'[94] The *Athenaeum*'s critic concurred with Elizabeth's judgement and wondered 'Whether the taste of the public for so refined a creation on the stage is yet formed'; but it was more a success than not — to the extent that it was taken on tour to Manchester where, as Robert wrote to Reuben Browning, 'everybody praised her [Helen Faucit] highly, which really delights me; the other actors seem poor creatures, and I won't admit that the play, with its Hero left out, is a play at all.'[95] That reviews of the play should be favourable was more important to the Brownings than Robert's insouciance about the production would suggest.

George Barrett, like Reuben Browning, had written to reassure them about the warm reception *Colombe's Birthday* had received. At the beginning of May, Elizabeth told George that she had insisted on going down with Robert the day before 'to get the letters and afterwards examine the newspapers at Vieussieux's [the Gabinetto Vieusseux, a library and reading-room in the Palazzo Strozzi open only to men: Elizabeth would not have been permitted to enter] before anyone else arrived — So frightened was I. Robert was calling on me to admire this bright light across the mountains — that black shadow on an old wall — but I couldn't look at anything for my part — My heart beat so I could hear it with my ears. Well! on the whole, I am satisfied. Your letter was a great relief — Then, the "Morning Post" was very satisfactory and flattering — we are only in advance of our age, that's all — Daily News favourable too — Times illnatured in its usual snarling way, but admitting a success. Oh — as you think, there won't be a run probably — but it's a "succès d'estime" and something more — and favourable to the position in literature, calculated to give a push to the poems.'

Chapman and Hall, according to Elizabeth, had taken no heed of Robert's suggestion about advertising his poems: 'They are worse than Moxon himself to my mind — For instance — how do you make out that from the sale of a large edition of my two volumes (above a thousand copies) at sixteen shillings, my share of the "half profits" should be only about a hundred pounds? Do you really imagine that booksellers pay themselves after the same fashion, and buy villas at Wimbledon out of such pay? I believe more easily in Rapping spirits.' Later in this letter to George, Elizabeth commented that 'Colombe is not likely to run into a gold mine.' The Brownings were constantly surprised — as authors continue to be — by publishers' balance sheets, when they could examine them. Throughout 1852 and 1853, Robert was reminding Edward Chapman of his promise to let them have up-to-date accounts on a regular basis — 'My wife and I are anxious to know what has been the exact success, so far, of cash sale — both hers and mine' . . . 'I should really be glad to have the account at once, if you can so far oblige me' . . . 'I should be glad to have the account, and to know how you get on with the new Edition.'[96]

Money being short, the Brownings decided to postpone their intended visit to Rome, and gave up any thoughts of London and Paris that year. They settled again in a house at Bagni di Lucca, further down the hill this year, in Casa Tolemei (or Dolemei — Elizabeth gives both spellings in her letters) at Alla Villa, the middle village, for the summer of 1853. Edward Lytton stayed with them from time to time. One day, in Florence, he had asked whether Pen could read. The answer, dreadfully, was no — though Elizabeth added, somewhat defensively, that he could write very well indeed. What he could write before he could read, she doesn't say. He was very good at playing and being shown off: visitors, until it was clear they had been sufficiently delighted, were treated to the spectacle of Pen's virtuosity with a tambourine and displays of his wonderful talent for impromptu dancing while Robert played a piano accompaniment for the golden-ringleted 'fairy King of a child'. Robert occasionally disapproved of such indulgence, but Elizabeth worried not at all, except to comment that 'His one fault is considerable vanity. Applause he can never resist in any form — that child of mine.'[97]

Lytton's inquiry, however, prompted her to teach Pen to read, though only because she wanted him 'to know how to read for his own pleasure's sake and that he may inherit the fat of fairyland, and not that I have the least notion of beginning a course of education'.[98] Since Pen's attention span lasted no more than five minutes, these lessons were fairly perfunctory. In any case, Elizabeth believed that a child learned more through play than through a formal effort to educate him. He liked to learn nursery rhymes, however. He had got some two hundred off by heart from Elizabeth and liked even better to recite them, 'using the most dramatic intonation and gesture to make up for the imperfect articulation. He means to have his father's memory.'[99] And so, despite efforts to teach Pen how to spell — 'D O G, dog; D O G, dog; D O G, dog. Says Robert, "What a slow business!"' — Pen played and pretty much pleased himself throughout the summer.

William Wetmore Story and his young wife Emelyn, with their own children, Edith (usually known as Edie), aged nine, and little Joe, aged six — both of an age to be friends for four-year-old Pen — were staying at the top of the hill, and they all went up and down on donkeys to drink tea and gossip. Elizabeth, with notable confidence, crossed a river on a 'picturesque sort of ladder-bridge of loose planks' that swayed and rocked alarmingly when she and Robert, holding her hand, were half-way across. 'A gallant colonel who was following us went down upon his hands and knees and crept.' Oh! The intrepidity of poets! 'I was so sick with fright that I could hardly stand when all was over, never having contemplated such a heroic act. "Why, what a courageous creature you are!" said our friends. So reputations are made . . .'[100]

Otherwise, aside from excursions on donkeys — once to Prato Fiorito to repeat their adventure of the first visit — and domestic entertainments, Elizabeth reported to Henry Fothergill Chorley in London that 'we are doing a little work, both of us'. Robert had shown her some of the poems intended for 'a volume of lyrics, and those seemed as fine to me as anything he has done. We neither of us show our work to one another until it is finished. An artist must, I fancy, either find or *make* a solitude to work in, if it is to be good work at all! This for the consolation of bachelors!' It was probably this summer, at Bagni di Lucca, that Robert wrote the dramatic poem-play (a little in excess of 900 lines) 'In a Balcony', and it is likely that the excursions, the first and the second, by the Brownings to Prato Fiorito inspired some romantic images in 'By the Fire-Side', a tender, forward-looking poetic contemplation of a happy marriage remembered in old age. The portrait of 'Leonor' in this poem is clearly of Elizabeth.

The Brownings returned to Florence in October, having been away some three months. Before leaving Florence they had engaged a new manservant, Ferdinando Romagnoli, a tall, strong, good-looking man, clearly pleasing to Wilson and — since he had taken a gun with him to Bagni di Lucca and knew how to use it, having been a veteran of battles for the reunification of Italy in 1848 — a hero figure to Pen, who adored Ferdinando and was much loved by him in return. The Brownings stayed only a few weeks in Florence to pack some personal belongings and necessary domestic equipment — they had not this time managed to sub-let the apartment — before setting off again in mid-November to spend the winter in Rome in lodgings engaged for them by the Storys. Robert had written to Story in October to make the necessary arrangements and to complain a little about the fag-end of the season at Bagni di Lucca: 'This poor place has given up the ghost now, and we really want to get away.' He was a little worried, nevertheless, that 'I hear more about the fever at Rome than I care to infect this paper with.' Travelling by way of Perugia, the great church of Assisi, and the spectacular Falls of Terni, they arrived in the city eight days later, Robert and Pen singing loudly, and found their rooms at 43 via Bocca di Leone, where the Storys had thoughtfully lit lamps and fires and were waiting, smiling broadly, to welcome them.

The next day, in a state of what Elizabeth characterized as 'bilious irritability ... from exposure to the sun or some such cause,' and a 'fit of suicidal impatience', Robert shaved off his entire beard and whiskers. 'I *cried* when I saw him,' wrote Elizabeth to Sarianna in May 1854. 'I was so horror-struck ... no human being was ever so disfigured by so simple an act.' She declared that unless Robert grew it all back, every hair, everything was at an end between them; so he conceded her preference. Growing or shaving a beard may be considered a radical act. Robert's fit of impatient irritability may well have derived from his feeling that he should shake off — or shave off — the stagnation of Florence, somehow revitalize or reinvent himself, perhaps even symbolically lighten the face he had presented for so long bewhiskered to the world. There may have been a touch of anxiety about reaching the age of forty,

and a thought of recovering a more youthful appearance — not simply
for the sake of vanity, but for the sake of the spirit in which he should
approach the lyrics for his next book. In any event, shaving may be
done impetuously, but it is not done lightly. The symbol is the thing.
Having shaved in a momentary crisis of reaction, there would be no
difficulty reverting to the familiar state of whiskerdom on demand. The
beard grew back. 'But it grew *white*,' reported Elizabeth to Sarianna,
'which was the just punishment of the gods — our sins leave their
traces.' Still, the 'argentine touch' of the new beard was considered more
becoming than not, 'giving a character of elevation and thought to the
whole physiognomy'. All in all, that winter, the consensus was that
Robert looked very well indeed, better than ever.

If the loss of Robert's beard on their first morning in Rome could
be considered to be portentous in any way, it certainly marked a tragedy.
The Brownings had not even sat down to breakfast before a manservant
was at their door with young Edie Story and a request for them to come
urgently to the Storys': 'The boy was in convulsions; there was danger.'
Leaving Edie with Wilson, they hurried to their friends' apartment.
There they found little Joe Story fevered and unconscious. He died that
night at about eight o'clock. Back at the Brownings' apartment, his sister
Edie was taken ill and, since the Brownings had no spare room, she was
put to bed in the apartment below by William Page, an American artist
and a good friend of the Storys. For two days Edie was seriously ill, to
the point that her life was despaired of, with the same illness that had
killed Joe — 'gastric fever, with a tendency to the brain'. Mr Page's
daughter Emma sickened, too, and the Storys' governess also fell ill.
Elizabeth, who had sat with Robert all the day by Joe's bedside and
watched the little boy — no more than two years older than Pen —
die so dreadfully, was anguished.

To Miss Mitford, on 7 January, she wrote: 'Now you will not wonder
that, after the first absorbing flow of sympathy, I fell into a selfish human
panic about my child. Oh, I "lost my head," said Robert; and if I could
have caught him up in my arms and run to the ends of the world, the
hooting after me of all Rome could not have stopped me.' But the
Brownings remained healthy: 'Robert is well, and our child has not
dropped a single rose-leaf from his cheeks.' In this letter, Elizabeth
confessed frankly her horror of even 'a common funeral', far less actual

corpses and fresh graves. Rome, for a while, was blackened and spoiled for her by her day's vigil — her first ever day of such a kind — at a deathbed. Robert, writing to Sarianna on 19 December 1853, hoped that the 'worst is past in all matters. The little girl was moved two days ago to her own house, and barring unforeseen relapses, is out of danger. The governess in much the same state, or not quite so well, perhaps: the father and mother going about their old life much in the old way, but effectually *struck*, of course.' Robert seems to have remained calm in these circumstances, but Elizabeth was constantly nervous, to the extent that she did not want to go so much to the Storys, though Robert told her that they must, for friendship's sake, spend Christmas in their company. And so they did, albeit Elizabeth feared that the day would be oppressive and Pen had been upset and tearful about Joe's death. In the event, there was some light relief. Pen 'fell sound asleep with his head on the table, between the turkey and the plum pudding. "Here's the pudding, Penini! wake up!" He woke up to eat the pudding and fell prostrate again; and was carried home in a state of unconsciousness which lasted till morning.'[101] Not ill — just over-tired and over-stuffed.

In the aftermath of this emotional drama, neither Elizabeth nor Robert felt much like doing any work. To Mrs Ogilvy, on 19 February 1854, Elizabeth wrote, 'the first effect of grief upon *me* is the striking of me dumb — and it's the same with Robert. We, both of us, wait for calms before we do anything with Art. Perhaps melancholy calms — but the state of calm is necessary to most artists, I think.' Elizabeth reported having fallen behind schedule by at least a month with *Aurora Leigh*, but 'Robert swears he shall have his book ready in spite of everything for printing in June when we shall be in London for the purpose . . . Mine won't be ready — what is left undone in Rome can't be done in London where we are regularly put into a mill and ground, body and soul.' The mill of Rome, however, was about to start grinding them pretty fine.

Tuscany had always attracted lotos-eating expatriates and tourists, northerners mostly, in flight from whatever most oppressed them in Britain, America, Germany, Scandinavia, and Russia — poverty, illness, climate, cultural stagnation, sexual prudery and social censoriousness, political and religious opinions and principles. Florence in particular had acquired a reputation as a paradise of exiles, not always to its credit. Mrs Jameson, a sensible woman of the world, had warned the Brownings in Pisa that Florence was swarming with feather-headed British pleasure-seekers, that the city was virtually a British colony, a *demi-monde* frivolous in its attitudes and verging on decadence in its hedonism. Shying away from reprehensible balls and parties, from high revelry and low gossip, the Brownings had loitered too long in the dull hinterland of Pisa. When they finally made up their minds to risk Florence, they were surprised, perhaps, to find it — against all warning and consequent expectation — slow and provincial rather than flighty and racy. First-rate Italian novelists and poets would flee a few years later to Florence to escape persecution elsewhere, but the resident amateur foreign poet-asters and dim romantic novelists, some of them eking out their small incomes, had chosen the city of their own free will. 'We are all poets in Florence,' wrote Elizabeth to Mrs Ogilvy on 28 August 1854. 'Not to rhyme would be a distinction.' She particularly cited Frederick Tenny-son, and 'young [Brinsley] Norton ... committed follies enough to win his poetical spurs before twenty one. His verses are not quite so convincing.' She had some hopes of Lytton, although 'At present he suffers in his imagination from the strength of his memory.' Miss Blagden 'is going to try to publish a book in America ... Then there's Mr Buchanan Read who has just finished a pastoral epic (toned between Thomson and Cowper — will *that do*?) of some eight thousand lines ... Also, Mrs Kinney, wife of the ex-minister (Turin), residing here now, has completed a narrative poem, a tragedy — I don't know what — we have plenty of Muses you see in Florence, though the "mediums," it is pronounced at New York, are for the present deficient.'

In respect of its foreign colony, Florence was undeniably second-rate compared to Rome, which at this time rivalled Paris as a European capital attractive to a large and heterogeneous enclave of vigorous and successful visiting and expatriated artists, writers, and theatrical person-ages. It is a characteristic of paradise that it should be beautiful but dull. The last thing one expects or desires in a paradise is to be shaken up and tumbled about by any disturbances to the easy flow of one's routine and peace of mind and spirit. The Brownings had not moved temporarily to Rome with any intention of being rattled, though certainly Florence, on their return from Bagni di Lucca, had seemed becalmed. They were in Rome principally for the sake of better winter weather (it was a consolation to hear that Florence was cold, and a gratification to read in Galignani's *Messenger* that London was even colder, snowbound and foggy besides), to see the principal sights of Roman antiquity, to finish their respective books, and perhaps to look for a little more novelty and social stimulation.

Paris had been pretty much a success, and Rome might have been better still had not the Grim Reaper met them on the doorstep, showering them with 'ghastly flakes of death', and had it not started immediately raining 'lords and ladies for the especial benefit of Thackeray perhaps', as Elizabeth wrote satirically to Arabel. Elizabeth never took very kindly to William Makepeace Thackeray. 'He is an amusing man-mountain enough, and very courteous to us — but I never should get on with him much, I think — he is not sympathetical to me.'[102] So far as Elizabeth was concerned, this tremendous literary personage, if he had not brought all of Vanity Fair with him, knew how to find it and stir it up in Rome and contribute his twopennyworth of small change: 'If anybody wants small-talk by handfuls of glittering dust swept out of salons, here's Mr Thackeray besides.'[103] Robert commented resignedly, and perhaps a little depressedly, to Sarianna on 19 December 1853, 'We shall be obliged to see some of the Christmas sights, I suppose, — midnight mass, etc. All the city will be illuminated with gas for the first time, — I don't care a straw about such things.'

Thackeray had brought his two chattering daughters, Anny [Anna Isabella] and Minny [Harriet Marion], aged fifteen and thirteen respectively, with him. They found 'everything delightful — "better than in Paris".' Robert thought his own initial indifference to Rome might disappear, but the sad business of the Storys had dispirited him. If he had been able to afford to move his household back to Florence, Rome being more expensive financially as well as emotionally than he had reckoned, he would have done so. This feeling wore off as the weeks passed, as grief altered from acute pain to chronic ache, and Rome began to exhibit better prospects. It was certainly rich in its opportunities for indulgence.

Thackeray had been ill in Rome and talked of leaving on the ground that the city didn't agree with him. Elizabeth suggested that it was 'the combination of dining out and Rome' that didn't agree with him — 'one at a time would answer perfectly' — and proposed that he should give up the dinners and remain in Rome. Thackeray declared it to be impossible: 'He can't live without dinners — he must have his dinners and two parties at nights, or in the mornings he finds it impossible to set to work on Vanity Fairs or Newcomes. The inspiration', she reported him as saying, 'dries without port.'[104]

Elizabeth may have known very well what Thackeray's habits were, but she was not inclined to be strictly fair to him at the expense of a good story. He was in fact working in the mornings and distractedly trying to take care of his two energetic adolescent daughters, who were sometimes taken out walking by Robert during the day and were regularly deposited with Elizabeth in the evenings when Robert went out to dinner or to the salons. Robert, writing to Sarianna on 19 December 1853, specifically identified Thackeray's severely acute illness as 'obstruction of the stomach'. It was 'smartly treated' and the patient recovered. He liked Thackeray well enough — 'very genial and kind' — and they were often thrown together in the social circles they both frequented in Rome. In Rome too, at this time, was John Gibson Lockhart, son-in-law and biographer of Sir Walter Scott and reputedly, as a reviewer for *Blackwood's Magazine*, the man responsible for the demise of John Keats — who had died in rooms on the nearby Spanish Steps — with his criticism of the 'Cockney' poets. Elizabeth enjoyed some little fun at the expense of Lockhart the Scots critic in her letter of 7 January 1854 to Miss Mitford: 'if anyone wants a snow-man to match Southey's snow-woman (see [Southey's poem] "Thalaba"), here's Mr Lockhart who, in complexion, hair, conversation, and manners might be made out of one of your English "*drifts*" — "sixteen feet deep in some places," says Galignani.' Tall, white-haired, pale, intellectually rigorous, ascetic, abstemious, and severe, Lockhart, who had come to Rome to recover his health, looked prematurely aged because he was in fact mortally ill and dying by degrees. He completed the process later in the year, at Scott's former home, Abbotsford.

Meanwhile, Lockhart could be regularly encountered at the fashionable Sartoris salon, where the Brownings first met him. Lockhart took kindly to Robert: 'I like Browning,' he said, 'he isn't at all like a damned literary man.' Elizabeth, reporting this encomium to Miss Mitford,

added, 'That's a compliment, I believe, according to your dictionary.'[105]
Lockhart and Elizabeth had an earnest discussion about Thackeray's
social habits. They agreed pretty closely: ' "Well" — said he to me —
with his lean frozen voice — "I am sorry to hear that Mr Thackeray is
ill." . . . "Dining out at Rome", he exclaimed — if a staccato effort of
the voice may be called an exclamation — "Why who *can* dine out at
Rome? *I* have never dined at all since I came — I have seen nothing I
could eat — And for the wine — nobody touches it unless in search
of poison — No — I will tell you what hurts Thackeray — Those girls
hurt him — Those girls annoy him and teaze [*sic*] him. If he wants to
be well, he should get a governess, or an aunt, and dispose of the girls."
I ventured a few words in extenuation of the girls who are nice and
frank, affectionate and intelligent — (and turn tables without touching,
moreover) but Mr Lockhart was in his snow — and after all, Thackeray
does complain that "domestic life is heavy on him –" *that* there's no
denying — and Lockhart understands why better than I pretend to
do.'[106]

If Elizabeth was pettish about the seeming glitter and unseemly
giddiness of Thackeray's social life, and the superficiality of his cynicism,
she was broad-minded about the desirability of Robert going out at
nights in search of agreeable company. His sociability in Paris and
London, she knew, had stimulated his spirits and his mind. Since Eliza-
beth usually thought better of risking adventures after dark, she encour-
aged him to leave her at home. He was the better for it, and — by
extension — so was Elizabeth, who delighted in his social pleasure and
affability in company. Robert would go as often as anywhere else to the
Storys. Being rich and well-connected, generous and genial, they were
well-acquainted with the city's best society and well-liked. Their apart-
ment was virtually a salon and a first resource for anyone of interest
passing through the city. Thackeray, who liked the Storys very much,
was often with them and endlessly ready to listen to them pouring out
their grief about Joe. He read *The Rose and The Ring*, not yet published,
aloud to Edie to comfort her when she was sick.[107]

It is easy enough, in dealing with this period in Rome, as it is with
the periods spent by the Brownings in Paris and London, to provide a
roll-call of their friends and acquaintances. They bustle along the streets
and through the shops of the Pincio, the piazza di Espagna, and the

piazza del Popolo; they gossip about their friends who are writers, painters, sculptors, musicians, actors and actresses; they visit one another morning, noon, and night; seek audiences with the Pope; tour the Vatican, the Coliseum, and the Forum; and often they pile themselves into fleets of carriages to go rolling and rumbling off for elaborate champagne and mayonnaise picnics in the surrounding Campagna.

Robert, in a letter to John Forster on 2 April 1854, lists picnic trips to Frascati, Ostia, and Valderano all in the course of just three weeks. Though Elizabeth could not go on every picnic, she told Miss Mitford in January 1854 that she had 'arrived at almost enjoying some things — the climate for instance, which, though perilous to the general health, agrees particularly with me, and the sight of the blue sky floating like a sea-tide through the great gaps and rifts of ruins'. She was comfortable in her sunny rooms, and she walked out most days as in an English summer. She reported that she and Robert 'do work and play by turns — having almost too many visitors — hear music at Mrs Sartoris's once or twice a week, and have Fanny Kemble to come and talk to us with the door shut, we three together'.

The Kemble sisters became particular favourites. Fanny Kemble, reputedly one of the greatest actresses of her day, was the divorced wife of an American planter, Pierce Butler, and spent the latter part of her life in America. Her sister Adelaide had given up a promising career as an opera singer to marry Edward John Sartoris, whereupon she launched herself upon another glittering adventure as an author and salonnière in Rome, Paris, and London. Elizabeth, to Miss Mitford in a letter of 19 March 1854, described Fanny Kemble as 'looking magnificent still, with her black hair and radiant smile. A very noble creature indeed . . . She thinks me credulous and full of dreams . . . Mrs Sartoris is genial and generous, her milk has had time to stand to cream, in her happy family relations. The Sartoris's house has the best society at Rome, and exquisite music, of course.' To Thomas Westwood, in February, Elizabeth had commented that a little society 'is good for soul and body, and on the Continent it is easy to get a handful of society without paying too dear for it. That, I think, is an advantage of continental life.'

Though continental life in Italy and France rarely involved much social contact with Italians or French themselves, the Brownings — who might have been expected to regard their fellow-countrymen abroad as a social resource — never took wholeheartedly to the English out of their own country, though there were some exceptions in the cases of Frederick Tennyson, Robert Lytton and Isa Blagden in Florence, and Lady Elgin and the Fraser Corkrans in Paris. In Rome, their special friends — the Storys, the Kembles, the artist William Page, and the young sculptor Hatty Goodhue Hosmer — were all either Americans by nationality or connected in some way, sometimes by marriage, sometimes simply by sympathetic feeling, with Americans.

Page, known to his admirers as 'the American Titian', painted a portrait of Robert which, though it later became blackened beyond either recognition or restoration, delighted Elizabeth so much that, in a princely gesture, the artist generously presented it to her. Robert later commented about this portrait, in a letter to Dante Gabriel Rossetti in October 1855: 'You must put it in the sun, for I seem to fear it will come but blackly out of its three months' case-hardening. So it fares with Page's pictures for the most part; but they are like Flatman the Poet's famous "Kings" in a great line he wrote — "Kings do not die — they only disappear!"' Page personally pleased Elizabeth very much, and he was forever in and out of the Brownings' apartment from his rooms downstairs. She greatly admired Page's portraits — 'like Titian's — flesh, blood and soul. I never saw such portraits from a living hand.' His technique was wonderful, then, and 'He professes to have discovered secrets, and plainly knows them, from his wonderful effects of colour on canvas.'[108] A pity, then, that these secrets included a technique of undertoning which the lapse of years destroyed. It didn't hurt his reputation with Elizabeth, or her confidence in him, that he was also an enthusiastic spiritualist.

Rome emptied a little of wintering tourists in the spring. The Thackerays went to Naples, where they all fell ill with scarlet fever; Lockhart departed with the Duke of Wellington who, fretting about how to manage Lockhart's funeral should he die untimely on the road, asked the company he found himself in on his last night — Robert included — whether it would be delicate to ask Lockhart if he would prefer his body to be sent back home or to be buried where he fell. Someone suggested that Wellington should consult with Lockhart about what he would do if death came to the duke instead on the journey.[109] Robert suggested 'that a similar question to [John Cam] Hobhouse about the relative advantages of being pickled and sent home, or consigned to the snug lying of the Abbey, had not been duly appreciated'.[110] But still there was enough to keep the Brownings occupied, including Robert and Pen sitting to an English artist called Fisher. Elizabeth approved her husband's portrait as an admirable likeness, but thought that Mr Fisher's sketch of her son, very pretty as it might be, failed to do justice to the delicacy of Pen's lower face — though of course nothing short of the artistry of Botticelli would have satisfied her in the depiction of that angel child.

William Page and Elizabeth were very thick together in Rome. At Mrs Sartoris's salon, they would sit together by the fire and discuss spiritualism over a slice of cake until Robert, 'who had been standing in the doorway of the quadrille-room, admiring the pretty women, and protesting that his own venerable age would prevent him dancing again', would come over 'to remonstrate with me for staying so late — "Anybody like *me* for dissipation he never had to do with"! Robert is charmed, you know, when he can accuse me of "dissipation" before a witness.'[111] At one of these salons, Robert was alarmed to see Mrs Sartoris sitting leafing through a book of his poetry. He was even more disturbed when she asked him to clarify a reference in one of the poems. Embarrassingly, he was quite unable to do so. Just as he usually forgot where or when a poem had been written, so he tended to forget the inspiration behind it and the references within it. What exactly he had meant by any verse or line or reference was often as much a mystery to Robert Browning as to the reader. Once he had finished with a poem, he rarely thought more about it beyond some technical tinkering with it later.

Pen, too, could be quite dissipated — children's parties were given in his honour; he had made no objections to going to the Thackerays when they were in Rome; was perfectly happy to be taken out by the Storys in their carriage without either parent or Wilson; and loved to be taken out to play by Ferdinando Romagnoli. Everything the child did was a delight, though even Elizabeth was 'a little surprised to hear him at Miss Blagden's soirée giving a "recitation" on the sofa with perfect presence of mind and calmness.' Pen, possessing no trace of reserve or shyness, talked fearlessly to everyone, even to Fanny Kemble who had a reputation for 'dashing' most people.[112]

Isa Blagden had come, like the Brownings, from Florence to Rome for the winter. Lily Wilson became friendly with Marianne, Miss Blagden's maid, and one day in early January, Wilson having taken Pen on a visit, the women fell to discussing spirit writing and experimenting a little. The pencil moved slightly in Marianne's hand, whereupon Wilson, who had always laughed at such things, suddenly decided to try her own luck. The pencil leapt in Wilson's fingers and wrote some legible letters, though no intelligible words. Ethereal spirits, in their eagerness to communicate, knew no mortal distinctions of social class in their choice of mediums. A *contadina* might be as receptive to the supernatural as a *contessa*, a gardener might be as acutely attuned to the spirit world as a Grand Duke, and a lady's maid might achieve as good a rapport with the beyond as her mistress — or even better.

When Elizabeth discovered that Wilson seemed to be a natural medium, able to receive and transmit spirit writings, she was astonished and delighted. Wilson, for her part, had been surprised and a little alarmed when she discovered her latent and unexpected talent. She remarked doubtfully to Elizabeth, 'I think there's something particular in that pencil of Miss Blagden's.' Elizabeth, immediately avid to test Wilson's abilities, gave her a Browning pencil, which performed admirably, Wilson's hand growing 'cold and stiff, while the pencil vibrates and moves itself — The hand simply supports the pencil — She has not the least consciousness of what is being written.'[113]

Elizabeth herself tried to imitate Wilson's psychic ability 'for a week together at fixed hours, holding a pencil in my hand for half an hour or more, and *always failed*, and when I had seen Wilson write — I said — "I will try no more. I am convinced that I am not fit to exercise the faculty. There's some reason against it."' To Isa Blagden, she had written in October 1853 that 'I shall get at Swedenborg in Rome, and get on with my reading. There are deep truths, in him, I cannot doubt, though I can't receive *everything*, which may be my fault … It strikes me that we are on the verge of great developments of the spiritual nature, and that in a philosophical point of view (apart from ulterior ends) the facts are worthy of all admiration and meditation.'

Writing to her brother George in January 1854, Elizabeth declared that 'Rational people should not put away these things without examination, nor should Christian people decide the whole work to be of the devil, when there's no devil's stamp upon it — They should take heed lest they be found fighting against God. These things are no miracles, properly so called, but a new development of Law.' This appeal to natural forces as the inspiriting nature of the phenomena is consistent with the scientific spirit of the Victorian age, however wrapped up in the traditional Christian values. Spiritualism, properly examined, would be found not only to be perfectly rational but congruent with God's will — which was not to say that scientific investigations might not be fallible. Michael Faraday, in a letter to the *Athenaeum* of 2 July 1853, had reported the results of a table-turning experiment that tended to prove that the table's motion was due to unconscious muscular actions on the part of persons in contact with the table. Elizabeth was indignant: 'I wish to reverence men of science, but they often will not let me. If *I* know certain facts on this subject, Faraday *ought* to have known them before he expressed an opinion on it. His statement does not meet with the facts of the case — it is a statement which applies simply to various amateur operations without touching on the essential phenomena, such as the moving of tables untouched by a finger.'[114]

She knew for a fact that tables had turned without human assistance — though some tables might be livelier than others. She had heard of tables becoming so reckless in their movements that they had actually to be held down! She did acknowledge the possibility of occasional fraud, however, and admitted the wickedness of some dishonest mediums. For Robert, trickery was the likely cause of most spiritualist phenomena; for Elizabeth, trickery indicated only individual cases of mediumistic vanity and venality. Her own amateur table-turning experiments had been as unsatisfactory as her attempts with a pencil. Arabel was informed that Frederick Tennyson, Edward Lytton, Robert, and Elizabeth had tried for quite twenty minutes to move a table in Florence, but, irritatingly, had failed. They blamed Robert's levity — he had been 'laughing the whole time'.[115]

His sister, on the contrary, gratifyingly took such matters more seriously. Sarianna, an admirably commonsensical soul in all conscience, and even inclined to scepticism, had been infected with the spiritualist fever. She had attended a séance in Paris where 'the table expressed itself intelligently by knocking with its leg, responses according to the alphabet'. She was 'not impressed', but 'being bound to speak the truth, she does not *think it possible that any trick can have been used*'.[116]

Throughout that winter in Rome, whenever Robert was out and the apartment was quiet, Elizabeth and Wilson wielded the spirit-inspired pencil, with varying results. On the evenings when the teenage Thackeray girls were confided to her care, they tried to shiver the timbers of a table. It seems unlikely that Robert knew the extent to which theoretical discussion of spiritualism had turned into active practice; he appears to have tolerated talk about spirits and their potentialities without making strenuous efforts to stop it. It is more probable that either he failed to enquire too closely about Elizabeth's interest in it at this time or that she discreetly concealed from him much of what she was up to in his absence.

In April, the Storys left to spend time in Naples. Edie had seemingly recovered from her illness, but — to their distress — relapsed, and they thought it best to remove her from Rome. Elizabeth saw them off with, probably, some relief. Joe's death had thrown a pall over the mild winter, and Edie herself had been a constant living reminder of a peril that might recur at any time. Elizabeth had been harrowed by a visit, soon after the funeral, with Mrs Story to Joe's grave in the English cemetery. As she wrote to Mrs Ogilvy on 24 January 1854: 'There's the Coliseum! — that's the temple of Vesta! — and that's little Joe's grave! — Ancient gods, renowned emperors, tumbled into the new grave and forgotten!! He's buried close by the heart of Shelley and away from his mother's . . . poor, good, dear, little Joe!' And now, before even reaching Naples, only a single night away from Rome, the Storys sent despairingly for Robert to come to them at Velletri, where Edie was again seriously ill. Robert rushed to them immediately, found Edie much better (though still unwell), sat up the night through with his friends, and returned in high spirits to his own family.

He had not gone to Velletri with Elizabeth's blessing. She had been enraged. Robert, she thought, had spent the entire winter fussing over the Storys, who had evidently become dependent upon him despite their own resources — two servants, three doctors, money aplenty, their own selves — what good could Robert do? What further help did they need? To Arabel, in plain contradiction of her professed scorn for 'masculine men', she condemned William Story's lack of 'manliness and fortitude'. Stunned by a 'concussion of nerves', she lay sleepless the whole night Robert was away, worrying about the risk of infection to Robert, who might in turn carry infection back to his own son. It was grossly irresponsible of him to leave them: their needs took precedence, surely, over anyone else's. She had begged Robert not to go, but he had gone all the same. Pen, hearing their argument, had screamed and sobbed piteously and uncomprehendingly as Robert's carriage was driven away.

Margaret Forster, in her biography of Elizabeth Barrett Browning, points out very acutely that 'In this attitude of hers there were many parallels to her father's reaction on similar occasions in the past when he too, in much the same way, had been incredulous that his wishes were not paramount among those he loved and who he believed loved him . . . The coldness of her tone was exactly like her father's, concerned with logic and facts and making no allowance for emotion.'[117] Elizabeth, certainly (according to her own philosophy and preferences), cursing Story's lack of masculinity and Robert's feminine sympathy, was not able, in the crisis of her shock and fear, to acknowledge Robert's innate compassion for the weak and the sick — though she had had ample evidence of it over the years and, in principle, admired it. She could admire it in these present circumstances only in retrospect, when she had recovered some sense and sensibility and was later able to write kindly, though somewhat acidulously, to sympathize with Mrs Story. It had been a very serious argument between Elizabeth and Robert, a genuine difference over a practical matter closer to the heart and the home than any theoretical dispute about politics or spiritualism or Pen's upbringing. There was no humour in it, no easy resolution of a dilemma that Robert had decided for himself, in his own manner and according to his own lights. That he had come back whistling and laughing had been the only good thing about it.

But, on the whole, the balance had not been all to the bad. There had been some good things in Rome — new friends, and reacquaintance with old ones particularly. Robert reported to John Forster in April 1854 that he had been 'talking on the Pincian to an acquaintance, when a stranger touched my arm and said in French, "Is that *you*, Robert?" It was my old friend Monclar, who, after an absence of seventeen years, had recognized *my voice* (my back being turned). He seemed not much changed, after a time.'[118] Whether the Comte Amédée de Ripert-Monclar could have said the same of Robert can only be guessed — but what he heard was instantly unmistakable. Though Monclar-Ripert swore to

Elizabeth 'that he was not changed for the intermediate years',[119] what he saw when Robert turned would have been a 'dark short man, slightly but nervously built with a frank open face, long hair streaked with grey and a large mouth which he opens widely when he speaks, white teeth, a dark beard and a loud voice with a slight lisp, and the best and kindest heart in the world'. That, at least, is the description left by Anne Thackeray of Robert in Rome. Such descriptions are accurate only up to a point: Miss Thackeray saw a short man where others saw a man of middle height or taller; she saw a dark beard where others saw a beard more 'argentine'; and she saw a dark complexion which others had perceived to be olive-skinned or sallow — though exposure to the Italian sun may have deepened its colour.

Robert's letter to Forster also briefly related the Story tragedy, remarking that 'This sorrow of theirs took us into its shadow also — and then the weather was unfavourable to my wife's power of enjoyment. Last, I have let myself be too much entangled with people's calls, card-leavings, and kindnesses of all sorts, having not been without social engagements for each evening for many a week now.' In May, Pen fell ill. The Brownings were 'forced three times to call in a physician'. It turned out to be nothing serious — 'just the result of the climate, relaxation of the stomach, etc., but the end is that he is looking a delicate, pale, little creature, he who was radiant with all the roses and stars of infancy but two months ago'.[120]

It was time to go. The Brownings would leave pestilential Rome for Florence in the last days of May without regret and, in Robert's words, 'after no very prosperous sojourn — the good we found being just what we had least expected, in an afflux of friends old and new. The place is ill starred, under a curse seemingly, and I would not live there for the Vatican with the Pope out of it.'[121] Elizabeth was of precisely the same mind: 'I don't like Rome, I never shall; and as they have put into the English newspapers that I don't, I might as well acknowledge the barbarism.'[122] She was even more forceful in her denunciation in her letter of 10 May to Miss Mitford: 'To leave Rome will fill me with barbarian complacency. I don't pretend to have a rag of sentiment about Rome. It's a palimpsest Rome — a watering-place written over the antique — and I haven't taken to it as a poet should, I suppose; only let us speak the truth, above all things. I am strongly a creature of association, and the associations of the place have not been personally favorable to me.'

To say that the Brownings were relieved to get back to Florence and Casa Guidi is seriously to understate their feelings. To Sarianna, at the end of May, Elizabeth wrote: 'We have arrived and see our dear Florence, the Queen of Italy, after all.' Pen, on the road, had been encouraged to improvise a poem. 'Without a moment's hesitation he began, "Florence is more pretty of all. Florence is a beauty. Florence was born first, and then Rome was born. And Paris was born after."' Which probably expressed the sentiments of the whole Browning family. To John Forster, in his letter of 5 June, Robert declared, 'This old Florence takes us to its breast like a friend after one defection — but I fear we can't stay in Italy and rest, as I am fain to do.' He thought Pen could do with some northern air to restore his health completely, and 'I must be in London, or Paris at farthest to print my poems.' Robert seems to say in this letter that from the writing of *Christmas-Eve* until 1853 he had written no poetry. This was not strictly true in fact, though in spirit it approximated to the truth of his perception. 'This is what I have written — only a number of poems of all sorts and sizes and styles and subjects — not written before last year, but the beginning of an expressing the spirit of all the fruits of the years since I last turned the winch of the wine press. The manner will be newer than the matter. I hope to be listened to, this time, and I am glad I have been made to wait this not very long while.'

Robert was referring to the poems he had already written that would be included in the book he next intended to publish, *Men and Women*. To William Story, on 11 June, he wrote, 'I am trying to make up for wasted time in Rome and setting my poetical house in order.'[123] And to Forster he predicted confidently: 'I shall be ready by the Autumn.' Elizabeth's *Aurora Leigh*, by now worryingly behind schedule, would be ready by the spring of 1855 — 'we count on it at least.' Then Robert asked Forster, 'Can one do anything with the American Booksellers, do you know? They tell us it is possible. But the talking usually blows a great round shiny bubble which a touch of the Yankee finger breaks promptly enough. You must know, — more, infinitely, than sanguine

American friends, — whether one *can* get a trifle for proofs in advance, etc.'[124] However humorously and delicately expressed, this inquiry — which had evidently first been canvassed around American friends in Rome — betrayed Robert's immediate anxiety about money.

It is clear that the possibility of such additional funds had been discussed with Elizabeth, who wrote to Miss Mitford on 6 June 1854 taking much the same line as Robert had taken with Chapman. 'Talking of American literature, with the publishers on the back of it, we think of offering the proofs of our new works to any publisher over the water who will pay us properly for the advantage of bringing out a volume in America simultaneously with the publication in England. We have heard that such a proposal will be acceptable, and mean to try it.' Rome had been expensive: 'Oh Henrietta!' Elizabeth had written to her sister the previous December, 'Rome is enough to ruin us with its dearness! We are reduced to live upon woodcocks, snipes, hares and turkeys because of beef and mutton being so high in price!'

Their financial situation was dire enough to worry even Elizabeth, and that took some doing. They were obliged to put off their trip to Paris and London: 'Our reason for not going to England has not been from caprice,' Elizabeth explained frankly to Miss Mitford on 20 July 1854, 'but a cross in money matters. A ship [the *David Lyon*] was to have brought us in something and brought us in nothing instead, with a discount; the consequence of which is that we are transfixed at Florence, and unable even to "fly to the mountains" as a refuge from the summer heat . . . That we should be able to sit quietly still at Florence and eat our bread and maccaroni is the utmost of our possibilities this summer.' John Kenyon had again been absent-minded about his twice-yearly gift of £50 — no reliance could be placed on that — and when all was paid and counted they reckoned they had only about £100 to last them for a little more than six months. On 1 July, Robert wrote to ask Edward Chapman if he would be so good as to give them 'the half year's account, which will be more interesting than usual just now?' Robert had to prompt Chapman for the account again on 5 August. For all that it brought them when it did finally arrive, it was hardly worth the trouble Robert had taken to get it.

And so, probably for better than for worse in terms of getting on with their poetry, the Brownings made up their minds to stay put at

Casa Guidi. They settled into a routine of work and play that enabled them to give their concentrated attention from mid-mornings to mid-afternoons to writing their books, to educating Pen — so far as that proved possible (he responded positively to Robert's discipline but took full advantage of Elizabeth's indulgence) — to reading and music for a couple of hours after breakfast, and to visiting and receiving friends in the evenings. Robert, with the aid of Isa Blagden, who acted happily and reverently as his amanuensis, wrote, dictated, and produced a fair copy of some eight thousand lines of poetry. When he set himself firmly to writing, he could produce great quantities in a short time. Elizabeth, with less speed and fluency, worked on through the long composition of *Aurora Leigh*. After their mid-afternoon dinner, Robert would show Elizabeth what he had done, and she would be properly appreciative. She would often, indeed, be profoundly proud and astonished. To Henrietta, on 27 April 1855, she wrote: 'Robert's poems are magnificent, and will raise him higher than he stands.' In September, the *David Lyon* finally paid ship money in the sum of £175, relieving the pressure of financial anxiety and allowing them to draw breath and work with calmer minds.

The world meanwhile turned and tipped visitors into Florence like water from a millwheel. If Florence was for Elizabeth the Queen of cities, Elizabeth was the Queen of Florence for many tourists, a sight to be seen. There was 'Lord Fordwich, Lord Cowper's son, and Lady Palmerston's grandson — a very gentlemanly unassuming young man, and intelligent up to a certain point. It was necessary to pay him atten-tion and he *took* to Robert apparently, as young men do.'[125] Another, mercifully unidentified, young man mesmerized Elizabeth 'into deep sleep by his miraculous stupidity, and commonplace'. There was also a cousin of Wordsworth's, and the previously mentioned Brinsley Norton, younger son of the poet and novelist Caroline Norton (later to become the model for George Meredith's heroine in *Diana of the Crossways*), married to 'a Capri girl without shoes and stockings (or beauty)'. Young Norton's self-contemplation, bordering on narcissism ('He is constantly on a pedestal, turning round on one heel before a glass'), did not endear him. At the Villa Torrigiani, Frederick Tennyson now and again set up a fourteen-piece orchestra to play the best German music for his friends; there were teas on Lytton's terrace; and of course Mrs Frances Trollope, having returned to Florence from her summer retreat at Bagni di Lucca, was again holding regular court at the Villino Trollope.

Elizabeth travelled across the city to call on Mrs Trollope, but found her not to be at home. This was to be regretted for one reason only — it frustrated Elizabeth's intention of reporting on her in her domestic habitat to Miss Mitford. 'From what I hear, she appears to be well, and has recommenced her "public mornings" which we shrink away from. She "receives" every Saturday morning in the most heterogeneous way possible. It must be amusing to anybody not overwhelmed by it, and people say that she snatches up "characters" for her "so many volumes a year" out of the diversities of masks presented to her on these occasions.'[126] Catch Elizabeth being 'snatched up' as a 'character' by Fanny Trollope! Not likely. Considering Thomas Trollope's abhorrence of the heterogeneity of the Grand Duke's receptions, he should have looked closer to home for a measure of social vulgarity — if we are to take Elizabeth's word for it. The Brownings had heard of Mrs Trollope as far away and as long ago as Pisa, when Robert was barring their door against the curiosity of casual visitors: '"There is that coarse, vulgar Mrs Trollope — I do hope, Ba, if you don't wish to give me the greatest pain, that you won't receive that vulgar, pushing woman who is not fit to speak to you." — "Well . . . now we are at Mrs Trollope! You will have your headache in a minute — now do sit down, and let us talk of something else." '[127]

More pleasantly, Mrs Sartoris stopped off in Florence on her way to Rome. That summer they met again the American actress Charlotte Cushman, who had already crossed their paths in London and Paris, and the young American sculptor Harriet Hosmer, who had intrigued them in Rome. Hatty, as she was usually known, was emancipated in every possible way. In his biography of William Wetmore Story, Henry James quotes a letter from Story of 11 February 1853 to James Russell Lowell in which he describes how 'Hatty takes a high hand here with Rome, and would have the Romans know that a Yankee girl can do anything she pleases, walk alone, ride her horse alone, and laugh at their rules. The police interfered and countermanded the riding alone on account of the row it made in the streets, and I believe *that* is over, but I cannot affirm.' Hatty had obtained a place in the Rome studio of the celebrated sculptor John Gibson — a great achievement since Gibson took very few pupils. In time, she set up her own studio and her own works fetched amazing prices — in at least one case, a thousand pounds.

Hatty Hosmer became a 'great pet' of the Brownings in Rome. She 'emancipates the eccentric life of a perfectly "emancipated female" from all shadow of blame by the purity of hers,' Elizabeth wrote admiringly to Miss Mitford in May 1854. 'She lives here all alone (at twenty-two); dines and breakfasts at the *cafés* precisely as a young man would; works from six o'clock in the morning till night, as a great artist must, and this with an absence of pretension and simplicity of manners which accord rather with the childish dimples in her rosy cheeks than with her broad forehead and high aims.' Hatty's particular friend was a Miss Hayes, described by Elizabeth to Henrietta back in December as 'the translator of George Sand, who "dresses like a man down to the waist" (so the accusation runs). Certainly there's the waistcoat which I like — and the collar, neckcloth, and jacket made with a sort of wag-tail behind, which I don't like. She is a peculiar person altogether, decided, direct, truthful, it seems to me.'

Miss Hayes' clothes — and Hatty's, which also featured boyish items — were too bohemian, too masculine in the Sand style, for Elizabeth's tastes, and perhaps too youthful. Elizabeth stuck to convention in her own dress, though convention had become more a disinclination to change her style other than in small details: her ringlets, bunched around her ears, were not now fashionable, and her dresses, however much care she took over them and however carefully they were made, were not modish. She might talk and write as animatedly about fashion as the next woman, but she kept to the style of the younger woman she had once been, with the effect perhaps of ageing herself more than she would have wished. Robert didn't seem to notice, but others did.

Miss Hosmer and Miss Hayes lived, in Rome, in rooms above those that had been occupied during the winter by Isa Blagden, and when they came to Florence that summer of 1854 they stayed with Isa (pronounced 'Eesa', in the Italian manner) at Bellosguardo. Isa had been born in 1816 — that, at any rate, is the date on her gravestone in the Protestant cemetery in Florence. Her father's name is recorded as Thomas Blagden, which sounds English, though her nationality for official purposes was Swiss. From her appearance — small, delicate, olive-skinned, black-eyed, and black-haired — most of the Florentine expatriate community assumed an Italian or, more likely, an Indian mother. She had first arrived in Florence in 1849, settling there permanently in 1854. From 1856 to 1861 she lived at the Villa Brichieri, where she entertained expatriate society to lunches and Saturday teas on her terrace — which were rather better in both quantity and quality than might have been expected on her exiguous income. The Brownings first met Isa in 1850 and over the years formed a close friendship with this little woman who wrote poetry that neither Robert nor Elizabeth discuss in their letters; later she began writing romantic novels for which Anthony Trollope helped to find publishers. Isa's broad acquaintance in Florence ranged from the Brownings at one end of the city to the Trollopes at the other, bridging the sublime and (in the Brownings' estimation, at least) the ridiculous.

The former Miss Theodosia Garrow, now Thomas Trollope's wife, was a particular friend of Isa's and both of them shared at least one thing in common with Elizabeth — a passionate commitment to the cause of Italian unity. Isa seems to have been everyone's darling. Warm-hearted, intelligent, vivacious — according to Thomas Trollope — she was universally liked and was universally obliging, hopping like a little bird from one friend and festivity to another. She seems to have fallen at least half in love with Edward Robert Lytton, her neighbour for a while at Bellosguardo; Lytton in turn, though fifteen years her junior, was apparently not indifferent, declaring that, 'A dozen or more good and dear women must have gone to the making of that one little body. I know of none so essentially loveable and absolutely to be loved, through and through.' Now approaching forty, Isa remained unmarried — a 'wandering English spinster', as Henry James characterized her[128] — but, for all the tenderness with which she was cherished by men and women alike, and for all the passion and sensuality she poured into her poetry and prose, there is no indication that she was a threat to any marriage.

She might have an affair in Rome, and she might fall romantically for young Lytton, and everyone might smile kindly, and Lytton might pay her charming attentions; but it was apparently perfectly safe for Robert, at Elizabeth's instigation, to visit Isa very regularly several times a week — these visits, every second day, with or without Pen, had begun in 1853 — while she stayed quietly home alone on her sprung sofas at Casa Guidi. Elizabeth indeed thought of Isa as 'a very affectionate friend of mine and very loveable on her own account'. Henry James has as good a word as anyone else to say for Isa Blagden's 'kindly little legend' in the 1860s: 'Above all she had befriended the lonely, cheered the exile and nursed the sick; given herself indefatigably, for instance, to the care of Robert Lytton, during a long illness . . . an eager little lady who has gentle, gay black eyes and whose type gives, visibly enough, the hint of East-Indian blood.'[129]

Isa was as fascinated by spiritualism as Elizabeth. They had talked and corresponded on the subject since at least July 1853, when Elizabeth wrote to Isa from Bagni di Lucca to declare, 'Oh, we are believers here, Isa, except Robert, who persists in wearing a coat of respectable scepticism — so considered — though it is much out of elbows and ragged about the skirts.' Florence was as infected with wonder-workers and seekers after spiritualist revelations as Paris, London, or Rome. Robert had already fallen in the way of ancient, fantastical, Faust-like Seymour Kirkup, a painter, archaeologist, and art historian — deaf as a post, and 'such a tragic face the old man has, with his bleak white beard', according to Elizabeth. Kirkup had removed to Italy for the good of his consumptive lungs. So much good did Florence do for him, indeed, that he lived to be a nonagenarian. He lodged near the Ponte Vecchio in rooms reputed to have been inhabited by Ariosto in an ancient palazzo said to have been a hospice of the Templars. He devoted himself to the study of magic and Dante, who, he claimed, often came to visit and pass a pleasant, chatty evening and whose portrait by Giotto he had discovered, at Dante's personal direction, in the Bargello. He collected books, demonological manuscripts, old pictures, occult and curious objects, and had lately become as much absorbed by spiritualism as by astrology and his other esoteric interests. Mrs Orr tells a story told her by Val Prinsep, an English artist, who, she says, got it from Robert Browning himself.

> One day Browning called on him to borrow a book. He rang loudly at the storey, for he knew Kirkup, like Landor, was quite deaf. To his astonishment the door opened at once and Kirkup appeared.
>
> 'Come in,' he cried; 'the spirits told me there was someone

at the door. Ah! I know you do not believe! Come and see. Mariana is in a trance!'

Browning entered. In the middle room, full of all kinds of curious objects of ''vertu,' stood a handsome peasant girl, with her eyes fixed as though she were in a trance.

'You see, Browning,' said Kirkup, 'she is quite insensible, and has no will of her own. Mariana, hold up your arm.'

The woman slowly did as she was bid.

'She cannot take it down till I tell her,' cried Kirkup.

'Very curious,' observed Browning. 'Meanwhile, I have come to ask you to lend me a book.'

Kirkup, as soon as he was made to hear what book he wanted, said he should be delighted.

'Wait a bit. It is in the next room.'

The old man shuffled out at the door. No sooner had he disappeared than the woman turned to Browning, winked, and putting down her arm leaned it on his shoulder. When Kirkup returned, she reassumed her position and rigid look.

'Here is the book,' said Kirkup. 'Isn't it wonderful?' he added, pointing to the woman.

'Wonderful,' agreed Browning as he left the room.[130]

On 2 February 1857 Elizabeth was writing to Mrs Jameson to say, 'There is a real *poem* being lived between Mr Kirkup and the "spirits," so called.' This may or may not have been meant satirically. By that time, Kirkup had been showing the Brownings 'various sketches of the evil and good, as spiritually discerned by friends of his — and there was an angel from a higher sphere, in a long floating garment of blue gleaming into rose-colour. The evil spirits are seen as through a dark veil.'[131] Two years previously, Kirkup had come to visit the Brownings with the news that a special revelation had been granted to him. As a consequence, he had thrown off his former creed that had been near enough to atheism, and he now wholeheartedly acknowledged a spiritual world and a future state for the soul. 'I confess it. I am convinced at last.' The revelation seemed to consist of loud rappings, articulate voices, and involuntary writings conveyed through the medium of Kirkup's clairvoyante. The rappings in particular had been so loud as to make the deaf old man jump.

Robert declared Kirkup to be a 'humbug', though he kindly neglected to tell him so. Even Elizabeth, finding herself surprisingly cool about the old man's enthusiasms, thought him 'somewhat hasty, after having heard in vain the mystical knockings at all the doors and windows of the universe his whole life long to come round suddenly through a rap on a door by means of a clairvoyante'. She knew that such supernatural phenomena occurred, but in this case she reserved judgement. 'Mr Kirkup is deaf, and though a man of great intelligence, he is not philosophical in his modes of carrying on experiment.'[132] Kirkup was not the only convert from atheism or to whom revelations had been granted. More credible was James Jackson Jarves, an American art critic, who had confided to Elizabeth 'that twenty or thirty persons, *of his own acquaintance*, have been brought to abjure atheism and materialism by these manifestations. The extraordinary things I am hearing day after day — for the thing makes progress — it would startle you to listen to.' Disappointingly, on the domestic front, Wilson's powers were beginning to fail after initial high expectations. 'Wilson still writes — but generally so illegibly and in so broken a way that we can't make much out of it. She is a weak medium — it is like trying to get a clear reflection in tremulous water.'[133]

Jarves, by contrast, was discovering the strength of his own mediumistic powers. From America, he wrote an 'extraordinary "spiritual"' letter to Elizabeth in the summer of 1855 to tell her of dramatic developments, as she reported to Henrietta: 'The spirits begin now to carry material objects from one place (out of the house) to another. They make themselves *partially visible* very often. Mr Jarves has become a medium himself — has the knocking sounds at night, and other manifestations. A chair in his father's dining room raised itself (without being touched by a finger) to the top of the table, and back again — and the table itself floating up into the air above all their heads. His watch was wound up without a key and went forty eight hours etc. etc. etc. He comes back to Florence in September. I think you know who he is — the author of a book on Art, the son of one of the most wealthy men in America. He himself is very rich — and what is more important to the subject, perfectly *veracious*. Even Robert admits this.'[134]

Jarves's own mediumistic abilities, he confided to Elizabeth, did not include the production of rapping sounds; rather, he could see spirits and hear 'the *spiritual voices* — which of course,' Elizabeth told Henrietta in November, 'demands very high mediumship'. Altogether, Jarves was highly satisfactory — young, intelligent, socially respectable, rich, sincere, and in full possession of a finely-calibrated aptitude for high level mediumistic contact with the spirits. In due course Jarves told them of the fashionable and gifted medium Daniel Dunglas Home, who, when Jarves stayed with him for a night, had been responsible — there could be no doubt — for the mysterious movement of a four-poster bed which 'was carried into the middle of the room — shadowy figures stood by the pillow, or lay down across the feet of those about to sleep — nothing threatening, everything kind; but, at best, extremely disturbing.'[135]

The winter of 1854–5 in Florence was generally a positive period for the Brownings. There were no serious quarrels about spiritualism — that matter mostly lay dormant between them — and the bickerings over Pen's education were partially resolved. Robert wrote to Edward Chapman on 11 January 1855, asking him to send a quantity of children's pamphlets suitable for a six-year-old child's first reading. Three of them were publications of the Religious Tract Society (*Joseph and His Brethren, History of Moses, Great Truths in Simple Words*), and three others were from a series of 'Rollo' books by an American schoolmaster who, at the progressive Mount Vernon School, preferred to rely on the honour and conscience of his pupils rather than the discipline of corporal punishment.

Very likely, given what we know about the Brownings' attitudes towards infant education, the 'Rollo' books were Elizabeth's choice, the rest Robert's. Elizabeth crowed to Mrs Ogilvy in March 1855 that Pen 'reads very well and with great animation — sometimes when a book's amusing, twenty pages at a time. We go through heaps of books — childish books — as high up, however, as [Hans Christian] Andersen and Grimm's fairy tales which he enjoys much.' To Henrietta, Elizabeth had noted proudly the previous November that Pen had written to John Kenyon, at his express request, 'a long letter . . . all about the rabbits and tortoises — every word the child's own. He has an ominous fluency in composition and really writes wonderfully.' In fact Pen's tendency was to stop whenever any difficulty impeded that fluency and throw his arms around his mother's neck — a ploy, he had learned, irresistible to Elizabeth.

Robert had been obliged to give up his preferences over Pen's appearance. Pen himself had asked to have his hair cut, but Elizabeth agreed only that the length should be slightly trimmed, just to keep the ends from splitting. The curls could not be sacrificed. 'When Penini is twelve years old, it will be time to think of such barbarisms, unless by that time the fashion of male heads should become less barbarised.' By that time, she hoped, men would be wearing their hair in Miltonic fashion, parted in the middle and grown long — much as Robert had worn his hair as a youth. Pen was still being fantastically dressed: 'Penini's costume is admired, I assure you — he was called "a little Vandyke" but yesterday.'[136] Robert had more success with musical instruction. Under daily paternal supervision, and with Elizabeth strictly forbidden to interfere, Pen was learning to play the piano. 'Think of those little fingers, Henrietta, running down the scales on the piano in the key of C, G and F! It *is* so funny! and the small heels kicking out.' Quite unprompted and untutored, he liked to sing a Verdi aria, *La Donna è mobile*, and a song of his own composition about Napoleon and the milkman. 'Penini thinks humbly he sings it "rather lite [*sic*] Mrs Sartoris".'

On 12 February 1855, Elizabeth was writing again to Henrietta to say that 'Penini has remarkable quickness; and we might, by a little *pushing*, make him do anything: but we won't push, be certain. Robert says that if he pushed him in music, for instance, he would make an "infant wonder" of him in two years. We want instead an intellectual man, of healthy development.' Pen was fluent in Italian and English, though Italian was his preferred language and he always called himself an Italian — '*io voglio essere Italiano*' [I want to be Italian].[137] His spelling was occasionally more inspired than correct, but he could be induced to persevere with getting it right. To Miss Mitford, in October, Elizabeth happily sighed in a letter, 'How young children unfold like flowers, and how pleasant it is to watch them!'

The reference to rabbits and tortoises in Elizabeth's letter to Henrietta was as much about a loss as a gain of livestock. Flush, elderly and almost hairless, had died shortly after the Brownings had returned from Rome. He was ceremonially buried in the courtyard of Casa Guidi. The once lively and beautiful spaniel had been old and tired, they explained to Pen, who was consoled by the acquisition of more rabbits and tortoises, which were housed on the balcony in hutches constructed by Ferdinando. These animals were only part of a menagerie that was being collected — there were snakes and other creeping and crawling things acquired at Bagni di Lucca,[138] for Pen who, much like Robert himself as a child, acquired a wide variety of domestic and garden pets.

In the last months of the year, Elizabeth heard that Miss Mitford was ill. It was difficult to believe, since Miss Mitford's letters seemed to betray no trace of infirmity. Nevertheless, and perhaps a little shadowed by the death of Flush, who had been a gift from Miss Mitford, Elizabeth's letters to her old friend became filled with the consolations of religious belief in an afterlife. A third calamity was an accidental injury to Elizabeth's father. She had been worrying in any case about reports from Arabel about Mr Barrett's bilious attacks and asthma; now she heard that he had been thrown from a hackney carriage and had broken his leg. Mr Barrett was now seventy years of age, and there had been — on that account alone — some ground for concern. In the event, he made a good recovery. Miss Mitford did not. She died, aged sixty-seven, in January 1855, much to Elizabeth's grief. It happened, too, that Elizabeth herself fell into bad health after Christmas.

The weather in Florence had been unusually severe. On the last day of October the Brownings lit fires and crowded chairs, tables, and sofas in a ring around the hearth. On 11 November 1854 Elizabeth wrote to Sarianna to report 'a horrible tramontana which would create a cough under the ribs of death, and sets me coughing a little in the morning'. In the succeeding February Elizabeth wrote to condole with Mrs Jameson, whose husband had recently died, leaving his widow in very straitened circumstances (though these were later relieved by a subscription among her friends and admirers that enabled her to live comfortably and continue writing her books). In this letter, Elizabeth admitted to 'a severe attack on the chest — the worst I ever had in Italy — the consequence of exceptionally severe weather — a bitter wind and frost together — which quite broke me up with cough and fever at night. Now I am well again, only of course much weakened, and grown thin. I mean to get fat again upon cod's liver oil, in order to appear in England with some degree of decency. You know I'm a lineal descendant of the White Cat, and have seven lives accordingly. Also I have a trick of falling from six-storey windows upon my feet, in the manner of the traditions of my race. Not only do I die hard, but I can hardly die. "Half of it would kill *me*," said an admiring friend the other day. "What strength you must have." A questionable advantage, except that I have also — a Robert, and a Penini!'

These assurances were repeated to her usual correspondents — Mrs Ogilvy, Mrs Martin, Henrietta, Arabel, and Sarianna — but they have an air about them of whistling against bad fortune. She acknowledged that these paroxysms of violent coughing, exhausting and painful, were as bad this time as they had ever been. Robert and Wilson nursed her twenty-four hours a day, piling and stoking the fires to keep her warm in the large open spaces of the apartment, making sure she ate a little to keep up her strength and drank spoonfuls of coffee to keep her from dehydrating. The image of the White Cat was not casual: Elizabeth had survived, prospered even, throughout the miscarriages and bronchitic attacks during her time in Italy, and she had not only herself to live for but her husband and son. Then, too, there was work still to do — *Aurora Leigh* to finish. Unthinkable, then, despite the deaths and accidents that had so recently claimed some of those close to her, that she herself should succumb.

She could fall on her feet again. Get to her feet again, at very least. Her letters dwelt less on her illness than on events in the outside world, as if she was determined to extend herself from the concentrated core of illness, from herself merely, to encompass the greater concerns of life. If she could do that, she would be well. She had said of Miss Mitford, in conventional tones of comfort, that death would be gain to her; but — for herself — she would gain more by living than dying. She took strength from the fact that she had not coughed blood, had not lost her voice, and that there had been no pain in her side. The illness had debilitated her, but not to the extent that she had 'wasted away' in the way she had done during previous attacks. This, more than anything, convinced her of her increased powers of resistance and of her continuing resilience. That resilience was probably more fancy than fact, since her rallying was due in part to a constant consumption of opium.

She had recovered well enough by the end of February 1855 to have started work again. Robert, working four hours a day, was pressing ahead and achieving quantities of verse, producing at least a first draft.

Elizabeth, however, looked despairingly at her own pages and, as she reported to Mrs Ogilvy in March, 'here are between five and six thousand lines *in blots* — not one copied out — and I am not nearly at an end of the composition even — Robert has at least all his rough work done.' Elizabeth and the weather had greatly improved by April. On the 20th she wrote to Mrs Martin to say she was 'alive again and prosperous . . . I was looking miserable in February, and really could scarcely tumble across the room, and now I am on my perch again — nay, even out of my cage door . . . I go out, walk out, have recovered flesh and fire — my very hair curls differently.'

She had not been in touch with Henrietta since the beginning of November, but wrote lengthily five months later, on 12 April 1855, to say she had been ill but was now pretty well recovered. She had been worried about Captain Surtees Cook, Henrietta's husband, in the circumstances of the Crimean War that had broken out in 1853 and had disturbed both Elizabeth and Robert. 'Robert has been frantic about the Crimea. The accounts turn one sick.' There was, nevertheless, a political gain from the Crimean War — the very welcome alliance between England and the France of Napoleon III against Russia in defence of the Ottoman Empire. To Sarianna, on 12 June, Elizabeth wrote that Robert was not only frantic about the Crimea, but about ' "being disgraced in the face of Europe," etc. etc. When he is mild he wishes the [English] ministry to be torn to pieces in the streets, limb from limb . . . Robert is a good deal struck by the generous tone of the observations of the French press, as contradistinguished from the insolences of the Americans, who really are past enduring just now. Certain of our English friends here in Florence have ceased to associate with them on that ground. I think there's a good deal of jealousy about the French alliance.'

Elizabeth, like everyone else at the time, knew the reality of victory achieved by the common soldiers despite inadequate supplies, scant training and preparation, lack of military intelligence, and leadership. 'But we have soldiers, and soldiers should have military education as well as red coats, and be led by properly qualified officers, instead of Lord Nincompoop's youngest sons. As it is in the army, so it is in the State.'[139] The Crimean War was right and necessary, no doubt, though 'How dismal, how full of despair and horror!' At stake was nothing less, in the Brownings' view, than the liberty and civilization of all Europe.

Elizabeth blamed England more than the French. The English state was rotten. It could be nevertheless redeemed from corruption: 'The results will, however, be good if we are induced to come down from the English pedestal in Europe of incessant self-glorification, and learn that our close, stifling, corrupt system gives no air nor scope for healthy and effective organisation anywhere. We are oligarchic in all things, from our parliament to our army. Individual interests are admitted as obstacles to the general prosperity. This plague runs through all things with us. It accounts for the fact that, according to the last marriage statistics, thirty per cent. of the male population signed with the *mark* only. It accounts for the fact that London is at once the largest and ugliest city in Europe. For the rest, if we cannot fight righteous and necessary battles, we must leave our place as a nation and be satisfied with making pins.'

This diatribe, simultaneously passionate and cold-blooded, is remarkable. To Mrs Martin, in April 1855, Elizabeth recommended 'that nothing will do for England but a good revolution, and a "besom of destruction" used dauntlessly'. What Robert thought of this can only be conjectured. He had watched revolutions in France and Italy from the same vantage points as Elizabeth, and had taken them more calmly. But he was observing as an outsider, as an Englishman in continental Europe, and was not required personally to take up arms in whatever cause was currently creating a commotion under his windows. Robert, from the little Elizabeth says about his reaction, seemed principally concerned about the possibility of England's humiliation in the eyes of her European friends and allies, though there is no reason to doubt that he considered the Crimean War honourable in its aims and principles and looked to victory for the alliance against Russia.

It is questionable, however — despite his reported ferocity in respect of the British government and the ministry of Lord Aberdeen — whether he went so far as Elizabeth in wishing for revolution in England against English oligarchs, for the tumbling down of vested and established interests, and the breaking up of influential cliques and controlling cabals. That there was a case for reform in all areas of public life, he would not have seriously disputed: Robert Browning was a middle-class English liberal who believed in gradual progressive processes according to law, in contrast to Elizabeth's zestful revolutionary desires to overturn the entire state of the nation and start again from first principles. Her interpretation of constitutional law, as evidenced by her arguments in favour of Louis Napoleon, was rather different from her husband's.

The Crimean War was finally concluded by negotiations, initiated by Louis Napoleon, that led to the Treaty of Paris on 30 March 1856. For the French, the war remains significant in popular memory for their victory at Sebastopol; for the English, it is mostly memorable for the courage and carnage of the Charge of the Light Brigade (immortalized in verse by Tennyson) and the work of Florence Nightingale, who went out from England to the Crimea to establish hospitals for the wounded. Elizabeth had met Miss Nightingale during the Brownings' last visit to London and honoured her from her heart as 'an earnest, noble woman' who had 'fulfilled her woman's duty where many men have failed'. But she questioned whether Miss Nightingale's efforts and achievements had been anything other than 'the most imperfect solution of the "woman's question" ... If a movement at all, it is retrograde, a revival of old virtues!' Princesses, she remarked in a letter to Mrs Jameson in February 1855, had been binding the wounds of fallen heroes since the siege of Troy. In latter days, 'Every man is on his knees before ladies carrying lint, calling them "angelic she's," whereas, if they stir an inch as thinkers or artists from the beaten line (involving more good to general humanity than is involved in lint), the very same men would curse the impudence of the very same women and stop them there ... I do not consider the best use to which we can put a gifted and accomplished woman is to *make her a hospital nurse*. If it is, why then woe to us all who are artists! The woman's question is at an end. The men's "noes" carry it.' Elizabeth recommended that Mrs Jameson should henceforward know her place and give up writing books of art criticism: 'I shall expect to hear of you as an organiser of the gruel department in the hospital at Greenwich.'

Again, this is powerful, if humorously ironic, stuff — a radical assessment of received opinion, a blast of the trumpet against the monstrous regiment of men who, sentimentally worshipping women in their traditional roles as carers, conceded no ground in the field of intellect, the arts, and — by extension — no part in political or cultural power. Elizabeth is writing far in advance of contemporary feminist thought and even challenges moderate feminist thinking in our own times. Robert, respectful of women in general, and of his wife in particular, would not seriously have quarrelled with any of this. Genius or foolishness were not, so far as Robert Browning was concerned, matters of gender. Elizabeth's advanced feminist stance, stimulated to expression by such intense thinking about Florence Nightingale's ambiguous contribution to female emancipation, may partly account for an astonishing incident that occurred at Easter 1855. It is only in recent years that it has come to light, first in a largely overlooked account by Mrs Kinney published by Edward McAleer, a Browning scholar, and subsequently picked up by Margaret Forster and later by Julia Markus, Elizabeth Barrett Browning's biographers.

Hatty Hosmer, dressed in her usual semi-masculine mode, called on Robert and Elizabeth at Casa Guidi. Also present on this occasion were William and Elizabeth Kinney, who had settled in Florence after Mr Kinney had ceased to be the US Minister to the Court of Sardinia-Piedmont at Turin. Robert started talking about some remarkable paintings at a nearby monastery to which only men were admitted. Elizabeth possibly still smarted from her first experience of being banished from the monastery at Vallombrosa, and the continuing inconvenience of being denied access, purely on the basis of her sex, to the books and daily papers at Vieusseux at the Palazzo Strozzi. Hatty Hosmer jumped up and declared that she *would* see the pictures. She suggested that the women should dress up as schoolboys and, escorted by Robert and Mr Kinney pretending to be their tutors, infiltrate the monastery. Hatty's high spirits gave the idea the air of a good lark, and Robert and Kinney agreed. Hiram Powers, let into the plan, provided full knee-length frocks belted at the waist and loose trousers, cloth caps, and wigs — garments more appropriate to Pen than his mother and her friends. A week after the scheme had been conceived, they all met at Casa Guidi and dressed themselves up as young male students.

Mrs Kinney, in her account of the adventure, commented that Hatty, only in her early twenties, being short and stout, and accustomed in any case to wearing men's clothes, looked like a fat little boy; Elizabeth's transformation, on the other hand, was astonishing. Like Elizabeth, Mrs Kinney favoured the rather ageing style of cascading ringlets that hung heavy around the face. With her hair hidden under a cap, 'Elizabeth really looked handsome . . . For the first time I saw her without those dark, heavy curls she always wore half concealing her cheeks, and the wig of short straight hair improved her looks: excitement gave her usually pale face a fine color, and her large black eyes an unwonted brightness.' Robert and Mr Kinney had gone out to look for a closed carriage while the women changed their clothes.

Elizabeth finished first, and rather than wait in the apartment for Hatty and Mrs Kinney, she went downstairs. But instead of loitering discreetly inside the gate, Elizabeth took it into her head to go out into the piazza Pitti and walk slowly up and down in her full masculine costume. Hatty and Mrs Kinney, looking out of the window, caught sight of her sauntering to and fro, apparently oblivious to the interest of passers-by. The two women rushed from the window, downstairs, into the street, and caught at Elizabeth's sleeve. The sudden appearance of two more peculiar-looking characters began to attract public attention. Elizabeth began to cry a little and whisper, 'Oh, Mrs Kinney, we shall be in the Bargello!' — in gaol, that is, which might have been the case had not Robert and Mr Kinney driven up and hustled the three women back into Casa Guidi, where Hatty and Mrs Kinney burst out laughing — probably from relief.

Robert was not amused. Robert indeed, white-faced with fright, was furious. Elizabeth burst into tears. Robert's principal alarm was nothing to do with playful transvestism — more that someone might call the police, with the result that the escapade might make it into the newspapers. Mr Kinney took it less seriously, Mrs Kinney kept on laughing, and Hatty, all fired up, called Robert a 'poltroon' and other names. But it was all now well beyond a joke, quite out of hand, and Robert called off the whole thing. There would be no expedition *en travesti* to the monastery, no matter how much Hatty or anyone else might want to see the paintings. What could have possessed Elizabeth? Mrs Kinney thought she knew: 'It must have been an extra dose of opium that pushed her to such a wild step!' Elizabeth's energy after her winter illness was not wholly due, apparently, to her wonderful powers of recovery: it was helped along on occasions, perhaps stimulated more frequently than she admitted, by the opiates she had tried from time to time to reduce when other considerations demanded.

Opium revived her energies, perhaps also released her inhibitions, and allowed her opinions sometimes to transcend what were then considered to be the bounds, not only of common sense but of common decency. Elizabeth's views on the 'woman's question', to take only one instance, had a quality of far-sightedness, of clarity that would not be achieved by most women for generations to come. Poetry, too, may benefit from a poet's consumption of drugs — there are plenty of instances, from Samuel Taylor Coleridge to Allen Ginsberg — but the capacity for thought leading to inspiration and revelation in more ordinary matters may often also be improved. It helps, of course, if the capacity for thought is already well-established and well-honed. Elizabeth's mind was the equal of anybody's, as Robert was the first to acknowledge. It is worth repeating, too, the profundity of Robert's respect for Elizabeth as a woman as much as a wife. Frances Kemble, observing his behaviour towards Elizabeth on a Roman picnic, declared that Robert Browning was the only man she ever met who treated his wife like a Christian. Whether they owed anything to Christian virtues or not, Robert's attitudes as a husband surpassed contemporary standards of common decency. He would hear nothing against his wife.

The Kinneys were decent, God-fearing Americans — that is to say, they were a little strait-laced, and acquaintance with Europe had not loosened the strings of their moral corsets. Elizabeth characterized this gracious couple to Arabel as being quite agreeable in most essential respects: 'Mrs Kinney is a pretty woman with torrents of ringlets and dresses perfectly — clever, literary, critical, poetical — just as you please.' If fault was to be found, it might be that she was 'rather over-lovely and not over-refined'. William Burnet Kinney was 'an admirable, thoughtful, benevolent person, as liberal in politics as an American diplomat is bound to be and much more religious'. Mr Kinney and Elizabeth agreed harmoniously on most things, including Louis Napoleon, though he drew the line, as a devout Christian, at Swedenborg.

Mrs Kinney drew her own line at George Sand. She was surprised, in the summer of 1853, just before the Brownings left Florence for Bagni di Lucca, to learn that Robert had kissed that notorious woman's hand in Paris. 'Pray, who is her lover now?' asked Mrs Kinney, though hardly wishing to know. 'I can't say,' replied Robert mischievously, 'since she has a new one every day.' Mrs Kinney supposed, more in hope than conviction, that Mme Sand had never loved but one — at least, one at a time. '*One?*' cried Robert. 'Their name is legion.' Mrs Kinney found herself in a difficulty. 'And *you* kiss the hand of such a woman — Robert Browning?' It was evidently an indelible stain on the poet's character that his lips had touched that sordid flesh. 'Yes, and *Elizabeth Barrett* Browning does the same, in respect to one of the greatest geniuses God ever made!' Robert was getting into his stride. This was worse news still. Elizabeth, that pure spirit, had been equally compromised by paying homage to immorality. 'Well, well,' said Mrs Kinney, 'the greater the genius, the greater the shame of yielding that body which should be sacred . . . to the "lust of the flesh": to me George Sand is the worst of women.' Elizabeth now piped up in defence of the great woman. 'Don't say that! She is not a *bad* woman, but, on the contrary, a good and charitable one.' Scenting open ground, sensing a triumph, Mrs Kinney plunged recklessly ahead. She now objected, 'Then what your husband said is not true.' Elizabeth had a ready answer. 'If it *be* true, it is only because she has fallen under the dominion of a sensual appetite, which she cannot control; but it is no more than gluttony, or intemperance; I *pity* her, more than I blame her for it. Her *mind* is none the less godlike.' Mrs Kinney was perplexed in her mind and troubled in her heart: the thought of the great woman's lasciviousness could hardly be compensated for by her goodness and charity, but she made a tremendous effort to be charitable herself. She conceded that George Sand might be excused an unlawful love if her husband had been uncongenial . . . at which both Brownings were inspired to the same ironic thought and exclamation. '*Love*! She never loved anyone but herself.'[140]

Mrs Kinney's scrupulous morality got her into trouble then with the liberal-minded Brownings, just as her impetuous defence of Mrs Browning would do the next year, in 1854. The Kinneys, less prosaic than Lockhart, liked their poets to be poetic — Robert, disconcertingly, didn't look like a damned literary man, but Elizabeth was gratifyingly soulful in appearance. She looked older than her husband, of course, but her large eyes were still lustrous in her pinched face, and her mouth was generously wide. In the autumn of 1855, Frederick Locker-Lampson remarked on Mrs Browning's physique as 'peculiar' and commented on her 'poor little hands — so thin that when she welcomed you she gave you something like the foot of a young bird'. Robert preferred to describe them as 'spirit-small hands'. An article in the *New York Home Journal*, describing Elizabeth as 'a crooked, dried-up old woman, with a horrible mouth', had come to Mrs Kinney's notice. As a former newspaper-woman, she dashed off an article in reply, insisting on Mrs Browning's 'beauty of spirit', though not denying that 'her frame is shattered by disease'. Robert was appalled. Mrs Kinney had thought him insensible to the fact of his wife's illness — '[he]never will allow that she is ill, but now he must see it and feel it' — and he retorted, very forcefully, that 'I see well enough yet without spectacles, and yet see nothing of the matter.' Mrs Kinney should have described Elizabeth, it seems, as being not only beautiful in mind, but as 'beautiful in person'.[141] Robert is said never to have forgiven Mrs Kinney, though Elizabeth's appearance also struck others — who kept sensibly quiet — as wasted.

Mrs Kinney had her reservations, too, about Robert's poetry. Mr Browning, she thought, indeed frankly said, 'labors in all he writes — not to *polish*, but to roughen it'. This was in the summer of 1853, before her journalistic intervention on Elizabeth's behalf, and Robert wrote kindly and complaisantly enough from Bagni di Lucca on 25 July to thank her for verses from her own hand she had sent him. 'As for your criticism, I take it thankfully from your hands — the "good nature" you appeal to, won't answer, because the business is not with *it*. What? Shall I be graced by not a few kind pats of encouragement on the cheek, and refuse to profit by the occasional lift of an admonitory finger? No, I shall mend my ways, I assure you, get as smooth as I can, and as plain as I can, and you shall re-criticise, if you will be so good, and take due credit to yourself for my improvement — which Ba (my wife) declares is manifest already.' By reliable scholarly line-counting, Robert had written only half — if that — of the poems that were to comprise *Men and Women* by August 1854. The two volumes would finally attain a length of just over seven thousand lines — 7,164, to be exact — though Robert had indicated on 25 August 1854 to his American publishers, Ticknor and Fields, that the book would 'contain about 5000 lines'.[142] By June 1855, according to Elizabeth, he had completed some eight thousand lines while she herself was short of some thousand lines of *Aurora Leigh*.

The Brownings thought it necessary to be in London during the summer of 1855 to see Robert's book through the publishing process. Money was still short, but the trip could not be postponed another year. In June, the rumour arose that cholera had broken out in a street behind Casa Guidi. Fourteen people had died, it was said. Elizabeth was frantic with worry, principally for Pen's health, and she insisted that they should pack up and be gone without delay. Robert calmed her as best he could, and she conceded a day's grace, whereupon it turned out that there was no cholera after all — people had fallen sick from eating too many fruit and vegetables. Nevertheless, Elizabeth was impatient to be gone to Livorno to catch the ship for Corsica and Marseilles on the first leg of their trip to London. At Marseilles, they bumped into Elizabeth's brother Alfred ('Daisy') staying in the same hotel. He had run away from Wimpole Street at the age of thirty-five to marry his cousin, Lizzie Barrett. There had been several objections to this match: Mr Barrett would not give his consent either to his son Alfred or to Lizzie, who had been his ward for thirteen years. Lizzie's mother had gone mad, and Alfred had no money — indeed was in debt. Nevertheless, Alfred and Lizzie went ahead and were married at the Paris Embassy at the end of July. Alfred was duly, and predictably, disinherited. Elizabeth, though she could not quite bring herself to approve of her brother's behaviour, was at least pleased to see him happy, and he had made a tremendous fuss of Pen.

From Marseilles, they went to Paris where there was another marriage to be negotiated. Lily Wilson and Ferdinando Romagnoli had become engaged in Florence, much to Elizabeth's surprise but not, at this stage, to her discomfiture. Ferdinando was a reliable, good-hearted fellow — 'A better man more upright and of a more tender nature it would be difficult to find,' Elizabeth wrote with great satisfaction to Arabel. The matter was, nevertheless, complicated. Wilson was a Protestant, Ferdinando a Catholic. Wilson was perfectly willing to raise any of her children as Catholics, Ferdinando was perfectly prepared to turn Protestant and could not understand why the Brownings wouldn't let him. The betrothed couple — *I promessi sposi* — could see no difficulty. Robert and Elizabeth, however, took the situation more seriously. They insisted that the marriage must be valid in the eyes of the Church in Italy and obtained an initial dispensation from the Archbishop of Florence. After a delay of some ten days, Wilson and Ferdinando were married in Paris, on 10 July, by a liberal priest; the next day, accompanied by Sarianna, they all took 'a hideous, rolling, heaving' passage to England, where the weather was depressingly familiar — 'cloudy, misty and raining'.

They settled in lodgings at 13 Dorset Street, a little west of Wimpole Street, and immediately got down to business. They were carefully reckoning their resources — squandering neither their days nor their guineas — during that English summer. They couldn't afford to visit Henrietta in Taunton (who in turn, besides being in ill health, couldn't afford a trip to London) and they declined other invitations, including one to stay with Sir Edward Lytton at Knebworth. Robert took the manuscript of *Men and Women* to Edward Chapman, and soon the proof sheets came rolling off the presses into the hands of the Brownings. Elizabeth's own work was set aside in favour of proof-reading: 'My book is not ready for the press yet; and as to writing here, who could produce an epic in the pauses of a summerset? Not that my poem is an epic . . . I flatter myself it's a *novel*, rather, a sort of novel in verse.'[143] In a letter of July-August to Mrs Jameson, Elizabeth reported that 'Robert has printed the first half volume of his poems, and that the work looks better than ever in print, as all true work does brought into the light.' Robert had read the proofs to William Johnson Fox, whose opinion was that 'the poems are at the top of art in their kind'. Elizabeth, admitting her partiality, considered that 'The poems, for variety, vitality and intensity, are quite worthy of the writer, it seems to me, and a clear advance in certain respects on his previous productions.'

A visit to London was welcome to Elizabeth for opportunities to see her sisters and brothers. This year, her father had commanded the complete redecoration of the Wimpole Street house and attempted to ship those of his children who still lived with him off first to Ramsgate and, when that project foundered, to Eastbourne. Arabel at first refused to go, then cravenly gave in, but plucked up her courage and returned to London to see Elizabeth. Occasionally, she was able to take Pen off Elizabeth's hands, and one day took him to Wimpole Street, where George was still in residence. Playing boisterously and loudly in the hall, George and Pen were interrupted by the sudden appearance of Mr Barrett, who watched them silently and intensely for two or three minutes. 'Whose child is that, George?' he asked. 'Ba's child,' said George. 'And what is he doing here, pray?' asked Mr Barrett, as though he didn't know very well what George and Arabel were up to. Pen was quickly taken back to his mother, who was pleased that her father had at least set eyes on his grandson, even if he would not willingly see his eldest daughter. He had never consented to see Altham, Henrietta's son, nor would he ever do so.

In late August, Wilson was obliged to admit what was becoming increasingly obvious — one of the reasons, indeed, that she had been in such a hurry to marry Ferdinando: her premature pregnancy. The baby was due sooner rather than later, in mid-October. More than likely, the prospect of Wilson's child did not much bother Robert except as another mouth to feed, but Elizabeth was curiously shocked and dismayed. She was cross that Wilson had not felt able to confide in her from the beginning (though it is hardly probable that Wilson would have frankly and unconcernedly confessed to sleeping with Ferdinando at Casa Guidi) and that the true state of affairs had been wilfully concealed from her. She was in no position — that admirer and defender of George Sand — to complain about immorality, but she felt justified in reprobating what she perceived as Wilson's deceit, which implied a lack of trust in her employer's willingness to tolerate, indeed to be sympathetic to, her condition. All this quite aside from the personal inconvenience to Elizabeth. Wilson, whose mother had died a couple of years before, was packed off to her sister in East Retford. She could have the baby there. Then some thought would have to be given to what should be done with the baby: there was no question that Wilson could be allowed to bring it back to Casa Guidi. There would be no room, and the Brownings couldn't afford the extra expense. That being a given, would Wilson herself return to Italy? No wonder the wretched Ferdinando had been mooning disconsolately around the rooms in Dorset Street, looking out at the grey streets and the rain, muttering *'Povera gente che deve vivere in questo posto'* [Poor people who have to live in this place].

Elizabeth set herself resolutely, in these circumstances of Wilson's betrayal, 'to think chiefly of her excellent qualities and of what she has done for me in affectionate service'. As well she might. Margaret Forster points out that 'Elizabeth failed Wilson as Wilson had never failed her. To take Wilson and her baby back to Italy would have been impractical, inconvenient, unreasonably charitable — but it would not have been impossible for people as resourceful and courageous as the Brownings.' She is the first of the Browning biographers fully to consider the implications of Wilson's pregnancy for Elizabeth and, by extension, for Robert, who, beyond commenting that it was wrong in principle to separate a man and his wife, probably left the practicalities of the matter in his wife's hands. If Wilson's fall from grace could be reproached in conventional terms of commonplace Victorian moral standards, Elizabeth's could just as well be faulted in terms of her own position as a poet in *Aurora Leigh*, in which the author so sympathetically concerned herself with the fictionalized plight of poor working women — in particular with the rape and pregnancy of the young and pure-hearted Marian Erle. Though Lily Wilson had consented to sexual relations with Ferdinando, and had certainly not been raped and abandoned, her real-life difficulty was not so different. The options open to Wilson, as presented to her by Elizabeth, were to stay in England with her baby but without her husband, or to board her baby with her sister and return to Italy with Ferdinando and her employers. In either case, the loss to Wilson would be intolerable. It occurred to none of them that the baby might just as well be boarded out in Florence as in England.

There had been consolations that had gone some way to mitigate the discomforts and disappointments of that summer — the Brownings had not wholly closeted themselves away from friends. The social traffic in London was as brisk as it might have been in Paris or Rome. Visits with Carlyle (whom they met, still forceful in his damnations, at John Forster's); Fox, whom Robert gratified by readings from his new book; the Kemble sisters, Frances and Adelaide, the one looking magnificent, the other beautiful; the Bryan Procters looking very well; and John Kenyon, who afterwards took himself off to the Isle of Wight. There were also new faces 'eager to see if Italy has cut off our noses or what!':[144] Alexander Kinglake, author of *Eothen*; John Ruskin, 'gracious and generous', who showed them the Turners hanging on the walls of his Denmark Hill house; Dante Gabriel Rossetti, who made studies for a portrait of Robert; and Frederick Locker-Lampson, who commented privately but disobligingly on Elizabeth's physical appearance.

Above all, there had been two days with Alfred Tennyson, who had come to London from the Isle of Wight. Calling on the Brownings at Dorset Street, Tennyson 'dined with us, smoked with us, opened his heart to us (and the second bottle of port), and ended by reading "Maud" through from end to end.' Her own heart full of this tremendous Tennysonian experience, Elizabeth wrote to Mrs Martin that, 'If

I had had a heart to spare, certainly he would have won mine. He is captivating with his frankness, confidingness and unexampled *naïveté*! Think of his stopping in "Maud" every now and then — "There's a wonderful touch! That's very tender. How beautiful that is!" Yes, and it *was* wonderful, tender, beautiful, and he read exquisitely in a voice like an organ, rather music than speech.' Robert concluded the evening's entertainment by reading aloud 'Fra Lippo Lippi' from his about-to-be-published book, *Men and Women*.

Maud was published in August 1855. Elizabeth conceded that the work was not without its faults; and, as she reported to Mrs Jameson, 'People in general appear very unfavourably impressed by this poem, *very unjustly*, Robert and I think. On some points it is even an advance.' Despite this, 'The sale is great, *nearly five thousand copies already*.' So: even for an imperfect poem, even for a poem that did not find general favour, great things were possible. The thought must have been in the Brownings' heads that Robert's book, as much an advance in poetic Browning terms as Tennyson's, whether or not it found favour — though there was no reason it should not appeal to a wide readership — could do just as well as, if not better than, *Maud*. Buoyed up by this atmosphere of poetic afflatus, and bathed in an atmosphere of poetic excitement and achievement, the Brownings' spirits were lifted to Parnassian heights. They looked forward with full confidence to publication of *Men and Women*.

It had been a difficult summer for the Brownings — 'most uncomfortable and unprofitable', as Elizabeth irritatedly characterized it, as though a wild animal had been let loose in the house. Wilson gone; Elizabeth at the mercies of a new maid and in low spirits; Pen missing his 'Lila' and bad-tempered; Ferdinando homesick, lonely and morose; the Barrett siblings for the most part inaccessible in Eastbourne and Taunton; the weather dampening everybody's spirits and taking the curl out of their hair; the publisher's proofs needing constant close attention at the expense of creative work; and the sociability of friends, however well-intentioned, a distraction rather than a welcome diversion. 'It's the mad bull and china shop,' Elizabeth later commented to Mrs Martin, 'and we are the china shop.'

There had been one other significant disturbance to the temper of the Browning household. Mr Daniel Dunglas Home happened to be in

London and Elizabeth had been determined to meet him. Just as she had pestered, cajoled, and bullied to meet George Sand, so she would not give up her opportunity to meet Home the celebrated medium. He was staying at Ealing, she heard, with Mr and Mrs J. S. Rymer, whose twelve-year-old son, Wat, had died some three years ago. Mr Rymer was a wealthy lawyer. Mrs Rymer happened to be a friend of Mrs Jameson, who provided an introduction. On the night of 23 July 1855, Robert and Elizabeth went by invitation to the Rymers's house in Ealing to attend a séance conducted by Mr Home.

They were both in much the same frame of mind as they had been on their way to meet George Sand: Robert apprehensive and prepared to be disapproving, Elizabeth hectic with anticipation and thrilled to the marrow. G. K. Chesterton makes the point that 'in all probability ... Browning's aversion to the spiritualists had little or nothing to do with spiritualism. It arose from quite a different side of his character — his uncompromising dislike of what is called Bohemianism, of eccentric and slovenly cliques, of those straggling camp followers of the arts who exhibit dubious manners and dubious morals, of all abnormality and of all irresponsibility ... Browning felt, and to some extent expressed, exactly the same aversion to his wife mixing with the circle of George Sand which he afterwards felt at her mixing with the circle of Home ... He did not dislike spiritualism, but spiritualists.'[145] As for Home, Chesterton himself despised 'the bragging, the sentimentalism, the moral and intellectual foppery' of Home's self-recommendatory writings.

Daniel Dunglas Home — later in his career he changed the spelling of his surname from the original Hume — was a tall, good-looking, well set up young man barely in his twenties, Scottish by birth. His family had emigrated to America, where he had first made his sensational mark as a medium capable of summoning spirit forces that could effortlessly move heavy furniture, materializing spirit phenomena in the form of hands and music, and self-levitation. His fame, spread to Europe by influential American admirers such as Jarves, was tremendous. The Rymers were not only convinced by him, they doted upon him, were besotted by him. Home, for all his infantile affectations, was no fool: he knew instinctively how to promote himself and his celebrity.

Talking with the young and mediumistic Miss Rymer in the garden before the Ealing séance, Home suggested that they should prepare a wreath of flowers. A chaplet of clematis was placed in the room to be used for the sitting, the curtains were drawn against the late evening light, and at nine o'clock the company seated themselves around a table. Elizabeth had thought to warn the Rymers in advance about Robert's scepticism — she remembered perhaps how his attitude of merry disbelief had foiled an attempt to move a table in Florence a couple of years before — and Mr Rymer sensibly requested that there should be no questions during the proceedings. The table began to vibrate and tilt. There were rappings that indicated to Home and the Rymers that Wat was present. The knocking sounds soon stopped, and Home advised that there were too many people in the room. Some were requested to leave, until only nine persons — Mr and Mrs Rymer, their son and daughter, two family friends, Robert and Elizabeth Browning, and Home himself — were left to form the circle.

Wat's spirit, in this diminished (and mostly familiar) company, became more confident. The Rymers felt his hand, and Elizabeth felt her skirt uplifted at her waist. The remaining light in the room was extinguished and Robert observed a hand clothed in white, loose, muslin-like folds appear from the edge of the table opposite himself and Elizabeth. The hand rose and sank down to the table's edge. Elizabeth took out her spectacle glass to look at it more closely. Home asked Elizabeth to leave her place and sit next to him, which she did; whereupon a larger hand appeared, pushed the wreath off the table and picked it up from the floor. The hand, which she noted to be of the largest human size, white as snow and very beautiful, thereupon placed the wreath on Elizabeth's head. Home later reported that she had been 'much moved'. He then requested Elizabeth to resume her seat by her husband. She asked that the wreath be transferred to Robert's head. The hand took the wreath and transferred it under the table. Robert felt himself 'touched several times under the table on one knee and the other — and on my hands alternately — (a kind of soft and fleshy pat) — but not so that I could myself touch the object. I desired leave to hold the spirit-hand in mine, and was promised that favour — a promise not kept, however.' Robert was allowed only to hold the accordion that the spirits played, not very tunefully, under the table.[146]

The large hand then disappeared. It belonged, said Home, after consulting the spirits and receiving taps in confirmation, to a relation of Elizabeth's. According to a prearranged code, the spirit would rap out the name. It rapped several names, none of which meant anything to the Brownings. Robert wasn't much surprised — 'Misses all.' Home then went into a state of apparent trance. Through Home as medium, the spirit began to address Mr Rymer in the character of his dead son, first whispering but then speaking in an affected tone of baby-talk that even Elizabeth found nonsensical. The Brownings and the two friends of the Rymer family were then asked to leave the room. They were called back after fifteen minutes to be treated to the sight of the table lifted and tilted some twelve inches from the ground while Home's hands remained plainly above its surface. A lamp on the table stayed steady, though Robert remarked that its base was heavy enough to keep it in place. He would have been better impressed had the spirits been able to prevent a silver pen from rolling around on the table top. But this scepticism annoyed the company: had Mr Browning not seen enough? Well, the answer to that was yes: quite enough of humbug; and no: nothing like enough of physical evidence. The séance concluded with some spirit-inspired rigmarole recommending the legitimacy of spiritualistic investigation.

After the performance, Elizabeth carefully preserved the wreath of flowers that had crowned her head that 'wonderful and conclusive' night. Robert acknowledged that 'the sitting was conducted in exact conformity to Mr Rymer's suggestions, which though polite were explicit enough, — that we should put no questions, nor desire to see anything but what the spirits might please to show us. I treated "the spirit" with the forms and courtesies observed by the others, and in no way impeded the "developments" by expressing the least symptom of disbelief — and so kept my place from first to last.'

Despite Robert's scrupulous suspension of disbelief, the sitting was not all that it might have been. Young Robert Lytton and his father had been at the Rymers's two nights before and had seen the spirit hand 'rise out of the *wood of the table*' instead of hovering at the table edge as if it had come out from under it. The Lyttons had, unlike the Brownings, been permitted to touch the spirit hands and had seen a 'spiritual (so called) arm elongate itself as much as two yards across the table and then float away towards the windows, where it disappeared'.[147]

Elizabeth was both elated and despondent after her wondrous experience. To Henrietta, she confided, 'Robert acquits the whole [Rymer] family of collusion, believes in their veracity, but cries out against Hume's *humbugging*. Oh! It is difficult to convince any man (even my Robert) against his will. I think that what chiefly went against the exhibition, in Robert's mind, was the trance at the conclusion during which the medium talked a great deal of much such twaddle as may be heard in any fifth-rate conventicle. But according to my theory (well thought-out and digested) this does not militate at all against the general facts. It's undeniable, and has been from first to last, that if these are spirits, many among them talk prodigious nonsense, or rather most ordinary commonplace.'

Of Home's integrity, Elizabeth had no doubt: 'I believe that the medium present was no more *responsible* for the things said and done, than I myself was.' Robert begged to differ. Home, so far as he was concerned, was entirely and personally responsible. Elizabeth, the Rymers, the Lyttons, and all the other believers in his charade were his dupes. Home was odious in himself: he looked older than twenty, Robert thought, however he might affect the manners of a little child. He preyed upon the Rymers by kissing them abundantly and nestling against them, playing up to them like a child himself in their loss and grief for their son. Home had not merely deceived the Rymers and Elizabeth, he had adroitly exploited their willingness to believe, and had thereby implicated them in a vulgar, meretricious fraud.

Writing to a Miss Gaudrian, who had asked him for an account of the night at Ealing, Robert later commented (oddly in the third person) 'that there can hardly be any opinion than his own on the matter — that being that the whole display of "hands," "spirit utterances," etc., was a cheat and an imposture'. He imputed no bad faith to the Rymers, and was sorry that they had been taken in. The 'best and rarest natures', Robert believed, could be led to 'a voluntary prostration of the whole intelligence before what is assumed to transcend all intelligence. Once arrived at this point no trick is too gross — absurdities are referred to as "low spirits," falsehoods to "personating spirits," and the one terribly apparent spirit, the Father of Lies, has it all his own way. Mr Browning had some difficulty in keeping from an offensive expression of his feelings at the Rymers; he has since seen Mr Home and relieved himself.'

This letter, when it was first published in *The Times Literary Supplement* on 28 November 1902, provoked a response from the adult Pen Browning, who, in a reply published the following week, corroborated the story as Robert Browning had given it to Nathaniel Hawthorne in June 1858. Robert, speaking of the wreath which had been placed on Elizabeth's head, 'avowed his belief that these hands were affixed to the feet of Mr Hume who lay extended in his chair, with his legs stretched far under the table. The marvellousness of the fact as I have read of it, and heard of it from other eye-witnesses, melted strangely away in his hearty grip, and at the sharp touch of his logic; while his wife, ever and anon, put in a little gentle word of expostulation.'

In the letter to Miss Gaudrian, Robert preferred 'to leave the business to its natural termination' rather than personally proceed to any formal exposure. He respected the feelings of the Rymers and his own wife. He had no intention of embarrassing them publicly. Nevertheless, he was privately prepared to give Home another chance to prove himself — and himself another chance to prove Home a fraud. Robert suggested that he might attend another sitting, and that this time he should be accompanied by Helen Faucit Martin — no doubt to give himself some freedom of movement in the absence of Elizabeth. The request was refused, but Home took the opportunity to call on the Brownings.

At first Robert was reluctant to receive him, even though he was accompanied by Mrs Rymer and her son, but was persuaded by Elizabeth that to refuse would be rude. Robert shook hands civilly with both Rymers, but pointedly ignored Home. Elizabeth, thrown into confusion — 'pale and agitated' according to Home's account of the meeting — anxiously clasped Home's hand. When they were all seated, Robert addressed himself specifically to Mrs Rymer, declaring that he was 'exceedingly dissatisfied with everything I saw at your house the other night, and I should like to know why you refused to receive me again with my friend'. Home spoke up for himself, saying that 'that was the time and place for you to have made objections regarding the manifestations, and not now. I gave you every possible opportunity, and you availed yourself of it, and expressed yourself satisfied.' Robert pointed out, 'I am not addressing myself to you, sir.' Home replied, 'No, but it is of me you are speaking, and it would only be fair and gentleman-like to allow me to reply.' Mrs Rymer supported Mr Home.

Robert, by this time, is said by Home to have been 'pallid with rage, and his movements, as he swayed back and forwards in his chair, were like those of a maniac.' Elizabeth, when Home and the Rymers stood up to leave, bleated, 'Dear Mr Home, I am not to blame. Oh dear! Oh dear!' We have only Home's account of the particulars of this meeting, from his own memoirs, but there is no reason to doubt their accuracy — except, of course, to bear in mind Home's natural preference for presenting himself in a good light. He would have liked to have made a convert of Robert Browning, to have basked in his friendship; but it was perfectly obvious that Robert's resistance to him was ferocious and implacable. By the time the story of this meeting had got around, and by the time the Chinese whispers had done with it, Robert Browning had all but kicked Mr Home downstairs and bounced him into the street.

The story of that night at Ealing had even longer reverberations and repercussions. Home, in the latter part of the 1860s, embroidered his account of the event by attributing Robert's disbelief to his 'ludicrous jealousy' of Elizabeth: the spirits had preferred to crown her as 'the Poet' and to pass over her husband. More, and yet worse, the rumour mill put it about that Robert had positively angled for the spirit coronation, hovering agitatedly behind Elizabeth's chair. In December 1863, hearing that Home had been in touch with the Storys at Rome, Robert wrote to Isa Blagden describing him as a 'dungball'. He never forgave Home. 'If I ever cross the fellow's path,' he wrote to Mrs Kinney in January 1871, 'I shall probably be silly enough to soil my shoe by kicking him, — but I should prefer keeping that disgrace from myself as long as possible.' What he did, finally, was tear the clematis wreath from the dressing table where Elizabeth had reverently, and perhaps a little defiantly, hung it and throw it out of the bedroom window into the street. For a while after the Ealing séance spiritualism was not a subject to be raised lightly — or at all — in the Browning household. Elizabeth warned Henrietta to be discreet even in letters: 'the subject is still *in suspense* in this house. Some of these days perhaps Robert will be a medium himself, and then he will believe. Till then I shall never stir the question more.'[148]

The question, however, continued to be stirred in quarters close enough to the Brownings to make it hard to ignore. Home took himself

off soon afterwards to continental Europe, where, for a season, he fasci-
nated their friends. He stayed in Florence with Fanny and Thomas
Trollope, impressing them for a while by apparently levitating and whirl-
ing round the rooms of the Villino Trollope. He held a session or two
at the house of Hiram Powers during which he conjured hands that
waved fans and that stuck the tip of a penknife into all too human
legs.[149] Powers considered Home a knave but a powerful medium. Eliza-
beth tended to the same opinion. In a letter to Mrs Martin of 21 February
1856 she wrote: 'it appears that Mrs Trollope has thrown over Hume
from some failure of his moral character in Florence. I have had many
letters on the subject. I have no doubt that the young man, who is weak
and vain, and was exposed to gross flatteries from the various unwise
coteries at Florence who took him up, deserves to be thrown over. But
his *mediumship* is undisproved, as far as I can understand. It is simply
a physical faculty — he is quite an electric wire. At Florence everybody
is quarrelling with everybody on the subject.'

If this admission is to be taken at face value, it seems probable that
Elizabeth and Robert might have achieved some temporary conciliation
in the matter of spiritualism. Pen Browning, in his letter to *The Times
Literary Supplement*, claims that 'towards the end of her life my mother's
views on "spirit manifestations" were much modified. The change was
brought about, in a great measure, by the discovery that she had been
duped by a friend in whom she had blind faith. The pain of disillusion
was great, but her eyes were opened and she saw clearly.' The 'friend'
was not Home himself, but another professed adept of spiritualistic
practice, Mrs David Eckley. Pen Browning does not say that his mother
lost her interest in spirit forces, but that she was readier to recognize
the possibility of fraud — which, to be fair, she had never wholly
discounted. Then, too, the constant force of Robert's disbelief must have
had some effect on her position. Elizabeth longed to believe — did
indeed believe until proof positive to the contrary was forced upon her;
Robert could not believe, but was not unwilling that the evidences of
the other side, on which rested the onus of proof, should be fairly
demonstrated and objectively examined.

Objective investigation might have explained some of Home's effects
in semi-darkness for a credulous audience as sophisticated illusions,
technically proficient trickery; but the characters of the spectators may

themselves be called into subjective question. What prompted them to belief more usually and readily than disbelief? To what personality traits did Home's illusions make such appeal, and what needs did his effects so readily satisfy? The Victorian scientific age evoked spiritualism in much the same way as our own technological age is balanced by ardent new-age beliefs, poetic rather than practical, inspirational rather than utilitarian. Betty Miller, in a much-discussed passage in her biography of Robert Browning, likens the medium's 'confidence trick' to that of the poet and suggests an affinity:

> Like the poet, the medium attempts, through the resources of his own craft, his own magic, 'to bring the invisible full into play'. Both claim to discern, beyond the natural frontiers of life, those 'mysteries of things' which, without their intercession, would remain unavailable to the great mass of mankind. But the gift of second sight, of inspiration, call it what you will, brings with it, so Browning always believed, obligations which the artist ignores at his peril. 'A poet's affair is with God, to whom he is accountable, and of whom is his reward: look elsewhere, and you find misery enough,' he wrote a few months later to John Ruskin. Now a poet who, looking elsewhere, has falsified, or even modified the burden of the message with which he is entrusted, is as culpable as a medium who simulates an experience which he knows to be beyond his own range: a guilt, a fall from grace, which over and over again in his poetry Robert Browning has chosen to analyse and defend.[150]

Robert Browning could be a great hater for the sake of conscience, but Betty Miller also suggests a sort of psychological shadow projection that inspired Robert's distaste for Home on a wholly personal level. Home's infantile attitude towards the Rymers was, says Mrs Miller, 'Distasteful, certainly: all the more so, perhaps, in that the situation contained a reflection, aggrandised into caricature, of another over-valued son, also of quite the ordinary bodily strength, who, readily embracing both Mama and Papa, as he "never broke the habit" of calling them, avowed himself incapable, to the day of his marriage, of packing his own carpet-bag, or of walking "into a shop" to "buy his own gloves".'[151]

It is true, on his wife's own testimony, that even during marriage

Robert had 'a sort of mania about shops, and won't buy his own gloves'. He had to be forced to go into a shop to buy a pair of boots for himself, and only then when the soles were worn to the point of letting in water.[152] In the ordinary things of personal life, Robert remained fearful, though not often to the point of such neglect. Quite the opposite, in fact: he would take the most elaborate precautions against disasters acutely apprehended and fully developed in his imagination. Elizabeth perceptively characterized the difference between herself and Robert in a letter to Henrietta written not much later, on 13 September 1855: 'Robert's prudence is apt to take fright at the flies. He sees afar off what may be — how a black cloud comes up in the wind, and how if we lock up the umbrellas we shall be sure to feel the want of them in the rain. It's all fear through far-seeing. As for me I am short-sighted — for my happiness. I am never afraid, and everything always turns out well I observe just as if I, too, had been ill with spasmodic terrors.' Her own terrors took a different turn.

Being freed from the prospect of an early grave by marriage — by happiness — she did not now look to death for any comfort. Elizabeth grudged the passing of the years. She disliked her own ageing, which she attempted to retard visually by dressing as she had done as a younger woman. She was vain of her husband's handsome, healthy appearance. She selfishly, short-sightedly, kept her son not only innocent and uneducated so far as possible, but in a style of dress and babyish appearance which gave an illusion that he, too, was younger than his years. It was important to her that death should be a continuation, which hope spiritualism seemingly served to confirm. Thus, naturally, she looked for, and was more easily persuaded, by material proofs of an afterlife — however elementary, however banal — that did not so readily impress Robert. He had, after all, in all probability rescued Elizabeth from a premature death.

Before Lily Wilson gave birth to a son, Oreste, on 13 October, she had helped Elizabeth pack up the household and had instructed her successor, Henrietta, who would be travelling with the Brownings to Paris in a few days' time. The Fraser Corkrans had found an apartment for their friends at 102 rue de Grenelle, in the Faubourg St Germain, the very street where Mr Browning and Sarianna lived. This proximity must have seemed appropriate, and — further persuaded by 'yellow satin furniture' — the Corkrans had taken the unsuitable rooms for six months. 'We shall probably have to dress on the staircase, but what matter? There's the yellow satin to fall back upon.'[153] The rooms faced east and Paris, though beautiful, was cold. There was one less bedroom than they needed, so that Pen was sleeping on the floor of his parents' room, and the trunks lay around still unpacked. Robert, writing to Dante Gabriel Rossetti on 29 October 1855, commented that 'We are in little, inconvenient rooms here, and I have been in continual hot water, the landlady, a "Baronne," profiting by the blunder of an overzealous friend, who took the apartments against my direct order.' Robert had hoped for 'a blessed quietude here after the London worry', but no such luck. There were eight hundred thousand demons in Paris. But he had 'lain perdu and seen nobody'.

Six weeks of discomfort had to be endured before the Brownings moved to better accommodation at 3 rue du Colisée, off the Champs-Elysées, 'where, as Robert says, we are as pleased as though we had never lived in a house before. Well, I assure you,' Elizabeth reported to Mrs Jameson on 17 December 1855, 'the rooms are perfect in comfort and convenience; not large, but warm ... Clean, carpeted; no glitter, nothing very pretty — not even the clocks — but with sofas and chairs suited to lollers such as one of us, and altogether what I mean whenever I say that an "apartment" on the Continent is twenty times more really "comfortable" than any of your small houses in England.' Elizabeth could never resist a dig at the physical discomforts of English domestic life. 'Robert has a room to himself too. It's perfect. I hop about from one side to the other like a bird in a new cage. The feathers are draggled and rough, though. I am not strong, though the cough is quieter without the least doubt. And this time also I shall not die, perhaps. Indeed, I do think not.'

Having been more or less reclusive in the rue de Grenelle, the Brownings now began to go out and about to meet old friends and make new ones. Putting their faces even into the street involved elaborate precautions: 'That darling Robert carried me into the carriage, swathed past possible breathing, over face and respirator in woollen shawls. No, he wouldn't set me down even to walk up the fiacre steps, but shoved me in upside down, in a struggling bundle — I struggling for breath — he accounting to the concierge for "his murdered man" (rather woman) in a way which threw me into fits of laughter afterwards to remember! "Elle se porte très bien! elle se porte extrêmement bien. Ce n'est rien que les poumons." Nothing but lungs. No air in them, which was the worst! Think how the concierge must have wondered ever since about "cet original d'Anglais," and the peculiar way of treating wives when they are in excellent health. "Sacre." '[154]

On their previous visit to Paris, though it had lasted no more than two weeks, they had caught up with Milsand, Thackeray and his daughters, and the Corkrans, and visited the painter Rosa Bonheur. They had gone to Mme Mohl's one evening where they encountered François Mignet, the liberal historian, and Prosper Mérimée, only three years older than Elizabeth, whose distinguished career as a novelist and playwright of the French Romantic school was now crowned by the favour of the Emperor Louis Napoleon and the Empress Eugénie. In the winter of 1855–6, the Brownings consolidated friendships in Paris that by now could be considered long-standing, even intimate.

Dante Gabriel Rossetti visited the city for ten days in mid-November, and Robert toured the Louvre with him. To Rossetti's wonderment, Robert displayed a 'knowledge of early Italian Art beyond that of anyone I ever met, — encyclopaedically beyond that of Ruskin himself'. For Carlyle, Robert dug into the Library of the Chamber of Peers to research some 'verifications' about Voltaire, the Marquis de Breteuil, and Talleyrand. In his letter to Carlyle of 23 January 1856, Robert also mentions a meeting in Paris with Charles Dickens. George Sand still held their interest: they read the eighteenth volume of her memoirs, which was more lively than the preceding volume, Elizabeth told Mrs Jameson, since it 'concludes with the views upon the sexes! After all, and through all, if her hands are ever so defiled, that woman has a clean soul ... Robert quite joins with me at last. He is intensely interested, and full of admiration.'[155] Richard Monckton Milnes, too, paid a visit to Paris early in 1856. Robert 'dined with him in company with Mignet, Cavour, George Sand, and an empty chair in which Lamartine was expected to sit. George Sand had an ivy wreath round her head, and looked like herself.'[156]

The Brownings were in Paris awaiting publication of the two volumes of *Men and Women* brought out in London by Chapman and Hall in mid-November 1855. When Ruskin had written to Elizabeth to praise her poetry she wrote in reply: 'I had to bear it — I couldn't turn round and say, "Well, and why don't you praise him, who is worth twenty of me? Praise my second Me, as well as my Me proper, if you please." One's forced to be rather decent and modest for one's husband as well as for one's self, even if it's harder.' Specifically of the contents of *Men and Women*, she told Ruskin: 'I consider them on the whole an advance upon his former poems, and am ready to die at the stake for my faith in these last, even though the discerning public should set it down afterwards as only a "Heretic's Tragedy."' To Henrietta, on 15 November, she wrote to say that 'we hear good news of the promise of success, "the trade" having "subscribed" (as they call it) largely — that is — having made large orders — so that the expenses were covered after three days. Robert will stand higher than ever through these poems ... they are his ablest works. They are making translations of nearly half of them for the "Revue des deux Mondes," and Mr Milsand told me quietly the other day, that he considered the poems "superhuman" — Mark that! Only superhuman.'

Robert had promised Chapman 'something saleable' in March 1853, and in February that year he had promised Milsand lyrics 'with more music and painting than before, so as to get people to hear and see'. He had certainly kept his promise to Milsand. *Men and Women*, which took its inspirations and subjects from art, love, and religion, was rich visually in its images and aurally in its imaginative metres. The title is generally supposed to have derived from a letter of 13 January 1845, Robert's second letter to Elizabeth, in which he had written: 'You speak out, *you* — I only make men and women speak — give you truth broken into prismatic hues, and fear the pure white light, even if it is in me, but I am going to try.' But there is another possibly apposite reference in Elizabeth's 'Sonnets from the Portuguese', Sonnet 26, where she writes,

> I lived with visions for all my company
> Instead of men and women, years ago.

In either case, there is the sense that the reality of living men and women informs the poems; that these are no shadows or phantoms, but creatures of quick blood and lively feeling. The last poem of the book,

'One Word More', written in London in September 1855, is dedicated 'To E. B. B.' and deliberately signed 'R. B.'. This unusual acknowledgement of authorship gives authority to the words. Here is one of the rare occasions on which, perhaps mindful of his letter to Elizabeth in which he looks up to her because 'You speak out, you . . .', Robert himself speaks out, 'him', in order to show how much he admires Elizabeth — indeed loves her and commits himself, heart and head, to her. The first four lines of 'One Word More' run thus:

> There they are, my fifty men and women,
> Naming me the fifty poems finished!
> Take them, Love, the book and me together:
> Where the heart lies, let the brain lie also.

Men and Women is shot through with elements of autobiography, of personal experience, of personal feeling, of Browning's most profoundly personal thinking, images, and ideas. Robert and Elizabeth Browning, both, had moved physically and psychologically, during the years of their marriage and their travels in continental Europe — through landscapes and peoples, ways of living and thinking, that had significantly altered and extended their former narrow horizons. Their experiences had opened them up to much that lay beyond the proprieties of repressed English life, and released them from perceptions hedged around with English middle-class ideals. The subjects in both Robert's and Elizabeth's poetry were drawn from a broader range than had been hitherto possible now that they were no longer cribbed, cabin'd, and confined by the madhouse cells in London that had driven them in upon themselves.

There were enough psychological monsters in the world without having to look for them exclusively in their own souls. These monsters could be identified and used objectively by the poet to personify or evoke conflicts rather than subjectively in himself (or herself) to resolve them. In an essay on Robert Browning, the Scottish poet and critic Edwin Muir makes this crucial point: 'He had to enter into the lives of people quite unlike himself before he could realise all the obstacles to his easy faith in things. But this is what he did; his work consisted in this.' From romantic Tennysonian contemplation of the natural order of life, simple and profound, Browning bravely and dramatically went that important step further: he entered into things to see where they would lead him, and in them he found complexity and contradictions, energy, change, and development. The 'infinite moment' was just a moment after all: it was not still — things moved on. There was no stasis, but instead a constant dynamic and a driving forward.

The world's monsters were psychologically complex, to the point that — some modern critics have rightly observed — Robert Browning's best monologues in *Men and Women* are susceptible to no single interpretation: a critic can dwell forever on any one poem and never finish his or her analysis of what exactly Robert intended. The very artistries and ambiguities, effects and illusions, of the poems are grounded in the difficult realities and enigmatic ironies of life — what we see and hear is not always what is shown and said. Robert Browning always said what he thought: there is no more honest poet; but what he thought was sometimes more than he said, and what he said was sometimes taken to be more than he thought. How he said what he did, and what he meant by what he said, is the subject of constant and ingenious literary criticism, giving pleasure and employment to many.

There are as many critical opinions of *Men and Women*, concerning its derivations, references, and qualities as literature, as there are critics. Maurice Baring, in *Have You Anything To Declare?*, has quoted a remark by Baring as applying 'equally well to Byron, Browning, Wordsworth, and many other poets': '*Des vers de haut vol, de ceux que le génie trouve et que le talent ne fabrique jamais quelque peine qu'il y prenne.*' ['Of those high-flying (or far-reaching) verses, those which genius finds and which talent can never make no matter what pains it takes.'] In this sense, of natural genius, Browning is one of the major poets of his own or any age.

Baring himself wrote: 'Someone wisely said that poets should be judged by their strongest links, and this is especially true of Browning. Sometimes in his chains the strongest link will come suddenly and unexpectedly. But sometimes, again, you will not be conscious of the links at all, but only of the strength of the chain when it is ended. I remember Vernon Lee [the pen-name of the critic and author Violet Paget] saying to me once that in Browning's poem *The Grammarian's Funeral* every line was atrocious, an ear-sore, but the whole was incomparable. She said the same was true of Shelley's *Cloud*: nearly every line was bad, but the whole was incomparable.'[157] Of Browning's links, particularly in his later poetry, Mrs Orr commented, 'He has never intended to be obscure, but he has become so from the condensation of style which was the excess of significance and of strength. Habit grows upon us by degrees till its slight invisible links form an iron chain, till it overweights its object, and even crushes it out of sight; and Mr Browning has illustrated this natural law.' In short, Browning was — as always — rarely conscious of what he knew that others did not know and might find puzzling.

W. H. Auden made much the same point as Vernon Lee: 'Browning's way is not mine, but I can admire him. The lyrics are atrocious, but the longer poems are not. *Bishop Blougram's Apology* is a tremendous achievement.' Auden considered that Browning 'doesn't become really good until he's read in bulk. *Bishop Blougram's Apology* is magnificent, but the magnificence is in the psychology. The shorter pieces are pretty awful. But the great ingeniousness of the work is undeniable.'[158]

Men and Women, as Robert described the collection to John Forster in a letter of 5 June 1854, was 'a number of poems of all sorts and sizes and styles and subjects . . . the fruits of the years since I last turned the winch of the wine press'. More poems were added between this date and the summer of 1855 bringing the total to fifty-one. Elizabeth characterized the collection as 'miscellaneous' (also as 'magnificent'). *Men and Women* may conveniently be grouped into thematic and stylistic sections by critics, but as a whole it is miscellaneous only insofar as Robert's own life may be described as a miscellany of influences and experiences during the years of the book's composition. London inspired one poem, Paris inspired several; but most of the poems in *Men and Women* are set in Italy, so that the proportion at least accurately reflected Robert's life since marriage.

There is a poem written in 1913 by the Alexandrian poet Constantin Cavafy, 'The Rest I Will Tell To Those Down In Hades':

> 'Indeed,' said the proconsul, closing the book,
> 'this line is beautiful and very true.
> Sophocles wrote it in a deeply philosophic mood.
> How much we will tell down there, how much,
> and how very different we will look.
> What we protect here like sleepless guards,

wounds and secrets locked inside us,
with an oppressive anxiety —
we will reveal freely and clearly down there.'

'You might add,' said the sophist, half smiling,
'*if* they talk about things like that down there,
if they bother at all about them any more.'
[translated by Edmund Keeley and George Savidis]

Cavafy's poem — not quoted here idly or at random — is very like Browning in tone and content, in its dramatic dialogue, its ironic inversion, its economy of erudition and expression, and in its intelligent conflation of several difficult ideas. The shorter poems of *Men and Women* prefigure this sort of twentieth-century poetry. The collection has many beautiful and true lines, written no doubt in a deeply philosophic mood; but Robert Browning dismisses the sleepless guards and openly examines those wounds and secrets he is disinclined to take to the grave and beyond. Since he does not believe in spirit writing and table tapping, he may as well, since it is his principal business to do so, speak out while he can.

Robert's distrust of spiritualistic forces and the consequences of dabbling in them is forcibly expressed in 'Mesmerism'. The narrator is, or has become, deranged, and imagines that he can summon a woman to him by the irresistible force of mesmeric power. For Robert, the individual soul is inviolate, sacred — though, as William Clyde DeVane points out,[159] the poem 'By the Fireside' seems to indicate that the soul of the beloved may be intuitively and healthily apprehended through love. 'Mesmerism' is not principally — if at all — a dig at Elizabeth's belief in the subject: Robert's theme is about belief in general, about personal delusion and the Faustian forfeits that illusions will inevitably — perhaps demonically — demand.

Madness is a principal theme of *Men and Women* — love, hate, passion, obsession, all manner of abnormalities turned on their heads. There are indeed 'many beautiful and true lines' in Robert's poems, but underpinning truth and beauty is mortal and moral fallibility; the implications of action and — worse — of inaction; the consequences of courage and cowardice, triumph and failure, success in striving and the accidie of apathy and abandonment, of the fine line between righteousness and right, repression and revelation. The macabre is never far from the surface, the grotesque grins out from behind the apparently respectable face of priest, prince, and peasant. These are not poetic abstractions. Robert often nails them to reality by telling dramatic short stories in verse, some of which can — without stretching critical credibility — be interpreted as autobiographical, as truth-to-feeling if not truth-to-fact: poetic fictions that are art and truth, art and lies.

> I only knew one poet in my life,
> And this, or something like, was his way.

Thus the two opening lines of 'How it Strikes a Contemporary'. The poet is supposedly Shelley, or at least the poem's reflections on the nature of the poet and poetry are influenced by the work Robert put into his essay on the spurious Shelley letters. It is legitimate to suspect, however, that a poet can truly know only one poet — himself. And so here we have a self-portrait — admittedly fanciful — of Robert Browning, beginning with his clothes:

> His very serviceable suit of black
> Was courtly once and serviceable still,
> And many might have worn it, though none did:
> The cloak, that somewhat shone and showed the threads,
> Had purpose, and the ruff, significance.
> He walked and tapped the pavement with his cane,
> Scenting the world, looking it full in the face,
> An old dog, bald and blindish, at his heels. [ll. 5–12]

The old poet of Valladolid maintains a shabby but respectable, presentable, even distinctive appearance: just so did Robert care about a good personal presentation, distinguished and a trifle dandyish. It is irresistible, of course, to identify the 'old dog, bald and blindish at his heels' with the elderly dilapidated spaniel, Flush. And as he walks, the poet's curiosity is stimulated by the least detail, his hat shading the object of his interest as he pokes with the ferrule of his stick at a piece of loose mortar on the façade of a building. The very fabric of things, their materiality, detains his attention. In similar terms, Robert's own intense practical interest in all manner of arts and crafts and trades is caught in a few vivid lines:

> He stood and watched the cobbler at his trade,
> The man who slices lemons into drink,
> The coffee-roaster's brazier, and the boys
> That volunteer to help him turn its winch.
> He glanced o'er books on stalls with half an eye,
> And fly-leaf ballads on the vendor's string,
> And broad-edge bold-print posters by the wall. [ll. 23–9]

The life of the street fascinates the old poet, who closely observes without seeming to pay direct attention. Unsettlingly, he seems to know more than is apparent to the unconsidering eye:

> He took such cognizance of men and things,
> If any beat a horse, you felt he saw;
> If any cursed a woman, he took note;
> Yet stared at nobody, — you stared at him,
> And found, less to your pleasure than surprise,
> He seemed to know you and expect as much. [ll. 30–6]

Just so, one feels, Robert walked the streets of London, Paris, Rome, and Florence. No wonder Thomas Trollope and others occasionally felt uneasy in Robert's company:

> We had among us, not so much a spy,
> As a recording chief-inquisitor,
> The town's true master if the town but knew!
> We merely kept a governor for form,
> While this man walked about and took account
> Of all thought, said and acted, then went home,
> And wrote it fully to our Lord the King
> Who has an itch to know things, he knows why,
> And reads them in his bedroom of a night. [ll. 37–46]

Lurid rumours about the scandalous private life of the poet circulated among the credulous:

... he ate his supper in a room
Blazing with lights, four Titians on the wall,
And twenty naked girls to change his plate! [ll. 75–7]

The reality, however, was quite prosaically otherwise:

Poor man, he lived another kind of life
In that new stuccoed third house by the bridge,
...
Playing a decent cribbage with his maid
(Jacynth, you're sure her name was) o'er the cheese
And fruit, three red halves of starved winter-pears,
Or treat of radishes in April. Nine,
Ten, struck the church clock, straight to bed went he. [ll. 78–87]

'How it Strikes a Contemporary' is significant not only from the point of view of how a poet's inspiration derives from the apparently mundane and the seemingly banal, but psychologically from the point of view that comprehends — one senses a certain element of counter-transference — the ordinary man and woman's anxiety, bordering on fear, that they are to be judged in their hearts by a perceptive poet, the agent of a higher, powerful authority. The poet is regarded not just as a spy, as 'a chiel among you taking notes', but as infected, or invested, with a dangerous glamour that is belied in reality by his very humdrum domestic circumstances. Nevertheless, the men and women in the street are not entirely wrong. The poet tells the truth about them and, in so doing, tells the truth about the poet himself. A risky procedure if, like the old poet of Valladolid he supposedly publishes solely for the eyes of 'our Lord the King'; or, as Robert wrote on 10 December 1855 to John Ruskin, 'A poet's affair is with God, to whom he is accountable, and of whom is his reward.'

The personal element is a running thread throughout *Men and Women*, and naturally the thread is tied at one end to Elizabeth. Robert's ideal of female beauty crops up again and again: lustrous, luxuriant dark hair, a 'pale brow spirit-pure', large dark eyes. His rightness in marrying Elizabeth, in urging deliberate and urgent action upon her despite her every hesitation lies behind Robert's treatment of the story of 'The Statue and the Bust'.

The ostensible two lovers of the poem are the Grand Duke Ferdinand di Medici, whose equestrian statue is a feature of the Piazza Annunziata in Florence, and the young woman he notices at a window of the Palazzo Riccardi overlooking the Piazza. She commissions a della Robbia bust of herself, a memorial to her youthful beauty, to be affixed to the wall of her house. Despite their love, they delay doing anything to consummate it. The days slip by, for the sake of others, for the sake of the city, for personal and political reasons, until their opportunity is lost. To all outward appearance, the Duke is a determined and successful man; the woman is a dutiful wife to a tyrannical, elderly bridegroom who has shut her up alone in a room. The tragic reality behind good appearance is quite other: they have both failed to save their souls, have disappointed themselves in their lives, have lost love through inaction.

The parallel with Robert and Elizabeth's own situation is clear: decided action, flight together, no matter what the world thought, no matter the effect their marriage might have on others, was — in Robert's view — the right thing to do. The poem caused some moral outrage. Its inverted morality was regarded as indecent and likely, if every woman and every man acted upon their base desires, to throw society into barbarism. Other poets might have interpreted the lovers' inaction as virtuous self-restraint, but Robert Browning would have none of such casuistry, such timid interpretation of cowardice and apathy as positive renunciation rewarded by redemption.

Men and Women is riddled with Robert's apparent moral perversities. 'The Patriot' begins with a hero's welcome:

It was roses, roses, all the way,
    With myrtle mixed in my path like mad: [ll. 1–2]

until, just a year later, the patriot is led to the gallows:

I go in the rain, and, more than needs,
    A rope cuts both my wrists behind.
. . .
Thus I entered, and thus I go!
    In triumphs, people have dropped down dead. [ll. 21–7]

The theme of reversal of fortunes had a grim relevance for Robert, and this poem surely expresses some personal experience of the fickle nature of public acclaim. This again prompts Robert's belief that the poet's responsibility is to higher things than conventional public morality. Devotion to a higher good is distinct from lip service to the common good. Best not to trust to human justice: the poet, like the patriot, must trust to God:

> 'Paid by the world, what dost thou owe
> Me?' — God might question; now instead,
> 'Tis God shall repay: I am safer so. [ll. 28–30]

These few examples, taken virtually at random from *Men and Women*, may serve here to indicate, however briefly, that Robert's whole experience of life from 1812 to 1855 is contained in fifty-one poems. They may have been collected together with an intention of pleasing a wide readership, but they first had to please Robert Browning the poet and be respectful of the truth they owed to God. Whatever else they may have been, the poems of *Men and Women* were no sops to an easy popularity, to a facile renown. No matter that they were ungenerously received on publication, they now exist in eternity as the real thing: God — or Robert Browning's moral adherence to personal integrity and poetic authenticity — has amply repaid the astonishing range and depth of thought that the poems demonstrate and the extraordinary development of poetic power that they evidence.

The most famous, and still controversial, modern criticism of Browning's work is contained in George Santayana's previously cited essay, 'The Poetry of Barbarism', published in 1900. Santayana criticizes contemporary poetry, and especially two poets, Walt Whitman and Robert Browning, as 'things of shreds and patches; they give us episodes and studies, a sketch of this curiosity, a glimpse of that romance; they have no total vision, no grasp of the whole reality, and consequently no capacity for a sane and steady idealization'. Of Browning in particular Santayana says:

Apart from a certain superficial grotesqueness to which we are soon accustomed . . . [Browning] easily arouses and engages the reader by the pithiness of his phrase, the volume of his passion, the vigour of his moral judgement, the liveliness of his historical fancy. It is obvious that we are in the presence of a great writer, of a great imaginative force, of a master in the expression of emotion. What is perhaps not so obvious, but no less true, is that we are in the presence of a barbaric genius, of a truncated imagination, of a thought and an art inchoate and ill-digested, of a volcanic eruption that tosses itself quite blindly and ineffectually into the sky.

Santayana's definition of 'the poetry of barbarism' is a touchstone by which we can still measure Robert Browning as a poet, though Santayana does admit the possibility that he makes a criticism 'which might seem needlessly hostile and which time and posterity will doubtless make in their own quiet and decisive fashion'. Time and posterity, as capricious in their judgements as God, have done just that.

Times have changed and criticism, contemporary or posterior, like any perception but unlike poetry, is not eternal. There is truth in Santayana's critical position, and it can still be defended; but a great deal of what he criticized in Robert Browning's work is what we now most value. To put it baldly, Santayana held the view that poetry at its finest aspired to 'the Highest Good', and 'Of this art, recommended by Plato and practised in the Christian Church by all adepts of the spiritual life, Browning knew absolutely nothing. About the object of love, he had no misgivings. What could the object be except somebody or other? The important thing was to love intensely and to love often. He remained in the phenomenal sphere: he was a lover of experience; the ideal did not exist for him.' This is easy enough to prove; any number of quotations from Browning's work will fit the case. In 'Fra Lippo Lippi', the artist's superiors in the Church take issue with Lippi's instinct to paint the world and its men and women precisely as he observes them in daily life and without much pious reference to their souls.

> Your business is not to catch men with show,
> With homage to the perishable clay,
> But lift them over it, ignore it all,
> Make them forget there's such a thing as flesh.
> Your business is to paint the souls of men.

To which Fra Lippo Lippi replies,

> Or say there's beauty with no soul at all —
> (I never saw it — put the case the same —)

If you get simple beauty and naught else,
You get about the best thing God invents;
That's somewhat; and you'll find the soul you have missed,
Within yourself, when you give thanks.

Lippi is a sensualist, passionate in his love for creation and wholly engaged with it. This, says the modern critic A.S. Byatt of another poem in *Men and Women*, is 'wholly admirable . . . It is in their engagement with the detail of the world of the senses that gives to Browning's theological monsters their engaging, and somehow redeemed, quality.'[160]

Santayana, however, would not have it so: Browning 'had no idea of anything eternal; and so he gave, as he would probably have said, a filling to the empty Christian immortality by making every man busy about it in many things . . . But it is a mere euphemism to call this perpetual vagrancy a development of the soul.' He finds little or no sense of redemption, no indication of developmental growth. He identifies Browning's poems as not only portraying passion, which is interesting, but betraying it, which is odious, and characterizes Browning's art as being 'still in the service of the will. He had not attained, in studying the beauty of things, that detachment of the phenomenon, that love of form for its own sake, which is the secret of contemplative satisfaction.' This is particularly in contrast to the intellectual work and art of Tennyson: Browning, wrote Santayana, 'threw himself too unreservedly into his creations . . . He did not master life, but was mastered by it.' Santayana admits the genius of Browning's barbarism — primitivism we might call it now — but points out that he could not 'even reach the intellectual plane of such contemporary poets as Tennyson and Matthew Arnold, who, whatever may be thought of their powers, did not study consciousness for itself, but for the sake of its meaning and the objects which it revealed'.

While Tennyson and Arnold conformed, in Santayana's view, to Platonic and Aristotelean ideals, marching along the broad high road towards the Higher Good, Robert Browning — by this yardstick — was forever on his knees fossicking in the ditch by the roadside, his hands grubby with the common clay and his nose in the mud. Robert Browning, it might be argued, however superficially, was of his materialist and metaphysical times and true to the spirit of the age. A. S. Byatt points out in her essay on Browning that the three principal subjects of his poetry — art, love, and theology — can be more closely associated with the whole contemporary shift of religious feeling that threw up the phenomenon of spiritualism as readily as the ideas of the German theological critics. Swedenborg's mystical, material visions were remarkably 'solid and carnal' and Swedenborg himself, 'who saw a life in stones', had been a mineralogist, a very material occupation. Spiritualism, says A. S. Byatt, 'was the religion of a materialist age' and inevitably partook of it. However much Robert Browning may have disbelieved in spiritualists and mediums, in slipshod eccentricity, as Chesterton puts it, he was not uninterested in spiritualism. Browning and spiritualism, in a sense, were not just two faces of one and the same poetic coin: they were much the same, the coin and the poem itself. In his reactions to spiritualism, Browning was positive in the sense that he would have welcomed proof, however disturbing.

No wonder the Pre-Raphaelites, including William Morris, Dante Gabriel Rossetti, and William Bell Scott, harbingers of future acclaim for *Men and Women*, loved Robert Browning: in the realistic precision of his images and details, in his truthful, vehement conviction that love is the supreme thing in life, he gave them in words a rich reflection of their own philosophies and mythologies, iconographies, pictures, and portraits. Carlyle admired the sharp observation and 'opulence of intellect' of *Men and Women*, while Joseph Milsand praised Browning's ability to focus on a single, perhaps seemingly trivial, event in a character's life that allowed 'great truths . . . to reveal themselves in miniature episodes'. He emphasized his friend's realism — the factual detail, sensuous imagery, conversational tone, rhythm and diction that melded together to give a physicality to human hopes, feelings, and thoughts. Milsand regarded the poems as more intellectual and more objective than Browning's great Romantic poetic predecessors, 'nearly the opposite of Wordsworth and his school'. Like Santayana, Milsand was also aware of Browning's fondness for the grotesque — which might too quickly and simplistically be perceived by contemporaries as ugly and sordid.

Santayana can be said to contrast Robert's miniaturist particularity with the cinemascopic sublimity of the Romantics, who conjured heights and depths, surveyed large landscapes, reeled at frightful grandeurs, and who sought to inspire a frightful thrill at natural vastnesses of all types. It is worth emphasizing that Robert saw, like T.S. Eliot, fear in a handful of dust. In 'My Last Duchess', for example, there is terror in every descending footfall made by the Duke, a horror in the *Neptune Taming a Sea-horse* by Claus of Innsbruck commissioned by the Duke. It is not manifest in these things themselves, but in the serenity of the man himself. Childe Roland, a young innocent, moves through a Romantically blasted landscape in which, at every point, he observes small things that are emblematic of terror. Robert's effects are, one might say, myopic. They are rich with accommodating detail. Poetically, they relate more to the close, densely packed paintings of, say, Richard Dadd than to the cloudscapes of Constable or the seascapes of Turner.

However, the first English critics of *Men and Women* were not so ready to overlook or accustom themselves to grotesqueries — or anything else, for that matter, that might cause them aesthetic pain and critical affront. Their difficulty, as William Irvine and Park Honan point out, 'was that they could not fit Browning's work into any satisfactory notion of what poetry ought to be or what an author ought to do'. Poetry was changing from the Romantic style of Wordsworth and from the traditional tone of Tennyson. Browning's was a major transitional voice that at first appeared to throw all that was civilized, contemplative, and familiar into chaos without any discernible — or, at any rate, comprehensible — rationale that showed a clear way forward. Browning, the critics perhaps dimly perceived, had taken a major step forward into new territory; but he was a Childe Roland travelling through a dark and ruined landscape of his own making towards some monstrous, unknown end that even the poet himself did not understand.

Browning was charged with a lack of unity and order, and again — the all-too familiar cry — with obscurity. The *Athenaeum*, predictably, was no very friendly partisan, lamenting 'energy wasted and power misspent', criticizing wit in a love poem as a painful blemish and complaining about veils of obscurity. *Fraser's Magazine*, somewhat anticipating Santayana's criticism by half a century, declared that Browning was a genius unfaithful to his trust; *The Christian Examiner* regretted that the poet showed no high, moral direction; whilst the *Rambler* was offended by Browning's 'keen enjoyment of dirt as such, a poking of the nose into dunghills ... accompanied by the peculiar grunt which expresses not only the pleasure experienced but also the nature of the experience'.

These reviews, and others like them, mixed praise and blame with occasional flashes of genuine critical penetration, like lightning dashes through dark storm clouds — the poems gambolled and raved, they were arcane and bizarre, the poet himself was grossly at fault. Initially elated by good sales of the book, Robert's and Elizabeth's spirits were dashed by the reactions of the reviewers and the fact that sales fell off quickly and steeply. The reason for this may not have been entirely due to critical disapprobation: first sales were very likely accounted for by admirers of Browning, and the sudden dropping away of sales can partly be attributed to Robert's lack of a high public profile in England. He had been away too long, perhaps, and none but friends and partisans in London knew him.

Then, too, the prevailing literary fashion was for the poetry of Alexander Smith, a Scottish lace-pattern designer who published his *Poems* in 1853. They were at first enthusiastically received but soon became a subject for satire, particularly in 'Firmilian' ('O! Firmilian, Firmilian! What have you done with Lilian!') by William Edmonstoune Aytoun, who identified Smith and other poets like him as the Spasmodic School. The Spasmodics, who briefly burned with a violent and extravagant poetic flame, took their introverted inspiration from Byron and Goethe. Their tortured poetry caught the public imagination by a combination of pathetic fallacy, intense interior psychological drama, and a violent verbosity that both assaulted and gratified the sensibilities of their readers. The Spasmodics were as popular as old-style barnstorming actors. They were immediately effective; sensation was the thing, and their heart-wringing appeals to the lonely and disillusioned produced sentimental knee-jerk reactions like a galvanic current. Aytoun's satires popped their inflated pig's-bladder effects, however. Deflated by sharp wit, they quickly subsided.

Elizabeth, in a letter to Fanny Haworth in June 1853, replied kindly to Miss Haworth's enthusiastic recommendation of the exciting new poet. 'Your Alexander Smith has noble stuff in him. It's undeniable, indeed. It strikes us, however, that he has more imagery than verity, more colour than form. He will learn to be less arbitrary in the use of his figures — of which the opulence is so striking — and attain, as he ripens, more clearness of outline and depth of intention.' This is nicely cautious. To another correspondent in September that year Elizabeth further commented that Alfred Tennyson had said of Smith, 'He has fancy without imagination', and she admitted that 'Certainly he is very rich and full of colour; nothing is more surprising to me than his favourable reception with the critics. I should have thought that his very merits would be against him.'

Like most writers, the Brownings suffered the pain of bad reviews more keenly than they were mollified by the balm of positive notices. George Eliot, writing in the *Examiner* in January 1856, professed some reservations: she complained at first of the subjectivity of the poems, considered them private in their subject matter, and was irritated by Browning's whimsical mannerism; but she acknowledged that they shook up the reader from 'drowsy passivity'. Generously, she conceded that 'in Browning's best poems he makes us feel that what we took for obscurity in him was superficiality in ourselves'. In a letter to Sarianna during the winter of 1859–60, Elizabeth wrote that

> The blindness, deafness and stupidity of the English public to Robert are amazing. Of course Milsand had heard his name — well the contrary would have been strange. Robert IS. All England can't prevent his existence, I suppose. But nobody there, except a small knot of pre-Raffaelite [*sic*] men, pretend to do him justice. Mr Forster has done his best, — in the press. As a sort of lion, Robert has his range in society — and — for the rest, you should see Chapman's returns! — While, in America he is a power, a writer, a poet — he is read — he lives in the heart of the people. 'Browning readings' here in Boston — 'Browning evenings' there. For the rest, the English hunt lions, too, Sarianna, but their lions are chiefly chosen among lords and railway kings.[161]

Robert's own reaction was pungently expressed in a letter to Edward Chapman. On 17 December 1855, he wrote: 'don't take to heart the zoological utterances I have stopped my ears against at Galignani's of late. "Whoo-oo-oo-oo" mouths the big monkey — "Whee-ee-ee-ee" squeaks the little monkey and such a dig with the end of my umbrella as I should give the brutes if I couldn't keep my temper, and consider how they miss their nut[s] and gingerbread.' He had been going to Galignani's reading-room almost daily to look more and more despondently through the English papers, and coming home to the hateful yellow satin furniture to sit despairing over the fire. On 5 December 1855 he had written to Chapman to wonder about sales of *Men and Women* and to ask about receipt of a cheque from Ticknor and Fields; he wrote again on 17 January 1856 to say that American publication of the book had been set for 10 December 1855. Robert asked Chapman for 'the Christmas account to put a little life and heart into the end of this bleak month'.

Mr Fields, in Robert's estimation, 'behaves handsomely altogether'. Fields had agreed to pay the asking price, £60, for proof sheets of *Men and Women*, and published the book in one volume simultaneously with the two-volume English edition. Two thousand copies were originally printed in America, then another five hundred early in 1856. American reviews, though there were few enough of them, generally came down in favour of the book. There were the usual charges of obscurity, though those by now had become pretty much automatic responses; but *Russell's Magazine* endorsed George Eliot's line that any seeming difficulty was worth the reader's effort, while the *Albion* and *Putnam's Magazine* both printed supportive reviews.

These approved Browning's accurate observation of nature and the poet's objectivity (as opposed to English dismay at his subjectivity), his genius as a dramatist was emphasized, and the nebulous matter that might at first be thought obscure revealed itself rather as 'constellations' that yielded at last 'a wonderful music and a profound coherency'. The *Albion* set *Men and Women* higher than new books by Tennyson and Longfellow: 'In no former volume has Browning shown so great a mastery over language. He does whatever he pleases with it. The words ring, and crack, and snap; the crabbed lines are alive.' *Putnam's* published a long overview of Browning's entire *oeuvre*, from *Paracelsus* to *Men and Women*, regretting 'so much general misconception as to the character and intelligibility' of Browning's work. Some poets, the reviewer remarked, are easier reading because they are easier thinking. 'To complain of Browning, because he is not so intelligible, at a glance, as Pope, is like complaining that Plato is not so easy as Steele.'[162] This comment reflects George Eliot's view that, 'Turning from the ordinary literature of the day to such a writer as Browning, is like turning from Flotow's music . . . to the distinct individuality of Chopin's Studies or Schubert's Songs.'[163] From this point, thanks to the efforts of a few enthusiasts, Browning's popularity grew gradually from obscurity to, within only five or six years, something of a rarefied cult among American *cognoscenti*, who formed Browning groups and societies and attended public readings of his work.

Meantime, the prospect of future fame was no consolation for the damping, distressing reality of present disappointment. Robert's first reaction was to give up poetry until Elizabeth, who was busy finishing *Aurora Leigh*, recommended that he fill his time by revising *Sordello*. This occupied him, a little desultorily, for a while, but his heart was never in it and he soon gave it up. He found better employment by joining his father on sketching visits to the Louvre. Elizabeth was at first enthusiastic about this creative displacement activity, and was thrilled that 'after thirteen days' application' Robert had 'produced some quite startling copies of heads'. But, like anything else Robert Browning undertook, he threw himself into this new hobby with such complete absorption that she became alarmed that he might throw over poetry altogether for drawing and art.

Social life took up another quantity of Robert's time in Paris that winter. Lady Elgin, to whom he and Elizabeth were sincerely attached, was now severely paralysed by a stroke and confined to a wheelchair. Robert went regularly to read poetry — beginning with Keats — to her. Elizabeth suggested Robert go off alone on a visit to Jerusalem and the Holy Land. This was a project very close to his heart, and it had been discussed on various occasions. But he refused. In any case, Elizabeth had been spitting blood and he was alarmed that this might indicate a deterioration in her health.

And so Robert settled to sketching, Elizabeth settled to writing, and gradually their life together fell back into a familiar and comfortable routine. In *The Brownings and France*, Roy E. Gridley points to several influences on Robert's poetry from contemporary French work, notably from poems by Alfred de Musset, and suggests that *Men and Women* would have been better understood on publication by the French rather than the English. The climate of Paris, cultural as much as meteorological, for the time being suited the Brownings better than that of England. Elizabeth gave an hour and a half to Pen's lessons in the mornings, and afterwards worked concentratedly at her poem. 'It's a sort of *furia*! I must get over so much writing, or I shall be too late for the summer's printing. If it isn't done by June, what will become of me? I shall go back to Italy in disgrace, and considerably poorer than I need be, which is of more practical consequence. So I fag.'[164]

From breakfast at nine in the morning until four o'clock in the afternoon, the Brownings saw nobody. Robert, if not working sadly at *Sordello*, or marvelling at the six books of *Aurora Leigh* that he had so far read (the last three were still being written), might go sketching with his father, while Elizabeth stayed peacably at home. Robert and Pen had had sore throats, but Elizabeth thought that regular exercise would keep them well. The rue du Colisée apartment was not ideal — the rooms were a little small and airless, and they missed the open spaces of Casa Guidi — but it would do. Elizabeth stopped spitting blood, her cough moderated, and she kept up her strength with cod-liver oil. She was tired, but not ill.

There was not much to provoke any disagreements between Robert and Elizabeth. Daniel Dunglas Home, they heard in mid-June, was in Paris when they had thought him to be in Rome. Elizabeth got into a panic, but Robert 'promised me he would be "meek as maid" for my sake, and that if he met the man in the street he would pass without pretending to see . . . On the subjects of spirits generally we are at peace, and one can hear oneself speak.' Spiritualism as a subject was not avoided, but mention of Hume himself was very definitely 'a bone in the lion's throat'.[165]

On the question of Louis Napoleon, the Emperor — who had recently introduced liberal reforms — seemed more popular than ever, though Robert drily remarked that he was an opportunist, 'a man of genius using his opportunities'. All was pretty much gilt and gingerbread until disturbing news arrived, in the first days of May 1856, that John Kenyon, now in his early seventies, had fallen seriously ill. 'He wanders much at times, and his vision appears troubled, tho' at intervals he is quite himself — aware of his precarious state, with occasional in-breaks of hope and rallying. There seem to be some good symptoms, but I am in great alarm and sadness about this dear kind generous friend, of course. Robert has twice offered himself as a nurse. The first time, there was a kind negative, but this second time we have not yet heard.' Mrs Jameson had urged Robert to go, but 'it is a *very delicate position*.'[166]

On 29 June 1856, the Brownings set out again for London. Kenyon, seemingly a little better since he had been moved to his house on the Isle of Wight, insisted that they stay in his town house at 39 Devonshire Place. It was from there that Elizabeth wrote to Henrietta on 9 July 1856. Though comfortable in the great house, and grateful for accommodation better than they were used to in London, they were faintly awed, careful about 'moving our elbows for fear of breaking something'. Kenyon's two servants kept the house clean, while the Brownings' two servants cooked and kept their employers in good repair. To Pen's great joy and Elizabeth's relief, Lily Wilson left her baby with her sister in East Retford and returned to stay with them in London. Elizabeth was still working, though more intermittently than in Paris: to Henrietta, she commented, 'you know what London is, how bells ring and knockers knock, — and you don't know how desperately in haste I am with poems not done and proofs not corrected. Almost frantic I grow sometimes, what with one thing and another.' Despite distractions, the nine books, amounting to some eleven thousand lines, of *Aurora Leigh* were written by the first days of July and completed ready for the printer by 3 August. A second copy had to be made for the American publishers, C. S. Francis, who had offered a useful though not magnificent £100 for publication in the United States simultaneously with Chapman and Hall's English edition.

Invitations had been mostly 'disregarded', though the Brownings had dined with the Procters and breakfasted with the Monckton Milnes, where Elizabeth was seated beside Nathaniel Hawthorne who was then the American consul at Liverpool. In his *English Notebooks*, scrupulously kept, Hawthorne described Elizabeth as belonging to 'that quickly appreciative and responsive order of women ... a quiet little person' in contrast to the 'shrill and strident' effect her poetry had made upon him. Robert struck Hawthorne as 'A younger man than I had expected to see, handsome, with dark hair, a very little frosted. He is very simple and agreeable in manner, gently impulsive, talking as if his heart were uppermost.' Elizabeth called, cautiously as usual, at Wimpole Street, where she found the Barretts were looking well, George particularly 'brilliant'. Henrietta, by now the mother of three children, was urged to come to London from the country.

It was always Elizabeth's intention to bring the whole Barrett family together, but, as on the last visit by the Brownings to London, Mr Barrett stepped in to frustrate such a reunion. Getting wind of Elizabeth's presence, he ordered Arabel and the rest of the Wimpole Street family to Ventnor in the Isle of Wight. This was not as inconvenient as he had reckoned: the Brownings took their opportunity to stay with John Kenyon, who was convalescing at West Cowes, and to be reunited with Arabel, George, Sette, and Occy. The Barrett uncles set themselves to toughening up their nephew Pen, who was thrilled by their rough and tumble and their encouragement of the natural boyish aggression that his mother played down.

Their fond attentions to him, and their good-natured attitude towards Robert, enabled Elizabeth to concentrate on the proofs of *Aurora Leigh* in comparative peace, although John Kenyon's health was still worrying. He appeared, distressingly, to be very ill — he was suffering in fact from cancer — and Elizabeth was more concerned than she would have been had he been younger. Since Henrietta was not able to join them in the Isle of Wight, the Brownings made a quick trip to Somerset in the last week of September to see her, Surtees Cook, and the children. Back in London, still surfeited with proof sheets, there was alarming news from Ventnor: Mr Barrett had fallen ill. Writing to Henrietta on 11 October 1856, Elizabeth was a little relieved that there had been better news of her father from Arabel. The damp and fog in Ventnor did not agree with him, however, and the fog and east wind in London was doing no good for his eldest daughter. Robert was urging a return to Florence, but there were eighty pages of *Aurora Leigh* still to be proof-read. Elizabeth began to cough, and her attention to the work in hand — as well as the labour of reading through the letters written to her by Miss Mitford to edit out all that was unfit for publication — became less precise: 'omissions *will* happen'. Writing to Isa Blagden some years later, in January 1870, Robert gave his own opinion of Miss Mitford's letters as 'worse than nonsense' and declared that 'Ba resolutely destroyed at least five out of six letters, and mutilated the rest wherever they needed it, — else dear friends . . . would have been treated to an odd sensation or two.' With the intention of returning next summer, the Brownings at last left London for Italy on 23 October 1856. Lily Wilson, who had decided to leave Oreste, her infant son, with her sister in England, went with them.

Aurora Leigh, dedicated to John Kenyon, was scheduled for publication by Chapman and Hall on 15 November. By that date, the Brownings were happy to be back in the Casa Guidi apartment, which had been sub-let during their absence, and happier still to find the rooms and the familiar things just as they had left them. They began buying new carpets and furniture so that they could increase the rent when they went away again; but aside from this forward-looking activity, 'the place is duller and quieter than Paris and London, and we seem to ourselves to have dropped suddenly down a wall out of the world'. Home the medium had been and gone from Florence, leaving behind conflicting opinions and sensational materials for considerable quantities of gossip. What the Brownings could not pick up from their friends about everything else, Pen supplemented with information of his own. To Henrietta, Elizabeth wrote on 18 November 1856, 'You can't think how learned Peni is already in all the gossip of Florence (he gets among the Italians and listens with erect ears) and how he translates to us most horrible stories.'

Aurora Leigh, Elizabeth's 'novel-poem' (as she herself characterized it), was a racy read for its times. She had laid out her intentions in only her fifth letter to Robert, on 27 February 1845, to write 'a poem as completely modern as "Geraldine's Courtship," running into the midst of our conventions, and rushing into drawing-rooms and the like, "where angels fear to tread"; and so, meeting face to face and without mask the Humanity of the age and speaking the truth as I conceive of it out plainly'. It took her ten years (however hurried at the end) to achieve this ambition, but the result, in terms of high sales and an avid readership, was gratifying. Queen Victoria read it, John Ruskin read it, everyone from duchesses to drudges read it. Mothers forbade their daughters to read it, whereupon daughters rushed to get their hands on it. The first edition was entirely sold out within a week, the second edition was quickly exhausted within a month. Chapman and Hall's presses hummed and thrummed and drummed out editions, though hardly fast enough to satisfy the public appetite. As a novel, it was poetic in style — high-flown and elaborate in its treatment of serious social themes; as a poem, it was novelistic — *Jane Eyre*, it was suggested, had inspired some of the sensational plot motifs, though Elizabeth, hurrying to re-read the novel, rejected any such facile comparison. In any case, *Jane Eyre* was only one of hundreds of intoxicating romantic novels in various languages — French, Italian, and German, as well as English — that she had read and digested over the years and that could just as well have left a substantial sediment in her mind.

The critics mixed blame with praise to such an extent that it was never clear to Elizabeth or Robert whether the overall tone of a particular review was favourable or not. What mattered most to Elizabeth, beyond brisk sales and pleasing notices, was whether the reviewers had understood *Aurora Leigh*, and on the whole she was persuaded that they had missed her essential 'metaphysical intention'. She wrote to Isa Blagden late in the year to complain about the *Athenaeum*: 'the analysis it gives of my poem is so very unfair and partial. You would say the conception was really *null*. It does not console me at all that I should be praised and over-praised, the idea given of the poem remaining so absolutely futile.' This review had been written by Henry Fothergill Chorley, of whom Elizabeth had expected more penetrating insights. Other friends were no better in their inflated compliments: Robert Lytton wrote to praise *Aurora Leigh* as 'the solitary epic of the age', superior in certain respects even to Dante and Milton. His hyperbole was worth little more than the ink it had cost him to write such an effusion.

Robert, for his part, was thrilled to the marrow by Elizabeth's success. He was forever running between Casa Guidi and the Villa Brichieri to keep Isa Blagden informed of good reviews and even better sales, and writing to Edward Chapman to resist any editorial intervention. 'There is nothing whatever to correct ... My wife made up her mind to it as it *is*, and for the present, as I say, I cannot reconsider the subject. All the "modern" passages, illustrations, are vitally necessary, she thinks, — and I think quite as strongly, — and could not be detached without capital injury to the rest of the poem.'[167] To Mrs Martin, in February 1857, Elizabeth confided the truth of the matter. 'The second edition was issued so early that Robert would not let me alter even a comma, would not let me look between the pages in order to [make] the least alteration. He said (the truth) that my head was dizzy-blind with the book, and that if I changed anything it would probably be for the worse;

like arranging a room in the dark.' Robert urged Chapman to keep printing and to pay no attention to reviews.

The letter to Chapman concludes with one of Robert's most notorious roars: 'I saw the *Athenaeum, Globe*, and *Daily News*, that's all, hearing of eulogy from the *Lit. Gaz.* and blackguardism from "The Press"; all like those night-men who are always emptying their cart at my door, and welcome when I remember that after all they don't touch our bread with their beastly hands, as they used to do. Don't you mind them, and leave me to rub their noses in their own filth some day.' Chapman himself came in for some stick. Never the most effusive letter-writer, nor the quickest with a reply, he had forwarded copies of *Aurora Leigh* to its author without a word of comment. The lack of an accompanying letter was branded by Robert as 'a shame of you, black and burning, not to have been at that trouble'.

The commercial failure of *Men and Women*, and the discouragement Robert had felt as he scoured the press for good notices, obviously still rankled. Now, looking at reviews of his wife's work, the fact that the likes of Chorley had eaten the Brownings' bread and, like dungmen passing their door, had left their loads on their doorstep, was intolerable. Robert felt betrayal sorely. He ground his teeth and snarled and held grudges warm under his tail until such times as he could repay the injuries in kind. Betty Miller, commenting on some lines from Robert's poem 'Andrea del Sarto' and Vasari's characterization of del Sarto in *Lives of the Artists* which Robert had relied on for his information, implies that Robert — if the lines are to be taken as autobiographical — may have felt some resentment at his wife's success, that Robert Browning's personality, like del Sarto's, displayed 'a certain timidity of mind, a sort of diffidence and want of force in his nature'. The inference is that Robert was under Elizabeth's thumb and that, far from inspiring him in his work, her 'stronger character' and 'lesser genius' held him back from the highest achievements.

Mrs Miller quotes Robert directly: 'Now, in marriage, he was to find "the personality of my wife . . . so strong and peculiar", that for many years he was unable successfully to assert himself in the face of it'. She rejects as romantic nonsense Elizabeth's image of the two poets having but 'one soul between them' and that 'we feel alike in many, many things — the convolvuluses grow together; twisted together'. A pretty conceit, perhaps, but Mrs Miller points out that the twin convolvulus plants 'threatened to become a stranglehold on the independent vision of each. Of the two, it was Browning who was in the greater danger', at first eagerly submitting his work to Elizabeth for commentary and in order to guide him 'and half put into my mouth what I ought to say'.[168]

Maisie Ward, by contrast, states firmly that '[Fra Lippo] Lippi is surely Browning on canvas, striking out new ways of seeing, doubted by his Prior as Browning was by his world. Anything odder than comparing him to Andrea del Sarto, the "faultless painter," I can hardly conceive. Browning's art was crammed with faults, roughnesses, elisions, obscurities.'[169] Julia Markus makes the further interesting suggestion that Robert's poetic portrait of Andrea del Sarto derived not from any subjective element of autobiography but from objective observation of the life of William Page, the American artist the Brownings had met in Rome: 'Both painters had had beautiful and difficult wives who also served as models.' Just as Page strove for a faultless technique, 'Andrea del Sarto's perfect technique was an artistic fault that was related to a moral fault. Del Sarto's obsession with style impeded him from striving for meaning in art and also allowed him to succumb to his wife and to become morally culpable in his dealing with the French king . . . One thing was sure. Both del Sarto and Page would have risen higher in their art if their wives' beauty had extended to their souls.'[170]

The two Browning souls accorded perfectly well in poetry and practice, allowing for differences of opinion over the French Emperor, spiritualism, money, and Pen. Quarrels and differences of opinion were natural between them: there would have been considerably more cause for worry if they had absolutely agreed on every little thing, or if they had evolved a convention of reserving their true opinions from one another, if they had not allowed themselves complete intellectual freedom and independence of expression. If Robert felt any pang of envy whatsoever, he concealed it so well as to render it indiscernible to Elizabeth and to everyone else. *Aurora Leigh*, so far as Robert was concerned, was only to be celebrated.

In particular, to Chapman on 5 January 1857, he wrote quoting a letter to Elizabeth from John Ruskin, who had praised *Aurora Leigh* as 'the greatest *poem* in the English language; unsurpassed by anything but

Shakespeare, *not* surpassed by Shakespeare's *Sonnets*, — and therefore the greatest poem in the language'. This was a more deliberate judgement than Lytton's, though just as high-flown. Ruskin, in an earlier exchange of letters with Robert about *Men and Women*, had good-naturedly tackled what he perceived to be the obscurity of Robert's wide range of references. Robert had replied that if clarity was what Ruskin wanted, he should read contracts for house leases or last wills and testaments. Instead of songs, Ruskin should read prose. Elizabeth took Robert's part: poems could not and should not be written on a principle of general, instant comprehension by their readers. Ruskin had the good grace to apologize, though humorously claiming that he saw no use in poetry and had a better use for his breakfast. At least Ruskin believed that *Aurora Leigh* was all Elizabeth's own work. Mr Jarves called to discover the truth of the feather-headed gossip that had got about in Florence: 'that "Aurora" was written by the "spirits," and that I disavowed any share in it except the mere mechanical holding of the pen!!! Think of that', wrote Elizabeth to Henrietta on 10 January 1857.

On 3 December 1856, John Kenyon died. Since his brother had only recently died, making John Kenyon his sole heir, it turned out that the will distributed two substantial fortunes. Kenyon's generous bequests were many and various, but the largest, to the Brownings, amounted jointly to £11,000: £6,500 to Robert, £4,500 to Elizabeth. News of Kenyon's death preceded news of the inheritance. Writing on Elizabeth's behalf to Mrs Kinney on the morning of 7 December, Robert thanked her for her sympathy: 'This has been a sudden misfortune for which she was all but absolutely unprepared. And even now it hardly seems to be more than a dream.' Elizabeth, in her normal attitude of distaste for intimations of mortality, had evidently put any idea that Kenyon's illness might be fatal to the back of her mind. When she heard of his death she was prostrated by grief. John Kenyon had, by his affection and generosity, largely taken the place vacated by her own father. He had been fond, too, of Henrietta, who also benefited by a disappointingly small legacy of £100 in his will. Surtees Cook, her husband, had hoped for more.

News of the great legacy got out quickly and circulated widely. Others, less sensitive than the Kinneys, were quick to write to congratulate the Brownings on what was generally supposed to be their good fortune. To Mrs Martin, on 29 December 1856, Elizabeth wrote, 'we are overwhelmed with "congratulations" on all sides just as if we had not lost a dear, tender, faithful friend and relative — just as if, in fact, some stranger had made us a bequest as a tribute to our poetry. People are so obtuse in this world — as Robert says, so "*dense*"; as Lord Brougham says, so "*crass*".' Elizabeth was grateful nevertheless for the inheritance, and particularly touched by the delicacy, Kenyon's 'sense of trust', with which it had been allocated between herself and Robert. The belief by some that the legacy had been given for literary merit, rather than friendship, was an opinion that Robert took trouble to disabuse.

It took about a year for the terms of the will to be implemented, and the Brownings put most of the money in the Tuscan funds, which paid about £550 per annum on the investment. For the rest, there was Elizabeth's personal income and whatever her royalties might amount to. In all, by the end of 1857, the Brownings could count on a joint annual income of something in excess of £700. They were not rich, but they were very comfortably off and — though by no means inclined to hedonism — could indulge some minor luxuries without anxious prompting of Chapman for accounts or worrying where the next guinea was to be found.

Kenyon's death depressed Robert and Elizabeth, but both individually had other reasons to feel a little flat that winter. Robert still felt the failure of *Men and Women* and, having given up on *Sordello*, was looking around for something to do with himself. He could afford to begin riding again, worked up an active social life, and turned his writing room into an artist's studio where he resumed such a passion for drawing that Elizabeth worried once more that he was neglecting his literary art. As usual, after breakfast, they both tutored the impatient, resistant Pen before he was taken out to be distracted by Wilson, but that was hardly stimulating or a day's work. Elizabeth, having unloaded *Aurora Leigh* into the public domain, felt deflated. She now had no major project to be working on. Writing might be physically exhausting, but it also energized her mentally, and without that emotional and creative stimulus she began to fret on her sofa and became easily bored even by reading. The weather turned cold, her cough returned, and she spent much of her days in the airless warmth of her bedroom. She stayed there for three months. Only Pen seemed happy — especially at Christmas when, loaded with presents, he declared himself to be '*exceptionally* happy. He has taken to long words,' wrote Elizabeth to Sarianna in January 1857.

Spring, and the end of a dull, depressed period, was marked by a *festa* described delightedly by Elizabeth to Sarianna in a letter of February 1857 and effusively to Henrietta on 4 March that year. Pen had been mad to go out into the streets wearing a domino, a long hooded cloak, which he insisted should be blue satin trimmed with pink. Though he was talked out of the pink into a blue trimming, 'the rapture of that child was beyond words'. Wilson often lost sight of him in the crowds as he ran around the streets and piazzas, talking to everyone; but she was under his strict embargo not to keep calling him back by name. The coddled child was perfectly able to take care of himself and talk his way out of difficulty.

Elizabeth herself — 'I, *I*, such as you know me, who had not stirred from the fire for three months, put on a domino and a mask and went to the masked ball at the opera and *came back* at two in the morning.' They had arrived at about half past ten. Robert was arrayed in a black silk domino, which Elizabeth coveted and planned to have made later into a black silk dress for herself, and stayed until four or half past four in the morning. Uncharacteristically and extravagantly anticipating the Kenyon legacy, Robert had taken a third tier box (which turned out to be a 'pretty little room') at a cost of two pounds and five shillings, plus the entrance fee, where they could entertain a few friends with champagne and a buffet supper prepared by Alessandro. Not satisfied with this elegant seclusion, Robert and Elizabeth 'elbowed our way through the crowd to the remotest corner of the ball below. Somebody smote me on the shoulder,' wrote Elizabeth later, 'and cried "Bella mascherina!" and I answered as imprudently as one feels under a mask.'

Not unexpectedly, Elizabeth compared the 'orderly and refined' Italian crowd favourably with the loutish English: 'Such things would be so impossible in England.' The Grand Duke, she noted, put in an appearance, 'poor creature, wretched man, though he couldn't bear it long, to mix with them as if he were innocent!' But she couldn't be bothered for long with political causes that night: 'The brilliancy and variety of the sight, were well worth coming for; and then I like to see characteristic things.' The next day, falling asleep over every book she took up, Elizabeth 'moralized and thought that if one went to a masked ball every night, one would lead a useless life — "proprio inutile" — as the Italians would say.' That would never do. But an occasional draught of pleasure after a dreary period was as good as a dose of opium. Then, too, she had surprised herself by holding up so long at the ball: 'The first time out after three months. It shows how little I have lost strength this winter.' Robert had only allowed her to go to the ball at the last minute, because the night happened to be warm. Nevertheless, she had not caught cold and felt the better for her brilliant adventure.

Otherwise, that spring, there was little to divert her. There was the prospect of a visit from Elizabeth Gaskell, whose novel *Ruth* has been suggested as an influence on *Aurora Leigh*, and whose biography of Charlotte Brontë Elizabeth was anxious to read. On three successive days in early April Harriet Beecher Stowe came to call at Casa Guidi. The famous American abolitionist, and author of the anti-slavery novel *Uncle Tom's Cabin*, published in 1851–2, was as celebrated a figure in Europe as in America. The lioness roared more softly than Elizabeth had expected. She was much taken with Mrs Stowe's sweet voice, and noted 'something strong and copious and characteristic in her dusky wavy hair', but was discontented physiognomically with the brow, which 'has not very large capacity; and the mouth wants something both in frankness and sensitiveness, I should say'.[171] For want of something better to do, Elizabeth set herself in April to writing a plea to the Emperor Napoleon that the novelist and poet Victor Hugo, exiled in 1852 and currently living in Jersey, might be forgiven and allowed to return to France. This letter, though sincerely felt and tenderly expressed, was never sent. The Brownings may have thought better of it; but in any event, not much later, they were thinking of nothing else but the death of Edward Barrett, which had occurred suddenly on 17 April after a short illness, and shortly before his seventy-second birthday.

To Mrs Martin, Robert wrote on 3 May 1857. 'We had the intelligence from George last Thursday week, having only been prepared for the illness by a note received from Arabel the day before. Ba was sadly affected at first; miserable to see and hear. After a few days tears came to her relief. She is now very weak and prostrated, but improving in strength of body and mind: I have no fears for the result.' Ten days later, Elizabeth felt able to write to Henrietta: 'I take up books — but my heart goes walking up and down constantly through that house of Wimpole street, till it is tired, tired.' Enclosed with this letter of 13 May was a note in Robert's hand: 'Ba has made an effort and written; she is no more shaken than was inevitable, and far less than I should have expected. How kind and good you were to write, disregarding your own grief, for the sake of hers. It has been very strange and sudden and mournful: but I think there are some alleviating circumstances about it.'

Her father's death had been quick and unexpected, leaving no time for deathbed reconciliation — even if such a thing had been likely. Hope of that had died in Elizabeth's mind a long while before, however much she tried to convince her heart otherwise. She had been remembered in his daily prayers, but piously rather than fondly: those prayers were more probably for her repentance than for her happiness in the life she had chosen with Robert. Mr Barrett's last words to a trusted family friend, Mrs Martin, some three months previously, had been supposedly a prayer for his family. Elizabeth clung to those words and urged Henrietta to do likewise. She wrote to Mrs Martin on 1 July 1857 to thank her for her sympathy and to reassure her that she was now 'much better, calm and not despondingly calm (as, off and on, I have been), able to read and talk, and keep from vexing my poor husband, who has been a good deal tried in all these things'.

Though her instinct was to lie on a sofa, never stirring or speaking, she was making an effort, at Robert's insistence, to go out most days for two or three hours in a carriage. She saw and spoke with Isa Blagden, and continued with Pen's daily lessons. 'If I could get into hard, regular work of some kind, it would be better for me, I know; but "the flesh is weak."' The Brownings had decided against going to England for the summer and for the funeral. John Kenyon was dead, Mr Barrett was dead: 'Oh, no, to have gone to England this summer would have *helped nobody*, and would have been very overcoming to *me*. I was not fit for it, indeed, and Robert was averse on his own account.' Instead, she became even more deeply interested in spiritualism than before — she could not have been reconciled with her father in this world, but she thought it would be possible in the next — and she started writing wistful but bossy letters to Henrietta and Arabel urging that the latter should remove herself instantly to Italy. It takes no great psychological insight to see these letters now as adopting something of her father's deep desire to corral the entire Barrett family together in one place and keep them together, but now, after his departure, within Elizabeth's (the eldest's) easy reach and, possibly, personal direction.

On or about 1 August, the Brownings took themselves off to Bagni di Lucca. They rented a house, Casa Betti, for the season at Alla Villa, where they were joined by Isa Blagden, her friend Miss Annette Bracken, and Robert Lytton, who stayed opposite them at a hotel. Lytton promptly fell ill with gastric fever and was tended by Isa, who, on the grounds of economy and personal devotion, refused to have a nurse to look after him — 'an imbecile arrangement . . . imagine what a pleasant holiday we all have!', was Robert's comment to Sarianna — and instead co-opted Robert and Elizabeth to sit with poor Lytton in shifts, night and day. By 22 August, to judge from a letter of that date from Elizabeth to Mrs Jameson, Isa had been talked into hiring a nurse for the nights, so relieving the Brownings a little from duty. Robert rode at dawn and dusk, bathed in the river daily at half past six every morning, and Pen too swam like a little fish and rode around on 'donkeys and mountain ponies . . . as bold as a lion'.[172] Though it was a pang to his mother's heart, she was forced to put him into 'white jean trowsers for him to ride in' since riding through rocks and briars tore Pen's satin and lace to shreds. These jeans, ugly and utilitarian, were — at Elizabeth's earnest desire — to be worn on no other occasions.

An irritating letter from Edward Chapman reached Robert that summer, suggesting that if he 'could but write bad enough' he might think about writing for the penny papers that were then making fortunes for their proprietors. Other authors had tried this tack, though not all successfully since some of them couldn't help but write well, which apparently did them and the papers to which they contributed no favours. One more item was added to the charge sheet against Bagni di Lucca: in mid to late September Pen fell ill with the same complaint that had felled Lytton and had to be put to bed. The illness was not severe, he soon recovered, but it had been worrying. The doctor had initially feared a form of typhus common in Tuscany. A vision of little Joe Story rose in Elizabeth's mind.[173] She was physically well herself, but thoroughly done in emotionally by 'a summer to me full of blots, vexations, anxieties'.[174] The Brownings, thoroughly disgusted with Alla

Villa, were glad to leave for Florence on 7 October, though not everything there was as rosy as might have been.

Wilson, now pregnant for the second time, had gone with them to Bagni di Lucca but had fallen ill and had to be put to bed. Since she was not much use as a maid in this condition a replacement, a lively, lovely young woman by name of Annunziata, was hired. Still feverish, seven months pregnant and tearful, Wilson was sent back to Florence alone. Ferdinando stayed with his employers. Supplied with a small loan of twelve pounds which Robert had obtained from Edward Chapman as part of monies owing on Elizabeth's royalty account,[175] Lily Wilson rented lodgings for herself next to Casa Guidi and fell to worrying about the effect that the absence of his wife and close proximity to pretty, amusing Annunziata might have on her husband. She was glad to have Ferdinando back in time for the birth of her second son, Pilade, on 11 November 1857.

It was a cold winter in Italy. Elizabeth reported snow as far south as Rome and Naples. In Florence the Arno, for the first time in ten years, had partially iced over. Both Robert and Pen took head colds, though Elizabeth suffered 'only losing my breath and my soul in the usual way, the cough not being much'.[176] Pen was delightedly distracted by Pilade. The baby was living next door with Wilson, who began to run her new lodgings as a boarding-house, while Ferdinando, to Pen's pleasure, remained at Casa Guidi. When he was not with Wilson and Pilade, who became like his baby brother, Pen was at home happily improving his proficiency on the piano and less contentedly learning his lessons, which by now included German and Latin as well as Italian, French, and English. Elizabeth, lying on her sofas and reading French and German romances, rarely stirring from the apartment, waited for the spring sunshine to revive her from an oppressive period of brooding on her father's death that 'seemed to have stamped out of me the vital fluid' and left her 'physically low'.[177]

Robert, also restless, with cause of his own to brood on the premature demise of all hope for *Men and Women*, brisked himself up by going out regularly to Isa Blagden's house at Bellosguardo, riding, and taking daily drawing lessons. A year before, on 21 March 1857, he had written to Edward Chapman to send him a shilling pamphlet entitled *Instructions in the Art of Figure Drawing* by C. H. Weigall. Whether this was for himself or Pen is not clear, but perhaps it did for both of them if Robert had it in mind to pass on his own interest in drawing to his son. After the Christmas of 1857, Robert brought home a complete skeleton, a wondrous object, fully articulated, the joints nicely finished with gutta-percha. These bones had recently held together the flesh of a young, thirty-six-year-old Florentine who had no doubt, and none too lately, walked past Casa Guidi. The head could be taken off and put back on with a wonderful facility. Robert was happy to demonstrate. Robert couldn't stop talking about it altogether, much to Elizabeth's disgust. If she could tolerate Robert's bones, she complained, he should be able to tolerate her spirits. And so, generously, he did, writing to Chapman on 4 January 1858 to remind him to send *Rollo's Travels in Europe* for Pen and, presumably for Elizabeth, 'one of that thing about "Spirit-Drawings" by Wilkinson which you are about to publish?'

Robert had evidently been unwell that winter, perhaps with the sick headaches to which he was prone as well as his head cold or — worse — influenza, because he was somehow converted to homoeopathy. He dosed himself from a homoeopathic medicine chest he acquired. He gave up wine; his appetite improved, and he felt very much better. 'If he begins by being an homoeopathist,' Elizabeth wrote mischievously to Henrietta on 4 March 1858, 'he will end by being a spiritualist, I prophesy to him.' Homoeopathy at least became a mutual interest for the Brownings: they planned to get the necessary bottles, a book on the subject, and Elizabeth even considered moderating her regular intake of opium.

On 9 June, Nathaniel Hawthorne dined at Casa Guidi with the Brownings. Robert had gone the day before to deliver the invitation. Hawthorne's notebooks are again wonderfully and pleasurably circum-stantial. In the entry for 8 June, Hawthorne records that Robert 'looked younger and even handsomer than when I saw him in London, two years ago, and his gray hairs seemed fewer than those that had then strayed into his youthful head'. In his entry for the next day, Hawthorne interestingly describes the 'spacious staircase and ample accommoda-tions of vestibule and hall, the latter opening on a balcony, where we could hear the chanting of priests in a church close by. Browning told us that this was the first church where an oratorio had ever been per-formed.' Of course, this was something Robert would have known —

he was unlikely likely to have missed something like that — from the very start of his tenancy of Casa Guidi and affably passed on to guests. Pen was introduced. Hawthorne was properly astonished. 'I never saw such a boy as this before; so slender, fragile and spirit-like, — not as if he were actually in ill health, but as if he had little or nothing to do with flesh and blood. His face is very pretty and most intelligent, and exceedingly like his mother's.' He had some reservations about nine-year-old Pen: the boy seemed 'at once less childlike and less manly than would befit that age . . . I wonder what is to become of him, — whether he will ever grow to be a man, — whether it is desirable that he should.' Pen was decidedly not like any child to which Hawthorne, himself a father, was accustomed. 'He was born in Florence, and prides himself on being a Florentine, and is indeed as un-English a production as if he were native of another planet.'

In contrast to Robert Browning, who 'talked a wonderful quantity in a little time' and who had already begun to put on the booming tone and display the confident, whooshing, energetic attitude of his later years, Mrs Browning seemed 'a pale, small person, scarcely embodied at all; at any rate, only substantial enough to put forth her slender fingers to be grasped, and to speak with a shrill, yet sweet, tenuity of voice. Really,' concluded Hawthorne after this encounter with the Brownings *en famille*, 'I do not see how Mr Browning can suppose that he has an earthly wife any more than an earthly child; both are of the elfin race, and will flit away from him some day when he least thinks of it.' Elizabeth seemed like 'a good and kind fairy, however, and sweetly disposed towards the human race, although only remotely akin to it'. Her black ringlets clustered down into her neck, making her face look the whiter by contrast. The 'certainty of her benevolence' particularly struck Hawthorne, who thought it more likely that 'there were a million chances to one that she would have been a miracle of acidity and bitterness'.

The conversation, which Robert kept going like a juggler by seeming to be here, there and everywhere in the room at once, prompting with his quick wit, logic, common sense and vitality, took a turn to spiritualism, which Hawthorne found wearisome. Among the guests served by Pen with cake and strawberries that night at Casa Guidi were the Eckleys, David and Sophia, rich young Americans who had taken a fancy to the

Brownings when they had met them the previous summer at Bagni di Lucca. Sophia, an ardent spiritualist and a creature of poetic inspirations, had swiftly fixed herself in her obsession like a limpet on Elizabeth's good nature and susceptibility. Elizabeth, writing to Arabel, thought that Sophia Eckley 'had taken it into that enthusiastic head of hers to fall into a sort of love' with her. David Eckley seems to have indulged his wife, no matter what her interests and devotions, and made himself inoffensively agreeable, riding out with Robert almost every day. Robert, though outwardly courteous and thankful to Mrs Eckley for her generosities — she showered gifts upon them — was privately cautious about her influence over Elizabeth, who had responded warmly during the winter to Sophia's earnest spirit practices and experiments, and her almost daily attendance at Casa Guidi. Mrs Eckley's enthusiasm worried Robert, who warned Elizabeth to beware of becoming — unusually for her — too intimate too quickly.

The Eckley connection was temporarily broken for the summer when the Brownings left Florence in the first week of July by way of Livorno, Genoa, and Marseilles, for Paris, where they stayed for two weeks in an apartment full of clocks at the Hôtel Hyacinthe, on the rue St Honoré, near the Tuileries. They had left Ferdinando and Wilson behind, much to Pen's distress, and took only Annunziata with them. Florence had been hot; Paris by contrast was cold even in the sunshine, so that Elizabeth could only occasionally drive out with Robert. But Paris! — Elizabeth in a letter of 8 July 1858 confessed to Fanny Haworth her '*weakness*' for Paris and her '*passion*' for Italy. There was everything to admire in the city, 'from cutlets to costumes'. Robert the homoeopath boasted of his great good health and his large appetite. William Allingham, a friend of the Pre-Raphaelites, recorded in his diary a conversation with Thackeray, who had met Robert in Paris at this time: '"Browning was here this morning," Thackeray said, "what spirits he has — almost too much for me in my weak state. He almost blew me out of bed!"'[178]

Robert was deeply comforted to have arrived in the city and to have seen his father on his birthday, 6 July, looking happy and younger than before. There were other pious duties to be attended to: not knowing Joseph Milsand was at home, Robert proceeded to his house twice to 'muse and bless the threshold'.[179] The Brownings also met with Mrs Jameson and visited Lady Elgin, who had recently suffered another stroke that had almost done for her completely. They sat with her, talking politics and other subjects, while Robert 'fed her with a spoon from her soup-plate, and she signed, as well as she could, that he should kiss her forehead before he went away. She was always so fond of Robert, as women are apt to be, you know — even *I*, a little.'[180]

Robert was attractive to both sexes, as it happened: young men sought out his company and, like Robert Lytton, Dante Gabriel Rossetti, David Eckley, Amédée de Ripert-Monclar and others, actively and earnestly sought his approbation and friendship. They walked with him, rode with him, talked with him, wrote about him and sketched him, gave up hours to him and took such hours as he could give them: he was a frank, affectionate, confident, and talkative friend and confidant whose solid common sense consoled them as much as his breadth and originality of imagination inspired them. Tomboys like Hatty Hosmer loved him. Women loved him. Robert himself was not so promiscuous in his loves, though generally he was at first more disposed to like than dislike and, once fixed in a positive attitude towards a friend, it was difficult to dislodge him from it except in cases where he perceived betrayal of that friendship in respect of whatever Robert Browning held most dear — whereupon he was capable of astonishing, implacable savagery.

To Isa Blagden, more than likely, he had confided whatever niggling doubts had been raised in his mind and feelings over the year, since the last holiday at Bagni di Lucca, by Sophia Eckley. Robert Browning needed women: no question about it. There is, also, no question that he loved his wife, was faithful to her, and that there existed between them the most profound confidence in the exclusive love that they possessed and were possessed by, the one for the other. It was in that confidence that Elizabeth could catch sight of Robert standing and looking happily at pretty girls and beautiful women in the doorway of the dancing-room at Mrs Sartoris's house in Rome and laugh at his dissipations. It was in that confidence that she could look indulgently on his conversational and occasionally petting flirtations with young Hatty Hosmer. It was in that confidence that she was happy to know that he was talking and taking tea and gossiping several times a week with Isa and pressing close on the sofa to whatever women friends happened to be staying with her at the Villa Brichieri.

Robert, as Hawthorne observed — and he was not the only one to notice — was not only younger than Elizabeth, but looked it: he was in his mid-forties, a healthy, good-looking man, captivating in conversation and engagingly sociable without being frivolous, naturally confident without pomposity or bombast. He was, too, it was well known by now, relatively and independently well-off. There might be those in Florence who raised an eyebrow or rattled a teacup over Mr Browning's hearty appetite for life outside Casa Guidi while his ailing, older wife (poor thing!), decrepit and wasted (she can't last!), lay on her sofa and doped herself with opium or morphine or laudanum or whatever laid her out these days. In four cases out of five, according to the scandalized morality of their social circle, they might have been correct in their speculations. The Brownings, nevertheless, were the exception that proved the rule.

Elizabeth pushed Robert out into the world because she knew very well that it suited him to be there. She was aware that her slow pace of life was not, could not, and should not be his. Robert went out into the world because it pleased Elizabeth to see him enjoying life and because, too, on his own account, it pleased him to be there. As she withdrew more and more, secluding herself at home, so he increasingly extended himself in company. He might flirt vigorously, and others might read more into this than was ever intended by Robert; but in his own mind, as much as in Elizabeth's, there was all the difference in the world between a man making a friend and confidante of a woman, married or unmarried, and making her his mistress. This arrangement, which would have wrecked a less well-founded marriage, evoked a gnawing jealousy in a less confident wife, and put irresistible temptations in the way of a less temperamentally loyal husband, succeeded because Robert and Elizabeth loved one another as deeply at the end as the beginning.

For the summer of 1858, the Brownings decided against a visit to England. For the sake of Elizabeth's health they went no further north than Le Havre after inspecting accommodation in the nearby coastal village of Étretat. The rooms they first looked at came expensive at two hundred francs a month for a view of a potato patch, but Robert 'in a fine phrenzy' had already taken them until forced to give them up at Elizabeth's vehement entreaty. He lost ten francs by his impetuosity, 'which was the only cheap thing in the place, as far as I observed anything', Elizabeth commented to Mrs Jameson. The countryside was not very pretty in Elizabeth's estimation, but they had come for the sea — which was 'open and satisfactory' — rather than for the surrounding views. At Le Havre, in the garden of the house they took, Maison Versigny at 2 rue de Perry, close to the sea, Elizabeth reported to Mrs Jameson that Robert had 'found a hole I can creep through to the very shore, without walking many yards, and there I can sit on a bench and get strength, if it so pleases God'.[181] Reporting to Isa in Florence in August 1858, Robert wrote that Elizabeth was taking healthful baths, filling her hip bath with sea water, and that her 'improvement in health is incontestable and rapid', that Pen was busy fishing for minnows, that he himself, though 'somewhat bilious and indisposed to salt water', intended to take, literally, the plunge — though not immediately. 'I shall begin tomorrow—'.

Sarianna and Mr Browning were with them in the house, both well in mind, body, and spirit. Mr Browning took advantage of a nearby library and subscription to a 'Casino — *salon de lecture*', which, so far as Robert could make out, entitled whoever cared to pay the fee 'to study one "Constitutionelle" three days stale, several numbers of the "Guide Dentaire" (full of information about curious teeth) — all the back livraisons of a certain Journal of useful inventions containing models of improved cheese-toasters, novel implements of use in drill-husbandry and the like, — the remaining three-quarters of the table being cleverly littered over with tradesmen's prospectuses, cards for a dancing-master's Ball and so on.' Not that intellectual or social diversion was the point of the holiday. For a while they saw nobody, went nowhere, and simply recruited their health. They were later joined by various Barrett relations, at first Arabel accompanied by George, then Elizabeth's brother Henry and his new wife Amelia Morris, endearingly known as Millikins.

It was a relief to Robert when his friend Joseph Milsand arrived from Dijon for ten days. Elizabeth was busy with brothers, sister, and catching up with family matters that interested her more than they held Robert's attention. Truth to tell, Robert had been frustrated in any mild intention to write, being a little overwhelmed by so much family and even a little bored: 'What is to say about such a dull life as this daily one of ours?' he wrote to Isa on 4 September. 'I go mechanically out and in and get a day through — whereof not ten minutes have been my own — so much for your "quantities of writing" (in expectation) — I began pretty zealously — but it's of no use now: nor will the world very greatly care.'

Arabel accompanied the Brownings back to Paris, to an apartment at 6 rue Castiglione, in late September for two weeks to continue gossiping and to do some shopping with her sister before Robert, Elizabeth, Pen, and Annunziata set out circuitously for Florence on 13 October. For reasons of ingrained economy, they travelled back by way of Lyon and Chambéry, where, 'for the sake of Les Charmettes and Rousseau', they stopped to visit the philosopher's house. There 'Robert played the "Dream" on the old harpsichord, the keys of which rattled in a ghastly way, as if it were the bones of him who once so "dreamed." Then there was an old watch hung up, without a tick in it.'[182] The journey home, unlike the easy, faultlessly comfortable journey out, was a nightmare of frustrated connections, debilitating cold on Mont Cenis, and finally a frightening storm arose at sea on an eighteen-hour voyage from Genoa to Livorno, where they rested to recover their spirits and energies before making the last leg to Florence, Casa Guidi, and only a short respite of two weeks before sunshine gave way to unexpected cold. Snow ('enough to strangle one', Elizabeth wrote to Sarianna) fell on the city, followed by rain. Dr Harding, their regular physician, had recommended that Elizabeth should be back in Florence no later than the end of September, but she had been inclined to linger in Paris.[183] The weather, and concern for Elizabeth's health, which had been done no good by the arduous conditions they had endured on the way from Paris to Florence, drove them within a fortnight to Rome for winter light and warmth.

They arrived on 24 November and settled again in the familiar rooms at 43 Bocca di Leone that they had occupied in 1853. Robert, richer now but still unweaned from the habit of carefully counting his small change, reckoned he had struck a good deal. The apartments had been newly cleaned, carpeted, and painted. Though prices in Rome had risen enormously, the rent (forty dollars for four months, just over £10 a month) was only ten dollars more than they had paid before and twenty less, 'in consideration of the desire the old landlady had to get us again', than would have been charged to anyone but the Brownings. The spendthrift Eckleys, by contrast, were paying a thousand dollars [over £200] for six months. 'One can't do *that*,' wrote Robert, properly shocked, to Sarianna on 26 November 1858. The Eckleys, who had been expensively waiting in a hotel for the Brownings to return to Florence in order to decide about their own plans, had insisted that Robert, Elizabeth, Pen, and Annunziata should travel to Rome in the second of their luxuriously appointed carriages.

Elizabeth had been embarrassed by the grandiosity of the Eckleys' generosity, and Robert had initially been inclined to refuse the offer altogether. 'The Eckleys were extravagantly good to us,' Robert commented to Sarianna, 'something beyond conception almost.'[184] But Elizabeth, in this same letter, was inclined to attribute the unaffected kindness of the Eckleys to their American character: 'Such generosity and delicacy, combined with so much passionate sentiment (there is no other word), are difficult to represent. The Americans are great in some respects, not that Americans are generally like these, but that these could scarcely be English — for instance, that mixture of enthusiasm and simplicity we have not.'

The 'delightful' journey, by way of Arezzo and Perugia, Spoleto and Terni — where Robert, David Eckley, and his mother-in-law got drenched visiting the waterfalls — was not without disturbing incident. According to information from Elizabeth, attached to Robert's less sensational letter to Sarianna, 'We were as nearly as possible thrown once into a ditch and once down a mountain precipice, the spirited horses plunging on one side, but at last Mr Eckley lent us his courier, who sate on the box by the coachman and helped him to manage better. Then there was a fight between our oxen-drivers, one of them attempting to stab the other with a knife, and Robert rushing in between till Pen and I were nearly frantic with fright. No harm happened, however, except that Robert had his trousers torn. And we escaped afterwards certain banditti, who stopped a carriage only the day before on the very road we travelled, and robbed it of sixty-two scudi.' Elizabeth had all but fainted at Robert's decisive intervention on the road.

Since he did not comment on the incident himself in known letters, not to Sarianna, nor to Isa, nor to make an amusing set-piece of it to anyone as he did to Fanny Haworth of his maritime adventures on the high seas earlier in his career, such records of Robert's intrepid activity are rare. When episodes of derring-do are displayed, we are reminded that Robert Browning was a physical man, actively interventionist when necessary. He was ready to face down anyone. When the American poet Julia Ward Howe, author of 'The Battle Hymn of the Republic', imagined some slight on the part of the Brownings in respect of a volume of her verse, *Passion Flowers*, which she had sent to them but had been too tardily personally acknowledged and apparently privately disparaged, she took her revenge by writing poems about them in *Words for the Hour*, published in 1858. A particularly offending reference to Elizabeth, was contained in verses entitled 'One Word More With E.B.B.':

> I shrink before the nameless draught
> That helps to such unearthly things,
> And if a drug could lift so high,
> I would not trust its treacherous wings;
>
> Lest, lapsing from them, I should fall,
> A weight more dead than stock or stone —
> The warning fate of those who fly
> With pinions other than their own.

Julia Ward Howe herself, evidently, just said 'no' to stimulants and virtuously repudiated any of opium's derivatives. Her poetry needed no artificial aids to inspiration and composition. She did not actually name the drug that Elizabeth famously used, but the implication was plain enough: Elizabeth's high poetic flights were due less to natural creative genius than to drug-induced fancy. Robert, discovering that Mrs Howe's sister was married to Crawford, the American sculptor in Rome, and that Mrs Crawford was herself in Rome, called on her 'in order to show her how much I despised her sister Mrs Howe who has written a couple of poems to Ba and me beginning "I have heard you do not praise me, Barrett-Browning, high inspired! Nor you, Robert! [with your manhood and your angels interlyred]" etc., and ending with saying Ba's poetry all comes from her use of a "nameless drug" and plenty of similar abuse — because we didn't *praise* her! Mrs Story seemed to think we must be writhing under such awful blows — but I find out people soon enough and know just what they will do one day to us, if they have the chance. Mrs C. looked black and disconsolate enough, poor thing.'[185] Mrs Crawford might quail more readily than her sister before the Browning blast, but Robert, characteristically, was not intending to neglect any opportunity to put matters straight for the future. As always, he nipped in the bud anything likely to be troublesome. No doubt Mrs Crawford would pass on the message. As it turned out, however, the Ward Howe feud with the Brownings continued for another ten years. In 1866, in *Later Lyrics*, Mrs Ward Howe returned to the attack with a poem entitled 'Kenyon's Legacy'. It began with a sharp reference to the two 'Poet-Bees' who had omitted to praise the 'honey' in her *Passion Flowers*:

> Good Johnny Kenyon's gone and done
> The best thing with his money:
> He's left it for two Poet-Bees,
> Who make the wasp-world honey.

Rome turned cold at Christmas. To Isa, who had gone to Madrid for the winter, Robert reported 'a fountain this morning one shagginess of huge icicles, and the others are similarly metamorphosized, I am told'. Elizabeth stayed at home in their 'little "poky" warm rooms' and fussed over Pen, who had developed a bad cold and a cough after 'playing late on the Pincian a week ago'. He was confined to the apartment 'lest it should harden into a habit'.[186] Robert, though he too caught a cold, rose at a quarter to six every morning, before first light, and walked or rode out for an hour or more with David Eckley, going 'all about Rome, up and down, in and out, the worst and best of it, so that I see it thoroughly on the outside and like it *so* much — so much more than last time'.[187] He came home ravenous, a wonder to his wife — 'this habit of regular exercise (with occasional homeopathy) has thrown him into a striking course of prosperity, as to looks, spirits, and appetite. He eats "vulpinely" he says — which means that a lark or two is no longer enough for dinner. At breakfast the loaf perishes by Gargantuan slices.'[188]

Robert took drawing lessons twice a week from a Mrs Mackenzie, who coughed and neglected her health; caught up with Hatty Hosmer, who was suffering from neck boils; and fell in again with the American actress Charlotte Cushman, who had contracted Roman fever. Nathaniel Hawthorne and his entire family had also fallen ill, with gastric fever, though none so seriously as fifteen-year-old Una Hawthorne, whose lungs had been affected. Half the expatriates in Rome, to judge by Robert's account to Isa, were coughing, sneezing, sniffling, and snuffling, falling down with gastric fever and Roman fever, nursing abscesses and rheumatism. Visiting friends was like taking a tour of a hospital out-patient department. Elizabeth was still worried about Pen's health.

But the shadow of little Joe Story had mostly evaporated, and she confessed that 'I like Rome better than I did last time . . . I have only heard of one English artist since we came, who arrived, sickened, died, and was buried, before anyone knew who he was.'[189] Nevertheless, sure of the buoyant spirits of the halt, the lame and the sick, the Storys were about to give a 'great dancing party' in the apartments at the Palazzo Barberini, on the slope of the Quirinale, where they had lived since 1856, and Robert thought that 'perhaps I shall go in the end'.

Try to keep him away from it, more likely. The ball was held on 12 January, and three hundred guests attended. Robert had quickly plunged back into the gaieties of Roman society, where he was immensely popular despite occasional gaffes when trying, none too deftly, to pay happy courtesies and give graceful compliments. To Isa Blagden, Elizabeth reported that 'He said the other day to Mrs Story: "I had a delightful evening yesterday at your house. I *never spoke to you once,*" and encouraged an artist who was "quite dissatisfied with his works," as he said humbly, by an encouraging — "But, my dear fellow, if you were satisfied, you would be so *very easily* satisfied!" Happy, wasn't it?'

While Elizabeth had read Swedenborg in bed, her husband had 'gone out every night for a fortnight together, and sometimes two or three times deep in a one night's engagements. So plenty of distraction, and no Men and Women. Men and women from without instead!'[190] There is the faintest hint of dissatisfaction in this comment — Robert was neglecting poetry for worldly pleasure. 'As to Robert,' Elizabeth wrote to Henrietta on 10 February 1859, 'he is lost to me and himself. If once a fortnight we have an evening together, we call it a holiday, both of us.'

She perhaps felt more personally neglected than she could openly admit, though confining herself only to the expression of a slight disappointment that Robert's hectic social activity, after they'd dined at five o'clock, 'has hindered us from having people here in the evening. I have no vocation for receiving alone, and if my husband is caught up out of the windows — what then?' She did not grudge him his Roman pleasures, though she would be better pleased to see an end to them as a permanent condition: 'It pleases me that he should be amused just now (not but that he denies being amused very often); and I think it's good for him — in an occasional winter like this. I wouldn't spend every winter at Rome though. Rome is too like a watering place — like a Cheltenham — the only difference being that the society is generally of a more aristocratical order generally here ... the Prince of Wales has arrived.'

The young Edward, Prince of Wales, only seventeen years old, was under strict instructions to attend to his studies, refuse invitations to 'go to any balls',[191] and meet only the most improving persons. Despite Elizabeth's anti-Englishness and republicanism ('I do hope the English may not make themselves absurd by carrying up addresses and the like, as really there is no occasion for toad-eating loyalty, and it isn't the way of this foreign world'), Robert accepted a royal request to dine — men only were invited — with the Prince of Wales, whose governor, Colonel Bruce, had called upon the Brownings to say that he *knew it would be gratifying to the Queen that the prince should make Mr Browning's acquaintance*.[192] To gratify Queen Victoria, Robert was obliged to give up an interesting invitation for that same night from William Cornwallis Cartwright, a liberal Englishman, to meet several notables, including the Marquis Massimo d'Azeglio, who, to Elizabeth's mind, was 'worth a hundred royalties — (always excepting the Emperor Napoleon's)'. At dinner, according to Elizabeth's report to Henrietta on 4 March, 'The prince did not talk much, but listened intelligently and asked several questions on Italian politics — to Robert's own great surprise and mine — (for he and I had only jested in supposing the subject possible) and he found himself talking quite naturally of the wrongs of Italy to an evidently sympathetic audience. Not that the prince committed his royal youthfulness in the least degree, but that he listened intently, and his suite did more than listen.'

Whatever the English, through the mouthpieces of their press and politicians, thought or said about the question of Italian independence or of Louis Napoleon's government was bound, so far as Elizabeth was concerned, to be plain wrong and reactionary or, worse, ill-intentioned. English opinion still bothered her, though more out of ingrained habit and long-standing grudge than from any remnants of embarrassed English patriotism. She declared to Henrietta on 10 February 1859, 'never did I feel myself so little English as now' and described herself and Pen as 'we Italians'. Robert, who retained an English identity, and having gone 'where British loyalty called', [193] had got away early enough from dinner with the Prince of Wales to rush to Mr Cartwright's party and make d'Azeglio's acquaintance after all; and d'Azeglio, that distinguished statesman and patriotic novelist, formerly Prime Minister of Piedmont from 1849–52, and currently the Piedmontese ambassador to Rome, had promised to call at 43 Bocca di Leone to see Elizabeth.

When he did so, he enchanted her by his admirable appearance and incontestable sentiments: 'A noble chivalrous head, and that largeness of the political *morale* which I find nowhere among statesmen, except in the head of the French government.' D'Azeglio's greatness, comparable only to that of Louis Napoleon, was confirmed in his political principles. He 'spoke bitterly of English policy, stigmatized it as belonging to a past age, the rags of old traditions. He said that Louis Napoleon had made himself great simply by comprehending the march of civilization (the true Christianity, said Azeglio) and by leading it. Exactly what I have always thought,' reported Elizabeth, full of fresh inspiration for Italian nationalist ambitions, to Isa Blagden on 27 March 1859. 'Azeglio disbelieves in any aim of territorial aggrandisement on the part of France. He is full of hope for Italy. It is '48 all over again, said he, but with matured actors.'

Elizabeth's faith in the moral virtue of Louis Napoleon's statesmanship was as unqualified as her devotion to the moral cause of Italian national unity. He had no irredentist ambitions, she could be sure. Robert, too, tended to believe that the Emperor's goodwill towards Italy was genuine. And so it was, all things considered — given that there were a lot of things to be considered by Louis Napoleon. Equally genuine was the Emperor's ill will towards the Austrians and his desire to rout them out of Italy. Louis Napoleon's considerings had been subtle, and foremost among them was his self-interest at the expense of both Italy and Austria. If he could benefit Italy at some cost to Austria, well and good; but his intervention was not altruistic — it came with a political price tag. Since the premature uprisings of 1848, Italy had been waiting for another opportunity. In 1855, Count Camillo Benso di Cavour, who had succeeded Massimo d'Azeglio as Prime Minister of Sardinia-Piedmont in 1852, had sent some fifteen thousand men to the Crimea in support of Britain and France against Russia. He thus gained a seat at the Paris peace congress of 1856, where he had taken his opportunity to assert the right of Piedmont, as much as Austria, to be interested in the rights and future of Italy.

Cavour, in his time, was the Bismarck of Italy. This pragmatic, opportunistic statesman was as well acquainted with French literature and English history as the culture and politics of Italy. The subtlety of his political manipulations was naturally regarded as Machiavellian. Europe was Cavour's natural habitat, and he masterfully exploited the various rivalries of Europe's great powers to his own advantage. His impressive internal reforms — economic, political, and civil — of Piedmont during the 1850s gave weight and authority to himself and the state he had strengthened as the natural leader of the movement towards national unification. That movement, Cavour saw clearly, required a powerful ally to assist him in his aim of uniting Italy under the monarchical rule of his nominal master, Vittorio Emanuele of the House of Savoy. Britain would have been ideal, since it could have made no territorial claims in Italy. British policy, however, was to keep the peace in Europe rather than to provoke or support any disruption of the status quo, and there were besides some strong English opinions that favoured Austria over Italy. And so Cavour turned to a more natural ally and closer neighbour, Louis Napoleon, who had come to power in 1852, the same year as Cavour himself, and like Cavour had created an impressively powerful state.

Cavour had met Louis Napoleon secretly at Plombières in July 1858. There, the two statesmen had agreed to provoke Austria into war, whereupon an allied army of French and Piedmontese troops, supported by forces from the rest of the Italian states, would invade Lombardy. The Austrians would be driven across the Alps, and Italy would become a federation of allied states ruled by Vittorio Emanuele II. The Kingdom of Northern Italy, which was what really interested Cavour, would consist of Piedmont, Lombardy, Venetia, and the Papal States east of the Apennines. Tuscany and Umbria would become Central Italy, the Pope would retain Rome, and the Kingdom of Naples would be given to the French Emperor's cousin, the unappetizingly fat and priapic Plon-Plon, Prince Jérôme, who would marry Vittorio Emanuele's daughter Clothilde, thus maintaining a dynastic French presence and interest in Italy. Savoy and Nice would be ceded to France. Cavour's theoretical liberalism and practical utilitarianism combined to make him more cautious than the utopian Mazzini, whose revolutionary republican insurrectionism conflicted with Cavour's plans for alliance with France. The idealistic Mazzini was sidelined and some of his more pragmatic supporters defected to Cavour.

The marriage of Prince Jérôme to the young Princess Clothilde, after some distinct hesitation on the bride's part — she first had to be persuaded to the view that he was not absolutely repellent — was celebrated at Turin Cathedral on 30 January 1859. Beforehand, on 1 January, Napoleon III had loudly and publicly regretted to the Austrian ambassador that bad relations existed between France and Austria. This was news to the other ambassadors present, who interpreted it as the unmistakable diplomatic signal it was intended to be. On 10 January, Vittorio Emanuele opened the Piedmontese parliament at Turin with a speech that referred to the *grido di dolore* — the cry of pain — that had reached him from every part of Italy. The Austrians concluded from these two remarks, and an inflammatory pamphlet about Napoleon and Italy published in Paris, that France and Piedmont were working together to provoke a European war. The British government was appalled. Privately, and rather *de haut en bas*, the Foreign Secretary, Lord Malmesbury, took exception to what he perceived as Piedmont's conceit and mischief-making and characterized the evident alliance between Cavour and Louis Napoleon as the ambitions of an Italian attorney and a tambour major.

It was becoming clear to Louis Napoleon that England and Austria's supporters would not tolerate a French or Piedmontese declaration of war. England, wary in any case of Louis Napoleon, urged a European Congress to discuss a general disarmament. Austria declined to participate in any such discussions. Cavour remained confident that Austria could be provoked into belligerence without much further prompting, and he was proved correct when, on 23 April 1859, Austria demanded Cavour's assent to unconditional disarmament and demobilization of the Piedmontese forces within three days. Cavour refused and waited for the trap to close.

On 29 January Austria declared war on Piedmont and crossed the Ticino, whereupon France declared war on Austria, promising a free Italy from the Alps to the Adriatic. On 4 June 1859, combined French and Italian troops defeated Austria at Magenta and the victors occupied Milan. On 24 June, at the cost of a bloody massacre of some seventeen thousand men, the Austrians were defeated at Solferino. Napoleon III's stomach turned at the carnage and his head recognized hard political realities. He had had enough blood and had gained enough politically. On 8 July he met the Austrian Emperor at Villafranca to agree an armistice in which Austria ceded Lombardy to France and France in turn ceded the territory to Italy. The French would gain Savoy and Nice in return for Lombardy. Much had been achieved, but the grand plan seemed to many in Italy to have fallen disappointingly short of its ultimate ends — as, from their own viewpoint, they had understood them to be.

Elizabeth's profoundest political conviction — her absolute faith in Louis Napoleon — and her deepest political ideal — Italian freedom and unification — had combined in the early stages of this revitalized Risorgimento. Anyone who questioned the French Emperor's honesty in respect of his aid to Italy or the rights of Italy to independence was given short shrift. Napoleon III's generosity and magnanimity were contrasted sharply, as ever, with the ignoble attitude of the English towards Italy.[194] Her letters during the first half of 1859 to Sarianna, Isa Blagden, and Henrietta are full of familiar effusions in favour of French virtue and expostulations against English ignominy. She spoke, after all, from first-hand experience that the hidebound English press and politicians could not confound: 'We who have lived in Italy all these years, know the full pestilent meaning of Austria everywhere ... Now, God be thanked, here is light and hope of deliverance ... We shall be perfectly satisfied here with French universal suffrage and the ballot, the very same democratical government which advanced Liberals are straining for in England.'[195] When *The Times*' correspondent fell ill of fever in Rome, she almost rejoiced at his misfortune, seeing it as a judgement on him and his hateful, lying newspaper.[196]

The Brownings and the Eckleys returned to Florence in the last days of May 1859. In their absence, Florentines and Tuscans, wearing the nationalist symbol of the tricolour in the form of cockades and ribbons, had taken to the streets of Florence to demonstrate in their thousands against Austrian rule. The Tuscan government resigned on 25 April, and two days later the crowds reassembled in the Piazza Maria Antonia, under tricolour flags and banners, to march to the Piazza della Signoria. At six o'clock in the evening of 27 April, the Austrian-nominated Grand Duke Leopoldo II left the city with his family, their carriages passing through the mostly silent crowds lining the Porta San Gallo and the via Bolognese. In Florence, it had been a peaceful, almost festive revolution. 'Not even a window broken,' remarked the awed French minister. Pen, entering the city, had hung out of the carriage windows shouting '*Viva!*' to the French troops camped in the Cascine. He had come from Rome equipped with tokens of dual nationalism — at one end of the Casa Guidi balcony he set up a French tricolour, at the other end he erected an Italian one. Between them he kept a smaller, portable flag that he intended to take out and wave from a carriage.[197]

Elizabeth's letter to Sarianna, written in May 1859, moved immediately from Pen's patriotic flags to Robert's political attitude:

> The melancholy point in all this is the dirt eaten and digested by England and the English. Now that I have exhausted myself with indignation and protestation, Robert has taken up the same note, which is a comfort. I would rather hear my own heart in his voice. Certainly it must be still more bitter for him than for me, seeing that he has more national predilections than I have, and has struggled longer to see differently. Not only the prestige, but the very respectability of England is utterly lost here — and nothing less is expected than her ultimate and open siding with Austria in the war. If she does, we shall wash our hands like so many Pilates, which will save us but not England.

By this account, Robert — whether to soothe Elizabeth, to keep the domestic peace within his own family, or from genuine distaste for England's possible adherence to Austrian imperial interests against Italian freedom — would seem to have ceded some of his natural sympathy for England's policies. In Rome, he had become friendly with

Odo Russell, later Lord Ampthill, a diplomat serving with the British Legation to Florence who maintained a residence in Rome and was popular in expatriate and Italian society there. Robert gleaned some inside news of political developments from Russell, though he made no comment in letters written at the time that give any indication of his true feelings towards England.

Elizabeth's excitement after the allied victories at Magenta and Solferino increased to the extent that she was hardly able to eat or sleep; she talked constantly and fervently and increased her daily dosage of opium. She was almost literally consumed by the holy cause of the war — she ate her heart out for Italy's freedom and gave what was left to Louis Napoleon and what she perceived to be his altruistic devotion to Italian liberty. When, on 8 July, at Villafranca, Louis Napoleon appeared to betray the trust she had placed in him by treating with the Austrians for peace, her entire, fantastical world collapsed, taking her with it. She wasn't alone. Young, strong Italian men, she heard, took to their beds, stricken by emotion. Elizabeth had been living on the reserves of what little energy she had recouped at Rome, insistent and fixed on the war that sustained her hopes and ideals. At Villafranca, as though he were her puppet master, Louis Napoleon cut the strings that held up her limbs and agitated her frail body.

For a moment, she doubted her hero. For a moment, she thought that all — after ten long years of brooding — was lost for Italy. Of the fatal date, 8 July, she wrote to Henrietta in the summer of 1859, 'I fell that day from the mountains of the moon where I had walked hand in hand with a beautiful Dream — now fled away. The grief, the despair overwhelmed us, none of you can imagine of. I *never will* forgive England for her part in these things — *never* — in helping Prussia and confeder- ated Germany, by a league of most inhuman selfishness, to prevent the perfecting of the greatest Deed given to men to do in these latter days.'

Elizabeth took to her bed for three weeks, worn out and ill. At the very end of July, Robert, on medical advice, was able to remove her to the cooler climate of the Villa Alberti at Marciano, a couple of miles outside Siena, for the rest of the summer. By then, almost in an attitude of denial, she had begun to reconsider and had contrived to forgive and exonerate Louis Napoleon, who, she saw now, had been beset by irresistible forces arrayed against him. His hand had been forced and his great intentions truncated by 'all the nations of the earth — selfish, inhuman, wicked'.[198] In the ground-floor rooms of the Villa Alberti, sitting quietly by its windows, and cooled by the winds that blew around the house, she wrote to Isa Blagden that 'I dreamed lately that I followed a mystic woman down a long suite of palatial rooms. She was in white, with a white mask, on her head the likeness of a crown. I knew she was Italy, but I couldn't see through the mask. All through my illness political dreams have repeated themselves, in inscrutable articles of peace and eternal provisional governments.' This fantastical dream introduced a welcome note of reality.

In a letter of 24 August 1859 to Fanny Haworth she seemed to rally from her despair: 'I believe entirely in the Emperor. He did at Villafranca what he could not help but do. Since then, he has simply changed the arena of the struggle; he is walking under the earth, but *straight* and to unchanged ends. This country, meanwhile, is conducting itself nobly. It is becoming worthy of a great nation.' By October, she had managed to reconcile herself, for the most part, to Villafranca. Writing at the end of that month to Mrs Ogilvy, she declared, 'Well, it is all past, I thank God. Now, if it were not for Venetia, whose future is not distinct, I should be almost glad for Villafranca. The war could not of itself have solved certain difficulties — and the peace has developed in these Italians the only qualities capable of solving them. How admirable have been the constancy, dignity, and energy of this people. What a ripening since 1848!' Remembering, perhaps, d'Azeglio's words to her, she noted, 'Afflictions do indeed instruct and mature men.'

The countryside around Siena was pretty enough, though not especially beautiful or otherwise distinguished, and the house was a 'wild, rough old villa',[199] but both countryside and house were pacifying and quiet. Pen drove cheerfully around on oxen carts between heaps of tomatoes, and his parents were well supplied with a piano, books, newspapers, and journals. They intended to hire a little carriage for local excursions during their two months' stay. Elizabeth, recovering — though she was at first unable to write letters or to walk more than three steps — wrote later in the summer to give these details to Henrietta, and to exclaim, 'Oh, I ought to give you an idea how good and devoted Robert has been to me through my illness — and it was wearing work at nights. I am very grateful to him, and may God enable me to prove it.' Writing to Mrs Eckley immediately on arrival on 2 August 1859, Robert remarked that Elizabeth had been eager to be removed from Florence. 'Let Ba but get well and strong, as I trust will soon be the case, and I shall be thankful to Siena indeed.' To Dr Grisanowski, the doctor who had attended Elizabeth in Florence and advised her removal to Siena, Robert wrote a report on 15 August: 'You will be glad to know that my wife is much better: her recovery seems slow, but all may be all [the surer] for that The cough is *gone* . . . She now takes her usual diet, in diminished quantity, and no medicine.'

The Storys had also taken a house outside Siena that summer, the Villa Belvedere. At a distance of only half a mile from the Villa Alberti, they were near neighbours. Writing to Charles Eliot Norton on 6 August 1859, William Wetmore Story reported the condition of his friends on arrival: 'He is well and full of life as ever, but Mrs Browning is sadly weak and ill . . . she cannot talk and every excitement must be avoided. When she came up she was carried in arms to the carriage and thence to the house, and looked like a dark shadow. Browning is in good spirits and has no fears now. Pen is well, and as I write I hear him laughing and playing with my boys and Edith on the terrace below my windows.' The Storys sat every evening with the Brownings 'on our lawn under the ilexes and cypresses and take our tea and talk until the moon has made the circuit of the quarter of the sky'. [200] The two families were often joined by Walter Savage Landor, now elderly and who — at Robert's request — had been staying since mid-July with the Storys at the Villa Belvedere. At the beginning of August he was installed 'in a pleasant little apartment in a villa hardly a stone's cast off. He will stay there,' Robert told Isa, 'till I have arranged everything with his English relatives.'[201]

Robert, preoccupied that summer of 1859 with the health of his wife and the management of his son (since Elizabeth could not give Pen her usual attention), as well as with sorting out the affairs of the octogenarian Landor, might have been forgiven some irritation and impatience. But he took it all pretty much in his stride, competently and for the most part uncomplainingly. Landor was on the run from a judgement against him the year before by an English court in the sum of one thousand pounds damages — the result of a libel suit brought by a clergyman's wife whom he had more or less accused of being a lesbian. He had fled from England to his wife and family in Fiesole, just outside Florence. Since he had pretty much walked out on them some thirty years before, they were disinclined to have him back and — after some bad-tempered disagreements — threw him out. The old man, possessed only of the clothes he stood up in and some small change in his pockets, walked back to Florence, for want of anywhere else to go, where he happened to meet Robert. Hearing his story, Robert took him in. Landor greatly admired him, and Robert was a long-standing admirer of Landor, whom he regarded as a great poet and whose poems, he said, had influenced his own works. Robert installed him temporarily in a hotel and inter-viewed Mrs Landor, who, with her children, remained adamantly opposed to having the old man back on any terms or to exerting them-selves for his benefit in any way whatsoever. A glass of water would be too much charity, declared Landor's daughter. Robert wrote to John Forster in London. Forster, he knew, was a friend and supporter of Landor's and could be in touch with Landor's brothers to arrange for funding. The brothers agreed willingly to pay, through Robert's agency, two hundred pounds a year for the rest of Landor's natural life.

Story, at first sight of the old man, decided that Landor's situation 'was the case of old Lear all over again; and when he descended from his carriage with his sparse white hair streaming out, and tottered into my house dazed in intellect with all he had suffered, I felt as if he were really Lear come back again'.[202] Charles Dickens famously rendered Landor rather too generously and too kindly in *Bleak House* in the character of Mr Boythorne — inventing a name that simultaneously implied a prickly personality and a perpetually childlike or adolescent personality. At Siena, Landor quickly recovered his spirits. His appetites returned, not only for large quantities of food — 'The plate was large, the eggs were four, He breakfasted — there was no more!'[203] — but for mischief. Towards the Storys, he was unimpeachably courteous, but on being moved to his own apartment he reportedly threw a dinner provided by his landlady, still hot on its plates, out of the window.[204] Since this was a regular habit of Landor's when the food served to him did not suit his taste, anyone rash enough to agree to take care of him was obliged to take his irascibility and its consequences into their calculations. He was eighty-three years old, and still liked nothing better than to nurse resentments and write inflammatory poems.

Story noted in his letter to Charles Eliot Norton that the latter-day Lear rose 'early in the morning, he reads and sometimes writes Latin alcaics, and since he has been here he has fired several bombs into Louis Napoleon's camp ... We hope still to have imaginary conversations from his pen, as we have real conversations from his mouth. We have found him most amiable and interesting, with certain streaks of madness running through his opinions, but frank and earnest of nature and a hater of injustice.' [205] Story was generous in hospitality and attitude, and Robert too found that Landor's 'three weeks stay at the Storys, who have treated him most kindly, enables one to dispose very summarily of the assurances of Mrs Landor that he is mad, ungovernable and so on'.[206] Robert was inclined to be over-indulgent towards Landor, whose long life had not been entirely blameless.

The ancient poet's lines against Louis Napoleon could of course be relied upon to irritate Elizabeth tremendously. In the peace and quiet of the villa, she had been writing poems of her own, quite opposed in their politics to those of Landor. Towards the end of her stay at the Villa Alberti, she wrote to Henry Fothergill Chorley that Landor 'is able to write awful Latin alcaics, to say nothing of hexameters and pentameters, on the wickedness of Louis Napoleon. Yes, dear Mr Chorley, poems which might appear in the "Athenaeum" without disclaimer and without injury to the reputation of that journal.' Landor moaned miserably over his exile from England, 'and I rather leant to sending him back', commented Elizabeth to Fanny Haworth.[207]

She was more wary than Robert of Landor's seeming good nature, apparent docility, and evident fondness for her husband: 'Robert always said that he owed more as a writer to Landor than to any contemporary. At present Landor is very fond of him; but I am quite prepared for his turning against us as he has turned against Forster, who has been so devoted for years and years. Only one isn't kind for what one gets by it, or there wouldn't be much kindness in the world.'[208] Forster's fault had been to attempt to restrain Landor from compounding the original libel, which had cost him a court judgement and his residence in England, with another. Even Robert, writing to Forster, Landor's biographer, eventually came around to the somewhat understated view that 'There is some inexplicable fault in his temper, whether natural or acquired, which seems to render him very difficult to manage.'[209]

The question of what to do with Landor on a permanent basis was solved at one inspired stroke by Robert when the Brownings returned to Florence in October. He suggested to Lily Wilson that he should live with her as a lodger. Robert would lend Wilson enough money to take a larger lodging-house, furnish a small set of rooms for Landor, and allow her thirty pounds a year for her trouble (Landor, he and Elizabeth acknowledged, would be a considerable trouble), as well as four pounds and ten shillings a month for Landor's keep. Wilson, considering the offer, decided to accept. This assured annual income, together with what she could make from other paying guests, would not only set her up in modest but secure circumstances, it would enable her to send for her elder son, Oreste, to live with her in Italy. She took a house in Oltranto, at what was then 93 via Nunziatini, now via della Chiese, backing on to the Church of the Carmine and not far from Casa Guidi, and Landor agreed to move in with her.

He continued his habit of throwing his dinner and most of the crockery out of the window when it displeased him, was easily provoked into tantrums, and generally could be relied upon to be disagreeable. Wilson earned her money the hard way. But her own mental state had been disturbed. When the Brownings had returned from Rome, Elizabeth had found Wilson to be perfectly mad. Jealous of Annunziata, whom she suspected of designs upon Ferdinando, separated from her husband and her first child, the one in Rome, the other in England, left alone with the second baby in her own house in Florence, she had resorted to a close reading of the Bible. What she took from her studies was a conviction that the world was about to end and that her two sons, Oreste and Pilade, were 'in the first fruits of the resurrection'. Her madness had moderated somewhat over the summer, but her hold on reality was still precarious. She tended to hallucinate visions; and churches, where she saw strange things, held a strong attraction for her.

The trouble of settling Landor comfortably delayed the Brownings' intention, on medical advice, to winter again in Rome, so that they did not leave Florence until 28 November. They moved reluctantly: Elizabeth had written to Sarianna from Siena to describe it as an 'undesirable expense . . . the taste for constant wanderings having passed away as much for me as for Robert'. Pen had preferred Paris to Rome, and Robert had proposed Palermo as a possible winter resort, though several considerations persuaded them against travelling to Sicily, including 'a rough sea to pass, and a risk of being made revolutionary mincemeat of at the end ... I should not fear at Rome,' Henrietta was assured by her sister.[210] Robert and Elizabeth, making the journey south with Pen, Ferdinando and Annunziata, were hampered this time by the business of transporting not only themselves but also a Sardinian pony they had bought at Siena for Pen (who was 'very coaxing') which travelled with them like a 'glorified Houyhnhnm' and required a second male servant to take care of him.[211] The war had emptied Rome, as it had also emptied Florence, of most of its visitors so that prices had fallen from the heights they had reached the previous year. 'Apartments here for which friends of ours paid forty pounds English the month last winter are going for fifteen or under — or rather not going — for nobody scarcely comes to take them.'[212] They settled on 3 December in rooms at 28 via del Tritone. This accommodation, *secondo piano*, consisted of two well-furnished salons, four sunny front rooms and a dining-room, all for a very reasonable fifty scudi.

At the Villa Alberti, Robert had grown a moustache to complement his beard, and Elizabeth remarked to Sarianna that he 'looks very picturesque. I thought I should not like the moustache, but I do. He is in very good looks altogether, though, in spite of remonstrances, he has given up walking before breakfast, and doesn't walk at any time half enough.' Elizabeth blamed herself: '*I* was in fault chiefly, because he both sate up at night with me and kept by me when I was generally ill in the mornings. So I oughtn't to grumble — but I do.' Robert was also putting on weight, filling out the middle-aged frame that had once been youthfully slim and elegant. He looked about in Rome for the usual 'dissipations' and found considerably fewer than he was used to. 'There is no Roman news, people are so scarce,' Elizabeth wrote to Fanny Haworth that winter. The Storys gave a ball, but for 'Italians, chiefly. We think of little but politics.'

It was politics that prompted an excursion to the premises of Castellani, the famous Roman jeweller, to admire two presentation swords which, as Elizabeth proudly wrote to Fanny Haworth, were 'subscribed for by twenty thousand Romans at a franc each and presented in homage and gratitude to Napoleon III and Victor Emmanuel'. The Pope, however, denounced 'all such givers of gifts as traitors to the [Holy] See' and the 'whole business had to be huddled up at the end'. The swords were to be packed up and tactfully hidden away. Before the vainglorious weapons disappeared from public view, the Brownings were picked up in a closed carriage one evening and driven to Castellani's, where they were received, Elizabeth reported to Fanny Haworth, 'most flatteringly as poets and lovers of Italy; were asked for autographs; and returned in a blaze of glory and satisfaction, to collapse (as far as I'm concerned) in a near approach to mortality. You see I can't catch a simple cold. All my bad symptoms came back. Suffocations, singular heart-action, cough tearing one to atoms.'

Robert, worried about Elizabeth's health, blamed himself, in a letter of January 1860 to Isa Blagden, for her relapse: 'all the evil came of a silly visit to Castellani's . . . I urged her to go, like a fool I was, and she caught cold on the stairs, here or there, — all which is pleasant to think of.' He was at a loose end socially in Rome, with nothing much to occupy his time and mind, forever plagued by letters of complaint about Isa Blagden and Lily Wilson from Landor and by letters from Isa, who was living at Casa Guidi in their absence, telling him about difficulties with Landor, whom she visited regularly in order to keep an eye on the old man. He was terrorizing Wilson, who in turn continued to have troubles of her own — her religious mania seemed no better. Robert wrote to Isa on 1 January 1860: 'We are grieved, indeed, about Wilson's illness and anxious to hear — by today's post, I hope, how she is now. That hysterical affection always possesses her poor foolish brain after looking steadily at pictures, and then she becomes aware of presentiments and so on. I wrote to her before your note arrived. I suppose Mr Landor plagues and frightens her: a grasshopper's is the stouter soul of the two. Mr Landor wrote a long sheetful to me yesterday, with rather fewer groans in it than usual.'

Hatty Hosmer had been ill in bed in Rome at the end of December, but revived and called with Charlotte Cushman to visit the Brownings in the evening of New Year's day. Robert renewed acquaintance with the sculptor John Gibson and his friend Penry Williams, a Welsh artist. To Isa, Robert described the familiar sight of 'dear old Gibson, blue velvet cap and all' and his work in progress, a tinted statue of Hebe. A certain mischievous pleasure informed Elizabeth's account to Fanny Haworth of Robert's falling in with a certain 'Mr Hazard, a spiritualist who believes everything, walks and talks with spirits, and impresses Robert with a sense of veracity, which is more remarkable. I like the man much ... Certainly enough Robert met him and conversed with him, and came back to tell me what an intelligent and agreeable new American acquaintance he had made, without knowing that he was Hazard the spiritualist, rather famous in his department.'

The young English artist Val Prinsep was in Rome that winter with the Pre-Raphaelite painter Edward Burne-Jones, who had been provided with an introduction to the Brownings by Rossetti. Prinsep confided to Mrs Orr an account of two high-spirited nights out with Robert at an *Osteria* in the Monte quarter of the city, where two rival Roman poets had met to challenge each other:

> Gigi (the host) had furnished a first-rate dinner, and his usual tap of excellent wine. (*Vino del Popolo* he called it.) The *Osteria* had filled; the combatants were placed opposite each other on either side of a small table on which stood two *mezzi* — long glass bottles holding about a quart apiece. For a moment the two poets eyed each other like two cocks seeking an opportunity to engage. Then through the crowd a stalwart carpenter, a constant attendant of Gigi's, elbowed his way. He leaned over the table with a hand on each shoulder, and in a neatly turned couplet he then addressed the rival bards. 'You two,' he said, 'for the honour of Rome, must do your best, for there is now listening to you a great Poet from England.' Having said this, he bowed to Browning, and swaggered back to his place in the crowd, amid the applause of the on-lookers.[213]

Describing the second occasion, Prinsep wrote that he and Burne-Jones were dining with Robert and William Story. A little orchestra consisting of mandolins, two guitars, and a lute entertained them.

> While they were playing with great fervour the Hymn to Garibaldi — an air strictly forbidden by the Papal Government, three blows at the door resounded through the *Osteria*. The music stopped in a moment. I saw Gigi was very pale as he walked down the room. There was a short parley at the door. It opened, and a sergeant and two Papal gendarmes marched

solemnly up to the counter from which drink was supplied. There was a dead silence while Gigi supplied them with large measures of wine, which the gendarmes leisurely imbibed. Then as solemnly they marched out again, with their heads well in the air, looking neither to the right nor the left ... When the door was shut the music began again; but Gigi was so earnest in his protestations, that my friend Browning suggested we should get into carriages and drive to see the Coliseum by moonlight ... In after-years, Browning frequently recounted with delight this night march. 'We drove down the Corso in two carriages,' he would say. 'In one were our musicians, in the other we sat. Yes! and the people all asked, "who are these who make all this parade?" At last some one said, "Without doubt these are the fellows who won the lottery," and everybody cried, "Of course these are the lucky men who have won." '[214]

Odo Russell, too, was in Rome. He had paid a visit to the Brownings during the summer, staying a couple of nights with them at the Villa Alberti, where he managed partially to appease Elizabeth despite her normal allergic reaction to English diplomats, politicians, and correspondents for the English press. It was in Russell's favour that he had 'the merit of being very appreciative of Robert — besides being, on his own part, acute and liberal (as liberal as the English can be) and extremely refined and amiable in manners.'[215] But he was less meritorious in his professional aspect: Elizabeth had seized her opportunity to complain directly to Russell ('flying at once at my guest like an exhausted blood-hound') about the ill behaviour of the English in respect of the war, to which he had mildly replied that at least the government wasn't doing much harm and that it had little power to do anything at all. Elizabeth said she wasn't talking about the government, which was as mischievous as any other, in or out of power, but about England generally. To which Russell replied that it was 'too true that England was perfectly without feeling for foreign nations'. On this point, Elizabeth reported to Henrietta, she was silent. She and Odo Russell were agreed. 'But the difference is that he admits it with a smooth accent and countenance, while I revolt against the fact, and call it intolerably hideous, a national sin crying out for judgement.'

Elizabeth had been preparing just such a judgement in poetry since the summer. To Isa Blagden, Robert wrote in January 1860 that 'Ba's proofs are on the road and, I expect, will arrive tomorrow: she sent off two additional poems, since the first consignment. Chapman don't say a word beyond hoping, for her sake, that the apartments in the Castle of St Angelo are comfortable ... Ba don't care, — and I think she has a right to say her say.' The prospects of imprisonment for political provocation in the Castello S. Angelo in Rome, or the Tower of London for that matter, were unlikely impediments to Elizabeth's determination to express herself forcibly about European politics in *Poems Before Congress*, published by Edward Chapman in London in March 1860.

Her letter to Mrs Martin of 29 December 1859, in response to charges that Elizabeth had put herself out of her 'natural place', sharply questioned what that natural place might be according to God and circumstances. She declared her love for Italy and France, and certainly, she said, 'I love England'; but she had broken through the narrow parochialism ('Little Pedlingtonism') of England, which she ranked as 'among the most immoral nations in respect to her foreign politics', and she was not about to exchange that larger view even for Italian *campanalismo*. Writing to Mrs Jameson in February 1860 to tell her of her 'thin slice of a wicked book', she admitted that everyone would hate her for it, but she urged Mrs Jameson, even if she should say 'it's mad, and bad, and sad', to concede 'that somebody did it who meant it, thought it, felt it, throbbed it out with heart and brain, and that she holds it for truth in conscience and not in partisanship'.

Her book had originally been intended as a joint publication with Robert, who had begun a poem about Napoleon but had torn it up or burned it. 'Robert and I began to write on the Italian question together, and our plan was (Robert's own suggestion!) to publish jointly. When I showed him my ode on Napoleon he observed that I was gentle to England in comparison to what he had been, but after Villafranca (the Palmerston ministry having come in) he destroyed his poem and left me alone, and I determined to stand alone.' He had made no attempt to urge Elizabeth to tear up her poems too. He thought, as he always did, that it was important that she should freely express her own opinions. His only measure was artistic: 'Robert would not have let me print what he considered below my own mark', she told her brother George.

Reviews of the eight poems comprising *Poems Before Congress* were pretty much as Elizabeth had anticipated. The English could hardly be expected to react favourably to an ode proclaiming the greatness of Napoleon III. The toughest toad they refused to swallow was the final poem, 'A Curse For a Nation', which Elizabeth said she had intended as a denunciation of slavery and an indictment of America where it was still practised. Henry Fothergill Chorley, in the *Athenaeum*, misinterpreted the 'curse' as applying to England and very strongly censured the poem, by an English writer, as improper and unpatriotic — a 'malediction against England'. When Elizabeth wrote to point out the injustice of his mistake, he grudgingly acknowledged that he might have been wrong but that he had put a natural interpretation on her words and sentiments. However, the damage had been done — to Elizabeth's discredit.

To Isa Blagden, at the end of March 1860, Elizabeth wrote that the poem had already been published in America and had only been included in the book at Robert's insistence. 'Robert was *furious* about the "Athenaeum;" no other word describes him, and I thought that both I and Mr Chorley would perish together, seeing that even the accusation (such a one!) made me infamous, it seemed . . . I never saw Robert so enraged about a criticism. He is better now, let me add.' Robert was showing symptoms, indeed, of that developing capacity for outrage which was to become a familiar aspect of his character. To Isa Blagden on 28 April 1860 he wrote to say, 'Chorley's cat-scratch was offensive from the creature's spitting at the same time.' He didn't object to honest reviews, but so long as there was no lying, he was beginning rather 'to enjoy the practice of "knagging" myself'. In June Elizabeth wrote to her brother George, who did not approve of the tone of his sister's latest volume, to tell him that 'Chapman junior says that I have not hurt myself by the Congress poems which promise to go soon into a second edition, and which people praise for "pluck".' The length and weight of abuse she had been accorded by the English had done more good for sales of her controversial book than harm to her reputation as a poet. By association with renewed interest in her name, sales of *Aurora Leigh* also increased and the work went into its fifth edition.

Robert's reluctance to publish a poem about Italy at this time was probably due partly to his disinclination to be an occasional poet. He rarely wrote to order (he refused requests to publish single poems in magazines, journals and newspapers) or instantaneously on the great political or social issues of the day. The Laureateship, even had it been offered to Robert, would not have suited his temperament. An obligation to write in the heat of the moment in a patriotic vein on significant public events and occasions would have caused him more misery than pleasure.

In April 1854 he had contributed, exceptionally, as a special favour, a short poem, 'The Twins', to a pamphlet inspired by Arabella Barrett for the benefit of the Ragged Schools. The sixteen-page pamphlet, entitled *Two Poems*, also contained a poem by Elizabeth, 'A Plea for the Ragged Schools of London'. The Brownings additionally contributed the cost of paper and publication by Chapman and Hall of the pamphlet, which sold disappointingly and made no money for the cause. 'The Twins', which was included in *Men and Women*, took as its theme '"Give" and "It-shall-be-given-unto-you"'. It was based on a passage from Martin Luther's *Table-Talk* and did not in fact directly address the subject of the social cause that had inspired the charity for whose benefit it was published.

Nevertheless, to judge by Elizabeth's remarks about the original idea of joint publication, Robert was keenly interested in public events and paid them close attention. The Brownings took in the Tuscan *Nazione* and the *Monitore*, as well as Galignani's *Messenger*, and shared the published news with half a dozen Tuscan expatriate friends of Ferdinando's who came to the via del Tritone to read the *Monitore*. They came secretly 'for fear of being convicted through some spy of reading such a thing and prayed to come to his house to read it ... We keep a sort of café in Rome, observe, and your "Monitore" is necessary to us,' Elizabeth wrote to Isa, who smuggled the paper out of Florence for them.[216]

On the whole, Robert was as fervid for Italian liberty as Elizabeth and strongly opposed to English Tory policy. These sentiments did not imply an automatic, corresponding admiration for Louis Napoleon. Though he destroyed the poem he had intended to write about 'the Italian question', he began to think of another, a long monologue based on the character of the Emperor Napoleon III, which was eventually to be published in mid-December 1871 as *Prince Hohenstiel-Schwangau,*

Saviour of Society. Robert himself noted in a letter of 1 January 1872 to Edith Story that 'I really wrote — that is, conceived the poem, twelve years ago in the Via del Tritone — in a little handbreadth of prose, — now yellow with age and Italian ink, — which I breathed out into this full-blow bubble in a couple of months this autumn that is gone — thinking it fair to do so.'

By April, Elizabeth and Robert were better able to judge the English reaction to *Poems Before Congress* and to adopt a positive, less defensive attitude. 'Dear,' she wrote to Isa Blagden that month, 'the abuse of the press is the justification of the poems.' Robert had called on Odo Russell, who had said to him, 'it's extraordinary, the sensation your wife's book has made ... The offence has been less in the objections to England than in the praise of Napoleon.' To Isa, Elizabeth then went on to comment on Richard Monckton Milnes, who had 'said a good thing when he was asked lately in Paris what, after all, you English wanted. "*We want,*" he answered, "*first, that the Austrians should beat you French thoroughly; next we want that the Italians should be free, and then we want them to be very grateful to us for doing nothing at all towards it.*" "This," concluded Russell, "sums up the whole question." Mark, he is very English, but he can't help seeing what lies before him, having quick perceptions, moreover. These men have no courage. Milnes, for instance, keeps his sarcasm for Paris, and in England supports his rifle club and all Parliamentary decencies.'

Lady Elgin died in the spring of 1860. Elizabeth wrote to Sarianna in March that year to say, 'It is impossible to have a regret for dear Lady Elgin. She has been imprisoned here under double chains so long.' A more serious shock was the death of Mrs Jameson on 17 March, at the age of sixty-six, 'from bronchitis ending in paralysis of the brain', as Robert reported it to Isa Blagden. He was annoyed that Mrs Jameson's daughter Gerardine, now married to a Mr Macpherson, had written directly to Elizabeth: 'such a note ought to have been addressed to me (I was out unfortunately)'. A third blow was the discovery that Sophia Eckley had betrayed her friendship with Elizabeth.

On 19 April 1863, in a letter to Isa, Robert wrote of John Jarves that he 'is without light inside or outside: there is some *hole* in his head, break in his moral constitution, that *does* for him: I always considered him to be the nearer madness ... Mrs E, devilishness.' Mrs E. is usually identified as Mrs Eckley. Robert's comments on Jarves' intense devotion to spiritualism, akin to madness, is so closely associated with Sophia Eckley's 'devilishness' in this letter that her own involvement in spiritualism is presumably the subject of Robert's damning use of the word. It has always been supposed that Mrs Eckley had been exposed at this time as a fraudulent medium, but others have suggested, more improbably, that she may have been found out in an extra-marital affair. Either proposition is likely, though neither can be proved with any certainty. Pen Browning refers only to his mother's betrayal by a friend in his letter to *The Times Literary Supplement*.

It is curious, however, that during their time from 1859–60 in Rome, the Eckleys, though they lived in the same street for six months, had kept their distance from the Brownings, with Sophia pretending to be devoting herself to scuplture. Referring to the rupture between Elizabeth and Sophia Eckley, Robert later commented to Isa, in March 1868, that 'When Mrs Eckley found herself discovered, she never made an effort to recover her place in Ba's liking — not to say love, still less esteem: she just asked leave to come and see her sometimes, — by way of hiding the separation from people. Ba wrote her *one* letter, which I read, — and which, depend on it, don't figure in the book [of letters from Elizabeth to Mrs Eckley which the latter intended to publish] as "finis" — and then, for the next year and a half, not a word: for "Where's Agnes?" — disguised in the circumstances for my sake — who always said, "For the husband's sake, — and because *you* really deserve some punishment in the matter, don't make an explosion."'

'Where's Agnes?' was Elizabeth's bitter poem against Mrs Eckley. Robert had persuaded Elizabeth to write of an Agnes rather than a Sophia to spare David Eckley's blushes, and he apportioned some blame to Elizabeth herself in the business. Whatever Sophia Eckley's offence may have been, Elizabeth had been credulous. That she had allowed herself to be deceived was as much a moral fault as the deceiver's own moral failure. To Fanny Haworth, Elizabeth wrote of Sophia Eckley, 'I don't think she knows what truth is, and why it should be cared for. In order to conciliate me she says she has given up her mediumship!! "Because mediums are always suspected."' And to Isa Blagden, Elizabeth commented, 'I feel inclined to grind my teeth and stamp. She sticks, dear, like treacle … once I praised the sweetness — now I feel very sick at the adhesiveness ... if she said she hated me how much easier I should feel.'[217]

'Robert deserves no reproaches,' wrote Elizabeth to Fanny Haworth on 18 May 1860, 'for he has been writing a good deal this winter — working at a long poem which I have not seen a line of, and producing short lyrics which I *have* seen, and may declare worthy of him.' It is difficult to resist the conclusion that Robert, happy to show his shorter poems to Elizabeth, deliberately concealed the long one from her. If such is the case, then its subject can only have been spiritualism and its title, 'Mr Sludge, "The Medium"'. Though the character of Sludge is readily identifiable as being based on Daniel Dunglas Home, who was never conclusively exposed as a trickster, the direct factor that instigated Robert's writing that winter was, more likely than not, Mrs Eckley's 'devilishness'.

The Brownings left Rome on 4 June and arrived five days later in Florence. In *William Wetmore Story and His Friends*, Henry James reproduces a letter of 8 June 1860 from Robert to William Story on the ground that, 'There attaches to the letter something of the charm of a document on the old romantic method of progression at a date when such documents were becoming rare. This is one of the last of them.' Since neither James's biography nor the letter are now readily accessible to the common reader, it would seem a pity not to publish it again here, not only for the reason that James suggests but as an example of Robert's bald and vigorous epistolary style. He writes from Siena, on the way to Florence from Rome:

> I said I would tell you how we found things and fared on the Orvieto road. We arrived at four yesterday afternoon and preferred resting here for four-and-twenty hours to going forward at once. We travelled 48 or 50 miles delightfully the first day and reached Viterbo early. Next morning we began the new part of the journey — continued 30 miles at a stretch and got to Orvieto through a pleasant placid country (much work of Luca Signorelli at the cathedral). On Wednesday we advanced to Ficulli; but for Ba's fatigue it would have been better to push on to Città della Pieve, where a fresco of Perugino's is worth the trouble of a longer journey and the comfort of the inn

would have been much greater. But it was our choice to divide the way so. We reached Chiusi early, having travelled all day through exquisite scenery. We felt the heat — not intolerably, however, nor before this third day, and there was never any dust to mention. We left Chiusi at nine, or later, yesterday (I got up early every morning and saw sights for about an hour or two), and reached Sinalunga by one o'clock. Had there been an endurable inn Ba might have rested sufficiently to proceed to Florence; but she was forced to choose between the kitchens and the carriage, and preferred the latter — so here we stopped, as I began by saying. We were perfectly served throughout, the *vetturino* caring for all things, and his charge for the three days and a half amounts to 19 scudi, 2 pauls. I paid the service myself; only this was not much. The end is, we have had a delightful journey which Ba has borne very well on the whole, though the whole business is far more fatiguing than by the short stages on the Perugia road.

In Florence, Elizabeth reported to Fanny Haworth on 16 June: 'We find Wilson well. Mr Landor also. He had thrown a dinner out of the window only once, and a few things of the kind, but he lives in a chronic state of ingratitude to the whole world except Robert, who waits for his turn.' She admired the old man's 'beautiful sea-foam of a beard . . . all in a curl and white bubblement of beauty' and was interested to hear that he had 'quite given up thinking of a future state — he had *had* thoughts of it once, but that was very early in life'. Seymour Kirkup, deafer than ever, had been trying 'in vain to convert him to the spiritual doctrine. Landor laughs so loud in reply that Kirkup hears him.'

It was perhaps just as well that the Brownings had not gone to Sicily at the end of 1859, though they might have sat in their usual fashion on a balcony to observe another revolution at first hand. On 14 May 1860 General Giuseppe Garibaldi and his thousand men landed in Sicily. Garibaldi, an Italian patriot who had been born in Nice, had been dismayed by the decision of the people of Savoy and Nice, who had voted in February, to be ruled by France rather than accede with the other Italian states to the Kingdom of Piedmont. He sailed with his supporters to Sicily three months later with the intention of overthrowing the Kingdom of Naples and the Two Sicilies. Rapidly taking possession of the island, he sailed for the mainland and on 6 September 1860 succeeded in driving the King of Naples, Francis II, from his capital to Gaeta. Elizabeth was entranced and adopted Garibaldi immediately into her pantheon of heroes. To Sarianna, she wrote in rodomontade in June 1860, 'We are talking and dreaming Garibaldi just now in great anxiety. Scarcely since the world was a world has there been such a feat of arms. All modern heroes grow pale before him.'

In early July, the Brownings returned to Siena, to the Villa Alberti, for the summer months of 1860. The Storys were there again too, a mile away in a neighbouring villa. Isa Blagden took a small 'cabin' nearby, and Landor was transported from Florence to a cottage 'hard by in the lane'[218] where he was looked after by Wilson, who was allowed to bring along her little son Pilade and to be with Ferdinando on a regular basis. Almost immediately came news that Henrietta was seriously ill. As Robert later learned, she was suffering from cancer of the womb.

The thought of Henrietta's pain was an agonizing hurt to Elizabeth. She herself had more often suffered acute discomfort than chronic pain, but she had seen John Kenyon staggering and heard him crying out in agony just before his death, and that memory may now have supplemented her vivid imaginings. To George Barrett, Elizabeth wrote on 6 September 1860: 'The thought of that pain is the worst thought I have to bear — If anything here ever approaches with me to a pleasurable feeling . . . if I look at the blue hills or hear Penini's musical chatter or get news even of our triumphant Italy, — instantly comes the idea . . . "My precious Henrietta is in great pain at this moment perhaps."' It was, however, out of the question that Elizabeth could go to England to be with her sister.

Her inability to go to Henrietta, even if only to hold her hand, depressed Elizabeth in a more general sense: she began to think more morbidly of her own mortality and to reflect dispiritedly on herself as a burden and hindrance to those she loved. In such a frame of mind, she wrote to Fanny Haworth on 25 August 1860: 'my "destiny" has always been to be entirely useless to people I should like to help (except to my little Pen sometimes in pushing him through his lessons, and even so the help seems doubtful, scholastically speaking, to Robert!) and to have only power at the end of my pen, and for the help of people

I don't care for. At moments lately, thanks from a stranger for this or that have sounded ghastly to me who can't go to smooth a pillow for my own darling sister.' To Sarianna she would write: 'I know my place; I am only good for a drag chain.'

The Brownings returned to Florence on 11 October. Though Elizabeth had no inclination to leave Casa Guidi again, Robert preferred that they should. 'As for me, I do as he likes,' Elizabeth wrote to George on or about 11 November. 'Robert says it is a duty for me to go to Rome.' Besides being in touch with George about Henrietta, it had become necessary to correspond with him on a matter of business. Joseph Arnould and Henry Fothergill Chorley had been appointed, fourteen years before, as trustees of the Brownings' marriage settlement that had been negotiated with Mr Barrett by John Kenyon. Since he had been appointed to the Supreme Court of Bombay in 1859, Sir Joseph Arnould, 'too busy and distant', now wished to retire from the duty. Robert and Elizabeth suggested that George should take Sir Joseph's place.

In the event, Arnould agreed to continue, but his proposed resignation had prompted Elizabeth to write firmly to George on 2 April 1861. She indignantly reviewed the history of the matter: 'When the first Deed was made fourteen years ago, I protested strongly, and yielded only to a representation of dear Mr Kenyon that I had no right to put my husband in a false position and to expose him to the shadow of a suspicion even for a limited time.' (The suspicion being that Robert was marrying for Elizabeth's money.) The terms of the deed of settlement, and far more that it should have been required in the first place, still rankled with Elizabeth. She took her opportunity to condemn it unreservedly and to point out its perfect uselessness in the light of her marriage to Robert, whose character in respect of money had proved unimpeachable. The letter dramatically but fairly sums up this aspect of their years together in Italy:

> I yielded — agreeing that the advantage we lost by the Deed, (being simply a money-advantage) was not worth that other risk — I point out to you, however, that we suffered for a great many years pecuniary disadvantage from the restrictions of the

Deed. We had to live on half the small income at best possible to us — and how much we were pinched and ground down through Robert's resolution to keep out of debt, none of you perhaps ever knew — If Mr Kenyon had not forced on us his hundred a year after three years, when Pen was born, the straight [*sic*] would have been increased.

Since his bequest, all this is of course altered — Through our prudence in not increasing the circle of our expences in proportion to the enlarged income, we never want to think of money — which is an infinite blessing to people like us — We are free to move our hands, and to please ourselves . . . Then — after fourteen years, we are above suspicion. Agreed that Robert will probably survive me, — agreed even, on my side, that he may remarry . . . being a man . . . nay 'being subject to like passions' as other men, he *may* commit some faint show of bigamy — who knows? But what is absolutely impossible for him is that under any temptation or stress of passion, he *could* sacrifice what belongs to Pen to another — Draw up the strictest legal document by the help of a confederation of lawyers, and I would rather trust Robert. Your deed may have a flaw in it after all — 'You can drive a carriage and four through any Act of Parliament!' But for Robert to fail *here* is IMPOSSIBLE. He has that exaggerated idea of virtues connected with money, which distinguishes the man from the woman. He is *rigid* about such things — I know him. He is far more capable of committing murder, than of the slightest approach to pecuniary indelicacy. That is beyond the circle of his temptations, be sure.

The end of all this is to prove to you how entirely motiveless it would be as an act of folly, if *I* consented to restrictions of the kind you hint at.

If you have the goodness, dearest George, to accept any trust for us, you will find everything laid as straight, and smooth for your hand as you could desire, — poets though we be — Property in Italy as in England, will be left clear — The worst we do is add to the principal — We had a temptation towards buying an exquisite villa close to Florence last autumn, but resisted on the ground of doubt whether the winters were not over-cold for me — To resist on the ground of the money's being tied up, would have been considerably more mortifying.

On 2 April 1861 Robert himself wrote to George to say that Arnould had agreed to continue his trusteeship and to confirm all that Elizabeth had said in her letter. Kenyon had suggested the deed of settlement, and so it had been done. After discussing some points and principles, Robert stated that 'We shall live in Italy always, and the convenience of our present arrangement causes us to bless ourselves every quarter day at least ... All that we save, after necessary expenditure, I invest and add to our capital, from which in fifteen years not a sixpence has been subtracted. The whole of this will go to Ba and her child after my death ... I repeat, that I leave Ba and my child not only all *her* money proper, in the law's eye, but all that I have got or saved or (in the exercise of an economy I pride myself upon) shall save or get: nobody else in the world has a fraction of a claim to it, and — for other causes or of incitements to injustice in testamentary dispositions, I shall only say that Ba and I know each other for time and, I dare trust, eternity: — We differ *toto coelo* (or rather, *inferno*) as to spirit-rapping, we quarrel sometimes about politics, and estimate people's characters with enormous difference, but, in the main, we *know* each other, I say.'

These two letters to George are more than statements of private moral principles in the daily conduct of financial affairs: they strongly and confidently affirm a broad and lasting mutual love and trust at a difficult time, a time when many objective observers might have considered the Browning marriage to be in decline. In any event, the fifteen-year association between a younger, healthy, sociable husband and an older, invalidish, reclusive wife was a wonder in itself. The Brownings themselves frankly acknowledged points on which they significantly differed day by day, but in terms of eternity these temporal squabbles hardly mattered. At the heart of the marriage lay a trustful familiarity strengthened by a constant communication. As Elizabeth remarked to Sarianna, 'the peculiarity of our relation is, that even when he's displeased with me, he thinks aloud with me and can't stop himself'.[219]

Robert and Elizabeth talked with one another and laughed together all the time; they listened to one another, they paid the most detailed attention to one another; and underlying all that talk was a solid foundation of mutual love and — no less enduring — mutual respect and a sense of what was right in the world at large. An offence to one was an offence to the other, in even the most minor matters. Writing to Isa Blagden on 27 December 1860, Robert referred to his current preoccupation with a sense of being short-changed by a woman in Florence who had engaged, on a commercial basis, to send books to the Brownings in Rome. 'Observe I tell you plainly, I don't think she treats Ba properly: we pay all she asks, and never get new books nor a quarter the good things that you do, for instance. I am always strict upon *right* in this world, and let generosity and all its derivative virtues and graces show themselves or keep quiet as they please — provided justice is done in the first place: and one doesn't find *that* (like blackberries and "decided genius") at one's right hand and left.'

The Brownings, after arranging with Isa Blagden that she would stay for the winter in the warmth of Casa Guidi, left Florence on 18 November 1860. After 'a wretched journey'[220] they settled in Rome for the winter at 126 via Felice 'in sunny rooms', as Elizabeth described them in a letter to Mrs Ogilvy in January 1861, 'too high up, but it is quiet ... which I care for chiefly.' Henrietta died on 23 November, though letters telling them the news were delayed until the first days of December. Robert had known that Henrietta's condition was more serious than some optimistic bulletins in October had led Elizabeth to hope and believe, and he had hurried her out of Florence before the inevitable could happen and prevent her, in her grief, from setting out for Rome. All letters from England were read by Robert before they were given to Elizabeth — 'She had the firmness to desire me to do so,' Robert told George.

Robert's letter also reassured George that Elizabeth 'has borne it, on the whole, as well as I should have thought possible — but the wounds in that heart never heal altogether, tho' they may film over. God bless her.' To Isa Blagden, Robert wrote on 8 December 1861 that 'Ba continues to suffer acutely, but not more than was to [be] expected, nor as to give serious apprehension at all — for she is good, and content to be "done for" — made to try and eat a little, listen to talking, attend to Pen, and so on.'

Elizabeth did not leave the rooms in the via Felice that winter.

Robert was 'very good in keeping people off,' she told Mrs Ogilvy in January 1861, 'so that I have had repose, and have learnt to live again, as we all must. To break out of the narrow personal life into the larger and higher, is the only secret of satisfaction in this world — and I have begun again to do it and to work a little in the healthy way.' To Fanny Haworth, the previous autumn, she had written of herself as 'very much in my corner, and very quiet . . . gloomy lionesses with wounded paws don't draw the public.' She consoled herself with writing maladroitly and self-interestedly to Surtees Cook to contest the extent of the loss both had suffered, saying her attachment to Henrietta had preceded his, suggesting arrangements he should consider for his children's sake, and making very little allowance for depth of grief and loss as distinct from width. Her Barrett egotism, her abstract concentration on arranging matters for family members without much reference to their own wishes, now and again got in the way of perfect sympathy for the feelings of others.

She turned again to spiritualism for comfort, though now even that faith wavered a little. To Mrs Martin she wrote in December 1860 that, 'One must live; and the only way is to look away from oneself into the larger and higher circle of life in which the merely personal grief or joy forgets itself . . . I believe that love in its most human relations is an eternal thing. I do believe it, only through inconsistency and weakness I falter . . . when the tender past came back to me day by day, I have dropped down before it as one inconsolable.' Where pious belief in the eternal failed to rally her spirits, practical politics supplied the deficit. As well as dwelling minutely on the European situation, she had begun to extend her range to the American Civil War — hardly to be avoided, in respect of moral and political principle and in the fact that many of the Brownings' American friends were deeply concerned with it.

In reality, politics had virtually kept Elizabeth alive. Her letters to her diminished company of correspondents throughout Henrietta's illness had dwelt less on personal matters than on great events and great persons. She had partly recognized this tendency during the summer at the Villa Alberti, rationalizing it to George: 'I put down something, not to send you an echo of your own sadness — and nothing is at hand but this';[221] and to Mrs Ogilvy: 'Private cares have been broken through for me by the press of public events on all sides.'[222] The energetic life of her son, too, diverted her attention and she displaced some of her cares into his education. Pen was being taught Latin by a young abbé, Robert was continuing to teach the boy music and arithmetic, and she herself helped to prepare his lessons and watched Pen's progress with her usual enchanted benevolence. He went out riding on his Sardinian pony and looked 'very rosy and well'.[223]

Robert, in Rome, also sought distraction. When he had assured himself that Elizabeth was able to withstand the intense emotions following Henrietta's death, he took up clay modelling at Story's studio. To Fanny Haworth, in the autumn of 1860, Elizabeth wrote to comment on Robert's novel pursuit and to contrast it with her own less active condition. 'He has copied already two busts, the Young Augustus and his Psyche, and is engaged on another, enchanted with his new trade, working six hours a day. In the evening he generally goes out as a bachelor — free from responsibility of crinoline — while I go early to bed, too happy to have him a little amused. In Florence he never goes anywhere, you know; even here this winter he has had too much gloom about him by far. But he looks entirely well — as does Penini. I am weak and languid. I struggle hard to live on. I wish to live just as long as and no longer than to grow in the soul.'

G. K. Chesterton regarded this apprenticeship in the plastic arts as significant to Robert's work as a poet. He was a 'strenuous amateur' of 'half a hundred things at which he can never have even for a moment expected to succeed'. On the general principle of amateurism, which Chesterton generously took to be informed by passion rather than tepidity:

> There is a large army of educated men who can talk art with artists; but Browning could not merely talk art with artists — he could talk shop with them. Personally he may not have known enough about painting to be more than a fifth-rate painter, or enough about the organ to be a sixth-rate organist. But there are, when all is said and done, some things which a fifth-rate painter knows which a first-rate art critic does not know; there are some things which a sixth-rate organist knows that a first-rate judge of music does not know. And these were the things that Browning knew ... he made himself to a very

considerable extent a technical expert in painting, a technical expert in sculpture, a technical expert in music ... he was precisely in the position, with a touch of greater technical success, of the admirable figure in [Robert Louis] Stevenson's story who said, 'I can play the fiddle nearly well enough in the orchestra of a penny gaff, but not quite.' The love of Browning for Italian art, therefore, was anything but an antiquarian fancy; it was the love of a living thing.[224]

Besides industrious application to art, Robert's was again a familiar face in and around Rome. In January 1861, Elizabeth wrote to Isa Blagden that 'Robert came home this morning between three and four. A great ball at Mrs Hooker's — magnificent, he says. All the princes in Rome (and even cardinals) present. The rooms are splendid, and the preparations were in the best taste. The princess Ruspoli (a Buonaparte) appeared in the tricolor. She is most beautiful, Robert says.' Her husband, in Elizabeth's estimation, was himself looking most beautiful — she and Robert had had their photographs taken, the 'sepia-coloured thing of last year' having been unsatisfactory: nobody liked it. By contrast, the newer pictures were definitive: 'we had even resolved (as we couldn't hope to grow younger) to stand or fall with posterity by this production. "Ecco!"'[225]

Sarianna, having inspected these marvels of photographic portraiture, had commented too tartly that Robert looked like an *épicier* — a sisterly remark that Elizabeth was at pains to refute very particularly: 'The clipping of the side whiskers, which are very grey, is an advantage, and as to the hair, it is by no means cut short. "Like an *épicier*?" No indeed. The *épicier* is bushy and curly about the ears (see an example in "Galignani"), and moreover will keep the colour of the curl "if he dyes for it" — an extremity to which Robert and I will never be driven — having too much the fear of attentive friends and affectionate biographers before our eyes.'

This letter to Sarianna, though lively, lightly witty, and amusingly gossipy, reveals Elizabeth's worries for herself and Robert one by one; she provides virtually a check list for her sister-in-law:

Robert is looking particularly well and young — in spite of all lunar lights in his hair ... He is not thin or worn, as I am —

no indeed — and the women adore him everywhere far too much for decency. In my own opinion he is infinitely handsomer and more attractive than when I saw him first, sixteen years ago . . . And as to the modelling — well, I told you that I grudged a little the time from his own particular art — and that is true. He has given a great deal of time to anatomy with reference to the expression of form, and the clay is only the new medium which takes the place of drawing. Also, Robert is peculiar in his ways of work as a poet . . . Robert waits for an inclination — works by fits and starts — he can't do otherwise he says. Then reading hurts him. As long as I have known him he has not been able to read long at a time . . . The consequence of which is that he wants occupation and that an active occupation is salvation to him with his irritable nerves, saves him from ruminating bitter cud, and from the process which I call beating his dear head against the wall till it is bruised, simply because he sees a fly there, magnified by his own two eyes almost indefinitely into some Saurian monster. He has an enormous superfluity of vital energy, and if it isn't employed, it strikes its fangs into him. He gets out of spirits as he was at [Le] Havre.

But Robert, as has been remarked, saw monsters everywhere and always in his habitual view of life as through the magnification of a telescope — a fly in the distance could seem like a monstrous creature already too close for comfort.

Elizabeth had pointed out that habits of regular work suited Alfred Tennyson, who 'shuts himself up daily for so many hours' and that, she thought, was a good discipline. In the via Felice, there was 'a bright room with three windows' consecrated to Robert's use, but he was never there, just as, the year before, 'he had a room all last summer and did nothing'. Instead of writing poetry, he had worked off his energy by riding three or four hours at a stretch every day. He had written a great deal of poetry the previous winter, but not this. Modelling in clay now utterly absorbed him. 'The modelling combines body-work and soul-work, and the more tired he has been, and the more his back ached, poor fellow, the more he has exulted and been happy — "no, nothing ever made him so happy before" — also the better he has looked and the stouter he has grown. So I couldn't be much in opposition against the sculpture — I couldn't in fact, at all. He has the material for a volume, and will work at it this summer, he says. His power is much in advance of Strafford, which is his poorest work of all. Oh, the brain stratifies and matures creatively, even in the pauses of the pen.'

Another reason for Robert's apparent reluctance — allowing for his sporadic habits of work — to confine himself to poetry may have been the public lack of appreciation of his efforts as a poet. Elizabeth recognized this subconscious motive. To Sarianna, she could write freely:

> At the same time his treatment in England affects him naturally — and for my part I set it down as an infamy of that public — no other word. He says he has told you some things you had not heard, and which, I acknowledge, I always try to prevent him from repeating to anyone. I wonder if he has told you besides (no, I fancy not) that an English lady of rank, *an acquaintance of ours* (observe that!) asked, the other day, the American Minister whether 'Robert was not an American.' The Minister answered, 'Is it possible that *you* ask me *this*? Why, there is not so poor a village in the United States where they would not tell you that Robert Browning was an Englishman, and that they were very sorry he was not an American.' Very pretty of the American Minister — was it not? — and literally true besides.

In America, true enough, Robert Browning's was a name held in respect by the younger generation, just as in England it would be the younger generation of Pre-Raphaelite painters and poets who would understand and respond to Browning's poetry, unlike those accustomed to the traditional Romantics and who conservatively preferred familiarity to innovation, distrusted the tendencies of new poetry to lead youth astray, and who feared the worst in what they found obscure. What they did not understand, they condemned.

In *Browning and America*, Louise Greer points out that 'by 1861 Browning had won in America an audience of the "fit though few" whom he professed to prefer. Practically every mention of his name was coupled with a reference to his lack of popularity; but his following made up in its quality and enthusiasm what it lacked in numbers. In numbers, moreover, it was increasing — very slowly but surely — and small impressions of around 280 copies were being issued from time to time. Thus, the third edition of *Poems* had been brought out in 1859 and a fourth was to appear in 1863, at which time *Men and Women* was to go into its third impression.' Greer considers that Elizabeth's letter to Sarianna somewhat exaggerates Robert's popularity in the United States in 1860–1 in relation to his reputation in England, but 'her contrast, in a general way, holds good and is supported by considerable contemporary testimony'.[226]

Elizabeth swallowed back her anxieties, striving to make a positive thing in her mind of sculpture as a truly creative displacement activity, and estimating to the highest degree the intelligent appreciation of American friends and supporters in respect of her husband's poetry. She was accustomed, in any case, to taking pleasure in Robert's happiness and its beneficial effect on his appearance while fretting about his lack of discipline. Elizabeth was more committed to habits of regular work than Robert. But if the child is the father of the man, many of Robert's habits of life in his maturity were founded in the circumstances of his childhood. Many children, clever and quick by nature rather than by routine application to their lessons, will not only be easily diverted by a multitude of other interests but will brilliantly throw off a project or succeed in an examination by a combination of almost unconscious absorption of lessons to which they hardly seem to be paying attention and intense eleventh-hour concentration on the matter in hand. Robert's perceived lack of discipline in his habits of work were not so uncommon: he could apply himself as well as Tennyson to regular hours of composition when he felt pressured to do so by the niggle of anxiety, by the nag of a deadline, and by numinous inspiration that impelled him to seize the moment.

Some ten years later, in 1871, putting his own words into the mouth of a semi-fictional character, Prince Hohenstiel-Schwangau, Robert would declare what had always been true of his own character since adolescence: 'I live to please myself.' If he didn't write poetry one day, he would do it another. It was no credit or consolation to Robert Browning as a man and as a poet to have to do anything according to a grinding schedule, except promptly pay his bills as and when they fell due.

Robert and his son had much in common. Pen's nature was more like his father's than his mother's. His childhood very remarkably resembles that of his father: the indulgent, almost indisciplined home education by an imaginative father and a soulful mother, both devoted to their son's welfare and his freedom of expression; the precocity in respect of music, drawing, poetry, languages, and little dramatic performances; the confidence in adult society; the voracity of Robert and Pen for information acquired almost randomly; the physical need for riding and running around freely (as Robert liked a country fair, so Pen loved a city *festa*); the strong attachment in early childhood to both parents — just as Robert never missed a night at home or a goodnight kiss to his mother, so Pen regularly slept at night in his mother's bedroom until the age of twelve.

In Rome in 1861, Pen met the man whose stories his mother had read to him: Hans Christian Andersen, who, as Elizabeth wrote to William Thackeray on 21 May, had been 'charming us all, and not least the children'. At a children's party given by the Storys, Andersen read aloud 'The Ugly Duckling', after which Robert 'struck up with the "Pied Piper"; which led to the formation of a grand march through the spacious Barberini apartment, with Story doing his best on a flute in default of bagpipes.'[227] To Isa Blagden, Elizabeth wrote a little later, 'Andersen (the Dane) came to see me yesterday — kissed my hand, and seemed in a general *verve* for embracing. He is very earnest, very simple, very childlike. I like him. Pen says of him, "He is not really pretty. He is rather like his own ugly duck, but his mind has *developed* into a swan." That wasn't bad of Pen, was it?'

Others had come to kiss or bow over Mrs Browning's little hand. By the first months of 1861 she had recovered sufficiently to entertain select visitors who could talk spiritualism or politics, including the liberal-minded Sir John Bowring, in Rome on a commercial mission from the English government. Bowring's advantage was that he could tell Elizabeth that the more liberty Napoleon III could give, the better he [Napoleon] would like it. This, veraciously, from the horse's mouth — '*He told Sir John so.*'[228] There came, too, Diomede Pantaleoni, the celebrated physician and agent in Rome for Cavour. He had been negotiating with some liberal Cardinals to persuade them that the Pope should resign his temporal power to strengthen the case, which Louis Napoleon supported, for Vittorio Emanuele as putative King of a united Italy.

A year before, in Florence on 15 March 1860, it had been announced that the people of Tuscany had voted for unification of the former Grand Duchy with the constitutional monarchy of Piedmont. Pen, mixing with French troops on the Pincio, had fallen in with some officers who were happy to talk with him about music and politics. When Pen got home, escorted by French troops 'because he was too little to come alone through the crowd', he reported like a secret agent to his mother. ' "They hoped," said Pen, "that *I would not think* they were like the Papalini, No indeed. They hoped I knew the French were different quite; and that, though they protected the Holy Father, they certainly didn't mean to fight for him. What *they* wanted was V.E. King of Italy. *Napoleon veut l'Italie libre.* I was to *understand that, and remember it.*" '[229]

As the winter in Rome turned to spring, the Brownings began to consider how and where to spend the summer. Elizabeth was less enthusiastic than in previous years about the prospect of Paris. She thought she might prefer the quieter, cheaper option of Fontainebleau, 'in the picturesque part of the forest.'[230] To Mrs Ogilvy, in a letter of May 1861, she acknowledged that Robert would be able to see his sister and father again after three years and that she could see Arabel, but confessed that the prospect of travelling to Paris or its environs disturbed her: 'I am very little "up" to this effort, either in my body or my soul, and am much averse to it. Only the *duty* of it is clear, ... seeing that my husband's father is not young, and I have already been the cause of the meeting being put off for a year — so I shall eschew farther responsibility, and shut my eyes and leap. Oh — how deeply my inclination is, ... never to set foot out of Italy again! I have grown to the soil. Everywhere else seems too loud and too light. I can live here my own way, and work my own work, and enjoy my own silence.' Arabel, Elizabeth wrote to Sarianna, wanted the Brownings to come to England, but 'my heart and nerves revolt from it now'. To Mrs Martin, in April 1861, she wrote candidly, warning her old friend not to repeat her admission, that not only did she dread the prospect of any journey whatsoever, but that 'I should like to go into a cave for the year.' The image of the wounded lioness is implicit in this confession. The need to lay up quietly, to rest and recoup, to tend to herself and heal her injuries would, she knew within herself, take time and solitude.

Work, too, was a healing thing for Elizabeth. To George Barrett, she wrote on 30 April 1861, 'Work, work, work — is the best we can get at in this world, we sons and daughters of men.' There had been some good news for Robert — she had been sending poems to America for good prices; and there had been an amusing exchange of letters between Elizabeth and Thackeray. The *North British Quarterly* had published an article about Robert. It was a straw in the wind that indicated, perhaps, some revival of interest in him. 'That gives hope for England', Elizabeth commented to Sarianna on 11 May. On her own account, she reported that 'Thackeray has turned me out of the "Cornhill" for indecency, but did it so prettily and kindly that I, who am forgiving, sent him another poem.'

Thackeray, who had become editor of a new literary magazine, the *Cornhill,* had solicited a contribution from Elizabeth and she had sent him 'Lord Walter's Wife'. He felt unable to publish it because it was 'an account of unlawful passion, felt by a man for a woman, and though you write pure doctrine, and real modesty, and pure ethics, I am sure our readers would make an outcry, and so I have not published this poem'.[231] Thackeray explained that the *Cornhill* was 'written not only for men and women but for boys, girls, infants, sucklings almost . . . there are things *my* squeamish public will not hear on Monday, though on Sundays they listen to them without scruple.'

On 21 April, Elizabeth replied lightly, spiritedly, but reserving her liberal opinions and her freedom to express them: 'I confess it, dear Mr Thackeray, never was anyone turned out of a room for indecent behaviour in a more gracious and conciliatory manner! . . . I am not a "fast woman." I don't like coarse subjects, or the coarse treatment of any subject. But I am deeply convinced that the corruption of our society requires not shut doors and windows, but light and air: and that it is exactly because pure and prosperous women choose to *ignore* vice, that miserable women suffer wrong by it everywhere. Has paterfamilias, with his Oriental traditions and veiled female faces, very successfully dealt with a certain class of evil? What if materfamilias, with her quick sure instincts and honest innocent eyes, do more towards their expulsion by simply looking at them and calling them by their names? See what insolence you put me up to by your kind way of naming my dignities — "Browning's wife and Penini's mother." '

The lioness still had some atavistic roar left in her, some admonitory thump in her tail. To Isa Blagden, in May 1861, she sent some transliterations from English into Italian she had been working on in Rome for the Italian poet and political revolutionary Francesco Dall' Ongaro: 'I'm the rag of a Ba. Yet I *am* stronger, and look much so, it seems to me.' Despite her efforts — though none too strenuous — to persuade Robert that it was her duty to enable them to see their families in France, the Brownings returned to Florence in the first days of June, with no immediate intention of going to Paris. Robert had 'made up his mind (helped by a stray physician of mine, whom he met in the street) that it would be a great risk to carry me north'.[232] It was more Robert's duty to look after his wife than to consider his responsibilities to his father and sister. The Brownings looked forward, rather, to a return to Rome later in the year, when they would take over apartments neighbouring the Storys in the Palazzo Barberini.

On 6 June, the day after they arrived back in Florence, they heard the shocking news that Cavour had died suddenly at the age of fifty. To Sarianna, on 7 June, Elizabeth wrote: 'I can scarcely command voice or hand to name *Cavour*. That great soul which meditated and made Italy, has gone to the Diviner country. If tears or blood could have saved him to us, he should have had mine. I feel yet as if I could scarcely comprehend the greatness of the vacancy. A hundred Garibaldis for such a man. There is a hope that certain solutions had been prepared between him and the Emperor, and that events will slide into their grooves. May God save Italy.'

The unity of Italy had mostly been achieved by Cavour before his death, but the great work was still incomplete. The death of the grand animating and controlling spirit was a considerable and unexpected personal blow, though not fatal to the political cause for which Cavour had worked. He was succeeded as prime minister of Piedmont by Bettino Ricasoli, who continued Cavour's policies. In a postscript to a letter written by Robert to the Storys on 13 June, Elizabeth wrote: 'what a return to Florence! — I have felt beaten and bruised ever since — though the banners are all out this morning for the as-good-as-official "recognition of Italy" — but there's a crepe on the flag, and the joy is as flowers on graves — may God save Italy without his angels.'

To the Storys, Robert wrote on 21 June to thank them for their negotiations on his behalf about the Palazzo Barberini apartments (though he doubted whether these would come off successfully), to report that Landor on a whim had completely shaved off the hair on his head and all his whiskers, and to tell them that 'Ba is stronger and better, but has not yet left the house.' He wrote again on 23 June to say that she had 'caught cold in some strange way two days ago, suddenly became much worse — and last night was alarmingly attacked by the old obstruction at the chest.' While Robert had been out, Isa Blagden had opened the windows, at Elizabeth's insistence, and she had sat for a while in a draught of air. 'I had to fetch a Doctor in the middle of the night who stayed with us till morning — it really seemed as if she would be strangled on the spot, — and that for six hours together! At five o'clock she began to get thro' it, and since then has been much better.'

On 26 June, he wrote a third time to the Storys to say, 'Ba has been very ill indeed but is better I hope and think, to-day . . . but her weakness is extreme tho' we do all we can to strengthen her.' Robert had thought it imperative, in his letter of 23 June, 'to leave this burning place as soon as she is able' and asked the Storys where they intended to spend the summer — Viareggio, Siena, Bagni di Lucca, or 'Corvigliajo, 30 miles hence on the Bologna mountains, said to be as cold as Switzerland, with one inn and no resources beyond its romantic scenery'. By 26 June, Siena seemed the more likely location as 'the easiest and coolest place . . . her recovery will be slow, — one lung is completely congested and useless . . . Ba can see no one, of course.'

Dr Wilson, 'a physician of great repute here, and specially conversant in maladies of the chest', who had been called out urgently by Robert at one o'clock in the morning, had applied a poultice and steeped Elizabeth's feet in a hot mustard bath. He had diagnosed 'that one lung was condensed (the right) and that he suspected an abscess in it'. He had prescribed morphine, which, William Wetmore Story states, 'she was obliged to take in larger quantities than she was accustomed to'.[233] Elizabeth's reaction was complacent: 'This is only one of my old attacks. I know all about it and I shall get better.'

Robert, with the assistance of Lily Wilson and Isa Blagden, the only visitors who were allowed to call daily at Casa Guidi, carried Elizabeth every day from her bedroom to the drawing-room, where she sat, still in her nightgown, in her own chair. A small bed, too, was carried into the drawing-room, and there she slept, Robert sitting wakefully by her side. She was not interested in solid food: a little wine or asses' milk, a few spoonfuls of broth, and occasionally a morsel of bread and butter were all she would take. She seemed not to be dispirited, reacting cheer-fully to efforts made by Isa and Robert to amuse her, though she could hardly respond 'with voice all but extinct'. To Isa, who bent over her to kiss her, she whispered, 'I am decidedly better.'

With Robert, Elizabeth discussed the future. 'We talked about our plans,' Robert wrote to Sarianna on Sunday, 30 June 1861, '— about the house, Casa Guidi, which had suddenly grown distasteful to both of us, noisy, hot, close — poor place we had liked so for fourteen years!' They talked about a villa — 'Villa Niccolini, for instance — that would just suit' — and Elizabeth caught at the idea with avidity: 'If you take it for three years you can send up our furniture and we can enter at once in it when we return next Spring.' Robert noticed 'a tendency to light-headedness in all this — as she did — complaining to the doctor, and telling me how she had strange thoughts, about the windows, which "seemed to be hung in the Hungarian colours" — And she smiled to Isa Blagden at eight on Friday, as she took the glass, "Oh, I not only have asses' milk but asses' thoughts — I am so troubled with silly politics and nonsense".' The light-headedness could possibly be attrib-uted, Robert thought, to the increased dosage of morphine.

He sent Isa away when she tried to relay some small political gossip, and she left in good humour, confident that Elizabeth was well enough. When Pen came in later to kiss his mother goodnight, he asked her three times whether she was really better. He may, earlier, have heard Lily Wilson contradicting the doctor, saying — from her long experience of nursing Elizabeth — that the congestion was in the left lung and that she would recover. Elizabeth assured Pen that she was much better.

Throughout the small hours of that night, when Friday gave way to Saturday, Robert sat by Elizabeth:

She coughed little, took the emulgent duly, and another medi-cine, but dozed constantly: if I spoke she looked, knew me —

smiled, said she was better, and relapsed. I continued this until past three in the morning, when the dozing made me very uneasy. She said 'you did right not to wait — what a fine steamer — how comfortable!' I called Annunziata, bade her get hot water, as the Doctor had done, and sent the porter for himself. I bade her sit up for the water — she did with little help — smiling, letting us act, and repeating 'Well, you do make an exaggerated case of it!' — 'My hands too' she said and put them in another basin. I said you know me? 'My Robert — my heavens, my beloved' — kissing me (but I can't tell you) she said 'Our lives are held by God.'

Robert brought a saucerful of a strong chicken jelly he had had made and put on ice beforehand, and Elizabeth was persuaded to be fed by spoonfuls. She ate a second saucerful, then took some more from a glass — 'she took all. She put her arms round me "God bless you" repeatedly — kissing me with such vehemence that when I laid her down she continued to kiss the air with her lips, and several times raised her own hand and kissed them: I said "Are you comfortable?" "Beautiful." I only put in a thing or two out of the many in my heart of hearts. Then she motioned to have her hands *sponged* — some of the jelly annoying her — this was done, and she began to sleep again — the *last*, . . . I saw. I felt she must be raised, took her in my arms — I felt the struggle to cough begin, and end unavailingly — no pain, no sigh, — only a quiet *sight* — her head fell on me. I thought she might have fainted — but presently there was the least knitting of the brows — and A[nnunziata] cried "*Quest' anima benedetta è passata!*" [This blessed soul is gone].' The time was four-thirty in the morning.

It was so. She is with God, who takes from me the life of my life, in one sense, — not so, in the truest. My life is fixed and sure now. I shall live out the remainder in her direct influence, endeavoring to complete mine, miserably imperfect now, but so as to take the good she was meant to give me. I go away from Italy at once, having no longer any business there. I have our child, about whom I shall exclusively employ myself, doing her part by him. I shall live in the presence of her, in every sense, I hope and believe — so that so far my loss is not *irreparable* — but the future is nothing to me now, except inasmuch as it confirms and realizes the past.[234]

PART 3

ROBERT AND PEN

1861–1889

Elizabeth's death coincided — 'was signalized' according to Mrs Orr[1] — with the unexpected appearance of a comet. Assuming the aspect of a Calpurnia, Mrs Orr impliedly invites us to reflect that, 'When beggars die, there are no comets seen;/The heavens themselves blaze forth the death of princes.' Or, in this case, the heavens themselves acknowledging the loss of a leading light of the Republic of Letters. Robert himself remarked on the phenomenon in a letter of 5 July to Sarianna. He had gone straight from Elizabeth's funeral service on 1 July to the Villa Brichieri, where, 'in the evening came the astonishing sight of the comet, which totally invisible before, it now appears had reached its nearest point to the earth on the *29th* — was first seen, next day, and on the third was over half the sky: it is rapidly going off, and on the 12th, a week hence, will be 36 million of miles away.' This evidently gave Robert pause for thought: he was always interested in significances and synchronicities, though in less troubled times he would perhaps have taken a more rational view.

Hearing of Elizabeth's death, the Storys had immediately hurried from nearby Livorno to Florence, where they found 'a sad house enough'.

> There stood the table with her letters and books as usual, and her little chair beside it, and in her portfolio a half-finished letter to Mrs [Jessie White] Mario, full of noble words about

Italy. Yes, it was for Italy that her last words were written; for her dear Italy were her last aspirations. The death of Cavour had greatly affected her. She had wept many tears for him, and been a real mourner. The agitation undoubtedly weakened her and perhaps was the last feather that broke her down.[2]

Robert and Pen were subdued. Nobody found them prostrated by grief[3] or hysterical with sobbing. They maintained a sober self-control, sustained, as Robert told friends, by the strength and resilience in life of Elizabeth herself. It had been difficult at first for them to comprehend their loss, to believe that Elizabeth was dead at all. She was more evidently simply at peace. 'After death,' Robert told Story, 'she looked . . . like a young girl; all the outlines rounded and filled up, all traces of disease effaced, and a smile on her face so living that they could not for hours persuade themselves she was really dead.'

Elizabeth had passed away quickly, quietly, unknowingly, and — much to Robert's consolation — without pain. He clung to this comfort and passed it on to others repeatedly as, he supposed, a solace for their own sorrow as it was for his own. Dr Wilson had assured him, Robert wrote to Sarianna, 'that she could never have recovered — to her old state of comparative health: she would have become confined to the room, then the bed, no travelling, no visitors *possible*. There was no pain — the little wandering was caused by the morphine, in an increased dose as was necessary: nothing could have helped, all I did was right, nothing omitted. The death was caused most probably by the breaking of a second abscess [which pierced?] the trachea. The first night's attack was the breaking one in an attack of asthma: he knew it was a grave case from the first, but never expected the end would be so near, — that is, he thought there would be more lingering and pain.'[4]

Dr Wilson's assurances that Robert could have done no more than he did were welcome, since his own reasons for hope, as well as the optimism of others, had at first led him to believe — against his instinct — that this last illness was no more serious than some others from which Elizabeth had recovered. To have taken it lightly at the last, to have omitted any little comfort for her, would have grieved him more than he could bear. Her death, now that he knew it had been inevitable, could be borne: self-blame for the least neglect could never have been forgiven.

At the end, as Robert wrote to George Barrett on 2 July 1861, Elizabeth had 'laughed with pleasure and *youth*, and I believe in some perfectly gracious way allowed by God suffered no pain whatever, even as she averred.' To Fanny Haworth, on the 20th, he wrote:

> Then came what my heart will keep till I see her and longer — the most perfect expression of her love to me within my whole knowledge of her — always smiling, happily, and with a face like a girl's — and in a few minutes she died in my arms, her head on my cheek. These incidents so sustain me that I tell them to her beloved ones as their right: there was no lingering, nor acute pain, nor consciousness of separation, but God took her to himself as you would lift a sleeping child from a dark, uneasy bed into your arms and the light. Thank God.

Robert's composure was a relief to his friends. Pen, perhaps even more surprisingly, behaved just as well. Father and son appeared to give their cues to one another, comforting and being comforted by some mutual, unprompted agreement. 'Pen has been perfect to me,' Robert told Sarianna the day after Elizabeth's death.

> He sate all yesterday with his arms round me; said things like her to me. I shall try and work hard, educate him, and live worthy of my past fifteen years happiness. I do not feel paroxysms of grief — but as if the very blessing, she died giving me, insensible to all beside, had begun to work already. She will be buried tomorrow. Several times in writing this I have for a moment referred in my mind to her — 'I will ask Ba about that.' The grief of everybody is sincere, I am told. Everybody is kind in offers of help — all is done for me that can be; and it is not a little just now. Isa came at the early morning and stayed till night, taking away Pen. I shall now go in and sit with herself — my Ba, forever ... How she looks now — how perfectly beautiful!

On 29 June, immediately after Elizabeth's death, Robert had written briefly to Sarianna and his father, 'Don't come, nor send nor be anxious.' Since the funeral was to take place on 1 July at 7 p.m. — on account of the heat, it could not be delayed — neither Brownings nor Barretts would have time to come to Florence. Arabel and George had been informed of their sister's death by telegram, but Robert had not yet written fully to either of them and would not do so until 2 July. The funeral service, at Robert's express wish, was conducted according to the forms of the Church of England, 'that I may hear those only words at the beginning'[5] — those words being from the Book of Common Prayer: 'I am the resurrection and the life, saith the Lord; he that believeth in me, though he were dead, yet shall he live: and whosoever liveth and believeth in me shall never die.'

The funeral itself did not impress William Story, who had expected better; but he had come too late to Florence to take any hand himself in the arrangements. He wrote resentfully and regretfully to Charles Eliot Norton on 15 August 1861: 'She was buried in the Protestant cemetery . . . many of her friends were there, but fewer persons than I expected and hoped to see. The services were blundered through by a fat English parson in a brutally careless way, and she was consigned to the earth as if her clay were no better than any other clay . . . I carried two wreaths — it was all I could do — one of those exquisite white Florence roses, and the other of laurel, and these I laid on her coffin.'[6] These wreaths made an impression on Robert, who referred to them in a letter of 5 July to Sarianna without identifying the mourner who had put them there: 'The coffin was carried with two great crowns, of laurel and white flowers, through the streets.' That the coffin was permitted to be carried through the streets at all, by a special dispensation, was an unusual honour generously granted by the city of Florence.

Robert, reporting to George the day after, in his letter of 2 July, had more favourable, though less detailed, memories of the funeral than Story and no complaints. Neither Robert nor Elizabeth had much liked funerals. 'I have a horror of that man of the grave-yard,' Robert had written to Isa Blagden in September. Mrs Orr comments that, 'For him, a body from which the soul had passed, held nothing of the person whose earthly vesture it had been.'[7] He regarded dust as dust, and where it was laid and what happened to it thereafter, should it happen even to be his own, was no great matter — 'I have no kind of concern as to where the old clothes of myself shall be thrown' — though he expressed the wish that, 'if my fortune be such, and my survivors be not unduly troubled', to be interred in the plot he had acquired for

Elizabeth.[8] Robert's 'habitual aversion for the paraphernalia of death' very probably accounted for whatever inattention to the observances and etiquette of interment that Story disliked and disapproved.

Robert's own recollection of the occasion was blurred and impressionistic. 'She was buried yesterday — with the shops in the street shut, a crowd of people following sobbing, another crowd of Italians, Americans and English crying like children at the cemetery, for they knew who she was — "the greatest English Poet of the day, writer of the sublimest poem ever penned by woman, and Italy's truest and dearest of friends." — as the morning and evening newspapers told them, "calling on the friends of Art and Italy, of whatever tribe and sect, to go and pay a last homage" — and so they did, I am told, for I saw nothing but for one minute a flash of faces — noble, grateful Italians.'

To Fanny Haworth, Robert reaffirmed: 'She was, is, lamented with extraordinary demonstrations if one consider it: the Italians seem to have understood her by an instinct.' The streets of Florence, already hung with black in mourning for Cavour, honoured also, now, the poet of the Risorgimento. In 1865, a monument designed by Frederic Leighton was erected over Elizabeth's grave, some years after the Florentine municipal authorities had placed a commemorative tablet on the via Maggio wall of Casa Guidi. The inscription, composed by the poet Niccolò Tommaseo, reads, complete with its misspelling of Barrett:

QUI SCRISSE E MORI
ELISABETTA BARRET BROWNING
CHE IN CUORE DI DONNA CONCILIAVA
SCIENZA DI DOTTO E SPIRITO DI POETA
E FECE DEL SUO VERSO AUREA ANELLO
FRA ITALIA E INGHILTERRA
PONE QUESTA MEMORIA
FIRENZE GRATA
1861

[Here wrote and died
Elizabeth Barret Browning
who in a woman's heart united
the learning of a scholar and the spirit of a poet
and of her verse made a golden ring

between Italy and England
This memorial stone was placed
by a grateful Florence
1861]

Writing to George was more of an ordeal than Robert had expected. He had already written lengthily, in the most minute detail, to Sarianna on 30 June, and the effort of going over the events again for his brother-in-law all but broke his composure. On the Wednesday, 3 July, he abruptly finished the letter: 'Dear George, I must write no more letters like this.' He would tell the Barretts everything when he saw them, but meantime, 'all brothers and relatives *must* forgive my not attempting to write to them . . . I cannot yet go over this again and again in letters.'

Among the mourners at the funeral had been 'Italian men crying like children, Villari the historian, dall' Ongaro the Poet, and many others unknown to me — but I will have done with all this,' wrote Robert to John Forster shortly afterwards, 'only, see if they are not grateful, this traduced people! Cavaliere Perruzzi [of a distinguished Florentine family] called on me a week ago: he said he and the Italians all were anxious I should not leave Florence, — or if that must be, yet that Pen might continue to be a "Tuscan"; he could go away for a year or two and come back — "only, let him try a career with us — we want those who were our friends in our ill days to share in our coming good fortunes — every thing will be open to him!" — Of course Pen is and will be English as I am English and his Mother was pure English to the hatred of all un-English cowardice, vituperation and lies — but so he spoke, and so I shall remember.'9 Robert had already written to Sarianna on 13 July 1861 to tell her of Ubaldino Perruzzi's plea and to say that, 'Of course, the answer is, we are English and the beauty of Ba's effort was in its being utterly disinterested and the just zeal of a stranger for right and truth: let Pen continue it.'

Elizabeth had felt herself empathetic to Italy, had given her words and soul to its great causes, and Pen had stated very plainly that he regarded himself as Italian. Pen might well have preferred to remain Italianate rather than become Anglicized; but, so far as his father was concerned, it was to be one or the other, and English for preference. In a letter of 20 August 1861 to William Story, Robert discussed his plans for Pen's schooling. These were to be put in hand without delay, lest 'I may lose the critical time when the English stamp (in all that it is good for) is taken or missed . . . I distrust all hybrid and ambiguous natures and nationalities and want to make something decided of him.'

Story, in a letter of 15 August 1861 to Charles Eliot Norton, seriously questioned Robert's character and intellect as an Englishman. If that was what Robert professed himself to be, then he was very untypical of Englishmen as Story had found them to be. He sorely regretted Robert's decision to leave Italy:

> I have lost my best friend and daily companion in Italy. You cannot imagine how I shall miss him . . . There is no one to supply his place . . . no one with whom I can sympathise on all points such as him, no one with whom I can walk any of the higher ranges of art and philosophy . . . Englishmen who think are very rare; they are generally ganglions of prejudices, which they call opinions, and what ideas they have are generally narrow and bigoted or developments only in a single direction. Their education is never general, but special, and outside their special- ity they are terribly barren . . . You and I know hundreds of such men. They are planted on their ground and can't speculate; they say 'Ouh! ouh!' to you when you hazard a theory or state a principle. The English mind is not a philosophic one; they are not of the air, but of the earth; in the good sense of the term, but still of the earth. Browning is by nature not an Englishman.[10]

Story's estimation of Browning may be contrasted with G. K. Chesterton's constant assertions that 'Browning . . . delighted, with a true poetic delight, in being conventional. Being by birth an Englishman, he took pleasure in being an Englishman; being by rank a member of the middle class, he took a pride in its ancient scruples and its everlasting boundaries.'[11] Chesterton — himself a stout Englishman of the middle class — rejoices over Robert's 'ardent and headlong conventionality'. He finds great goodness in Robert Browning, though that in itself would be insufficient to explain the regard felt for Robert by Story and such disparate, difficult men as Carlyle and Landor.

Rather, says Chesterton, 'when a man is loved by other men of his own intellectual stature and of a wholly different type and order of eminence, we may be certain that there was something genuine about him, and something far more important than anything intellectual'.[12] An Englishman may be highly esteemed as being good and genuine without being prized for genius. And, of course, vice versa. Chesterton's regard for 'something genuine' as a spiritual benefit, as a primary and worthy virtue, does not of itself invalidate Story's assessment of the English as being 'not of the air, but of the earth', as essentially non-intellectual at best when not positively anti-intellectual at worst; Robert Browning was exceptional for being a man of broad learning and constant curiosity, genuinely thoughtful, generously open-minded and good-heartedly philosophic.

Pen, in Robert's regard, was essentially 'perfect in his goodness',[13] genuine in his affections, and lacked only learning. Robert claimed afterwards to have talked with Elizabeth about Pen, and that what he did with the boy in the week after his mother's death would have had her blessing. Writing to Fanny Haworth on 20 July 1861, he said: 'You know I have her dearest interest to attend to at *once* — her child to care for, educate, establish properly — and my own life to fulfil as properly, — all, just as she would require were she here.' Writing to Sarianna on 5 July 1861, Robert described the transformation: 'Pen, the golden curls and fantastic dress, is gone just as Ba is gone: he has short hair, worn boy-wise, long trousers, is a common boy all at once: otherwise I could not have lived without a maid. I can now attend to him completely myself, — so all pins, worked collars and so on, are gone and forgotten. He behaves perfectly — has grown a dear, considerate boy of a sudden, will come to nothing but good, I am convinced.' The fantastical Pen, like Elizabeth's physical presence and the happiness of the family's life in Italy, was consigned to the past.

Robert was impatient to move on. It irked him to stay a moment longer than necessary in Florence. 'The cycle is complete,' he said to William Story, who stood with him as he looked round the drawing-room at Casa Guidi and turned the years in his mind:

> Here we came fifteen years ago; here Pen was born; here Ba wrote her poems for Italy. She used to walk up and down this verandah in the summer evenings, when, revived by the southern air, she first again began to enjoy her out-doors life.

Every day she used to walk with me or drive with me, and once even walked to Bellosguardo and back; that was when she was strongest. Little by little, as I now see, that distance was lessened, the active out-doors life restricted, until walking had finally ceased. We saw from these windows the return of the Austrians; they wheeled round this corner and came down this street with all their cannon, just as she describes it in 'Casa Guidi.' Last week when we came to Florence I said: 'We used, you know, to walk on this verandah so often — come and walk up and down once. Just once,' I urged, and she came to the window and took two steps on it. But it fatigued her too much, and she went back and lay down on the sofa — that was our last walk. Only the night she went away for ever she said she thought we must give up Casa Guidi; it was too inconvenient and in case of illness too small. We had decided to go away and take a villa outside the gates. For years she would not give up this house, but at last and, as it were, suddenly she said she saw it *was* too small for us and too inconvenient. And so it was; so the cycle was completed for us here, and where the beginning was is the end. Looking back at these past years I see that we have been all the time walking over a torrent on a straw. Life must now be begun anew — all the old cast off and the new one put on. I shall go away, break up everything, go to England and live and work and write.[14]

The past, nevertheless, could take him by surprise: now and again it overwhelmed his seeming composure and dealt him enough of a blow to make him bellow in pain. Isa Blagden had been taking motherly care of Pen at the Villa Brichieri and Robert himself slept there overnight, returning to Casa Guidi for breakfast and to make preparations for their departure.[15] He had fallen ill the day after the funeral. To Sarianna, he reported, 'in the afternoon of Tuesday ... I found myself of a sudden with my head on the table and sense out of it for some few moments.' This was alarming enough to set him walking up to the Villa Brichieri, where Isa dosed him with some medication, but 'in the night I had a couple more closings of the throat, or something of the kind, and I really thought I might not get thro' the next — so I told her two or [three] things necessary to be known for Peni, and consequently, more at ease about that, got safely thro' the night, took more physic and was soon better and well ... I am quite well now, understand — Pen has always been so.' It was only with Isa Blagden that he could give way to his grief, weep frantically, cry out, 'I want her! I want her!' Nobody saw or knew of these moments of release but Isa. Afterwards, a little embarrassed by the display, Robert would pull himself together. To the rest of the world, in person or in his letters, he presented a sombre, controlled surface.

All that was left to do in Florence was close up the rooms of Casa Guidi. He had intended to have the interior photographed,[16] but instead the customary appearance of the drawing-room, 'just as she disposed it and left it', was very precisely recorded in a painting.[17] Only then could the apartment be cleared. Robert would keep some 'few old articles that we are used to at Casa Guidi' — furniture, books, and household items to be carefully crated and stored before being sent to London — the rest would be sold. 'The staying at Casa Guidi was not the worst of it,' he wrote to William Story on 30 August 1861. 'I kept in my place there like a worm-eaten piece of old furniture looking solid enough, but when I was *moved*, I began to go to pieces.'

The biographical and critical consensus is that Robert Browning broke precisely into two pieces, the one public, the other private. The polished surface of Robert's urbane life after he left Florence has long and consistently been perceived as a veneer. 'He,' wrote Chesterton, 'closing the door of that room behind him, closed a door in himself, and none ever saw Browning upon earth again but only a splendid surface.'[18] This wonderfully dramatic image artfully summarizes Henry James's irresistible analysis of Robert after he quitted Italy for England:

> The writer's London period was in fact to be rich and ample, was to be attended with felicities and prosperities of every sort that cast the comparatively idyllic Italian time into the background and seemed, superficially, to build it out. But thus, really, was generated, in the personal, social, intellectual way, the wonderful Browning we so largely were afterwards to know — the accomplished, saturated, sane, sound man of the London world and the world of 'culture,' of whom it is impossible not

to believe that he had arrived, somehow, for his own deep purposes, at the enjoyment of a double identity.[19]

Henry James's polished concept of two Robert Brownings is more plausible in its novelistic genius than in the more complex reality. The idea was in fact fictionally expressed in a short story, 'The Private Life', written by James and published after Robert's death when, as Leon Edel puts it in his biography of James, he 'allowed his imagination to play over the image of a great poet who could be deadly prosaic'.[20] The story tells of an urbane, sociable dramatist, Clare Vawdrey, who has promised to write a play for an actress. The narrator of the story, incredulous that such a man is capable of writing a play, discovers that Clare Vawdrey has a double who keeps out of sight and writes the great man's works for him.

Edel says that James had, from his first meetings with Robert, 'been struck by his double personality — the poet incarnated in an individual as hearty and conventional and middle-class as any of the numerous privileged with whom he and Henry dined out constantly during the late seventies . . . The world had seen always the commonplace Browning. The genius was in his books. Browning had been all "private life" and had no life in public, save the usual and the expected.' James had been disappointed in Tennyson's performance of his own poetry. He had gone to lunch with the old Laureate and heard him growl through *Locksley Hall* from beginning to end and not very well. On another day, James had gone 'to Lady Airlie's to hear Browning read his own poems — with the comfort of finding that, at least, if you don't understand them, he apparently understands them even less. He read them as if he hated them and would like to bite them to pieces.' Browning might be harsh in his delivery, but unlike Tennyson, 'the result was that what he read showed extraordinary life'. Henry James concluded from this contrast: 'When I feel disposed to reflect that Tennyson is not personally Tennysonian, I summon up the image of Browning, and this has the effect of making me check my complaints.' What Tennyson lacked in youthful fire, Browning possessed in personal involvement with the internal life of his poetry.[21]

Over the years, Henry James watched Robert Browning in London as the poet bustled around town with 'prompt responses and expected opinions and usual views'. He noted his 'intellectual eagerness to put himself in the place of other people; and there was in him "a restlessness of psychological research".' Robert Browning was a psychological study in himself for an inquiring acquaintance, and James made the most of him.

'It was not easy to meet him and know him without some resort to the supposition that he had literally mastered the secret of dividing the personal consciousness into a pair of independent compartments. The man of the world — the man who was good enough for the world such as it was — walked abroad, showed himself, talked, right resonantly, abounded, multiplied his contacts and did his duty; the man of "Dramatic Lyrics," of "Men and Women," of "The Ring and the Book," of "A Blot in the 'Scutcheon," of "Pippa Passes," of "Colombe's Birthday," of everything, more or less, of the order of these, — this inscrutable personage sat at home and knew as well as he might in what quarters of *that* sphere to look for suitable company. The poet and the "member of society" were, in a word, dissociated in him as they can rarely elsewhere have been ... Such at least was the appearance he could repeatedly conjure up to a deep and mystified admirer.'[22]

James's biography of William Wetmore Story, in which this portrait appears, was first published in 1903, some five years before Marcel Proust began, in 1908–9, writing the essays that were posthumously published in 1945 as *Contre Sainte-Beuve*. James would have been fully aware of the French literary critic Charles Augustin Sainte-Beuve, who had died in 1869 and whose short essays, collected as *Premiers Lundis* and *Causeries du lundi*, continued to be influential. The centenary of Sainte-Beuve's birth, commemorated in 1904, was an occasion for pious celebration of the great man's literary authority and complimentary reverence for his peerless discernment. In his attack on Sainte-Beuve, who had promoted the autobiographical interpretation and subjective evaluation of literary works, Proust complained that the critic had failed to distinguish between the writer as a social being in everyday life and the writer as someone who creates his work in solitude. Like Browning, Sainte-Beuve had enjoyed a full social life. Proust, though he had been equally sociable, contrasted what he perceived to be the language of mere superficial literary conversation — what Gore Vidal has disparagingly defined as 'book chat' — with the language appropriate to the deep and serious business of literature.

In his draft essay, translated as *The Method of Sainte-Beuve*, Proust quotes from one of Sainte-Beuve's *causeries* ('chats') on Chateaubriand:

> For me, literature is not distinct or at any rate separable from the rest of the man and of his organization . . . We cannot go about it in too many different ways or from too many different angles if we are to get to know a man, something more than a pure intelligence, that is. Until such time as one has put to oneself a certain number of questions about an author, and has answered them, be it only to oneself and under one's breath, one cannot be sure of having grasped him entire, even though the questions may seem quite foreign to the nature of his writings: What were his religious ideas? How did the spectacle of nature affect him? How did he behave in the matter of women, of money? Was he rich, poor; what was his diet, his daily routine? What was his vice or his weakness? None of these questions are irrelevant if we are to judge the author of a book or the book itself, provided that book is not a treatise on pure geometry, if it is a work of literature above all, one, that is, which brings in everything, etc.

Proust, on the contrary, distinctly separated the social self, the persona publicly displayed by a writer, from the deep self, what he termed the '*moi profond*', which the writer kept secret to himself and by and from which the great literary work was created. The difference resided in language, the medium in which the externalized public self and the contemplative private self were materialized: 'At no time,' says Proust, 'does Sainte-Beuve seem to have grasped what is peculiar to inspiration or the activity of writing, and what marks it off totally from the occupations of other men and the other occupations of the writer. He drew no dividing line between the occupation of writing, in which, in solitude and suppressing those words which belong as much to others as to ourselves, and with which, even when alone, we judge things without being ourselves, we come face to face once more with our selves, and seek to hear and to render the true sound of our hearts — and conversation!'

In the case of Robert Browning, his public and private use of language, of words, is markedly differentiated according to the media employed for expression — speech and writing. The literary critic Clyde De L. Ryals points out that 'Nearly every one of Browning's monologists has a near obsession with words. The duke of Ferrara [in "My Last Duchess"] constantly refers to speech: what people do not ask . . . what Fra Pandolf said, how the duchess talked or would have talked, what he himself said, could not say and is now saying . . . It is as though the monologists, who are never at a loss for words, see themselves as mouthers of scripts in theatrical situations.'[23]

Sainte-Beuve, wrote Proust,

> continued not to understand the unique, enclosed world, incommunicado with the outside, which is the soul of the poet . . . And not having seen the gulf that separates the writer from the society man, not having understood that the writer's self shows itself only in his books, that he only shows society men (even those society men that other writers are, when in society, who only become writers again once on their own) a society man like themselves, he was to launch that famous method which, according to Taine, Bourget and so many others, is his claim to fame, and which consists, in order to understand a poet or writer, in questioning avidly those who knew him, who frequented him, who may be able to tell us how he behaved in the matter of women, etc., that is, on all those very points where the poet's true self is not involved.[24]

In contrast to Sainte-Beuve, who believed, said Proust, 'that the salon life which he enjoyed was indispensable to literature', Robert Browning had no such illusion that membership of literary cliques and coteries contributed substantially to the creation of poetry. He took cues from the psychological quirks of the world he moved in, of course; he was vitally interested in the people he met — how they talked and what they gossiped about; and he was gratified by their acclamation. 'A great many literary persons', wrote Chesterton, 'have expressed astonishment at, or even disapproval of, this social frivolity of Browning's. Not one of these literary people would have been shocked if Browning's humanity had led him into a gambling hell in the Wild West or a low tavern in Paris; but it seems to be tacitly assumed that fashionable people are not human at all.' But for 'humanitarians of the highest type, the great poets and philosophers . . . the nearest drawing room is full of humanity, and even their own families are human.'[25]

Robert had no objection to salon life; indeed, despite privately regarding it as an activity he calculatedly and cold-bloodedly indulged, he displayed a seeming relish for it and was a lively participant in its rituals. Nevertheless, on the face (or the two faces) of it, he would, like Proust himself, seem to be the perfect exemplar of Proust's thesis. More than most, beginning in youth, Robert Browning hid himself behind masks. Clyde De L. Ryals dates the defining moment as the night of 22 October 1832, when the twenty-year-old Robert saw Edmund Kean act on stage. He saw more than a performance: he saw 'the sight of his own future as an artist: the acting of roles would bridge the chasm between what he was and all he "would be". Henceforth his was to be a world of theatre.'[26] This is not simple speculation, considering Robert's professed ambition at that time to write a series of different literary works under different names. History became spectacle in the commonest life as in the highest art. In his preface to *Strafford*, he had insisted on 'Action in Character, rather than Character in Action' in theatrical dramas. He lived just such a principle in his own life — depending, of course, on which character, the man of the world or the poet in purdah, was currently being exhibited.

This is more or less consistent with Proust's insistence that the poet has his being at two levels of existence — in the character of the urbane man of the world and in the '*moi profond*'. This was true of Robert Browning perhaps, in the view of Henry James, more obviously than most of his kind. At both levels, if Proust and James are to be believed, Browning lived a continuous series of performances, in which case only the literary critic can come close to the true depth of Browning's character through the study of his works — what Browning liked to regard as his dramatic performances. These certainly contain references we may now interpret as pertinent to his personal feelings about identifiable persons in public and private life and to significant contemporary events. By implication, nothing to which John Forster, the Flower sisters, Anne Thackeray, Mrs Orr, the Storys, any other close friend, or a hundred more interested acquaintances of Robert Browning can testify can have any more relevance to the life of Robert Browning than the best efforts of dramatic critics commenting on polished performances by a consistently good actor.

Nevertheless the literary and subjective biographer, as distinct from his strictly critical and objective brother, must take the side of Sainte-Beuve and warm to his methods. He must believe that Browning's, or any other creative writer's works, are informed by his character and express it; that 'Action in Character' can be examined for consistency; and, too, that 'Character in Action' will confirm patterns of life. Since the door is banged in the biographer's face when Robert Browning retires into creative solitude, into his deep self, the biographer must believe that there is value in comparing, sometimes contrasting, the inner creative self as expressed in his works with the outer self as expressed in society, in an effort to identify some synchronicities and thereby some consistent characteristics.

Maisie Ward pauses at this point: 'Here we touch another element in criticism where we should surely walk cautiously: the support of a doubtful interpretation of Browning's prose by bringing in his poetry. Poetry tells us much about the poet's self, but I wonder how much of brute fact goes into it. A poem may as easily be written about action repudiated as action taken ... And critics who accept personal interpretations will almost violently repudiate the conclusions of other critics concerning the same poem.'[27] Chesterton, on the other hand, cautions to the contrary, suggesting that 'critics have been misled by the fact that Browning in many places appears to boast that he is purely dramatic, that he has never put himself into his work, a thing which no poet, good or bad, who ever lived could possibly avoid doing'.[28]

Like a busy Boswell in pursuit of Dr Johnson, the conscientious biographer must regard everything as relevant: he must not only read the works but also run around his great subject in different ways and at different angles, finally sighing, like Boswell, 'You cannot imagine what labour, what perplexity, what vexation, I have endured in arranging a prodigious multiplicity of materials, in supplying omissions, in searching for papers, buried in different masses — and all this besides the exertion of composing and polishing. Many a time have I thought of giving it up. However, though I shall be uneasily sensible of its many deficiencies, it will certainly be to the world a very valuable and peculiar volume of biography, full of literary and characteristical anecdotes ... told with authenticity and in a lively manner.' Like Boswell, the plain biographer is glad to know that Samuel Johnson wore latchets in his

William Wetmore Story and family;
photographed in Rome, *c.*1861.

Sarianna Browning, the poet's sister.

Browning's owl.

Elizabeth Barrett Browning, photographed in Rome in May 1861 a month before she died.

Monument to Elizabeth Barrett Browning, designed by Count Henry Cottrell and Sir Frederick Leighton, erected over her grave in the Protestant Cemetery in Florence, photographed 1866

Robert Browning and his son Pen, photographed in May 1870.

Sketches of Browning reading at Naworth Castle, September 1869, by William Wetmore Story.

The Consolers: Julia Wedgwood.

Louisa, Lady Ashburton
(with her daughter Maisie)
from a Landseer portrait
of 1862

Joseph Milsand
(with Browning in 1882).

The Great Man, Caricatured: 'Mr Robert Browning Taking Tea with the Browning Society', a drawing by Max Beerbohm. Emily Hickey is seated foreground at Browning's knees; F. J. Furnivall, bearded, is in the first row of the circle to the left of Browning.

Browning caricatured as the Pied Piper of Hamelin, 1873.

Depicted in *Punch* magazine by Linley Sambourne in July 1882 wearing a Red Cotton Night-Cap which students had humorously dropped on his head during a ceremony in which the honorary award of D.C.L. was conferred by Oxford University.

Perseus & Andromede –
this picture hung above
Browning's desk.

Browning's study in his house
at De Vere Gardens, London;
and the house's exterior.

Fannie Coddington, Pen's wife,
photographed in 1872.

Browning in Asolo, 5 September 1889.

Robert Browning and his son Pen photographed in Venice, 1889.

The End: 'The Last Life-Picture of Robert Browning', sketched in Venice, 24 November 1889, by G.D. Giles – the inscription is Browning's own.

Here I'm gazing, wide awake,
Robert Browning, no mistake!
Venice, Nov 24. 89.

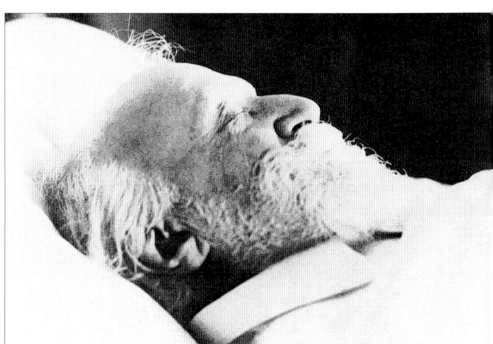

Browning photographed in Venice after his death, 1889.

shoes or that the soles of Robert Browning's boots, on at least one occasion, had a hole in them. Such peculiar and particular biographical details may at least be usefully 'characteristical'.

It is, of course, perfectly possible that Robert's distrust of 'all hybrid and ambiguous natures and nationalities' may have implied some unease about his own hybrid nature, his own dual personality. Whether or not he felt any such thing, he would have regarded it either as nobody else's business or as nothing abnormal. He would, it is perfectly clear from his earnest efforts to suppress publication of his own and Elizabeth's letters, have sided with Proust over Sainte-Beuve. His instinct, as always, was to value memory without vain regret and look to the future, to live necessarily in the moment but not exclusively for it. When Florence had ceased to be of any importance to his personal life, he abruptly tore his own and Pen's lives up by the roots and planted them in London.

To move dramatically and definitively would resolve at least one ambiguity. Maisie Ward, in the second volume of her biography of Robert Browning, comments on the 'sharp contrast between the English criticism of Browning as Italianate and the long-resisted pull on him of what can only be called homesickness. He was to an unusual degree a man of two countries, longing for his homeland yet loving Italy ... And you have only to read *Aurora Leigh* to realize that, with all her enthusiasm for the Italian cause, Elizabeth's roots too had been elsewhere. Only their son "Pen" could say, with no reservations, "*Sono Italiano*".'[29] It is certainly true that, quite aside from the tenor of her poetry, Elizabeth's constant vehemence in letters and conversation against England as a nation of smooth-faced villains, either ignobly supine or actively malevolent in the Italian causes she had espoused, could only have derived from a rooted, residual Englishness that reprobated the betrayal of everything fine and honourable in that nationality. Robert, she admitted, retained more nationalism and respect for the English than she did herself.

Robert later confirmed that he felt culturally more at home in England, in its literature and mode of thought, and that his decision to leave Florence had been correct. He summed up his attitude to Italy and Italians retrospectively in a letter of 19 May 1866 from London to Isa Blagden:

I agree with you, and always did, as to the uninterestingness of the Italians individually, as thinking, originating souls: I never read a line in a modern Italian book that was of use to me, — never saw a flash of poetry come out of an Italian *word*: in art and action, *yes*, — not in the region of ideas: I always said they *are* poetry, don't and can't *make* poetry, — and you know what I mean by *that*, — nothing relating to rhymes and melody and *lo stile* [style]: but as a nation, politically, they are most interesting to me, — I think they have more than justified every expectation their best friends formed of them, — and their rights are indubitable: my liking for Italy was always a selfish one, — I felt alone with my own soul there: here, there are fifties and hundreds, even of my acquaintance, who do habitually walk up and down in the lands of thought I live in, never mind whether they go up to the ends of it, or even look over them, — *in* that territory, they are, — and I never saw footprint of an Italian there yet.

Pen, however, was more thoroughly Italian than either of his parents. He had often associated with British and American children in Italy, but he had been born in Italy, Italian was the first language he heard from the *balia* and habitually used for personal preference; and he had hero-worshipped the wonderful Ferdinando Romagnoli and thought of Lily Wilson's Italian-born son as a brother. He had run around the streets of Florence and Rome eavesdropping the local gossip, and helpfully contributing to it himself. By contrast, most of his experiences in England had not been positive. Pen's 'goodness' in his wish to please his father was natural. He would not have objected to his hair being cut short, nor to being put into proper hard-wearing trousers and plain jackets — he had begged for these himself for years. Being turned overnight into a regular boy would not have bothered him, indeed might well have caused him some relief. But we hear little or nothing, in the immediate aftermath of his mother's death, of Pen's feelings about being uprooted from the distinctive Italian and European culture and society he had known in his earliest, formative years. His own homesickness, as distinct from his father's, would be for Italy. For the time being, however, Pen was proving himself not only amenable and amiable, but adaptable.

The painting Robert had commissioned of the drawing-room at Casa Guidi was the only thing that held him up for more time than was tolerable. He considered the immediate future: putting Florence behind him, he would go to London with Pen. Isa Blagden, generously setting aside her own engagements in Florence, would go with them — first to Paris to see Sarianna and Mr Browning and stay with them a day or two, then go to Arabel for a few days. Thereafter, as Robert wrote to Sarianna on 13 July 1861, 'we can all go quietly into the country together — if such a thing were possible, to the sea-side . . . I should much like some quiet place wherein to arrange my thoughts, and attend to Pen . . . Pen is changed and so good: the loss cannot be to him what it is for me — on the other hand, he could not get the comfort out of it that I do: he will have new objects, desires etc. every week and day.'

By mid-July, Robert had comforted himself with the thought that 'all has been for the best' for Elizabeth 'in the painless end, absolute ignorance of the parting that was to be and of anxiety, in the immunity from the sad dark days that *must* have followed very soon, if her health had continued to decline without this abrupt close: everything would have been miserable in that case.' A lingering half-life for all of them in Florence would have done none of the Brownings any good. Pen, Robert wrote to Sarianna, 'being just of this age, a boy, and just the kind of boy he is, will help immensely: and in my case, *writing* being the only thing I have always been used to do absolutely by myself. However, I am not too sure I shall be able to do all the wise things I profess — only, I will try — and I have done some hard things already, for which I feel the better.' Activity, facing up to things, dealing with them promptly, nipping trouble in the bud always reassured Robert and did him good.

Robert and Pen, 'encumbered with Peni's pony', finally left Florence on 1 August[30] after Pen had taken heartbroken leave of Lily, Ferdinando, and the Romagnoli boys. The last thing they heard, says Betty Miller, was the crash of crockery behind them. Landor had thrown another dinner out of the window of Wilson's boarding-house. Isa accompanied Robert and Pen only as far as Paris, whence she proceeded alone to England to see friends before meeting the Brownings later in London. Robert had thought better of his plan to visit Arabel in London. He told William Story on 20 August that 'the process of going over the old ground, stopping at the old Inns etc. was too much — and I found it impossible to go farther: Paris is also unbearable to me, and I only breathe freely since we arrived at this wild, primitive and lonely place — by St Malo — with a solitary sea, bays, sands and rocks, and green, pleasant country.' They had fetched up — Robert, Pen, Sarianna, Mr Browning, and the pony — at St Enogat, close to Dinard on the northern coast of Brittany. This letter to Story shows him true to his intention 'to arrange my thoughts, and attend to Pen'. Robert recognized that sending Pen immediately to school after they had got to London 'would have been desirable had Peni been brought up in England from the first', but instead he preferred to think about engaging a 'very good English Tutor, capable of preparing Pen for the University without, if possible, necessitating the passage thro' a Public School.'

Meanwhile, Pen was allowed to do pretty much as he pleased and was attending to himself very capably. Robert, to his credit, took the opportunity of their holiday together to observe his son closely. What he saw was altogether pleasing. To Isa, on 9 September, he declared that Pen 'shows me many things about him which I am glad to discover. He has a great power of suiting himself to circumstances.' To the Storys, Robert had reported that 'Pen is quite well, strong, red as a brick, and amusing himself all day with his grandfather, who, at the age of seventy-nine is absolutely unchanged. I see no difference whatever except in the greyer hair, and a touch or two of rheumatism which does not prevent three long walks a day. Pen rides, bathes and does well generally. My sister is better, and finds the loneliness and roughness of the place to her taste.' As to Robert's own plans, they were unchanged: 'London may suit me better than a brighter place for some time to come — but I shall have no ties, no housekeeping, nothing to prevent me from wandering about, if circumstances permit. I want my new life to resemble the last fifteen years as little as possible.'[31]

By 30 August, when Robert wrote once more to the Storys from St Enogat, he was again beginning to 'feel impatient at doing nothing, and long to begin with Pen'. He had taken time during the summer to correspond with friends in London — 'Forster, Procter, and others — for help and advice about . . . the apartment, the tutor and room. I shall be in London by October, I dare say, for I am feverish to begin in earnest.'[32] Robert recognized, nevertheless, that it would be better to bide his time, let Pen build up as great a stock of health and strength as possible — 'it will all come into use presently in our grim London'.[33] He had no rosy illusion that London would be any great, good place: it was necessary to be there only for the benefit of Pen's education and grounding as an Englishman.

Aside from the lively prospect of 'so many kind friends proposing to put light into the coming gloomy winter', he evidently regarded the life to come in London as a duty towards Pen rather than an opportunity for himself. He would set up no household that could not be abandoned in a minute, tie himself down to as little as possible, give himself room for quick manoeuvre and — when and as possible — flight and escape to places less dolorous and that held no painful associations, places that might lift the spirits with a little light and colour. He had turned his back on Florence, which, though he did not know it then, he would never see again, but he had no thought of giving up on Italy entirely. Robert's letter to Isa Blagden of 9 September 1861 makes this clear: Italy 'should be open to *me*, I know, if the least duty to go there presented itself: even if my own health imperatively required my return, I would go — knowing that I ought.'

The Brownings left St Enogat towards the end of September to return to Paris, where Robert and Pen stayed only a couple of days before setting off for Boulogne on their way, finally, to lodge for a week or so with Arabel at 7 Delamere Terrace in London. They arrived on 29 September, though not without delays on account of the pony. Robert, as usual, had informed himself minutely in advance about train times and boat connections. There are certain incidents in Robert's life so perfectly illustrative of his character that they demand quotation in full. Robert's account of his difficulty *en route* is one of them. In a letter to George Barrett of 30 September 1861, Robert wrote:

> Do you know what an escape we had on Thursday? I was informed by a timetable and the railway official that a train would leave Paris for Boulogne at 6. in the morning to arrive at 1½; (any other train would arrive too late for the customhouse, without a permission from which Pen's pony could not be

embarked — I should therefore be delayed 36 hours at Boul-
ogne.) On the faith of this information I brought the horse to
the station at 5. a.m. — and found no train was to go: the next
available for horses would start in the afternoon and I must wait
till then — horses on no account could go by the 'express'
which alone would arrive in time. I reasoned with the officers
for above two hours, declaring quietly I would prosecute the
company — they admitting the blunders and calling them inex-
plicable. At the last minute (there was not even time to pay for
him) they gave in. The horse was attached to the express ('for
the first time') to the wonder of everybody along the line. So I
gained my point and got off by the boat at 2 past midnight.
Had they persisted, I should have been forced to go by the 8.
p.m. train, arriving at 12: and, as you see by the papers, at 11
there was the dreadful accident and loss of life on the line at
Amiens.

Robert's quick irritation at plans that went awry was just as often
tempered by a dogged persistence in setting them right again, and this
occasion recalls his earlier battle to transport his wife, son, and Thomas
Carlyle from London to Paris. Such incidents are very representative of
his resilience and resourcefulness when, despite all precautions to avert
delay or disaster, chaotic, unpredictable life set the poet and his plans
at an obtuse angle to the orderly universe. This incident was rehearsed
again by Robert, in a letter to the Storys on 10 November, elaborating
the circumstances a little and marvelling at the adventure, the upshot
of which had possibly — providentially as it might be — spared their
lives, which could have been lost had they got on 'the "proper train for
me", which I certainly should have taken had they beaten me, and which
was run into by another train at Amiens having "22 wounded and 10
or 12 killed," said the "Times" two days after'.

Among the dead and injured might not have been just one poet,
but two. Robert happened to put his head out of the carriage window
at Amiens, and who should he see but Tennyson boarding the train,
great-bearded but instantly recognizable. This was a cause of wonder
to Robert, since he had been 'thinking much of the meeting I had with
Tennyson ten years ago when he was the first person I chanced upon

in Paris — I must have told you, for it always impressed me'. In this instance, not having seen an English friend since he left Florence, the sighting of Tennyson was serendipitous or synchronous enough to strike Robert as significant. But this time, Robert was in no mood to make himself known to his friend: when he spotted him again, and confirmed to his satisfaction that it was indeed Tennyson in the train doorway at Boulogne, 'I kept out of sight.' Nevertheless, Robert wrote to the Storys, on the quay from which the Folkestone boat was due shortly to leave, he said to Pen, ' "I'll show you Tennyson" — and presently he came forward with his wife and two beautiful children — they seated themselves a few yards from me: I pulled my hat over my face, — not that they would have recognized me' — nor would they have recognized the abruptly transformed Pen — 'and so saw them off. Odd, is it not, to leave Florence, twice, and twice meet, for the first English face — Tennyson's! I wonder whether he, also, had missed the afternoon train and its smash.'

For the first nine months in London, Robert and Pen stayed in lodgings at 1 Chichester Road, just off Westbourne Terrace. Revising his resolution to give up housekeeping, Robert then moved with Pen to 19 Warwick Crescent, a substantial house in Little Venice. The convenience of the Chichester Road lodgings had been that they were close to Isa Blagden, who was staying nearby. The house in Warwick Crescent had the advantage of being close to Arabel's abode in Delamere Terrace, and its windows looked out over the Grand Union Canal, which widened at that stage in its career to include a tiny island, sparsely furnished with trees. Not far away was a bridge across the canal. To this bridge, Robert liked to say, Byron dragged his publisher, John Murray, to show him the spot where a publisher had drowned himself.[34]

It was a pretty-enough situation — for London — but the prettiness, says Mrs Orr, who could be condescending in the manner of her times and social class, 'was neutralized for him by the atmosphere of low or ugly life which encompassed it on almost every side'.[35] Chichester Road had been worse: 'There had been nothing to break for him the transition from the stately beauty of Florence to the impressions and associations of the Harrow and Edgware Roads and of Paddington Green.' Nevertheless, though he took it temporarily, as he then thought, Robert was to find the house in Warwick Crescent convenient and comfortable. He was to make it his home for twenty-five years, 'in spite', wrote Mrs Orr, 'of the refuse of humanity which would sometimes yell at the street corner, or fling stones at his plate-glass'. Over the years, she claimed, Robert 'learned by degrees to regard London as a home; as the only fitting centre for the varied energies which were reviving in him; to feel pleasure in its increasingly picturesque character'.[36]

On 21 January, from the Chichester Road address, Robert wrote to William Story:

> Of myself — so little to say; my life is as grey (or yellow) as this sky, one snow-bank above head at this minute. I make up my mind from week to week — *next* Monday I will begin and call on my friends . . . *Next* week I still say. I see hardly anybody, but mean, I assure you, to alter all that for abundance of reasons . . . My end of life, and particular reward for myself, will be, one day years hence, to just go back to Italy, to Rome, and die as I lived, when I used really to live. If you knew — but you *do* know, and can conceive, how precious every mud-splash on the house-walls of Rome is, how every minute of those last six months in Rome would *melt up* into gold enough for a year's use now, if I had it. But I have *not*, and must think of something else — as that you at least are there, where you were, as you were.

He seems, from this letter, to have exchanged what some had perceived as a homesickness for England in Italy, for a homesickness for Italy in England. The view from Warwick Crescent, say William Irvine and Park Honan, 'on sunny days, suggested Venice'.[37] If it did, by an effort that would stretch even the most romantic poetic imagination, it might have struck Robert as pinchbeck rather than gold, a failed alchemical attempt to transmute the desolating bridge of the suicidal publisher into the Bridge of Sighs or, more happily, the Rialto.

Failing in these early days to rally his resolution to face his friends, Robert took long, slow, solitary walks through the squalid neighbourhoods that so distressed Mrs Orr and through the more salubrious London parks. He missed Isa, who was visiting friends in Kent, and on 6 February 1862 Robert wrote to her of his London walks as 'dreary'. For the time being, he applied his energies immediately to his reason for being in London — Pen's education. There were difficulties finding suitable tutors, as he wrote to William Story on 10 November 1861, and he was undecided 'whether to send him to Eton before Oxford . . . "the advantage at Eton is *not* of getting scholarship, but of-of-of" — why, getting aristocratic connexions and friendships, which in England is the chief end of man! . . . meantime, all the teaching falls on me . . . I see nobody — have only called on people about business — the main business being about Pen.' There was also some business, from 21 December 1861 to 2 January 1862, the date of two letters from Robert to George Barrett, about 'the investment of the proceeds of the sale of the "David Lyon" on Peni's account'. The *David Lyon*, one of the Barrett ships in the West India trade, had paid the Brownings an annual dividend, and the asset had, on Elizabeth's death, been applied to Pen's benefit. The point of these letters was a technical matter of trusteeship which Robert, punctilious in financial matters to the point of pedantry, rather blew up beyond its proper proportions.

At this time, Robert's only sociable daily visits had been to Isa, living virtually opposite, and to Arabel, who was in a poor state. Quite aside from her own chronic rheumatic complaint, she was distressed that Octavius Barrett's wife had died a week after a confinement, and also that a Barrett uncle had recently passed away. In the first week of January 1862, Pen came down with what Robert at first, alarmed, thought might be smallpox, but turned out to be chicken pox. The boy recovered, continued his lessons, and seemed, gratifyingly, to be 'growing fast in every way and wants to understand serious work: his behaviour is very satisfactory, — he gets good habits of attention and diligence daily — and continues as childlike and docile as before — rather grows more so'.[38]

By mid-February, Robert was feeling more lively. As he had pulled himself together by an act of will at Bagni di Lucca after his mother's death, he now made a conscious resolution after the death of his wife to confront the business of getting on with life and getting into life, not just for his own good but for the good of his family — for his son — and for the sake of those friends he had, to their concern, been avoiding. He had seen an edition of Elizabeth's *Last Poems* through Chapman's presses (dedicating the volume, in graceful allusion to the memorial tablet that had been placed on the wall of Casa Guidi, to 'grateful

Florence'); he had more or less resolved the matter of tutors for Pen; and he now began, tentatively, to be sociable in London as he had been in Rome and Paris. 'I go out a little, — have called on friends, old and recent, — mean to accept all invitations henceforth: am just made a member of the "Athenaeum," by the committee' — the Athenaeum, in Pall Mall, possessing a fine library, was a well-established gentleman's club, highly regarded as a resort of distinguished men, and Robert took full advantage of its opulent facilities — 'and in short am like one of those well-appointed cockney sportsmen who are accoutred from head to heel in sporting gear, with the primest of guns and perfectest of pointers, and who only want nerve to pull the trigger.'[39]

This would have been welcome news to the Storys, who had urged him, as Elizabeth had constantly done, to go out into society for his own good. Pen's welfare had been Robert's first priority: until the boy's schooling was settled, there had been no time to think about his own well-being. The discussion in detail of all the possibilities and probabilities of Pen's education in Robert's letter to the Storys had evidently been short compared to the conversations on the subject that Robert had had with Isa. By 25 March 1862, he commented: 'Don't fear, dearest Isa — I shall never become a "monomaniac" about Pen's education: I made an effort because it was wanted; and it is already so successful as to admit of my going out *every evening*, with time enough at other parts of the day: had I done less he would have gained less. I shall always have plenty of anxiety, but none unduly — nor do I ever put my hand to the machine a minute after it is really working by itself: and when more of my time is my own I shall have plenty to do with it as of old.'

His first excursions were a mixed benefit. He called on Dante Gabriel Rossetti, whose wife, Elizabeth Siddal, had died early in February of an overdose of laudanum. Robert did not know it at the time, but the overdose had been deliberate. He visited Mrs Twistleton, the wife of another friend, 'young, so pretty, so full of sympathy, so good to me — has one of those horrible internal complaints, — just such a case as Henrietta's', as he reported to Isa. Mrs Twistleton was to die just three months later. Robert had heard, too, that Lady William Russell, Odo Russell's mother, was seriously ill. There is a certain desperate relish in Robert's writing with such news to Isa. 'So one lives! And so would I *not* live, if this life were all, — no, indeed!' But, once out and about,

Robert's sociability acquired an irresistible, self-perpetuating momentum: once swept up into London society, he had little thought of retiring from it. Nevertheless, just as he had tired of society as a young man and professed to go about in it mechanically and for professional benefit, so he now wrote to the Storys on April 10 1862, 'I go out every night to dine in a cold-blooded way'; and in a letter of 18 January 1863 he told them, 'I can't chronicle all these people that come and go before me, and whose very names I forget next day: why do I like so much to hear gossip from you and fancy that London news can no more interest you than it does me? You throw bits of porphyry and marble pavement from Rome, and I have only London mud, that's the fact.'

When Isa left London to return to Florence, she and Robert agreed to write to one another on set days every month — he on the 19th, the anniversary of the date on which Robert and Elizabeth had first left London for Italy, Isa on the 12th, the anniversary of the Brownings' marriage. These letters seldom touched more than the surface froth and bubble of their lives. 'All this tittle-tattle', Robert wrote, 'is intended to resemble what will be lost to us for many a year — the old chats and gossip: I can never, — shall never try to go an inch below the surface — but what need is there of that with you?'[40] This might have been taken as a backhanded compliment, but both Robert and Isa knew very well that everyday trivia might often be more consoling, compelling even, than page after page of earnest, introverted self-examination. Robert and Isa knew, too, the limits of their relationship.

This was no romance; they were loving towards one another, but they were not in love. 'Dearest friend,' Robert wrote to Isa on 19 July 1862, 'no one has ever been to me all you have been. I shall find no new friends even of a lower grade nor do I want them — kind acquaintances I continue to make every day: you are my — nearly one, certainly best, woman-friend. God bless you, — we will be "snakes" together yet, if He please.' As 'snakes', Robert and Isa would end their lives together in Italy as a latter-day Cadmus and Harmonia. 'Last will come the pythons incubating their addled eggs in Italy, — eh?'[41]

But even to such a close and trusted friend as Isa, Robert felt impelled to spell out one primary condition of their correspondence: 'To begin and to end, these notes are *always private*, you know, and I trust.'[42] He reinforced this embargo two months later in his letter to Isa on 18 August: 'Remember I read your letters, twice, and then burn them: mine, I trust, — earnestly conjure you will never show: but you will not.' In March, Thornton Hunt, the son of Leigh Hunt (who had died in August 1859), had requested a letter from his father to Robert for publication in a book of Hunt's edited correspondence. The letter was 'locked up in Florence' but Robert was perfectly willing to permit publication as and when it could be obtained. Instead, lacking that letter, Thornton Hunt published, without permission, a letter from Robert and Elizabeth to his father, 'full', as Robert wrote to Isa on 7 March 1862,

> of intimate talk about our child's illness, and other things which give me real pain to read — the whole improved by such a series of blunders in the copying my letter (being unused to my handwriting, I suppose, that the result is unintelligible beyond even *my* unintelligibility. He confesses it probably needs correction!) Think of doing this without one word of enquiry as to whether I would allow such a liberty — which means, taking care not to receive the inevitable refusal. Once I should have been angry enough — now, I seem hardly to care after the first feeling of disgust and annoyance — it is as if some clownish person had thrown open the door of a bathing-machine in which I was undressing — the whole company on the beach probably stare and laugh — and a very young lady would be mortified enough, — but I shall not break my heart, depend on it. What clownishness, however!

Elizabeth had herself expressed a desire that her letters should be private until after her death. Robert, even more cautious about public exposure of his private life, in fear of albums and memorials and the like being published in his lifetime and after, had already made determined attempts to retrieve or suppress his own letters. He cared about such revelation very intensely, though if the thing was done and beyond help, he might get over the annoyance quickly enough. But he would take care to avoid it in the first place. He was forever turning down requests for letters and other materials begged by would-be biographers of Elizabeth. On 19 January 1863, he fulminated in a letter to Isa about a Mr George Stampe of Great Grimsby who had got his hands on Elizabeth's letters to Hugh Stuart Boyd and was canvassing friends of the Brownings for 'details of life and letters for a biography he is engaged in'. Robert, in the heat of a very considerable passion, could not contain himself:

> Think of this beast working away at this, not deeming my feelings, or those of her family, worthy of notice — and meaning to print letters written years and years ago, on the most intimate and personal subjects, to an 'old friend' — which, at the poor, old blind, forsaken man's death fell into the hands of a complete stranger, who at once wanted to print them — but desisted thro' Ba's earnest expostulation enforced by my own threat to take law proceedings — as fortunately letters are copy-right . . . But what I suffer in feeling the hands of these blackguards (for I forgot to say, *another* man has been making similar applications to friends) — what I undergo with their paws in my very bowels, you can guess and God knows!

This letter would impliedly have warned Isa again, if warning were needed, what the consequences would be should she ever contemplate publication of the monthly letters exchanged between them: Robert would, if necessary in the case of Stampe, 'be forced to advertise in the Times and obtain an injunction'. The threat was not especially directed at Isa, but the heat of Robert's rage clearly made him oblivious to any tactful phrasing: 'No friend, of course, would ever give up the letters: if anybody is ever forced to do that which *she* would have so utterly writhed under — if it ever *were* necessary, why, I should be forced to do it, and, with any good to her memory and fame, I should *do* it at whatever cost: but it is not only unnecessary but absurdly useless — and, indeed, it shall not be done if I can stop the scamp's knavery — along with his breath.' At least the previous owner of Elizabeth's letters to Boyd, who had sold them to Stampe merely, as he'd thought, for the interest and value of the autographs, had promised to do his best to retrieve them.

Stampe, the scandalous would-be biographer of Great Grimsby, was not the egregious first and would not be the loathsome last. Letters were one thing — copyright — but the confidences of friends were another: they should keep their counsel as close as their correspondence. To Isa,

Robert begged: 'Warn anyone you may think needs the warning of the utter distress in which I should be placed were this scoundrel or any other of the sort, to baffle me and bring out the letters. I can't prevent fools from uttering their folly upon her life, as they do on every other subject, but the law protects *property* — as these letters are.' Robert's suspicion of false and foolish friends was justified. A few years later, in a letter to Isa of 19 March 1868, he worked up another fine head of steam at the prospect of a volume of Elizabeth's letters to Mrs Eckley that the latter was touting around in hopes of publication. She should have known better. As early as 28 March 1862, in response to a letter from Sophia Eckley asking Robert's help in finding a publisher for her poetry, he had declined — though not in so many words — to be of assistance. His letter to her had contained the words, enigmatic in the context of their correspondence but unambiguous in the context of their past history, 'Depend on it, I forget nothing and nobody — whether to my greater happiness or misfortune, I really don't know.'

Mrs Eckley's reappearance with another literary project was no big surprise, and Robert could only sigh to Isa that it had been mostly Elizabeth's fault: 'not only I knew she would make a show of those letters, and said so, — but Ba was the first to say so, when she found her out — *at last*. I used to reply (for she mentioned her belief more than once) — "of course she will parade them, and you must make up your mind to it: the very uselessness which yourself feel of making any appeal to her, shows what you now understand her to be — the love, the honesty you were once confident in the existence of, — yourself laugh now at the notion of finding a trace of those to appeal to. It is a punishment you must bear — that of having her name associated with yours: you should have believed *me* so far at least as to use your own faculties and so get to believe for yourself." So I say still, — with hardly additional pain.'

Sophia Eckley's second betrayal was hardly worse than the first, except that Robert had the measure of her that Elizabeth had lacked. Resignedly, Robert admitted to Isa, 'Of course there is no possible way of preventing her doing as she likes with her own, — as the letters are. She cannot *print* them (in England at least) — and if she does so in America, she will have to explain why they end abruptly, and what she won't explain, letters of Ba, to other people, *will* — to say nothing of what I may contribute.'[43] In the event, the letters were not published.

Though Robert had written to the Storys on 18 January 1863 to complain that there was nothing very interesting to pass on about London society gossip, he did add: 'I cannot say I am dull here — I work, or, at least, am employed all day long.' His confidence had been boosted over the previous year by a surprising offer. On 19 March 1862 he had written to tell the Storys that Thackeray had recently resigned the editorship of the *Cornhill* and that it had been offered to '— *me!* I really take it as a compliment because I am, by your indulgence, a bit of a poet, if you like — but a man of the world and able editor, hardly! They count on my attracting writers, — I who could never muster *English* readers enough to pay for salt and bread!' Robert tried, a little, to play down the compliment, but his exhilaration could hardly be repressed. He was — the only word for it — cock-a-hoop.

His first, prompt answer to Thackeray, 'that my life was done for and settled, that I could not change it and would not', was, however, a refusal. He was asked to think again, which he did over the course of a week and wavered: he was flattered 'to figure as a man actually capable of choosing better articles from the quantity always on hand than have illustrated the Cornhill', and £2000 a year, the same as Thackeray had earned — Robert would accept not a farthing less — was tempting as a salary 'which Pen might find something to do with'. It might, too, be interesting to 'try what the business [of editing] is like'. On the other hand, what did Robert want with more money? And the expense of time would be considerable: 'the little to do ought to be honestly done, might take more of my time than I choose to part with'. These thoroughly enjoyable reflections occupied Robert very pleasurably — 'I have my little piece of satisfied conceit' — until he again declined the offer.

The little irony was, as he confessed to the Storys, 'now that I care not one whit about what I never cared for too much, people are getting goodnatured to my poems'. John Forster and Bryan Waller Procter were already busy editing *Selections from the Poetical Works of Robert Browning*, which was to be published on 22 December 1862 by Chapman and Hall. Forster and Procter, champions both of Robert Browning and his works, claimed Browning, in their preface to this volume, as 'among the few great poets of this century'; and so, when it was published,

Robert suddenly became. The book, intended 'to popularize my old things', was exciting interest well in advance of publication. To the Storys, on 19 March 1862, Robert airily remarked that, 'so and so means to review it, and somebody or [other] always was looking out for such an occasion, and what's his name always said he admired me, only he didn't say it, though he said something else every week of his life in some Journal. The breath of man!' Robert himself was busy preparing a new three-volume edition of his complete works — everything except *Pauline*, that is — which, dedicated to John Forster, was published in 1863. To this he added the happy labour of reprinting Elizabeth's early contributions to the *Athenaeum*, which were collected and published in March of the same year as *The Greek Christian Poets and the English Poets*.

These books might have seemed to be memorials as much as anything: enshrining the past, sealing it like flowers in the still, stale atmosphere of a bell-jar. And yet — and yet — currents of air from the old life stirred and scented the stale atmosphere of a London summer. The Storys, flushed with the prodigious and long-awaited success of the great sculptor's two new pieces — a Libyan Sibyl for which he had refused a princely £1500 (it finally sold for £2400) and a Cleopatra (borrowed as an image by Hawthorne for his novel, *The Marble Faun*), which would leave another buyer £2400 the poorer — swept into London in June 1862. They were followed a week later by Hatty Hosmer and John Gibson, in England that summer, like the Storys, for the important London Exhibition that could make or break, promote or petrify, artistic reputations in Europe and America. Pen, too, was visited by a friend from Florence, young Alessandro, 'the red-headed boy Peni so liked to play with', wrote Robert to Isa on 19 June 1862, 'coming here on a visit, — to his grandmother who lives at Highgate! He walked over a fortnight ago, and I was amazed at hearing a chatter of Tuscan and seeing emerge his unmistakable locks!'

Mrs Orr deigns to notice Alessandro in what amounts to a virtual footnote and comments with heavy humour on a friendship she can hardly bring herself to admit as appropriate for Pen but is obliged to recognize as 'testimony to the moral atmosphere into which the child had been born'. Pen, she says, 'was sometimes allowed to play with a little boy not of his own class — perhaps the son of a *contadino*'. The word '*contadino*' is in itself demeaning in terms of English class-consciousness. 'The child was unobjectionable, or neither Penini nor his parents would have endured the association; but the servants once thought themselves justified in treating him cavalierly, and Pen flew indignant to his mother, to complain of their behaviour. Mrs Browning at once sought little Alessandro, with kind words and a large piece of cake; but this, in Pen's eyes, only aggravated the offence; it was a direct reflection on his visitor's quality. "He doesn't tome for take," he burst forth, "he tomes because he is my friend." How often, since I heard this first, have we repeated the words, "he doesn't tome for take," in half-serious definition of a disinterested person or act! They became a standing joke.'[44]

Robert encouraged young Alessandro to visit as often as possible, and took particular pleasure in hearing the two boys 'chatter away in the dear old language just as they did at Siena or Florence'. Another surprise visit was made by the first of the Brownings' servants, Alessandro; and another friend, the Italian poet Villari, came to lunch, to Robert's great pleasure. Correspondence with Isa, the regular exchange of gossip between London and Florence, also mended the bonds with the past. The regularity, indeed, with which they were reinforced was all to the good: not all had been tied and knotted. Besides the letters from Isa, there was a regular bombardment of cursing and complaining correspondence from Landor, which Robert stoically withstood and even, writing to Isa on 19 November 1862, weakly defended: 'Mr Landor is, I hope, hardly to be blamed for what he does. He has been trying hard of late to annoy us all here as much as possible: if he were to be judged by his actions, it would be sad indeed. He wrote to me three days ago that he should die this year — but what folly and falsehood does he not write?'

On 2 August, Robert bolted from London, surfeited with society: 'I never quitted a house so precipitately — my engagements were continual to the last: I look forward to the quiet October and November in London: fortunately I have so many invitations to go into the country that I shall best extricate myself by pleading the impossibility of accepting one without offending another — I shall go *nowhere*.'[45] With Pen he travelled first to Paris, thence with Sarianna and Mr Browning to Sainte Marie — 'a wild little place in Brittany' — where they had taken the mayor's house for two months for their summer holiday. Pornic, 'full and gay enough', was only half an hour away by foot. The lonely little hamlet, a dozen houses by the sea, reminded Robert of St Enogat, where they had spent their holiday the year before, and suited his mood: 'I have brought books, and write: I wanted a change,' he told Isa. Elizabeth and Florence remained much on his mind. Frederic Leighton had proposed designs for the monument to be erected over Elizabeth's grave, and there were some practical matters to be settled in respect of the foundations, the commissioning of a local artist to make the monument, and the inevitable disagreements about taste that arose among all the interested parties and some who felt a personal interest in the project.

To Isa, in his letter of 18 August 1862, Robert confided a great secret: 'I shall go to Florence whenever the erection takes place of the monument — ... for that and nothing else.' He 'could not live at Florence, now or at any time — unless perhaps in old age: but Italy, — Rome or Naples, I will go to the moment I can — and when will that be?' In this state of mind, Robert told Isa: 'If I could, I would stay just as I am for many a day. I feel out of the very earth sometimes, as I sit here at the window — with the little church, a field, a few houses, and the sea; on a week day there is *nobody* in the village: plenty of haystacks, cows and fowls — all our butter, eggs, milk are produced in the farm-house. Such a soft sea and a mournful wind! I wrote a poem yesterday of 120 lines — and mean to keep writing, whether I like it or no.'[46]

As so often, it is unclear which poem Robert was writing at any particular time. He provided Isa with neither the title nor any detail that would definitely identify this one, but the two candidates are 'Gold Hair: A Legend of Pornic', which in its final version comprised 135 lines, or part of the longer poem, 'James Lee's Wife', at a length of 311 lines — though this might just as likely have been written a year later at Sainte Marie.

Though the poem at times recalls the mood of Tennyson's *Maud*, it is suggested that 'James Lee's Wife' [entitled 'James Lee' until 1868] may have been prompted as a response to George Meredith's tragi-comic *Modern Love*, a sequence of fifty short lyrics published in June 1862. Robert is known to have received a copy from Meredith in July and to have admired it. The male narrator of the themes and events of *Modern Love*, disillusioned in his idealization of women, cruelly and cynically analyses the failure of his marriage in which, as passionate love gives way to jealousy, discord, and misery, two lives are ruined. Meredith's poem differs not only in form from Browning's but also in emphasizing the pressures of external social conventions as significant elements in the disintegration of the marriage. The dramatic or novelistic instinct would be to find in the sections and stanzas of 'James Lee's Wife' a summation of, or at least a meditation on, Robert the widower's feelings about life with and without Elizabeth. If it is in that sense autobiographical or subjective, it is so in an internalized, reflective manner. Meredith's poem is written and narrated by and for a man of the world: Browning's poem is written by and from the '*moi profond*' and, notably, as the reverie of a young woman. There are no external forces leading to the separation of the lovers: the internal tensions that drive them apart derive from temperamental differences.

'James Lee's Wife' was not entirely a new poem. Six stanzas, signed 'Z' (Robert's *nom de plume* at the time), had been published in May 1836 in the *Monthly Repository*; but its landscape in the full version is recognizably the bleak turf and rock of the Brittany coastline. An exquisitely realized sense of autumnal melancholy suffuses the poem: there is regret and resolution in its lines, an acknowledgement of failure, and — unusually for a Browning poem — no obvious pleasure or joy. A quiet, dull acceptance rather than any positive affirmation permeates its lines: more dispiritedly than in 'Christmas-Eve and Easter-Day', the higher consolations of Art and God are recommended as a solace for disappointed love. Robert later, in December 1864, commented on the poem, saying that he had meant James Lee and his wife to be 'people newly-married, trying to realize a dream of being sufficient to each other, in a foreign land (where you can try such an experiment) and finding it break up — the man being tired *first*, — and tired precisely of the love: — but I have expressed it all insufficiently, and will break the chain up, one day, and leave so many separate little round rings to roll each its way, if it can.'[47]

The poem is probably more expressive of Robert's feelings of understandable but unusual lassitude and ennui at the time of composition rather than of any profound dissatisfactions during his own marriage — although, looking back upon it, he may have recognized deficiencies and difficulties, irritations and discontents, that could only now, in retrospect, be identified as having been personally restrictive. But to read 'James Lee's Wife' simply as a comment by Robert on his marriage to Elizabeth is to interpret it at the level of a literary *causerie*, in terms of literary salon chat. It may be suggested, nevertheless, that marriage to another poet may have hindered or stalled Robert's own poetic development. He had hoped, at the beginning, that his union with Elizabeth would provoke them both to even greater heights of creative achievement; but Elizabeth, throughout the marriage, had been the more commercially successful writer, as well as the more productive, and her work had been more esteemed by critics and the public than her husband's.

Her celebrity had always eclipsed Robert's. For his part, he had consistently supported her in her work and rejoiced in her triumphs. To a friend who had preferred his poetry to Elizabeth's, Robert protested: 'You are wrong — quite wrong — she has genius; I am only a painstaking fellow. Can't you imagine a clever sort of angel who plots and plans, and tries to build up something — he wants to make you see it as he sees it — shows you one point of view, carries you off to another, hammering into your head the thing he wants you to understand; and whilst this bother is going on God Almighty turns you off a little star — that's the difference between us. The true creative power is hers, not mine.'[48]

The Brownings' marriage, like any other, had been tested by differences of temperament. In a letter to Isa Blagden of 19 September 1867 Robert admitted 'seven distinct issues to which I came with Ba, in our profoundly different estimates of thing and person: I go over them one by one and must deliberately inevitably say, on each of these points I was, am proved to be, right and she wrong.' Edward McAleer, commenting on this, speculatively identifies the seven issues as spiritualism, Napoleon III, Mrs Eckley, Mrs Trollope, the method of raising Pen, the subscription for Mrs Jameson's sisters, and their own marriage.[49] The Brownings' marriage had occasionally been strained by internal tensions, and there are some who have attempted to make a case for the decline of the marriage in its final months. It is a matter of debate whether Elizabeth's death had been timely, whether she had died just before what is generally perceived to have been the perfect passionate union of two souls could deteriorate into something more prosaic.

There were contemporaries of the Brownings who thought so, and Elizabeth herself had given the decline of her health and strength some thought in the context of its effect on Robert, who, in the immediate circumstances of her death, fell into what we can recognize as a depressed state of mind during which, nevertheless, he had dealt with practical matters very ably and conscientiously. He had considered and consulted, and by and large he felt he had done right. He had come to terms, so far as possible, with the knowledge that Elizabeth's quick and peaceful death had spared her any prolonged suffering. But of course, despite all the earnest resolutions and deliberate efforts he had made to fashion a new life for himself and Pen, there were moments — just as in the last days in Florence — when the past, the loss of the old life, overwhelmed him.

From Sainte Marie, on 19 September 1862, two weeks before he and Pen were due to return to London, Robert wrote in a restless mood to Isa:

With respect to Florence, I cannot tell how I feel about it, so do I change my feelings in the course of a quarter of an hour sometimes: particular incidents in the Florence way of life recur as if I could not bear a repetition of them — to find myself walking among the hills, or turning by the villas, certain doorways, old walls, points of sight, on a solitary bright summer Sunday afternoon — there, I think that would fairly choke me at once: on the other hand, beginning from another point of association, I have such yearnings to be there! Just now, at the approach of Autumn, I feel exactly like a swallow in a cage, as if I *must* go there, have no business anywhere else, with the year drawing in. — How thankful I am that all these foolish fancies never displace for a moment the solid fact that I can't go but have plain duty to do in London, — if there could be a doubt about that, I should drift about like a feather at times (to give you a notion of what I might do if free to be foolish) I seem as if I should like, by a fascination, to try the worst at once, — go straight to the old rooms at Casa Guidi, and there live and die! But I shake all this off — and say to myself (sometimes aloud) 'Don't be afraid, my good fellow, you'll die too, all in good time.'

The notion in these last few lines is plain: to return to Florence, to harrow hell, to seek out an old love, to eke out an old life, would be to embrace not only Elizabeth's death but his own. Indeed, on Monday 20 October 1862, adding to his monthly letter, dated Saturday the 18th, he declared to Isa just such a thought: 'Oh, me — to find myself there [by a wall close to Isa's villa], some late sunshiny Sunday afternoon, with my face turned to Florence, — "ten minutes to the Gate, ten minutes home!" I think I should fairly end it all on the spot.' When, late in 1862, the memorial tablet to Elizabeth was finally placed on the wall of Casa Guidi, Robert wrote to Isa from London on 19 November that year: 'I can't tell you the thrill of pain and pleasure I feel about it: the presence of Her is now habitual to me, — I can have no doubt that it is my greatest comfort to be always remembering her, — the old books and furniture, her chair which is by mine, — all this is comfort to me — but in this case, it was as if, besides my feeling on my own account the deepest gratification at this act, determined and carried into effect, — I also sympathized with her pride and pleasure ... all I can say is, I shall love the dust of Florence, the letters which make up its name, every man, woman and child it holds. There — I've done.'

Robert's feelings about the finality of his separation from Elizabeth seemed to become as fixed as the tribute. He was able to write to Isa, 'I am certainly not unhappy, any more than I ever was ... In many ways, I can see with my human eyes why this has been right and good for me — as I never doubted it was for Her — and if we do but rejoin one day, — the break will be better than forgotten, remembered for its uses.' His clear duty was to live in the present for his own sake and look to the future of his son.

Pen's development is pretty well summarized in Robert's letters from 1862–4 to Isa Blagden and to the Storys. Robert and Pen had been accompanied to Sainte Marie for August and September 1862 by Mrs Bracken, a widow and friend of Isa's, and her teenage son Willie. On July 18 1858, Elizabeth had written to Isa from Paris to say that the Brownings had seen Isa's brother, Mrs Bracken, and Willie who 'is charming I think — with a graceful head, and curls, sheared a little ... much fairer than Peni's. He is taller too by nearly a head.' By 1852, Pen was as tall as Willie. Both boys had shot up in height, and both were energetic. They swam together, Pen 'quite well, in the deep sea — with a *baigneur* swimming beside, for my assurance — so that he has gained a good thing.' Writing thus to Isa on 19 September 1862, Robert also reported favourably on his son's moral character: 'he may be depended on, is very undemonstrative and very sensitive — has good sense and self-command.'

Robert was sustained by the thought that his management of Pen was self-evidently successful. To Isa, in the same letter, he commented that Pen 'is doing well, on the whole, with me. The health and strength of him are extraordinary, and indeed, perfect . . . The air, neighbourhood of the sea, extreme solitariness of the place, suit us all — Pen having Willy and my father to his heart's content.' By the time the Brownings and the Brackens were ready to leave Sainte Marie, on 2 October 1862, Robert was proudly reporting to William Story that 'I go away with Pen in prodigious force — he has taken his fifty-first good swim in the sea, is brick-coloured and broad-shouldered.'[50]

Robert's only niggling anxiety was that Pen's moral, intellectual, and physical development might be slow. Set against this, however, was the consolation that it was '*sure* — [he] retains all he has learnt and digests it, as I am surprised to find: is undemonstrative, but feels deeply as I have had occasion to observe'; and this might be better than a 'clever precocious immaturity to be admired and then forgotten . . . I shall be able to manage him easily, I believe, and already have not half the difficulty that I had last year.' Robert admitted to Isa that life without Pen would be hardly worth living. 'I see increasingly every day, that were he not *here*, I should be "no where": life is, as you describe Mr Landor's dressing gown, "all the colour washed out of it" — but, with the particular incentives I retain, I hope to fight a good fight and finish my course.'[51]

By 19 November, the date on which Robert next wrote to Isa, Pen's tutor had commended his pupil's 'confirmed habit of attention' and a steady improvement which even the Browning servants noticed. Robert 'might give him holidays enough — but *he* does not desire it, — in fact he *thinks* now: he has taken to earnest reading . . . of [Captain Frederick] Marryat's novels! I can hardly get him to lay them down.' Pen took his nose out of books of adventure stories long enough, nevertheless, to attend, with Robert, a ball given by Lady de Grey in February

1863, and, as Isa was informed, 'he would go to another to-morrow but for the cold — the same reason keeps him from accepting an invitation to dine with Lady Westmorland tonight and go to Fechter — I won't have it.' Charles Albert Fechter was an actor-playwright who had recently leased the Lyceum Theatre. Already, even before his fifteenth birthday, it looked as though Pen was taking his social cues from his father, who in this same month — far from forbidding himself any diversions — was back in his routine of regular evening engagements, dining on the night of 19 February with Lady William Russell, then going to Lady Salisbury's, the next night invited to Mrs Sartoris's, and the day after that to Lady Palmerston's.

Still and all, London's amusements were occasionally less than satisfactory. The episode of Dickens' van had been simply irritating. On 10 March 1863, Edward, Prince of Wales, married Princess Alexandra, daughter of the King of Denmark, and that night there were to be tremendous illuminations. In a letter of 31 March 1863 to the old actor William Macready, Charles Dickens described the treat he had intended for some of his friends and family. 'Having two little boys sent home from school "to see the illuminations" on the marriage night, I chartered an enormous van, at a cost of five pounds, and we started in majesty from the office in London, fourteen strong. We crossed Waterloo Bridge with the happy design of beginning the sight at London Bridge, and working our way through the City to Regent Street. In a by-street in the Borough, over against a dead wall and under a railway bridge, we were blocked for four hours. We were obliged to walk home at last, having seen nothing whatever.'

Among Dickens' guests was Robert Browning. Robert's account of the night to Isa, in his letter of 19 March 1863 from Paris, where he and Pen had gone to see Mr Browning and Sarianna, was peevish: 'We saw the sights, I ought to tell you — he [Pen] from the War Office in Pall Mall, I from Devonshire House: the illuminations I went to see with Dickens — we left Waterloo Bridge in a Van at 7 o'clock — were to go by a by-way to Southwark Bridge in order to do the thing superiorly: spent *five* miserably cold and black hours in trying vainly to do so, got out in despair, and walked back — by which means I saw little — far more, however, than was worth seeing: the English can't manage anything of the kind — I notice every night that the illuminations here of the Place de la Concorde and all round are so strangely superior that I can't understand how people with the love of fireworks and lights in their large souls don't go to Paris and return — at less expense than Dickens' Van which cost £5!'

Pen's activities were not merely — indeed, perhaps not principally — bookish. He was athletic, cutting a fine figure when riding in Rotten Row in Hyde Park and attending the Ascot races, rowing on the nearby Grand Union Canal and being present at the Oxford and Cambridge Boat Race, fencing and boxing with Willie Bracken, skating in winter, swimming in summer. A healthy body satisfied Robert and Pen just as much as a healthy mind. Pen's mind, when fixed on the studies in hand, was exercised by a broad range of subjects: besides German, drawing, dancing and music (supplemented with regular visits to concerts by the violinist John Ella and the pianist and conductor Charles Hallé), he received instruction in the essentials that would, with luck and application, earn him entry to Oxford University — French, Italian, Greek, Latin, and Mathematics.

Planning ahead, Robert wrote to Isa on 19 February 1863 of his intention to 'enter Pen, if I can, at Balliol, under Jowett — one must do it for years beforehand'. It was quickly and pleasingly done: to the Storys, on 5 March 1863, Robert wrote of Pen, 'I have just succeeded in entering him for residence at Balliol, Oxford, in 1867, if we live and do well. It is the best college at Oxford, by all testimony, being *Jowett's* — a reading college exclusively — and conferring great honour on those of its inmates who distinguish themselves. His name was most kindly put down simultaneously by Jowett and Dr Scott, the Master, each signifying to me his intention of being useful and kind to Pen when he should need it. I believe I have done the best in the course I decided on: he learns more than at school, seems to enjoy himself quite enough, and proves really so good, conscientious and respectable, that I am content with things as they are.' Robert's hope, expressed to Isa in his letter of 19 March, was that Pen should rise to Balliol's 'high standard of scholarship', and in this expectation he was encouraged by Joseph Milsand's estimation of Pen in Paris as being 'much more mature'.

By any standards, Robert Browning was now fully mature in a body that had filled out to the prosperous proportions of middle-age — many thought he looked more like a financier than a poet — and in a mind that was constantly fattened by voracious reading at all levels in foreign and English literatures, from newspapers to literary reviews, from the latest philosophical tracts to books of poetry, all more easily and quickly obtainable in London than in Florence or Rome. Finding a mind to match his own among his male peers was not difficult, though it took several at one time to span the breadth and plumb the depths of Robert's remarkably all-encompassing intellect: Thomas Carlyle, Charles Dickens, Matthew Arnold, John Ruskin, William Allingham, Dante Gabriel Rossetti, John Forster, and many others encountered at the Athenaeum, at dinner parties and balls where, too, there were many more lightweight men and women who buzzed brightly and gratifyingly like bees around the hives, feeding the great spirits of the age who dwelt among them and lent their lustre to social occasions. There were letters constantly received and constantly written — to the Storys and to Isa in particular, though those were light in tone and largely domestic in content, rarely touching on intellectual topics.

Pen was always there, young, eager, quick to assimilate impressions and information, showing promise but hardly, yet, attainment. Another constant daily companion was Arabel, the charitable angel of the Ragged Schools. Her spiritual devotion to the Bedford Street Chapel and to the sermons of a Welsh preacher, Thomas Jones, was pious and touching. Robert accompanied her to services there every Sunday. Arabel's mind, largely given to God and social issues, was absorbed by good works and best intentions. She was a Barrett, which counted for much, but of a different type from her sister. Elizabeth's quick, darting wit and her humorous, feminine intelligence had supplied the foil to Robert's own weightier, more measured and masculine intellect. He missed his wife. He missed Elizabeth's teasing truthfulness, her endless interest in the impressions and information he had brought home to her, her critical enthusiasms, her occasional waywardness, and her joyful spirit. He missed, above all, the intimacy and continuity of their endless conversations.

Feelings of intellectual isolation were largely relieved by regular, solid work; emotional loneliness was sublimated into constant attention to the needs of Pen and Arabel. Robert had spent his entire married life taking care of his wife, and now he took assiduous care of his son and his sister-in-law. To Isa, Robert remarked: 'As for Pen, I love him dearly, but if I hated him, it would be pretty much the same thing.' He took particular care even of Pen's pony. Writing to Isa in May 1863, Robert referred to 'the poor little pony' as 'a source of real sorrow to me, — he is at his prime, not six yet, — fuller than ever of spirit, so pretty, — but *so* small now that the season must be his last with Pen: of course I shall never sell him, but care for his comfort to the last: where shall I ever find such a trusty little brute?' Had his father and Sarianna been able to live in London, he would have taken daily care of them too. His perception of the needs of others — Landor, constantly troubled and troublesome, being a notable example — always filled a large part of Robert's own need to be needed.

In this condition of mind and emotion, he met Miss Frances Julia Wedgwood, the great-granddaughter of Josiah Wedgwood the famous Staffordshire potter and china manufacturer. In this young woman, Robert perceived echoes and elements of Elizabeth that she more or less deliberately presented to him. Robert was already an acquaintance of the Wedgwood family. He knew Hensleigh (a founder-editor of the Oxford English Dictionary) and Frances Wedgwood, Julia's parents, and probably James, her brother: he had dined with them, and in December 1863 had certainly called at their house at 1 Cumberland Place, close to Regent's Park. The acquaintance was sufficiently established to the point that, on 8 February 1864, he had provided Mrs Wedgwood with an introduction, in the event unused, to Isa Blagden in Florence and, two days earlier, a letter of recommendation to Hattie Hosmer in Rome.

Julia, known to her family and intimates as 'Snow', was the eldest of six children. She had been born on 6 February 1833. Robert was fifty-one when he met her; Julia was thirty, going on thirty-one years of age, unmarried, chronically hard of hearing, socially conventional, and formidably serious-minded. The Wedgwoods were rich enough to be considered upper middle-class. Their forebears were more or less distinguished in English life: Hensleigh's grandfather's name was a byword for the neo-classical design he had imposed upon English ceramics; Frances's grandfather was the Rt. Hon. Sir James Mackintosh Bt., MP, a politician and political philosopher; Charles Darwin had married a sister of Hensleigh Wedgwood, thus becoming uncle to Julia.

Hensleigh himself being an eminent philologist and etymologist, family friends had naturally included a fair number of literary intellectuals — among them, Carlyle, Thackeray, Wordsworth, Harriet Martineau, and — since the Wedgwoods were fervent for Italian nationalism — Mazzini.

The first known letter from Julia to Robert, dated 14 May 1864, thanks him for his interest in the condition of her beloved brother, James Mackintosh Wedgwood, known as 'Bro', who was at that time close to death. 'The knowledge of your sympathy,' she wrote, 'has been a great comfort to me.' Julia refers directly to Robert's 'own unparalleled loss'. She commiserates with him and writes of the comfort she has derived from his poetry: 'You were an old friend to me long before I saw you, so that it does not seem unnatural to me to express the deep sympathy which I long have had for such a loss as yours, and which is now brought out afresh, with the thought of all such separation, as the dark shadows close around us.' It is unlikely that Elizabeth's loss of a greatly loved brother, coincidentally also known as 'Bro', would have been lost on Robert's emotional memory.

James Wedgwood, little more than a year younger than his sister, died on 24 June. The day after, Julia wrote again to Robert. Her remarkable letter is as direct in its appeal to Robert's generous attention as Robert's first letter to Elizabeth had been direct in its appeal to her heart. Addressing him as 'Dear and kindest friend', Julia wishes to say directly to Robert what has been hitherto 'implied in every word of mine to you ... A woman who has taken the initiative in a friendship with a man, as I have done with you, has either lost all right feeling or has come to a very definite decision on the issue of all such friendships.' Julia, maintaining all right feeling, is definite and decisive. Though she values Robert's friendship, she could bear to give it up — not now, but in due time — without 'unreasonable pain, for any reason but one, for any good reason at least. That one exception would be if your kind heart checked you in any approach to me with a fear of the consequences to myself.' This was daring stuff for Julia Wedgwood, snowed into her determined spinsterhood.

The extent to which she thought it daring — or likely to be interpreted as such — prompted her to take the precaution of showing Robert's reply of 25 June to her mother in order to forestall any inappropriate speculation: 'without explanations she might have made the natural mistake which I wished to guard against. She was startled at the unusual course I had taken, hers is a mind to perceive very clearly the many objections to it, but as she saw I had lost nothing in your eyes by it she was satisfied.'[52] Robert, in his reply to Julia, wrote: 'I am glad that you showed my letter to Mrs Wedgwood. You know well what is the way of the world with any exceptional mode of proceeding: if one wears a white tie instead of a black one, or calls at a house at 10. rather than 5:p.m. — it has something to say and smile about.' Robert had been caught out before, and would be again. It took no more than the bidding of a hostess to take a lady down to dinner — 'and when the lady told me she would not sit by so and so, I let her sit away from him'[53] — to set tongues wagging about Mr Browning's intentions towards women.

On 3 May 1864, Robert had written amusedly, and perhaps a little bemusedly, to the Storys about 'floating reports' — which had evidently even reached Rome — of his supposed romantic attachments. Among the rumoured objects of his affections was Miss Mary Ann Virginia Gabriel, a composer. Another was Hilary Bonham Carter, a sculptress. A third presumed romance was with the poet Jean Ingelow, with whom he had exchanged no more than a few blameless words. And there were others, including Amelia Harriet Otter, daughter of the Bishop of Chichester. All such encounters were mostly taken out of context by gossip and inflated by ribaldry beyond any probability. Regarding Miss Gabriel, Robert knew 'well enough how that bubble was blown, Lady Westmorland having told me the other day: it was simply a cackle of our dear Lady W's at the egregious joke of an "*angelic attraction*" — helped by a piece of impertinence of [Richard Monckton] Milnes! who was at a dinner where she would not sit near him, as she told me, but at the other end of the table by me — of course, seeing that I was bidden take her downstairs — so he went grinning monkey-fashion about my "attentions" — in the company of some twenty other guests!'

The temptation, from the modern perspective of our less censorious society and lighter morality, is to make fun of Julia Wedgwood as an emotionally repressed and sexually prudish spinster, a cautious, unmarried bluestocking, straitlaced into what we assume to be the corseted Victorian mould of maidenly virtue — though the inquiries and revelations of the social historian and psychologist Peter Gay, in several substantial and authoritative volumes, have recently obliged us to reassess the received wisdom on the emotional psychology and sexual activity of Victorian women. Nevertheless, Julia seems to have possessed none of the flirtatious fun and feminine sensuality of, we might say, Madame du Châtelet, Voltaire's mathematical and astronomical mistress, or the self-possessed and philosophical Belle de Zuylen, Boswell's 'Zélide' and the lover of Benjamin Constant. We have a lively sympathy for both these women, who combined an eighteenth-century love of learning and literature with the romantic arts of love to the detriment of neither.

Few Browning partisans have much patience with plain, pedestrian Julia, whose photograph, possibly less than flattering, shows her in uncompromising profile. Her high, prominent brow seems to hang over her large jaw. These features are not improved or softened by the style in which she wears her straight dark hair scraped back from her face and above her ears, balled tightly in a bun at the nape of her neck. Her low, rather bushy eyebrows cast a shadow over her small eyes. Her mouth gapes open. She is neither positively ugly nor positively pretty. At best a *jolie laide*, she betrays no sense of personal vanity about her appearance. Perhaps the camera did not like Julia Wedgwood; certainly Julia seems not to have liked the camera, judging by her reluctance to satisfy Robert's requests for her photograph and her comments on the celebrated photographer Julia Margaret Cameron as 'a dreadful friend', though Robert mildly replied that she exaggerated 'the horrors of Mrs Cameron'.

Inevitably, Julia Wedgwood's character and appearance do not bear comparison with the unconventionality and charm of Elizabeth, the nonpareil. Nor does Julia appear, on the face of it, likely to appeal to Robert, who appreciated a pretty woman and was responsive to an accomplished feminine wit. 'Her limitations must have been apparent enough to Browning,' writes Betty Miller, who disparages Julia wittily but wickedly as 'a touch of earthenware where he had long known only porcelain'.[54]

Julia was learned — in July 1861, in *Macmillan's Magazine*, she had published a critically acute review of Charles Darwin's *Origin of Species* which pleased and impressed the author, her uncle; Julia was pious — she later wrote an ethical history of civilization, *The Moral Ideal*, which she dedicated in 1888 to Robert Browning; Julia was moral — in her mid-twenties she had published two novels under the pseudonym Florence Dawson, *Framleigh Hall* and *An Old Debt*, which recommended and sanctified self-sacrifice in love. Her letters to Robert are contrasted, by Maisie Ward, with the letters to Isa Blagden and the Storys: 'one feels overwhelmingly that Browning did not expect or receive much intellectual response from either ... the Wedgwood letters are very different, with their references to books, casual Latin phrases, discussion of ultimates. Browning is at home in these letters — that restful and stimulating feeling one gets only with people who themselves are at home in a library and can toss ideas to one another as readily as gossip. And while there is on Browning's side no faintest note of patronage there is on hers not the least subservience.'[55]

Like Elizabeth Barrett Browning, Julia Wedgwood was notably intelligent. Her lively mind was, however, debilitated or depressed by a morbid dwelling upon death, which she imminently anticipated for herself and others. Unlike Elizabeth, who could be shaken out of morbid feelings or otherwise deal more or less realistically in her own mind with intimations of mortality, Julia was not notably merry, not often mischievous, and she was not likely to be distracted by a fancy or to make a friendship that might confound conventionality. 'I know,' she wrote to Robert on 27 June 1864, 'there is in me an exacting spirit that dries up all the love and kindness which it needs so terribly.'

Both Julia and Robert edged warily around one another in their first letters and meetings, she careful to play down any sense of physical attraction — 'My sphere is the intercourse of spirit with spirit ... and this is my excuse for this fearlessness towards you'[56] — he respectful and conciliatory of her dry desires: 'I am lifted by past experiences above the temptation to be false and selfish and vain in such a relation as ours — do I want you to wear like a ring round my neck-tie as the fashion is? — I am older than to care to look fine *so*. There would be real matters for regret, if I tried to find the real obstacles at all likely to seriously inconvenience us ... You see the disjointed way of writing — I am unused to this way of direct transfusion of souls. Understand what you can — and you will.'

Underlying the serious philosophical themes and literary subjects of the correspondence between Julia Wedgwood and Robert Browning is this pussyfooting around the relationship between a man and a woman, between an older, experienced man and a sexually immature, very likely virginal, younger woman. Julia understands and writes candidly, 'With what a wonderful fearlessness of misconception I am writing to you! I did not think such utterance was possible while we were clothed in flesh, but with you I have invincibly a sense of that emergence being past.'[57] Soul speaking to soul, spirit speaking to spirit, may often be a denial or displacement of physicality, and throughout the letters is a powerful repressed eroticism which subtly reverses the usual mode: Julia's rather heavy masculinity comes across strongly, while Robert's lighter, creative femininity and subconscious flirtatiousness is irresistibly evoked in his reaction to it. He cajoles Julia, rallies her out of despondency, and appeals to whatever embryonic sense of coquettishness she may possess — though her petticoats remain pretty much unruffled.

Robert's letters to Julia — there are thirty in all, in response to forty-two of hers — continued until the early days of March 1865. On 1 March that year, Julia suddenly wrote to ask him to pay her no more visits. She is known to have written two drafts of the letter before sending the third and final version which read: 'it would be better that we did not meet again just now, at least that you did not come here ... I have reason to know that my pleasure in your company has had an interpretation put upon it that I ought not to allow. I have no doubt the fault has been mine, in incautiously allowing it to be known that I made an object of your visits.' She fully absolved Robert from any responsibility — 'remember I invited you' — and he accepted this: 'I left you always to decide (as only yourself could) on what length into the garden I might go: and I still leave it to you.' Nevertheless, he resignedly and unquestioningly accepted the cessation of an interesting friendship: 'My dear friend, this comes to me as no surprise: I thought from the beginning it was too good to last, and felt as one does in a garden one has entered by an open door, — people fancy you mean to steal flowers.' He doubted, with some awareness of how the world wagged, 'that to snap our outward intercourse off short and sharp will hardly cure the evil, whatever it be: two persons who suddenly unclasp arms and start off in opposite directions look terribly intimate. But you know all the circumstances.'[58]

In this letter, agreeing to say goodbye, Robert wrote kindly but somewhat distantly: 'As to the past, it was only incomplete thro' my wife's absence: she never had any woman-friend so entirely fit for her as you would have been — I told you so sometimes.' He had often spoken to Julia of Elizabeth, of the persistence of her lively presence in his living memory. The correspondence was resumed a couple of years later, by Robert in a letter of 17 May 1867, and it continued intermittently, courteously but without intimacy, until July 1870. It is unlikely that Julia and Robert ever met again after 1865. She saw him twice in the street thereafter, and deliberately avoided him. For whatever reasons of piety or sentimentality, she kept the letters from Robert Browning, which only came to public attention in 1935 on the death of Julia's younger sister. Julia's own letters came to light the year after.

Julia's two sentimental novels of disappointed romance, both published in 1858, predated but perhaps anticipated her correspondence with Robert Browning. Her attitudes had already, and early, been set in aspic. She could never have fled for Italy with a lover. She took the world she lived in pretty much for granted, more or less unquestioningly. Believing in its shibboleths, and reciting them, she gave up her poet partly for love of him, partly for her own self-respect. In *Robert Browning and Julia Wedgwood*, his edition of the correspondence, Richard Curle publishes an extract from a letter written to Julia by her confidante, Julia Sterling, in response to a letter of 5 March 1865 with which Julia Wedgwood had enclosed a copy of Robert's undated letter and perhaps — though this is less certain — a copy of Julia's own letter of renunciation to Robert of 1 March.

Miss Sterling remarked: 'Such a friendship the longer it is indulged, the more absorbing it becomes in the nature of things — and now your heart must be torn out by the roots ... what a real effort you must have made in your appeal to him to conceal the fact that your heart had betrayed you. If he guesses the truth, he certainly most honourably ignores it — and makes the path easy to you which you now have chosen.' The word 'indulged' seems sadly indicative of the attitude of both Julias to emotional feelings as self-indulgent and a distraction from 'all right feeling' which Julia Wedgwood had initially feared. Robert seems, for his part, to have been genuinely regretful that the suspicious and censorious world of the flesh and the devil had come between them — though he too acknowledged that its proprieties had to be observed.

Did he acknowledge it too readily? Some have thought so. Some have thought that Robert desired nothing more than friendship with Julia, whereas Julia's heart was subverted by feelings beyond friendship that, once acknowledged, she decisively uprooted. It may be suggested that Robert had also recognized Julia's feelings and, cautious in his own way, was willing enough that they should be forestalled. The psychological acuteness of his poetry, particularly those poems that reveal the depth of his insights about the relations between men and women, might tend to give substance to this view. Robert's own feelings may have been warmer at the beginning than they were towards the end: there was enough of Elizabeth in Julia to recommend her initially to his instinctive affections.

The letters themselves may be endlessly analysed. They are enigmatic in many respects and susceptible to all manner of interpretations. What lay within the hearts of Robert Browning and Julia Wedgwood is not always plainly laid out on the pages of their circumspect correspondence that sometimes refers to, sometimes skirts, possible embarrassments. They are never unguardedly trustful love-letters. Nor, for all the surface resemblances, are they a latter-day version of the courtship correspondence between Robert and Elizabeth: the letters between Julia and Robert start from rectitude and finish in renunciation. From the beginning, there is a blighting worm in the bud that consumes the friendship and kills any possibility of a full flowering.

On 17 October 1864, Robert had written to Julia to assure her of Pen's health and his own: 'I am pale and used to be thin, and never had a serious illness in my life . . . Yet I have just heard that Trollope was so struck by my altered looks last year that he warned George Barrett of what was to soon come, who wrote to his sister Arabel to enquire, who replied that she didn't notice anything particular.' There is no mention of Robert's pallid portliness as a problem in his letters to Isa, and in fact, to Julia, Robert had commented on the history of his normally sound health. But perhaps the cumulative effect of the poet's socializing and his immediate concern about publication by Chapman and Hall

on 28 May of *Dramatis Personae* had rendered his appearance less rosy than usual. There would have been some nervousness, at least, about critical reaction to his latest book of poems. Nevertheless, 'here am I spared to read the "Edinburg" [*Edinburgh Review*] this morning. The clever creature rummages over my wardrobe of thirty years' accumulation, strips every old coat of its queer button or odd tag and tassel, then holds them out, "So Mr B. goes dressed now!" — of the cut of the coats, not a word.'[59]

The 'Edinburg' particularly vexed Robert. Two days after reading the notice of his book, in a letter to Isa of 19 October 1864, he referred again to the review 'that says all my poetry is summed up in "Bang whang, whang goes the drum."' The reviewer, in the October 1864 issue of the *Edinburgh Review*, did not believe that the poems of *Dramatis Personae* 'will survive except as a curiosity and a puzzle'. The hapless critic, who clearly did not keep up with changing poetic fashions and the varying fortunes of literary reputations, was a singular dissenting voice quickly throttled by other, high-ranking reviewers.

Dramatis Personae, which was also published three months later in an American edition by Ticknor and Fields in Boston, consisted of eighteen new poems, described by Robert to William Wetmore Story in a letter of 5 September 1863 as 'men and women — but under some other name, to please the publisher'. He spoke no less than the truth when he referred to the poems of *Dramatis Personae* as an accumulation of thirty years' observation, experience, and thought — though they were, too, an accumulation of eight years of actual composition. They can also be seen as marking the borderline between Robert's previous life and the altered circumstances in which he was to live the rest of it. The poems were something old, something new, a summation and a step forward. The book had been long in the making, begun well before the death of Elizabeth, who, in letters, had commented in May 1860 about having seen Robert's short lyrics and that he had been working at a long poem of which she had not seen a line.

He had continued working in the three years since leaving Florence, writing poems informed by his loss, inspired by contemporary issues, and coloured by his fascination with the local legends of Pornic and the Brittany coast. As in *Men and Women*, the poems of *Dramatis Personae* are about love, human nature, art, and, significantly for

Robert's own time and society, religion. The love poems — among them 'James Lee's Wife', 'The Statue and the Bust', 'The Worst of It', 'Too Late', 'Prospice', and 'Dîs Aliter Visum; Or Le Byron de Nos Jours' — are generally expressive of regret for lost love and for wrong choices that betray love. Love thwarted by or denied in favour of worldly considerations is a familiar theme, universal in its truth and modern in terms of the society in which Robert Browning and Henry James (some of whose novels echo Browning's themes) both moved and in which both were closely observant of its dramas.

The poem of which Elizabeth had not seen a line was probably 'Mr Sludge, "The Medium"'. The model for Sludge was largely, of course, Daniel Dunglas Home, who had so fascinated Elizabeth and been so despised — to the point of detestation — by Robert. The poem is a dramatic monologue by David Sludge, justifying himself and his profession to one Hiram H. Horsefall, who has accused Sludge of common trickery, of lying and cheating. With breathtaking acumen, Robert uses the poem to examine his own vocation as a poet and poetry as a medium. The name Sludge is expressive, in an onomatopoeic, Dickensian manner, of a man earthbound, bogged down in the cloying mud of the world and unable to rise above it to the higher planes he claims to perceive and make perceptible.

Sludge is surprisingly candid from the start. He admits to Horsefall that his mediumship is false, that those who believed in him, who thought they saw and heard true spirit manifestations, were deceived. He then proceeds to confound the hard-headed, rational, outraged Horsefall by asking what is certainty, what is truth? Did not those who believed in him have cause — the evidence of their own senses — to give credence to his performances and to interpret what he showed them as reasonable, as genuine spiritual experiences? If reason convinces as well as reason deceives, how then can reason be taken to be the test of truth? May it not be that faith is the better test? May it not be that Sludge himself is merely the medium through which God works in His mysterious way to inform and enlighten the faithful, to confirm them in their faith?

It is at this point that Robert enters upon the wider question of religious faith and, as in other poems in *Dramatis Personae*, examines the contemporary issues that had been raised by theological scholars, particularly the matter of biblical authenticity and the common humanity of Jesus, which had been analysed and insisted upon by Ernest Renan in his *Vie de Jésus*, published in France in 1863 and in an English translation in 1864. Robert had read Renan's book in the French edition. In a letter to Isa he wrote that Renan's arguments had not convinced him: he had found the book 'weaker and less honest than I was led to expect. I am glad it is written: if he thinks he can prove what he says, he has fewer doubts upon the subject than I — but mine are none of his ... Take away every claim to man's respect from Christ and then give him a wreath of gum-roses and calico-lilies.'

'Mr Sludge, "The Medium"', consisting of 1,525 lines, is the longest poem in the collection. 'A Death in the Desert', 688 lines, and 'Caliban upon Setebos', 295 lines, precede it and introduce the religious views that pervade the entire collection. 'A Death in the Desert' directly addresses Renan's doubts about whether St John was the actual author of the fourth Gospel and about the reliability of the narrative attributed to the apostle. Robert's daring standpoint is to have John admit that he was not present at the Crucifixion and that he was not personally responsible for a miracle claimed in his Gospel. John, now an old man, is not at all bothered by 'plain historic fact' — he has moved beyond truth-to-fact; what now concerns him is truth-to-faith. Historicity has become irrelevant. He is beyond reason: the Christ story, too, moves beyond reason that once served a temporal purpose, beyond reductivist historical proofs. When John, the last living man to have seen the Christ, dies, so will historical truth — and the necessity for it — die with him. What will survive is God's love, and in that spirit will John's Gospel, as a testament to that love which is the essence of Christian faith, continue to be read as truthful. Those who cannot believe, who cannot love, will read it in the irreverent, irrelevant spirit of academic criticism. What remains of value to faithful Christians will be visceral truth rather than intellectual truth.

'Caliban upon Setebos; or, Natural Theology in the Island' adopts Shakespeare's Caliban, from *The Tempest*, as its protagonist. Caliban is beset by Setebos, a minor divinity conceived by Caliban in his own image. Setebos cruelly torments Caliban, a primitive, monstrous creature, with all of humanity's sufferings. Here Robert Browning takes issue with Darwin's *Origin of Species*, in which man's divine origins were questioned, and with the Higher Critics of Christian theology who posited that God is created in the image of man. Primitive man, Browning's contemporaries were urged to believe, lived in a state of nature and naturally derived his knowledge of God from observation of the natural world. If a state of nature might be considered wicked — or at least inimical and unpredictable to human life — so would God be conceived by natural man as wicked and malicious at worst, at best capriciously cruel.

Nevertheless, if the natural man is capable of progress, of looking forward beyond the immediate moment, he might conceive of a higher nature within himself and thus, through the enlightenment of self-consciousness, of a God who is beyond simple antagonism and indifference to the suffering of His creatures. Such a God is indeed imagined by Caliban, dimly perceived as 'the Quiet'. Caliban, as conceived by Shakespeare, is resolved at last to 'seek for grace': so Robert Browning permits his own Caliban the imagination to conceive of God as a moral principle and, as Caliban himself aspires to grace, so will Setebos grow in goodness. The ultimate condition of both Caliban and Setebos will be to achieve the revelation of love as the moral and Christian principle.

Park Honan makes an important and convincing case for the influence of Theodore Parker on the gestation of 'Caliban upon Setebos'.[60] Through the Storys, the Brownings had met Parker, a Unitarian minister of Boston, in Rome, whence he had come, like J.G. Lockhart, in hopes of recouping his health — though he was soon to die of tuberculosis in 1860 in Florence. A letter of 9 October 1859 from Charles Sumner to Mrs Story recommended Parker to her care: 'Pray watch him and send him home strong and well to preach great sermons and hold aloft the scales of justice.'[61] Parker and Browning would be bound to take to one another: says Honan, 'In many ways, the two men were much alike. Both were dynamos of energy, geysers of aspiration. Parker was a Unitarian. Browning had long been friendly to Unitarians. Both detested theology and scorned Calvinism. Both believed that man had an intuition of perfect, impersonal deity, though whereas Browning held that man needed deity also to be human and incarnate, Parker maintained that he anthropomorphized deity through a want of intelligence or culture — and the more so the lower in the evolutionary scale he stood, for Parker had just been reading Darwin's *Origin of Species*, published in November 1859.'

On the basis of an article by C. R Tracy,[62] Honan believes that Robert 'seems to have understood Darwin only later, if at all', but that Parker's plan to write *A Bumblebee's Thoughts on the Plan and Purpose of the Universe* — an attack on theological homocentrism, 'a satire of the narrow, vindictive anthropomorphism of the Calvinists', and a denial of 'characteristically Darwinian ideas' — was the immediate source of 'Caliban upon Setebos'. However, Browning's poem is more moderate than Parker's own work. Browning, says Honan, 'held that, on its highest level, anthropomorphism is natural and proper for man. Man must not only revere God as an abstract principle; he must love Him as a person. Christianity is unique in permitting man, at least ultimately, this double faith.' Honan perceives 'Caliban upon Setebos' as 'another optimistic study of evil. Thoughts that grovel in the slime may yet reach to the stars. If Caliban's soul lies in the grip of the biblical and Miltonic Belial, it may yet win release from horrendous shackles.'

Dramatis Personae also and notably includes the poem 'Rabbi Ben Ezra'. Its first, best-known verse runs thus:

> Grow old along with me!
> The best is yet to be,
> The last of life for which the first was made:
> Our times are in His hand
> Who saith, 'A whole I planned,
> Youth shows but half; trust God: see all nor be afraid!'

It is generally assumed that Rabbi Ben Ezra speaks for Robert Browning, who, with this poem, provided a counterweight of optimism to the pessimistic, hedonistic philosophy of *carpe diem* propounded in Edward FitzGerald's translation of the *Rubáiyát of Omar Khayyám*, published in 1859, and to the suffering stoicism of Matthew Arnold's *Empedocles on Etna*, published in 1852. Robert, in optimistic mode, looks confidently to the future: there is progress, there is achievement, there are possibilities. The famous biblical image of the Potter's wheel is introduced in verses 25 and 26:

> Thoughts hardly to be packed
> Into a narrow act,
> Fancies that broke through language and escaped;

All I could never be,
All, men ignored in me,
This, I was worth to God, whose wheel the pitcher shaped.

Ay, note that Potter's wheel,
That metaphor! and feel
Why time spins fast, why passive lies our clay, —
Thou, to whom fools propound,
When the wine makes its round,
'Since life fleets, all is change; the Past gone, seize today!'

Things change, of course, undeniably: hot, fleshly Youth has its hedonistic day, but with Age comes a clearer perception of life's 'whole design' and perfect plan. To seize the moment, to be reckless of continuation, is the prerogative of Youth; to acknowledge futurity, to live in the moment but not for the moment, is the privilege of Age. If 'Rabbi Ben Ezra' was written in 1862, as is generally believed, it was a remarkable effort by Robert, as by any fifty-year-old man, to move forward after the death of a beloved wife, to believe in futurity, to acknowledge loss and — the poem says as much — to relinquish youth and the flesh and to project 'soul on its lone way' into age.

The poem 'Apparent Failure' complements the themes of 'Rabbi Ben Ezra': the corpses of three suicides lie in the Paris Morgue, apparently miserable failures who opted for the completion of death over the continuation of life. Robert himself inspects them — men thwarted in political and military ambition, in ideals of social equality, and in passion for women — imagining that their reach exceeded their grasp. If so, then they are to be praised rather than pitied; for what was of good and value in them will remain:

That what began best, can't end worst,
Nor what God blessed once, prove accurst.

The critics were more or less kind to *Dramatis Personae*. It was more positively received than any of Robert's previous books and it was generally agreed that his creation of Caliban surpassed even Shakespeare's conception of the creature. Robert had sounded depths in which there were acknowledged to be things as profoundly unsettling as they were deeply satisfying. The critics, affected perhaps by the rapture of these deeps, recognized pathos and power in the poems; they enjoyed the poet's ironies and inversions; they greeted his grotesqueries with enthusiasm and invested them with significances. If they were still sometimes stumped by the poet's intellectualism, his allusions and allegories, they attributed their own shortcomings to Robert Browning's own difficult and puzzling brilliance. In short, he was now given the great benefit of that critical doubt which had hitherto damned him.

Partly, this reaction was due to the fact that Robert, returned from his self-imposed exile in Italy (to the extent that no poems in *Dramatis Personae* were identifiably set in Italy), had become a notably ornamental and accessible figure in London literary society. His wife was dead, and as her poetic star inevitably dimmed a little — though there was still a demand for her work — so his began to dazzle. He was greatly liked, much respected, perfectly approachable and knowable as a man, even if, as a poet, sunk into the *moi profond*, he was less accessible, less comprehensible, less superficial than in person. But it could be taken that his internal, impenetrable density was like the core of a great planet that shone in the firmament and illuminated its surroundings, eclipsing even Tennyson, the Laureate, whose most recent production, *Enoch Arden*, had been generally judged a disappointment.

Robert himself had his doubts about how much good it had done him to be in London after so long away, however frankly he had admitted to putting himself about in society for fear of missing 'some unknown good'. Though he was conscious of the coincidences of society that might lead to unexpected benefits, he had difficulty squaring his present renown with previous disregard. Mrs Orr, commenting on Robert's letter to Isa of 19 August 1865, acutely remarks: 'We cannot wonder at the touch of bitterness with which Mr Browning dwells on the long neglect which he had sustained';[63] but even she has sense enough to appreciate that 'His presence in England had doubtless stimulated the public interest in his productions; and we may fairly credit *Dramatis Personae* with having finally awakened his countrymen of all classes to the fact that a great creative power had arisen among them.'[64] Robert had written thus to Isa:

I suppose that what you call 'my fame within these four years' comes from a little of this gossiping and going out, and showing myself to be alive: and so indeed some folks say — but I hardly think it: for remember I was uninterruptedly (almost) in London from the time I published Paracelsus — till I ended that string of plays with Luria: and I used to go out then, and see far more of merely literary people, critics etc. — than I do now, — but what came of it? There were always a few people who had a certain opinion of my poems, but nobody cared to speak what he thought, or the things printed twenty five years ago would not have waited so long for a good word — but at last a new set of men arrive who don't mind the conventionalities of ignoring one and seeing everything in another: Chapman says, 'The orders come from Oxford and Cambridge', and all my new cultivators are young men: more than that, I observe that some of my old friends don't like at all the irruption of *outsiders* who rescue me from their sober and private approval and take those words out of their mouths 'which they always meant to say', and never *did*. When there gets to be a general feeling of this kind, that there must be *something* in the works of an author, the reviews are obliged to notice him, such notice as it is: but what poor work, even when doing its best! — I mean poor in the failure to give a notion of the whole works, — not a particular one of such and such points therein. As I began, so I shall end, taking my own course, pleasing myself or aiming at doing so, and thereby, I hope, pleasing God. As I never did otherwise, I never had any fear as to what I did going ultimately to the bad, — hence in collected editions I always reprinted everything, smallest and greatest.

Except, of course, Pauline, which was not included in the collected works until 1868.

The reprinting, in an edited selection and in a collected edition, of Robert's poetry in 1862 and 1863 had certainly been beneficial, re-acquainting the public mind with old work and preparing it for a new book. By 19 December 1864, the date on which he wrote to Isa Blagden, Robert had become increasingly confident about his vocation, even if he felt his life to be less fixed in a pattern. 'I am certainly not unhappy, any more than I ever was: I am . . . if the phrase were now to be coined first . . . "*resigned*" — but I look on everything in this world with altered eyes, and can no more take interest in anything I see there but the proof of certain great principles, strewn in the booths at a fair: I could no more take root in life again, than learn some new dancing step. On the other hand, I feel such comfort and delight in doing the best I can with my own object of life, poetry, which, I think, I never *could* have seen the good of before, that it shows me I have taken the root I *did* take, *well*. I hope to do much more yet: and that the flower of it will be put into Her hand somehow.'

It is always difficult to know why and how the works of a poet, or any other creative artist, will suddenly 'take' with critics and the public, like egg whites being beaten for long enough until, aerated by the Zeitgeist, they begin to solidify and assume a substantial shape. They don't always: some impurity, such as a drop of yolk, will prevent, despite all tiring effort, the thickening process. Robert had been right, in this sense, to take his own course, please himself, refuse to adulterate his work in hopes of popular success. This purity paid off, finally. It paid off when the time was right, when the originality of his work had been subversively influential, in part, in forming the poetic taste that succeeded the literary, political, and social attitudes that had hitherto found their most perfect expression and greatest satisfaction in the works of Wordsworth and Tennyson.

Before these major and respected poets had achieved full recognition, Wordsworth had been worryingly revolutionary, Shelley had been shocking, Keats had been dismissed as a common Cockney, Byron had been thought of as a thrillingly bad lot and a worse influence. At least Robert Browning had generally been considered simply incomprehensible rather than vicious. Inevitably, when readers and critics learned to read his language, to discern reason and beauty where they had previously seen only chaos and ugliness, the style and themes of Robert's poetry became more apparent. In the cumulative effect of poetic production over the long term, readers were at last able to perceive forms and patterns and meaning.

The *Athenaeum* review of 4 June 1864, often quoted, identified Robert as 'a great dramatic poet' and recognized his uniqueness: 'No one ever thought Mr Browning like unto any other poet. He could not be if he would, and he would not be if he could. He pioneers his own way, and follows no one's track for the sake of ease and smoothness. His music is not as the music of other men. He frequently strikes out something nobly novel; but it is not to be quickly caught, for we have not heard the like before, and at first the mind of the reader finds it difficult to dance to the beat of the time. He has a horror of all that is hackneyed in poetry, and so he goes to the antipodes to avoid it, and finds things on the other side of the world with which we are not commonly acquainted.'

Dramatis Personae succeeded so surprisingly well that it went into a second edition, not just on the word of Robert's peers, contemporaries, and the critics, but importantly — as Robert himself was made aware by Chapman, his publisher — on the enthusiastic acclamation of a younger generation of writers, poets, artists, and scholars who were rising on a wave of literary and artistic revolution against, among other things, 'the tyranny of Tennyson'. They carried Robert Browning along with them. It did Robert no harm, indeed possibly did him a great deal of good, that he had hitherto languished in relative obscurity until, now, his genius could be understood and appreciated. As Tennyson and others sank in their middle age and settled to middling achievements, so did Robert rise with his greatest, most complex and most powerful work still in progress.

In *A Browning Handbook*, commenting on the reception of *Dramatis Personae*, William Clyde DeVane attributes Robert's success to his contemporaneity:

> Written over a period of eight years, in such different places and changing circumstances, it is not surprising that the poems in the volume are so disparate in tone. A number of lyrics express the mood of lost love. But the chief characteristic of *Dramatis Personae* is this: that in an age when the poets were mainly interested in escaping to the past — Tennyson to Arthur's medieval kingdom, Arnold to Greece, Rossetti and Morris to the Middle Ages, the young Swinburne to Greece and Elizabethan England — Browning almost alone wrote of contemporary ideas and contemporary life, often in colloquial

language and contemporary phrase. The true topics of *Dramatis Personae* are such live and pressing problems as science, higher criticism of the Scriptures, recent tendencies in the religious life of England, spiritualism, social conditions in the 1860's, and modern love.[65]

Nobody seriously disagrees with this assessment, and Robert himself prefigured it in his private comments; yet it does not entirely account for the enthusiasm of the antiquarians, medievalists and others for a modernity they did not themselves endorse or express. The attraction perhaps lay in Robert's imagery and language, which continued, as ever, to be suffused with what the critic Walter Bagehot in *The National Review* perceived to be a 'grotesque realism' — the stock-in-trade of Swinburne, Morris, Rossetti and the rest, but which Robert refused to bury entirely in the mythic past of gods and gargoyles. Instead he energetically and with great gusto applied it to the present moment, creating a fantastic naturalism from the materials of modern life just as the medievalists made devils and dragons from the stuff of mythology.

Robert's own assessment of his contemporaries was summarized first in a letter to Isa of 19 January 1870 and in subsequent letters over the next few months:

I go with you a good way in the feeling about Tennyson's new book [*The Holy Grail and Other Poems*, published in December 1869]: it is all out of my head already. We look at the object of art in poetry so differently! Here is an Idyll about a knight being untrue to his friend and yielding to the temptation of that friend's mistress after having engaged to assist him in his suit. I should judge the conflict in the knight's soul the proper subject to describe: Tennyson thinks he should describe the castle, the effect of the moon on its towers, and anything *but* the soul. The monotony, however, you must expect — if the new is to be of a piece with the old. [William] Morris is sweet, pictorial, clever always — but a weariness to me by this time. The lyrics were the 'first sprightly runnings' — this that follows is a laboured brew with the old flavour but not *body*. So with Tennyson — the old 'Galahad' is to me incomparably better than a dozen centuries of the 'Grail,' 'Coming of Arthur,' and so on.

I ought to be surprised to find myself thinking so, since it seems also the opinion of everybody: even the reviews hardly keep on the old chime of laudation.

A couple of months later, in his letter of 22 March to Isa, Robert took another swipe: 'As to Swinburne's verses, I agree with you — they are "florid impotence," to my taste — the *minimum* of thought and idea in the *maximum* of words and phraseology. Nothing said and done with, left to stand alone and trust for its effect in its own worth.' Rossetti, too, came in for criticism: 'Yes, I have read Rossetti's poems — and poetical they are, — *scented* with poetry, as it were — like trifles of various sorts you take out of a cedar or sandal-wood box: you know I hate the effeminacy of his school, — the men that dress up like women, — that use obsolete forms, too, and archaic accentuations to seem soft — fancy a man calling it a lilý, liliés and so on: Swinburne started this, with other like Belialisms — witness his harp-playér, etc. It is quite different when the object is to *imitate* old ballad-writing, when the thing might be; then, how I hate "Love," as a lubberly naked young man putting his arms here and his wings there, about a pair of lovers, — a fellow they would kick away, in the reality.'[66] Robert had the grace to end this diatribe with the abrupt acknowledgement, 'Goodbye, for I am getting ill-natured.'

As in poetry, so in painting: Robert valued, above all, authenticity and a strong, honest pictorial presence and artistic vision. In a letter to Isa of 26 November 1866 Robert had praised Simeon Solomon as the 'painter of the best picture in the Exhibition [*Habet!*, exhibited at the Royal Academy Exhibition in 1865]. By 1870, he could not spare the time to take up Solomon's invitation to view his latest pictures: though 'full of talent,' Robert admitted to Isa in February 1870, 'they are too affected and effeminate. One great picture-show at the Academy, — the old masters' exhibition, — ought to act as a tonic on these girlish boys and boyish girls, with their Heavenly Bridegrooms and such like.' It is unlikely that Robert knew of Solomon's homosexuality, however much he sensed and disliked the hybrid natures and sexual ambiguities in his paintings. Even of a good friend, Anne Thackeray, whose prose and poetic work could not be ranked with Tennyson or the Pre-Raphaelites or Swinburne, Robert could be critically uncompromising:

'I read, for a wonder, Miss Thackeray's "To Esther" — the praises of her having been long buzzing round me, — surely that is poorer than the poorest of Miss Mitford's sketches! I cannot conceive of anybody, acknowledged intelligent, writing worse. *That* sort of thing will not last very long, depend on it!'[67]

In the prime of his own poetic life, amid his gods and monsters, gravid with a sense of futurity for his work, the poet Robert Browning himself walked and talked — a well-fed, well-dressed, well-bred, well-informed, well-intentioned member in good standing of the English and European society he so ruthlessly analysed and convincingly caricatured. The general perception of Robert Browning in June 1865 was summed up by Benjamin Jowett, Robert's junior by only five years: 'It is impossible to speak without enthusiasm of his open, generous nature and his great ability and knowledge. I had no idea that there was a perfectly sensible poet in the world, entirely free from enmity [or vanity], jealousy, or any other littleness, and thinking no more of himself than if he were an ordinary man. His great energy is very remarkable, and his determination to make the most of the remainder of his life.'[68]

Jowett, then Regius Professor of Greek at Oxford, would naturally have warmed to Robert Browning's readiness to run head-on at the great theological debates of the day and contribute to the contentious intellectual disputes of his contemporaries. Jowett's liberal views as an able and highly-regarded classical scholar and clergyman of the Church of England had caused a stir in 1860 when, as a youngish Oxford don, he had contributed an essay, 'On the Interpretation of Scripture', to *Essays and Reviews*. Some who read this notorious piece interpreted it as a manifesto of theological Liberalism that argued against the evangelical High Church movement of John Henry Newman, who received the cardinal's hat from Pope Leo XIII in 1879.

Jowett's reputation, not only as an original theological thinker and able Greek scholar, but also as a charismatic teacher and moral mentor who took a strong personal interest in his pupils and impressed his stamp upon them, had attracted Robert's attention in relation to Pen's further education, and in this regard he was gratified by Jowett's earnest interest and assistance. To his favourable remarks about Robert Browning, Jowett added that, 'Of personal objects he seems to have none, except the education of his son, in which I hope in some degree to help him.' Gratification led to a mutual high personal regard between these two great men and, as the years wore on, and despite difficulties with Pen's career as a scholar, a close friendship developed and was strengthened by many expressions of academic honour and personal esteem.

Meantime, Robert and Pen, on 3 August 1864, broke their routine of recouping themselves in Brittany and proceeded to Paris, where they stayed for a week to pick up Mr Browning and Sarianna before setting off on holiday for Cambo, near Bayonne in the Pyrenees. From there, Robert wrote to Isa Blagden and to Julia Wedgwood on 19 August 1864, and to the Storys three days later, with a woeful tale of having found Arcachon too over-developed, too *mondaine* — 'a toy-town with boulevards traced through the sand-hills' — and 'crammed with strangers'; of having tried 'St Jean de Luz and Biarritz to no better purpose', the former pretty but no rooms to be had there, the latter too noisy and expensive; and of quiet little Cambo, 'in repute for its mineral waters, but out of the season now', thankfully and finally suiting their purpose: 'the Basque peasantry are somewhat interesting, anyhow; here we stay a month'.

The countryside was perhaps too reminiscent of Bagni di Lucca, 'the mountains just like the Tuscan ranges, with plenty of oak and chestnut woods, and everywhere the greenest of meadows'. 'It is very saddening to me,' wrote Robert to Isa, 'to feel the Southern influence again'; but, writing again to Isa on 19 September from Biarritz, he reported that Pen had enjoyed himself, that Sarianna — who had never been so far south before — was delighted with everything, and that 'I have got on by having a great read at Euripides — the one book I brought with me [though to Julia Wedgwood he also mentioned having brought and read "a volume of George Sand's plays and The Travels of Rabbi Benjamin of Tudela"], besides attending to my own matters, my new poem that is about to be; and of which the whole is pretty much in my head — the Roman murder story you know.'

The 'Roman murder story' had been in Robert's mind for four years, since June 1860, when he had first happened upon an old book in a Florence market and eagerly read therein the source materials for what would be his longest and most accomplished work. By October 1862, having tried unsuccessfully to offload it on other writers, the story had established itself in his head as a probable subject for a poem of his own, and now, at Cambo, he seemed finally to have settled on a firm plan for its execution. From Cambo, the Brownings had travelled to inspect a famous mountain pass, '*le pas de Roland*, so called because that Paladin kicked a hole in a rock, which blocks the way, to allow Charlemagne's army to pass: very striking and picturesque it was, while the meadows by the river-side were delightful'.[69] On 27 August Sarianna sketched the great lozenge-shaped cleft in the cliff face, the rubble of great boulders at the foot of it and, through the gap, a landscape of trees and hills.[70]

William Clyde DeVane[71] cautiously infers from the diary of William Michael Rossetti, to whom Robert spoke in March 1868 of his visit to the Bayonne mountain-gorge, that Robert was inspired by Roland's great feat to break suddenly through the impasse of his thoughts and 'there laid out the full plan of his twelve cantos, accurately carried out in the execution'. But another, later, account by Robert to a friend, Rudolph Lehmann, is quoted by DeVane: 'When I first read the book, my plan was at once settled. I went for a walk, gathered twelve pebbles from the road, and put them at equal distances on the parapet that bordered it. These represented the twelve chapters into which the poem is divided and I adhered to that arrangement to the last.'[72]

Neither version may be strictly true. Robert took at least two years, from 1860–2, to decide to use the materials of the old book as the basis for *The Ring and the Book*, and the image of the heroic Roland kicking through rock is a neat conceit, a poetic *Eureka*! moment. Park Honan reasonably concludes that 'Browning had considered the organisation of *The Ring and the Book* much earlier. Yet Roland's feat seems to have unloosened some obstacles in his mind.'[73] DeVane, puzzled by Robert's discrepant accounts — though Robert was ever liable to give variant stories, not all of them strictly compatible — supposes that 'the vivid event of the twelve pebbles . . . may have happened at the Pass of Roland in August, 1864, when Browning was at last free to turn his mind fully to his next poem'.[74]

What is certain, nevertheless, is that on a day in June 1860 Robert 'Gave a *lira* for it, eightpence English just',[75] and thus acquired the square, battered old book, 'Small quarto-size, part print part manuscript',[76] which he later came to call 'the Old Yellow Book'. It had been lying on a market stall, one of many junk-strewn booths that littered the teeming Piazza di San Lorenzo in Florence and which were famous for touting dusty, dilapidated, disregarded second-hand goods to the noisy, jostling, heat-weary crowds who searched

> 'Mongst odds and ends of ravage, picture-frames
> White through the worn gilt, mirror-sconces chipped,
> Bronze angel-heads once knobs attached to chests
> (Handled when ancient dames chose forth brocade)
> Modern chalk drawings, studies from the nude
> Samples of stone, jet, breccia, porphyry
> Polished and rough, sundry amazing busts
> In baked earth (broken, Providence be praised!)
> A wreck of tapestry, proudly-purposed web
> When reds and blues were indeed red and blue
> Now offered as a mat to save bare feet
> (Since carpets constitute a cruel cost)
> Treading the chill scagliola bedward.
>   [*The Ring and the Book*, I, ll. 53–65]

Browsing and rummaging through the broken and tattered detritus of this bazaar, hard by the steps of a Medici palace, Robert had found the book tucked between four others:

> A dog-eared Spicilegium, the fond tale
> O' the Frail One of the Flower, by young Dumas,
> Vulgarized Horace for the use of schools,
> The Life, Death, Miracles of Saint Somebody,
> Saint Somebody Else, his Miracles, Death and Life, —
> With this, one glance at the lettered back of which,
> And 'Stall!' cried I: a lira made it mine. [I, ll. 77–83]

He leaned for a while against some low railings, by a statue and a fountain, leafing through the pages of his find, before setting off, still reading, to walk slowly and circuitously back to Casa Guidi. By the time he arrived, he had concentratedly worked his way through most of the book's printed pages and browsed in the pamphlets, legal documents, and manuscript letters — 'pure crude fact', in Latin and Italian — bound between its 'crumpled vellum covers'.

Still read I on, from written title page
To written index, on, through street and street,
At the Strozzi, at the Pillar, at the Bridge;
Till, by the time I stood at home again
In Casa Guidi by Felice Church,
Under the doorway where the black begins
With the first stone-slab of the staircase cold,
I had mastered the contents, knew the whole truth
Gathered together, bound up in this book,
Print three-fifths, written supplement the rest. [I, ll. 110–19]

The story Robert had read was very sensational. He summarized it shortly as:

'*Romana Homicidiorum*' — nay,
Better translate — 'A Roman murder-case:
Position of the entire criminal cause
Of Guido Franceschini, nobleman,
With certain Four the cutthroats in his pay,
Tried, all five, and found guilty and put to death
By heading or hanging as befitted ranks,
At Rome on February Twenty Two,
Since our salvation Sixteen Ninety Eight:
Wherein it is disputed if, and when,
Husbands may kill adulterous wives, yet 'scape
The customary forfeit.' [I, ll. 120–31]

Either then or later — though it is difficult to imagine Robert bottling up his excitement over his find, so more than likely on reaching home — he tried to show the book and outline some of its 'pure crude fact' to Elizabeth, who, wrote Robert to Julia Wedgwood on 21 January 1869, 'never took the least interest in the story, so much as to wish to inspect the papers. It seems better so to me, but *is* it better?' His wife's unenthusiastic reaction may have damped Robert's excitement in the short term, but it did not extinguish it since he continued to study the papers and consider the narrative of facts. Over the years, Robert read the record of the case in the Old Yellow Book 'fully eight times before converting it into the substance of his poem'.[77] He doesn't specify what

Elizabeth's objections were to the story, but the letter to Julia implies that it offended some female sensibility. Perhaps Elizabeth had found the story personally distasteful, morally repellent, fit only for the police court.

Robert was more likely than his wife to discover beauty and significance in the dark alley, in the morgue, in the police court. Betty Miller remarks: 'His wife, he knew, had never shared his passion for the "curious depth below depth of depravity" which he found "in this chance lump taken as a sample of the soil" of human nature.'[78] There were some, including Julia Wedgwood, having later read what Robert finally made of the Roman murder story in *The Ring and the Book*, who would have agreed with Elizabeth. Nevertheless, despite her complete lack of interest in the Old Yellow Book, Elizabeth is ineluctably linked with the poem from first line to last in the image of the Ring: 'Do you see this Ring?', the poem begins. ' 'Tis Rome-work, made to match / (By Castellani's imitative craft) / Etrurian circlets . . .'. The Ring is the image, literal and metaphorical, of a valuable Castellani ring given to Elizabeth by Isa Blagden. The last two lines of the poem — 'Thy rare gold ring of verse (the poet praised) / Linking our England to his Italy!' — refer to the '*aureo anello*' uniting Italy and England that is mentioned in Tommaseo's lines on the commemorative plaque to Elizabeth's memory fixed to the wall of Casa Guidi.

Robert and Pen were back in London by 11 October and both settled to work. It had been a satisfactory holiday, by and large, though Robert wrote to Julia Wedgwood that the heat had been 'only too Southern, none of us are "braced", as by the Breton rough procedure, but slackened rather'. In this letter of 3 October from Biarritz, Robert remarked that Landor had died in Florence 'without pain, and, at the last, very patient . . . I wish him well with all my heart: he wrote to me a month ago — "probably about to die in a few weeks or days," but he had cried "Wolf!" so often. Five years care about him, and now he is past me.' Robert's generosity towards Landor, says Chesterton, 'was fully repaid in his own mind for his trouble by the mere presence and friendship of Landor, for whose quaint and volcanic personality he had a vast admiration, compounded of the pleasure of the artist in an oddity and of the man in a hero.'[79]

Robert understood that neither his own opinion of Landor's work

— 'He has written passages not exceeded in beauty and subtlety by any literature that I am acquainted with' — nor his tolerant estimation of the old man's contentious personality was shared by everyone. The date of Landor's death had been 17 September 1864: 'he was followed to the grave by two of his sons, and nobody else — the grand old solitary man, beset by weaknesses just as, in his own words, "the elephant is devoured by ants in his inaccessible solitudes." Bless us, if he had let the world tame him and strap a tower on his broad back, what havoc he would have made in the enemy's ranks! — as it was, they let off squibs at him and he got into a rage and ran off, topsy-turveying his friends right and left.' That Robert himself was to take on something of this elephantine element in later years, indulge in rampaging rages when fires were lit under his feet, may perhaps partly account for his tolerance of Landor. He understood irritation very well, and had hitherto dealt with it deliberately, even if his increasing tendency was to react to it less continently and cautiously than before.

The letter to Julia ends, 'I have got the whole of that poem, you enquire about, well in my head, shall write the Twelve books of it in six months, and then take breath again.'[80] The poem was to take a great deal longer than six months to compose. To Isa, Robert wrote no more than a fortnight after the letter to Julia Wedgwood that he hoped 'to have a long poem ready by the summer, my Italian murder thing',[81] and on 1 November 1865, speaking to William Allingham, he estimated that he had by then achieved 15,000 lines of what was to be the final total of 21,116 lines of blank verse.[82] William Clyde DeVane estimates that the great bulk of the work was done 'in the year from October, 1864 to November, 1865'.[83] By 18 March 1865, when he wrote to Isa, Robert was fairly launched on The Ring and the Book: 'I am about a long poem to be something remarkable — work at it hard.' He was writing for at least three hours every morning as well as continuing to research the story.

On 17 October 1864 he had written to Frederic Leighton to beg a favour: 'Go into the church St Lorenzo in Lucina in the Corso — and look attentively at it — so as to describe it to me on your return. The general arrangement of the building, if with a nave — pillars or not — the number of altars, and any particularity there may be — over the High Altar is a famous Crucifixion by Guido. It will be of great use

to me. I don't care about the *outside*.'[84] In a letter to George Barrett of
28 January 1867, Robert was still seeking particulars: 'By the bye, —
should you happen to come across any old postal map of the road
between Arezzo and Rome, via Perugia, — containing the names of *all*
the little villages by the way, — of the year 1700, a little earlier or later,
— I should be glad to have such a thing.'

Earlier still, Isa had been instrumental in obtaining some sup-
plementary materials. In 1862, a Mrs Georgina Baker had promised to
lend Robert a manuscript account of the trial of Count Francesco Guidi
for the murder of his wife, which Robert was 'anxious to collate with
my own collection of papers on the subject',[85] but she had already loaned
it to Thomas Trollope. Robert requested Isa to ask leave of Mrs Baker
that the papers, if they 'really related to *my* Count Francesco Guidi of
Arezzo', should be sent or brought to him from Florence. In the event,
the account of the trial — 'The Death of the Wife-Murderer Guido
Franceschini, by Beheading' — was found to be so relevant when it
reached Robert's hands in October 1862 that it is now known to literary
scholars as the 'Secondary Source', the Old Yellow Book being regarded
as the 'Primary Source'. 'Pray thank Mrs Baker for her kindness,' Robert
wrote to Isa on 18 October 1862, 'and say it will be particularly useful
to me: it would be of little use to anybody without my documents, nor
is it correct in certain respects, but it contains a few notices of the
execution etc. subsequent to my account that I can turn to good: I am
going to make a regular poem of it.'

Robert may have taken the Old Yellow Book with him to Rome for
the winter of 1860–1, with the intention of re-reading it and — he
claimed — of making inquiries about its story there and in Arezzo in
the spring of 1861. It was continually on his mind, though he made
seeming attempts to give it away — the reasons for this apparent gener-
osity are unclear — to others. It may be that he had not yet definitely
decided to use it for his own purposes: Elizabeth's lack of enthusiasm
possibly influenced him at this time. William Allingham wrote in his
diary for 26 May 1868 that Robert at lunch that day had said he had
offered the book to Thomas Trollope (though some say to Anthony
Trollope, Thomas seems more likely) to turn into a novel. When Trol-
lope couldn't manage it, Robert had thought, 'why not take it myself?'

This does not quite square with Robert's letter of 19 September 1862 to Isa, in which he wrote, a few weeks before obtaining the 'Secondary Source' himself, that Mrs Baker had loaned the papers about the trial to Thomas Trollope 'along with other documents which she thought might interest him, and that he had found nothing in this subject to his purpose'. To a Miss Ogle, a novelist, Robert had suggested it as a subject for one of her fictions — but she could make nothing of it — 'and for poetic use, I am almost certain, to one of his leading contemporaries', says Mrs Orr.[86] Park Honan identifies this intended beneficiary as none other than Tennyson.[87] Robert even went so far as to offer the book to his friend William Cornwallis Cartwright so that he could write a historical account of it. Cartwright, who declined the offer, could not be sure whether Robert had brought the book with him to Rome or had left it behind in Florence.[88]

On 16 March 1865 Pen attained the age of sixteen years: 'A great boy — or rather young man — I took him to a party last Monday,' Robert wrote to Isa on 18 March 1865, 'and, woe's me, he figured in coat and white tie!' To the Storys, on 11 April 1865, he reported that 'Pen is a great fellow now, with incipient moustaches . . . his whole great soul was wrapped up in the Boatraces last Saturday, when Oxford beat Cambridge, the cool long and strong stroke against the spurt and spasmodic dip: the English do best by sticking to the English way.'

Edie Story was in England that summer, staying with family friends at Walton-on-Thames, and of course she was keen to see Pen and his father. But pressures of social life and working life prevented a meeting: 'I have no time, — can never call, much less leave town for a day, but I neither am forgetful nor ungrateful, I hope: It is now the end of the season, (and *my* working season, besides — for I have written *8400* lines of my new poem since the autumn, — there's for you) — and there is a little breathing-space before going away.'[89] Right through July, Edie and the Brownings failed to meet: 'Regattas — what has a grey owl like me to do with Regattas and the lovers of the same? No, no! the dark for me!'[90] Three days later, after declining the delights of a regatta, Pen and Robert were on their way to Paris before travelling to Pornic for their summer holiday, staying with old Mr Browning, Sarianna, Mrs Bracken and Willie at the mayor's house as usual until 1 October.

It had been a vexatious six months up to Christmas 1864 when Robert wrote to Isa, on 19 December, to say, sadly, 'Yes, dearest Isa, it is three Christmasses ago — *fully* now: I sometimes see a light at the end of this dark tunnel of life, which was one blackness at the beginning. It won't last for ever. In many ways I can see with my human eyes why this has been right and good for me — as I never doubted it was for Her — and if we do but re-join any day, — the break will be better than forgotten, remembered for its uses.' The memory of Elizabeth lingered in Robert's life, and in his personal Christian belief he looked forward, with a cautious optimism, to being reunited with her.

Meanwhile, life had become a competitive sport. Isa had written to Robert to advise him that 'college acquirements and fame' did little or nothing to prove a man's quality of soul. Robert agreed with her in principle, 'but a race is a race, and whoever tries ought to win'. In this less than Corinthian spirit, Robert was referring, in his letter of 19 January 1865, to Pen and his efforts towards Balliol matriculation — though as a matter of success in life he no doubt identified some competitive spirit within himself. Poetry was art, for sure, and Robert Browning did his best in that art, sticking consistently to his own poetic principles and models.

Whether or not there was some element of active competition in his feelings towards other poets, the thought of glittering prizes and poetic progress was in his mind. While Pen was working diligently to acquire the scholastic resources to pass the entrance examination for Balliol, his father was applying himself on a regular basis to the composition of *The Ring and the Book*. The parallels between the ambitions of father and son at this point are not difficult to discern. If Pen, he told Isa, 'means to try, why I want him to get the reward of it, though that be only a help to something better . . . Well, two years more, and then — I shall not break my heart in any case. He grows, is happy, and good — clear gain!' This is realistic, and probably designed to allay Isa's concern about what she had perceived as Robert's 'monomania' about Pen's education. What it says about Robert's own feelings on his own efforts and prospects may be reasonably inferred.

Though his greatest fame was still in the future, Robert Browning was now sufficiently a celebrity to attract occasional parasites. An advertisement in the *Athenaeum* on 8 April 1865 announced a new publication, the *Shilling Magazine*, edited by one Samuel Lucas, who promised in his prospectus a contribution to its pages from Browning. To this piece of impertinence Robert replied in the next issue of the *Athenaeum* that 'my name occurs in a list of the promised contributors to a new magazine ... in spite of a distinct notice on my part of my inability to contribute'. Lucas rather lamely admitted the *faux pas* not as his but as 'the mistake of my publisher'.

Rather more exotically, in 1862, the former Dublin *demi-mondaine* Laura Bell, now married and converted to become the evangelical, charismatic street preacher Laura Bell Thistlethwayte — 'the canting hypocrite', Robert called her — had passed off some verses she had written as addressed to her from the hand of Robert Browning. 'She thought I was still in Italy,' Robert wrote to Isa on 19 April 1865, 'and that she could show this impudent forgery with no risk of detection — but I got to see a copy of it, and wrote underneath my denial of having perpetrated a syllable of it: whereupon she wrote two flaming letters inviting me to dine with her — which I never answered: I thought she might want to get my handwriting and really forge something like it. There's a Magdalen for you! It answers perfectly, of course — crowds of people go to hear her, and take her by the hand, — like the exquisite fools they are — born for Laura Bells, Humes [Daniel Dunglas Home] and such vermin. So is the world made, and we have got to live in it.'

At Sainte Marie during August and September 1865 things were reassuringly quiet and familiar: 'Nothing is changed — Pornic itself, two miles off, is full of company, but our little village is its dirty, unimproved self — a trifle wilder than before, if possible.'[91] Mary Bracken, too, was unchanged — 'a woman of a mild mournful voice over minute grievances, chiefly culinary, but really devoted to Willy' — and so was the weather: 'rain every day, with intervals of sun, a contrast to the wonderful Biarritz and Cambo blaze of last year: at the same time it suits me, and I think the others, better by far: the sea is the great resource'. The sea air, it occurred to Robert a year later, on a subsequent holiday, 'seems to wipe out all my ailments and set the brain to rights, I come back aged sixteen'.[92]

He bathed safely every day in a creek and liked to watch Pen and Willie swim more frequently and strongly than ever, competing in deep-sea swimming races which Robert, holding an open umbrella in one hand, timed with his watch in the other. Even the mayor and his family were wonderfully unchanged: 'The people here are good, stupid and dirty, without a touch of the sense of picturesqueness in their clodpoles. The Mayor and master of this house, — for instance, — is good and abundantly rich, — has houses and land and other incomings, — yet out of pure preference for piggishness, he sleeps in one room with his son and three daughters, the eldest being fifteen, and — the somewhat less ugly than usual maid servant of about nineteen or twenty, — who is lately take into service, — four beds in a row — and the notion that such arrangement is queer will not enter a head in the village for the next fifty years.'[93]

While Mrs Bracken moaned softly and Mr Browning groaned aesthetically as he sketched the recent ruins of the Sainte Marie church, Pen and Robert worked daily through several books of Virgil at the rate of a hundred lines an hour. Robert liked to tease Isa a little in his letters to her: on 19 May 1865, he had written from London of being 'on a staircase the night before last, so dense was the double current, coming and going, — I stood on the landing, jammed between two ladies, and laughed at my friends lower down.' It is a vivid little picture of Robert Browning at play, at his happiest, sandwiched between two women, their scent in his nostrils and their sophisticated silks rustling against his suit. At Saint-Marie, by contrast, he bade Isa 'fancy the buxom servant girl, aged some 20, washing clothes before my window (on the pianterro, dressed in a blue gown and nothing else, I can see, just covering the naked legs below the knees — and so kilted, turning her back to me and burying herself with linen she has to stoop for on the ground! Primitive manners!'[94] If the girl had this effect upon Robert's imagination, what did the sight of her do to the adolescent fantasies of Pen Browning and Willie Bracken? If the thought entered Robert's head, he did not confide it to Isa.

By the time Robert and Pen returned to London, William Story and his wife had joined Edie at Walton-on-Thames, but circumstances conspired against their meeting with Robert. In a letter to the Storys on 21 October, he wrote, 'the reason I do not leave Town, when once fairly settled in it, is, as I have always truly declared, because I *cannot*: I take the longest possible holiday, and, that over, shut my eyes to any diversion in my business from this place.' There are few letters from this period, though whether few survive or Robert was writing fewer than usual can only be supposed. But in any case, work had been resumed on *The Ring and the Book*, and even the most punctilious correspondent will tend to write less letters when conscientiously engaged on creative work.

By May 1866 Robert told Isa that his 'poem is nearly done — won't be out for a year or perhaps more. I shall go about and sell my books to the best bidder, and I want something, decidedly for this performance: 16,000 lines or over, — done in less than two years, Isa!'[95] About anything else, 'I have nothing to tell you,' he had written candidly to Isa in February, though 'I go out a great deal.' His constant excursions into society made little permanent impression upon Robert, little enough worth comment, though he refers in this letter to Isa to a pleasurable dinner with Tennyson and his wife: 'she is just what she was and always will be — very sweet and dear: he seems to me better than ever'. He met the Tennysons again, soon after, at a party attended — surprisingly — by Carlyle, 'whom I never met at a "drum" in my whole life, till now'.

By 19 March, when he wrote again to Isa, Robert was 'just now getting very tired of the early season, all but at an end now, happily: and long to go to Paris, as I hope to do next Saturday week or thereabout: the weather is still vile here, and unholidaylike, as is the way when Easter is so early.' It had become Robert's habit to visit his father and sister for Easter. The year before, his visit had happily coincided with his friend Joseph Milsand's marriage. This year, he was disturbed to find his father seriously unwell. In his letter to Isa of 19 April 1866, Robert reported that he had gone nowhere, made not a single call on anyone during his two weeks in Paris 'lest I might be induced to spend an evening away'. He devoted his entire time and attention to the good old man, who was suffering from 'an internal varicose vein, — very painful and debilitating at his age, — and from the want of his usual exercise his diges-tion suffers'. Mr Browning's mind, however, was as sharp as ever. 'The other day,' Robert told Isa on 19 May, 'when I wanted a point of infor-mation about medieval history, he wrote a regular bookful of notes and extracts thereabout.' What he had particularly asked his father to investi-gate was 'the history of one of the Popes — (I did it to interest him mainly)'.[96] By the time Robert returned to London, Mr Browning seemed better and subsequent reports from Sarianna were good.

Their father was in fact at his last gasp. He died of internal haemor-
rhaging and a tumour on the morning of 14 June 1866, three weeks
before his eighty-fifth birthday and just twenty-four hours after Robert,
urgently summoned by a telegram from Sarianna, arrived at his father's
bedside in the small apartment in the rue de Grenelle. Robert had found
him 'in a kind of convulsion-fit, and insensible' at 8 o'clock in the
morning of 13 June, though he 'recovered presently, and knew me and
spoke like his old self'. Reporting these circumstances to Pen in a letter
dated the same day, Robert went on to write: 'He told me, with just
the usual air, that he was perfectly well — and seemed to wonder that
we found anything to grieve about: he is in the full possession of his
senses and every now and then asks Sarianna to read a chapter in the
Bible to him — mentioning the particular one, and what verses he
wishes to hear. He is in the most complete peace of mind, and as
unconcerned about death as if it were a mere walk into the next room.'

Robert relieved Sarianna's bedside vigil — she had been sitting by
her father for two days — and even persuaded her 'not to witness the
last struggle'. Mr Browning had been conscious almost until the last
moment, solicitous of any distress he might be causing his son. He
seemed wonderfully oblivious of any anxiety about his own condition.
'All the time he kept up that divine gentleness and care for others that
made him by far *the Finest Gentleman* I have ever known: — "Shall I
fan you?" I said — "If you please, dear — I am only afraid of tiring
you" — and so on: this, in the very agonies of death.'[97]

Mr Browning was buried in the Père Lachaise cemetery at noon on
Saturday 16 June. To Isa, on 20 June 1866, Robert wrote: 'So passed
away this good, unworldly, kind hearted, religious man, whose powers
natural and acquired would so easily have made him a notable man,
had he known what vanity or ambition or the love of money or social
influence meant. As it is, he was known by half a dozen friends. He
was worthy of being Ba's father — out of the whole world, only he, as
far as my experience goes. She loved him, — and he said, very recently,
while gazing at her portrait, that only that picture had put into his
head that there might be such a thing as the worship of the images of
saints.'

Robert's letters to Pen in London, besides relaying detailed accounts
of the sad events in Paris, were full of concerns for his son's well-being.

Pen was earnestly advised not only to read in the Bible those last chapters which Mr Browning had asked Sarianna to recite aloud to him a few hours before his death, but also to walk and row more than usually, as though devotional and physical exercise might not only distract his mind but assure his good health. Maisie Ward regards Robert's uneasiness for his son as unusual. Very credibly, she suggests that his concern for Pen was less definite and more profound at this time than his normal anxieties about his son's education and adolescence: 'For five years Browning had been congratulating himself and praising Pen, but it looks as though a shiver had just gone through him.'[98]

On the Tuesday after the funeral, Robert returned to London, leaving Sarianna to settle her own affairs in Paris before she, too, travelled to London. It had been agreed that she would live permanently with Robert and Pen at 19 Warwick Crescent: 'you will like that as much as I,' Robert told Pen. 'My sister will come and live with me henceforth,' he wrote to Isa. 'You see what she loses, — all her life has been spent in caring for my mother, and, seventeen years after that, my father: you may be sure she does not rave and rend her hair like people who have plenty to atone for in the past, — but she loses very much.'

A head and shoulders photograph of the middle-aged Sarianna Browning is not very informative. Her face is round; her eyes are like two currants in a bun. Her black hair is parted in the centre of her head, worn back and above her ears — rather like the style favoured by Julia Wedgwood, though not as severely trained or tightly bound. Another photograph, apparently taken earlier in her life, shows — in profile — a stronger chin, a firm line to the lips, and an unflinching look in the sharp, dark eyes. Her hair, this time worn in ringlets falling almost to her shoulders, does not much soften her appearance.[99] Though her face is not pretty in photographs, and seems characteristic of her capable personality, it is likely that Sarianna was more lively and displayed more charm in real life. Indeed, Alfred Domett in 1872 was struck by her 'frank and energetic style', which had not altered since he had last met her, some thirty years before, as a young woman.[100]

Sarianna had remained close friends with the Fraser Corkrans throughout her residence in Paris, and Mr Browning had been indulgent and kindly to their children, Henriette and Alice. According to an account by Henriette Corkran in *Celebrities and I*, published in 1905,

Sarianna was very short and very talkative. When in full flood, in animated anecdote, she would stand on tiptoe. Though her head is more round than square, she probably resembled her mother in looks; her character, however, seems more formidably assertive. Like her brother, she had learned to be careful about money: towards the end of his life, she had rationed the amount her father could carry about in his pockets when he went bargain-hunting for books and pictures in Paris. Sarianna herself was not personally extravagant in any sense. Henriette Corkran found her 'a splendid character, a staunch friend', but 'not expansive or demonstrative; indeed there may be a lack of *outward sympathy*; she does not caress or purr'. For all Sarianna's reliability and delightfulness as a companion, Henriette Corkran is obliged to admit one weakness: Sarianna was a snob. She never liked to hear her father talk about having been a clerk in the Bank of England, and would tread on his toes to stop him — which only confused old Mr Browning, who would apologize and thus make matters worse.

And so it probably suited Sarianna very well, when she brought her chairs and the considerable quantity of her father's books and pictures with her to London and settled herself in a little room which Robert had made comfortable,[101] to associate in person with all those grandees who had visited her brother and sister-in-law, and about whom, says Miss Corkran, Sarianna had loved to talk. To be fair to Sarianna, she seems to have been a good and sensible woman, intelligent and well-regarded by those who knew her, who had willingly and without complaint spent her entire life in the service of her mother, father, brother, and — latterly — her nephew. What Sarianna herself gained from this arrangement was financial security and social status — though at what cost to her own ambitions cannot be said since she is not known to have had any beyond the conscientious discharge of family responsibilities she took upon herself and her aspirations towards acquaintance with superior and celebrated persons. Unlike Isa Blagden, she would never have to eke out a small and uncertain living as a minor romantic novelist. It seems probable, however, that her self-imposed duties as the Browning family housekeeper and hostess satisfied her domestic nature and her strong sense of loyalty, not only to her father, who had occasionally been exasperatingly other-worldly, but also to her brother.

In later life, she was an indefatigable and apparently precise source of information about Robert and Elizabeth Browning for anyone with a legitimate interest in them. At least, she was always very definite in her recollection, more reliable than Robert could ever be about the details of his own life and work, though her interest was also in giving lustre to the Browning name. Sarianna never married. As Henriette Corkran remarked, perhaps not quite artlessly, 'Her wonderful affection and admiration for a Browning was touching, nothing that any of them said or did could be wrong, it was all perfection.' Robert, very sincerely, expressed the same sentiment: 'She has always been perfect in her relation to everyone she was naturally a help to.'[102]

That summer, the Brownings and the Brackens took their holidays as usual in Brittany. Robert had solicited an introduction from Richard Monckton Milnes to Victor Hugo, who was then still living in exile in Guernsey: in the event, he did not visit Guernsey but travelled instead with Pen and Willie by way of Jersey to visit his old friend Frederick Tennyson and his family. 'I enjoyed it all greatly,' Robert wrote to Isa on 7 August 1866, 'and, but for the arranged plan, would have spent our holiday there. Mrs T. told me he is wholly addicted to spirit-rapping and writing — in which she also believes — moreover he is "quite changed" (from what?) and "is of the faith of the New Jerusalem" — i.e. Swedenborgianism: she said a word or two on both subjects, but no more — and the fewer the better . . . I groan over such a noble, accomplished man being as good as lost to us all.'

This letter to Isa tells how the holiday-makers had first found Dinard unsuitable and, after a few days at St Malo, had settled at fashionable Le Croisic, which, on account of a rumoured outbreak of cholera, had been deserted by the usual crowds. The Brownings had the place 'nearly to ourselves: we are in the most delicious and peculiar old house I ever occupied, the oldest in the town, — plenty of great rooms, — nearly as much space as at the Villa Alberti: Mrs Bracken is well-lodged too, close by: the little town, and surrounding country are wild and primitive, even a trifle beyond Pornic perhaps: close by is Batz, a village where the men dress in white from head to foot, with baggy breeches, and great black flap hats, — opposite is Guerande, the old capital of Bretagne, — you have read about it in Balzac's Beatrix, — and other interesting places are near: the sea is all round our peninsula, and on the whole we expect we shall like it very much.'[103]

The correspondence between Robert and Isa had recently dwelt upon the shortcomings of their publishers, Edward Chapman and his son Frederic, who seemed in matters of business to be as bad as his father. On 19 March 1865, Robert had written to Isa of 'Chapman's carelessness ... I have suffered nearly as much from his peculiarities ... He is honest, but a scatter brain creature, — forgets, makes excuses, and worse — but the *worst* he is not, and you will certainly get your money tho' you have been most shamefully kept out of it — and might have suffered inconveniences enough.' The next letter, from Robert to Isa of 22 April 1866, more or less repeats these comments and congratulates Isa on having got her money from Chapman and Hall and having delivered her next novel to them. By 13 July, there was another dispute about the sum of £75, which Chapman had declared to have been paid to Isa three years previously.[104] On 26 and 27 June 1866 Robert, prevented from calling personally to discuss matters with his publishers, had written irritatedly to Edward Chapman. Grievances had been aired and, up to a point, wounded feelings had been patched; but relations remained tricky: Robert always liked precision and required punctuality in matters of personal business. Though Chapman and Hall had normally paid up after prompting, and had never been dishonest in business, in other respects, notably the promotion of its products, the firm had often been dilatory and inattentive.

Robert distrusted Edward Chapman professionally without disliking him personally. He complained that *Dramatis Personae*, 'a publication from which we were entitled to expect considerable results had proved a comparative failure, and it did strike me that my trees of this sort would gain by changing the soil. I desire no better than that you show me I was wrong.' Mildly qualifying this muted but premonitory threat to change publishers, Robert professed no 'inordinate expectation of gain ... But really my income may be seriously affected by affairs in Italy, and I ought to care a little about what most of my fellows of the pen care abundantly for.'[105] Money was not Robert's primary interest, though a better financial return on his books would at least provide some material evidence that they were of value to the public. More than money, Robert valued reputation. If Chapman would not jump to the stick of an author who regarded himself as underrated and undervalued by his publisher, he might more readily rise to the bait of improved profit. But, all things considered, Robert was not convinced that the relationship could be repaired, far less improved.

To Isa, in his letter of 19 May 1866, Robert had expressed some concern about money: 'Suppose I am ruined by the loss of my Italian Rents — how then? I shall go about and sell my book to the best bidder . . . .' His feelings were that Chapman and Hall had never demonstrated sufficient confidence in his work and had done too little to promote his books, neglecting opportunities that Robert's rising reputation should have provided. On June 20 1866, he had written frankly to Isa what he did not yet confide to Chapman: 'I am profoundly discontented with him, and shall dissolve our connection, — on my own account, not yours only.' Robert did write to his publishers on 26 June. The Chapmans responded the same day, with uncharacteristic alacrity, making promises and proposals that satisfied Robert for the time being; but there was no question in his mind that Chapman and Hall should get its inept and pusillanimous hands on *The Ring and the Book*.

The holiday at Le Croisic had been a mixed benefit for Robert. Though he felt 'a real attachment to the place', it had rained for 'three full weeks' in September, in contrast to the 'two months of golden days' the previous year at Pornic. But 'I was resolute not to return to Pornic, full of my poor dear Papa — as I never broke the habit of calling him: I wonder whether Pen will long come and kiss me, morning and night, as he now does.'[106] These whiskered kisses — these twice-daily brushes of Browning moustaches — were important: they meant that Pen, now well into his seventeenth year, was 'quite a boy still', though, as Robert wrote a few months later to Seymour Kirkup in Florence, 'you will hardly recognize the curly little creature that was'.[107] At Le Croisic, Robert began more consciously to recognize the natural changes in his own and Pen's linked lives that he had only dimly perceived at the time of his father's death and that had prompted his advice to Pen to take care of his spiritual and physical health.

That he had his doubts about Pen is clearly marked in his admitting to Isa, in September 1866, that 'I don't in the least know how he will turn out *eventually*: he is still to all intents, growing, — a boy: he seems to me able to do many things for which at present he has little or no inclination, — and that inclination may arrive at any moment: but the bases of a good and strong character, on the other hand, are more than indicated, — they are laid: he is good, kind, cautious, self-respecting, and true. I ought to be satisfied with these qualities which are valuable enough. I want him to be what I think he may be: next year or two will decide perhaps if I am to be disappointed or no.'[108] To Seymour Kirkup, on 19 February 1867, Robert characterized Pen as 'strong, healthy, inordinately given to boating, quite a boy still, but good, truthful, *loyal* — I may safely say: all depends on the turn he may take just now.'

For all Robert's loyal insistence on Pen's beautiful and admirable moral qualities, there is a distinct sense in his letters of paternal anxiety — perfectly natural and justified — about his son's development as a scholar. He noted in the adolescent Pen no spontaneous interest in books or unprompted pleasure in the miscellaneous learning that he himself, and his own father, had possessed all their lives, and which had needed no force of discipline to develop. Whatever 'turn' Pen might take in the future, for the time being he would have to be kept pretty strictly on the straight and narrow path that led to Balliol. On their return to London, Robert and Pen buckled down — at the cost of time that Robert could give to his own work on *The Ring and the Book* — to the serious work of preparing for the Balliol matriculation on 2 May. On 25 March, at Jowett's invitation, Pen went to Oxford for a week and returned to London with Jowett's depressing verdict that he was 'up to the mark in Latin, hardly in Greek'. Any prospect of matriculation was postponed until October at the earliest. The Brownings set themselves determinedly to a further few months of intensive tutorials.

Perhaps too ironically, Oxford decided at this time to heap academic honours upon Robert. Matthew Arnold proposed to relinquish the Poetry Professorship at Oxford in June. According to Robert's letter to Isa of 19 February 1867, 'a number of young men at Oxford made a request that *I* might be their Poetry Professor', and Jowett also proposed to Robert that he should offer himself as a candidate. The difficulty was that Robert did not possess an MA degree. This was an unexpected and unfortunate long-term consequence of Robert's exclusion as a Nonconformist from Oxford and from having dropped out of London University in his youth. It was suggested that the university should qualify him for the position by conferring on him the degree of MA as required by statute, but 'the Council declined to do this, as unfair to the Candidates already in the field'. Robert thought this 'very fair and just'.

For the sake of being able to keep an eye on Pen at Oxford, he would have accepted ('Had they wished me to blacken their boots instead of polish their heads, I should not have demurred, you understand, in the prospect of possible benefit to Pen'), though the drawbacks would have been considerable, 'in the shape of the curtailment of liberty for the next five years, when I should perhaps want to dispose of my time otherwise. Moreover, the three Lectures in the year would take as much trouble to write as three tragedies, — for I try to do things thoroughly.' Robert's freedom never to have to do anything on any particular day was as deeply ingrained as his taste for doing whatever he did choose to do very thoroughly. It had been for Pen's benefit that he had considered, even briefly, Thackeray's offer of the editorship of the *Cornhill* a few years before, and for his own benefit that he had declined it.

In mid-June 1867, Robert made what had become an annual trip to Oxford to visit Benjamin Jowett and be 'pleasantly entertained for three days'. The day after his return, on the 18th, a telegram arrived from Jowett, who arrived himself in London that same night and hurried straight to Warwick Crescent with 'something of importance' to tell. On the 19th, immediately after Jowett's departure, Robert wrote to Isa. 'He came to tell me a long story of which the short is this — they (somebody unknown) proposed me at Oxford for the D. C. L degree: no opposition was made, only nobody having been apprised, there were not the proper two-thirds, but a simple majority of votes, — so the motion was lost. This transpiring, there was a [*sic*] another sort of motion from the members of congregation calling on the council to give me a M. A. degree by Diploma, — a very rare distinction said to have only happened in Dr Johnson's case! It is much better than the D. C. L. because it gives all the rights of the university, voting, etc. — while the other is a mere right to wear a gown and put the letters after your name ... I have just telegraphed and written to say I accept ... There is better still, — for they are going, once the degree is given, to elect me Honorary Fellow of Balliol!!!'[109] The degree of MA was awarded on 26 June, and the Honorary Fellowship conferred in October 1867.

Though Robert's whooping glee in the letter to Isa is spontaneous, irrepressible, he immediately damped it down and displaced his pleasure: 'Of course it is purely for Pen's sake — though I am not insensible to the strange liking for me that young and old Oxford seems to have — WHY?' That 'WHY?' is unconsciously ambiguous: why should Oxford have a strange liking for Robert Browning? or why should Robert Browning care twopence for being liked? The former is the obvious interpretation, the latter less likely were it not for Robert's remarks to Isa a few lines later in his letter: 'Years ago I only wanted a notice in a Review, and did not much want that. Now, all I want *for myself* is to be forgotten in some out of the way place in Italy or Greece, with books, a model and a lump of clay and sticks ... Poor Papa was buried last year about this time: I should have enjoyed the thing for his sake.' When Isa began to address her letters to him as 'Mr Robert Browning M. A.' he put a stop to such foolishness — 'unless as a joke, which I don't mind'.[110]

That can be reasonably interpreted as natural modesty, but Robert's self-deprecation went deeper. He had a healthy-enough sense of himself — as a man and as a poet — that gave him distinction in society and dignity in literature, but his deepest confidence had been wounded too early to heal entirely. Something of this seems very likely to have been displaced into his regret that his father had not lived to see his son being honoured, as well as his anxiety for Pen's fate in life. Possibly as a matter of ingrained lack of expectation — born of professional humiliations in youth and barely repressed resentments in maturity that had recently been expressed in his relationship with Chapman — Robert invariably chose to play down his own achievements and dedicate them, perhaps as offerings to capricious Fortune, for the benefit of his son, who needed all the help he could get: 'You see the advantage it will be to me to be in that position while Pen is there.'

Old ghosts came back at this time to haunt and taunt Robert's memories of the past. On 19 June 1867, to Isa, Robert had written: 'Here is the sixth year completed, next 29th. Time does go certainly. The years they come and go — The races drop in the grave — But *never* the love does so!' Mindful of Elizabeth's death, and just before the usual holiday period, Robert asked in his letter of 19 July to Isa whether she had heard 'anything about the trial of Mr Hume which is coming on?' Daniel Dunglas Home had lately fascinated Jane Lyon, the widow of Charles Lyon, a grandson of the eighth Earl of Strathmore. The Lyon family was closely connected by family blood to Queen Victoria. In 1866, Jane

Lyon, then aged seventy-five, adopted Mr Home and first settled £24,000 on him, then £6,000 more when he took the name Home-Lyon, and finally gave him another £30,000 before changing her mind about these benefactions and filing a bill against him in the Court of Chancery on the grounds of extortion and undue influence.

In April 1868, Mrs Lyon won her case, though at the expense of being directed to pay Home's costs. Much to Robert's satisfaction, Home had actually been arrested and thrown into prison. He was only released 'on condition of his giving up all the deeds, papers, etc. to be used in the case. He will be tried "for getting money under false pretences," — pretending he was inspired by a spirit when there was none.'[111] Robert had got his information from Mrs Lyon's counsel in the case, who told him that Home had 'wanted in the first place to marry Mrs Lyon', which, Robert disobligingly remarked, would have been 'a misfortune' for several other spiritualistic society women 'and such like vermin' who were devoted to Home.

Lily Wilson, too, had turned up — in trouble again. She was now living with her family in East Retford, but spoke of wanting to return to Florence. Robert was exasperated both with Wilson and her sisters and had not moderated his words to one of the latter: 'I have no sort of patience with the sister who allows, if she does not encourage Wilson in the notion of going to Florence, — just to get rid of her. The sister is to blame in the highest degree for advising Wilson to set up for herself as a lodging-keeper, as if there were any chance of her doing that in England which she could not do in Florence with fifty fold the advantage. I have told this to the sister in the plainest words I could use — written words — and, of course, affronted her, — to judge by the way she last wrote to me, — on the occasion of Wilson's wanting to return to Florence — where she will infallibly go mad. The sister could very well have taken her as assistant or partner in her millinery business. But the behaviour of them all (except poor Ferdinando, who has had to painfully expiate his old faults) is too exasperatingly imbecile.'[112]

As a last-ditch measure to save Wilson from destitution and madness, Robert 'would have taken both Wilson and Ferdinando into my service, tho' intimately convinced I should be nearly ruined by one or the other of their incapablenesses — but fortunately for me, they, or she would not come. She hesitated at first between taking a cigar-shop and a pastry cook shop! Imagine the imbecility of her brother and sister in putting such nonsense into her head, or allowing it to stay there for a moment.'[113] A cheque, whether from Isa or Robert, was dispatched to East Retford, but for his trouble Robert 'got an impertinent, improper letter in reply' from Wilson's sister 'saying Wilson was quite able to take care of herself, and had been found so as long as she was of any use, — "when worn out in the service she was to be thrown on other people," and more of this sort of thing'.[114]

Robert replied in ripe terms, the consequence of which was a visit from Wilson herself, 'to my mind, mad *now* — so utterly irrationally did she talk. "Ferdinando *must* keep her, or why did he marry her?" — I asked what she was going to do? Now this, now that. "Keep a shop, lodgings, take in needlework"; with what? "Nothing — all the money was spent." She did not deny that her sisters, whose trade is doing needlework, would have nothing to do with her. The fact is, they have been determined she should do for herself, — just what she can't do, — never did nor will. It is all deplorable, and I expect the worst will come of it in every way.'[115] Robert's patience with anyone who made a *pasticcio* of their lives, and thus disturbed or distracted his own, was always short: his intolerance for perceived incompetence, and his ready irritability at weakness or lack of spirit in others, was easily provoked and familiar enough even to close friends, including Isa, who knew his 'ogre-fashion', and Julia Wedgwood, who recognized Robert as 'the most impatient man in the world'.

All this, of course, only a few weeks after the point of greatest worry about whether Pen, who had paid his visit of a week to Jowett at Oxford at the end of March, would be able to do for himself — and perhaps that was just what he couldn't do, never would be able to do. Then, too, Robert had been trying to sell, so far unsuccessfully, a picture on behalf of an old and ailing friend, Count Cottrell, who was hard up for money in Florence. In the same letter to Isa, only a few lines after his account of Wilson's difficulties, he wrote: 'How hard it is for people to get money! I don't wonder they grow misers: It is so terrible to have to leave all your soul's business and set about getting fifty pounds — even your sorrows you would have to give up.'[116]

It is not unambiguously clear how far Wilson's difficulties, or even the peril to her soul, were compounded, in Robert's mind, with those of Count Cottrell. In his letter of 21 March 1867 to Isa, Robert had remarked, 'after all five or six hundred pounds contribute materially to oil the wheels of life, in the case of folks of moderate means'. Isa, for her own part, would have known this all too well. It is unlikely that the cheque to Wilson amounted to anything like so much. Some five years later, on hearing that George Barrett had offered to pay Wilson an annual pension of £10, Robert's conscience was pricked and he repented his neglect. Writing to Isa on 19 February 1872, he admitted that 'Wilson ought to be a care to me rather than to anyone else, much less you.' Evidently Isa had been helping Wilson out from her own meagre resources and George, too, had supplied money for Wilson's benefit. 'I have done wrong in putting her out of my thoughts, of late — but there was some excuse in the impertinent letter which her sister wrote to me as a wind-up . . . George is, as always, most generous, — but I can't allow him to take my business on himself . . . if he pleases to give something in addition, I have nothing to say of course.' But Robert washed his hands of any responsibility for Ferdinando Romagnoli: 'Ferdinando, though quite as good in his way, is not my concern.'[117]

The letter of 23 April 1867 to Isa concluded with some shrewd financial calculations of Robert's own prosperous prospects: booksellers were already making him 'pretty offers' for his new poem, even before he finished it. At this date, some five thousand lines short of the final length of 21,116 lines, Robert wrote to Isa of that 'R B who for six months once did not sell one copy of the poems. I ask £200 for the sheets to America and shall get it, — or rather, Pen will.' Robert is sometimes accused of, at best, close-fistedness with money, and at worst, with miserliness; but if that was how it seemed to others, and may still seem to some now, it was not for himself but always for Pen that he felt the need to make the fullest possible financial provision.

The summer of 1867 was spent again at Le Croisic, in the same accommodation — the house Robert judged big enough for a dozen families — as the year before. The weather was better this year: 'fifty consecutive fine days here', during which Robert developed his swimming skills: 'I could only swim a few strokes in my youth, — only took to the sea at Pornic five years ago . . . now it seems to suit me better than any other exercise, at any hour and for any time.'[118] Besides swimming daily for up to three-quarters of an hour at a stretch, Robert walked long distances. At least once he and Sarianna walked nine miles in two hours along the sands from Guerande. Pen and Willie 'swim and shoot and enjoy themselves. Mrs Bracken and Miss Smith are always here, and enjoy the place.'[119]

Miss Smith was Annie Egerton Smith, Mary Bracken's sister, who had also been at Le Croisic with the Brownings in 1866 and had become a good friend whose company Robert much enjoyed and valued. The landscape of Le Croisic, brushed by gusting wind and flooded by rushing water, was as inspirational to Robert as the lives of the Croisickese (Browning's spelling), whose legends, few enough but dramatic, he found in a local guidebook, *Notes sur le Croisic* by *Caillo jeune*. Some of these he saved up for later use, but one — the romantic story of a Croisic naval hero, Hervé Riel — became the eponymous subject of a poem dated 30 September 1867. Robert was never starved of materials to spark his imagination. Ten years later, in 'The Two Poets of Croisic', he wrote:

> Anywhere serves: for point me out the place
> Wherever man has made himself a home,
> And there I find the story of our race
> In little, just at Croisic as at Rome. [ll. 137–40]

'The whole district is wild, strange and romantic, with a fine fierce sea and driving sands,' Robert wrote to Seymour Kirkup on 19 February 1867. Responsive to the particular tastes of his correspondent, he further confided to Kirkup, the old necromancer of Florence, what he did not divulge to Isa: that 'Croisic is the old head-seat of Druidism in France ... the people were still pagan a couple of hundred years ago, despite the priests' teaching and preaching, and the women used to dance round a phallic stone still upright there with obscene circumstances enough, — till the general civilization got too strong for this.'

This wild, underlying paganism of the Bretons perhaps had its subliminal effect on Robert, whose eye for a young woman and a finely-turned female leg was often whetted while on holiday. Pen Browning's more urgent, youthful sexuality seems not to have been entirely sublimated into swimming, racing, and wrestling with Willie Bracken. Despite Robert's high regard for his son's admirable caution, Pen became possibly over-excited by phallic dolmens epitomizing the primacy of sexual desire. His hormones got the better of his discretion, his sensuality overrode his sense, if we are to believe Frances Winwar, who, in the London edition of her book *The Immortal Lovers: Elizabeth Barrett and Robert Browning*, published in 1950, alleges that Pen fathered 'two illegitimate daughters by different mothers, peasant girls of Brittany' before his nineteenth year. Though Robert occasionally and pleasantly referred to his own innocent little gallantries, if and when he ever discovered the consequences of Pen's bold philanderings and confessed them to anybody, it was not — so far as can be known — to Isa, his closest confidante after Sarianna.

Back in England after the summer, Pen was behaving impeccably. He had been packed off to Oxford to enjoy a preliminary taste of university life before matriculation. According to his regular letters home, he was having a wonderful time. Robert rejoiced: 'the experiment turning out exactly as I had hoped: the impulse gained by a glimpse, or rather good gaze into the life of young men with a purpose to study, has done him great good. He writes me often, — enjoys himself much, having his own boat there. Indeed, people are only too kind to him, and the magnates have him to breakfast etc. in an unusual way.'[120] Jowett had already noted Pen's instant popularity with everyone on his first, shorter visit. Pen himself attended Jowett lectures in Greek and paid respectful attention to other tutors who coached him intensively.

Even allowing for the curious deficiency of Pen's memory, and the fact that he seemed strangely unused to writing in English, Jowett expressed to Robert a comfortable confidence towards the end of the year that his pupil would be ready for the examination at the beginning of the Easter term. Robert looked forward to Pen's success, as much for his own sake as for his son's. It was always in his mind that he stayed in London only for Pen's benefit. By 19 January 1868 he told Isa that he'd had enough of 'this black rainy beastly-streeted London world' and his 'whole soul' turned to Italy — 'how I wish myself there, out of all this ugliness'. Once Pen was safely settled for several years as a student at Balliol, Robert would feel free to please himself about what to do, where to be.

Pen's temporary residence in Oxford meanwhile relieved Robert of his own duties as a tutor, enabling him to give the early hours of the mornings to work on his poem. All that winter he took a disgust to dining out, refusing what invitations he possibly could: 'I want my life for myself, what remains enough: do you know I get up, — have got up all winter at 5? and even so, I can't get thro' my work.'[121] To Edward Dowden, on 16 October 1867, he had written: 'I am finishing the exceedingly lengthy business, and hope to be rid of it in a few months more.' In anticipation of that great event, Robert had broken entirely with Chapman and Hall, confiding future publication of his works to the publishers Smith and Elder, and in particular to George Murray Smith, with whom he had been on friendly terms for twenty years. Robert liked and trusted George Smith, who confidently, competently, and with exemplary tact and patience, supervised a very distinguished list of successful writers, among them Anthony Trollope, Charles Darwin, Matthew Arnold, and John Ruskin — all of these rich, respected, and happy writers being Robert's personal friends. Joining Smith and Elder was as good as joining the Athenaeum Club.

To Isa, Robert wrote: 'I part from Chapman, pursuant to my resolution taken when you were last in England, and go to Smith and Elder — who bring out a new Edition presently.' This handsome six-volume edition of Robert's complete works to date would include, for the first time, *Pauline*. Smith insisted, and Robert gave in much against his will — with 'extreme repugnance', indeed — but resignedly since the fact of his authorship was already known to the *cognoscenti* and could not be concealed indefinitely from the rest of the world. The authoritative Smith and Elder Edition, sonorously entitled *The Poetical Works of Robert Browning, M. A., Honorary Fellow of Balliol College, Oxford*, was published in 1868, neatly timed to provoke critical and public interest just before publication of *The Ring and the Book* at the end of the year.

As to that prospect, wrote Robert to Isa, 'I have had strange offers for the Poem, — which I shall give to Smith in all probability.' He provided Isa with details of his new publisher's munificence — 'Smith gives me exactly five times for an edition, — an arrangement which is preferable' — and of Chapman's miserable incompetence: 'Chapman's behaviour was characteristic to the last: he apprised me "he had fifty-copies on hand" (as it was stipulated he should, it being a bad thing to let a book get quite out of print). I sent for one of these copies (to reprint by) — no answer, — at last I sent a servant to bring one, —

then came the avowal — all were gone. What do you say to that? I am well rid of such a publisher, *I* think.'[122]

On 2 April 1868, Pen sat and failed the Balliol matriculation examination. What was to be done? Jowett pointed out that Pen often and easily tackled the most difficult questions but miserably botched the simplest. It wasn't a question of Pen's aptitude or application — he had demonstrated both perfectly adequately — but more a matter of carelessness. Jowett's sole concern was for the reputation of Balliol: nothing else mattered, neither personal interest nor personal friendship. Jowett had already done everything within his considerable power to help Robert and Pen, but Balliol men were trained to be masters of the universe, and special favours or attempts to influence the incorruptible examiners were out of the question. A stumble at the starting block was not to be countenanced for any prospective student.

Nevertheless, Jowett liked Pen, and found his contradictions — undoubted cleverness qualified by an unfathomable forgetfulness — interesting. He perceived qualities and potential in the young fellow, and perhaps for once he allowed a limited personal indulgence to get the better of his academic judgement. To that extent he permitted Robert to believe that a second attempt in October could be successful. For his own part, Robert had no complaint against Pen's tutors and attributed the boy's failure simply to nervousness, despite Pen's denial that he had suffered any such thing. Robert recommended renewed discipline; and so Pen buckled down once again to a six-month grind of study, first with a competent tutor, a Mr Gillespie, and later in the year with Jowett himself — as a special privilege — for five weeks during the autumn of 1868 at a reading party at St Andrews.

That year was one of particular gain and poignant loss for Robert Browning. In June, his sister-in-law Arabel died. Mrs Orr attributes the death to 'a rheumatic affliction of the heart'. Arabel had been taken ill on Wednesday 10 June, but her doctor had seen no danger. Robert, never wholly trustful of doctors, called for a second opinion from 'a second wise man, who saw with the eyes of the first, and a third was to come and help on Thursday at 3 o'clock; there was a superabundance of female attendance, and though I had my own convictions (rather than fears) from the beginning, I was not warranted in breaking the usual engagements.'[123] Robert went that evening to hear the Russian pianist Anton Rubinstein play at a party and did not return home until late.

He was urgently summoned by Arabel's servant the next morning at six o'clock (by which time Robert would in any case have been awake and dressed). When he arrived at her house, he found Arabel 'in a deplorable state. I stayed till the Doctor came, who repeated that there was no immediate danger, and that he was anxious she should not look worse than she really was when the other Physician arrived at 3 o'clock. So he went, and, five minutes after, I raised her in my arms where she died presently.'[124] In his account to Isa, Robert repeated the lines from Heine that Elizabeth had translated and which he had first quoted to her about Elizabeth in a letter of 19 June 1867: 'The years they come and go — The races drop in the grave — But *never* the love does so!'

Since George Barrett, 'the useful brother', was inconveniently away 'touring it in Ireland',[125] there devolved on Robert in practical terms 'every sort of sad business that seems duty, and I am as full as a sponge of vinegar and gall just now'.[126] George, who was 'in perfect ignorance of her being other than quite well', was contacted by telegrams thoughtfully worded so as to ensure his speedy return but without causing too much anxiety. 'He is alarmingly susceptible, and may find the blow too much,' remarked Robert to Isa. George was informed in person of Arabel's death and burial by Robert and one of the other Barrett brothers only when they met him at the railway station on his return early in the morning of 20 June. This occasion more or less terminated the Brownings' intimate involvement with the Barretts. Even George, the brother with whom Robert was on best terms, had never been — and could never be — as close a friend or confidante as Arabel.

The correspondence between George and Robert continued intermittently until 22 October 1889, but it pertained to what Robert perceived as family matters, and was never regular. There were ties of blood between Pen and the Barretts, but even Pen was never as close to his uncles as he was to his Aunt Sarianna. The tone of Robert's letter to George of 28 July 1868, informing him of the Brownings' imminent departure on holiday for two months, is not wholly conventional in its sentiments: Robert hoped earnestly that George was 'through the worst of it' and regretted that he had 'not been in a condition to render any service, — but I have sympathized with you however fruitlessly. If now, by any of the strange chances of the world, I still can be of any service, you will count on me, I think. I just write this to give you a day in case there is anything you would say: in any case, it is equivalent to a good shake of the hand, if I don't find you at the Club presently. God bless you.' Nevertheless, there is a sense in the letter, despite its warmth, that Robert did not seriously expect his offer of service (though sincerely tendered) to be taken up by George, whose material resources were adequate and whose emotional needs were more likely to be better satisfied elsewhere, and with more than a good shake of the hand from a fellow clubman.

Writing to Isa on 16 June 1868, Robert, quoting from a sonnet by Elizabeth to Hugh Stuart Boyd, characterized Arabel as 'the one "steadfast friend who never did my heart or life misknow".' Far and above Julia Wedgwood, or any other woman of his acquaintance, Arabel had been a constant solace and support. She had been the daily link with Elizabeth during Robert's seven years in London and the closest to him among the surviving Barrett siblings. Her death was another of those synchronous events that tested Robert's incredulity: 'You know I am not superstitious', he remarked in his letter to Isa of 19 June, but 'here is a note I made in a book [his own copy of Elizabeth's *Poems Before Congress*], "Tuesday July 21, 1863. Arabel told me yesterday that she had been much agitated by a dream that happened the night before, Sunday July 19: she saw Her [Elizabeth], and asked, "When shall I be with you?" The reply was "Dearest, in five years," whereupon Arabel woke. She knew in her dream it was not to the living she spoke, and her question referred to her own death. In five years, within a month of their completion. I had forgotten the date of the dream, and supposed it was only three years ago, and that two had still to run. Only a coincidence, but noticeable.' He might have noticed as coincidental, too, that in the space of just seven years he had lost his wife, his father, and his sister-in-law all in the mortal month of June.

Robert's letter to Isa of 19 July appears to be missing. The next we hear of him is in a letter to her dated 28 August from Audierne in Finistère: 'you never heard of this place, I daresay . . . Look on the map for the most westerly point of Bretagne . . . there is niched Audierne, a delightful quite unspoiled little fishing town, with the open ocean in front, and beautiful woods, hills and dales, meadows and lanes behind and around.' With Sarianna, Robert walked for hours at a stretch, and they bathed, 'but somewhat ingloriously, in a smooth creek of mill pond quietude . . . unlike the great rushing waves of Croisic: the water also is much colder: but the general effect is admirable'. They were still there, very late in the season, on 19 October when Robert wrote again to Isa to say that 'Miss [Egerton] Smith most benevolently chose to come here. I hope she don't repeat it, — the place suits me very well, but for reasons in which I don't expect everybody to sympathise.' He had been thinking sadly of Arabel: London would 'be sad to return to, with no more Arabel — dear Arabel!' He had been minded even to 'take another house, — but after all it matters so little. There are many advantages in mine, and it is cheap. I shall be put to more than enough trouble by any move — and to what end? One must have a pied-à-terre — and the less it costs, the more money for travelling about. I think it will not be Florence I return to, however, — except for a day or two: all which lies on the knees of the gods, as Homer says.'

Pen seems not to have been with his father and aunt in Brittany during the summer of 1868, and certainly in the early autumn he was in Scotland with Jowett, who wrote to Robert on 8 October to express some doubt about whether Browning *fils* would make it through his second attempt at the matriculation examination for Balliol. Jowett's fears were justified. Robert's correspondence with Julia Wedgwood had resumed on 30 October 1868, and on 5 November that year he wrote to tell her, 'My son is well — just not going to Balliol, alack, as I hoped would be, — *why* after all? — but to the more congenial Ch[rist] Church: he will never be an adept at grammatical niceties, which are the daily bread at Balliol . . . So, having let the Ch. Ch. matriculation pass by, this term, he will go up at Christmas.' As to his own plans, 'This place is *bearable* — it was never *more* than that. I may stay till the Boy leaves College.'

Isa, in Robert's letter of January 1869, was advised that the nineteen-year-old Pen had matriculated at Christ Church a few days before, on 15 January, and 'did it easily and creditably, just because he fancied the thing would be as easy as he fancied the Balliol business an awful affair . . . They have give him good rooms at once, and he is enjoying himself extremely.' Robert's buoyant attitude of pleasure matched Pen's — 'because *now* Pen is having exactly what he wanted to drive away the stupid "nervousness"', though in his soul Robert may privately have been writhing with disappointment. Balliol had been his fixed ambition, his *summa cum laude*, for Pen: Christ Church could by no means match it for academic excellence or the calibre of its students. Christ Church men tended to be sportsmen and hearties, academic *flâneurs* and flannelled fools who took philosophically (or, more probably, with no philosophy at all) the likelihood that they would never proceed to graduation. Nevertheless, it was still an Oxford college and Pen's name was inscribed on its books. As for Robert, from June he would have the use of rooms at Balliol he had chosen for himself — 'side by side with Jowett's . . . it will be pleasant, won't it?'[127] From this rarefied eyrie he might keep a weather-eye on Pen.

With Pen settled, Robert could turn his attention to the business of publishing *The Ring and the Book*. George Murray Smith, casting a judicious editorial eye over the monstrous length of the manuscript, proposed to issue the poem by instalments in four monthly volumes rather than the two volumes originally intended. Robert had rejected any idea of publishing the poem serially in a magazine. To William Allingham, he remarked, 'I want people not to turn to the end, but to read through in proper order. Magazine, you'll say: but no, I don't like the notion of being sandwiched between Politics and Deer-Stalking, say.' Since he had so rarely published in magazines before, it perhaps did not seem sensible to start now. The thought 'of bringing it out in four monthly volumes, giving people time to read and digest it, part by part, but not to forget what has gone before', seemed a decent compromise on which poet and publisher came to terms: £1,250 for a five-year lease of English publication rights. Robert made a separate deal with Fields, his American publisher, who insisted on publication in two volumes and an advance of £200, raised from a first offer of £50 that Robert had properly rejected.

In the summer of 1868, the title of the poem was still undecided. *The Franceschini* was Robert's first and preferred thought. It may have sounded, to his ears, rather reminiscent of Shelley's *The Cenci*, and certainly there were some superficial similarities between the stories told in Shelley's poem and Robert's. For one thing, Shelley's and Robert's

ill-used heroines both shared an unfortunate fate. An alternative sugges-
tion, *The Book and the Ring*, sounded 'too pretty-fairy-story-like' and
was perhaps too close to Thackeray's fairy story, *The Rose and the Ring*,
published in 1855. But Robert came round to a variation on that title
— *The Ring and the Book* — thus pleasingly reflecting the circular form
of the twelve monologues and alluding to the image of the ring that
signified Elizabeth as the muse of the poem. And so the twelve-part
poem of just over 21,000 lines of blank verse was published in four
volumes, one each month, from November 1868 to February 1869.

A novel normally occupied only three volumes. What sort of story
(and poetry, at that) could it be that required a fourth? Carlyle's crabby
judgement that the poem seemed to be 'all made out of an Old Bailey
story that might have been told in ten lines and only wants forgetting',
not to say his earlier advice that Robert and other poets should stick to
prose, was forestalled and defended by Robert towards the end of *The
Ring and the Book* where he wrote:

> Why take the artistic way to prove so much?
> Because, it is the glory and good of Art
> That Art remains the one way possible
> Of speaking truth, to mouths like mine, at least.
> [XII, ll. 837–40]

Art of course transformed the raw materials of the seventeenth-
century Franceschini affair, and it is Robert's account of that *cause
célèbre*, rather than the actual historical murder and trial, that concerns
us here, however much literary and historical critics have since compared
the two in the minutest detail and continue to discover notable differ-
ences. Briefly, then:

On the night of 2 January 1698, Pietro and Violante Comparini were
stabbed to death at their house in Rome by Count Guido Franceschini
and four accomplices. The putative daughter of the Comparinis, Pompi-
lia, was mutilated and left for dead. She lasted four days — long enough
to make a deathbed deposition that identified her assailants to the
authorities. Guido and his henchmen made a run for Arezzo, but were
discovered, arrested, put on trial, and executed.

Carlyle asked for ten lines — there it is in just about half that
amount. As a pitch to a Hollywood producer it is probably three or

four lines too long: as a summary of the poem it is nothing like enough. Behind this baldly-told sequence of events lies a lurid story of financial cupidity, aristocratic arrogance, disputed parentage, physical abuse, alleged adultery with a priest, and the sensation of the trial itself, which was ended by a controversial final verdict by Pope Innocent XII.

The tragedy was set in train in 1693 when Count Guido Franceschini of Arezzo in Tuscany, a dilapidated (*decaduto*) nobleman of no great social rank and even less moral reputation, married the young (thirteen- or fourteen-year-old) Francesca Pompilia, the declared daughter of Pietro and Violante Comparini, an elderly, moderately well-off Roman couple. On both sides, the marriage was apparently advantageous: the Comparini gained status, the Franceschinis gained an heiress. Guido, Pompilia, and the rest of Guido's family thereafter all lived unhappily together at Arezzo for some three years. The Comparini couple, who had accompanied Pompilia to Arezzo, returned to Rome after a few months claiming grievous ill-treatment at the hands of the Franceschini. Violante then publicly confessed that Pompilia was no daughter of hers — she and Pietro had bought her clandestinely as a young child from her natural mother, a common prostitute, and passed her off as their own.

Pietro and Violante's purpose had been to gain full control of a valuable inheritance that was dependent on their having a child. The Comparini sued Guido for return of Pompilia's dowry; Guido in turn claimed that the Comparini were lying and that Pompilia was in fact their legitimate daughter. Pompilia, trapped between these two factions, was treated even worse than before by Guido and the Franceschini. After several unsuccessful attempts to run away, Pompilia finally made her escape with the help of Giuseppe Caponsacchi, a young canon of the Church with whom she had become friendly. They had all but reached Rome when Guido caught up with the luckless pair at an inn at Castelnuovo, where they had stopped to rest. At Guido's behest, they were arrested on a charge of adultery.

In the event, when they were tried at Rome, adultery could not be proved, but Caponsacchi was banished to Civita Vecchia for three years and Pompilia was committed to a nunnery, a convent for fallen women. When she was discovered to be pregnant, she was released into the care of Pietro and Violante. On 18 December 1697 — eight months after her flight from Arezzo — Pompilia gave birth to a son. Whether the boy was Guido's or Caponsacchi's became an item of considerable public speculation, and a matter of grave personal concern to Guido Franceschini. On 2 January 1698, Guido and four hired men gained entry to the Comparini house on the pretext of delivering a message from Caponsacchi. Guido hacked at Pietro and Violante, who both died there and then. Guido assumed he had also murdered Pompilia who had been stabbed twenty-two times.

Guido and his men immediately took off for Arezzo. Since Guido had neglected to obtain a permit to hire horses, they were forced to struggle along, increasingly exhausted, for some twenty miles on foot before being caught and arrested. Pompilia had survived and had been able to identify her assailants to the authorities. She died of her wounds four days later, though not before making a full deathbed confession and deposition. Guido and his four henchmen were accused of murder and brought to trial in Rome. There was no question that Guido had been responsible for the death of his wife and in-laws, but there was a legal question as to 'whether and when a Husband may kill his adulterous wife without incurring the ordinary penalty'.

Guido's lawyers threw themselves industriously into the job of exculpating their client. It was argued on his behalf that Pompilia had committed adultery with Canon Caponsacchi (the contrary had not been proved beyond doubt at her trial), that the Comparini had attempted to defraud their son-in-law, that the birth of Pompilia's child had finally unhinged the dishonoured Count Franceschini and provoked him to extreme measures. The prosecution lawyers argued that Guido Franceschini's sole motivation had been money rather than honour: he had married for money and he had murdered for money. The death of the Comparini would cause all their lawsuits against him to fall, and Guido, as Pompilia's widower and legal father of her son and heir, would walk away with the Comparini fortune intact and his noble honour redeemed.

Guido and his co-accused were found guilty and sentenced to death — Guido to be beheaded, his henchmen to be hanged. Guido appealed to the Pope on a technicality: since he held a minor office in the Church, he claimed that he was therefore subject to the jurisdiction of the Church rather than to the civil authorities of Rome. It was confidently expected that the Pope would allow the appeal and show mercy to the appellant. To everyone's surprise, Innocent XII confirmed the sentence. Guido and his accomplices were duly put to death on 22 February 1698. Pompilia was exonerated of all blame, her virtuous reputation posthumously restored, and her infant son, Gaetano, was confirmed as the rightful heir to his mother's property.

The twelve sections of *The Ring and the Book* are cast in the form of consecutive dramatic monologues. In each instance, a single speaker gives his or her account of the Franceschini affair. The first to speak is Robert Browning who, in Book I, explains the title of his poem by reference to the gold Etruscan ring worn by Elizabeth and gives a summary of the principal elements of the story to be told. The authorial voice leaves the reader in little doubt as to where Robert's sympathies lie in the tragedy: firmly with the gentle-mannered, much-abused, and horridly murdered heroine, Pompilia, and her heroic, gallant St George, the priest Caponsacchi.

Books II to IV are given over to three voices representative of gossiping public opinion, which knows the case only by hearsay (which is not evidence, and can be misleading to the point of perversity): 'Half-Rome', a married man who is experiencing some marital difficulties, speaks up for Guido and the rights of wronged husbands; 'The Other Half-Rome', a bachelor beguiled by the victim's beauty, fiercely takes Pompilia's side; and 'Tertium Quid', a sophisticated nobleman, is less exercised by the grievous fate of the human victims than by the shocking improprieties that have been committed against property rights and the social order. Marriage, in the view of this Very Superior Person, is a commercial transaction. The Comparini and the Franceschini, by their attempts to cheat each other, have been hoist by their own petards.

Books V to VII are given over to statements of their respective cases by the three principals of the drama — Guido, who very capably and almost convincingly addresses the judges in his own defence as a man more sinned against than sinning; Caponsacchi, who makes a poignant, grief-stricken speech passionately appealing for justice that reveals him as a chivalrous defender of virtue, a man whose moral perceptions have been heightened to the utmost degree by pure love (Chesterton points out that Caponsacchi's attempted rescue of Pompilia bears some resemblance to Robert's flight with Elizabeth from the Barrett household);

and Pompilia, whose deathbed deposition is admitted in evidence: her dying speech, delivered in a tone of dignified pathos, is devoted to protecting her infant son and burnishing 'the lustrous and pellucid soul' of Caponsacchi (Mrs Orr acutely points to Pompilia's love for her son and her rescuer as reflecting Elizabeth's love for Pen and Robert).

The following two Books, VIII and IX, are devoted respectively to the courtroom speeches being composed by Guido's defence counsel, Dominus Hyacinthus de Archangelis (Arcangeli), and the counsel for the prosecution, Juris Doctor Johannes-Baptista Bottinius (Bottini). The two lawyers are somewhat comedic caricatures, Dickensian and Chaucerian, concerned less with the personal tragedies of the case than with the interesting intellectual challenges of the forensic process, less with justice than with law. Their indifference to the truth is absolute; their major concern is to put on a good show, to present themselves rather than their clients in the best possible light. It hardly stretches credibility to suppose that Robert here took his opportunity to pay back, a little, the embarrassment caused by the humorous courtroom exchanges between counsel in the case of Von Müller v. Browning.

In Book X, the octogenarian Pope — Innocent XII, Antonio Pignatelli of Naples — sums up the case and delivers his verdict. Here we are given shrewd, humane wisdom derived from long personal experience of the world and a devotion to justice over the casuistical cleverness of legal counsel. The Pope's judgements are generally acknowledged to adhere very closely to Robert Browning's own attitudes towards the case and the protagonists. Robert took his opportunity in this Book to put his own theology, as evolved in poems such as *Christmas-Eve and Easter-Day*, 'Saul', 'Cleon', 'Karshish', and 'A Death in the Desert', in the mouth of a seventeenth-century Pope. As William Clyde DeVane points out, 'the particular kind of theology offered is not papal, nor is it of the seventeenth century'. But then, 'If *The Ring and the Book* were history the objection would be well taken, but since the poem is, properly speaking, Browning's reading of life, one ought not to complain of this noble and masterful presentation of the poet's theological position.'[128]

Book XI gives Guido, condemned and incarcerated in a prison cell, another opportunity to speak out. The general critical view of Guido, as a creature of the poet rather than of historical fact, is that he is a magnificent, deep-dyed, and intellectualized villain created from the unpromising clay of the rather weak, impulsive, and degenerate nobility of the historical Guido. The fictional Guido is fit to rank beside Shakespeare's Iago in the annals of dramatic infamy. Robert was so delighted with his slippery villain that he could not resist giving Guido a second opportunity to reveal himself entirely, albeit in the extreme colours of black and white. The Pope's verdict has been pronounced, Guido faces certain death, he has nothing left to lose except his mask of hypocrisy — and that last defence and refuge is finally cast away by this evil man in a crescendo of self-interested casuistry and naked, abject terror.

The final Book, XII, like the first, is Robert's own monologue as the last narrator and impresario of the entire poem. Completing the circle, like Giotto making a perfect freehand 'O', Robert ties up loose ends and introduces four reports concerning the aftermath of the trial. The first, a zestful letter describing Guido's execution, is written from Rome by a giddy-headed Venetian gentleman; the second and third are also letters, one on the Franceschini case to Arcangeli and commented upon by him, the other by Bottini, who is angered by a sermon preached by an Augustinian monk. These letters give the lawyers' true opinions (as distinct from their pleadings) of the case; the fourth is a sermon on the subject of the Roman murder case preached by the Augustinian, Fra Celestino, at the church of San Lorenzo. Fra Celestino dwells movingly upon the innocence of Pompilia, the triumph of virtue, the vindication of right, and laments the number of Guidos who walk about unpunished, the number of Pompilias whose victimization is unheard and unavenged. How often, says Fra Celestino, has God spoken no word! And of course we are prompted to think not only of Pompilia but of poor, innocent, strangled Porphyria, her yellow hair wound three times tight around her little throat — 'And yet God has not said a word!'

Robert prefaced *The Ring and the Book* with a somewhat nervous, combative laugh, at once defensive and provocative:

> Well, British Public, ye who like me not,
> (God love you!) and will have your proper laugh
> At the dark question, laugh it! I laugh first.
> Truth must prevail, the proverb vows; and truth

> — Here is it all i' the book at last, as first
> There it was all i' the heads and hearts of Rome
> Gentle and simple, never to fall nor fade
> Nor be forgotten. [I, ll. 410–17]

Robert had been wounded before by the British Public: he had not forgotten *Sordello*, even if the public had. The truth about Robert Browning must surely prevail if he continued, heart and head, to work to the highest ideals, to communicate his own pleasure in an idea or a story, to transcend the base materials and create a work of Art, a thing of value and beauty, as a goldsmith with craft and soul creates a ring. The Old Yellow Book was the gold, its very leaves medicinable:

> From the book, yes; thence bit by bit I dug
> The lingot truth, that memorable day,
> Assayed and knew my piecemeal gain was gold, —
> Yes; but from something else surpassing that,
> Something of mine which, mixed up with the mass,
> Made it bear hammer and be firm to file.
> Fancy with fact is just one fact the more;
> To wit, that fancy has informed, transpierced,
> Thridded and so thrown fast the facts else free,
> As right through ring and ring runs the djereed
> And binds the loose, one bar without a break.
> I fused my live soul and that inert stuff,
> Before attempting smithcraft, on the night
> After the day when, — truth grasped and gained, —
> The book was shut and done with and laid by
> On the cream-coloured massive agate, broad
> 'Neath the twin cherubs in the tarnished frame
> O' the mirror, tall thence to the ceiling-top. [I, ll. 458–75]

And so, the poem is declared to be the truth of the matter — of the Roman murder case — and 'Fancy with fact is just one fact the more': the poet, the maker, becomes annealed indissolubly with the matter of the case, with his materials, which are thereby strengthened.

The Ring and the Book is, by and large, faithful to the facts as Robert knew them. Thorough historical and literary critical research continues to turn up more original contemporary materials about the Franceschini affair. The characters of Guido, Pompilia, Caponsacchi, and the rest are now known to be not wholly consistent with Robert's interpretation of them, and his understanding of the case as a whole is increasingly undermined by new evidence. Since Robert claimed to be true to fact (actually he altered at least one date for symbolic effect) and to have invented nothing (though he said nothing of *suppressio veri* — the omission of inconvenient materials), that claim has become more and more difficult to sustain. And yet, as Daniel Karlin has pointed out,[129] as the historical accuracy of the poem is weakened, so the importance of the autobiographical aspects and elements of the poem are increased; and to the extent that the foreground story fades, the background emotional investment put into the poem by the poet correspondingly becomes more apparent and relevant:

> In Book I, Browning speaks of Guido as the man who 'determined, dared and did / The deed just as he purposed'. Not only does the phrase 'determined, dared and did' reappear in this particular poem (at IV 1106 for example: 'murder was determined, dared and done') but it resonates throughout Browning's work because it comes from one of his favourites, Christopher Smart's *Song to David* (1763), which concludes its exultant paean of divine glory with a flourish of self-praise: 'And now the matchless deed's achieved, / DETERMIN'D, DAR'D, and DONE.'

This 'phrase designating supreme artistic achievement' was taken and used by Browning, says Karlin, 'to describe the accomplishment of a brutal crime'. But it also designates, in Robert Browning's own life, occasions on which firm and decided action — which might have been reprobated by rigorous moralists — led to success and happiness, led to the natural justice and the moral truth of the matter. Marriage to Elizabeth — 'determin'd, dar'd and done' — had been a supreme achievement of love. Neither he nor Elizabeth had betrayed love, and in that love they had not betrayed one another. And so, too, in poetry: Robert and Elizabeth had 'determin'd, dar'd and done' and recked not the consequences. Popular success, in Robert's case, had long been elusive, but Art had been served and his own soul had been saved.

Well, if — in the pious phrase — virtue is its own reward, Robert was at last rewarded over and above that soul-satisfying return by the ego-feeding success, both critical and popular, of *The Ring and the Book*. The poem had resignedly concluded its round with Robert's ripe raspberry to all who had bad-mouthed and ignored him over the years:

> So, British Public, who may like me yet,
> (Marry and amen!) learn one lesson hence
> Of many which whatever lives should teach:
> This lesson, that our human speech is naught,
> Our human testimony false, our fame
> And human estimation words and wind. [XII, ll. 831–6]

So, British Public, you like me not — tough! *tant pis*! You like me — words and wind! Fame and fortune — it mattered, maybe, once upon a time. There are other, better things worth thinking about now. My poem? Take it or leave it, just as you like. But it's worth taking and the poet may please you yet. Beyond a mere story, an agglomeration of facts, Art may show the truth, artistry may reveal it:

> Art may tell a truth
> Obliquely, do the thing shall breed the thought,
> Nor wrong the thought, missing the mediate word.
> So may you paint your picture, twice show truth,
> Beyond mere imagery on the wall, —
> So, note by note, bring music from your mind,
> Deeper than ever the Andante dived, —
> So, write a book shall mean, beyond the facts,
> Suffice the eye and save the soul beside. [XII, ll. 855–63]

But the British Public did take *The Ring and the Book*, and took suddenly to Robert Browning too. Critics recognized the merits of the work and praised its author; readers paid good money for the books and acclaimed the writer. The *Athenaeum*, in its issue of 20 March 1869, gasped out hyperbole: 'We must record at once our conviction, not merely that *The Ring and the Book* is beyond all parallel the supremest poetical achievement of our time, but that it is the most precious and profound spiritual treasure that England has produced since the days of Shakespeare.' The reviewer was Robert Buchanan, the Spasmodic poet, a self-confessed idolater of Robert Browning, who was given to such exuberant expressions of undiluted enthusiasm.

But in this case, Buchanan's was not a lonely voice: it was just one swelling a large chorus harmoniously singing an anthem of praise. The important papers, with few exceptions, could find little or no fault with Robert's *magnum opus*. Size had something to do with this reviewers' rapture: four volumes, after all, implied some serious poetry; and epic length always inspires a certain respect even before a word of it has been read. His constant production, his great accumulation of a substantial body of work over the years, may additionally have had something to do with the glad reception given to *The Ring and the Book* — a critic never likes to think he may have missed something tremendous unawares, and sheer volume in itself provokes a certain awe. Then, too, Robert's bereaved status — by now it had become almost legend — provoked some natural sympathy.

The reading public, though naturally influenced by positive reviews, more than likely were also induced to buy the book by word of mouth recommendations. A literary sensation is partly self-fuelling. The more a book is talked about, the more interest it accumulates, like a snowball precipitating an avalanche. The story in itself was a traditional crowd-pleaser, featuring the marriage of a low-born girl to a nobleman, an evil villain, a spotless and much-wronged heroine, a romantic lover, violent murder, a sensational trial (with comic counsel), a wise judge — spectacularly, a Pope — who cut through the knots of evidence to dispense justice, and finally a satisfactory beheading of the guilty party and the pathetic death of the heroine. All the above set in a seductive location, Italy, in a time *lointain* and somewhat *féerique*, hallowed by Shakespeare and Shelley, but infused with a brutality familiar to Victorians. With all its Gothic and Romantic paraphernalia, *The Ring and the Book* was as good as a period novel by Sir Walter Scott, and as grisly as a fairy tale by the Brothers Grimm.

The popular Victorian taste for reading lengthy newspaper accounts of colourful criminal and civil trials (such as that of the Tichborne Claimant, for example) also contributed, no doubt, to the poem's success. All human life and passion may be exhibited in a courtroom, and justice — natural or contrived — may be seen to be done. The spectacle simultaneously provokes our prurience and satisfies our moral outrage.

In the gossips and spectators of seventeenth-century Rome, Victorian readers may have recognized, dimly, a little of themselves. At any rate, they recognized that Robert had brought a profound and powerful imagination to bear on a complicated story of pride, passions, and prejudices.

Of course the poem contained difficult allusions, deep moral subtleties, complex social contrasts, and an idiosyncratic theology — all the usual elements thrown up by Robert's depths of learning and breadth of interests, but this time lightly worn though firmly embedded in the narrative. Thus *The Ring and the Book* was enriched for responsive scholars who dug themselves into the text in search of such jewels; the common reader, however, scampering along the surface of the compelling narrative to find out what happened next, would hardly be impeded by any inconvenient obstructions. Robert had learned to keep up a lively pace and to tack down any bumps and ridges in his poetic carpet so that it lay smooth and displayed the full, multi-coloured pattern laid out in twelve bold sections, each with its complex interior ornamentation.

'I find the British public is beginning to like you,' wrote Julia Wedgwood, a little tongue-in-cheek, to Robert. 'Yes, the British Public like, and more than like me, this week,' Robert replied on Monday, 8 March 1869:

> They let their admiration ray out on me, and at sundry congregations of men wherein I have figured these three or four days, I have seen, felt and, thru' white gloves, handled a true affectionateness not unmingled with awe — which all comes of the Queen's having desired to see me, and three other extraordinary persons, last Thursday: whereupon we took tea together and pretended to converse for an hour and twenty minutes; the other worthies, with the wives of such as were provided, being Carlyle, Grote and Lyell. This eventful incident in my life — say, the dove descending out of heaven upon my head — seems to have opened peoples' [*sic*] minds at last: and provided the Queen don't send for the Siamese Twins, the Beautiful Circassian Lady, and Miss Saurin [the plaintiff in a much-discussed suit for libel brought against the Lady Superior of a convent]

as her next quartette-party, I am in a way to rise: you see, I am not disposed to contest that some 'resources' *are*!

Carlyle noted that the Queen had asked Robert, 'Are you writing anything?' Under his breath, Carlyle might have answered for him: 'he has just been publishing the absurdest of things!' However, in her private journal for the day, 4 March 1869, Victoria noted that Mr Browning was 'a very agreeable man. It was, at first, very shy work speaking to them.' As well it might have been — Carlyle noting that the short, plump little Queen 'came softly forward' and 'acknowledged with a nod the deep silent bow of us male monsters'.

Carlyle's reservations about *The Ring and the Book* were expressed to William Allingham, who fairly noted that Carlyle rated the poem as good in parts, and better than anything else Robert had produced. This respectful position was fatally undermined, however, by Carlyle's dismissal of what he considered to be the absurd basis of the story. He was in no doubt that Pompilia had been no better than she ought to have been; that she and Caponsacchi had clearly been lovers. To Robert, Carlyle said 'that of all the strange books produced in this distracted earth, by any of the sons of Adam, this one was altogether the strangest and the most preposterous in its construction: and where,' asked Carlyle, 'do ye think to find the eternal harmonies in it?' Robert, said Carlyle, 'did not seem to be pleased with my speech, and he bade me good morning'. So much, maybe, for Robert's professed disdain for public opinion and his lofty devotion to Art and God.

One test of a major work is whether it provokes imitations and, better still when the original work is inimitable, parody. Robert's work attracted at least two able parodists — Charles Stuart Calverley, a writer of light verse, who published 'The Cock and the Bull' in *Fly Leaves* in 1872, and Rudyard Kipling, who sent it up in 'The Flight of the Bucket'. A more important litmus test, of course, is whether the work attracts the regular attention, in the long term, of heavyweight critics. Just as Thomas Carlyle regretted Robert Browning's partiality for poetry over prose, so Henry James addressed himself to the subject of 'The Novel in "The Ring and the Book"', the title of an address given to the Royal Society of Literature in 1912, the centenary year of Robert Browning's birth.

From far back, from my first reading of these volumes, which took place at the time of their disclosure to the world, when I was a fairly young person, the sense, almost the pang, of the novel they might have constituted sprang sharply from them; so that I was to go on through the years almost irreverently, all but quite profanely, if you will, thinking of the great loose and uncontrolled composition, the great heavy-hanging cluster of related but unreconciled parts, as a fiction of the so-called historic type ... as a work of art, in other words, smothered in the producing.

James had begun his address with a characteristically smothering impression — what may, with a little licence, be described as sensual onomatopoeia — of *The Ring and the Book* as

so vast and so essentially gothic a structure, spreading and soaring and branching at such a rate, covering such ground, putting forth such pinnacles and towers and brave excrescences, planting its transepts and chapels and porticos, its clustered hugeness or inordinate muchness, that with any first approach we but walk vaguely and slowly, rather bewilderedly, round and round it, wondering at what point we had best attempt such entrance as will save our steps and light our uncertainty, most enable us to reach our personal chair, our indicated chapel or shrine, when once within.

This phantasmagoric heaping up of images to present to us the poem at first sight as 'the first, the affronting mass' is preparatory to James's admission that 'I cling to the dear old tradition that Browning is "difficult".' Nevertheless, when all is (mostly) said and done, the poem is 'a great living thing, a great objective mass', and Browning's method — for all its seeming confusion and multitudinousness — is justified:

To express his inner self — his outward was a different affair! — and to express it utterly, even if no matter how, was clearly, for his own measure and consciousness of that inner self, to *be* poetic; and the solution of all the deviations and disparities or, speaking critically, monstrosities, in the mingled tissue of this work, is the fact that whether or no by such convulsions of soul and sense life got delivered for him, the garment of life (which for him was poetry and poetry alone) got disposed in its due and adequate folds.

James continued, lengthily, to characterize Browning's poetry as looming closer to us than any other poet's, so that we tend to back away from it a little, from 'the affronting mass' that 'is too much *upon* us and thereby out of focus', in order to get the whole into a comprehensible perspective. 'Browning is "upon" us, straighter upon us always, somehow, than anyone else of his race; and thus we recoil, we push our chair back, from the table he so tremendously spreads, just to see a little better what is on it.'

This sense of a precipitate, pressing poetic presence irresistibly conjures Robert Browning himself. James, with a sly wit, conflates the two Robert Brownings he had always perceived: Robert's inner poetic self, his *moi profond*, whose imagination and intellect constructed majestic, monstrous cathedrals of words; and his outward social self, the inveterate diner-out and confident conversationalist whom Disraeli condemned as 'a noisy poet', who crowded up intimately and confidentially against pretty women at dinner parties, whose clarion voice could be heard announcing its approach from the next room, who filled every inch of space he occupied with a presence apparently larger than his actual size, whose bonhomous physicality and boom of talk so pressed itself upon one that involuntarily one pushed back one's chair, or took a step back, to clear a personal space between oneself and — there is no image more apt — Robert's 'affronting mass'.

James presses Robert's physicality in poetry, and impliedly in person, yet further: 'The Rome and Tuscany of the early 'fifties had become for him so at once a medium, a bath of the senses and perceptions, into which he could sink, in which he could unlimitedly soak, that wherever he might be touched afterwards he gave out some effect of that immersion. This places him to my mind quite apart, makes the rest of our poetic record of a similar experience comparatively pale and abstract. Shelley and Swinburne — to mention only his compeers — are, I know, a part of the record; but the author of *Men and Women*, of *Pippa Passes*, of certain of the Dramatic Lyrics and other scattered felicities, not only expresses and reflects the matter; he fairly, he heatedly, if I may use such a term, exudes and perspires it.'

And so Henry James answers the question that perplexed many of Robert's contemporaries and has exercised many since — including a bewildered Thomas Hardy, who thought he looked like a smug grocer: how could such a man be a poet? There, on the other side of the street, Robert could be observed, walking and talking, well heeled and well disposed, looking like a superior butler or a self-satisfied grocer or a prosperous banker. The answer being that there was essentially no difference between the private poet and the public man: the poetry partook of the man, the man of the poetry. In that one phrase, 'the affronting mass', lies the telling image. The poems and the poet pressed themselves upon you in precisely the same manner, were upon you with the same enormity, with the same warm and confidential breath in your face, with the same conversational splutter leaving its mark on your coat lapels, so close that the poet's perspiration was a sharp scent in the nostrils.

In America, the first of the two volumes of *The Ring and the Book* had been published, by Fields, Osgood, & Co., simultaneously with the first volume of Smith and Elder's English edition, on 1 December 1868. The second volume was published on 1 March 1869, simultaneously with the fourth volume of the English edition. The *Atlantic Monthly* matched the *Athenaeum* in its praise of the poem, and magazines such as the *North American Review*, which had ignored Robert's publications for twenty years, sat up and took notice. Reviewers expressed some reservations about Robert's style and form but generally agreed that the poem, though rough reading, amounted to a remarkable intellectual achievement and displayed the poet's powerful creativity to wondrous advantage.

Longfellow's opinion would have gladdened the heart of Thomas Carlyle: he found the work 'very powerful but very obscure', whilst Charles Eliot Norton described it as a 'monstrous thing'. William Dean Howells, though deploring the repetitious nature of the narrative, nevertheless described it as 'a great story, and unfolded with such a magnificent breadth and noble fulness, that one who blames it lightly blames himself heavily'. That was something, if substantial and influential critics had begun to blame themselves rather than Robert for any shortcomings.

It was recognition, at least, that imperfect critical understanding was not absolutely attributable to poetic incoherence. These and other impressions confirmed, perhaps influenced, Henry James in his characterization of *The Ring and the Book* as an 'affronting mass'.

In *Browning and America*, Louise Greer quotes American critics at fascinating length and gives an overview of the publishing history of the poem: 'Each of the two American volumes of *The Ring and the Book* was printed, in two impressions, in more than 2,000 copies in its first two years: 2,750 of Volume 1 and 2,190 of Volume 2, figures which compare favourably with the number of copies printed in England. In the English edition there were 3,000 copies in the first impression of each of the first two volumes and 2,000 of the last two, while no more were issued until 1872, when the last two volumes were reprinted, the first and second not being reprinted until 1882 and 1883, respectively.'

Robert's stock stood so high in 1869 that not only were friends and acquaintances avid of their connections, remote or close, to the poet but also of possessing particular copies of the poem. Even Isa, in January 1869, succumbed to feeling 'very jealous of Lady Portsmouth who has your Poem on her table beautifully bound from the Author'. She was also feeling a little miffed, and had said so in a recent letter, that Robert, in her estimation, did not really care for her novels, even though over the years he had virtually acted as her agent with Chapman in London (indeed, there is a case to be made that Chapman published Isa Blagden only, or mostly, to keep Robert Browning on his list); he had also given considerable thought (which Isa admitted) in his letters to useful criticism of the composition of her fiction — though this, to judge by the advice, was as much a recommendation of his own dramatic style of poetic composition as a comment upon hers. In his reply of 19 February 1869, Robert set Isa's soul at rest and smoothed over their tiff: 'I never gave Lady Portsmouth a book, bound or unbound, nor anything else in my life.'

He then proceeded to an elaborate explanation of his precise allocation of the copies of *The Ring and the Book* that George Murray Smith had given him: 'I gave away all my twenty copies to twenty people who seemed to have a right to them, — not one "Lady" among them, — except Lady W[illiam] Russell, who collects books specially, and deserves mine, if she did not.' Robert's own copy, 'beautifully bound', had been given by his own hand to Mr Gillespie of Balliol as a gift to the college library, which also possessed the six beautiful volumes of the Collected Poems, an earlier donation by Robert. There were, indeed, no more copies for Robert to give away. The first edition had sold out: 'I have no copy, nor has Sarianna . . . shall stipulate for *more* copies on another occasion — the next edition, for instance. I ought to have done so *now*, but what is past is past: you see, I never was in the position before of one who had *"sold out all the books:"* Chapman gave me fifty copies at least — but he did not pay for the remainder like Smith.'[130]

In his letter of 19 February, Robert took elaborate pains to assure Isa of his regard for her: 'I am very happy that you should now be convinced that, after all, I dearly love you, — which to *me*, does not seem a thing that needs fresh conviction about, at this time of day.' The letter ends with a caution about believing gossip, whether about books or women: 'There is a curious lie flying about *here* — concerning poor me, I am going to marry Miss A. daughter of Lady B. mother also of Lady C. etc. etc. I heard of it three times last week. I never even heard that there was such a person as any one of the three, — never heard their names even. You will soon have it retailed to you as indubitable fact.' This resurgence of speculation about Robert's romantic inclinations and marital prospects coincided, not unnaturally, with the increase in his celebrity. It evidently seemed unlikely to tender-hearted ladies and roguish-minded gentlemen that Robert Browning should be innocent of any sentimental attachment. That such an eligible widower should still be unmarried amounted almost to a social scandal.

But Robert had so far declined even to contemplate the possibility of engaging himself to another woman, far less to marry again. On 19 September 1867 he had written to Isa of his spotless reputation: 'It is funny people think I am likely to do nothing naughty in the world, neither rob nor kill, seduce nor ravish, — only honestly *marry* — which I should consider the two last, — and perhaps two first, — naughtinesses united, together with the grace of perjury.' Having given his heart once, he had not another to spare. He gave his head and his loyalty willingly enough, however, and his love for Pen, to Oxford: so much so that when St Andrews University attempted to seduce him with the offer of the Lord Rectorship in 1868, in succession to John Stuart Mill, he declined the honour — shrinking, said Edmund Gosse later and realistically, from the 'vague but considerable extra expense' of the position. He regularly declined all such offers, including two from Glasgow University, for years afterwards.[131]

The tone of Robert's letters to Isa in April and May 1869 is a little edgy, a little irritated, as though life was constantly full of too much life. Some of this may be accounted for by the fact that the disagreements between Isa and Robert had rumbled on for some months, requiring another reassuring letter from Robert on 19 June when Isa, most unusually, had not written on the appointed date in May. Robert liked things cut and dried, he liked to make dark places light; he did not relish difficulties and, when a problem promised to become too difficult entirely, he was quite liable to pluck it out like a thorn in his foot — though Isa was unlikely to be so dealt with. With Sarianna, Robert paid a visit of some four weeks to Paris, where not much pleased him or patched his ragged nerves — neither a meeting with the theological philosopher Ernest Renan nor an encounter with the illustrator Gustave Doré, though 'Milsand made amends for everything and everybody'.

Two days after their return, the Brownings went to Oxford for the last of the rowing races. Pen, Isa was informed in a letter of 16 May 1869, 'steered the Ch. Ch. boat, and great was his praise seeing that ... they "bumped" five times: Pen was never seen by any of us to such advantage, — at least in his *manly* character: he was most affectionate and assiduous in his attention: he will come home in a fortnight for the long vacation, — I don't know what we shall do.' Robert emphasized Pen's 'manly character' and filial devotion in the absence, probably, of his academic distinction, which merits no mention.

In the event, what the Brownings did was go to Scotland for the summer. From Loch Luichart, where — with the Storys — they were staying with Louisa, Lady Ashburton, Robert wrote to Isa in August 1869: 'Through circumstances unforeseen and quite out of my control I am not in Brittany but here: having been bothered in the last three weeks beyond most folks' bearing: never mind, the worst is over and here, at an old friend's I am comfortable altogether: Sarianna and Pen (for whose sake I came) are here — I don't know for how long. I *could not* write till now, — in the hideous confusion of three weeks' constant inconstancy, and flitting from bad place to worse. However, all goes well now in this beautiful place. Pen has got what he wanted — shooting and deer-stalking: he began operations the day before yesterday and, much to his credit as a hunter, shot a splendid stag — "royal": the head of which will glorify his rooms at Ch. Ch.'

There had been vexations before the date of the August letter to Isa. A friend In Florence had welshed on a debt ('But I spit at him and have done with it'), and Lily Wilson had to be rescued from destitution now that she was back in Florence (Robert contrasted her poor behaviour with the admirable enterprise of Annunziata).[132] These were neither 'circumstances unforeseen' nor 'quite out of my control'; they were irritations, and familiar ones, that naturally bothered Robert, though hardly beyond bearing. His letter of mid-July to Isa is missing, if it ever existed. Their quarrel had been patched up well enough, so there is no reason on that score for Robert not to have written to her as usual. It seems, to judge by the August letter, that he had not written at all to Isa in July, and for quite other reasons. Then, too, Robert had braced himself earlier in the year for an encounter in Paris with the infamous Sophia Eckley, from which he had come away curiously softened towards her and somewhat more indulgent than before. He still distrusted her, but did not now believe that Sophia, who offered to give him Elizabeth's letters to her, 'intended for a minute to print or sell anything'.[133]

Park Honan remarks of this point in Robert's personal life, 'Impatient with the famous, Browning developed curious sympathies for the infamous.'[134] But this, as G. K. Chesterton tells us, had always been true of his poetry and increasingly became so. A result of his meeting with Sophia Eckley was a saddening and disappointing confirmation of his view that Elizabeth had been wilfully blind to Sophia's undoubted faults: 'My sole concern, charge against her, or whatever it be called is — that she cheated Ba from the beginning — and I say, in the bitterness of truth, that Ba deserved it for shutting her eyes and stopping her ears as she determinedly did.' For his own part, Robert dismissed Mrs Eckley as an inveterate fabulist and was not deceived: 'I always knew how to play with a snake, and could manage a dozen like her.'[135]

By the time the Brownings left for Scotland, Robert was 'thoroughly worn out and unwell . . . so much so that a stranger I met on the day of my departure confessed (afterwards) he thought me dying: but my tallowy hue soon grows russet when allowed the free play of the air, — and I am bound to confess that, — whether travel in Scotland *please* me or no, — it does me more good in one week than Brittany in eight.'[136] If Robert was indeed in Scotland for Pen's sake, the *prima facie* interpretation is that he was generously giving way to Pen's novel taste for 'shooting and deer-stalking'. But there is another, less indulgent explanation for the Brownings' absence from Brittany in 1869. Park Honan plausibly suggests that deeply disappointing news had reached Robert from Oxford that Pen's career there might be cut short, and that 'it was during this spring that Robert learned of his son's sexual waywardness at Le Croisic'.

The revelation of 'Pen's Croisic daughters would help to explain much in the late spring and summer of 1869: Browning's unusual dissatisfaction with Pen, his repugnance for Pen's summer companion Willy Bracken, his sudden cancellation of a Breton holiday, his nervous exhaustion, pallor, forgetfulness, refusal to see his old friends, and, early in September, his extraordinary behaviour at Loch Luichart, which had considerable consequences for his poetry. In 1869, Pen's academic failures in themselves were no longer a novelty.'[137] To Mrs Frederick Lehmann, on 27 July, Robert apologized for withdrawing from a dinner invitation: 'I was unwell, having been so for some time — and feel the grasshopper a burden all day long in the house, from which I never stirred.' He frankly confessed to 'being frightened by all this bad luck'.[138]

The 'hideous confusion of three weeks' constant inconstancy, and flitting from bad place to worse', was caused, if Henry James's account of the matter is to be credited, by Lady Ashburton's absent-mindedness. The Brownings and the Storys had been invited to Loch Luichart, but when they got there they found their hostess 'far from home at the date of the appointment'. The weather was cold. Making the best of being benighted, the Brownings and the Storys made impromptu shift for themselves — or, as Henry James more positively glosses it, 'her guests made merry, for the time, instead, at a little inn, then described as "squalid," on Loch Achnault, near Garve, with assistance from picnics (of the four) in the neighbouring heather, where, the rough meal not unsuccessfully enjoyed, Browning loudly read out "Rob Roy." '[139]

Sarianna, in a letter of 27 August to Annie Egerton Smith, alternatively suggests that the Brownings and the Storys had embarked upon a tour of Scotland and that Lady Ashburton had suddenly appeared, a *deus ex machina*, to rescue them from the squalor of local Highland inns. By 'main force' they were carried off to nearby Loch Luichart Lodge, where they were obliged — despite their politest protestations, no doubt — to accept her offer of lavish Scottish baronial hospitality. 'The worst is over,' Robert wrote to Isa in August, 'and here, at an old friend's I am comfortable altogether . . . all goes well now in this beautiful place.'[140]

In 1851, Robert and Elizabeth had deposited Thomas Carlyle at the Hôtel Meurice with his hosts, the immensely wealthy second Baron Ashburton and his first wife, the former Lady Harriet Mary Montagu, who died in 1857. Being in want of a wife, in 1858 Lord Ashburton married a Scotswoman, the young and lively Louisa Caroline Mackenzie, twenty-eight years his junior and a considerable heiress in her own right, who became his widow in 1864. Robert and Louisa had very likely met socially before the death of Lord Ashburton: a reference to her occurs in a letter written by Robert to William Story of 10 April 1862 — 'Tonight I dine at the Milmans and meet people (the Ashburtons I believe)' — and on 17 July 1863 he wrote again to Story to say, 'I sent all your photographs to the proper people, except Lady Ashburtons [*sic*] — she has not been in town and I keep it till the last thing, at all events.'

In 1869, Louisa Ashburton, mother of a nine-year-old daughter, Maysie, was forty-two years old. She was a force of nature and a woman of fashion: tall, handsome, dark-haired, amply-proportioned, energetic, driven by high spirits, violent emotions, and curious contradictions that often led to confusions. Her tastes were for high culture and distinguished minds. Equipped with all the resources of her beauty, money, intelligence, and charismatic character, she went tuft-hunting and won many notable scalps, including Carlyle's. Few could resist her opulent personality and lavish hospitality.

At first sight of Louisa Ashburton, Hatty Hosmer had immediately fallen in love with her. Of their first meeting in Rome in 1867, she wrote: 'it seemed to my bewildered senses that the Ludovisi Goddess in person, weary, perhaps, of the long imprisonment of Art, had assumed the stature and state of mortals and stood before me. There were the same square-cut and grandiose features, whose classic beauty was humanized by a pair of keen, dark eyes, lovely smile, and then a rich, musical voice of inquiry . . . Such was the personality of the lady whose acquaintance I made on that auspicious day and which ripened into a friendship that throughout her life knew no shadow of change.'[141]

Henry James more tactfully, more discreetly — less susceptible to goddesses and only partly seduced — allusively and elusively described Louisa as 'This so striking and interesting personage, a rich, generous presence that, wherever encountered, seemed always to fill the foreground with colour, with picture, with fine mellow sound and, on the part of everyone else, with a kind of traditional, charmed, amused patience — this brilliant and fitful apparition was a familiar *figure* for our friends, as, throughout, for the society of our time, and I come, in my blurred record, frequently upon her name.'[142] Like most rich, generous people, Louisa could be impulsive and unpredictable — in a word, difficult. James considered her character to be more fit for fiction than biography: in 'a sort of glow of remembrance', he subtly and diffusively cast upon her a 'friendly light' that 'rests on occasions, incidents, accidents, in which a liberal oddity, a genial incoherence, an *expected*, half funny, half happy turn of the affair, for the most part, appears to declare itself as the leading note'.[143]

There occurred one such occasion, incident or accident, in the summer of 1869 at Loch Luichart, which resulted, wrote James with considerable delicacy and the lightest brush of the pen, in 'more interesting passages of personal history than may here be touched upon'.[144] And there, on the threshold of revelation, he quietly closed a door that he had barely opened. What went on privately behind it then, and became the subject of speculation later when the door was flung open to the gossiping world, remains confused. It was first supposed, and then taken more or less for granted, that Robert had proposed marriage to Louisa Ashburton on some date between 5 and 19 September and that the form of the proposal was so offensive to her that she had angrily refused it.

Virginia Surtees, in *The Ludovisi Goddess*, her 1984 biography of Louisa Ashburton, brought to light fresh evidence proving almost certainly that the proposal had been Louisa's and that Robert had not immediately turned it down. He had been surprised and noncommittal, but had been willing to think it over. It was worth thinking over, perhaps. Pen's interests were forever at the forefront of Robert's mind, and there were worrying signals that, left to his own devices and diversions, to boating and billiards, his son's prospects were not likely to be good. Robert's pessimistic instincts, rather than his more optimistic aspirations, were contending in his head. Looking forward for probable trouble, as he often did, and making provision for the worst, as seemed sensible, it appeared more than likely that Pen would always have to be provided for, and that a wealthy, socially well-connected stepmother would be a considerable advantage to him.

Before Virginia Surtees published her findings, most male biographers, critics, and commentators had fully credited the supposition that the proposal of marriage had come from Robert's mouth. Some perceptive, intuitive women, however, had expressed their doubts. Maisie Ward, in her psychologically acute biography of Browning, took into account an underrated aspect of Robert's well-established character — 'his strange inability, often noted with amusement by Elizabeth, to relate any happening other than backwards or standing on its head'[145] — and so thought to query the conventional interpretation of relevant passages in two letters written by Robert to the Storys in 1872 and 1886. Not only in conversation or letters was Robert liable to turn an event inside out or stand an idea on its head: he did it in poetry, too, just as readily.

Maisie Ward drummed up in support of her view a letter to the magazine *Time and Tide* in which Dame Myra Curtis had asked: 'Who actually proposed to whom? We know from all the records that women were attracted to Browning and that he thoroughly enjoyed the superficial relation of admiration (and affection) known as a flirtation. A successful flirtation engages both parties and the atmosphere was favorable. Scotland in the autumn: the glory of sun and water and heather, the long idle country-house days, the happiness and well-being of an adored but troublesome son, the flattery of admiration poured by a beautiful woman on a man not unsusceptible either to beauty or flattery — moreover a woman who wants . . . well what *did* she want?'[146] That question — what did Louisa Ashburton want? — had not hitherto troubled Browning's male critics, had hardly even occurred to men who supposed they knew what Robert Browning wanted and that nothing else was much to the purpose. What women wanted was an old question, too difficult, even had they thought to raise it, to which no man had ever puzzled out a satisfactory answer.

The Loch Luichart party broke up, seemingly in good humour, after some three weeks of luxurious leisure. The guests, who also included Lady Marian Alford (an old friend of Robert's from the days in Italy), her son Lord Brownlow, and Sir Roderick Murchison, had been regaled with readings by Robert from *The Ring and the Book* (it is said he tended to favour some of the more affecting passages from the section devoted to Pompilia), and other occasional poetry had been extemporized in a round robin to which they all contributed, which Robert wrote out, and which was sent to Hatty Hosmer in Rome. The Storys seem to have noticed nothing unusual in the atmosphere, no strained relations between Robert and their hostess. Pen had been in high spirits, banging away with his gun at anything that could run or fly. Sarianna had been floating, no doubt, in a nirvana of high social rapture.

By mid-September, Pen had gone to Hampshire, Sarianna had returned to London, and Robert was installed at Naworth Castle in Cumberland as the guest of George and Rosalind Howard, the Earl and Countess of Carlisle, close friends of the Storys, who accompanied him. On 19 September, from Naworth, he confided to Isa that his "worry" — presumably about Pen's academic career — 'is increased to pretty nearly the last degree'[147] and cautioned her to keep the matter secret between themselves. At Naworth, according to another guest, the young Sidney Colvin, who had won the Chancellor's medal for English verse at Cambridge in 1865, Robert broke down in tears during a strident recitation from the 'Pompilia' section of *The Ring and the Book* — though the stridency which Colvin thought notable recalls Henry James's observation that Browning recited his verses as though he should like to bite them to pieces.

On 19 September, Story sketched Robert hunched over at the waist, leaning forward over the book, holding it close to his bearded face, reading from it near-sightedly, concentratedly, and with knitted brow. Colvin's impression of Robert was of a man perfectly cordial, free with 'confidential and affectionate gestures', though his conversation was inconsequential. He might at least have been thought distracted while observing — with all his long experience of social etiquette — the conventions of an aristocratic house party. William Story seems by this time to have become aware of his old friend's anxiety and covered for him by drawing him out conversationally with reminiscences, prompting anecdotes from Robert that recalled happier days.

In two letters to Edie Story and her parents, written from Warwick Crescent on 28 September 1869, Robert referred to weariness and disturbed sleep patterns on his return from Scotland. He was back in Scotland briefly in mid-October in bitter weather before setting out on a tour of English country houses. From Blickling Hall in Norfolk, he wrote on 16 November to Edie Story: 'The fact is, the holidays are over, with (for me) an end of boys'-play, which, — it is said, — men ought to know when to leave off: and "left off" it all is, I very sincerely assure you. I am seeing all my sober friends, and still have visits to pay before I settle down to my work in London — whatever that work is to be.' He then provided Edie with details of his itinerary — from the Marquis of Lothian at beautiful Blickling Hall to Earl and Countess Cowper at Wrest Park, near Ampthill in Bedfordshire, thence to Highclere Castle near Newbury, Berkshire, to visit the Earl of Carnarvon, then 'home, I hope. Pen is working for "Smalls": he has an ugly cold which he can't shake off.' Robert himself was 'bilious and out of sorts — but shall be quiet and collect my scattered forces'.

By 24 February 1870, when he next wrote to Isa, he had been 'very unwell and quite unable to write . . . biliousness bothers me, as of old, — and now gives me an unpleasant turning of the brains which must be got rid of somehow. If I tide over the next season, I shall try and wash all away with divine salt water, "which cures all pollution" says the ancient.' Sarianna, too, had been unwell, but Pen had taken a surprising turn: he seemed to be '*at last* round the corner of his career and fairly with his head the right way — I do trust! His last years have been possibly a sort of battle for his own individuality, — and, now that I was fairly giving up my part of the strife, — *what* do you suppose? What that should, most of all things imaginably, stupefy me? Why, — *between us*, — he has once more broken out in violent poetry! He wrote, a few weeks ago, a poem in some six hundred lines about an adventure he had at Croisic — You know very well how little sympathetic I am to poetry of most sorts — nor would I give much for this —

this as an ultimate product: but considering the boy's all but absolute ignorance of poetry, it was a very welcome proof indeed of what may be still in him.'

To Robert's regretful lack of sympathy for the poetry of Tennyson in his later style, of William Morris, Algernon Swinburne, and Anne Thackeray, he now added a splenetic distaste for the works and person of the vain, irascible poet and critic Alfred Austin. In his letter of 22 March 1870 to Isa, Robert rued the delay in writing to her 'because of a press of calls on my time, — and things hardly mend as the season grows exacting'. This was the usual business — his underlying weariness with the social life to which he was by now so habituated that he felt unable to give it up lest he should, as he had said in the past, lose some unexpected good.

'If I spend my old age my own way, quietly alone, — how odd and dreamlike will all the people come and go in my memory! I suppose it is, on the whole, a gain in some respects to the soul to have seen so many people: I mainly care about human beings, yet I feel weary of the crowd I chose to fancy it would do me good to see.' Inevitably, Robert's social success evoked enmities and provoked jealousies: but even those, when he became aware of them, were gnat bites. He felt only 'an ignoble touch of satisfaction when I think that, after all, it "riles" such a filthy little snob as Mr Alfred Austin to read in the Morning Post how many dinners I eat in good company.'

Robert took his opportunity to retail to Isa a funny, derogatory, and highly satisfactory story about Austin's attempt to sell an article to Thackeray as editor of the *Cornhill* and being fobbed off by the great man with half a crown as an act of charity.[148]

For fully six months, in his letters to Isa, Robert had been cavilling at the poetry of his contemporaries and complaining of minor ailments, both personal and within his own household — biliousness, headaches, colds. The impression given is of worry and unease displaced into diseases of both body and soul. He worried about Isa's health, Sarianna had been ill during the winter, and Pen had came home from Oxford 'very unwell'.[149] Even the Brownings' pet owl had fallen ill. By 15 April 1870, the date of a letter from Robert to Sarianna, who was then visiting

Paris, the little bird seemed better, 'though very helpless still: he seems paralysed in some degree. I feed him against his wish, poor fellow.' The weather, too, had been 'abominable beyond precedent'.

Altogether Robert's letters at this time gave an idea of non-specific, generalized discontent that displayed itself in a perception of pervasive ill-health and an ill-natured snapping at anyone and anything within reach of his teeth and the point of his pen. He became aware himself of these attitudes, writing apologetically to Isa in July: 'the time of the year always weighs upon me, — most of my troubles happen in June . . . Nine years ago, completed on the 29th.' And again, as usual, Robert quoted the familiar words: 'The years they come and go — the races drop in the grave — But *never* the love doth so.'

June 1870 did not alter the pattern of Robert's troubles. In that month, Pen failed his Oxford examinations, the 'Smalls', and — no help for it this time — he was required to remove his name from the College books and leave Christ Church. Remarkably, Robert did not immediately pour out his disappointment to Isa or the Storys. It was to George Barrett that he turned in three letters: the first, dated 17 June; the second dated 1 July, which re-stated and elaborated the first; and the third, undated, probably written a few days after the second. Perhaps he regarded Pen's disgrace and the prospects for his future as a family matter; possibly it seemed not coincidental that the fatal month of Elizabeth's death was the same as her son's downfall. Some salt may have been rubbed in the wound by the fact that Altham Cook, Henrietta's son, also at Christ Church, had passed the 'Smalls' that Pen had ploughed — despite eight or ten weeks of intensive cramming, which were not, however, in his father's estimation, 'enough to overcome nine years of idleness'.[150]

Oxford had been sympathetic to Pen: 'the Dean intimated that should Pen apply for leave to try again, he would give the application every attention,' wrote Robert to George on 1 July 1870, 'but, to what use?' He was beyond exasperation. His sympathy was exhausted, his efforts were pointless: 'though I might possibly get him yet another respite, I shall not dream of doing so.' There was another matter, no less grave, that seriously alarmed Robert: Pen had been spending money at a ruinous rate. 'Pen's outlay impossible to be sustained: his expenses for the last term, of some five weeks barely, were something like £150 or 160 — multiply that by 4, add seven months of holidays to be provided for, and you will judge whether I am justified in trying to go on with the experiment.' Pen could not be made to see 'that he should follow any other rule than that of living like the richest and idlest young men of his acquaintance, or that there is any use in being at the University than to do so: and if I tried the experiment for the fiftieth time the result would be the same.'[151] Pen had declared as much: in the presence of his Uncle Occy, he had said 'that he would not have consented to be at Ch. Ch. at any less expense than he had been incurring, and that he considered getting a first class no brilliant thing at all.'[152]

This lordly insouciance, this callow, quasi-aristocratic *me ne frego* disdain, presumably acquired from his fellow-students at Christ Church, snapped the last thread of Robert's tolerance. Pen's tutors had constantly given him hope that Pen was capable of academic attainment and now, apparently, all was ashes: 'I am quite at my wits' end and hopeless of doing anything to the boy's advantage. He is unfit for anything but idleness and pleasure.'[153] The most complete despair had come upon Robert, who saw his own hard-won principles and dearly-held ideals smashed like idols and swept to the ground by an unthinking hand: 'You see that all my plans are destroyed by this double evil — the utmost self-indulgence joined to the greatest contempt of work and its fruits ... I am ready to make all possible sacrifice that may end in something like success: I can hardly make a greater than I have done — of the last nine years of my life, which have been as thoroughly wasted as if they were passed in playing at chuck-farthing. All I can do, — except to give money, — is done and done in vain.'[154]

To George, Robert miserably rehearsed and immediately dismissed the usual options for a scapegrace: 'The diplomatic service is out of the question now: nobody *in* it but wishes he were out of it as a *profitable* career.'[155] Far from increasing income, diplomacy merely drained it. A military career, a sure road to profligacy, was not to be thought of either in terms of morality or money: 'I will not hear of such a life, — first of all, hateful to his Mother: next, as hateful to me, — finally, involving all the worst temptations to every sort of weakness.' A third option presented itself to Robert: he could hand Pen over to George, a former barrister.

The poor boy is simply WEAK — not bad in any way, — clever, quite capable of doing all I ever had the hope he would do, singularly engaging to all his friends with whom he is as popular as possible, and quite docile and amenable to reason with a comparative stranger: I believe were he with *you*, he would conduct himself with the utmost propriety, even self-restraint: but I am merely the manger at which he feeds, and nothing is more certain than that I could do him no greater good than by dying tonight and leaving him just enough to keep him from starving: I believe it will end in my making him an allowance, going abroad, and so doing the next best thing.[156]

By the time Robert had written his third letter to George, he was a little calmer. He had been turning over the idea of 'Pen becoming a barrister . . . in some respects it seems a promising scheme'. While still admitting Pen's disinclination to do anything like work, 'I don't see why he might not cut a respectable figure as a pleader under certain conditions: I am told that nothing could exceed his coolness and readiness at improvising in the charade at Lord Houghton's, — himself remarking that he felt no embarrassment at all. He is really shrewd, quick enough at rendering a reason, and able to take his own part volubly when it would seem a difficult matter.'[157] If there was ever an image of a man clutching at a straw before disappearing under deep water for the third time, this is surely it. Sarianna, wedded to an ideal of gentility, thought well of the notion. Pen, however, had not been apprised of it before Robert sent him to his uncle the same night the letter was despatched; but perhaps, when it was revealed to him, he reacted as passively as he did in all things. What the sensible, professionally useful George thought of a career at the bar for Pen can only be imagined.

Maisie Ward, in her short, fascinating biography of Pen Browning, reverses — with an ingenuity worthy of Robert Browning himself — the idea of Pen's unfitness for life and applies it to his father: the revelation about Pen's idleness in Robert's letters to George could just as much be said of Robert's 'own unfitness to cope with life in the world to which he had returned, after fifteen years of devotion to one purpose in a climate created by himself and the other poet who was his wife'.[158] This displacement is a little harsh, to the extent that Robert had applied himself diligently to poetry since his return to London and achieved significant successes; but it contains an element of truth that Robert himself acknowledged. When he wrote so bitterly to George of nine wasted years, he might have recalled his letter of late February 1869 to Julia Wedgwood, responding to her letter of 21 February in which she had more or less judged the time spent writing *The Ring and the Book* as a mistake: 'yes, I have give four full years to this "mistake," but what did I do with my fourteen years in Italy?' The answer very likely being, in his own estimation, not much.

He had certainly earned very little money from the fitful poetic efforts he had made in Italy. Had it not been for John Kenyon's twice-yearly gift of £50 and his final substantial legacy, Elizabeth's share of which accrued to Robert after her death, he would have been hard pressed for many years to make even a barely adequate living, far less maintain the gentlemanly style to which he and Pen had become accustomed in London. His devotion to nothing but poetry had been made possible only by the generosity of others — his father, his wife, and his friend John Kenyon. Even in 1870, at the height of his success, his annual income from poetry amounted only to £100, more or less, in comparison with the princely sum of £5,000 and more said to be earned in a year by Tennyson. Robert had managed his life by a necessarily acquired and by now habitual caution in financial matters. Though he was not averse to occasional extravagances, and would contribute generously enough for a creditable cause, it pained him to see hard-earned money dissipated on frivolities.

If Sarianna was socially aspirational, and Pen was aristocratic in his social ambitions, Robert was at least liable to be particular about social niceties. On 5 November 1887, he wrote to George Barrett mentioning a correction he had taken the trouble to make: 'on the occasion of a notice in the "Times" many years ago, of the new pictures in the "National Portrait Gallery," the likeness of Ba had, appended to the catalogue, quoted in the "Times," the information "Daughter of &c West India Merchant." I at once wrote to the editor of the Catalogue, and to the "Times," correcting the error just as you have done, and for the same reason, that a fact is a fact.' An amendment was obligingly made, describing Elizabeth not as 'the daughter of a London merchant' but 'of a private gentleman'. Just so, Sarianna had winced and trod on her father's foot when he had referred to himself as formerly a Bank of England clerk. And just so, Jeannette Marks, when researching the Browning and Barrett family history among its descendants, discovered a long-standing emphasis on the gentility of both families.

In *The Tragi-Comedy of Pen Browning*, Maisie Ward makes a point — perfectly valid — of Robert's pleasure in Pen's social success and distinction in field sports, despite the fact that Robert and Elizabeth had 'agreed in hating' such activities.[159] Sarianna had been thrilled at Loch Luichart by Pen's prowess in bringing down that first stag, describing it as a 'great event' in Pen's young life. Despite, or because of, his middle-class origins, Robert fully colluded with the prevailing social snobbery and class distinctions of his times. Ancestry mattered very much: 'Browning's grandfather was said to have kept an inn. This might exclude him — but far worse, because closer and more recent, was his *father's* employment as a clerk. And even if he, by his poetry and his social gifts, had crossed the line, the admission of his son might have remained more than doubtful. About this Browning seems to have been far too greatly concerned.'[160]

Robert's attitude, wholly conventional in public, rather more critical in private, was light-heartedly summarized in a letter to Isa on 25 January 1872. Kate Field, an American journalist, and an old friend from the days in Florence and Rome, had turned up in London and had expressed some astonishment at the narrow niceties of the English class system and the petty, precise pecking-order of social precedence. Kate had arrived 'probably primed and loaded with book-stuff about England, and perfectly ignorant of course'. He went on:

The thing that quite warrants a revolution in England is, I find, the atrocious fact, she has some difficulty in believing, that at a dinner party a 'mere baronet' would take precedence of R B in the passage to the dining room: in answer I told her that an orderly procession, with no scrambling, was desirable, and that I should prefer an alphabetic arrangement of the guests to none at all — as in an American dinner I was present at some weeks ago, when everybody made a rush, and I chose to stand stock still till it was over, and go in last of all. In vain I also told her that the said abominable baronet was likely to take precedence of me in any other fashion, once the table was reached. It was simply an abomination. I finally assured her that Princess Louise [Queen Victoria's daughter, the Princess Royal, Empress of Germany] made her husband go and tell me 'I had met her' because I did not at once step forward and speak: all to no use!

This account to Isa of Robert's explications to Kate Field comes across as semi-humorous, tongue-in-cheek: but behind it lay the republican, democratic principles of both Robert and Elizabeth Browning, their experience and admiration of more democratic, meritocratic American and Italian societies, and of course the entire absurdity of the whole system of social precedence at the lower end of its long and precisely calibrated scale from the Queen of England at the top to the Esquires of Little Pedlington at the bottom.

In mid-July, Pen came down for the second time in his life, and perhaps not surprisingly, with a severe attack of measles. He was put to bed, physicians were summoned, and Sarianna fussed over the invalid.[161] He recovered fairly quickly. By 9 August, the date of a letter from Robert to Isa, he was well enough to go and stay with his tutor at Ollerton in Nottinghamshire while his father and aunt took themselves off for a holiday in France, at St Aubin-sur-Mer, Calvados, where, as Robert wrote to Isa on 19 August 1870, Joseph Milsand had a house — 'a cottage with a nice bit of garden, two steps off, and we occupy another of the most primitive kind on the sea-shore — which shore is a good sandy stretch for miles and miles on either side, — I don't think we were ever quite so thoroughly washed by the sea air from all quarters as here.' Robert had got his desire to 'try and wash all away with divine salt water, "which cures all pollution"'. But he had not, perhaps, fully reckoned on a rapid conclusion to the war that had broken out in mid-July between France and Prussia and which, coming to a head just six weeks later, dramatically smoked the Brownings out of their holiday haven.

Despite their intention to linger on at St Aubin-sur-Mer until the end of September, Robert and Sarianna were forced to make a premature, precipitate, and in the end undignified run for England. Mrs Orr provides the details:

One morning M. Milsand came to them in anxious haste, and insisted on their starting that very day. An order, he said, had been issued that no native should leave the country, and it only needed some unusually thick-headed Maire [mayor] for Mr Browning to be arrested as a runaway Frenchman or a Prussian spy. The usual passenger-boats from Calais and Boulogne no longer ran; but there was, he believed, a chance of their finding one at Havre. They acted on this warning and discovered its wisdom in the various hindrances which they found on their way. Everywhere the horses had been requisitioned for the war. The boat on which they had relied to take them down the river to Caen had been stopped that very morning; and when they reached the railroad they were told that the Prussians would be at the other end before night. At last they arrived at Honfleur, where they found an English vessel which was about to convey cattle to Southampton; and in this, setting out at midnight, they made their passage to England.[162]

The ostensible reason for Louis Napoleon's war with the Prussian Kaiser Wilhelm and his Chancellor Otto von Bismarck was an attempt to prevent Prince Leopold of Prussia ascending the Spanish throne, which had become vacant following the deposition of Queen Isabella. The declaration of war was just what Bismarck had wished for as a pretext for uniting the German states in a cause demanding national unity. As a result of several quick and famous Prussian victories, the consequence of which was a thorough rout of French troops, the Second Empire fell following a decisive French defeat at the battle of Sedan. The next day, 2 September 1870, Louis Napoleon surrendered his sword, himself, and 80,000 of his men.

A Parisian mob invaded the Paris Assembly on 4 September, the Third Empire was declared by public acclamation, and a Government of National Defence was formed by republicans and radicals at the Hôtel de Ville. Soon after these events, the desperate siege of Paris began. It lasted for four months until the Parisians, destituted by starvation, more dead than alive from bitter cold, demoralized by Prussian bombardment, capitulated in January 1871. The Empress Eugénie, who had been deeply implicated in fomenting the political fervour for war, fled to England. She arrived at Hastings on 8 September 1870 and there she found her son, the Prince Imperial, who had preceded her by two days. Six months later, in March 1871, they were joined by Louis Napoleon, who died on

9 January 1873 at Camden Place, Chislehurst, where he had set up his penniless little court in exile and had occupied his time writing his memoirs.

Robert was deeply interested in the Franco-Prussian war of 1870. He had no doubt that Prussia had been scheming for it just as much as France. To Isa, on 19 July, the date that war was officially declared, he wrote: 'All I trust is that Italy will get Rome easily and naturally.' He had never sympathized with Louis Napoleon's 'dynastic ambition for his son [the Prince Imperial], — who has no right to be anybody in France ... I think, in the interest of humanity'. So far as Louis Napoleon himself was concerned, in Robert's view he 'wants a sound beating this time and probably may get it: ... Oh, oh, Ba — put not your trust in princes neither in the sons of men, — Emperors, Popes, Garibaldis, or Mazzinis, — the *plating* wears through, and out comes the copperhead of human nature and weakness and falseness too!'

On 19 August 1870, Robert's letter to Isa reflected further on the war. He thought 'that Napoleon is far from his old self' — which was true in the physical sense: the Emperor was now sixty-two years old and riddled with diseases scarcely fit to be mentioned in polite society — 'and these indecisions succeeded by rashnesses have tried the world's temper too long, — I don't think he has a chance of re-entering Paris as Emperor.' Robert's 'sorrow that France should be so humiliated is quite independent of, — or rather, all the more increased by, — her folly and ignorance in this matter': which was not to say that his sympathies were much with the Prussians either. Even before the spring of 1871, when Kaiser Wilhelm I was proclaimed Emperor of Germany by the King of Bavaria in the Hall of Mirrors at Versailles, Robert had commented to Isa: 'The effect will be, that we shall all be forced into the Prussian system, of turning a nation into a camp; nothing but soldiering to concern us for the next generation.' His principal interest was, as ever, for Italy. On 19 September 1870, he wrote to Isa: 'The one sweet and comfortable thought is the advance on Rome, which indemnifies one for much sorrow in other respects. How poor Florence will like the change is hardly a question: what a fall in rents may you expect! — also a pause to the pulling down and building up.' Rome was taken on 20 September, whereupon Florence ceased to be the capital city of Italy.

On 19 October, Robert expressed to Isa his view that Napoleon 'should simply be blotted out of the world as the greatest failure on record. The "benefits of his reign" are just the extravagant interest which a knavish banker pays you for some time till he, one fine day, decamps with the principal, — and then where are you? ... As for Rome, — had he kept his word to Italy, this occupation would now be an old affair, and he would have had an Italian army to help him two months ago: but "who can control his fate?" — and his was only to be nearly a great man.' Despite Robert's disapproval of the effects that Louis Napoleon's reign had wrought on France, his sympathy was strong for the French people. He was so distressed by the suffering of Parisians in the winter of 1871 that he permitted George Murray Smith, against his usual authorial practice of refusing to publish individual poems in magazines, to offer *Hervé Riel* as a contribution to the March 1871 issue of the *Cornhill* and donated his fee, 100 guineas, to the French Relief Fund.

Louis Napoleon had for long years figured largely in Europe, and more directly in Robert's life, than, possibly, he would have wished. His complex feelings, a mixture of sympathy and contempt, for the Emperor were expressed in a long poem, *Prince Hohenstiel-Schwangau, Saviour of Society*, based on 'the little handbreadth of prose' that, as he related to Edie Story, he had made in the Via del Tritone in Rome in 1860, and that was now, twelve years later, 'yellow with age and Italian ink'.[163] The poem, which he claimed to Edie that he 'really wrote — that is, conceived' in 1860, was 'breathed out into this full-blown bubble' in Scotland during the summer and autumn of 1871. It is likely that Robert was prompted to take up the notes he had made and to work them up into a poem by a conviction that Louis Napoleon's career had run its course, that he was finally a spent force — that there was now nothing left for the old political operator to do, no further mischief he could get up to. By 1 October that year the poem had swollen to 'about 1800 absolutely new lines or more, and shall have the whole thing out of hand by the early winter, — what *I* can't help thinking a sample of my very best work'.[164] Taking the form of a monologue, the tone of the poem was described by Robert as 'a sort of political satire', and when it was published in early December 1871 it finally consisted of 2,155 lines.

Four months before, on 8 August 1871, Robert had published *Balaus-*

tion's Adventure: Including a Transcript from Euripides. This poem, much
admired as a whole by Browning scholars, as well as by classicists, who
rate very highly Browning's translation of Euripides within the poem,
amounted to a modest 2,705 lines. It was quickly written in May 1871
(contrary to Robert's own dating of it in the manuscript: 'Begun and
ended in May, 1872') as 'the most delightful of May-month's amuse-
ments' at the behest of Katrina Cecilia, Countess Cowper, to whom it
was gratefully and gracefully dedicated. Though its dedication was to a
living woman, the published poem itself was a memorial to Elizabeth
shortly after the tenth anniversary of her death. Commentators on
Balaustion's Adventure have noted resemblances to Elizabeth not only
in the circumstances of Balaustion's life — an overbearing parent, an
addiction to poetry — but, just as markedly, in the intelligence and
effervescence of Balaustion's pretty, girlish character, which is also remi-
niscent, in certain respects, of Pippa and Pompilia.

Maisie Ward makes the interesting observation that 'to no one
except Browning would the wife he had known only as an invalid and
middle-aged reappear as a young and beautiful woman. Yet the convic-
tion is well founded — this was how Browning had seen her ... when
Mrs Kinney aroused his wrath by talking of the beautiful mind and the
ravaged face.'[165] It is true enough that, in Robert's eyes, Elizabeth had
always seemed youthful in looks and sparkling in spirit. To Robert,
immediately after her death, she had looked 'like a young girl'; and it
would be surprising, in the years following, if he did not think now and
again of the line by Keats, from his 'Ode on a Grecian Urn': 'For ever
wilt thou love, and she be fair!'

The source of *Balaustion's Adventure* was *Alkestis*, a play written in
or about 438 BC by Euripides, a dramatist much admired by Elizabeth.
An account of a performance of the play in 413 BC, during the latter
half of the Peloponnesian war between Athens and Sparta, is narrated
by the Rhodian girl Balaustion, whose name means 'wild pomegranate-
flower' — a subtle allusion, it may be thought, to Elizabeth and her
first reference to the 'blood-tinctured' fruit in acknowledgement of her
admiration for Robert's *Bells and Pomegranates*. The poem contains, as
usual, some Browning reflections upon the nature and transforming
power of poetry, and draws upon his own Christian faith for its conclud-
ing redemptive moral. But above all, in any subjective interpretation,

there are plain parallels between the dramatically-presented marriage of the poetic protagonists, Alkestis and Admetos, and the real-life marriage of the poets Robert and Elizabeth.

The original Euripidean character of Admetos, King of Thessaly, in the play is somewhat altered in the poem. Interpreted by Robert as conventional and self-centred, Admetos is gradually brought to an adequate appreciation of the noble, self-sacrificing Alkestis, his wife, and at her death he insists on not remarrying. Balaustion, an original-minded girl, possessed of imagination and seized by sympathy, is dissatisfied with Euripides' play. She adds her own commentary: since Admetos was willing to let Alkestis die for him, it is surely unlikely that, when retrieved from death by the god Herakles, she would be willing to return to her selfish husband. Balaustion's better idea is that Apollo should so transform the character of Admetos that he becomes an ideal king, ruling honourably for the good of his people. Though Alkestis has obtained Apollo's consent to her own death in place of her husband's, Admetos is unwilling to accept her sacrifice. When Alkestis does indeed die, she is returned to life not by a redeeming god but — vitally — by the strength of their love:

> And so, before the embrace relaxed a whit,
> The lost eyes opened, still beneath the look;
> And lo, Alkestis was alive again,
> And of Admetos' rapture who shall speak? [ll. 2648–51]

And so they lived happily ever after. Of Robert's intention in his poem, Balaustion clearly speaks to 'reinforce, recognisably, the contrition of Admetos, unworthy husband of a supremely worthy wife'.[166] It was commonly assumed, without firm evidence but on a balance of probabilities, that *Balaustion's Adventure* expressed Robert's regret over the proposal he was supposed to have made to Louisa Ashburton: more likely now, in the light of what we know with more certainty, it may be taken as expressing his regret for having considered the Ashburton proposal in the first place and affirming his resolution to refuse it. Robert would not remarry.

At the invitation of an old friend, Ernest Benzon, a rich German-American businessman whose wife was the sister of Rudolph and Frederick Lehmann, Pen and Robert went to stay for the summer of 1871 at Little Milton, a shooting-lodge in the hills above Loch Tummel. The lodge was some 'three rugged miles' from Benzon at Allean House near Pitlochry, on the shooting estate which their host had recently acquired. Sarianna had opted to visit Joseph Milsand and his wife in France and to visit 'poor Paris, which she found melancholy enough'.[167] By 19 August, when Robert wrote to Isa, Pen was wholeheartedly in the grip of the licensed murderous spirit that had come upon him on 'The Glorious Twelfth': 'Pen enjoys the shooting much: shot, by himself, to-day 14½ brace of grouse, 4 hares and a plover — on the eighth day of shooting, — that is, when the birds have been, two thirds of them, shot, and the rest effectually frightened. A poor business, and one I could wish him to hate as much as I do: but "who can control his fate?"'[168]

Pen's character had lately been somewhat rehabilitated, if only by comparison with worse behaviour by Willie Bracken — characterized by Robert as a 'selfish young piece of worthlessness'[169] — who intended to marry and was currently defying his mother's resistance to the match. Robert was by now 'to a certain degree ... relieved about Pen by knowing the very worst of the poor boy, to-wit that he won't work, or perhaps can't. I shall go on, now, as long as I am able, and do the best for us both, taking the chances of this world. He is clever and in the main very good and very conscientious: everybody likes him. He would never treat me as Willy is treating his mother, — to be sure, I would not be treated so.'[170] It had become Robert's habit by now to perceive the good in Pen and thereby redeem, so far as possible, his shortcomings. His illusions of academic achievement for his son had been thoroughly dashed, and so it might be better to reconsider Pen's positive points in an effort to turn those to the young man's benefit and his own consolation. He had been tried, in these past few months, almost beyond endurance.

To Isa, Robert confessed that 'The strain of London life is too much for me, or rather *has* been too much, when added to the other strain of cares and fears which, I hope, are over now. I don't know whether I am "vivacious" as ever, but I am susceptible enough of pain, —

perhaps, pain which I make for myself by unnecessary anticipation, — still, pain no less.' The point of this might be that the questions looming about Pen's future were still no nearer being answered and that Robert looked forward — as he habitually did — to difficulties that he could not yet readily see how to resolve. Despite his distrust of those who advocated a philosophy of *carpe diem*, Robert's circumstances in a remote Highland shooting-lodge, alone for most of the day while Pen was out with the guns, were such that he found 'an impulse to write'.[171] He seized the day and his pen.

He was thinking, in this solitude, of Elizabeth. To Isa he wrote on 19 August, 'the simple truth is that *she* was the poet, and I the clever person by comparison: remember her limited experience of all kinds, and what she made of it — remember, on the other hand, how my uninterrupted health and strength, and practice with the world have helped me.' Such words were by now a familiar threnody in Robert's song about his late wife. In this frame of mind, Robert settled to work. With Elizabeth in his thoughts, she inevitably moved from being a motivating force behind *Balaustion's Adventure* and entered in memory — as she had vitally intruded in life — into Robert's reflections on the career of Louis Napoleon and his assessments of the Emperor's character.

The subject was timely — decidedly *dans le vent*. In January 1871, Robert Buchanan had already published a poem, 'Napoleon Fallen', and had sent a copy to Robert, who replied, 'I think more savagely *now* of the man, and should say so if needed.'[172] Swinburne, too, had been considering a poem about Napoleon III and reckoned that Victor Hugo — who had good reasons of his own to maul the deposed Emperor — was also sinking his 'lion claws' into the man. The consistent pace that Robert had achieved with *The Ring and the Book* was matched in the composition of *Prince Hohenstiel-Schwangau, Saviour of Society*. The steady rhythm he maintained was a wonder to a member of the reading party being led in the neighbourhood that summer by Benjamin Jowett. Robert was observed to be 'perpetrating "Hohenstiel Schwangau" at the rate of so many lines a day, neither more nor less'.[173]

The observer was not, but might have been, Swinburne himself, who, before being sent down from Oxford, had been one of Jowett's students. He was a member that year of the Scottish reading party under the strict supervision of Jowett who had been charged with the responsibility of keeping Swinburne and intoxicating liquor strictly apart. For recreation and light relief from the task in hand, Robert 'walked over to see Jowett one afternoon, very keen about a fanciful rendering he had imagined' for a word in the *Alkestis*.[174] To Isa, on 1 October 1871, Robert reported, 'I never at any time in my life turned a holiday into such an occasion of work: the quiet and seclusion were too tempting . . . is not that edifying conduct for a holiday-maker?' The manuscript of *Prince Hohenstiel-Schwangau, Saviour of Society*, was given to George Murray Smith on 8 November and published on or about 16 December 1871.

One might be tempted to think, concerning Robert's views on Louis Napoleon, that the poem speaks for itself. Insofar as it may be said to do so, the critics heard two distinctly different things. The deeply ironic title should have given the game away right from the start, but it passed without impediment through most critical English heads. Just as Elizabeth's *Poems Before Congress* had been misinterpreted by at least one critic as unpatriotic, so was *Prince Hohenstiel-Schwangau* identified on the one hand as a eulogy for the Emperor, on the other as an attack on him. In fact, it was neither. In fact, it was both. In fact, it was an attempt by the author to come to terms not only with Louis Napoleon's antithetical character, but, equally, with his own opposed feelings and perplexed perceptions about his subject.

The differing interpretations that were made of the work derived from the duality of the poem itself, its even-handed admixture of private psychology and public politics, its complex balance of sympathy and distaste, its disturbing shifts from first-person to third-person narratives, its ironies and inversions, its casuistries and contradictions, its recognition of the differences between what the Prince self-confessedly 'never was, but might have been'. All these things should by now have been familiar to *aficionados* of Robert's work, who had seen Mr Sludge, the Medium, and other notable charlatans and characters in the Browning repertory company, treated in much the same ambiguous way that was, essentially, a symptom of the subjective poet's fair-minded striving for objectivity.

Robert's declaration to Robert Buchanan that 'I think more savagely *now* of the man, and should say so if needed' was moderated as he settled into writing about Louis Napoleon. Isa, in Robert's letter to her of 29 December 1871, was asked to judge for herself 'whether I make the best or the worst of the case'. Isa, he knew perfectly well, had agreed wholeheartedly with Elizabeth in her estimation of the Emperor. 'I think in the main,' wrote Robert, 'he meant to do what I say, and, but for the weakness, — grown more apparent in these last years than formerly, — would have done what I say he did not. I thought badly of him at the beginning of his career, *et pour cause*, better afterward, on the strength of promises he made and gave indications of intending to redeem, — I think him very weak in the last miserable year.'

In the event, Isa seems to have approved of what she had read. Like the editor of the *Edinburgh Review*, Henry Reeve, she interpreted the poem as being favourable to Louis Napoleon. Reeve, with less respect than Isa for the Emperor, and with even less of her benevolence for the poet he took to be the imperial eulogist, declared: 'The "Prince of Hohenstiel-Schwangau, Saviour of Society" . . . is a rhapsody, without much metre or meaning, for the glorification of Napoleon III — the "one wise man" — and the Second Empire.' Reeve went on to 'regret that Mr Browning should entertain and express such false and unworthy sentiments and opinions on modern politics: and we prefer to see him in the classical garb of antiquity'. To Isa, Robert refuted the idea that the poem was a eulogium, any more than it was what 'another wiseacre affirms to be a "scandalous attack on the old constant friend of Eng-land"'. The poem was, said Robert, 'just what I imagine the man might, if he pleased, say for himself'.[175]

Balaustion's Adventure had been critically well received and by 25 January 1872, the date of Robert's letter that month to Isa, had sold out its first edition of 2,500 copies, 'a good sale for the likes of me!'. Neverthe-less, Robert had met the poet Henry Taylor at dinner, 'and he said he had never got anything by his books, — which surely is a shame, — I mean, if "no buyers" mean "no readers."'[176] This pinched at an old nerve in Robert's system, recalling his first approach to Edward Moxon, who had published Taylor's *Philip van Artevelde* in 1834, and who had taken a sadly pessimistic view of poetry as a paying proposition. Robert was now in the comfortable position of being able to care more for a wide readership than for large royalties.

It had not always been so. *Prince Hohenstiel-Schwangau*, he reported to Isa on 29 December 1871, was 'succeeding: sold 1400 in the first five days, and before any notice appeared: I remember that the year in which I made a little rough sketch of something of the kind in Rome, '60, my account for the last six months with Chapman was — *nil*, not one copy disposed of! I have just consented, after a long delay, that Tauchnitz [the Leipzig publisher of English-language authors] shall print our works: it hurts the English sale somewhat, but one writes to be read, and I don't care.' The character of Balaustion caught and charmed the public imagination and *Balaustion's Adventure* went into a second and then a third edition; the *Prince* did not, for years afterwards, exhaust its first edition. The initial brisk sales tailed off and then ceased almost entirely.

Prince Hohenstiel-Schwangau has hitherto not been rated very highly by Browning critics, though Chesterton greatly admired it as 'one of the finest and most picturesque of all Browning's apologetic mono-logues'.[177] In his short biography of Browning, he paints a quick, vivid picture of Louis Napoleon as a duplicitous villain, a man who 'deceived Europe twice — once when he made it think he was a noodle, and once when he made it think he was a statesman ... deceived a third time, when it took him after his fall for an exploded mountebank and nonentity'. Chesterton perceptively noted 'something peculiarly charac-teristic of Browning in thus selecting not only a political villain but what would appear the most prosaic kind of villain. We scarcely ever find in Browning a defence of those obvious and easily defended publi-cans and sinners whose mingled virtues and vices are the stuff of romance and melodrama — the generous rake, the kindly drunkard, the strong man too great for parochial morals. He was in a yet more solitary sense the friend of the outcast. He took in the sinners whom even sinners cast out. He went with the hypocrite and had mercy on the Pharisee.'[178]

Before publication, Robert had regarded *Prince Hohenstiel-Schwangau* as an important poem, as one of the best things he had done. After it appeared, however, he seemed to revise this estimation when he wrote to Edie Story on 20 December 1871: 'I expect you not to care three straws for what, in the nature of things, is uninteresting enough, even compared with other poems of mine which you have been only too good to. What poetry can be in a sort of political satire, made the milder because of the present fortunes of the subject? So, all you are to understand by the gift of the thing is that, for want of better, it is my best at present.' The political subject of the poem, the deposed Emperor and his circumstances, might have compromised the basic humanitarian and philosophical theme of the poem. Robert's underlying purpose had been to analyse the psychological and practical paradoxes of antithesis, to examine the contradictions and compromises implicit in the character of a man whose ideals and actions were frequently at odds, to tread the dangerous edge where personal principles and political pragmatism were insecurely welded together.

The Prince's initial self-justification and self-apology leads inevitably to self-examination and self-awareness in which he is forced to admit that his idealism, his first good intentions, may be warped in practice and become but excuses for his failures. Throughout the career of Louis Napoleon, Robert saw the fluctuation of much good and much bad in the man, until, at the end, as he wrote of the Prince/Emperor to Edie Story on 1 January 1872, 'I don't think ... you will find I have taken the man for any Hero — I rather made him confess he was the opposite, though I put forward what excuses I thought he was likely to make for himself, if inclined to try. I never at any time thought much better of him than now; and I don't think so much worse of the character as shown us in the last few years, because I suppose there to be a physical and intellectual decline of faculty, brought about by the man's own faults, no doubt — but I think he struggles against these; and when that is the case, depend on it, in a soliloquy, a man makes the most of his good intentions and sees great excuses in them — far beyond what our optics discover!'

The theme of best intentions thwarted was too good to abandon because of a relative critical and financial failure. It had not succeeded in *Prince Hohenstiel-Schwangau* as well as Robert had hoped, and so he immediately tackled it again in a poem he began energetically to write in December 1871. He completed this poem in 2,355 lines, not counting the paraphernalia with which it is topped and tailed, by 11 May 1872.

The new work greatly shocked Mrs Orr. Her biography had lately been loitering along, unhindered by any tactless revelation of personal difficulties in her subject's private life: 'It would be hard to imagine from Mr Browning's work during these last ten years that any but gracious influences had been operating upon his genius, any more disturbing element than the sense of privation and loss had entered into his inner life.'[179] But now she was obliged to perceive that 'Some leaven of bitterness must, nevertheless, have been working within him, or he could never have produced that piece of perplexing cynicism, *Fifine at the Fair* — the poem referred to in a letter to Miss Blagden, and which appeared in the spring of 1872.'

'Perplexing cynicism' are two strong words in Mrs Orr's vocabulary. Put together, they are bonded in a judicious phrase that understates her distress. She bravely continues, 'while *Dramatis Personae, The Ring and the Book*, and even *Balaustion's Adventure*, represented the gradually perfected substance of his poetic imagination, *Fifine at the Fair* was as the froth thrown up by it during the prolonged simmering which was to leave it clear. The work displays the iridescent brightness as well as the occasional impurity of this froth-like character. Beauty and ugliness are, indeed, almost inseparable in the moral impression which it leaves upon us.' Mrs Orr's none too subtle culinary analogy made her opinion plain: *Fifine at the Fair* was like the frothy scum that formed on the surface of a pot of stock. To clarify the substance of the simmering stock, the surface scum should be scooped away by the conscientious cook and discarded as unpalatable waste matter.

In letters to Isa Blagden, Robert had briefly referred three times to *Fifine at the Fair* — though without identifying the poem by its title, which even Robert may not then have known. The first Isa heard about a new work, in the letter from Robert of 29 December 1871, was only that he was 'half way thro' another poem of quite another kind'. On 25 January 1872, he wrote, 'Spite of all my ailments and bewailments I have just all but finished another poem of quite another kind, which shall amuse you in the Spring, I hope!' Two months later, on 30 March, he wrote to say, 'I have been hard at work, the poem *growing* under me, and seeming worth attending to: it is *almost* done: but I am very tired and bilious.'

Robert had been feeling under the weather for some three months. In January he had caught a cold from Pen, who had taken to his bed for two weeks, suffering also from a rheumatism that his father attributed to the 'hateful and to be hated' English climate, 'rainy and rainy again, till one is saturated even through brick walls, and by the fireside'. These miserable matters became worse: 'then, staying home on that account,

[I] got bilious, — then increased the cold — then added to the bile, — till I was sick of both, and nearly everything into the bargain.' Added to the exasperation of being 'really unwell', Robert had been 'bothered beside with no end of calls on my scraps of time'.[180] Pen continued to be unwell — 'very ill' indeed, 'confined to his room these five weeks' — and Robert himself endured being 'bilious and out of sorts' until, by 19 February, when he gave this invalidish report of conditions at Warwick Crescent to Isa, he seemed to be improving — although biliousness returned in March and he confessed himself 'very tired'. On 30 March he left London to spend a recuperative week with Lord and Lady Brownlow, Lady Marian Alford's son and daughter-in-law, at Belton, their house in Lincolnshire.[181] Pen, who was feeling very much better, went to Scotland for a month with Ernest Benzon.[182] In May, the Browning family took themselves off to stay with Lord Shrewsbury at Alton Towers for another respite.

Fifine at the Fair, when it was published on or about 4 June 1872, gave rise to some serious misunderstanding. If *Prince Hohenstiel-Schwangau* had been irritatingly enigmatic, *Fifine* was plainly perverse. The character of the 'fizgig' Fifine had been inspired by the sight, probably in 1865, of a 'fine fierce'[183] gypsy woman, an acrobatic rope-dancer, at the fair of St Gilles at Pornic. Into the carnival scene strolls handsome Don Juan, the narrator of the poem, and his spiritual, beautiful wife Elvire. This latter-day Lothario is a young man of the mid-nineteenth century, a Don Juan *de nos jours*, circumscribed in his activities by rigid middle-class moral conventions of respectability. In the course of their stroll on an autumn afternoon, Don Juan and Elvire visit the village fair, pass the church of St Gilles, cross a bridge, and walk along the sands to watch the sun set over the church of Sainte Marie. They walk on further, Don Juan wishing — for his own libidinal reasons — to look upon those Breton menhirs and dolmens of the district that had caught Robert's attention and prompted his description of them to Seymour Kirkup. When the couple reach home at twilight, Don Juan leaves the pale, ethereal Elvire and returns to the fair to dally with the dark, sensually beautiful gypsy girl Fifine, who had earlier caught his eye. Despite Don Juan's casuistical monologue — his subtle, insidiously ingenious defence of infidelity, of the fleeting charms and claims of the flesh, and of his desire for sexual freedom, for freedom itself — he inevitably forfeits, by his inconstancy, the constancy of Elvire's moral beauty and, by his deception, loses the deep pleasures of domestic happiness.

Robert had anticipated some difficulties with public appreciation of the poem, which he rated as his boldest and most metaphysical work since *Sordello*. What he had not bargained for was that he himself would immediately be publicly identified with Don Juan, his hero, as a devil's advocate in defence of the indefensible. What made matters worse was that Robert's Don Juan had put up a very good case for adultery, and that his lonely comeuppance at the end of the poem was nothing like as definitely emphatic as could have been desired. Worse, perhaps, the adulterer could be forgiven and redeemed by the wife he had betrayed. Robert and the poem, both, came in for some considerable critical and moral stick. The *Westminster Review* declared that *Fifine at the Fair* 'might just as well have been written in Sanscrit. There are such breaks, digressions, involutions, crabbed constructions, metaphysical hair-splitting, that reading becomes a positive fatigue.' *Fifine*, in short, was judged to be as obscure as *Sordello*. In those penetrable parts that the critics did find 'clear, ingenious and brilliantly illustrated', the apparent apologia for adultery was found 'questionable'.

Against this reaction, Robert privately and scornfully set two passages in Greek, written later in holograph on the manuscript of the poem before he gave it to the library of Balliol College; one, from the *Choephoroe* of Aeschylus, read: 'And reading this doubtful word he has dark night before his eyes, and he is nothing clearer by day' — to which he added, in plain English, 'if any of my critics had enough in him to make the application!'; the second, from the *Thesmophoriazusae* of Aristophanes, read: 'To what words are you turned, for a barbarian nature would not receive them. For bearing new words to the Scaeans you would spend them in vain.'[184]

Many have read much into *Fifine at the Fair*. It is undoubtedly a difficult poem, and, like all of Robert Browning's poetry, indubitably contains a great deal of subjective matter that can be interpreted biographically. From the thick, dense rope that Robert plaited, there is a great quantity of oakum to be picked. Some have reasonably perceived an expression of Robert's continuing desolation at the revelation of Shelley's philosophy of free love and callous treatment of his wife. In the character of the Byronic voluptuary Don Juan (who is also inspired by a character in a drama by Molière), they see Robert Browning. In the spiritual character of Elvire they see Elizabeth Barrett Browning, and in the butterfly fluttering over a sea-bather (an 'amphibian') they see a metaphysical, sun-suffused winged symbol of her soul — her psyche. In the seductive character of Fifine, they see the dark allure of the temptress Louisa, Lady Ashburton. In the tone of the poem, they discern a deep division between a longing to satisfy sexual desire and a repression or denial of lawless libido — an expression of Robert's own sensual, sexual frustration, no doubt. It is clear that Robert and Elizabeth had enjoyed a fully satisfactory sexual and spiritual life together, and in this sense of fulfilment on all emotional levels Elizabeth may be as much the sensual Fifine as she is the etiolated Elvire. *Fifine at the Fair* contains all these elements on such a basic level, but raises them, also, layer by layer, to the highest degree of personal reverie and poetic revelation.

Of course Robert is Don Juan; of course Elvire is Elizabeth; of course Louisa is Fifine. They are themselves and more, much more: they are archetypes of life and love, of modern morals and practical philosophy. The world is a carnival, its men and women merely players, moved by their material needs and their metaphysical aspirations. In the end, housebound and bored, aged and inactive, Don Juan sits waiting for death. He is visited in a sort of waking dream not by the vengeful and damning ghost of the Commendatore but by the gentle, forgiving spirit of Elvire, his lost wife, to whom he complains about the conditions and circumstances of his life since she left him.

> 'If you knew but how I dwelt down here!' quoth I:
> 'And was I so better off up here?' quoth She.
>
> ['Epilogue', ll. 23–4]

Together, Don Juan and Elvire — Robert and Elizabeth — compose an epitaph:

> 'What i' the way of final flourish? Prose? verse? Try!
> *Affliction sore long time he bore,* or, what is it to be?
> *Till God did please to grant him ease.* Do end!' quoth I:
> 'I end with — Love is all and Death is naught!' quoth She.
>
> ['Epilogue', ll. 29–32]

In the poem, Robert is plainly working out, almost cathartically, the relationship between himself, Elizabeth, and Louisa. He claims forgiveness. There was in his mind too, probably, another gaudy booth at this fair — the 'bigamous' betrayal of Robert's mother by his father, who had thought to remarry. Writing the poem did him good. It clarified, practically and philosophically, morally and metaphysically, the crisis of conscience he had suffered; it restored him to his senses; it brought balance to his thoughts and reaffirmed his fidelity to his wife. The sensual colour, the intellectual energy, the rhythms and energy of the poem — all these are evidence of a faithful widower's increasing confidence. The final affirmation, that 'Love is all and Death is naught', restores his zest for life until it is requited in death, in reunion with the beloved who is with and within God. For all the poem's dark mood, these are not the dispirited, black cinders of a man sitting by a burnt-out fire, sifting through the ashes of his life in hopes of a little warmth and comfort. Much of the darkness in Robert's soul was probably due to his long, enforced residence in bleak, black, gloomy London, denying himself for duty's sake the soft sensuality of Italian warmth and colour for which he so constantly longed and of which he wrote so often and so reminiscently to the Storys and to Isa.

Mrs Orr, who had been suspicious and censorious from the first of Robert's youthful admiration for a fair, probably figured any such carnal, carnival attractions as a temptation to immorality: if so, she was not — in her anticipation of the Don Juan finally emerging in *Fifine* — far wrong. The 'leaven of bitterness' she detected in the poem is attributed in her biography to a 'disturbing cause . . . of long standing'. She infers this cause to be the death of Elizabeth, and after publication of *Fifine* she is pleased to note that things quieten down, that the 'uncongenial mood of Mr Browning's mind' caused by the 'chemistry of human emotion' subsides as the poet 'learned to meet life as it offered itself to him with a more frank recognition of its good gifts, a more grateful response to them. He grew happier, hence more genial, as the years advanced.'[185]

This is Mrs Orr's gloss on circumstances about which, surely, gossip had informed her and close personal knowledge of her subject would have confirmed. The river of her biography glides past any reference to Lady Ashburton, stranding her like an oxbow, cutting her off like a meander, from the full flood. And, though there were to be fewer personal crises to shake him fundamentally, and though he could certainly be genial, Robert's temper did not notably mellow with age — indeed it would increasingly be liable to passionate eruptions. Nevertheless, it would be, as Mrs Orr suggests, a long time before Robert recognized the full extent of criticism to which publication of *Fifine* had exposed him. 'The belief conveyed in the letter to Miss Blagden that what proceeds from a genuine inspiration is justified by it, combined with the indifference to public opinion which had been engendered in him by its long neglect, made him slow to anticipate the results of external judgement, even where he was in some degree prepared to endorse them.'[186] Just as Don Juan could casuistically justify his activities as a lover, Robert could creatively justify his purity as a poet while also acknowledging the prevailing moral climate that might uncomprehendingly condemn him. But in the end there would inevitably be a reckoning.

The fall-out from *Fifine* was considerable. Louisa Ashburton considered herself for ever afterwards as a woman scorned. On 2 October 1871, Robert had washed his hands clean[187] of any prospect of what Elizabeth would have lightly referred to as 'some faint show of bigamy'. He had considered Lady Ashburton's proposal and had turned it down. The manner of his rejection and his reasons for it had been unfortunate, perhaps, or too directly declared. From Belton Robert wrote to Edie Story on 4 April 1872:

> I suppose that lady A[shburton]. did not suppress what she considered the capital point of her quarrel with me when she foamed out into the couple of letters she bespattered me with, — yet the worst she charged me with was, — having said that my heart was buried in Florence, and the attractiveness of a marriage with her lay in its advantage to Pen — two simple facts, — as I told her, — which I had never left her in ignorance about, for a moment, though that I ever paraded this in a gross form to anyone else is simply false; but had it been true, — does Hatty instantly practice impertinence on any friend of hers

who intends to make an ambitious or mercenary marriage? as for her devotion to Lady A., begetting this chivalrous ardour in her, — Lady A. has got plenty of friends quite as intimate, who never fancied for a moment that they were called on to fight her battles ... So now I have done with Hatty, for once and always.

Untangling these remarks, it seems clear that Louisa Ashburton had been less sensitive than Robert had expected when she was made to understand two principal points: his continuing devotion to the memory of Elizabeth and his constant commitment to the interests of Pen. But, as Elizabeth had noted on several occasions, Robert's way with men and women rarely pandered to their finer feelings and frequently offended their *amour propre*. His attempts to pay a graceful compliment often backfired. No offence was intended, but offence could easily be taken. And in Robert's poetry, his struggles towards objectivity in portraying character more often than not caused confusion that resulted in outrage. Just as what he had written was not always what was read, so what he said was not always what was heard.

An account, evidently garbled, plainly glossed, of what had transpired between Robert and Louisa had reached Hatty Hosmer — (possibly, Robert thought, by way of gossip from Mrs Sartoris, since she had in recent years fallen out with him), who had jumped fully-armed to the side of her heroine and goddess. Since Hatty had taken no trouble to ask Robert the truth of the matter, and to hear his side of things as readily as she had listened to Louisa's, she was henceforth cut forever out of Robert's life — 'so shall our relation be, and no otherwise, to the end of time'.[188] Robert himself had been discreet — his horror of being an object of gossip, of having his private life paraded for the amusement of others, was by now ingrained. Besides, embarrassment is a much underrated emotion. He was advised by the Storys to keep Louisa Ashburton's intemperate letters and others relevant to the matter in case of any future difficulty. A breach of promise suit was not likely, perhaps, but best to be on the safe side and refrain from committing useful evidence to the coals of a fire at Warwick Crescent.

To Edie Story, in his letter of 1 January 1872, Robert had considered himself well out of the imbroglio: 'The whole business has turned out too blessedly for me to much concern myself as to how it happened, and by means of whom.' Nevertheless, it still rankled in the noses of Louisa and her partisans. Louisa continued for two years to try to bring Robert round. He was having none of it. To William Story he wrote on 19 June 1886 to acknowledge the return of some copies of letters and, in this connection, to re-state his own well-founded position: a denial of the gossiping charge that it was he who had tried to renew the relationship with Louisa, and a rehearsal of her true character as he had subsequently discovered it to be. These letters were still painful, and difficult to re-read:

> Had I mustered courage enough to look at the originals — undisturbed in their repose of fourteen years since I copied them for you — I should probably have given neither you nor myself further trouble in the matter — but my memory was hazy as to the precise charge which I intended they should meet — and fancied they were more than they proved to be — a simple answer to the assertion (if it was really made) that I had been making endeavours to renew a relation of even ordinary acquaintance, instead of resisting cajoleries and pathetic appeals, for two years together, that I should do so. As bearing on the writer's veracity this was evidence enough. And even with respect to the calumnies which Lady A. exploded in all the madness of her wounded vanity — I was not aware at that time of what I have had abundant knowledge of since — how thoroughly her character as a calumniator was understood by those most intimately connected with her — and how little credit would be given to assertions of this sort in my case ...
> I found that her nearest relatives had undergone precisely similar treatment.

Nothing could shake Robert's distrust or soften his dislike of Lady Ashburton. The sight of her in society was inevitable, but close contact was to be avoided. To the Storys, on 9 June 1874, he had written: 'I see every now and then that contemptible Lady Ashburton, and mind her no more than any other black beetle — so long as it don't crawl up my sleeve.'

In *Two Robert Brownings?* Maisie Ward quotes a letter dated 15 June

1888 from Lord Acton to his daughter. Even nineteen years after the episode between Robert and Louisa Ashburton at Loch Luichart, the matter remained of the greatest interest to anyone who had ever heard of it: 'I find I was wrong about R. Browning and Lady Ashburton. He asked her to marry him about ten years ago. She refused, and he went away to Italy. Then she asked him to come back. He came, and they were engaged. Suddenly she broke off, and sent Hamilton Aïdé for her letters. Browning returned all but one, which he said he would keep till he died, that he might have a defence against her — a thing scarcely excusable under any imaginable circumstances. This explains the fury of her language about him last night: it was a storm unappeased.' The chronology and just about everything else in this letter is wrong, but Acton had got his information from Louisa in a tempest at the dinner table. Her passionate rage against Robert was unabated and would remain unappeased: it was matched by Robert's, though he kept his mouth shut in public and reserved his fury and his fire for poetry.

It is suggested, with no convincing contradiction, that Louisa Ashburton is evoked, dreadfully, in some lines from the 'With Daniel Bartoli' section of *Parleyings with Certain People*, published in January 1887, and that she is vanquished with the concluding lines that invoke Elizabeth's reviving power:

> Who bade you come, brisk-marching bold she-shape,
>   A terror with those black-balled worlds of eyes
> That black hair bristling solid-built from nape
>   To crown it coils about? O dread surmise!
> Take, tread on, trample under past escape
>   Your capture, spoil and trophy! Do — devise
> Insults for one who, fallen once, ne'er shall rise! [ll. 287–93]
> . . .
> Black eyes, black every wicked inch of those
>   Limbs' war-tower tallness: so much truth lives there
> 'Neath the dead heap of lies. [ll. 324–7]
> . . .
> Some day, and soon, be sure himself will rise,
>   Called into life by her who long ago
> Left his soul whiling time in flesh-disguise.

> Ghosts, tired of waiting can play tricks you know!
> Tread, trample me — such sport we ghosts devise,
>   Waiting the morn-star's reappearance — though
> You think we vanish scared by cock's crow? [ll. 336–42]

By 19 August 1872, in the aftermath of the disappointing reception given to *Fifine*, Robert was in St Aubin-sur-Mer. Writing to Isa on that date, he breathed a little easier: 'Dear Milsand is here, and the sea, and a rough little house, and that's all and quite enough.' At St Aubin, Robert mended a friendship that had cooled between himself and Anne Thackeray on account of some speculations she had made in public about his marriage prospects. She happened then to be staying nearby at Lion-sur-Mer. Sarianna, who had not been well, seemed the better for her holiday. Pen was in Scotland, blazing away with his guns and walking prodigious distances in search of something to kill: 'so I suppose his rheumatism has disappeared', was Robert's comment.

By 19 September, Robert and Sarianna were at Fontainebleau and Pen, in addition to shooting, had been 'riding and dancing the Eightsome Reel' in Scotland and driving in a pony-chaise that came to grief at the foot of a bridge over a ravine, with the result that Pen was tumbled out over the bridge and through a tree which broke his fall. There was news, too, of Willie Bracken, who had married and rewarded his mother for her pains exactly as Robert had realistically expected: 'the sooner *he* breaks his neck, the better'.[189]

Robert's short letter to Isa on 1 November 1872 was the last: she died on 28 January 1873. After her death, some of her poems were collected together and Alfred Austin — that 'literary cad',[190] who had become a friend of Isa's in 1865 — was invited to edit them. He agreed to prepare an edition and preface it with a memoir, the book to be financed by a subscription to which Robert was invited to contribute. Anything with which Alfred Austin was connected was anathema to Robert, who — despite his long and intimate friendship with Isa — refused to have anything to do with the project. To Madame Mazini, the friend in Florence who had looked after Isa at the end, he wrote savagely on 5 June 1873:

> I am sure you mean nothing but kindness to Isa Blagden's memory, and kindness to myself also, in the scheme of repub-

lishing her poems and in this application to add my name to
the subscription-list . . . I shall only assure you as briefly but as
emphatically as I can, that I will be no party to the association
of a dearly-loved name with that of Mr Alfred Austin. When
the book is perpetrated, — I *may* buy it, and, by help of penknife
and ink-blotting, purify and render it fit to be read — for so
I understand the 'mark of friendship' you expect of me.[191]

Alfred Austin, a diminutive literary critic of small poetic ability, had
already sunk his little rodent teeth into Tennyson, estimating him as
third-rate, before he had turned to attack Robert Browning, whose grey
hairs, he wrote in the June 1869 number of *Temple Bar*, would last just
about as long as the 'trumpery tinsel wreath' stuck on his head by 'small
London coteries, and large London salons'. The assault was as risible as
a rat jumping at a Rottweiler, but the bite still stung and there was a
danger of secondary infection. Then, too, the rat was persistent. Any
chance he could get, Austin was in with a fast nip, niggling and back-
biting, defiling and defaming the serious work of Robert's lifetime,
denigrating it as prose dressed up as poetry. Finally, enraged beyond
endurance, Robert picked up his heaviest and most lethal weapon —
a poem. In 1876, loading his sling with a work entitled 'Of Pacchiarotto,
and How He Worked in Distemper' — a wittily punning title — Robert
let fly not only at Austin but at the whole seething, crawling, pullulating
tribe of critics who had so long beset him and his best efforts and his
most honest intentions.

Justifying the Byronic venom of 'Pacchiarotto', Robert wrote of
Austin, 'He has been flea-biting me for many years past in whatever
rag of a newspaper he could hop into.' To George Barrett, in May 1875,
he remarked:

> Whenever there is a funny piece of raving against me in a
> newspaper you may be sure my little bug of an Austin is biting
> his best . . . 'Dwarfs', Dickens tells us, 'are mostly sarcy —' and
> if this particular Quilp gets any good, beside the penny-a-line,
> out of his 'sarce,' he has my full leave: but even dwarfs need
> not be blackguardly: and this one has a trick of 'giving an
> instance of Mr Browning's unintelligible stuff' which he makes
> so indeed by altering my words to his own, — leaving out a

whole line, for instance, and joining two broken ends! He did this in the 'World' a fortnight ago. In the same article he said 'my whole poem [*Aristophanes' Apology*] was a transcript from Jowett' — whom I have not seen these four years, and who never opened his mouth on that, or any other subject of the same sort, in his whole life: All this bug-juice from a creature *I* never saw in my life, and whose scribblings, except when they related to myself, I never read a line of! But — as the poet sings —

Who would be satirical
On a thing so very small?

In a letter to Edmund Gosse, on 19 August 1876, Robert gave chapter and verse from his works for particular misquotations and misrepresentations Austin had made in critical articles, and after this careful nitpicking launched into a flood of vituperation against Austin, who stood no more than five feet tall but whose tiny, Tom Thumb stature was compensated for by a colossal egotism: 'One particular piece of blackguardism headed "Men of Letters: R. B" — could only save its author from a kicking by the charitable hope that he was too small for that treatment. I never was unlucky enough to set eyes on the man: if he *is* physically as well as morally and intellectually a dwarf — you may be sure I should have considered him a pygmy had his stature been that of Goliath.'

There were some who doubted the wisdom of this kind of poetic flyting and deplored the poet's loss of dignity in such brutal abuse. One of these was Alfred Domett, who had returned to London in February 1872. Domett had been away in New Zealand for thirty years — and had to ask who Austin was: 'A scurvy little fellow who always abuses me' replied Robert.[192] News of Browning, though evidently not of Austin, had penetrated to the Antipodes, and in the absence of any first-hand information, Domett had kept up with his old friend's career through newspapers and magazines. Fresh in London, he had only an address that, for all he knew, might be out of date, but he turned up anyway on the doorstep at 19 Warwick Crescent on the last day of the month.

Robert was not at home, but Sarianna was, and presently she came hurrying down the stairs, looking not very much altered after thirty years.[193] There was 'an emphatic exclamation "Mr Domett!"', for Mr Domett it was, in the prosperous flesh. He was speedily introduced to Pen, who 'seemed a frank amiable young fellow, with his mother's arched eyebrows and grey eyes'. The next day, Sarianna wrote to invite Domett to lunch rather than dinner on 4 March, Robert being, she explained, 'a man of many engagements and unfortunately is engaged every evening next week'.[194] Delivered, too, the same day, was a note from Robert: 'How very happy I am that I shall see you again! . . . come and let us begin all over again.'

To Isa, on 30 April 1872, Robert had written: '*Waring* came back the other day, after thirty years absence, the same as ever — nearly: he has been prime minister in New Zealand for a year and a half, but gets tired, and returns home with a poem [*Ranolf and Amohia*, published by Smith and Elder at Domett's own expense].' Domett had written to Robert on the occasion of Elizabeth's death, but had received no reply. In exculpation, Robert said that he had carried the letter 'always about with me abroad in order to muster up courage some day which never came: it was too hard to begin and end with all that had happened during the last thirty years.'[195]

More to the point, perhaps, was that Robert had had other things to think about than 'What's become of Waring?'; and the difficulty of relating 'What's become of Browning?' had been too immense to tell in one letter when there had been so many other letters, much more pressing and necessary, to write. Then, too, except for the long-term habit of his monthly letters to Isa, Robert was not much inclined to unnecessary correspondence, and so the friendship with Domett had lapsed. Now it was somewhat revived.

The use by Robert of '*Waring*' rather than Domett in the letter to Isa may have been psychologically telling. Park Honan, in *The Book, the Ring and the Poet*, humorously makes a case for Robert's constant evasion of Domett, his continual giving the slip to a worthy-enough man who was inclined to stick with a dog-like devotion to his old friend. When Domett called at the house, Robert was out. When the Brownings went on holiday for several weeks in September 1872, Robert left no word for Domett. It might well have seemed bathetic to Robert that Domett should have returned at all. The point of his poem, 'Waring', was that the eponymous subject had definitively departed. He'd given everyone the slip, and who'd have guessed it? Waring, no matter how much missed, however much regretted, however much one might give for a day of his company, had gone. The old Waring was irretrievable. Waring had become mythical, a man invested with the dreams and fantasies of everyone he had left behind in London. Waring! —

> And so he went off, as with a bound,
> Into the rosy and golden half
> O' the sky, to overtake the sun
> And reach the shore, like the sea-calf
> Its singing cave. [ll.251–5]
>
> . . .
>
> Look East, where whole new thousands are!
> In Vishnu-land, what Avatar? [ll. 261–2]

And now here was Waring, no mistake, large as life and 'the same as ever — nearly'; as respectable and solid in his early success as a farmer as in his more recent reputation as a colonial statesman, as physically present and persistent in his late ambition as an epic poet as in his black boots, sober frock coat, and glossy top hat walking the London streets again with a furled umbrella.

On 9 December 1875, Alfred called on Robert who, despite being house-bound with a bad cold that had caused some hoarseness, seems — on the evidence of Domett's diary entry for that day — to have been as talkative as usual. The conversation touched on the poetry of the Pre-Raphaelites and Robert said that he 'did not much admire Rossetti's poetry; "hated all affectation". We laughed at the cant about the "delicate harmony" of his rhymes about the "Haymarket" which Swinburne affects to think beautiful. Browning quoted Buchanan's parody or imitation of them, adding a line or two of his own similarly rhymed — such as "But grog would be sweeter, And stronger and warmer, etc."'.[196] Beneath this bonhomous literary humour, however, lay a stratum of poetic tragedy: between them, Robert Browning and Robert Buchanan had all but driven Dante Gabriel Rossetti mad.

Fifine at the Fair had mostly, perhaps principally, dealt to Robert's satisfaction with the difficulty over Louisa Ashburton's proposal, though the poem had done nothing to appease the lady herself when she read it. But *Fifine* had a secondary effect: when Rossetti read it, knowing little or nothing of its true inspirations and intentions, he identified it as an attack upon himself. They had been friends for years, Robert and Rossetti; they had not often met, but when they did — in London, Paris, and Italy — it had been with the utmost cordiality. Rossetti greatly valued what he regarded as his intimacy with 'the glorious Robert' and his acquaintance with Robert's family and friends. Rossetti greatly admired, too, *Men and Women* and *The Ring and the Book* — there were elements in both books that spoke to him of his own pleasures and pains, of his gains and losses, so that he felt more than a friendship with Robert; he experienced a comforting kinship, a profound poetic and emotional fellow-feeling.

It was all the more wounding, therefore, when Rossetti received a copy of *Fifine* from Robert and perceived in it, when he read the poem on 4 June 1872, a plain attack upon himself and his own poem, 'Jenny', which had been obsessively written and rewritten between 1847 and 1870 — allowing for a gap of some seven years during which it had lain in the earth with the body of his wife, Elizabeth Siddal, tucked 'between her cheek and her beautiful hair'. Persuaded by friends and his own desires to retrieve 'Jenny' and the rest of his then unpublished poems, the coffin was disinterred in 1869. After this grisly exhumation of the rotting manuscripts, Rossetti came to feel that his work was cursed. Neither chloral nor whisky could console his conscience, so that by the end of 1871 he was sodden with drugs and drink, corroded by guilt, and suffused with a self-loathing which convinced him that there was a conspiracy 'to hound him from the society of honest men'.

Rossetti was in a condition of mind, therefore, to find verification of a conspiracy theory in the coincidence of two things: first, an attack on the sensuality of his work by Robert Buchanan, initially in an article entitled 'The Fleshly School of Poetry', published under the pseudonym 'Thomas Maitland' in the *Contemporary Review* for October 1871, and then amplified in a pamphlet, *The Fleshly School of Poetry, and Other Phenomena of the Day*, published in May 1872; secondly, the character of the 'hero' in *Fifine at the Fair*, who — not unreasonably — can be compared with the young monologist of Rossetti's own poem, who picks up Jenny, a pretty young prostitute, at a dancehall and spends the night with her in her lodgings — though all he does is soliloquize while Jenny sleeps with her head on his knees and in the morning, after putting some gold in her hair, leaves with an innocent and compassionate heart. Buchanan identified the young man with Rossetti himself and, in his personal vindication in an article, 'The Stealthy School of Criticism', in the December 1871 issue of the *Athenaeum*, Rossetti seems to have accepted Buchanan's identification.[197]

There are symbols and situations, characters and circumstances, in *Fifine* that Rossetti interpreted as being similar to those not only in 'Jenny' but also in 'The Blessed Damozel' (republished in 1870) and that struck him as confirming the condemnatory attitude Buchanan had adopted. In particular, according to Rossetti's niece, Helen Rossetti Angeli, one line in the epilogue to *Fifine* pierced Rossetti to the heart — 'Darker arts that almost struck despair in me?'. This, he thought, referred directly to his avid interest in spiritualism and his attempts to make mediumistic contact with his wife. To his clouded mind wrapped in despair, to his aching heart grieved by his loss, to his guilty conscience that perceived, solipsistically, any relevant reference as a piece of mud thrown at him by an ill-disposed society, it must have seemed that Browning and Buchanan had conspired to hound him, humiliate him, and punish him for his sins.

Robert cannot entirely be acquitted of blame in this episode. Though he did not go so far as Buchanan, who spoke — on Tennyson's word — of the 'filthiness' of Rossetti's poetry, it is pointed out that Robert had written to Isa on 19 June 1870 of his dislike of the 'effeminancy of Rossetti's school of poetry', of its '*scented*' quality and its deliberate archaisms, and to Alfred Domett, in the context of the Pre-Raphaelite style, he had spoken brutally of how he hated 'all affectations'. Though Robert did not rate Buchanan's poetry too highly, he mostly took his side during the Buchanan-Rossetti literary dispute of late 1871 — at which time he was writing *Fifine*. It is not unreasonable to suppose that the feud jogged his mind and may have brought back some memories of having read 'Jenny', and that Rossetti's work may have influenced him, if only subconsciously. Robert was never an imitator of anyone, far less a plagiarist; but — like any writer — he had acquired the habit of picking up, perfectly unconsciously, and brushing up, equally unconsciously, whatever literary flotsam and jetsam, shreds and shards of information, had glinted at the corner of his mind's eye and had been stored away in his head for future reference.

It can be said with confidence, however, that when Robert sent *Fifine* to Rossetti, he did so oblivious of any injury it might cause. He had nothing against Rossetti personally, beyond a distaste for his poetry, that came even remotely close to the hatred he nursed against the person of Alfred Austin. At most, Robert was perhaps insensitive and thoughtless — though probably he was not fully aware of the deep damage that Rossetti had been doing to himself and its paranoid consequences. Rossetti's brother, William Michael Rossetti, did not believe that *Fifine* was intended to harm Dante Gabriel, who had become half-crazed and delusional — in 1876, he even took Lewis Carroll's *The Hunting of the Snark* as a personal attack. In addition to breaking off a friendship with Robert that had lasted a quarter of a century, Rossetti also broke his close friendship with Swinburne. His hostility, which remained mostly impenetrable to Robert, who soon got tired of Rossetti's resentful insolence, continued for the rest of his life, for the ten years remaining to him until his death in 1882.

In May 1872, Robert had turned sixty years of age. Maisie Ward, whose psychological assessments of Robert Browning remain reliable, believes that a 'considerable change took place somewhere around his sixtieth year, 1872 . . . several of his best and worst poems lie on each side of a year that marks a beginning of dullness rather than mere occasional obscurity, a partial loss of vision accompanied by a wearisome ratiocination undermining his own profoundest philosophy of love through knowledge . . . As a whole, I would take *Fifine* as marking the divide between greatness and decline.'[196]

At St Aubin, in the summer of 1872, Robert conceived a new poem, dedicated to Anne Thackeray who had suggested its title — *Red Cotton Night-Cap Country; or Turf and Towers* — in which Robert altered the original white of the cotton that was used for local bonnets to a more dramatic red. Its plot had been brought to his attention by Joseph Milsand. The story had seized Robert so much that he had begun energetically to research it there and then. On 19 September, in his letter from Fontainebleau to Isa, he had crowed: 'I bring back with me, for winter-work in London, a capital brand-new subject for my next poem.' To Alfred Domett, in London, he said, 'I have got *such* a subject for a poem, if I can do justice to it.' After his return to London, Robert sat down on 1 December 1872 to write it in such a fervour that its 4,247 lines were accomplished by 23 January 1873. *Red Cotton Night-Cap Country* was published by Smith and Elder in the first week of May 1873. Writing to T. J. Nettleship on 16 May 1889, Robert described the genesis of the poem:

> I heard, first of all, the merest sketch of the story on the spot. Milsand told me that the owner of the house had destroyed himself from remorse at having behaved unfilially to his mother. In a subsequent visit (I paid one every year while Milsand lived there) he told me some other particulars, and they at once struck me as likely to have been occasioned by religious con- siderations as well as passionate woman-love, — and I con- cluded there was no intention of committing suicide; and I said at once that I would myself treat the subject *just* so.
>
> Afterward he procured me the legal documents, I collected the accounts current among the people of the neighbourhood, inspected the house and grounds, and convinced myself that I had guessed rightly enough in every respect. Indeed the facts are so exactly put down, that, in order to avoid the possibility of prosecution for Libel — that is, telling the exact truth — I changed all the names of persons and places, as they stood in the original 'Proofs,' and gave them as they are to be found in Mrs Orr's Handbook.

Red Cotton Night-Cap Country was another poem derived from the files of the police-court. Robert's partiality for this sort of yellow press shocker was quite to the taste, too, of G. K Chesterton, who regarded Robert as 'one of those wise men who can perceive the terrible and impressive poetry of the police-news, which is commonly treated as vulgarity, which is dreadful and may be undesirable, but is certainly not vulgar. From *The Ring and the Book* to *Red Cotton Night-Cap Country* a great many of his books may be called magnificent detective stories.'[199] Chesterton admits that the story Robert had taken up 'is somewhat ugly, and its power does not alter its ugliness, for power can only make ugliness uglier.' There arose an almost unanimous chorus that this time Robert had served up a dish that obliged his readers to sup full, and once too often, with horrors; that here, more than in *The Ring and the Book*, was pure perversity dressed up as poetic truth.

The title, *Red Cotton Night-Cap Country*, seemed innocuous — a bedtime story for children, perhaps, though readers of Browning's verse by now should have been wary of letting down their guard. The poem begins quietly enough, evoking the 'apparent innocence and primitive simplicity and other quiet-seeming qualities of the white-cotton-capped inhabitants of that part of France'[200] that Robert and Anne Thackeray had agreeably remarked in their conversations together, 'while all the time such a tragical series of events, of the *bonnet-rouge* style had occurred at a Chateau in sight. "His poem had terrible things in it,"' Robert said.[201]

The suggested somnolence of the landscape of northern France is shattered in Robert's poem by the suicide of a Parisian jeweller, Léonce Miranda, who throws himself from his high tower to the turf below. The act itself, the violent moment, was not very interesting to Robert — he could leave Tennyson and others to wring such incidents dry of dramatic images and poetic metaphor; the motives that lay behind it, the state of mind that had precipitated the act, were more significant and provided a field on which Robert could lay out his multi-coloured carpet of ideas about love and sex, religion and redemption, community and culture. Critics point to Robert's love for the realistic novel and his devotion in particular to Balzac. *Red Cotton Night-Cap Country* is a realistic — almost a naturalistic — novel in blank verse.

The sub-title, *Turf and Towers*, acquires a metaphysical meaning. Miranda's life is divided between sacred and profane love, between aspirations to the spiritual life, symbolized by the tower of his home that he has adorned with the finest examples of art, and the earthy life of the flesh, represented by the turf to which he falls when he steps off his own tower in the expectation of a miracle that will save him — a belief that angels will catch him in mid-air and transport him to the tower of La Ravissante, which contains a statue of the Virgin decked with the brilliant jewels he has given her. Miranda is generally regarded by locals as insane for having put his whole faith in the Virgin:

'Angels would take him!' Mad! [l. 3603]

The narrator of the poem, who can be taken to be Robert, contrarily reckons Miranda to be of sound mind and to have acted in accordance with his belief. He shows that black is white, and — further — that white is red:

> No! sane, I say.
> Such being the conditions of his life,
> Such end of life was not irrational.
> Hold a belief, you only half-believe,
> With all-momentous issues either way, —
> And I advise you imitate this leap,
> Put faith to proof, be cured or killed at once!
> Call you men, killed through cutting cancer out,
> The worse for such an act of bravery?
> Better lie prostrate on his turf at peace,
> Than, wistful, eye, from out the tent, the tower,
> Racked with a doubt. [ll. 3604–15]

The poem was based on the actual suicide of a jeweller, Antoine Mellerio, in Normandy in 1870, and a subsequent court case in 1872 contesting the suicide's will, which bequeathed a life interest in his property to his mistress and the rest to the Church, on the grounds of insanity. The court upheld Mellerio's sanity and confirmed the will. Mellerio's plunge from the tower on his own property was so recent, and still so sore in living memory, that publication of the poem was postponed for a short time so that the real names of the characters, which Robert had recklessly used in his original text, could be changed — at the insistence of George Murray Smith and on the legal advice of Sir John Duke Coleridge, the Attorney-General[202] — to avoid possible libel. General Robert Cumming Schenk, a lawyer, assured Robert that 'he would give me a Bill of Indemnity against any results in America'.[203]

It was these circumstances, perhaps (though Robert had 'gone through the whole poem, softening the roughnesses, and taking out all direct sting'[204]), that gave *Red Cotton Night-Cap Country* the raw contemporaneity which, quite as much as the sordid subject-matter, shocked readers and repulsed critics. The Mellerio case as the source of the poem was instantly recognizable: the *Athenaeum* commented in its issue of 10 May 1873: 'It is upon this well-known story of violence, called in France the Mellerio Debacher case, that Mr Browning's poem is based, and the disguise is so thin that it would be false delicacy in us if, being well acquainted with the facts of a story so easily accessible in the French law reports, we should follow Mr Browning in his alteration of names.'

William Clyde DeVane states that 'The poem was generally disliked ... *The Daily News* for May 5 expressed best the general opinion, that the theme and motive of the poem were outside the sphere of true and healthy art. [Richard] Hutton, the editor of the Spectator, told Domett that he did not think there was a single line of poetry in *Red Cotton Night-Cap Country*.'[205] DeVane himself recoils with a shudder from the poem, from the 'vulgar, contemporary' story on which it was based, and from 'the figures of a diseased man and a most ordinary woman for hero and heroine'; and he cannot resist quoting Carlyle, who, according to an entry for 12 May 1873 in William Allingham's *Diary*, remarked that 'there are "ingenious remarks here and there; but nobody out of Bedlam ever before thought of choosing such a theme"'. The next day, with what sounds like *esprit de l'escalier*, Carlyle made the famously witty but disobliging observation that quickly circulated among the literary coteries and social salons: 'Browning *will* very likely do [the Tichborne] Claimant by and by ... and call it *Gammon and Spinach* perhaps.'

Red Cotton Night-Cap Country contained a brief character study that was a generous tribute to Joseph Milsand. DeVane seizes upon this with relief as a 'noble expression of friendship'.[206] Robert's normally indulgent biographers W. Hall Griffin and H.C. Minchin regard it, 'so far as character is concerned, the sole relief in a desert of moral ugliness'.[207]

In her biography, Mrs Orr expresses some minor stylistic criticism of *Red Cotton Night-Cap Country*, but avoids any extended discussion of the subject matter and refrains from moral judgements: she concludes, as though briskly snapping a cotton thread between her teeth, that Robert's 'poetic imagination, no less than his human insight, was amply vindicated by his treatment of the story'.[208] It is only fair to add that, in an unpublished review, Mrs Orr defended the morality of the poem. In his lifetime, Robert looked to her not only as a supportive ally and constant friend, but also as a conscientious critic and a just moral arbiter.

Without having seen her review, Robert was confident that Mrs Orr's 'notion of the morality of the poem, — which I need no examination to accept as fair and favourable'[209] might be 'put in evidence' against charges in the *Daily News* that the poem lay beyond the sphere of what critics considered to be true and healthy art.

Mrs Orr was born Alexandra Leighton (the sister of Frederic, later Lord Leighton) in St Petersburg in 1828 and was named after her godmother, the Empress Alexandra. She and Robert had first met in Paris in 1855, two years before her marriage to Colonel Sutherland Orr, who died just months later in 1858. According to Edward McAleer's account, 'In 1869 she settled in London and became in the course of the years Browning's confidential friend. According to Thomas Hardy, some of Browning's friends believed "that there was something tender between Mrs Orr and Browning. 'Why don't they settle it?' said Mrs Procter." . . . Julian Hawthorne described her as "a little creature in black: her fingers and shoulders jerked nervously, her face twitched, her forehead was bulbous, her eyes very far apart; she was an intellectual woman, a Positivist, but told me she had been forbidden by her doctor to use her brain; when one looked her in the face, her eyes seemed to rush away to right and left: she adjured me not to write at night — else I would perish in my youth." . . . In 1881 she generously supported the Browning Society; in 1885 she published her *Handbook to the Works of Robert Browning*; and in 1891 she published her *Life and Letters of Robert Browning*.'[210] Mrs Orr died in 1903.

Like Maisie Ward, Mrs Orr noticed a change in or about 1872, though in more positive mood she judges the years following *The Ring and the Book* to be 'the fullest in Mr Browning's life; it was that in which the varied claims made by it on his moral, and above all his physical energies, found in him the fullest power of response'.[211] Robert rose early and went to bed late — 'this, however, never from choice'; he filled 'every hour of the day with work or pleasure', being alternately sucked into the whirlpool of London society and then thrown out into the 'fashionable routine of country-house visiting'. Though tiring, these activities fuelled, says Mrs Orr, 'the imaginative curiosity of the poet' and fulfilled 'for a while the natural ambition of the man'. These were 'social experiences which brought grist to his mill'.[212]

At this time, in a companionable, unromantic friendship with Annie

Egerton Smith, Robert was plunging himself into music in London just as he had taken to studying and collecting pictures in Florence, drawing with his father at the Louvre in Paris, and learning to model in clay under the tutelage of William Wetmore Story in Rome. Robert never took to a new art half-heartedly or revived an interest in an old one without a passionate commitment. He had neglected serious attention to music for years (music lessons and occasional concert-going with Pen hardly counted in this regard), but 'now,' says Mrs Orr, 'in addition to the large social tribute which he received, and had to pay, he was drinking in all the enjoyment, and incurring all the fatigue which the London musical world could create for him . . . It would scarcely be an exaggeration to say that he attended every important concert of the season . . . His frequent companion on such occasions was Miss Egerton-Smith' [sic], whose carriage regularly rolled up to Warwick Crescent to transport the poet with his friend to a concert. Betty Miller suggests that the bond of music between Robert and Annie Egerton Smith recalled the mutual interest in music that had existed between Robert and his mother.[213]

Robert and Annie Egerton Smith had first met through Isa Blagden and her friend Annette Bracken in Florence, but there was another synchronous association that reached far back into Robert's youth: the Egerton Smiths had been close friends of the Flower family and of William Johnson Fox. Annie Egerton Smith was no great beauty like Louisa Ashburton, no serious intellect like Julia Wedgwood, and no judicious critic of art and literature like Mrs Orr. Her mind was a little narrow and her responses were a little slow; her frame was tall, spare, and often racked with neuralgia; her facial expression was earnest. She was a rich woman through part-ownership of an important provincial newspaper, the *Liverpool Echo*, and her proprietorial influence there gave prominence to any article, news item, or feature that was well disposed towards Robert Browning and his works. Her nature is said to have been shy, almost reclusive; but in Annie Egerton Smith Robert found not merely an informed enthusiast for the finest music, but additional sympathetic qualities of quietness and goodness that endeared her to him. In Annie, Robert perhaps also found a companion more restful than others of his acquaintance: a woman who lived the retiring life for which he himself often longed.

Maisie Ward remarks on Robert's perplexing contradictions and inconsistencies:

Any one of us introspective enough to analyze his own moods would realize how often they change. And in the thoughtful and the sensitive such changes can be bewildering ... So it was with Browning who had, like [Cardinal] Newman, a deeply intuitive outlook, an intense sensitivity. His wife compared his feelings to the black and white of a chessboard. He could long for Florence yet never return there, could hate London and linger on, could feel that not even an angel's bidding would drag him to a country house yet thoroughly enjoy himself at Belton, Loch Luichart, or Hatfield. 'Frenetic to be free' in one mood, he would in another fasten on himself the bonds of society.'[214]

Mrs Orr makes much the same point: 'The conviction renewed itself with the close of every season, that the best thing which could happen to him would be to be left quiet at home; and his disinclination to face even the idea of moving equally hampered his sister in her endeavour to make timely arrangements for their change of abode.'[215] Robert went gadding about as usual, cramming two or three engagements into an evening when one would have been enough for any man, and the result — which worried Mrs Orr, who saw him frequently and observed him closely — was that 'each winter brought its searching attack of cough and cold; each summer reduced him to the state of nervous prostration or physical apathy ... which at once rendered change imperative, and the exertion of seeking it almost intolerable'. Even on holiday in the early 1870s, Robert worked almost obsessively and allowed himself no respite: 'Mr Browning subsequently admitted that he sometimes, during these years, allowed active literary occupation to interfere too much with the good which his holiday might have done him: but the temptations to literary activity were this time too great to be withstood.'[216] Robert's own letters confirm this diagnosis.

Anne Thackeray, to whom *Red Cotton Night-Cap Country* had been dedicated, felt — though she expressed her feelings so delicately and allusively that they mystified Robert — personally tarred by her association with a poem that had been piously savaged in a review in the

Daily News of 5 May 1873 by a Mrs Trimmer, who inquired 'whether psychological puzzles are fit subjects for poetry, or whether explorations in the mournful phantom-haunted borderland between Illusion and Guilt are the best exercises of the poet's genius'.[217] Robert took some trouble to mollify Anne Thackeray, and in a letter reminded her that if anyone was being got at, it was principally the poet himself. Nothing new in that: 'everybody this thirty years has given me his kick and gone on his way'.

His next poem, *Aristophanes' Apology*, kicked back. It would be, as Park Honan characterizes it, 'a theoretical defence of his excursion among naturalistic horrors'. As with most of Robert's longer poems, it is difficult to date, though most of it seems to have been written, if we are to take Robert's word in the manuscript as accurate, on holiday at Mers in Picardy between mid-August and early November 1874. Parts of the work, particularly the 'Herakles' section within the poem, had been completed by 17 June 1873, and the 'Thamuris Marching' lines had also been written earlier. The poem, published on 15 April 1875, finally amounted to 5,711 lines of mainly blank verse.

Aristophanes' Apology, Including a Transcript from Euripides; Being the Last Adventure of Balaustion cannily reintroduces the popular character of Balaustion of Rhodes. She has things to say to the dramatist Aristophanes, who, slightly drunk, has burst in on Balaustion and her husband to discuss the merits or otherwise of the tragedian Euripides, news of whose recent death had just reached them. Balaustion's husband takes notes of the debate between his wife and Aristophanes in which she more than holds her ground in defence of Euripides. The poem has been generally regarded as — in Swinburne's judgement — 'a libel on Aristophanes', and, as DeVane puts it, 'an erudite, garrulous piece of special pleading for Euripides against his mocker Aristophanes'. But Robert himself protested to Swinburne that he 'was no enemy of that Aristophanes — all on fire with invention, — and such music! I am confident that Euripides bore his fun and parodying good humouredly enough ... but a friend of Euripides, — above all a woman friend, — feels no such need of magnanimity: when I had done with her, I had *all but* done with anything like enmity to him.'[218]

The critical comparison between the works of Aristophanes and Euripides in *Aristophanes' Apology* is partly a vehicle for Robert's speculation on a new type of poetry and drama. Just as the poet Browning had resisted the conventions of poetry, so the dramatist Euripides had become dissatisfied with the limitations imposed by the division of drama into tragic and comic and had thought to make experiments in combining them. Robert's own innovations in the form of the dramatic monologue had been startlingly novel. His first thinking on the subject of progress in poetic form had been put forward, as a sort of manifesto, in his 'Essay on Shelley', in which he had questioned the standard critical division of poetry into the subjective and the objective. The poet, like a craftsman in precious metals forges a perfect shield of gold and silver, might combine the subjective and objective in a wondrous and beautiful form that displays both to perfection. *Aristophanes' Apology*, while appealing to other poets to take up the challenge where Robert Browning himself leaves off, is itself as far as Robert himself could go in the form he had begun to create. It is the last of Robert's great, innovative long dramatic monologues.

Euripides, recognizing the need for change in his own times and his own art, had also attempted a new literary form, a drama that

> Fain would paint, manlike, actual human life,
> Make veritable men think, say and do. [ll. 1312–13]

and that others, coming after him, would in turn move forward. Euripides envisaged

> The new adventure for the novel man
> Born to that next success myself foresee
> In right of where I reach before I rest. [ll. 1322–3]

Aristophanes' Apology is the apogee of Robert Browning's experiments with the dramatic monologue. The poem plays spectacular tricks with the form: the technique is breathtaking; the argument is as erudite as learning and as authentic as wide reading in the Greek classics can make it; and the translation of Euripides' *Herakles* within the poem is regarded as one of the finest in English.

Perhaps Balaustion's first adventure had been more amusing: at any rate, in this second (and last) adventure she had become tiresome to her public. On or about 16 June 1875, Alfred Domett talked with Robert about 'his new book *Aristophanes' Apology* and how some of the "critics" had abused it. The most virulent of these was a writer named Austin who, he said, had written attacks upon it in three different papers or periodicals, misquoting passages and designedly leaving out words or lines so as to make absolute nonsense of them. It is the old story "Folly loves the Martyrdom of Fame." [219] Domett, though far from siding with Alfred Austin, had been himself a little confused by the poem and offered some judicious comments. He remarked upon 'the large demands Browning makes in this book on his reader's knowledge', and pointed out that nobody but a classical scholar in the habit of reading Aristophanes daily would understand all the allusions in the poem without explanatory notes that Robert refused to provide. 'Browning thus wilfully restricted the number of his readers to a comparatively few.' [220]

This was an old complaint that harked back to Robert's earliest work, of 'taking it for granted that the ordinary or general reader must be as thoroughly proficient in a subject as the writer who has made it his particular study'. Robert 'said it could not be helped, but he was not likely to try anything of the sort again'. Whereupon an awe fell upon Alfred Domett, who commented: 'And here is this wonderfully fertile genius, after thirty additional years of varied productiveness, still working away — writing as vigorously if not always as fascinatingly as ever — and still making resolutions as to what is to be avoided in his *future* creations!' [221]

Carlyle liked *Aristophanes' Apology* well enough (he was probably one of the few who understood its complex arguments and recondite references) but would have preferred as usual, from the point of view of style, that Robert had told it 'in a plain straightforward statement'. Domett, taking this as 'a bit of Carlyle's banter', asked Robert what he thought of it: to which Robert sensibly replied, 'As if this did not just make all the difference between a poet's treatment of a subject and a historian's or a rhetorician's.' [222] The subject of *Aristophanes' Apology* was not simply an argument about the relative merits of Aristophanes and Euripides. The classical scholar and critic John Addington Symonds, reviewing the work in the *Academy* of 17 April 1875, noted perceptively that 'The point of view is modern' and that the poem expressed 'the views of the most searching and most sympathetic modern analyst'. Only a great modern poet would have been capable of such a viewpoint. But most critics were left floundering. Robert, foaming at 'how greedily the little men will catch up and carry about a little lie in the shape of a charge of plagiarism', wrote later in a letter that 'somebody, wholly a stranger to me, reviewing it in *The Athenaeum*, observed (for fun's sake, I suppose) that it was "probably written after one of Mr Browning's Oxford Symposia with Jowett." . . . Such a love of a lie have the verminous tribe!'[223]

Robert's next poem, *The Inn Album*, was, if anything, even more grotesque than *Red Cotton Night-Cap Country*. It was written quickly within two months — according to a note on the manuscript, between 1 June and 1 August 1875. In 3,080 lines, it took the form of a series of monologues within a dramatic narrative, and its subject was once again based — as he told Alfred Domett — on 'actual fact: he had heard it told 30 odd years ago of Lord de Roos [*sic*], a notorious cheat at cards; who having lost money to a young acquaintance, shewed him the portrait of an exceedingly beautiful woman, offering to procure her for him on condition of being released from the debt: she having previously been seduced by himself and married to a clergyman'.[224] Robert 'had intended originally to write a tragedy on the subject, but hearing Tennyson was engaged upon one, (*Queen Mary*) gave up the idea'.[225] In fact, Robert seems to have first heard the story of the elderly roué and cardsharper Baron de Ros in the context of *An English Tragedy*, a play written about him by Fanny Kemble, which she offered to Macready in December 1838. Macready, uneasy with the subject, had declined to produce the play.[226]

Robert might also have read the story even earlier, in *Paul Clifford*, a novel by Edward Bulwer-Lytton published anonymously in 1830, and recognized the dissolute Lord de Ros in the fictional character of Henry Finish, a swindler and soldier of fortune. In any case, the story of the 21st Baron de Ros had been recently resurrected in *The Greville Memoirs: A Journal of the Reigns of King George IV and King William IV* that, in the teeth of Queen Victoria's disapproval, had been published in three sensational volumes in 1874. *The Inn Album*, true to Carlyle's caustic prediction, also drew upon elements in the early life of the defendant in the famous case of the 'Tichborne Claimant' that lasted from 1871 until final judgement in 1874 against Roger Charles Tichborne, who thereby lost his claim on a great estate and was sentenced to fourteen years penal servitude for perjury and other crimes.

All in all, Robert's poem was a thoroughly modern piece of work, both in the subject that Greville had lately revived in readers' minds and the recent court case that had gripped the public's attention; it was modern, too, in its topical references to Victorian politicians, writers, and painters, and in the formal experimentation that combined melodrama with novelistic narrative. Clyde de L. Ryals finds the text almost Pirandellian, as if written by the characters themselves.[227] *The Inn Album* was published in late November 1875 and quickly sold, according to Smith and Elder, 1,100 copies out of an edition of 2,000.[228]

Critics were divided as to the merits of the poem. *The Athenaeum* ranked it higher than *The Ring and the Book* and thought it as good as *Pippa Passes*. Swinburne thoroughly, satirically, enjoyed 'the new sensation novel' and thought it 'a fine study in the later manner of Balzac, and I always think the great English analyst greatest as he comes nearest in matter and procedure to the still greater Frenchman'. Robert was pleased that his old friend John Forster liked it: 'That . . . you estimate my performance as you do — makes me proud,' he wrote. On the other hand, John Addington Symonds, in the *Academy*, did not care for the poem's grotesquerie or the poet's device of making each character 'a mouthpiece for his casuistic and psychological expertness', and A. C. Bradley, in the February 1876 issue of *Macmillan's Magazine*, echoed this view 'that the author is using his actors as vehicles for his own reflections'.

Henry James, in *The Nation* on 20 January 1876, confessed to some difficulty with *The Inn Album:* he could not 'say very coherently' what he had just read and which he felt had been too hastily written. It seemed to James to be 'a series of notes for a poem' in which he heard 'that hiss and splutter and evil aroma which characterise the proceedings of the laboratory'. For an admirer such as James, who recognized Robert Browning's 'great genius', it was disappointing to have to admit 'his wantonness, his wilfulness, his crudity' and to have to say, 'It is not narrative, for there is not a line of comprehensible, consecutive statement in the two hundred and eleven pages . . . It is not lyrical, for there is not a phrase which . . . chants itself, images itself, or lingers in the memory."'

On the day, 9 December 1875, when Alfred Domett had visited Robert Browning and recorded their conversation (Domett as Boswell to Browning's Dr Johnson) he was surprised when they 'were interrupted by a great screeching at the back of the house. "Ah! they are my pets" said Browning. They were 4 geese! "They are such affectionate creatures — and I am sure it is not for what one gives them." '[229] Two of them, according to legend, were named 'Edinburgh' and 'Quarterly' after the hissing and screeching periodicals that had regularly and viciously pecked at Robert's poetry. His own, as well as metaphorical, geese were on his mind when, in 1877, Robert wrote to a correspondent who had sent him some pert reviews from a provincial newspaper: 'I am quite sure you mean very kindly, but I have had too long an experience of the inability of the human goose to do other than cackle when benevolent and hiss when malicious; and no amount of goose criticism shall make me lift a heel at what waddles behind it.'

He was as devoted to birds and animals as he was intolerant of critics. He could write with equanimity of the worst crimes and grotesque characteristics of men and women, but he could never bear cruelty to animals and he was a committed anti-vivisectionist. On 3 February 1874, Domett and Robert had dined with the philanthropist and author Frances Power Cobbe, ' "a powerful writer — and advocate of the Rights of Woman" etc . . . She and Browning got into a lively discussion as to good or evil preponderating in human life generally; Browning taking an optimistic view of the matter and ending "Well, I can only speak of it as I have found it myself" which did not satisfy Miss Cobbe.'[230] But on the subject of vivisection, Robert and Frances Cobbe were in full agreement: 'I would rather,' he had said to her in Florence, 'submit to the worst of deaths, so far as pain goes, than have a single dog or cat tortured on pretence of sparing me a twinge or two.'[231] Three poems — 'Tray', published in Dramatic Idyls in 1879; 'Donald', published in Jocoseria in 1883; and 'Arcades Ambo', published in Asolando in 1889 — express 'how much I despise and abhor the pleas on behalf of that infamous practise — Vivisection'.[232] Indeed, so strongly did he feel about the suffering of animals that he became Vice-President of the Victoria Street Society for the Protection of Animals.

'Browning seemed to think,' noted Alfred Domett after a conversation between them as they strolled across Hyde Park on 16 July 1873, 'that it was Shakespeare's established preeminence of reputation that made the public accept murder scenes and revolting circumstances from him without disgust. I doubted this.'[233] But Robert was not convinced by Domett's arguments, citing in particular the *Herakles* of Euripides, which contained an account of the murder of his own children by Herakles in his madness but which was redeemed by 'the pathos of the scenes ... particularly of that where Herakles becomes conscious of what he has done, and his passionate comments upon it to Theseus'. Robert might flinch at the torture of a cat or a dog, but the 'stamping out of the eyes' in *King Lear* or the murder by Herakles of his children caused him less grief. And the torture by a poet of his critics caused him positive glee.

Robert's reputation had risen during the 1860s. On his return from Italy, publication of selections had stimulated a flagging interest in his previous poetry. During his years in London, collected editions and well-received new work had brought him serious critical attention and a celebrity he had not known since the sensation of *Paracelsus*. The day of the poet reached its high noon in 1869 on full publication of *The Ring and the Book*. In the following years, during the 1870s, the light of Robert's reputation began to fade: *Prince Hohenstiel-Schwangau*, *Fifine at the Fair*, *Red Cotton Night-Cap Country*, and *The Inn Album* had received a mixed reception — the latter two being regarded very much as Robert himself described them to Julia Wedgwood as 'morbid cases of the soul'. Critics began to nag again, to find fault and to pull him down from Parnassus.

Pacchiarotto and How He Worked in Distemper; with Other Poems was published on 18 July 1876. It was a blast that Robert could no longer restrain against his critics. The poem was principally directed with satirical Aristophanic and bold Byronic humour against Alfred Austin, who, according to Robert, wrote his lying articles 'for malice rather than the fun of the thing'.[234] Austin had already been characterized in *Aristophanes' Apology* as 'the Dogface Eruxis'. Robert had found Jacopo Pacchiarotto, an undistinguished Sienese artist and unsuccessful politician, in Vasari's *Lives*. Pacchiarotto's turbulent temper perfectly suited his purposes — it matched his own; and the man's conspiratorial and self-interested malice matched Austin's.

Pacchiarotto is the title poem in a book of eighteen poems which includes 'Hervé Riel'. This volume put an end to Robert's discretion about his private feelings and his silence in response to his critics, who had been biting at him for the past forty years, and to all those who had attempted to pry into his and Elizabeth's private lives. May Day is the morning Robert chooses in 'House' for the chimney-sweeps (the critics) to come to the householder, to the house that he has made and painted exactly to his taste, disturbing his privacy, trailing the dirt of their sooty trade, trampling his flower garden, and offering him house-keeping services he doesn't want and can well do without. These tradesmen are warned off: they may not enter and see the householder at home. That is, they may look at the house, and they may like what they see, or not — what they think of its external appearance is a matter of indifference to the householder: the house is not the man who lives within it.

And so critics may pinch and bite at Robert's work, but they cannot know the man, cannot reach the '*moi profond*', cannot trample and defile Robert himself, the poet who transcends all attempts to know who he is behind his own door and what he does within his own house. It is no business of the poet, or any other man, to redeem the world: his business is to attend to his own work and his own home, to look to himself and his own salvation. Critics may need Robert Browning: Robert Browning has no need of critics. The poet can speak very well for himself, if anyone takes the trouble to listen properly and has the capacity to understand what is being said. In short, along with intrusive biographers and all other mendacious gossips, they can bugger off and take the tools of their filthy business with them.

To George Barrett, Robert wrote on 12 August 1876 to say, 'I am glad indeed that you care at all about anything in the new little book. It was not worth while, perhaps, even to amuse myself for once (first and last time) with my critics — I really had a fit of good humour — and nothing worse — when the funny image of Austin, "my castigator," as he calls himself, struck me in a vision of May-morning: a "castigator" should be prepared for an appropriate reception from the "castigated" one.' The various short poems that were bundled together under the name of the title poem constituted the first book of Robert's short poetry since *Dramatis Personae* — which is not to say that the poems were miscellaneous. In one way or another, whether providing illustrations of success or failure in the business of making and maintaining an earthly house, they all contributed to the overall theme of man's existence in the flesh and the preparations he must make for the life of the spirit.

The critics failed to understand that Robert was amusing himself: and, up to a point, they were right. What was begun as a piece of poet's fun rather tended to end in a poet's fury. They were disinclined to take his banter in good part and saw no reason to laugh at themselves. When, like Xanthippe, Pachiarotto's housemaid, Robert poured water on their heads as they danced under his window, they took it badly rather than with good humour. It was one of their own, poor little Austin, bullied and bruised and bespattered by a horrid poet, that they picked up from the dust and brushed down with soothing words. They rubbed balm into their sorrowful wounds and bound up their injured dignity by uttering articles of burning reproof against their tormentor.

Critics took their opportunity to condemn what seemed to them yet another piece of Browning perversity when, on 15 October 1877, Robert published his translation — or transcription, as he preferred to call it — of *The Agamemnon of Aeschylus*. Carlyle, who — with reservations — had liked *Aristophanes' Apology*, had recommended that Robert 'ought to translate the whole of the Greek tragedians — that's your vocation'.[235] If he was not prepared to take it up as a vocation, translation had so far been well received critically, and Robert was always inclined to indulge — if not always agree with — Carlyle and his prescriptive advice. His method was to translate so literally, as he wrote in his preface, as to make 'a mere strict version of thing by thing' and 'to furnish the very turn of each phrase in as Greek a fashion as English will bear'.

This was Robert's response to a suggestion by Matthew Arnold that Greek literature provided the highest models of expression, that Greek authors were the unapproached masters of the grand style, and that they should be imitated by contemporary English poets. English could scarcely bear Robert's literal translation at all: it creaked and groaned very terribly under the burden of the Greek. Carlyle, when he read the *Agamemnon* translation, told William Allingham that Robert Browning was 'a very foolish fellow. He picks you out the English for the Greek word by word, and now and again sticks two or three words together with hyphens; then again he snips up the sense and jingles it into rhyme! I could have told him he would do no good whatever under such conditions.'[236]

A critic in the *Spectator* annoyed Robert by apparent unfairness and seeming ignorance in a review of the *Agamemnon*, but he decided that to complain was not worth while.[237] Alfred Domett, scratching his head over the book, asked Robert whether it might not have been 'reasonable to give English notes to his translation, that English readers might understand it?', and Robert 'agreed that notes might be necessary and said that he had no objection to any one else making them'. Robert admitted that his transcript of Aeschylus might be difficult: 'He mentioned that while engaged on the translation he met "one of the first Greek scholars in England, who asked him if what he heard was true, that he was translating the *Agamemnon*?" Browning answering in the affirmative, the other said, "And you understand it? for I have known it these twenty years and *I* can't." '[238]

Robert, however, understood the *Agamemnon*, and he understood Aeschylus, and he understood very well what he was doing with both of them. The play struck him as another opportunity to take issue with his critics by proving that his knowledge of Greek and Greek classical literature owed nothing to Jowett. He would revive Aeschylus the playwright (with whom Robert the poet identified himself as translator) from charges of obscurity; and deal in practice with Arnold by proving, as he wrote in his preface to the translation, that 'learning Greek teaches Greek, and nothing else: certainly not common sense, if that have failed to precede the teaching'. What was needed were new forms, new thinking. A reverential return to the past was unthinkable.

Elizabeth had perfectly agreed with him in this. In one of her first letters to Robert, she had written: 'I am inclined to think we want new *forms*, as well as thoughts. The old gods are dethroned. Why should we go back to the antique moulds, classical moulds, as they are so improperly called? If it is a necessity of Art to do so, why then those critics are right who hold that Art is exhausted and the world too worn out for poetry ... Let us all aspire rather to *Life*, and let the dead bury their dead.'[239] In the very failure (as it was perceived) of his translation, Robert may be said to have proved his point that old forms could only succeed if they were reinvented and reinterpreted as he had tried to do in *Balaustion's Adventure* and *Aristophanes' Apology*. Nevertheless, he was perversely pleased with his transcription, even though it had done him no positive good.

Things had been looking up for Pen over the last few years while his father had been pouring out great quantities of poetry, and Robert was feeling better about the boy. Now that they had both accepted that Pen had no aptitude for an academic life, it was a pleasure to discover that Pen had an inherent ability for art — for sculpture and painting. John Millais, happening to look over at some water-colours by Pen, who was improving the shining hour on a country house visit by dabbling beside him, had been impressed by the quality of his work and suggested some formal training. Robert took advice from an artist friend, the consequence of which was that in the spring of 1874 Pen had been sent to Antwerp to buckle down to studio work under the strict tutelage of the painter Jean-Arnould Heyermans, who had exhibited a painting in the Royal Academy show in 1874 and occasionally showed in London at the Grosvenor Gallery and elsewhere.

Robert reported to William Story in a letter of 9 June 1874, 'I can see that he is happier than he ever was in his life. What a load this lightens me of. Who can judge better than you? He has never once budged from his butcher's-shop lodging, and it is *I*, this time, who begin to be anxious that he should change the air and otherwise relax a little.' In January 1875, Robert wrote to George Barrett to say that 'Pen has indeed done capitally, — made remarkable progress for a student of less than a year's standing. Millais came to see his pictures last week, and said all we could hope or wish: there wants nothing but a continued application — such as he has shown he can easily manage. We (my sister and I) visited him in Antwerp and made acquaintance with his admirable master, Heyermans, to whom we owe everything. Millais said — under *nobody* in England could Pen have made such progress. I bought a little picture, which Pen had seen him paint, — most charming, "perfect in its way," declared Millais.'

Pen had come back to London at Christmas 1875, bringing with him a 'study' of a priest reading a book. Rudolph Lehmann glad-handedly offered 150 guineas for it, but Pen refused, embarrassed by such a huge sum of money for a work he knew to be inadequate. Lehmann insisted. Pen temporized, offering instead a future picture which, Lehmann said, by that time would be beyond his purse. 'I must have this one,' declared Lehmann, whereupon Robert exasperatedly burst in, 'Pen, don't be a fool — take it as offered.' Another friend of the Brownings, a lady, offered 40 guineas for a portrait, 20 guineas down and the balance on completion. Whereupon Robert said, 'I tell you what it is, Pen; you will be quite spoilt with all this; you had better get back to Antwerp as fast as you can.' Alfred Domett, who recorded all this in his diary entry for 30 March 1876, suspected — probably quite rightly — 'a little *practical flattery* to the poet in all this. Nevertheless Browning's manifest delight in his son's success, was very human (as Carlyle would say) and interesting.'

For their own change of air and relaxation, Robert and Sarianna, with their dear friend Annie Egerton Smith, had taken a holiday in 1876 at Lamlash on Arran off the west coast of Scotland. The next August, again with Annie, who by now had become as good as a member of the family, the Brownings settled for the summer of 1877 in La Saisiaz (which Mrs Orr says means 'the Sun', but Park Honan convincingly proves to be a Savoyard patois word for a rock-cleft or fissure), a substantial villa or chalet at the foot of Mount Salève, in the Jura Mountains some four or five miles from Geneva. On the morning of 15 September, Annie Egerton Smith suddenly died. Walking with Robert the evening before, 'in exceptionally good health and spirits', she had happily been discussing arrangements for a picnic the next day. When Annie did not put in an appearance at breakfast, Robert walked out and noticed that no figure was visible through the thin curtains at the windows of Annie's rooms.

In a letter to a friend, Mrs Charles Skirrow, Robert wrote immediately on 15 September 1877: 'I looked through an opening in the curtain, and saw her kneeling on the ground — which her poor dead head had touched. I called my sister, who ran in — cried to me — and brought me to her side. She was quite warm — but dead.' A doctor was called from Geneva, 'but no sort of assistance would have been of any avail: it was a case of the most thorough "apoplexie fondroyante": she must have died *standing*, and fallen as we found her. So I have lost one of the most devoted friends I ever had in my life — a friend of some five-and-twenty years standing: I have been much favoured in friendships — especially from women: no one ever was more disinterestedly devoted to me who grieve to remember how little I was ever able to do in return for so much.' Annie's brother and sister were urgently sent for, and Robert took charge until their arrival which, he expected, 'will relieve me of much anxiety and responsibility. The formalities to be observed here are precise and troublesome, but I believe I have arranged tolerably.' The funeral was conducted at Collonge, the neighbouring village, in an atmosphere of general and profound depression.

According to Mrs Orr, Robert had been depressed in any case, even before his holiday, and his condition was not much improved by 'the want of the sea air which he had enjoyed for so many years, and to that special oppressive heat of the Swiss valleys which ascends with them to almost their highest level'.[240] He was naturally not much better when he returned to London where, on 9 November, he completed a poem, entitled 'La Saisiaz'. Published on 15 May 1878 with 'The Two Poets of Croisic', it was dedicated to Mrs Sutherland Orr. The poem is generally taken to be Robert's contribution to a symposium, current at the time of Annie Egerton Smith's death, on the soul and immortality. She and Robert had both been vitally interested in, and had discussed, the symposium papers that were appearing at regular intervals in a new journal, the *Nineteenth Century*.

'La Saisiaz' is an elegy, a metaphysical reflection on death and immortality — on whether the soul survives the body. The poem advances the ideas first considered in 'Easter-Day', though now with rather more immediacy since Robert had by now turned sixty-five years old. 'The Two Poets of Croisic', the companion poem to 'La Saisiaz', is a more lively, amusing reflection on fame — which, Robert concludes, being an external, objective estimation, cannot be a valid criterion for valuation of a poet's authentic worth. It has perhaps a continuing and particular relevance in modern times in respect of our pervasive contemporary cult of celebrity and the avidity of the talentless for even temporary public attention.

Robert had never courted fame: on the contrary, he positively spurned it. An impression of impressive remoteness, of a high intellectuality, protected him from wide popular acclaim and all the promotional paraphernalia of his poetry and of himself as a poet that went with it. He made no public speeches, undertook no lecture tours, refused public recitals of his work (though privately, among groups of his own friends and acquaintances, he could be persuaded), turned away requests to publish individual poems in newspapers or periodicals, gave no interviews, and denied access to letters and other materials to would-be biographers. He offered no comment on social or political issues of the day, wrote to newspapers or periodicals only to correct matters of fact that had been misapprehended by others, and protected his own and his family's privacy with the constant vigilance of a goose guarding the Capitol. He avoided the phenomenal public adulation that Tennyson attracted — the old man could hardly leave his house in the country to catch a train without being mobbed: Robert could walk the streets unmolested. He gave no lavish dinners — unlike Dickens, who presided over great feasts: Robert preferred to be an inveterate and entertaining guest, even if placed below the salt as a poet, rather than a constant and convivial host.

And yet Robert Browning became invested with a celebrity he never sought. Almost everyone he ever met confided stories and anecdotes about him to their diaries, letters, and journals. Acquaintances dined out on their impressions and experiences of him. Every glance he made in the direction of a woman, every hand he laid on a shoulder or an arm, became an item of gossip and spiralling speculation about his romantic inclinations and marital intentions. Aspirant poets sent him their work, autograph seekers bombarded him with begging letters (most of which were ignored or torn to pieces), hostesses besieged him with invitations to more dinners than even the most dedicated diner-out could eat. Though Robert chose to live his life within narrow limits, he filled every inch of that space. The atmosphere around him crackled, almost literally, with his personal charge. William Sharp, one of his first biographers, remarked that he had often heard people say that a handshake from Browning was like an electric shock. This was pleasant or otherwise, depending on how one felt about such an exciting sensation.

Maisie Ward sums up the impression Robert made, not just in his latter years but throughout his adult life that had begun after his marriage: 'his was a strong, sometimes overwhelming, personality; he was loved, he was detested. Mrs Orr speaks of the "hysterical sensibilities which for some years past he had unconsciously but not unfrequently aroused in the minds of women, and even of men." Elizabeth had written with pleased amusement that many women loved him too much for decency — "perhaps, a little, I also." '[241]

Men, as Thomas Trollope and others in Florence could have testified, occasionally felt a little intimidated and condescended to: George

Russell 'describes how, when intensely bored by a man asking questions about his poetry, Browning "laid his hand on the questioner's shoulder saying 'But, my dear fellow, this is too bad. I am monopolising you,' and skipped out of the corner." '[242] However, if Robert was in high good humour he could be incomparable company. In *Memoirs of Life and Literature*, the novelist and political writer W. H. Mallock described how Robert 'held out both his hands to me with an almost boisterous cordiality. His eyes sparkled with laughter, his beard was carefully trimmed, and an air of fashion was exhaled from his dazzling white waistcoat. He did not, so far as I remember, make any approach to the subject of literature at all, but reduced both Jowett and myself to something like complete silence by a constant flow of anecdotes and social allusions, which, although not deficient in point, had more in them of jocularity than wit.' Robert's poetry might be intellectual, but often the poet was not.

Not everyone liked to be steam-rollered in this way. Mary Gladstone famously complained in her diary that she was always seated at dinner beside 'old Browning', who 'always places his person in such disagreeable proximity with yours and puffs and blows and spits in your face. I tried to think of Abt Vogler but it was no use — he *could* not have written it.' Like Henry James, she might have imagined another, more spiritual, Robert Browning sitting at home writing poetry while his egregious, all too physical *alter ego* sat nudging up to her and spluttering in her eye. Maisie Ward mischievously points out that Mary Gladstone later changed her mind: when celebrity had laid its social glamour over Robert, she admitted to having gone 'Browning mad'.[243]

Robert had recovered, in the social, professional and economic prosperity of his later years, the dapper and somewhat dandified surface that he had displayed in his youth. A newspaper expressed surprise that 'the crabbed and mystical poet is identical with the possessor of the compact little figure' and commented on Robert's 'urbane and genial bearing, the well made clothes'. Julian Hawthorne, Nathaniel Hawthorne's son, who remembered Robert from his time in Italy, was interested to see that 'Browning had become another Browning', that he had adopted the cultural camouflage of Piccadilly and Pall Mall: 'staid, grave, urbane, polished; he was a rich banker, he was a perfected butler, no one would have suspected him of poetry'.[244]

Hawthorne's snobbish little reference to Robert looking like a 'perfected butler' was just as grudging as his social observation that Robert also resembled a 'rich banker'. There were some, like John Churton Collins, who considered Robert to be vulgar and sycophantic, 'a man eager to be of a grade to which he did not belong'.[245] The place for a pomaded poet, perhaps, should be Camberwell rather than at the dinner-table of the mighty, and the appropriate dress for a poet should rather be the soft blue shirt that Robert had worn with pride in his poverty when writing first to Elizabeth than the starched, diamond-studded white waistcoat of those born to property and *politesse*.

In August 1878, Robert edged a little closer to Italy than he had managed to do, despite all his professed longings to return, in the past seventeen years. With Sarianna, he took his annual late summer holiday at Splügen, in the Swiss Alps, a little village 'with not a single shop in it, — much less a habitable house'.[246] Through 'exquisite scenery' the sexagenarian Brownings walked 'daily for some four or five hours at a stretch — generally managing seventeen miles about, in that time'. Robert felt refreshed by rambling and mountain air — which, more than sea bathing and salt air, he now felt to be his 'proper resource when fagged at the end of a season ... this sort of savagery is the suitable thing. We have newspapers, however, good cookery, absolute cleanliness, and *such* quietude.'[247]

Robert and Sarianna travelled on into Italy, resting for a night at Lake Como, taking two days to tour Verona, and stopping at Asolo before making for Venice. It had been forty years since Robert had last seen Asolo, the pretty little hill-top town of silk-makers, the scene in which he had set *Pippa Passes*, and he visited the ruined tower on the hill-top to see if he could still make the clear air ring with an echo, 'and thereupon it answered me plainly as ever, after all the silence'.[248] Sarianna had been charmed by Asolo, and Venice thrilled her to the marrow. There were gondola trips along the canals by moonlight and the pleasures of the great Piazza San Marco where, for a fortnight, she delighted to take tea to the accompaniment of music with new acquaintances among the rich and leisured, well-dressed and well-mannered, English and American community, as well as with old friends from London, Florence, and Rome among the summer visitors.

Their hotel, the Albergo dell' Universo, on the shady side of the

Grand Canal, just below the Accademia, had been recommended to the Brownings as cool and quiet. 'It accommodated few persons in proportion to its size,' according to Mrs Orr, ' and fewer still took up their abode there; for it was managed by a lady of good birth and fallen fortunes whose home and patrimony it had been; and her husband, a retired Austrian officer, and two grown-up daughters did not lighten her task. Every year the fortunes sank lower; the upper storey of the house was already falling into decay, and the fine old furniture passing into the brokers' or private buyers' hands. It still, however, afforded sufficiently comfortable, and, by reason of its very drawbacks, desirable quarters to Mr Browning.'[249] It is tempting to think that Robert may have been struck by the very Balzacian or Dickensian quality of the Albergo dell' Universo because he returned there every year until its final decrepitude, after which it was turned into an art gallery.

He had not been idle on holiday: he had worked, indeed, to the point that Sarianna became concerned for his health. Robert had set out for rest and recreation less willingly than usual that year, being worried and more than a little depressed by Pen, who had apparently given up work in Heyermans' studio for the charms of a young Belgian woman, to whom he had made a proposal of marriage. If this latest exploit was representative of what his son's life was likely to be, Robert didn't want to know. He and Pen were not currently on speaking terms. 'I am increasingly lazy,' Robert had written from London to Mrs Fitzgerald. 'I confess to having been quite idle of late.' He revived in the stimulating air of Switzerland and was consoled by the soft atmosphere of Italy to the extent that by the time he returned to London he had completed five of the six short narrative poems which were to comprise *Dramatic Idyls*, published by Smith and Elder on 28 April 1879.

It has been suggested that Robert thought, with these less intellectualized poems, to achieve some of the popular success Tennyson had enjoyed with his idyllic poems. In the public mind, and very likely also in Robert's, the Browning *Idyls* would be naturally associated with the *Idylls* of Tennyson and classed as much the same thing. Tennyson certainly thought so, objecting mildly to the theft of his word. Robert's definition of an *Idyl* was 'a succinct little story complete in itself: not necessarily concerning pastoral matters ... These of mine are called

"Dramatic" because the story is told by some actor in it, not by the poet himself.'[250]

The half-dozen relatively brief, readable poems were received with relief by critics and ordinary readers, who responded enthusiastically to Robert's tales of judgement, stricken conscience, and heroic deeds. 'Praised be heaven!' cried the reviewer in the July 1879 issue of *Fraser's Magazine*. 'This time he comes with no basket of mud, no screech owls fly.' The book was perceived as a welcome return to the style of *Dramatis Personae*. Sales were so good that a second edition was called for and they also prompted a second series, comprising eight new poems, published in June 1880, though to rather less acclaim. This second collection was perceived to be less thematic and less substantial than the first, though, as with much of Robert Browning's work, later critics have found much to admire in it.

A man does not generally become a public institution without some prophet having prepared the ground, just as a statue of a public hero does not stand without a plinth under its feet. Unbidden, a 'subtle moulder' presented himself to Robert and proposed to represent him in 'brazen shapes' by the formation of a society dedicated to the study of his works and days. Dr Frederick James Furnivall had previously performed such significant services for Shakespeare (in the form of the New Shakspere Society) in 1873 and Shelley (the Shelley Society) in 1886. He had industriously launched and guided the English Text Society in 1864, the Chaucer and Ballad Societies in 1868, and the Wyclif Society in 1886.

Furnivall was known to Robert. The men had met at Tennyson's house in May 1874, and possibly through Hensleigh Wedgwood, with whom Furnivall had collaborated in the first planning stages of the *Oxford English Dictionary*. In 1879, Furnivall had persuaded Robert to accept the honorary presidency of his New Shakspere Society. Furnivall was an enthusiast for the restoration and rehabilitation of English literary texts through the application of modern scientific method. The insistence on authenticity and accuracy was something of a novelty, somewhat at odds with the prevailing antiquarian taste for the discretionary alteration of texts, like the eighteenth-century antiquary Thomas Percy, who had produced his editions 'to please both the judicious antiquary and the reader of taste . . . to gratify both without offending either'. The likes of Bishop Percy deeply offended the purist principles of Furnivall, who demanded the 'very words of the manuscript'.

Robert's elevation to the presidency of the New Shakspere Society in 1879 had prompted Algernon Swinburne, an aesthetic Shakespearean scholar, offended by Furnivall's critical approach, to swipe at Furnivall's management of the Society and to cast serious aspersions on his positivist moral scholarship, which did not always adhere very strictly to the scientific rationalism he professed. Furnivall could too easily become, indeed, as fanciful as the antiquarians he criticized, and the speed with which he insisted on issuing allegedly authentic texts too often resulted in inaccuracies. The upshot was very shocking: the row descended into a slanging match between Swinburne and Furnivall, both of whom were excitable and intemperate men. It had begun mildly enough in 1876, and had rumbled on for three years before finally coming to a furious head over an essay written by Swinburne in which he ridiculed the 'New Shakespearean Synagogue' and its 'New Shakespeare' as 'sham Shakespeareans'. Furnivall replied energetically, accusing Swinburne of 'shallow ignorance', and — in a rudely punning reference to his name — calling him 'Pigsbrook'. Swinburne ripely returned the vulgarly punning insult, calling Furnivall ' Brothelsdyke Flunkivall'.

The details of this literary quarrel hardly matter now, though they still amuse scholars in their jauntier moments. In any case, the original basis of the row soon became inextricably entangled with personal animosities, and Robert was obliged to distance himself almost formally from what amounted to a prodigious frenzy of vituperation, not only between Swinburne and Furnivall but between anyone either of them could press into serving their respective positions. In a letter to an associate of Swinburne's, J. O. Halliwell-Phillipps, Robert wrote on 27 January 1881: 'My position with respect to the [New Shakspere] Society is purely honorary, as I stipulated before accepting it, nor have I been able hitherto to attend any one of its meetings; and should I ever do so, my first impulse will be to invoke the spirit of "gentle Shakespeare" that no wrong be done in his name to a member of the brotherhood of students combining to do him suit and service.' In spite of Furnivall's tinderbox touchiness, his fast and furious character, or perhaps partly because of it, Robert liked the man, liked his spontaneity and his fraternizing with the immortal figures of English literature as though they were his most intimate friends. Furnivall walked and talked with Tennyson and Browning as cheerfully and candidly as he did with Shakespeare and Shelley.

Miss Emily Hickey, a genteel Irish essayist and poetess, had joined the New Shakspere Society, and had developed a talent for dramatic reading at the Society's evenings. On one of these occasions, Miss Hickey had expressed her profound and sincere admiration for Mr Browning, and so it was that on 3 July 1881, a Sunday, she found herself being hurried along by Furnivall at a fast pace (he never did anything slowly) through Regent's Park on their way to 19 Warwick Crescent to visit the poet. Furnivall had decided that the time had come to form a society for the study of a living poet, and asked Miss Hickey whether she would help him found a Browning Society. This seems to have been a sudden, on-the-spot inspiration of Furnivall's: Robert had not yet been apprised of the idea. Miss Hickey wondered whether Mr Browning would approve and what Furnivall would do if Mr Browning was discouraging: 'Go on all the same and not mind him,' said Furnivall.[251]

At least he had the courtesy to consult Robert, who laughed loudly and joked at the idea but, significantly, turned the talk to another matter without first refusing to have anything to do with it. When Furnivall returned home, he reportedly sat up all night writing to suitable people to solicit their membership of his new society. By one account, he wrote enough letters — two hundred and more — that Sunday night to account for a pound's worth of penny stamps. By Monday evening Furnivall had enrolled the first members of the the Browning Society. He announced the formation of the Society in an advertisement in the *Academy*, and published a prospectus dated 27 July 1881. Furnivall was a fast worker. Robert began to feel a little uneasy: he was heard to murmur in French, 'Il me semble que ce genre de chose frise le ridicule.' [It seems to me that this sort of thing borders on the ridiculous.] But too late, too late: Furnivall was busy working up a full head of steam. The aims of the Browning Society, as set out in the prospectus, were: the study and discussion of the poet's works; publication of papers on the works; the formation of Browning reading clubs; the performance of Browning's dramas by amateur companies; the writing of a Browning primer; the compilation of a Browning concordance or lexicon; and generally the extension of the study and influence of the poet.[252]

Like most of Furnivall's ventures, the standard of scholarship was variable. The published papers of the Society found in Browning's works mostly what they wanted to find — no great difficulty about that, since the ambiguities of the works lent themselves as readily as the Bible to a multitude of subtle interpretations. These Society papers are marginally interesting now more as reflections of the social and moral preoccupations of the Society's membership than for their critical value. The close textual criticism produced by the Society's members beggared even Robert's belief: 'I write, airily, "Quoth Tom to Jack, one New Year's Day," and one "Student" wants to know who Jack was, — another sees no difficulty there, but much in Tom's entity, — while a third, getting easily over both stumbling blocks, says — "But *which* New Year's Day?"'[253] Robert added that, 'Since all this must be done for me by somebody, I congratulate myself on having somebody so energetic as Mr Furnivall to do it.'

The Society quickly became, embarrassingly, something of a joke. A duke (unnamed) suggested to Furnivall that the Browning Society had been founded three hundred years too early. Initially, Tennyson agreed to become its first president, but then — fearing mockery — withdrew. Furnivall himself became president in June 1887. Robert was a little taken aback that the membership included so few of his close friends. To Miss E. Dickinson West, he wrote on 12 November 1881 to state his own position and feelings:

I will tell you what I feel about the Society. It was instituted without my knowledge, and when knowledge was, I do not think acquiescence had need of being asked for. I write poems that they may be read, and — fifty years now — people said they were unintelligible. If other people in the fullness of days, reply 'we understand them, and will show that you may, if you will be at the pains,' I should think it ungracious indeed to open my mouth for the first time on the matter with 'Pray let the other people alone in their protested ignorance.' I see a paragraph in *The World* to the effect that none of my personal friends figure in the list of members. Had I persuaded them to do so, the objection would have been more cogent, 'only a clique — the man's personal following!'

Exactly what has touched me is the sudden assemblage of men and women to whose names, for the most part, I am a stranger, who choose to incur the ridicule sure to come readily to the critics who dispose of my works by the easy word 'unintelligible,' instead of saying safely to themselves '*I* understand it — or something of it — anyhow!' That there would be exaggeration in the approval was to be looked for, they exaggerate a good deal.

As for Dr Furnivall, I am altogether astonished at his caring about me at all. I suspect it is a late discovery with him, like that of Fontenelle when, chancing upon some out-of-the-way literature, he went about asking everybody, 'Do you know Habbakuk? He's a genius!' I think him most warm-hearted, whatever may be the mistakes about me of which his head is guilty; and as Lear's last instance of ingratitude is that of the mouth biting the hand for lifting food to it — so, it seems to me, would as signal an one be, the writer of books that are commonly pronounced unintelligible objecting to the folk who propose to try that question.

Occasionally, the Society could cause Robert some embarrassment. There was the time when Furnivall put about as a fact that Pen had married a Belgian girl, an innkeeper's daughter. Robert had to stamp on that pretty firmly. Park Honan makes the interesting point that the debates by the Browning Society about Robert's poetry were useful to him as diversions from speculation about his private life:

Privately, he viewed the debate over his work as a public debate over himself. As such, the debate obscured much of his past life and simplified his entire life, as he looked retrospectively over the years. The problem of his betrayal of Elizabeth's faith and trust, his possible obtuseness and wrong-headedness with Pen, his earlier defection from radical ideals, and many other issues and episodes of the past were conveniently blurred or blotted out in the starkly colourful challenge between Browningites and anti-Browningites — between those who simply affirmed and those who denied the value of everything he had ever done.[254]

Robert's friends had kept their distance from the Society on the assumption, mostly, that Robert could not possibly want this absurd form of homage. The attitude of the press, too, probably stopped them in their tracks: the general journalistic tone was sceptical when not outright merrily malicious. There was any amount of good fun to be got from the Browningites, who were perceived, even caricatured (as in a famous satiric cartoon by Max Beerbohm), as intense bluestockings, mostly adoring old maids and spiritually-inclined spinsters, and earnest aesthetes, theologically-minded curates, and greenery-yallery young men, all obscurely debating the unintelligible and blindly idolizing the rosy, self-satisfied poet who drank in their admiration with the same equanimity as he would drink down a cup of tea. There was irony in how these bloodless creatures drooped and wilted around the notoriously robust poet. The most famous Browning Society anecdote, attributed to E. F. Benson, is Robert's acceptance of an invitation to take tea and buttered muffins with the girls of Newnham College, Cambridge, who, after he read one of his poems to them, crowned his head with a wreath of pink roses.

But, as the letter to Miss West clearly shows, Robert was in no frame of mind to knock a Society dedicated to increasing public awareness of his works and to burnishing his reputation. He protested to Miss West that he himself was 'quite other than a Browningite', admitted that the Society was possibly premature, and that it had its grotesque elements. He declined to attend the monthly Society meetings, refused to correct critical papers written by its members (though he did correct its major publications), and to a great extent dissociated himself formally from the Society's proceedings. Informally, however, he was amiable and available to members and modestly received their expressions of admiration with no great displays of embarrassment or inclination to decline these evidences of high regard. The Browning Society, as it developed, took on the character almost of a cult, particularly in America, where a rage for the colour brown was associated with Robert Browning, editions of his books sold out wherever a Browning Society was established, and, says Park Honan, a Sordello Club was founded in St Louis.

The Browning Society continued for eight years, until 1891. It never formally declared itself ended, but membership had dwindled in its last two or three years and it simply fell into desuetude. Occasional meetings were held informally in members' houses, but the monthly meetings at University College ceased. It is easy to make fun of the Browning Society: the very fact that it took itself so seriously is faintly ridiculous, the personality of Furnivall, its founder, gives it a flavour of absurdity, and a great deal of its supposed critical work was amateur and incompetent and dwelt too much on a theology informed by an emphasis on moral uplift and optimism, support for which members increasingly strained their intellects and ingenuity to discover in Robert's works.

On the credit side, the Society produced the first decent bibliography of Robert's works that he himself proof-read and corrected. Variations in the poetic texts were analysed and authenticated, and Robert did make an effort to provide the Society with first-hand information (though not always absolutely reliable) about the dating, circumstances of composition, and meanings of poems when requested to do so. Then, too, he credited the activities of the Society with significantly increasing his readership — no small consideration for Robert. It should also be remembered that the Society's membership eventually included personal friends of Robert's who had joined out of loyalty to him, as well as some very notable names who joined for intellectual reasons — Frederic Leighton, Henry Irving, Joseph Milsand, Eleanor Marx, Miss Beale and Miss Buss (the formidable educational reformers), and George Bernard Shaw, who, when he joined, had allegedly not read a word of Browning but speedily made up the deficit and developed his first debating skills at meetings of the Society. In the *Star*, in October 1888, Shaw described the Browning Society as 'probably the most pugnacious body of its size in existence'.

Daily life at 19 Warwick Crescent was conducted according to a settled domestic pattern ruled by Sarianna but dedicated to Robert's convenience, comfort, and habits of work. William Grove, Robert's valet and manservant for seven years, gave an account of the poet's life to the *Pall Mall Budget* in December 1889. By 7 a.m., Robert was already awake and out of bed, eating an apple or some other fruit that he kept in his room and reading aloud from a book in Greek. He stayed in his bedroom until eight o'clock, then immersed himself in the bath that

Grove had drawn. Bathing involved violent splashing and loud singing and finally a crashing shower of water from an overhead tank. When he had dressed, Robert sat down to a light breakfast, after which he amused himself by reading his mail, *The Times* and the *Daily News* and playing the piano until 10 o'clock, when he went to his study to write poetry and deal with his correspondence until lunch time. Here Grove would sometimes photograph Robert in a characteristic pose — 'his head leaning on his hand. He would sit like that for half an hour sometimes, and then take up his pen to jot something down.'

Lunch at one o'clock was never substantial. In the afternoons, Robert walked out across Kensington Gardens to pay calls on friends or visit art galleries and artists' studios. In the evenings, he dined out and drank a little port or claret, and afterwards went on to a ball or a party where everyone was familiar with the sound Edmund Gosse described as Robert's 'loud trumpet note' of welcome to friends and 'the talk already in full flood at a distance of twenty feet'. Back home by half-past midnight, the bonhomous poet and booming *bon viveur* fell into bed and slept soundly.

Robert's routine was almost invariable: one could have set one's watch and marked one's calendar by it. On Saturdays he went to his club, the Athenaeum, to read the weekly papers; on Sundays he visited his friend Mrs Fitzgerald; on Mondays he dined with Arthur Penrhyn Stanley, Dean of Westminster; on Tuesdays and Fridays he visited Mrs Orr. His friends? 'Well,' said William Grove. 'I should have to give you a list of two or three hundred. Carlyle was a great friend, and so was Dean Stanley, Mr Gladstone, Mr Mundella, Sir Frederic Leighton and his sister [Mrs Orr], Watts, Tadema and a host of others. Tennyson came two or three times a year, and always on Show Sundays, to see Mr Barrett Browning's pictures.'

The house in Warwick Crescent was — no help for it — condemned by the Regent's Canal Bill to be demolished. Robert paid £5,000 for a large, several-storeyed house at 29 De Vere Gardens, right across the street from Henry James, who lived at number 34. The Brownings moved on 17 June 1887. Anne Thackeray recalls paying a visit one weekend to Robert at the new house and being marshalled by Sarianna, who steered her clear of the dining-room: 'there are some ladies waiting there; and there are some members of the Browning Society in the drawing room. Robert is in the study, with some Americans who have come by appointment.'

Considering this level of constant social activity, it is hardly surprising that for three years, from 1880 to 1883, Robert wrote hardly a word of poetry until he produced, in March 1883, another book of ten dramatic idylls entitled *Jocoseria* over which modern critics draw a veil (though contemporary reviewers and readers liked it) and which Robert himself, in a letter to Furnivall, described as 'this Olla Podrida', a collection of 'things grav*ish* and gay*ish* — hence the title *Jocoseria* — which is Batavian Latin, I think'.[255] Robert recognized the poems as 'light enough' and, perhaps tiring of the form, thought they would be 'probably the last of the kind I shall care to write'.[256] Nevertheless, the book was a gratifying success: it immediately sold out its first edition of 2,000 copies and was reprinted.

Robert and Sarianna had given up northern France as their summer resort. Every year from 1877 they preferred to take long walks — hours and miles surprising to modern generations, which equate leisure with idleness — and breathe in great lungfuls of bracing, healthful, Swiss-Italian alpine air, at St Pierre de Chartreuse in 1881 and 1882, at Gressoney St Jean in the Val d'Aosta in 1883, and at St Moritz in 1884. 'We feel renewed like eagles,' Robert had written to Mrs Charles Skirrow from Splügen on 12 September 1878. Thus healthfully recruited, they would descend upon Venice for the autumn season. On 12 September 1883, at Gressoney, Robert had begun to write the playful 'Prologue' to his next poem, *Ferishtah's Fancies*. The 'Epilogue' was dated 1 December 1883 and as from the Palazzo Giustiniani-Recanati in Venice, where Robert and Sarianna were the guests of Katherine C. de Kay Bronson. Most of the poem had been composed between these dates, though it was finished in London in January 1884 and published on 21 November that year. The unusual delay was probably due to George Murray Smith's inclination to give *Jocoseria* as long a run as possible.

Ferishtah's Fancies caught a favourable wind of the prevailing Western taste for Orientalism. Ferishtah, an imaginary Persian sage, is an ingenious but — as the poet himself admitted — thin disguise for Robert Browning, who relates his twelve 'fancies' — his dozen heroic tales and fables — and speaks his great mind on moral and philosophical questions of the day, lightly peppering the text with Hebrew quotations and Persian allusions and leavening the lump with appropriate love lyrics attached to each section of the poem. The result is a mature summation of Robert's religious views and theological speculations be-ribboned with enough romantic and exotic paraphernalia to render the poem palatable to a wide public taste. Despite some critical complaint that the preaching outweighed the poetry, *Ferishtah's Fancies* sold well.

Alfred Domett, however, found some difficulty getting through and making sense of the volume. On 2 December 1884 he wrote delicately to Robert to thank him for the book: 'I see that it is so full of subtle and profound thoughts on abstruse and difficult subjects, couched in racy and ingenious metaphors or allegories, that it would take a little time to read it so as to be able to speak of it at all becomingly afterwards ... "Out with your *nut-crackers*, you Browning Societies!" '[257] Modern critical opinion is sharply divided as to the value of *Ferishtah's Fancies*. Park Honan asks 'Why did Browning write so badly in 1883?', while Clyde de L. Ryals and Ian Jack consider that the poem 'recalls Kierkegaard' and that its 'structure — "fancy" incarnated in "fact" — is well suited to one who believed that "a poet's affair is with God"'. Or, as Robert himself wrote to John Ruskin in 1855, 'all poetry being a putting the infinite within the finite'. The poem was perceived in its time as optimistic — always a good selling point — and achieved second and third editions in 1885.

In one of her reminiscences, 'Browning in Venice', published in the *Century Magazine* in February 1902, Katherine Bronson merrily noted Robert's and Sarianna's 'approving especially of the cook's manner of treating ortolans, of which "mouthfuls for cardinals" the poet writes so amusingly in the prologue to "Ferishtah's Fancies".' Mrs Arthur Bronson, wrote her good friend Henry James, 'sat for twenty years at the wide mouth, as it were, of the grand Canal, holding out her hand, with endless good nature, patience, charity, to all decently accredited petitioners, the incessant troop of those either bewilderedly making or fondly renewing acquaintance with the dazzling city.' Katherine Bronson, an American lady, had acquired the Ca' Alvisi, directly opposite the church of S. Maria della Salute, and for the convenience of her friends she rented an adjacent property, the ancient fifteenth-century Palazzo Giustiniani-Recanati, which Robert and Sarianna were invited to regard as their own home during their visits to Venice. Her attachment to Robert Browning, remarked Henry James, revealed the 'serious thought and serious feeling' that Katherine Bronson cherished behind a surface of social facility. 'Nothing in all her beneficent life had probably made her happier than to have found herself able to minister, each year, with the returning autumn, to his pleasure and comfort.'[258]

Katherine Bronson's health was delicate: most of her day was spent reclining on a sofa, from which she would receive guests. Her principal occupations were smoking cigarettes, popping peppermint creams into her little rosebud mouth, writing comedies in Venetian dialect, and attending to a pack of a dozen small, ornamental dogs — pugs and a special breed of Chinese spaniel — which lay in litters of two or three at a time at her feet. Having saved her strength during the day, Mrs Bronson would exert herself in the evenings at little literary dinner parties for six, or else at theatrical performances provided for the entertainment of guests in one of the smaller drawing-rooms that had been converted into a bijou theatre where her daughter Edith and her friends would act short plays.

'Browning in Venice' is an affectionate memoir based on Katherine Bronson's close observation of Robert's habits, not only in Venice but also in Asolo, where, mostly on the strength of her admiration for *Pippa Passes*, she acquired a property, La Mura, at which the Brownings were always welcome. Robert's days in Italy, as in London, were ruled 'with a precision and regularity such as one would more naturally attribute to a mathematician'. At Asolo, Robert rose at seven, rolled around in a cold bath, ate a simple breakfast punctually served at eight, and then went out walking with Sarianna. On their return, Robert would read English newspapers and write letters before a light lunch of Italian dishes and Italian wine. After lunch, he would write and read again until three o'clock when he was ready for tea, which he did not normally take in London in the afternoons. At Asolo, 'He liked to see and hear the hissing urn on a table in the middle of the loggia, and he would accept a cup of tea and a biscuit with the greatest pleasure, as he did so saying, "I think I'm all the better for this delicious drink, after all." ' After tea, Mrs Bronson and the Brownings, wrapped up in rugs against the late afternoon autumnal chill, went bowling out in a carriage, exploring the countryside for miles around.[259]

In Venice, Robert walked the narrow *calles* and toured the canals in a gondola with Katherine's daughter Edith as his guide, familiarizing himself with the art and architecture of the city and regretting modern alterations. Often, too, he would travel out to the Lido to walk briskly around for hours enjoying the light, the air, and the life around him. It hardly crossed his mind in these years to make a sentimental journey back to Florence or Rome. Venice so enchanted Robert that he resolved in 1885 to buy a palazzo for Pen, who had by that time also become a regular visitor to Venice. The house in De Vere Gardens had been bought for Pen, rather than rented, as a safe investment for the young man's future — a substantial property that he could not easily fritter away. Now Robert fixed his sights on the Palazzo Manzoni, a place where Pen could live, work, and become part of the Venetian artists' colony.

To F. J. Furnivall, on 17 November 1885, Robert wrote: 'I have been kept thus long here by the business of buying a Venice Palace, the Manzoni Palazzo ... the most beautiful house — not the biggest nor most majestic — in Venice. I buy it solely for Pen, who is in love with the city beyond anything I could expect, and had set his heart on this particular acquisition before I joined him, quite unaware that I had entertained a similar preference for it years ago ... Pen will have sunshine and beauty about him, and every help to profit by these, while I and my sister have secured a shelter when the fogs of life grow too troublesome.' But the Manzoni Palazzo slipped from his grasp. The Austrian owner thought he could get a better price from another prospect and failed to produce the relevant documents. Robert attempted to sue, but withdrew when he learned that the walls of the beautiful property were seriously cracked and that the foundations were so shaky that the whole building might collapse into the canal.

It was in Robert's mind, too, that Pen might fall in love with Edith Bronson — and she with him — and that his future might be further secured by marriage to this charming, considerable heiress. It wasn't very likely. The golden Florentine boy, the little prince of Casa Guidi, had filled out into a plump, short-legged, hearty, heavily mustachioed, balding 36-year-old spendthrift with a minor talent for painting and sculpture and a reputation, if gossip could be credited, for discreditable promiscuity. His chief claim to attention was his paternity. It is surmised that Robert's none-too-subtle angling for the hand of the beautiful and elegant Edith to be joined to Pen's caused some coolness between Katherine Bronson and the Brownings and that it was not just a wretchedly rainy season in Venice in 1885, or the disappointing failure to obtain the Palazzo Manzoni, that resulted in Robert's sudden dissatisfaction with Venice and his absence from the comforts of Ca' Alvisi for three years until his return, in happier circumstances that resolved the difficulties of both marriage prospects and palazzo purchase, in 1888.

There was no decisive break with the Bronson women. Katherine and Edith met Robert in London in 1886, and the correspondence between them continued, although the frequency diminished and the tone of the letters fell away from the regular high excitements they usually exhibited. In 1886 and 1887, holidays were taken in Switzerland and — for reasons of Sarianna's health, says Mrs Orr: 'Miss Browning was not allowed to leave England'[260] — at the Hand Hotel, Llangollen, in Wales where Mrs Theodore Martin, formerly Helen Faucit, found Robert unusually quiet at luncheon: 'Conversation there is none.'

Always impatient with people who did not look after their health, Robert was probably depressed by — among other things — not only Sarianna's serious illnesses in 1884 and again in 1886 (from which she recovered) but by the passing of many old friends. Carlyle had died in 1881, Fanny Haworth in 1883. Thackeray, Dickens, Dean Stanley and his wife, Lady Augusta Stanley (the daughter of Robert's old friend Lady Elgin), 'Barry Cornwall' (Bryan Waller Procter), John Forster, Alfred Domett, Richard Monckton Milnes (Lord Houghton) — Mrs Orr gives the dolorous roll call[261] — all these and many others had gone. One of the greatest losses, on 4 September 1886, was Joseph Milsand, to whose memory Robert dedicated *Parleyings with Certain People of Importance in their Day*, which was published on 28 January 1887.

William Clyde DeVane characterizes this last major poem as 'notes for Browning's mental autobiography'.[262] In the seven monologues that constitute the body of the poem, Robert confronts and directly addresses — now, at last, without the thin poetic disguise of an interlocutor or a melodramatic theatrical mask — old ghosts called up from his past. 'The revision of the work,' says Mrs Orr, 'caused him unusual trouble. The subjects he had chosen strained his powers of exposition; and I think he often tried to remedy by mere verbal correction, what was a defect in the logical arrangement of his ideas. They would slide into each other where a visible dividing line was required. The last stage of his life was now at hand; and the vivid return of fancy to his boyhood's literary loves was in pathetic, perhaps not quite accidental, coincidence with the fact.'[263]

Robert's choice of the characters to represent the seven major interests of his life — philosophy, history, poetry, politics, painting, the classics (Greek), and music — were: Bernard de Mandeville (English satirist, author of *The Fable of the Bees*, first published in 1714, which paradoxically affirmed that 'private vices are public benefits'); Daniel Bartoli (seventeenth-century Italian Jesuit and author of *De' Simboli Trasportati al Morale*); Christopher Smart (English religious poet who died insane in 1771); George Bubb Dodington (Irish-born eighteenth-century politician, patron, and wit who frequently changed his political allegiance); Francis Furini (seventeenth-century Florentine painter of the nude who later became a priest); Gerard de Lairesse (Dutch painter and, after becoming blind, author in 1690 of *The Art of Painting*); and Charles Avison (English composer, author in 1752 of an *Essay on Musical Expression*). All these men 'had in some way been influential, usually in Browning's youth, in shaping his ideas upon their respective subjects: with one exception [Francis Furini], the works of these men had been the boyhood books of the poet.'[264]

Pressure on Robert for an autobiography had been applied by members of the Browning Society who, in their endless speculations about the object of their adoration, their reverent analyses of Browning poetry, and their avidity for any scrap of personal detail about the life of the poet, wished for the writer's own word that would shed ineluctable light upon the darkness in which they thrashed in their search for ultimate meaning. Robert was not disposed to be of such positive assistance, though he would conscientiously correct any misstatements, gross or minor, that were made in articles or published in proceedings of the Society. It was not difficult to feel too honoured by the Browning Society: its attentions could become intrusive. The *Parleyings* were, to quote Park Honan, 'a vast elegant bone for the Browning societies to chew, and a hostage to the future in a continuing skirmish with biographers yet unborn'.[265]

While the Browningites gnawed and growled at each other over the *Parleyings*, Robert was making a bonfire of anything that might over-excite their passions and set their gastric juices flowing for the flesh of more direct revelations. In 1887, Thomas Wise, a young and dedicated Browningite (and future literary forger), watched in mute horror as Robert crouched over an old trunk and ruthlessly pulled out handful after handful, bundle upon bundle, sheaf after sheaf, of letters and manuscripts, the product of sixty years and more of his personal life and professional work, and fed the fireplace at De Vere Gardens with priceless proofs and evidences, irreplaceable materials that would have kept a score of Browning Societies at work for a score of years.

It took Robert a week to reduce his personal papers to ashes (notably his letters to his family, from his youth up to the death of his father) — all but the letters to her correspondents from Elizabeth, which he left largely unread and untouched. The letters between himself and Elizabeth, he could not bear to destroy: 'As for the letters to myself, — and for months before our marriage I received one daily, — these which are so immeasurably superior to any compositions of the kind I have any experience of, — would glorify the privileged receiver beyond any imaginable crown in the world or out of it — but I cannot, any more than Timon, "cut my heart in sums — tell out my blood."'[266]

Those letters that were left edited or intact were for his son, and what he cared to do with them after his father's death was up to Pen — even though they dwelt upon embarrassing matters, such as Elizabeth's devotion to spiritualism and her reliance on morphine, that still worried Robert and that he had sought and fought in his lifetime to suppress from wide public knowledge. There existed letters from Elizabeth to Henrietta and to Arabel that he could not readily get at. 'There will not be found in the whole of the correspondence one untrue, ungenerous word, I know,' wrote Robert to George Barrett on 2 May 1882, 'but plenty of sad communication which has long ago served its purpose and should be forgotten. Unfortunately the unscrupulous hunger for old scandals is on the increase — and as the glory of that most wonderful of women is far from at the full — I cannot help many forebodings — which you share with me.'

Pen's progress as an artist was nurtured and managed by his father with as much determined energy as he had applied to furthering his son's academic career. Robert would stop at nothing, would black any boots and polish any heads, if that would bring Pen to sympathetic attention and his artistic works to the point of an exhibition and a sale. To his credit, Pen had been working hard, pouring out a stream of drawings, engravings, prints and paintings, portraits — an ancient tradesman at work cobbling boots and an elderly, dapper, white-bearded poet, Robert Browning to the life — and studies of *nature morte* such as grotesque skulls and dead furry animals on damask tablecloths. These were technically accomplished — there could be no denying Pen's facility with chalks and pens, pencils and stencils, engraving tools and brushes. So far, so good. Robert was satisfied that Pen had become serious, had settled to a productive and profitable profession that was no disgrace to social standing and was gratifying to the artistic sensibilities of good society.

From Heyermans' studio in Antwerp, Pen had begun to branch out with excursions to the Black Forest and Dinant (where he had become attached to the daughter of an innkeeper), then to Paris where he studied, apparently, under the historical painter Jean-Paul Laurens and the sculptor Auguste Rodin. Laurens, it seems, had given Pen short shrift, to judge by a letter from Joseph Milsand in Paris to the Brownings in London. Tactfully, Milsand had written, 'We must bear in mind his hopes and good intentions, crushed by M. Laurens; we must bear in mind too Pen's moral state. Whether through his own fault or not, he is like a man who has been thrown two or three times from a housetop onto the pavement.'[267]

Milsand braced himself to the embarrassing duty of talking directly with Pen, not just about his duty to work diligently but also of his obligations to his father and aunt. Filial responsibility to his own mother — for whose sake he had set aside his marriage for ten years — had figured largely in Milsand's own life. To Sarianna, he had written:

I understand perfectly your feelings and Robert's. It is cruel indeed to be disappointed in one's hopes, desires, the very purpose of one's life. But you know what I went through. I was unable in conscience to bow to the wishes of my mother: I merely postponed my marriage and it would be impossible for me to persuade any man to break or keep engagements which he alone can weigh. I shall advise Penn [*sic*] to work, I will do my best to make him understand and respect your feelings. I have told him that his father had a perfect right to demand that the sacrifices made to further his career should not be directed to any other purpose — above all one contrary to his wishes. It was up to him, Penn, to profit by the opportunity given him for life studies. But I could not and would not go further than to tell him I thought his primary duty was to concentrate on establishing himself in a profession.[268]

Pen's proposed marriage to the Dinant innkeeper's daughter seems to have coincided with his disappointment in Paris. The engagement was broken and Robert, in a letter of 5 January 1882, commenting on rumours put about by Furnivall that Pen had taken a Belgian wife, wrote: 'It is mere gossip grown out of just this fact that more than four years ago [Pen] formed an attachment to a young lady of perfectly unexceptionable character and connexions. I objected to a marriage on many accounts quite irrespective of these, and communicated with the lady's father (who parenthetically is wealthy) and the project was dropped on both sides. This occurred at a time when Robert's [i.e. Pen's] pictorial career was just begun and would seriously have affected it: and wholly dependent on myself as he was with little prospect of becoming otherwise, he had no right to dispose of his actions in that matter: and my objections were felt to be reasonable — I believe on both sides.'[269]

The rich innkeeper, being informed by Pen's father that the young Flash Harry, the plump and cheerful little painter consorting with his daughter, had little or no money of his own and was entirely reliant on Robert Browning's largesse, and no doubt mindful of his own money, promptly agreed that marriage would be a mistake and very likely talked to the young lady in terms less tactful than those employed to Pen by Milsand. In 1878 the lovers were separated. Robert's worry that Pen would always be dependent on him was mitigated — though not entirely — by Pen's first successes. In 1877, one of Pen's large pictures had been accepted by the Royal Academy and on the very first day of the exhibition a Mr Fielden, Member of Parliament for a Yorkshire constituency, had inquired about its price. Robert consulted with Leighton and Millais, who recommended that £300 should be asked. 'The price was somewhat extravagant, all things considered,' confided Alfred Domett to his diary on 13 June 1877, 'the friendship of the artist-assessors for the father had no doubt some influence on their estimate. But Browning was naturally highly gratified.'

Robert's address book was put fully at Pen's disposal: invitations were sent out, with a note written in Robert's own hand at the top, for a private exhibition of Pen's pictures to be held on 30 March 1879 in a room loaned by George Murray Smith at 17 Queen's Gate Gardens. A great number of Robert's women friends attended, so many that Alfred Domett observed Robert 'handing in a rather finely dressed lady with some ceremony and much profession at seeing her, etc., apparently having forgotten who she was, but presently afterwards recognising her. As I passed him, he whispered to me, "That was *my cook*, but I didn't recollect her." '[270] On 12 June 1880, Domett was recording, a little perfunctorily, a visit to 'the usual little exhibition of young Browning's pictures' which that year included 'a picture of two horned owls he made pets of, the female of which had often laid eggs, and had now hatched three'. Domett was among the guests on 27 March 1881 who had assembled to see Pen's pictures for the Royal Academy Exhibition. Among those who inspected a painting of 'a monk or officer in the Inquisition standing over a naked heretic chained to the dungeon floor' was Oscar Wilde, 'foppishly dressed; long hair to his shoulders, light brown overcoat with curly-furred collar etc.'.[271]

On 6 February 1883, Robert was able to tell Alfred Domett that 'Pen had made £1200 last year by his pictures. That of the "Girl before the Inquisitors" he (Browning Senr.) had sold for £300 to a Philadelphian Museum of Art . . . had also sold the "Monk pulling the bell" and two landscapes . . . Pen was "working away" at Paris, employed upon a statue (Dryope?) six feet high, subsequently exhibited at the Grosvenor Gallery.'[272] Things were looking up for Pen, though it still seemed to Robert and Sarianna that encouragement should be tempered with some caution: Sarianna thought it a good idea that Pen should have a studio in whatever house the Brownings bought after they left Warwick Crescent and that he should live with them. On 1 April 1884, the day that Sarianna confided this plan to Alfred Domett, he noted Pen to be 'rosy-looking, goodnatured and unassuming as ever, — beginning already to get a little bald on the top of his head'.[273]

The critics approved of Pen's work, which won significant prizes. It was generally considered to be vigorous and technically admirable, and it also impressed by its size — a fault, perhaps, but a magnificent, extravagant, magnanimous fault. Pen's pictures covered the walls of his father's house, and Robert redoubled his efforts to promote his son. As Pen's manager, agent, and intendant, he was shameless in his appeals to anyone who could do Pen some good. In collusion with Sarianna, Robert held exhibitions at their own house and arranged others elsewhere, pestered every artist of his acquaintance for hints and cues about how best to exhibit and sell work, dropped delicate hints to everyone — including Tennyson — that if they should happen to drop by, at any time of day, they would be surely gratified by the sight of a new painting. When simple cajolery failed, he would go to the extent of weeping at the Grosvenor Gallery, which, against its policy of accepting works rejected by the Royal Academy, recognized the distinguished poet's distress and accepted Pen's monumental life-size bronze, *Dryope Fascinated by Apollo in the Form of a Serpent*, which had cost Pen a thousand pounds to cast and cost the model long and anxious hours posing with a live python draped around her naked body.

Robert and Sarianna were on holiday at St Moritz in August 1887 when a letter reached them from Pen. In it, he announced his engagement to Fannie Coddington, who had rejected Pen's first proposal fourteen years before but, for whatever reasons, had now thought better of the offer and accepted it. Robert, according to a letter of 21 October 1887 to the Revd J. D. Williams, had known the Coddingtons for years, having first met them through Dean Stanley. Two letters from Robert to Mr and Mrs Coddington, dated 24 May and 14 November 1873, testify to a long-standing acquaintance. The senior Coddingtons — American, rich — had died. Fannie, now orphaned and possessed of a large fortune, had only recently returned to England with her sister Marie for the sake of Marie's health. Robert wrote rosily to Williams:

> Now it happens, that I could have chosen, within the circle of my acquaintance, no young person more qualified, so far as I can judge, to make Pen eminently happy — the match presenting every advantage without a single drawback: what was to be done, therefore, but accept and be thankful? Fannie, my

daughter in love and law, is good, true, sympathetic in every way, — a few years younger than Pen, — very pretty, we think, devoted to him, we know, — and having been an admirable daughter and sister will presumably become as fitting a wife. She has all the ambition for his sake which I could wish, and is eminently distinguished for common sense: so that — I repeat — how can I be other than thankful? I ought to add that the means of comfortable life are abundant in this case — indeed Pen might become independent of my own assistance, did either he or I permit of such an arrangement.

The letter to Williams dwells principally on the benefits to Pen of marriage to Fannie. On 19 August 1887, from St Moritz, Robert had written frankly to Pen to remind him that he should make every effort to deserve his good luck.

You know very well I have never had any other aim than your happiness in all I have done: the kind of life you have been forced to lead for these last years always seemed comfortless and even dangerous to me, — whatever might be said for it as helpful to your art (and *that* it no doubt was) — you must know it had lasted long enough for the purpose, and could not, in the nature of things, continue as you advance in years ... I do approve of your choice with all my heart: there is no young person I know at all comparable to Miss C. She has every requisite to make you happy and successful if you deserve it — as I believe you will endeavour to do. If the lady had been unknown to me, — or one of the innumerable pleasant parties to a flirtation and utterly useless for anything else, I should have given you up for lost ... Miss C. has spoken to me with the greatest frankness and generosity of the means she will have of contributing to your support — for my part, I can engage to give you £300 a year: this, with the results of your work — if you manage to sell but a single picture in the year — will amply suffice. Of course, at my death you will have whatever I possess: and meantime if any good fortune comes to me — well, it will be, as it ever has been, your good fortune too.

Sarianna, adding her own few prim words to this letter, affirmed in her customary short order everything that Robert had written: 'I am very happy indeed to think you are going to be married. Hôtel life is very comfortless as well as very expensive, and you have now had quite enough of it. You will not, I trust, work less well for having a happy home. I am sure I shall be very fond of Fannie, and altogether approve of your choice. This afternoon I went over to her, and we had a long talk. She is very different from the fast American girls who abound here. You have every prospect of happiness — God bless you.'[274]

Pen and Fannie were married at Hawkwell Place, Pembury, near London, on 4 October 1887, and thereafter travelled first to Venice on honeymoon before proceeding to America, 'where the lady must needs settle her affairs before returning to Europe: the aftercourse, and eventual subsidence, — that I leave', wrote Robert to J. D. Williams on 21 October, 'to their own judgment — sure that a well-weighed and all-considerate judgment there will be somehow.' In this trustful frame of mind, Robert settled to his own proper business, which consisted, in 1887 and 1888, of revising his published plays and poetry and correcting the proofs of a monumental sixteen-volume edition of his complete works. These volumes were issued at monthly intervals, between April 1888 and July 1889, by Smith and Elder. True to his principles, Robert declined, after giving the matter some thought, to provide notes to his poems. On 12 November 1887, he wrote to George Murray Smith to say that 'I am so out of sympathy with all this "biographical matter" connected with works which ought to stand or fall by their own merits quite independently of the writer's life and habits, that I prefer leaving my poems to speak for themselves as they best can — and to end as I began long ago.'[275]

Robert and Sarianna joined Pen and Fannie in Venice in the autumn of 1888. The newly-weds had returned from America in March. Fannie had been so thoroughly seasick on the voyage out that she had suffered a miscarriage shortly after arrival in America.[276] Pen had returned with laryngitis and an 'ugly and teazing cough'. Robert himself, in London, had not been well during their absence. He had not been well in 1887, though a holiday in the pure air of the Engadine 'got rid in a trice of all the ugly consequences of some nine months stay in London'.[277] On 14 January 1888, however, in a letter to Pen and Fannie, Robert wrote of having recovered from the recurrent symptom of a 'cough, which is *spasmodic*, not originating in anything worse than my old trouble of the liver' and a new one — rheumatic pain.

Fannie suffered another miscarriage in Venice in January 1888, and the state of her health continued to be uncertain by the time Robert and Sarianna made a return to Venice that year. To be in the city again, and staying again at the Palazzo Giustiniani-Recanati on good terms with Katherine Bronson was a tonic, not to say the excitement of Pen's acquisition — with Fannie's money — of the fantastically baroque Palazzo Rezzonico and hearing of his plans for its elaborate refurbishment. To Mr and Mrs Charles Skirrow, on Christmas Day 1888, Robert wrote from De Vere Gardens to reminisce: 'I never enjoyed Venice — the place — so much: I cared to see nothing but be on the lagune, — landing, as I did every day, at Lido for a long walk on the sand. Then the doings of my couple, Pen and his wife, were always calling on me for notice. The latter has again had a disappointment [miscarriage]: indeed the uncertain state of her health is all that seems to stand between them and happiness.'

On a happier note, Robert continues: 'My last news is favourable, I am glad to say. You know Pen has bought the huge Rezzonico Palace, — one of the best in Venice, — and he finds it not a bit too big, but is occupied all day long in superintending a *posse* of workmen who fit the rooms into comfortable inhabitedness . . . It is an excellent purchase, — and surprises everybody now that it has been effected: for the mere adornments might be sold tomorrow for the price of the palazzo itself. You know how unwell I was at the end of my stay here, — Venice cured me speedily — but I am far from reconciled yet to the fog and impure air one breathes — or coughs at.' To Marie Coddington, too, on 28 December 1888, Robert lamented the loss of 'such a succession of wonderful days of the finest weather imaginable: three months of glory with only two rainy days — in sad contrast to the grim aspect of things in London. You will be amused, and I think greatly interested when you see the famous palazzo their property, which Pen is doing his best to make as comfortable as it is magnificent.'

In June 1889, Edmund Gosse sat and talked for more than two hours in a garden at Trinity College, Cambridge, with Robert and was surprised that 'although, on occasion, he could be so accurate an observer of nature, it was not instinctive with him to observe. In the blaze of summer, with all the life of birds and insects moving around us, he did not borrow an image from or direct an allusion to any natural fact about us.' But the old poet's attention was not on the present:

> He sat and talked of his own early life and aspirations; how he marvelled as he looked back, at the audacious obstinacy which had made him, when a youth, determine to be a poet and nothing but a poet ... Then, with complete frankness, he described the long-drawn desolateness of his early and middle life as a literary man; how, after certain spirits had seemed to rejoice in his first sprightly runnings, and especially in *Paracelsus*, a blight had fallen upon his very admirers. He touched, with a slight irony, on the entirely unintelligible *Sordello*, and the forlorn hope of *Bells and Pomegranates*.

Gosse, marvelling as Robert played with an idea for a poem, quickly and with practised dexterity turning a straightforward story about a Tuscan nobleman inside out to 'suggest the non-obvious or inverted moral of the whole', reflected that 'it was not his strength only, his vehement and ever-eruptive force, that distinguished him, but to an almost equal extent his humanity'. Then, too, Browning demanded no tributes of sympathy, admiration, or amusement: 'He rather hastened forward with both hands full of entertainment for the new-comer, anxious to please rather than hoping to be pleased ... to Robert Browning the whole world was full of vague possibilities of friendship.'

On the reverse side, Gosse admitted that Robert Browning threw a shadow: 'No one resented more keenly an unpleasant specimen of humanity, no one could snub more royally at need, no one was ... more ruthless in administering the *coup de grâce*; but then his surprise gave way to his indignation. He had assumed a new acquaintance to be a good fellow, and behold! against all ordinary experience, he had turned out to be a bore or a sneak. Sudden, irreparable chastisement must fall on one who had proved the poet's optimism to be at fault.'[278]

Chastisement, sudden and irreparable, fell like a bolt of Jovian lightning upon the shade of Edward FitzGerald just a month after Gosse had conducted this interview with Robert. A selection of the *Letters and Literary Remains of Edward FitzGerald*, edited by Aldis Wright, had recently been published, some six years after FitzGerald's death in June 1883. On 7 July 1889, Robert was reading through the book when he came across a reference, in a letter of 1861, to Elizabeth. The words that Robert read were these:

> Mrs Browning's death is rather a relief to me, I must say; no more Aurora Leighs, thank God! A woman of real Genius, I know: but what is the upshot of it all? She and her Sex had better mind the Kitchen and the Children; and perhaps the Poor: except in such things as little Novels, they only devote themselves to what Men do much better, leaving that which Men do worse or not at all.

Enraged and outraged, Robert dashed off a poem that he sent the next day, white hot, to the *Athenaeum*, which, despite Robert's attempt to retrieve it, published it a few days later above his signature on 13 July 1889. The verses, under the title 'To Edward FitzGerald', ran thus:

> I CHANCED upon a new book yesterday:
> I opened it, and where my finger lay
>   'Twixt page and uncut page, these words I read
>   — Some six or seven at most — and learned thereby
> That you, FitzGerald, whom by ear and eye
>   She never knew, 'thanked God my wife was dead.'
>
>   Ay, dead! and were yourself alive, good Fitz,
> How to return your thanks would task my wits:
>   Kicking you seems the common lot of curs —
> While more appropriate greeting lends you grace:
> Surely to spit there glorifies your face —
>   Spitting — from lips once sanctified by hers.

To Furnivall, Robert wrote somewhat contritely on 16 July 1889, that he'd have done better to leave the thing alone: 'like all impulsive actions, once the impulse is over, I believe I might preferably have left the thing to its proper contempt. But there was something too shocking in a man, whom my wife never even heard of, "feeling relieved at her death, he must say" — and I too said what I must.'

Aldis Wright wrote to a mutual friend of his and Robert's to say that he 'was not aware of the exact form of the offending paragraph' but was 'confident it had been twisted from its true meaning'.[279] There was an exchange of letters between Wright and the *Athenaeum*, between Robert and offended parties, and things were smoothed over quickly enough, except that beneath the conciliatory words and phrases Robert still smarted under a complex set of self-inflicted wounds: not only from the insult in the original published passage but from a feeling that his haste had got the better of his temper, that he had risen to the bait of nothing more than a worm, and had succeeded mostly in getting himself gaffed on a hook that experience should have told him was better avoided. Worst of all, he was galled by a feeling that the ultimate result of his flash of vituperation had been to humiliate not only himself but Elizabeth before people who might, but for his reaction, have never heard of FitzGerald's miserable, misogynistic insult.

The incident had done Robert no good, and, as Sarianna wrote on 17 July 1889 to Pen, 'I need not say I knew nothing of the verses, or their cause, till I saw them in print — Your papa was quite ill with the pain it gave him.' By 16 August, when Robert wrote to Pen, he was feeling better for having given up dining out since the end of the previous month and for having taken advantage of some pleasant weather to treat 'London as the bracing place' and walk out for two hours daily. Sarianna, adding a few words to this letter, confirmed to Pen that Robert was now in good health, 'but he may change'. For Robert's sake, and for her own, she was keen to get him away to Asolo and Venice now that London had emptied of people and amusements. And so it was that on 4 October Robert was writing to Fannie from La Mura in Asolo to congratulate her on her second wedding anniversary.

On 15 October, from Asolo, Robert sent George Murray Smith the manuscript 'of my new volume', which he described the same day in a letter to Mrs Charles Skirrow as 'some thirty poems long and short, — some few written here, all revised and copied. There was an advertisement which mentioned "The" Poem or "A" Poem — I don't know how the mistake occurred. It was said too to be "in the Press" — really being in my portfolio till a couple of hours ago.' The title of the collection of short poems, published on 12 December 1889, would be *Asolando* in honour of the little town to which he had returned fifty years after it had first taken his fancy. 'I was right to fall in love with this place fifty years ago, was I not?' Robert asked Katherine Bronson. 'We outlive some places, people, and things that charmed us in our youth, but the loveliness of this is no disappointment; it is even more beautiful to me now than then.'[280]

The poems in *Asolando* had mostly been written over the past three years, and on publication they were acclaimed as brilliant in their simplicity. The little book is said to have sold out on the first day, and nine reprints of the first edition were quickly issued to meet the demand that arose in the particular circumstances of its first publication.

Pen paid a quick visit to his father in Asolo and was reassured to find him, in the good care and cheerful company of Sarianna and Mrs Bronson, looking well and contented. Robert's coughing had stopped, and regular exercise had eased his shortness of breath. In the morning, Robert rambled around the town with Sarianna; after tea in the afternoon they drove out in a carriage; and after dinner he played on Mrs Bronson's spinet that she had brought from Venice. He noticed a small piece of ground, a piece of municipal property on which stood an unfinished building, and resolved to buy it. The notion so excited Robert that he could hardly think about anything else: he planned the house he should build, and particularly insisted on a loggia even bigger than the one at La Mura. And 'It shall have a tower,' said Robert, 'whence I can see Venice at every hour of the day, and I shall call it "Pippa's Tower."' To invite Mrs Bronson to dinner, he would have flag signals. 'The telephone is too modern; don't you think so?' And then Robert would turn grave: 'It may not be for me to enjoy it long — who can say? But it will always be useful for Pen and his family. They can come here so easily from Venice whenever they need rest or change of air . . . But I am good for ten years yet. I am perfectly well.'[281] Towards the end of their stay in Asolo, Robert and Sarianna greeted the Storys, who had turned up for a few days to see them. Writing later to Pen, on 13 December 1889, William Story recalled how Robert had said to him, 'We have been friends for forty years — aye — more than forty years — and with never a break.'

On 31 October Robert and Sarianna arrived in Venice, where Pen had worked miracles of internal construction and interior decoration in the Palazzo Rezzonico. No longer was Fannie turning delicately blue and freezing genteely to death in great, echoing, empty spaces: Pen had installed a system of central heating. To George Barrett, Robert had written on 24 February 1889 to report on what he had heard about the sensitive restorations and renovations Pen and Fannie had made: 'it is pleasant to hear how grateful the old Venetian families are at the palace having fallen into such reverent hands ... not being destined to vile uses, turned into an hotel, or the like'. In another letter, on 22 October from Asolo, Robert exclaimed again that 'their palazzo excites the wonder of everybody — so great is Pen's cleverness and extemporized architectural knowledge, as apparent in all he has done there ... Have I told you that there was a desecrated chapel which he has restored in honor of his Mother — putting up there the inscription by Tommasei now above Casa Guidi?' Pen, Robert told George, would take up painting and sculpture again, 'having been necessarily occupied with super-intendence of his workmen — a matter capitally arranged I am told'. As for Fannie, 'if her health will but allow the consummation of their happiness, I don't know what else to wish for them'.[282]

Lodged at the Palazzo Rezzonico, Robert occupied himself with reading and correcting the proofs of *Asolando*. He paid little mind to the gorgeousness of his room, seventy-two stairs up from the ground floor, its painted ceiling by Pen depicting an eagle struggling with a snake in reference to Shelley's *The Revolt of Islam*. More interesting and inspiring was the perfect view from the Rezzonico he had enjoyed so often at Casa Alvisi: 'the still grey lagune, the few seagulls flying, the islet of S. Giorgio in deep shadow, and the clouds in a long purple rack, behind which a sort of spirit of rose burns up till presently all the rims are on fire with gold, and last of all the orb sends before it a long column of its own essence apparently: so my day begins.'[283]

Robert rose at 6 a.m., read for a couple of hours before breakfast at eight, and then took himself off to the Lido for his customary walks along the sand. Now that Robert knew every canal and *calle* in Venice, he confidently wandered the city by day, informing himself even more minutely than before on every particular of art and architecture, and in the evenings the warm rooms of the Rezzonico clattered with the sound of heels on the marble floors, scarcely muffled by silken drapes and damasked walls: visitors by the score thronged to marvel at the changes Pen's imagination and Fannie's money had wrought and to make a fuss of Robert Browning, who returned the compliment by dining out and singing for his supper by reciting poetry as inveterately as he had ever done in London.

Robert took some trouble to conceal the fact that his breathing was becoming more laboured. He even tried to conceal it from himself: he would not rest in bed, he would not stop in his routine of work, walking, writing letters and sociability. He hardly paused to draw what halting, shallow breath he could take. On 9 November he wrote from Venice to a correspondent, Miss Keep: 'Yesterday, on the Lido, the heat was hardly endurable: bright sunshine, blue sky, — snow-tipped Alps in the distance. No place, I think, ever suited my needs, bodily and intellectual, so well. The first are satisfied — I am *quite* well, every breathing inconvenience gone: and as for the latter, I got through whatever had given me trouble in London.'[284]

On 29 November, Robert wrote to a friend in London to say that he had caught a cold, felt sadly asthmatic and scarcely fit to travel, but he hoped to set out for London sooner rather than later: there was the business of a collected edition of Elizabeth's works to oversee. He dosed himself with some medicine that relieved his chest, and he blamed himself for neglecting his 'provoking liver'. Robert thought little enough of bodily ills that he had dosed before with patent medicines. When his liver played up, he put himself on a reduced diet for a while and had been none the worse for it. But this time, the symptoms of illness and unusual frailty had become perfectly obvious and a matter of anxiety to everyone at the Palazzo Rezzonico.

Robert was moved to an entresol apartment, just above the ground floor, which allowed easy access to the dining-room. But he refused to see a doctor and insisted on carrying out social engagements he had entered into. On 30 November, after a severe bronchial attack, he finally consented to see Dr Cini, who had been called in by Pen. Cini immediately understood the gravity of the illness — severe bronchitis compounded by an irregular heart action. Robert was put to bed in Fannie's large room: here fires were kept burning, the ventilation assured a good circulation of air, and the windows let in all the bright winter sunshine and the light from the Grand Canal.

A trained Venetian nurse, Margherita Fiori, was employed to relieve the ministrations of Sarianna, Pen, Fannie, and Evelyn Barclay, a friend of Fannie's who happened to be staying at Palazzo Rezzonico. Together, making poultices and taking it in shifts to provide the best care for Robert, their efforts seemed to have a positive effect on the patient, who appeared to recover strength, so much so that Sarianna wrote and posted encouraging bulletins to friends about his apparent recovery. It may be that she believed what she was writing. What she saw was Robert the model patient: he did as he was told, took food and medicine without complaint, continually thanked everyone for their kind attentions, and assured them that he was not suffering.

And so it went on, regularly and quietly, for ten days. On 10 December 1889, Robert experienced a syncope of the heart. It looked like the end. Evelyn Barclay ran for brandy, and Pen called for doctors. Three of them — Dr Cini, Dr da Vigna, and Dr Minich — consulted together on 11 December and expressed their opinion that recovery, though possible, was improbable. Copies of *Asolando* had arrived that day at Palazzo Rezzonico, and they were brought to Robert, who stroked one of the books, murmuring that the binding of dark red cloth was a pretty colour. Late in the afternoon of Thursday, 12 December, Robert said to Margherita Fiori, 'I feel much worse. I know now that I must die.'[285] At about 6.30 that evening, Pen came to his father's bedside with a telegram from George Murray Smith and read it aloud. It said that the reviews of *Asolando*, published that very day, had been 'most favourable' and that the edition was 'nearly exhausted'. To this news, Robert is said to have softly responded, 'More than satisfied'; and to Pen he whispered, 'I am dying. My dear boy. My dear boy.' At ten o'clock, just as the clock at San Marco's struck the hour, Robert Browning died.

The verses of the epilogue to *Asolando* are the last Robert Browning ever published. They have since stood, as well as anything he ever wrote, as his epitaph:

> At the midnight in the silence of the sleep-time,
>   When you set your fancies free,
> Will they pass to where — by death, fools think, imprisoned —
> Low he lies who once so loved you, whom you loved so,
>   — Pity me?

Oh to love so, be so loved, yet so mistaken!
    What had I on earth to do
With the slothful, with the mawkish, the unmanly?
Like the aimless, helpless, hopeless, did I drivel
    — Being — who?

One who never turned his back but marched breast forward,
    Never doubted clouds would break,
Never dreamed, though right were worsted, wrong would triumph,
Held we fall to rise, are baffled to fight better,
    Sleep to wake.

No, at noonday in the bustle of man's work-time
    Greet the unseen with a cheer!
Bid him forward, breast and back as either should be,
'Strive and thrive!' cry 'Speed, — fight on, fare ever
    There as here!'

Emelyn Story's immediate reaction on hearing from Pen of Robert's death was to telegraph to Henry James in London, not simply with the news but with an appeal to 'help poor Pen, who wants to have his father buried at Florence beside his mother'. The next day, she wrote: 'I feel sure that if he expressed any wish it must have been to be buried beside his ever-beloved wife at Florence. No Westminster Abbey could in his loyal heart have had an allurement to be named beside that dear Florentine grave.'[286] Only that summer Robert had indeed spoken to Sarianna of his own wishes: if he should die in England, he wished to be buried with his mother; if in France, with his father; and if he should die in Italy, he wished to be buried with his wife.[287]

Sarianna prompted Pen to seek permission to bury Robert next to Elizabeth in Florence, but it turned out that the Protestant Cemetery was closed. A recent decree had prohibited any further interments there, and nothing but an Act of God or the Italian Parliament — and the one was as unlikely as the other — could open up the ground to receive the mortal remains of Robert Browning. Venice recommended itself as an appropriate resting place: the city authorities would welcome the great poet as a permanent prize and offered all possible honours in a public funeral. Pen was tempted, but Florence won his heart and he had made up his mind to use every influence to secure his father's burial there when a message arrived from the Dean of Westminster offering an interment in the Abbey.

The original intention of the Abbey authorities had been only that a memorial service would be held on the day of Robert's funeral, but pressure had been applied, notably by George Murray Smith and Frederic Leighton, for this offer to be upgraded and a tomb to be provided. A suitable spot for Robert's reception was found in the crowded Abbey space, just below Chaucer's tomb and close to Spenser's. Pen willingly gave his assent, and arrangements were quickly made for transport of the body from Venice to London.

A private service was conducted for a large congregation of mourners — family, friends, visitors, residents, and Venetian municipal officials — in the great Sala of the Palazzo Rezzonico by the British Chaplain. At two o'clock on the afternoon of Sunday 15 December 1889, the coffin containing the body of Robert Browning, crowned with a wreath of bay leaves, was sealed. The coffin was borne down the steps of the Palazzo on the shoulders of eight local firemen — *pompieri* — dressed in their blue uniforms and laid on the impressively decorated and canopied black and gold funeral barge to be transported to the Isola San Michele, the mortuary Island of the Dead.

Heaped with wreaths, including a wreath of laurel leaves placed by Pen, the coffin was attended on the barge 'by four *uscieri* in "gala" dress, two sergeants of the Municipal Guard, and two of the firemen bearing torches'.[288] The barge was towed away by a steam launch commanded by an admiral of the Royal Italian Marine. Pen, Fannie, and Sarianna boarded another launch; the city officials, friends, and other mourners stepped into their black gondolas; and the entire funeral fleet slowly followed the barge in solemn procession down the Grand Canal and into the rose and gold light of the *laguna*. On arrival at the Isola San Michele, the firemen again took up their burden and bore the coffin to a reserved place in the chapel, where it rested for two days until it was transported, discreetly, privately, by night, to the railway station and placed on a train to be taken home, accompanied by an English manservant, to De Vere Gardens. Pen, Fannie, and Sarianna travelled quickly to London the day after.[289]

It had been suggested to Pen that he might make a formal application to have Elizabeth's remains re-interred in Westminster Abbey: if his parents could not rest together in Florence, they should be placed forever together in England. The idea did not appeal to Pen, who could not bear the thought of his mother's grave being disturbed. She had rested in Florence so long that the spot where she lay had become sanctified by her presence. And so it was that Robert alone was laid under the flags of Poets' Corner on 31 December 1889.

Six hundred distinguished ticket-holders queued from early morning, in freezing fog, to attend the official funeral ceremony. The pallbearers included Benjamin Jowett, the Master of Balliol; Henry Montagu Butler, the Master of Trinity College, Cambridge; Frederic Leighton; George Murray Smith; Archdeacon Farrar; and Hallam Tennyson, representing his father, Alfred Tennyson. Sarianna was too ill to attend, so Pen alone led the procession into the Abbey and the great obsequies began in the flicker of candlelight and fragments of fog that fitfully lit and shadowed the immense spaces crowded with the official representatives of art and literature, philosophy and learning, law, government, and others who had come out of simple love and liking for their old friend.

The last thing they heard before they departed from the celebration of death into the light of midday and their own lives was the sound of the choir singing a setting of three verses from Elizabeth Barrett Browning's poem 'The Sleep'.

In Venice, a memorial tablet was affixed to the wall of the Palazzo Rezzonico.

A

Roberto Browning

MORTO IN QUESTO PALAZZO

IL 12 DICEMBRE 1889

VENEZIA

POSE

Open my heart and you will see
Graved inside of it, 'Italy.'

EPILOGUE
Pen in Italy

Pen's marriage to Fannie survived his father's death by only two years. When Robert Browning died, a substantial hawser of Fannie's attachment to Pen was loosed. Pen, by various accounts friendly to him in later life, loved Fannie very sincerely and felt a true delight when she showed herself to best advantage. She possessed at least one distinct advantage in Venice — her beautiful Titian hair. Fannie, for her part, however fond she may have been of Pen, also loved the social and intellectual prestige that marriage into the Browning family had conferred upon her. As Pen's wife, she was now the first lady of the family and may have regarded herself, in whatever terms, as the natural successor to Elizabeth Barrett Browning. She might have been satisfied to be the wife of a distinguished artist whose paintings were admired as respectfully as the Tiepolo ceiling at the Rezzonico which Pen arranged to have carefully restored, or whose sculptures were as highly regarded as those of William Wetmore Story and fetched just as high prices. It might be, however improbably, that he would break out again into violent verse. But Pen's energies, even before the death of his father, were being enthusiastically diverted into the restoration of the Rezzonico at the expense of his artistic work for private collectors which provided an income and for exhibitions which offered the possibility of prizes and critical attention.

Not that Pen gave up his work entirely — he painted a vast design on canvas for another ceiling at the Rezzonico and occasionally committed himself to a sculpture. Fannie's embarrassment and moral outrage was considerable when he posed nude statuary of female models to best effect in situations around the Rezzonico where, naturally, they were intended to catch and gratify the eyes of visitors. When Fannie, who had imbibed a narrow Christian outlook from her parents, expressed her horror at the indecent display of these works (by Pen himself), he put them behind curtains in his studio so that the fronts were modestly shrouded but the backsides were exposed. Short of dressing them in fashionable frocks or classic draperies, what more could be done to hide them? Why, indeed, should they be concealed at all?

There was at least one good reason: Fannie is supposed by some partisans to have taken exception to one bust of a pretty girl. This sculpture was called 'Hope' and the model had been Ginevra Biagiotti, a young woman who had been brought into the household by Fannie herself and who was rumoured to be Pen's own daughter — perhaps one of the illegitimate children he was said to have fathered in Brittany, though the name is hardly Breton. And if she was not Pen's bastard, then she was alleged to be Pen's mistress. When Ginevra was promoted by Fannie to the post of virtual housekeeper at the Rezzonico, Sarianna and Fannie's sister Marie are said to have strongly objected, urging the dismissal of Ginevra. Pen was mortified by the gossip that quickly accumulated around himself and Ginevra, complaining angrily and bitterly that he was made out to be such a villain as to be capable of insulting his wife and aunt by making a mistress of his housekeeper. On the other hand, to send Ginevra away would be to stain the character of a girl his wife had taken up and who had trusted Fannie in all good faith. As a result of this moral dilemma, Ginevra stayed and eventually married Cantoni, the intendant of Pen's manufactory of silks, lace and linens when he set up that modest business in Asolo.

Fannie's peace of mind was disturbed not only by unclothed statuary or by gossip about her husband and her housekeeper — she was horrified, too, by the snakes (among them a boa constrictor) Pen liked to keep around him and, in the tradition of his father, the menagerie of other birds and animals he had collected since childhood. Shades, too, of his grandfather: Pen is said to have been more worried about the welfare of his birds and animals on his wedding day than the comfort of Fannie who screamed at the omen of ill luck when he gave her a peacock's feather with which to sign the register. Her invalid sister Marie, who seems to have enjoyed ill health in a thoroughly manipulative and self-serving manner, took violently against Pen over the matter of Ginevra in particular and lost few other opportunities to denigrate Pen's character to Fannie. Throughout her sister's marriage, she made vigorous attempts to persuade Fannie against him. The motives fuelling her implacable ill will are not readily decipherable. Some jealousy may be inferred, perhaps an innate acidity of character, and her chronic invalidism may point to some deep-seated egotism, intolerance and attention-seeking.

Fannie herself seems not to have minded too much about meeting her husband's expenses, though the vengeful and vitriolic Marie minded more about Fannie's indulgently generous attitude towards Pen, and it may be that Marie's attitude would have influenced Fannie to object more than she might have done on her own account. Then, too, gossiping Venetian and European society, ever willing to lend an ear to whispers of possible perversity, liked to reprobate Pen's extravagance with Fannie's money. They admitted his informed, exquisite taste in the matter of his redecoration of the Rezzonico in which Pen took a proper pride — little or no fault to be found there — but they adopted a more jaundiced view when pointing to the magnificence of his gondola and the elaborate costumes — red tunics, banded on the arms with gold and silver — of his two handsome gondoliers. All such grandiosity had been well and good, perfectly appropriate, when sanctioned by the sacred presence of the venerable Robert Browning, but Pen commanded less personal prestige and so his reputation fell when no longer protected by the authority of his father.

Fannie's health seems to have been delicate or simply indifferent. She and Pen remained childless after the first miscarriage, and there are stories — admittedly ambiguous — that might tend to confirm a tendency towards hysteria. Edie Story, who had married and become Contessa Peruzzi, related an account of a dinner at the Rezzonico which went off very genially until Fannie rose from her chair, disappeared into her room and, from behind the door, deaf to all entreaties to lure her out, could be heard apparently lying on the floor and kicking her heels. On another occasion, at the very end of the marriage, a guest heard Fannie shrieking so hysterically that the Rezzonico rang with the piercing sound. Pen explained this as 'a sudden fit of illness'. Sarianna, too, wrote of 'Fannie's *fits* of hysteria, screaming and crying, one could hear her down the street.' Like Marie Coddington, Fannie's dominant character was too often expressed indirectly through manipulative ill health.

Both Pen and Fannie seem, on the face of it, to have been difficult, ill-matched personalities, and it may be that nothing in particular but everything in general conspired to drive them apart. There was no great final rift, no dramatic denouement — they drifted further from one another until Fannie left one day for America. Pen made efforts to retrieve her, and Fannie responded to these attempts at reconciliation, but none that proved permanent. She talked now and again about the marriage to several friends who have left diverse accounts of what she had to say and their own interpretations of the matter. Some emphasised Fannie's jealousy over Ginevra, some shuddered sympathetically in horror over the snakes, some took offence on Fannie's behalf at Pen's extravagance with money not his own. What nobody got was Pen's account. Pen chose never to be confidential with anyone about his marriage or Fannie. Pen had been brought up as a gentleman; Pen did not kiss and tell. One element of Pen's legacy from his parents was a personal discretion that has done him some credit — though his decision to publish the letters between his father and mother provoked some hostility in the public perception of his filial duty towards their memory and, in particular, horrified many in the wider Barrett family.

But he defended himself vigorously in this regard, and Pen's qualities of faithfulness, sense of personal honour and generosity of spirit emerge most strikingly in the latter years of his life. Sarianna stayed on with her nephew, stout as ever in her devotion to what was left of the Browning family, until her death at the age of eighty-four, and Pen added Lily Wilson and Ferdinando Romagnoli to his household in their declining years. Wilson occasionally attended Fannie as her maid and made herself useful in small ways. Her apparent fits of madness or delusions in Florence seem to have abated, and it is pleasing to know that, to the end, she was well loved and well taken care of by Pen who never ceased in his affection for her. To Edie Story, too, who fell on hard times, suffered personal tragedies and lost her beauty, he remained a good friend, reliable in respectful sympathy and frequently generous in financial support. To the memory of his mother and father, Pen devoted an almost religious attention. He bought Casa Guidi and, so far as possible, restored it to the condition in which it had been when they lived there.

When Fannie disappeared to America to contribute generously to charitable works such as improving the conditions of slum children in New York and financing Christian missionary work, she distanced herself from the broad, easy-going bohemianism of the Rezzonico household that had scandalised her sense of social propriety and personal morality and returned to the comfortingly narrow certainties and quietly pious perspectives of the Dutch Protestant religious faith in which she had been raised by her parents. When the Rezzonico was disposed of in 1906 (it was bought by Baron Lionello Hirschell de Minerbi, a dealer in art and antiquities whose style of life at Ca' Rezzonico for twenty-five years surpassed Pen's for extravagance), it was ruthlessly stripped by Marie of whatever she could get her hands on.

Pen retired to Asolo where he acquired a property, Casa Browning, affectionately or disparagingly known as 'Palazzo Pigsty' where he installed himself, his seven or more hounds and dachshunds, the high-spirited horses he capably drove in tandem or four-in-hand, and his birds — shrieking peacocks, cacophanic macaws, full-throated doves, conversational cockatoos, clucking chickens, gobbling turkeys, and screeching geese. Pen himself was apparently known to his Barrett cousins as 'Cochon', and it has to be admitted that in his later years Pen became portly and liked to dress in loud checks that did little or nothing to minimise his appearance as a piggish, apple-shaped, red-cheeked English country squire. Pen thus dismayed some who had looked for a more poetic, romantic persona. Like his father, Pen didn't look like 'a damned literary man' or even a damned artist.

The feeling seems to be that Pen was proud of his parents and respectful of their literary achievements but modest to the point of diffidence about his own merits, personal and professional. There are some who may think he had much to be modest about, but he carried a heavy burden of expectation from those who, after Robert Browning's death, looked for a renaissance of poetic or artistic genius in the son and were cruelly disappointed. But Pen also bore an almost crushing weight of parental hopes and aspirations that he had for long enough and for the most part doggedly attempted to fulfil in his youth. As a mature man, Pen discovered his true talent for architectural and

decorative restoration. He had a sure, instinctive judgement and pro-
fessionally informed eye for aesthetics, and achieved successes in dis-
covering the potential in old properties which he carefully and truthfully
stripped of modern additions and restored, in a modern English attitude
of historical conservation, to historical verisimilitude.

At Asolo, a poor though picturesque village that had inspired 'Pippa
Passes', one of Robert Browning's earlier and most creatively innovative
poems, about a little silk worker on her rare day off, Pen bought the
property, the Torre all'Antella, known as Pippa's Tower, that his father
had wished to purchase just before his death. In time, he bought and
remodelled several other properties that came with substantial tracts of
farmland included in the price. In the village, Pen provided much-
needed employment for local women who produced characteristic Asolo
silks, lace and linens in work rooms open to the air. Pen never remarried,
and some, like the traveller Freya Stark, who also lived in Asolo, assumed
that Pen practised *droit de seigneur* over these girls and women, and
didn't much mind whether he did. But Pen's relations with the people
of Asolo seem to have been amiably democratic, without pomp or
ceremony, and no plausible suggestions of promiscuity have been
reported. Rather, Pen's reputation in Asolo has come down, in several
first-hand accounts, as generous in many ways — to give only two
examples, he gave away a dole of food on a regular basis and kept
rents low on his properties. In contrast to his earlier habits of prodigal
expenditure, his extravagances were minor, and it is to his credit (and
his own pride) that he paid back the cost of the Rezzonico to Fannie.

Pen died on 8 July 1912, a few weeks after the centenary of his father's
birth. The 'Cavaliere Browning' was buried in the Antico Cimeterio at
Asolo, mourned by all including the Mayor who commanded shops to
be shut and flags to be flown at half-mast. Pen left no will. The sole
document discovered left a legacy of 15,000 lire to a young woman,
Carolina Betti, whom he had taken under his wing when he had found
her in distressed circumstances some years earlier. Fannie, under Italian
rules of intestacy, as his widow, inherited one third of Pen's estate.
Sixteen Barrett cousins inherited the rest of the property which included
all the relics of his parents that Pen had accumulated and their personal
papers that he had preserved. The value of these materials was promptly
assessed, liquidated at a Sotheby's auction and the proceeds divided

between the heirs. A decade later, Fannie had Pen's body expensively removed to Florence for reburial. And so he was returned to the city of his birth, to lie there with his mother and his Aunt Sarianna. Marie Coddington died in 1929 and Fannie herself, who survived her husband by many years, died on 20 September 1935.

BIBLIOGRAPHICAL NOTE

Auden says in 'Hic et Ille', an essay in *The Dyer's Hand*, that the private papers of an author must, if they are to satisfy the public, be twice as unexpected and shocking as his public books. This has been largely true of Philip Larkin, a poet of the middle classes; it is not true of Robert Browning, another poet of the middle classes, whose works are twice as unexpected and at least twice as shocking as any private papers that survived his attempts to incinerate them. Any attempt to edit one's own life by destroying compromising correspondence is generally futile; one only succeeds in erasing one's own side of whatever controversy is conducted and discussed in retrieved letters, private journals or personal diaries. Other people are not so discreet — they like to hoard souvenirs of public personalities and, when motivated to do so, to publish these interesting relics. No doubt some occasional holograph items by Robert Browning will turn up even now or in the future — but there are no good reasons to expect that they will qualify anything other than known or supposed facts. They will not substantially alter our perceptions of the character of Robert Browning. In this biography I have relied upon several collections of Browning letters published by John Murray. The first groundwork was done by a devoted Browningite, Thomas Wise, in *Letters of Robert Browning* and extended by William Clyde DeVane and Kenneth Leslie Knickerbocker in *New Letters of Robert Browning*. John Murray also published the Browning love letters at the request and with the approval of Pen Browning. The collection of letters between Robert Browning and Julia Wedgwood was judiciously edited by Richard Curle. Leonard Huxley edited *Elizabeth Barrett Browning: Letters to Her Sisters*, and these were supplemented by *The Unpublished Letters of Elizabeth*

Barrett Browning to Mary Russell Mitford, edited by Betty Miller who also wrote a biography of Robert Browning published by John Murray. In 1897, Frederic G. Kenyon edited *The Letters of Elizabeth Barrett Browning* in two substantial volumes for Macmillan, and in 1906 Mr Kenyon also edited the invaluable *Robert Browning and Alfred Domett* for Smith, Elder & Co. These collections are well known and have been widely relied upon in this work: any biographer of the Brownings must be grateful for access to their riches.

Of course, they are not complete: further first-hand materials have turned up since the original publication of these books in the first half of the twentieth century. Edward J. McAleer, a Browning scholar, edited *Dearest Isa: Robert Browning's Letters to Isabella Blagden* in 1951 for the University of Texas Press, and for the Wedgestone Press, in 1985, Michael Meredith ably edited *More Than Friend: The Letters of Robert Browning to Katherine de Kay Bronson*. The Wedgestone Press is currently publishing what will become, when the project is completed by dedicated editors, a definitive text of all known letters by Robert and Elizabeth Browning. The latest two volumes, published in 2002 and edited with great distinction by Scott Lewis, substantially supplement the collection of letters to her sisters Henrietta and Arabella edited by Leonard Huxley. In due course, the Wedgestone edition will incorporate and annotate Elizabeth Barrett Browning's letters to Mrs David Ogilvy which are presently available in a volume edited by Peter N. Heydon and Philip Kelley, published by The Browning Institute, and *Letters of the Brownings to George Barrett*, edited by Paul Landis, published by the University of Illinois Press. I have drawn from these collections for this biography, and could hardly have done without them. I am personally grateful to the Wedgestone Press for what can only be called a work of devoted love as much as of impeccable scholarship.

I have already noted in my prologue the previous biographies of Robert Browning on which I have relied not only for supplementary information but also for useful — often inspired — critical and psychological commentary. I have given there my short evaluation of the usefulness of these books, but let me here reiterate my respect for their scholarship, and gratitude for the sheer pleasure they have given me. I hope that their authors will forgive any liberties I have taken with their words and opinions. First of all, *Life and Letters of Robert Browning* by

Mrs Alexandra Sutherland Orr remains a prime secondary source so long as it is read judiciously, particularly in the light of evidences published by William Irvine and Park Honan in *The Book, the Ring, and the Poet: A Biography of Robert Browning* published by Bodley Head in 1974. For some quarter of a century, this has remained the standard life of Robert Browning and its value to Browning scholarship has not yet been exhausted. Another biography with no sell-by date and that shows no sign of decaying in its long shelf life is of course *Robert Browning* by G. K. Chesterton, published by Macmillan in 1903 and from which I have quoted copiously. The fourth biography which was constantly at my elbow is *The Life of Robert Browning* by W. Hall Griffin and H. C. Minchin, published in 1938 by Methuen. I gratefully acknowledge my debts to these four important works.

Critically, many academic advances have been made in recent years by researchers and writers. My personal preference has been for *The Life of Robert Browning; A Critical Biography* by Clyde de L. Ryals, published by Blackwell in 1993. I acknowledge several critical cues which I have taken from Ryals and run with — not too far or too fast, I hope. I have also relied upon *The Brownings and France* by Roy Gridley, published by Athlone Press in 1982, a book which rigorously but entertainingly emphasizes the extent to which the Brownings surrendered to Francophilia and to which Robert Browning's poetry was admired by the French well in advance of its full acceptance by the English. It is a book valuable as much for its biographical as its critical commentary. In respect of Robert Browning's reputation in America and details of his publishing history there, I am grateful to have read and unhesitatingly relied upon *Browning and America* by Louise Greer. Most of all, I was impressed by the tenderness mixed with tough love with which Daniel Karlin commented critically on the love letters in *The Courtship of Robert Browning and Elizabeth Barrett*, published by the Clarendon Press in 1985. I hope I may be forgiven if I have exceeded the bounds of fair usage in my enthusiastic quotation from this book. Time and again, Karlin gets it right both critically and emotionally: he leaves little or no wriggle room for argument. He is consistently convincing.

One of my principal secondary sources has been Henry James: it took very little resistance for me to be persuaded to the Jamesian view of Robert Browning in essays contained in books such as *The Critical*

Muse edited for Penguin Books by Roger Gard, in *English Hours*, published by Oxford University Press, *Travelling in Italy with Henry James* edited by Fred Kaplan, and particularly in James's biography of William Wetmore Story. I hope, again, I have not exceeded the quota of permissible quotation from these works. If I have, I can only plead reverence for the materials I have plundered.

From others who once knew Browning plain, I have taken details given by Cyrus Mason in *The Poet Robert Browning and his Kinfolk* edited by W. Craig Turner; from Edmund Gosse's *Portraits from Life* edited by Anne Thwaite; from *The French and Italian Note-books of Nathaniel Hawthorne* and from *The Diary of Alfred Domett 1872–1885* edited by E. A. Horsman. In the first section of my biography, I have been more than happy to excavate the *Diaries of William Charles Macready* (edited by William Toynbee): they are, as a whole, magnificent. Only by reading Macready's Diaries through, every page, can one form an assessment of his great character and thus put true faith in his comments upon Browning and others.

Tennyson once remarked that 'the worth of a biography depends on whether it is done by one who wholly loves the man whose life he writes, yet loves him with a discriminating love.' Not only 'he' but she: the two volumes of biography by Maisie Ward, *Robert Browning and His World: The Private Face* and *Two Robert Brownings?* contain perceptive comments on Browning's psychology, as does *Robert Browning: A Portrait* by Betty Miller. These writers have for many years been gadflies on the body of Browning scholarship, biting with their psychoanalytic assessments. When it seemed appropriate to do so, I have quoted from them — judiciously, I hope. My epilogue — my account of the later life of Pen Browning — also owes much to Maisie Ward's *The Tragi-Comedy of Pen Browning* published by The Browning Institute. I have trustingly taken some assessments of Elizabeth Barrett Browning at particular points in her life from *Elizabeth Barrett Browning* by Margaret Forster. It is as necessary for a biographer of Robert Browning to consult her very thorough and moving biography of EBB as it is for him (or her) to read the Irvine & Honan biography of Browning. Both are indispensable.

I should like particularly to acknowledge the critical assistance I gleaned from *Passions of the Mind* by A. S. Byatt who, in that book, comments on Browning's poetry. I hope, in my own gloss upon her words, I have not misrepresented her views. In that same frame of mind, I hope I have not misconstrued the points made by Marcel Proust in *Against Sainte-Beuve and Other Essays* translated and edited for Penguin Books by John Sturrock. I hope my quotations from both these works fall within the limits of fair usage.

The question of which edition of Robert Browning's poetry to use as the text to be relied upon throughout this biography was decided early. It seemed to me important that the reader of this biography should be able conveniently to acquire a reliable, comprehensive annotated edition at moderate cost. The obvious choice was *Robert Browning: The Poems*, in two volumes, edited by John Pettigrew and Thomas J. Collins. The only omission by Pettigrew and Collins is *The Ring and the Book* which, fortunately, is also published by Penguin Books in a single volume edited by Richard D. Altick. There is no question of these editions being second-best: they are as near as dammit definitive and benefit from the best modern scholarship. All quotation from Browning's poetry in this book is taken from these three volumes.

I should like to say, finally, that few things in my professional life have given me greater pleasure these past few years than the background reading and research for this present biography. It is a pleasure as much as a duty to thank, very sincerely, all the authors whose works are acknowledged here. It is in this spirit of personal pleasure that I urge anyone interested in pursuing Browning beyond these pages to read at least some of the sources I have relied upon and from which — to the great benefit of this biography — I have gained so much. It should go without saying — but let me say it anyhow — that any errors of fact and all misapprehensions of anything else are mine alone. Nobody else can be held responsible for what Samuel Johnson frankly confessed, when challenged about an undeniably wrong definition in his Dictionary, as 'Ignorance, madam, pure ignorance.'

ABBREVIATIONS AND SHORT CITATIONS
OF PRINCIPAL SOURCES

Chesterton	G. K. Chesterton, *Robert Browning* (English Men of Letters series, 1903)
DeVane	William Clyde DeVane, *A Browning Handbook* (1956)
Domett	*The Diary of Alfred Domett*, ed. A. E. Horsman (1953)
EBB	Elizabeth Barrett Barrett/Browning
EBB/Mitford	*Elizabeth Barrett to Miss Mitford: The unpublished letters of Elizabeth Barrett Browning to Mary Russell Mitford*, ed. Betty Miller (1954)
Forster	Margaret Forster, *Elizabeth Barrett Browning: A biography* (1988)
Gosse	Edmund Gosse, *Robert Browning: Personalia* (1890)
Greer	Louise Greer, *Browning and America* (1952)
Gridley	Roy E. Gridley, *The Brownings and France: A chronicle with commentary* (1982)
Griffin & Minchin	W. Hall Griffin and H.C. Minchin, *The Life of Robert Browning. With notices of his writings, his family, and his friends* (1938)
Hawthorne	Nathaniel Hawthorne, *Passages from the French and Italian Note-Books of Nathaniel Hawthorne* (1871)
Hood	*Letters of Robert Browning, Collected by Thomas J. Wise*, ed., with introduction and notes, by Thurman L. Hood (1933)
Irvine & Honan	William Irvine and Park Honan, *The Book, the Ring, and the Poet: A biography of Robert Browning* (1974)

Jack	Ian Jack, *Browning's Major Poetry* (1973)
James	Henry James, *William Wetmore Story and his Friends*, vols i and ii (1903)
Karlin	Daniel Karlin, *The Courtship of Robert Browning and Elizabeth Barrett* (1985)
Kenyon	*Robert Browning and Alfred Domett*, ed. F.G. Kenyon (1906)
Kintner	*The Letters of Robert Browning and Elizabeth Barrett Barrett*, ed. Elvan Kintner (2 vols, 1969)
McAleer	*Dearest Isa: Robert Browning's letters to Isabella Blagden*, ed., with an introduction, by Edward J. McAleer (1951)
Macready	*The Diaries of William Charles Macready, 1833–1851*, ed. William Toynbee (2 vols, 1912)
Markus	Julia Markus, *Dared and Done: The marriage of Elizabeth Barrett and Robert Browning* (1995)
Martineau	Harriet Martineau, *Autobiography* (3 vols, 1877)
Mason	Cyrus Mason, *The Poet Robert Browning and his Kinfolk* (1983)
Meredith	Michael Meredith (ed.), *More Than Friend: The letters of Robert Browning to Katherine de Kay Bronson* (1985)
Miller	Betty Miller, *Robert Browning: A portrait* (1952)
New Letters	*New Letters of Robert Browning*, ed., with introduction and notes, by William Clyde DeVane and Kenneth Leslie Knickerbocker (1951)
Orr	Mrs Alexandra Sutherland Orr, *Life and Letters of Robert Browning* (1891); new edition, revised Frederic G. Kenyon (1908)
RB	Robert Browning
Ryals	Clyde de L. Ryals, *The Life of Robert Browning: A critical biography* (1993)
Sharp	William Sharp, *Life of Robert Browning* (1890)
Story	William Wetmore Story, *Conversations in a Studio* (1890)
Trollope	Thomas Trollope, *What I Remember* (1887)

Ward i	Maisie Ward, *Robert Browning and his World: The private face (1812–1861)* (1967)
Ward ii	Maisie Ward: *Robert Browning and his World: Two Robert Brownings? (1861–1889)* (1969)
Ward/PB	Maisie Ward, *The Tragi-Comedy of Pen Browning, 1849–1912* (1972)
Whiting	Lilian Whiting, *The Brownings: Their life and art* (1911)

NOTES

PROLOGUE

1 Joseph Brodsky, 'In the Shadow of
  Dante', in *Less Than One: Selected
  Essays* (1986) Penguin, London,
  1987.
2 John Keats to Richard
  Woodhouse, 27 October 1818. *The
  Letters of John Keats, 1814–1821*, ed.
  Hyder Edward Rollins (2 vols,
  1958), i, 387.
3 Joseph Brodsky, 'On "September
  1, 1939" by W. H. Auden', in *Less
  Than One*, op. cit.

PART 1

1 *Domett*, 212.
2 *Orr*, 19.
3 *Domett*, 212–13.
4 *Griffin & Minchin*, 50, n. 3.
5 Ibid., 53.
6 *Chesterton*, 3.
7 *Domett*, 213.
8 *Griffin & Minchin*, 8.
9 RB, 'Garden-Fancies', ll. 1–8.
10 Ibid., ll. 31–2.
11 *Domett*, 73.
12 Ibid.
13 *Griffin & Minchin*, 31.
14 *Chesterton*, 12–13.

15 *Griffin & Minchin*, 30.
16 *Miller*, 8.
17 *Domett*, 132.
18 *Orr*, 43.
19 RB to EBB, 3 March
   1846.
20 RB to Fanny Howarth, 30
   December 1841.
21 RB, 'Essay on Shelley', in the
   spurious *Letters of Percy Bysshe
   Shelley* (1852).
22 *Orr*, 48.
23 Ibid.; *Sharp*, 33.
24 *Orr*, 44.
25 Ibid., 49; *Griffin & Minchin*, 55.
26 *Griffin & Minchin*, 56.
27 *Orr*, 46.
28 *Griffin and Minchin*, 36.
29 *Sharp*, 96.
30 *Orr*, 37.
31 Ibid., 38.
32 Ibid., 82.
33 Ibid., 92.
34 Ibid., 54.
35 *Griffin & Minchin*, 58.
36 *Orr*, 59.
37 *Griffin & Minchin*, 44.
38 *Sharp*, 53.
39 Ibid., 54.
40 *Orr*, 64.
41 *Griffin & Minchin*, 63.
42 *Century Magazine*, vol. lxiii.

43 *Orr*, 65.
44 *Ward i*, 50.
45 *Hood*, 1.
46 *Griffin & Minchin*, 54, 80.
47 *Orr*, 66.
48 Ibid., 71.
49 Ibid., 72.
50 Ibid., 71.
51 Ibid., 70.
52 Ibid., 70–1.
53 Ibid., 77.
54 *Ryals*, 31.
55 RB to F. J. Furnivall, 11 October 1881; *Hood*, 199.
56 *Ryals*, 31.
57 *Macready*, i, 226.
58 Ibid., i, 267.
59 Ibid., i, 281.
60 Ibid., i, 318–19.
61 *Griffin & Minchin*, 77.
62 RB, 'The Lost Leader', ll 1–4.
63 *EBB/Mitford*, xiii.
64 *Orr*, 88; *Gosse*.
65 RB to William Charles Macready, 28 May 1836.
66 *Macready*, 9 April 1837.
67 Ibid., 15 April 1837.
68 Ibid., 28 April 1837.
69 Ibid., 9 May 1837.
70 *Sharp*, 80.
71 *Orr*, 91.
72 *Sharp*, 80.
73 *Griffin & Minchin*, 110.
74 Ibid., 94–5, n. 1.
75 *Orr*, 100.
76 *Hood*, 1–3.
77 *Orr*, 101.
78 Ibid.
79 *Sharp*, 59.
80 *Orr*, 95.
81 Ibid., 104.
82 *Sharp*, 109–10.
83 Ibid., 106.
84 *Chesterton*, 34.
85 Ibid., 37.
86 *Macready*, 17 June 1840.
87 *Chesterton*, 40–1.

88 *Griffin & Minchin*, 92.
89 *Orr*, 109.
90 Ibid., 104.
91 Ibid., 105.
92 Ibid., 78.
93 Ibid., 78.
94 RB to Fanny Haworth, May 1840; *Griffin & Minchin*, 113.
95 *Macready*, ii, 23.
96 Ibid., 6 August 1840.
97 Ibid., ii, 80.
98 *Griffin & Minchin*, 117.
99 *Macready*, 4 June 1846.
100 *Orr*, 117–125.
101 *Griffin & Minchin*, 117–18.
102 *Orr*, 118–121.
103 Ibid., 123.
104 Ibid., 121.
105 RB to Christopher Dowson, 10 March 1844.
106 *Orr*, 112.
107 Ibid., 114.
108 EBB to RB, 17 February 1845.
109 *Macready*, 5 May 1840.
110 *New Letters*, 263.
111 *Griffin & Minchin*, 135.
112 *Macready*, 27 March 1839.
113 *Miller*, 93–4.
114 *Chesterton*, 26.
115 *Jack*, 93.
116 *Griffin & Minchin*, 137.
117 EBB to RB, 3 February 1845.
118 *Kenyon*.
119 *Orr*, 136.
120 Ibid.
121 *Karlin*.
122 RB to EBB, 13 January 1845.
123 *Karlin*.
124 RB to EBB, 10 January 1845.
125 Ibid.
126 EBB to RB, 11 January 1845.
127 EBB to RB, 15 January 1845.
128 EBB to RB, 17 February 1845.
129 *Forster*, 22.
130 *Miller*, 90.
131 *Karlin*, 25.
132 *Forster*, 64.

133 *Chesterton*, 59, 74.
134 *Karlin*, 70.
135 EBB to RB, 16 May 1845. [NB Karlin dates this 15 May]
136 EBB to RB, 17 May 1845.
137 EBB to RB, 11 August 1845.
138 RB to EBB, 21 May 1845.
139 EBB to RB, 22 May 1845. [NB Karlin dates this 21 May]
140 EBB to RB, 24 May 1845.
141 *Karlin*, 80.
142 RB to EBB, 24 May 1845.
143 EBB to RB, 19 May 1846.
144 EBB to RB, 18 July 1845.
145 *Karlin*, 89.
146 RB to F.J. Furnivall, 15 April 1883.
147 *Karlin*, 90.
148 *Forster*, 155.
149 *Karlin*, 97.
150 EBB to RB, 25 August 1845.
151 *Karlin*, 99.
152 RB to EBB, 30 August 1845.
153 EBB to RB, 31 August 1845.
154 EBB to RB, 25 September 1845.
155 EBB to RB, 16 September 1845.
156 RB to EBB, 3 June 1846.
157 RB to EBB, 31 August 1846.
158 EBB to RB, 1 September 1846.
159 *Miller*, 125.
160 Ibid., 125–6.
161 Ibid., 126.
162 *Chesterton*, 77.
163 *Orr*, 144.
164 *Karlin*, 166.

PART 2

1 EBB to Arabella Barrett, 21–4 April 1846.
2 EBB to Henrietta Barrett, 30 April 1847.
3 EBB to Henrietta Barrett, 16 May 1847.
4 RB to Anna Maria Hall, 5 December 1848.
5 *Hawthorne*, 4 June 1858.

6 *Griffin & Minchin*, 163.
7 EBB to Mary Russell Mitford, 8 December 1847.
8 EBB to Henrietta Barrett, 16 May 1847.
9 EBB to Henrietta Barrett, 21 February, 2–4 March 1848.
10 *Griffin & Minchin*, 162.
11 EBB to Henrietta Barrett, 21 February, 2–4 March 1848.
12 *Trollope*.
13 EBB to Henrietta Barrett, 7 March–1 April 1848.
14 Ibid.
15 EBB to Mary Russell Mitford, 15 April 1848.
16 EBB to Mrs Martin, 20 June 1848.
17 *Miller*, 145.
18 *Irvine & Honan*, 250
19 EBB to Mary Russell Mitford, 10 October 1848.
20 EBB to Mrs Martin, 3 December 1848.
21 *Domett*, 212.
22 EBB to Mary Russell Mitford, July 1849.
23 *Griffin & Minchin*, 169.
24 EBB to Mary Russell Mitford, July 1849.
25 EBB to Mrs Jameson, 11 August 1849.
26 EBB to Henrietta Barrett, 19 September 1849.
27 Ibid.
28 *Miller*, 152.
29 Ibid.
30 RB to John Kenyon, 29 July 1850.
31 EBB to Henrietta Barrett, 2–5 May 1849.
32 A.S. Byatt, 'Robert Browning: Incarnation and Art', in *Passions of the Mind: Selected writings* (1993).
33 *Irvine & Honan*, 267.
34 *James*, i, 6–8.
35 Ibid., 31–2.
36 Ibid., 171–2.

37 Ibid., 128.
38 *Griffin & Minchin*, 170–1.
39 EBB to Mary Russell Mitford, late April 1850.
40 EBB to Mary Russell Mitford, 24 September 1850.
41 *Orr*, 211.
42 EBB to Mary Russell Mitford, 4 June 1851.
43 EBB to Henrietta Barrett, 7 July 1850.
44 EBB to Mary Russell Mitford, 4 June 1851.
45 EBB to Mrs Ogilvy, 2 July 1851.
46 EBB to Mary Russell Mitford, 22 October 1851.
47 EBB to Mary Russell Mitford, 12 November 1851.
48 *James*, i, 366.
49 EBB to Mary Russell Mitford, 22 October 1851.
50 EBB to Henrietta Barrett, 1 December 1851.
51 EBB to Mary Russell Mitford, 24 December 1851.
52 EBB to Mary Russell Mitford, 15 February 1852.
53 EBB to John Kenyon, 15 February 1852.
54 Ibid.
55 EBB to Mrs Jameson, 26 February 1852.
56 EBB to Mary Russell Mitford, 7 April 1852.
57 *Orr*, 178–9.
58 Ibid., 181.
59 EBB to Mary Russell Mitford, January-February 1852.
60 RB to Edward Chapman, 17 December 1851.
61 *Orr*, 182–3.
62 *The Times*, 2 July 1852.
63 EBB to Henrietta Barrett, 1 December 1851.
64 EBB to Mrs Jameson, 12 April 1852.
65 *Forster*, 265.
66 *Ward i*, 205.
67 *Miller*, 165–6.
68 EBB to Mary Russell Mitford, 9 May 1852.
69 Eric Hobsbawn, *The Age of Capital, 1848–1875* (1975), 277.
70 EBB to Mrs Ogilvy, 24 January 1853.
71 *Forster*, 268.
72 EBB to George Barrett, 28 February 1852.
73 *Orr*, 198.
74 *Mason*, 109.
75 EBB to Mrs Ogilvy, 5 October 1852.
76 *Irvine & Honan*, 299.
77 RB to John Kenyon, 16 January 1853.
78 RB to William Charles Macready, 23 September 1852.
79 *Orr*, 191.
80 EBB to Mrs Ogilvy, 5 October 1852.
81 *Ward i*, 204–5.
82 EBB to Mrs Ogilvy, 24 January 1853.
83 *Forster*, 276.
84 *Griffin & Minchin*, 189.
85 RB to Edward Chapman, 5 March 1853.
86 *Greer*, 72, 255.
87 *Whiting*, 261.
88 EBB to Henrietta Barrett, 32 July 1852; EBB to Mrs Ogilvy, 2 June 1853.
89 *Griffin & Minchin*, 189.
90 EBB to Mrs Ogilvy, 2 June 1853.
91 EBB to Mrs Ogilvy, 8 June 1854.
92 *Orr*, 193–4.
93 Ibid., 194.
94 Ibid., 194–5.
95 RB to Reuben Browning, 18 July 1853.
96 RB to Edward Chapman, 16 January 1852; 14 September 1852; 24 August 1853.

97 EBB to Henrietta Barrett, 14 May 1853.
98 Ibid.
99 EBB to Mrs Ogilvy, 5 October 1852.
100 EBB to H.F. Chorley, 19 August 1853.
101 EBB to Henrietta, 30 December 1853.
102 EBB to Henrietta, 30 December 1853.
103 EBB to Mary Russell Mitford, 7 January 1854.
104 EBB to George Barrett, 10 January 1854.
105 EBB to Miss Mitford, 19 March 1854.
106 EBB to George Barrett, 10 January 1854.
107 *James*, i, 287.
108 EBB to Mary Russell Mitford, 7 January 1854.
109 EBB to Sarianna Browning, March 1854.
110 RB to John Forster, 2 April 1854.
111 EBB to George Barrett, 10 January 1854.
112 EBB to Sarianna Browning, March 1854.
113 EBB to George Barrett, 10 January 1854.
114 EBB to Mary Russell Mitford, 15 July 1853.
115 *Forster*, 280.
116 EBB to Mary Russell Mitford, 15 July 1853.
117 *Forster*, 291.
118 RB to John Forster, 2 April 1854.
119 EBB to Sarianna Browning, late May 1854.
120 EBB to Mary Russell Mitford, 10 May 1854.
121 RB to John Forster, 5 June 1854.
122 EBB to Sarianna Browning, March 1854.
123 *James*, i, 288.
124 RB to John Forster, 5 June 1854.
125 EBB to Henrietta Barrett, 27 April 1855.
126 EBB to Mary Russell Mitford, 19 October 1854.
127 *Irvine & Honan*, 224.
128 *James*, ii, 95.
129 Ibid.
130 *Orr*, 219.
131 EBB to Henrietta Barrett, 10 January 1857.
132 EBB to Henrietta Barrett, 12 February 1855.
133 EBB to Henrietta Barrett, 6 November 1854.
134 EBB to Henrietta Barrett, 30 August 1855.
135 EBB to Henrietta Barrett, 28 April 1858.
136 EBB to Mrs Ogilvy, 6 March 1855.
137 EBB to Mrs Ogilvy.
138 *Orr*, 212.
139 EBB to Sarianna Browning, 12 June 1855.
140 *Ward i*, 224; *Markus*, 177–178, quoting from a journal by Mrs Kinney.
141 *Ward i*, 244.
142 *New Letters*, 78, n. 2.
143 EBB to Mrs Martin, July-August 1855.
144 Ibid.
145 *Chesterton*, 93.
146 RB to Mrs Kinney.
147 EBB to Henrietta Barrett, 17 August 1855.
148 EBB to Henrietta Barrett, 27 August 1855.
149 *Hawthorne*, 28 August 1858.
150 *Miller*, 186.
151 Ibid.
152 EBB to Fanny Haworth, 29 January 1856.
153 EBB to Mrs Martin, October 1855.
154 EBB to Mrs Jameson, 17 December 1855.
155 Ibid.
156 EBB to Mrs Jameson, 2 May 1856.

157 Maurice Baring, *Have You Anything to Declare? A note-book with commentaries* (1936), 173.
158 *The Table Talk of W. H. Auden*, ed. Alan Ansen (1991), 38.
159 *DeVane*, 226.
160 A. S. Byatt, 'Robert Browning: Incarnation and Art', in *Passions of the Mind: Selected writings* (1993).
161 *Orr*, 233.
162 *Greer*, 76–8.
163 George Eliot, *Westminster Review*, January 1856.
164 EBB to Mrs Martin, 21 February 1856.
165 EBB to Henrietta Barrett, 12 June 1856.
166 EBB to Henrietta Barrett, 7 May 1856.
167 RB to Edward Chapman, 2 December 1856.
168 *Miller*, 175–8.
169 *Ward i*, 230.
170 *Markus*, 189, 194.
171 EBB to Mrs Jameson, 9 April 1857.
172 EBB to Sarianna Browning, 18 August 1857.
173 EBB to Henrietta Barrett, 12 October 1857.
174 EBB to Fanny Haworth, 14 September 1857.
175 RB to Edward Chapman, 1 September 1857, 5 October 1857.
176 EBB to Sarianna Browning, February 1858.
177 EBB to Mrs Martin, 27 March 1858.
178 *Gridley*, 198.
179 EBB to Isa Blagden, 8 July 1858.
180 EBB to Fanny Haworth, 23 July 1858.
181 EBB to Mrs Jameson, 24 July 1858.
182 EBB to Fanny Haworth, October 1858.
183 EBB to Henrietta Barrett, 9 July 1858.
184 RB to Sarianna Browning, 26 November 1858.
185 RB to Isa Blagden, 7 January 1859.
186 Ibid.
187 Ibid.
188 EBB to Isa Blagden, 7 January 1859.
189 Ibid.
190 Ibid.
191 EBB to Henrietta Barrett, 10 February 1859.
192 EBB to Henrietta Barrett, 4 March 1859.
193 Ibid.
194 EBB to Sarianna Browning, February 1859.
195 EBB to Sarianna Browning, April 1859.
196 EBB to Isa Blagden, 27 March 1859.
197 EBB to Sarianna Browning, May 1859.
198 EBB to Sarianna Browning, July-August 1859.
199 RB to Isa Blagden, 2 August 1859.
200 *James*, ii, 16.
201 RB to Isa Blagden, 7 August 1859.
202 *Story*.
203 RB to Isa Blagden, 7 August 1859.
204 *James*, ii, 19.
205 Ibid., 15.
206 RB to Isa Blagden, 7 August 1859.
207 EBB to Fanny Haworth, 2 November 1859.
208 EBB to Sarianna Browning, December 1859.
209 John Forster, *Walter Savage Landor: A biography* (2 vols, 1869), ii, 569.
210 EBB to Henrietta Barrett, 13 September 1859.
211 EBB to Sarianna Browning, December 1859.
212 Ibid.
213 *Orr*, 235–6.

214 Ibid., 236–7.
215 EBB to Henrietta Barrett, 13 September 1859.
216 EBB to Isa Blagden, April 1860.
217 *Ward i*, 292–3.
218 EBB to Mrs Martin, 21 August 1860.
219 EBB to Sarianna Browning, late March 1861.
220 RB to George Barrett, 3 December 1861.
221 EBB to George Barrett, 6 September 1860.
222 EBB to Mrs Ogilvy, 12 September 1860.
223 EBB to Mrs Martin, December 1860.
224 *Chesterton*, 84–5.
225 EBB to Sarianna Browning, late March 1861.
226 *Greer*, 85.
227 *James*, i, 286.
228 EBB to Mrs Martin, April 1861.
229 EBB to Isa Blagden, 20 March 1861.
230 EBB to Sarianna Browning, late March 1861.
231 W.M. Thackeray to EBB, 2 April 1861.
232 EBB to Sarianna Browning, 7 June 1861.
233 *James*, ii, 63.
234 RB to Sarianna Browning, 30 June 1861.

PART 3

1 *Orr*, 245.
2 *James*, ii, 64.
3 RB to Frederic Leighton; *Orr*, 248.
4 RB to Sarianna Browning, 5 July 1861.
5 RB to Sarianna Browning, 30 June 1861.
6 *James*, ii, 66.
7 *Orr*, 252.
8 Ibid., 253.
9 RB to John Forster, July 1861.
10 *James*, ii, 68–9.
11 *Chesterton*, 100.
12 Ibid., 102.
13 RB to George Barrett, 2 July 1861.
14 *James*, ii, 65–6.
15 RB to Sarianna Browning, 13 July 1861.
16 RB to Sarianna Browning, 5 July 1861.
17 RB to Sarianna Browning, 22 July 1861.
18 *Chesterton*, 104.
19 *James*, ii, 88.
20 Leon Edel, *The Life of Henry James* (2 vols, 1977), i, 848.
21 Ibid., 573–4.
22 *James*, ii, 88–9.
23 *Ryals*, 73.
24 Marcel Proust, *Against Sainte-Beuve and Other Essays*, introduced and translated by Robert Sturrock (1994).
25 *Chesterton*, 111.
26 *Ryals*, 12.
27 *Ward ii*, 72.
28 *Chesterton*, 110.
29 *Ward ii*, 4.
30 RB to William Wetmore Story, 20 August 1861.
31 Ibid.
32 RB to Isa Blagden, 22 August 1961.
33 RB to William Wetmore Story, 30 August 1861.
34 *Griffin & Minchin*, 226.
35 *Orr*, 254.
36 Ibid.
37 *Irvine & Honan*, 386.
38 RB to William Wetmore Story, 21 January 1862.
39 RB to William Wetmore Story, 13 February 1862.
40 RB to Isa Blagden, 19 July 1862.
41 RB to Isa Blagden, 19 June 1862.
42 Ibid.
43 RB to Isa Blagden, 19 March 1868.

44 *Orr*, 213.
45 RB to Isa Blagden, 18 August 1862.
46 Ibid.
47 RB to Julia Wedgwood,
   31 December 1864.
48 *Orr*, 244.
49 RB to Isa Blagden, 19 September
   1867.
50 RB to William Wetmore Story,
   1 October 1862.
51 RB to Isa Blagden, 18 October
   1862.
52 Julia Wedgwood to RB, 27 June
   1864.
53 RB to Julia Wedgwood, 27 June
   1864.
54 *Miller*, 228.
55 *Ward ii*, 20.
56 Julia Wedgwood to RB, 23 July
   1864.
57 Ibid.
58 RB to Julia Wedgwood, undated.
59 RB to Julia Wedgwood,
   17 October 1864.
60 *Irvine & Honan*, 369–71.
61 *James*, ii, 49.
62 C.R. Tracy, 'Caliban upon
   Setebos', *Studies in Philology*, xxxv
   (1938), pp. 487–99.
63 *Orr*, 270.
64 Ibid., 280.
65 *DeVane*, 282.
66 RB to Isa Blagden, 22 June 1870.
67 RB to Isa Blagden, 19 January
   1870.
68 *Life and Letters of Benjamin
   Jowett*, ed. Evelyn Abbott and
   Lewis Campbell (2 vols, 1897), i,
   400–1.
69 RB to Mrs Story, 22 August
   1864.
70 *Hood*, illustration facing p. 80.
71 *DeVane*, 322.
72 Ibid.
73 *Irvine & Honan*, 406.
74 *DeVane*, 323.
75 RB, *The Ring and the Book*, l. 39.

76 Ibid., l. 85.
77 *Orr*, 281–2.
78 *Miller*, 231.
79 *Chesterton*, 103.
80 RB to Julia Wedgwood, 3 October
   1864.
81 RB to Isa Blagden, 19 October
   1864.
82 *DeVane*, 318, 323.
83 Ibid., 323.
84 *Orr*, 284.
85 RB to Isa Blagden, 19 September
   1862.
86 *Orr*, 261.
87 *Irvine & Honan*, 409.
88 *Griffin & Minchin*, 234.
89 RB to Edith Story, 8 July 1865.
90 RB to Edith Story, 26 July 1865.
91 RB to Isa Blagden, 19 August 1865.
92 RB to Isa Blagden, 19 March 1866
   [but see comment in text]
93 Ibid. [see previous]
94 RB to Isa Blagden, 19 October
   1865.
95 RB to Isa Blagden, 19 May 1866.
96 RB to Seymour Kirkup,
   19 February 1867.
97 RB to Pen Browning, 14 June
   1866.
98 *Ward ii*, 35.
99 *Hood*, illustration facing p.102.
100 *Domett*, 45.
101 RB to Pen Browning, 17 June
    1866.
102 RB to Seymour Kirkup,
    19 February 1867.
103 RB to Isa Blagden, 7 August
    1866.
104 RB to Isa Blagden, 13 July 1866.
105 RB to Edward Chapman, 26 June
    1866.
106 RB to Isa Blagden, 24 September
    1866.
107 RB to Seymour Kirkup,
    19 February 1867.
108 RB to Isa Blagden, 24 September
    1866.

109 RB to Isa Blagden, 19 June 1867.
110 RB to Isa Blagden, 19 July 1867.
111 Ibid.
112 RB to Isa Blagden, 29 March 1867.
113 Ibid.
114 RB to Isa Blagden, 23 April 1867.
115 Ibid.
116 Ibid.
117 RB to Isa Blagden, February 1872.
118 RB to Isa Blagden, 19 September 1867.
119 Ibid.
120 RB to Isa Blagden, 19 November 1867.
121 RB to Isa Blagden, 19 January 1868.
122 RB to Isa Blagden, 31 December 1867.
123 RB to Isa Blagden, 19 June 1868.
124 Ibid.
125 Ibid.
126 RB to Isa Blagden, 16 June 1868.
127 RB to Isa Blagden, January 1869.
128 *DeVane*, 335.
129 Daniel Karlin, 'Resurrection Man', *London Review of Books*, 24, 10.
130 RB to Isa Blagden, 19 February 1869.
131 *Griffin & Minchin*, 238.
132 RB to Isa Blagden, August 1869.
133 RB to Isa Blagden, 19 April 1869.
134 *Irvine & Honan*, 443.
135 RB to Isa Blagden, 19 April 1869.
136 RB to Isa Blagden, 28 August 1869.
137 *Irvine & Honan*, 444, 571.
138 *Griffin & Minchin*, 242.
139 *James*, ii, 197.
140 RB to Isa Blagden, 28 August 1859.
141 *Hood*, 329.
142 *James*, ii, 196.
143 Ibid., ii, 197.
144 Ibid., ii, 198.
145 *Ward ii*, 71.
146 Ibid., 70.
147 RB to Isa Blagden, 19 September 1869.
148 RB to Isa Blagden, 22 March 1870.
149 RB to Isa Blagden, 21 April 1870.
150 RB to George Barrett, 17 June 1870.
151 Ibid.
152 Ibid.
153 RB to George Barrett, 1 July 1870.
154 RB to George Barrett, 17 June 1870.
155 RB to George Barrett, 1 July 1870.
156 Ibid.
157 RB to George Barrett, July 1870.
158 *Ward/PB*, 58.
159 Ibid., 51.
160 Ibid., 53.
161 RB to Isa Blagden, 19 July 1870.
162 *Orr*, 288–9.
163 RB to Edith Story, 1 January 1872.
164 RB to Isa Blagden, 1 October 1871.
165 *Ward ii*, 88–9.
166 *Miller*, 252.
167 RB to Isa Blagden, 8 November 1871.
168 RB to Isa Blagden, 19 August 1871.
169 Ibid.
170 Ibid.
171 Ibid.
172 *DeVane*, 359.
173 *McAleer*, 366.
174 Ibid.
175 RB to Isa Blagden, 25 January 1872.
176 Ibid.
177 *Chesterton*, 121.
178 Ibid., 122.
179 *Orr*, 294.
180 RB to Isa Blagden, 25 January 1872.
181 RB to Isa Blagden, 30 April 1872.
182 RB to Isa Blagden, 30 March 1872.
183 *Domett*, 54.
184 *DeVane*, 370.
185 *Orr*, 298.
186 Ibid.
187 RB to Isa Blagden, 19 August 1871.
188 RB to Edith Story, 4 April 1872.

189 RB to Isa Blagden, 19 September 1872.
190 RB to Isa Blagden, 22 March 1870.
191 *McAleer*, xxvi–xxvii.
192 *Domett*, 67.
193 Ibid., 45.
194 Ibid.
195 Ibid., 46.
196 Ibid., 164,
197 *DeVane*, 366.
198 *Ward ii*, 82.
199 *Chesterton*, 123.
200 *Domett*, 75.
201 Ibid.
202 *Domett*, 78; RB to George Smith, 31 May 1873.
203 RB to George Smith, 26 March 1873.
204 Ibid.
205 *DeVane*, 374–5; *Domett*, 105.
206 *DeVane*, 375.
207 *Griffin & Minchin*, 252.
208 *Orr*, 299.
209 RB to George Smith, 9 May 1873.
210 *McAleer*, 382.
211 *Orr*, 301.
212 Ibid., 303.
213 *Miller*, 262.
214 *Ward ii*, 94.
215 *Orr*, 305.
216 Ibid., 307.
217 RB to George Smith, 9 May 1873.
218 RB to Algernon Charles Swinburne, 5 February 1891.
219 *Domett*, 149.
220 Ibid., 150.
221 Ibid.
222 Ibid., 161.
223 RB to John H. Ingram, 11 February 1876.
224 *Domett*, 162.
225 Ibid.
226 *DeVane*, 386–8.
227 *Ryals*, 200.
228 *Domett*, 163.
229 Ibid., 165.
230 Ibid., 116.
231 *Griffin & Minchin*, 254.
232 Ibid.
233 *Domett*, 99.
234 RB to Annie Egerton Smith, 16 August 1873.
235 *Griffin & Minchin*, 256.
236 *DeVane*, 418.
237 *Domett*, 209.
238 Ibid.
239 EBB to RB, 20 March 1845.
240 *Orr*, 315.
241 *Ward ii*, 169.
242 Ibid., 170–1.
243 Ibid., 169.
244 Ibid., 170.
245 Ibid.
246 RB to Mrs Charles Skirrow, 12 September 1878.
247 Ibid.
248 RB to Mrs Thomas Fitzgerald.
249 *Orr*, 327.
250 *DeVane*, 430.
251 *Irvine & Honan*, 500.
252 William Benzie, *Dr F. J. Furnivall: Victorian scholar adventurer* (1983), 222; *Browning Society Papers*, i (1881–4), Appendix 1.
253 RB to Mr Williams, 24 September 1886.
254 Irvine & Honan, 504.
255 RB to F. J. Furnivall, 9 January 1883.
256 RB to J. D. Williams, 10 March 1883.
257 *Domett*, 298.
258 Henry James, 'Recollections of Katherine de Kay Bronson', *Cornhill Magazine*, February 1902.
259 *Meredith*, 130.
260 *Orr*, 363
261 Ibid., 365.
262 *DeVane*, 491.
263 *Orr*, 367.
264 *DeVane*, 492.

265 *Irvine & Honan*, 510.
266 RB to George Barrett, 21 January 1889.
267 *Ward ii*, 194.
268 Ibid., 195.
269 Ibid., 196.
270 *Domett*, 226–7.
271 Ibid., 238, 242.
272 Ibid., 248.
273 Ibid., 292.
274 Sarianna Browning to Pen Browning, 19 August 1887.
275 *Ryals*, 235.
276 RB to George Barrett, 28 March 1888.
277 RB to J. D. Williams, 21 October 1887.
278 Edmund Gosse, *Portraits from Life*, ed. Ann Thwaite (1991), 46–7.
279 *Hood*, 378.
280 *Meredith*, 130.
281 Ibid., 134–5.
282 Ibid.
283 *Orr*, 408.
284 Ibid., 424.
285 Ibid., 427.
286 *James*, ii, 283–4.
287 *Orr*, 427.
288 Ibid., 429.
289 Ibid., 429–31.

INDEX

The following abbreviations are used: EBB = Elizabeth Barrett Browning; RB = Robert Browning; RBs = Elizabeth Barrett and Robert Browning (together)

Works by Robert Browning (RB) appear directly under title; works by others under authors' names

Empire declared, 614; *see also*
Franco-Prussian war
Franceschini, Francesca Pompilia,
582–9, 593
Franceschini, Gaetano, 585
Franceschini, Count Guido, 553, 556,
582–9
Francis II, King of Sicily, 465
Francis, C.S. (US publishers), 418
Franco-Prussian war (1870), 613–15
Franz Josef, Emperor of Austria-
Hungary, 284
Fraser's Magazine, 412, 666
Fuller, Margaret *see* Ossoli, Margaret,
Marchesa d'
Furini, Francis, 679
Furnivall, Frederick James: on
Browning family pedigree, 33; and
EBB's gift of 'Sonnets from the
Portuguese' to RB, 281; founds
Browning Society, 666–70, 672;
disagreement with Swinburne, 667;
on Pen's supposed marriage to
Belgian girl, 670, 682; letter from RB
on *Jocoseria*, 674; RB writes to on
purchase of Venice palazzo, 677; and
RB's poem attacking FitzGerald, 689

Gabriel, Mary Ann Virginia, 531
Gagarin, Prince, 77
Garibaldi, Giuseppe, 284, 464–5
Gaskell, Elizabeth Cleghorne, 427
Gaudrian, Miss, 391–2
Gay, Peter, 531
Genoa, 215
Gibson, John, 365, 455, 518
Gillespie, G.K. (Pen's tutor), 577, 598
'Give a Rouse' (RB), 136
Gladstone, Mary, 663
Gladstone, William Ewart, 45
Goethe, J.W. von, 50, 413
'Gold Hair: A Legend of Pornic' (RB),
520
Gosse, Sir Edmund: on RB's mother's
bookbuying, 20; RB tells of father's
poetry, 22; on RB's poetic vocation,
64; on RB's application, 65–6; RB
gives account of *A Blot in the*

'Scutcheon to, 122, 127–8; RB tells of
gift of EBB's 'Sonnets from the
Portuguese', 281; RB complains of
Alfred Austin to, 636; on RB's voice,
673; on RB's lack of observation,
687–8
Graham-Clarke, Arabella ('Aunt
Bummy'), 159
'Grammarian's Funeral, The' (RB), 401
Gray, Effie *see* Ruskin, Effie
Great Exhibition (1851), 301
Greer, Louise: *Browning and America*,
474, 597
Greville, Charles Cavendish Fulke:
Memoirs, 652–3
Gridley, Roy E.: *The Brownings and
France*, 416
Griffin, W. Hall and H.C. Minchin:
biography of RB: on portrait of
Margaret (Tittle) Browning, 29; on
paucity of art galleries in London,
46; on title of RB's *Incondita*, 48; on
RB's fondness for country fairs, 57;
on RB's schooling, 60; on RB's visit
to Russia, 75–7; on Pritchard, 79; on
Wordsworth's praise of RB, 93; on
RB's *Sordello*, 114; on Corkran's
relations with RB, 311; on RB's *Red
Cotton Night-Cap Country*, 645
Grisanowski, Dr E.G.T., 450
Grosart, Revd Alexander B., 93
Grosvenor Gallery, London, 683–4
Grote, Goerge, 592
Grove, William, 672–3
Grundy, Mrs (fictional figure), 46
Guardia Civica, 250
'Guardian Angel, The: A Picture at
Fano' (RB), 261–3
Guercino: *L'Angelo Custode* (painting),
261–3
Guerrazzi, Francesco, 267–9, 282
Guidi, Count Camillo, 241
Guidi, Count Francesco, 556

Hallé, Charles, 527
Halliwell-Phillipps, J.O., 667
Harding, Dr Henry, 269–70, 294, 437
Hardy, Thomas, 596, 646